D0622131

The Imperialist

Canadian Critical Editions

General Editors

John Moss and Gerald Lynch

Canadian Critical Editions offer, for academic study and the interested reader, authoritative texts of significant Canadian works within a comprehensive critical setting. Where appropriate, each edition provides extensive biographical and bibliographical background, reprints of documents, commentary to illuminate the context of its creation and the history of its reception, new essays written from a variety of critical perspectives, and a bibliography. These critical editions provide an excellent opportunity for appreciation of the works themselves, for understanding their place in the developing tradition, and for participating in the critical discourse surrounding each work. Making the best accessible, this is the key concept behind Canadian Critical Editions.

*Market square, Brantford, 1899, courtesy
Brant County Museum and Archives.*

Sara Jeannette Duncan (1861-1922) was one of the most adventurous Canadian women of her time. Born in Brantford (the
city on which the "Elgin" of *The Imperialist* is modelled), she
worked as a journalist for several years, joining the staff of
such newspapers as the Washington *Post*, Toronto *Globe*, and
Montreal *Star*. In the fall of 1888, she began a round-the-world
trip with another woman journalist. She met her future husband
in India, and lived there mainly for the next twenty years. *A
Social Departure* (1890), a lively account of her trip, launched
her career as a writer of books, and she wrote over twenty
others, though only *The Imperialist* is set in Canada.

Photo courtesy National Archives, C-46447, early 1890s

The Imperialist

Sara Jeannette Duncan

A Critical Edition

Edited by
Thomas E. Tausky

The Tecumseh Press
Ottawa, Canada
2008

Copyright © by The Tecumseh Press Ltd., 1996.
editorial matter by Thomas E. Tausky
Reprint 2008
Copyright permission has been sought for all reprinted items: see notes in
Backgrounds and Contexts, and Critical Interpretations, sections. For any
omissions, please contact the Publisher.

Previous publications include: *The Queen: The Lady's Newspaper*, Eng-
land, 1903, serially; *News*, Toronto, 1903-1904, serially; D. Appleton,
America, 1904; Constable, England, 1904; Copp Clark, Toronto, 1904;
McClelland and Stewart, Toronto, 1961, 1971; Tecumseh, Ottawa, 1988,
Tocumseh, Ottawa, 1996.

*All rights reserved. No part of this book may be used or
reproduced in any manner whatsoever without written
permission except in the case of brief quotations embodied
in critical articles and reviews.*

*The Publishers gratefully acknowledge the financial support of
Department of Canadian Heritage, and of the Smallman Fund,
Faculty of Arts, the University of Western Ontario.*

Canadian Cataloguing in Publication Program

Duncan, Sara Jeannette, 1861-1922
        The Imperialist

(Canadian critical editions ; 2)
Includes bibliographical references.
ISBN 1-896133-36-3 (bound).—
ISBN 1-896133-38-X (pbk.)

        I. Tausky, Thomas E., 1943-   II. Title.
III. Series.

PS8455.O8515 1996   C813'.4   C96-900687-X
PR9199.2.C68I5 1966

*Cover photo, Colborne St., Brantford, c. 1905, courtesy
Brant County Museum and Archives.*

Printed and bound in Canada

Contents

Preface

Take the train to Brantford, Ontario, and you get off at the imposing late Victorian station in which Sara Jeannette Duncan must have waited as she looked forward to leaving her home town for Toronto, New Orleans, Montreal, Ottawa, Washington, Vancouver, Japan, India, Britain—the world. A short walk takes you to the elegant Italianate house that was her childhood home. Not very far away are Zion Church, where her family worshipped, and the parsonage where her minister, Dr. Cochrane, lived for decades. Nearby is the statue to Joseph Brant, the Mohawk leader; Duncan was present at the statue's unveiling.

In short, alongside present-day Brantford are the traces of an older Brantford Duncan knew, and a visitor can imagine her walking streets that, some of them, retain their Victorian character today. But the inner life of that city, and of life in Ontario at the turn of the century, is more elusive, less easily captured. Duncan's *The Imperialist* is the key that unlocks the door to that past.

The Imperialist is the finest expression of Duncan's interests as a writer of fiction. She was fascinated by the mixture of idealistic and self-serving motives disclosed in political combat; her personal experience led her to explore the struggles of imaginative protagonists trapped in social worlds which seek to suppress their individuality; as a close observer of several societies, she felt drawn to the question of national differences. In *The Imperialist*, more than in any of her other novels, she succeeded in finding a narrative which fully developed the potential human drama of these subjects. Duncan had learned to examine the inner workings of society by writing several penetrating novels about the British community of urban India before she turned to the setting of what she hoped would be "her best book" (letter of 18 Sept. 1902 to John Willison). *The Imperialist* is a novel in which the social background matters as much as the foreground of individual endeavours. The novel begins with the rituals of Elgin's celebration of Queen Victoria's Birthday, and continues with scenes that in their detailed observation make us feel we are there having high tea with the minister, observing the haggling in the Elgin market and taking a seat at the partisan political rallies that absorb the town's attention.

At the same time, as *The Imperialist* unfolds, we become increasingly aware that the novel is also the story of one family, the Murchisons. This is a family whose members, the narrator tells us, "were too good for their environment." Their "quality," we are told, "marked them with a difference." Much of the novel's plot is anticipated in the narrator's grim warning that difference is "the one thing a small community, accustomed comfortably to scan its own intelligible averages, will not tolerate."

It is worth noting that the narrator warmly includes *all* the Murchisons in her praise. An observant reader may find herself evaluating the claims of each Murchison to this pride of place. Lorne Murchison, the imperialist of the title, radiates sincerity and idealism, and his passionate desire to find a political basis for our national identity has a renewed interest as we continue to grapple with that unresolved problem. But many readers may be drawn at least as much to his sister Advena. The town does not value her nearly as highly as her brother, but along with intellectual gifts, she has insight into her own feelings that her brother lacks. Her limited destiny contrasts sharply and tellingly with the bright future that seems to be open to Lorne. Advena Murchison is more radical than her brother in her difference from the community. By dedicating himself to politics, Lorne makes a choice that is honourable and honoured; in dedicating herself to books, Advena makes a choice that is incomprehensible to most in Elgin. Given the opportunity to spy upon Advena and Hugh Finlay in the Murchisons' library, the narrator elects "to follow the recognized tradition of Elgin, which would never have entered the library." Advena is a near relation of the many imaginative young women who are to be found throughout Duncan's fiction, and she shares childhood experiences and character traits with her creator. Yet she is not given one of the glamorous new occupations for women (journalist, doctor) that Duncan herself so admired, perhaps because there would be little opportunity for such professions in a small community. It is not easy to be a New Woman in Elgin, and Advena, unlike Duncan, turns her thoughts to that older ideal for women, romantic love.

In a letter to an admirer of *The Imperialist*, Duncan confided that she wondered if "I had forgotten my country's note" (letter of 4 May 1905 to Archibald McMechan). Her shrewd analytical grasp of Ontario small town society in the process of making a nation reveals that she had remembered well.

The text of this edition is that of the British and Canadian first editions, published by Constable and Copp Clark respectively. The text also exists in several other versions—it was first published as a serial in *The Queen*, a British periodical, and subsequently appeared as a serial again in *The Toronto Daily News* and then was published in an American edition by D. Appleton (for more information on the novel's publication history, see the "Textual Appendix" and "The Writing of *The Imperialist*" elsewhere in this volume). This revised version of an edition first published in 1988 has provided an opportunity to reprint some of the best essays that have appeared on *The Imperialist* in the past twenty years, a period which has seen the publication of over two dozen essays on the novel.

It was fortunately possible to convert the materials from the previous edition into a current word-processing programme and thereby retain the very accurate version of the text prepared by Launa Fuller. I am grateful to the Department of English at the University of Western Ontario and the former Dean of the Faculty of Arts, Thomas M. Lennon, for a grant which covered the word-processing costs. I am also greatly indebted to my colleague, Richard J. Shroyer for his generous assistance in taking charge of the desktop publishing dimension of that edition. The present edition has received a very timely and much appreciated grant from the current Dean of the Faculty of Arts, James M. Good, using funds provided by the Smallman Fund. Three graduate students in the Department of English—Alison Calder, Sarah Caskey and Susan Terry—made important contributions to the edition through proof-reading and/or advising about the essays to be selected.

Thomas E. Tausky
University of Western Ontario

Titles in the Canadian Critical Edition Text Series available from Borealis-Tecumseh Press

Stephen Leacock, *Sunshine Sketches of a Little Town*, editor Gerald Lynch, 1996.

Sarah Jeannette Duncan, *The Imperialist*, editor Thomas E. Tausky, 1996.

Susanna Moodie, *Roughing It in the Bush; or, Life in Canada,* editor Elizabeth Thompson, 1997.

John Richardson, *Wacousta*, editor John Moss, 1998.

Early Canadian Short Stories: Short Stories in English Before World War I, editor Misao Dean, 2000.

Stephen Leacock, *Arcadian Adventures with the Idle Rich*, editor David Bentley, 2000.

Frances Brooke, *The History of Emily Montague*, editor Laura Moss, 2001.

Charles G.D. Roberts, *Charles G.D. Roberts: Animal Stories*, editor Terry Whalen, 2002.

A Northern Romanticism: Poets of the Confederation, editor Tracy Ware, 2002.

J.G. Sime, *Sister Woman*, editor Sandra Campbell, 2003.

Ethel Wilson, *Swamp Angel*, editor Li-Peng Geng, 2004.

Frederick Phillip Grove, *Settlers of the Marsh*, editor Alison Claire Calder, 2005.

Titles in Preparation

Duncan Campbell Scott, *In the Village of Viger*, editor Robert May.

Frederick Phillip Grove, *Over Prarie Trails*, editor Alison Claire Calder.

Thomas Chandler Haliburton, *The Clockmaker*, editor Jeremy Lalonde.

Susie Frances Harrison, *Crowded out! and Other Sketches*, editor Tracy Ware.

Ernest Buckler, *The Mountain and The Valley*, editor Marta Dvorak.

The Imperialist

by

Sara Jeannette Duncan

Chapter I

It would have been idle to inquire into the antecedents, or even the circumstances, of old Mother Beggarlegs.[1] She would never tell; the children, at all events, were convinced of that; and it was only the children, perhaps, who had the time and the inclination to speculate. Her occupation was clear; she presided like a venerable stooping hawk, over a stall in the covered part of the Elgin market- place, where she sold gingerbread horses and large round gingerbread cookies, and brown sticky squares of what was known in all circles in Elgin as taffy. She came, it was understood, with the dawn; with the night she vanished, spending the interval on a not improbable broomstick. Her gingerbread was better than anybody's; but there was no comfort in standing, first on one foot and then on the other, while you made up your mind—the horses were spirited, and you could eat them a leg at a time, but there was more in the cookies—she bent such a look on you, so fierce and intolerant of vacillation. She belonged to the group of odd characters, rarer now than they used to be, etched upon the vague consciousness of small towns as in a way mysterious and uncanny; some said that Mother Beggarlegs was connected with the aristocracy and some that she had been "let off" being hanged. The alternative was allowed full swing, but in any case it was clear that such persons contributed little to the common good, and, being reticent, were not entertaining. So you bought your gingerbread, concealing, as it were, your weapons, paying your copper coins with a neutral nervous eye, and made off to a safe distance, whence you turned to shout insultingly, if you were an untrounced young male of Elgin, "Old Mother Beggarlegs! Old Mother Beggarlegs!" And why "Beggarlegs" nobody in the world could tell you. It might have been a dateless waggery, or it might have been a corruption of some more dignified surname, but it was all she ever got. Serious, meticulous persons called her "Mrs." Beggarlegs, slightly lowering their voices and slurring it, however, it must be admitted. The name invested her with a graceless, anatomical interest, it penetrated her wizened black and derisively exposed her; her name went far indeed to make her dramatic.

Lorne Murchison, when he was quite a little boy, was affected by this, and by the unfairness of the way it singled her out. Moved partly by the oppression of the feeling and partly by a desire for information, he asked her sociably one day, in the act of purchase, why the gilt was generally off her gingerbread. He had been looking long, as a matter of fact, for gingerbread with the gilt on it, being accustomed to the phrase on the lips of his father in connection with small profits. Mother Beggarlegs, so unaccustomed to politeness that she could not instantly recognize it, answered him with an imprecation, at which he, no doubt, retreated, suddenly thrown on the defensive, hurling the usual taunt. One prefers to hope he didn't, with the invincible optimism one has for the behaviour of lovable people; but whether or not, his kind attempt at colloquy is the first indication I can find of that active sympathy with the disabilities of his fellow beings which stamped him later so intelligent a meliorist. Even in his boy's beginning he had a heart for the work; and Mother Beggarlegs, but for a hasty conclusion, might have made him a friend.

It is hard to invest Mother Beggarlegs with importance, but the date helps me—the date, I mean, of this chapter about Elgin; she was a person to be reckoned with on the twenty-fourth of May. I will say at once, for the reminder to persons living in England, that the twenty-fourth of May was the Queen's Birthday. Nobody in Elgin can possibly have forgotten it. The Elgin children had a rhyme about it—

> "The twenty-fourth of May
> Is the Queen's Birthday;
> If you don't give us a holiday,
> We'll all run away."

But Elgin was in Canada. In Canada the twenty-fourth of May *was* the Queen's Birthday; and these were times and regions far removed from the prescription that the anniversary "should be observed" on any of those various outlying dates which, by now, must have produced in her immediate people such indecision as to the date upon which Her Majesty really did come into the world. That day, and that only, was the observed, the celebrated, a day with an essence in it, dawning more gloriously than other days and ending more regretfully, unless, indeed, it fell on a Sunday, when it was "kept" on the Monday, with a slightly clouded feeling that it wasn't exactly the same thing.[2] Travelled persons, who had spent the anniversary there, were apt to come back with a poor opinion of its celebration in "the old country"—a pleasant relish to the more than ever appreciated advantages of the new, the advantages that came out so by contrast. More space such persons indicated, more enterprise they boasted, and even more loyalty they would flourish, all with an affectionate reminiscent smile at the little ways of a grandmother. A "Bank" holiday, indeed! Here it was a real holiday, that woke you with bells and cannon—who had forgotten the time the ancient piece of ordnance in the Square blew out all the windows in the Methodist church?—and went on with squibs and crackers till you didn't know where to step on the sidewalks,[3] and ended up splendidly with rockets and fire-balloons and drunken Indians vociferous on their way to the lock-up. Such a day for the hotels, with teams hitched three abreast in front of their aromatic barrooms; such a day for the circus, with half the farmers of Fox County agape before the posters—with all their *chic* and shock they cannot produce such posters nowadays, nor are there any vacant lots to form attractive backgrounds—such a day for Mother Beggarlegs! The hotels, and the shops and stalls for eating and drinking, were the only places in which business was done; the public sentiment put universal shutters up, but the public appetite insisted upon excepting the means to carnival. An air of ceremonial festivity those fastened shutters gave; the sunny little town sat round them, important and significant, and nobody was ever known to forget that they were up, and go on a fool's errand. No doubt they had an impressiveness for the young countryfolk that strolled up and down Main Street in their honest best, turning into Snow's for ice-cream when a youth was disposed to treat. (Gallantry exacted ten-cent dishes, but for young ladies alone, or family parties, Mrs. Snow would bring five-cent quantities almost without asking, and for very small boys one dish and the requisite number of spoons.) There was discrimination, there was choice, in this matter of treating. A happy excitement accompanied it, which you could read in the way Corydon clapped his soft felt hat on his head as he pocketed the change. To be treated— to ten-cent dishes—three times in the course of the day by the same young man gave matter for private reflection and for public entertainment, expressed in the broad grins of less reckless people. I speak of a soft felt hat, but it might be more than that: it might be a dark green one, with a feather in it; and here was distinction, for such a hat indicated that its owner belonged to the Independent Order of Foresters, who would leave their spring wheat for forty miles round to meet in Elgin and march in procession, wearing their hats, and dazzlingly scatter upon Main Street. They gave the day its touch of imagination, those green cocked hats;[4] they were lyrical upon the highways; along the prosaic sidewalks by twos and threes they sang together. It is no great thing, a hat of any quality; but a small thing may ring dramatic on the right metal, and in the vivid idea of Lorne Murchison and his sister Advena a Robin Hood walked in every Independent Forester, especially in the procession. Which shows the risks you run if you, a person of honest livelihood and solicited vote, adopt any portion of a habit not familiar to you, and go marching about with a banner and a band. Two children may be standing at the first street corner, to whom your respectability and your property may at once become illusion and your outlawry the delightful fact.

A cheap trip brought the Order of Green Hats to Elgin; and there were cheap trips on this great day to persuade other persons to leave it. The Grand Trunk had even then an idea of encouraging social combination for change of scene, and it was quite a common thing for the operatives of the Milburn Boiler Company to arrange to get themselves carried to the lakeside or "the Falls" at half a dollar a head. The "hands" got it up themselves, and it was a question in Elgin whether one might sink one's dignity and go as a hand for the sake of the fifty-cent opportunity, a question usually decided in the negative. The social distinctions of Elgin may not be easily appreciated by people accustomed to the rough and ready standards of a world at the other end of the Grand Trunk; but it will be clear at a glance that nobody whose occupation prescribed a clean face could be expected to travel cheek by jowl, as a privilege, with persons who were habitually seen with smutty ones, barefaced smut, streaming out at the polite afternoon hour of six, jangling an empty dinner pail. So much we may decide, and leave it, reflecting as we go how simple and satisfactory, after all, are the prejudices which can hold up such obvious justification. There was recently to be pointed out in England the heir to a dukedom who loved stoking, and got his face smutty by preference. He would have been deplorably subversive of accepted conventions in Elgin; but, happily or otherwise, such persons and such places have at present little more than an imaginative acquaintance, vaguely cordial on the one side, vaguely critical on the other, and of no importance in the sum.

Polite society, to return to it, preferred the alternative of staying at home and mowing the lawn, or drinking raspberry vinegar on its own beflagged verandah; looking forward in the afternoon to the lacrosse match. There was nearly always a lacrosse match on the Queen's Birthday, and it was the part of elegance to attend and encourage the home team, as well as that of small boys, with broken straw hats, who sneaked an entrance, and were more enthusiastic than anyone. It was "a quarter" to get in, so the spectators were naturally composed of persons who could afford the quarter,[5] and persons like the young Flannigans and Finnigans, who absolutely couldn't, but who had to be there all the same. Lorne and Advena Murchison never had the quarter, so they witnessed few lacrosse matches, though they seldom failed to refresh themselves by a sight of the players after the game, when, crimson and perspiring, but still glorious in striped jerseys, their lacrosses and running shoes slung over one shoulder, these heroes left the field.

The Birthday I am thinking of, with Mrs. Murchison as a central figure in the kitchen, peeling potatoes for dinner, there was a lacrosse match of some importance, for the Fox County Championship and the Fox County Cup, as presented by the Member for the South Riding. Mrs. Murchison remains the central figure, nevertheless, with her family radiating from her, gathered to help or to hinder in one of those domestic crises which arose when the Murchisons were temporarily deprived of a "girl." Everybody was subject to them in Elgin, everybody had to acknowledge and face them. Let a new mill be opened, and it didn't matter what you paid her or how comfortable you made her, off she would go, and you might think yourself lucky if she gave a week's warning.[6] Hard times shut down the mills and brought her back again; but periods of prosperity were very apt to find the ladies of Elgin where I am compelled to introduce Mrs. Murchison—in the kitchen. "You'd better get up—the girl's gone," Lorne had stuck his head into his sister's room to announce, while yet the bells were ringing and the rifles of the local volunteers were spitting out the *feu de joie.* "I've lit the fire an' swep' out the dining-room. You tell mother. Queen's Birthday, too—I guess Lobelia's about as mean as they're made!" And the Murchisons had descended to face the situation. Lorne had by then done his part, and gone out into the chromatic possibilities of the day; but the sense of injury he had communicated to Advena in her bed remained and expanded. Lobelia, it was felt, had scurvily manipulated the situation—her situation, it might have been put, if any Murchison had been in the temper for jesting. She had taken unjustifiable means to do a more unjustifiable thing, to secure for herself an improper and unlawful share of the day's excitements, transferring her work, by the force of circumstances, to the shoulders of other people, since, as Mrs. Murchison remarked, somebody had to do it. Nor had she, her mistress testified, the excuse of fearing unreasonable confinement. "I told her she might go when she had done her dishes after dinner," said Mrs. Murchison, "and then she had only to come back at six and get tea—what's getting tea? I advised her to finish her ironing yesterday, so as to be free of it to-day; and she said she would be very glad to. Now, I wonder if she *did* finish it!" and Mrs. Murchison put down her pan of potatoes with a thump to look in the family clothes-basket. "Not she! Five shirts and *all* the coloured things. I call it downright deceit!"

"I believe I know the reason she'll *say*," said Advena. "She objects to rag carpet in her bedroom. She told me so."

"Rag carpet—upon my word!" Mrs. Murchison dropped her knife to exclaim. "It's what her betters have to do with! I've known the day when that very piece of rag carpet—sixty balls there were in it, and every one I sewed with my own fingers—was the best I had for my spare room, with a bit of ingrain in the middle. Dear me!" she went on with a smile that lightened the whole situation, "how proud I was of that performance! She didn't tell *me* she objected to rag carpet!"

"No, Mother," Advena agreed, "she knew better."

They were all there, in the kitchen, supporting their mother, and it seems an opportunity to name them. Advena, the eldest, stood by the long kitchen table washing the breakfast cups in "soft soap" and hot water. The soft soap—Mrs. Murchison had a barrelful boiled every spring in the back yard, an old colonial economy she hated to resign—made a fascinating brown lather with iridescent bubbles. Advena poured cupfuls of it from on high to see the foam rise, till her mother told her for mercy's sake to get on with those dishes. She stood before a long low window, looking out into the garden, and the light, filtering through apple branches on her face, showed her strongly featured and intelligent for fourteen. Advena was named after one grandmother; when the next girl came Mrs. Murchison, to make an end of the matter, named it Abigail, after the other. She thought both names outlandish, and acted under protest, but hoped that now everybody would be satisfied. Lorne came after Advena, at the period of a *naive* fashion of christening the young sons of Canada in the name of her Governor-General. It was a simple way of attesting a loyal spirit, but with Mrs. Murchison more particular motives operated. The Marquis of Lorne[7] was not only the deputy of the throne, he was the son-in-law of a good woman, of whom Mrs. Murchison thought more, and often said it, for being the woman she was than for being twenty times a Queen; and he had made a metrical translation of the Psalms, several of which were included in the revised psalter for the use of the Presbyterian Church in Canada, from which the whole of Knox Church sang to the praise of God every Sunday. These were circumstances that weighed with Mrs. Murchison, and she called her son after the Royal representative, feeling that she was doing well for him in a sense beyond the merc bestowal of a distinguished and a euphonious name, though that, as she would have willingly acknowledged, was "well enough in its place."

We must take this matter of names seriously; the Murchisons always did. Indeed, from the arrival of a new baby until the important Sunday of the christening, nothing was discussed with such eager zest and such sustained interest as the name he should get—there was a fascinating list at the back of the dictionary—and to the last minute it was problematical. In Stella's case, Mrs. Murchison actually changed her mind on the way to church; and Abby, who had sat through the sermon expecting Dorothy Maud, which she thought lovely, publicly cried with disappointment. Stella was the youngest, and Mrs. Murchison was thankful to have a girl at last whom she could name without regard to her own relations or anybody else's. I have skipped about a good deal, but I have only left out two, the boys who came between Abby and Stella. In their names the contemporary observer need not be too

acute to discover both an avowal and to some extent an enforce-
ment of Mr. Murchison's political views; neither an Alexander
Mackenzie[8] nor an Oliver Mowat [9] could very well grow up into
anything but a sound Liberal in that part of the world without
feeling himself an unendurable paradox. To christen a baby like
that was, in a manner, a challenge to public attention; the faint
relaxation about the lips of Dr. Drummond—the best of Liberals
himself, though he made a great show of keeping it out of the
pulpit—recognized this, and the just perceptible stir of the
congregation proved it. Sonorously he said it. "Oliver Mowat, I
baptize thee in the Name of the Father—" The compliment should
have all the impressiveness the rite could give it, while the Murchison brothers and sisters, a-row in the family pew, stood on one
foot with excitement as to how Oliver Mowat would take the drops
that defined him. The verdict was, on the way home, that he
behaved splendidly. Alexander Mackenzie, the year before, had
roared.

He was weeping now, at the age of seven, silently, but very
copiously, behind the wood-pile. His father had finally cuffed him
for importunity; and the world was no place for a just boy, who
asked nothing but his rights. Only the wood-pile, friendly mossy
logs unsplit, stood inconscient and irresponsible for any share in
his black circumstances; and his tears fell among the lichens of the
stump he was bowed on till, observing them, he began to wonder
whether he could cry enough to make a pond there, and was
presently disappointed to find the source exhausted. The Murchisons were all imaginative.

The others, Oliver and Abby and Stella, still "tormented." Poor
Alec's rights—to a present of pocket-money on the Queen's Birthday—were common ones, and almost statutory. How their father,
sitting comfortably with his pipe in the flickering May shadows
under the golden pippin, reading the Toronto paper, could evade
his liability in the matter was unfathomable to the Murchisons; it
was certainly illiberal; they had a feeling that it was illegal. A little
teasing was generally necessary, but the resistance to-day had
begun to look ominous, and Alec, as we know, too temerarious,
had retired in disorder to the wood-pile.

Oliver was wiping Advena's dishes. He exercised himself
ostentatiously upon a plate, standing in the door to be within ear-

shot of his father.

"Eph Wheeler," he informed his family, "Eph Wheeler, he's got twenty-five cents, an' a English sixpence, an' a Yankee nickel. An' Mr. Wheeler's only a common working man, a lot poorer'n we are."

Mr. Murchison removed his pipe from his lips, in order, apparently, to follow unimpeded the trend of the *Dominion*'s leading article. Oliver eyed him anxiously. "Do, father," he continued in logical sequence. "Aw, do."

"Make him, mother," said Abby indignantly. "It's the Queen's *Birth*day!"

"Time enough when the butter bill's paid," said Mrs. Murchison.

"Oh, the *butter* bill! Say, Father, aren't you going to?"

"What?" asked John Murchison, and again took out his pipe, as if this were the first he had heard of the matter.

"Give us our fifteen cents each to celebrate with. You can't do it under that," Oliver added firmly. "Crackers are eight cents a packet this year, the small size."

"Nonsense," said Mr. Murchison. The reply was definite and final, and its ambiguity was merely due to the fact that their father disliked giving a plump refusal. "Nonsense" was easier to say, if not to hear, than "No." Oliver considered for a moment, drew Abby to colloquy by the pump, and sought his brother behind the wood-pile. Then he returned to the charge.

"Look here, father," he said, "*cash down*, we'll take ten."

John Murchison was a man of few words, but they were usually impregnated with meaning, especially in anger. "No more of this," he said. "Celebrate fiddlesticks! Go and make yourselves of some use. You'll get nothing from me, for I haven't got it." So saying, he went through the kitchen with a step that forbade him to be followed. His eldest son, arriving over the back yard fence in a state of heat, was just in time to hear him. Lorne's apprehension of the situation was instant, and his face fell, but the depression plainly covered such splendid spirits that his brother asked resentfully, "Well, what's the matter with *you*?"

"Matter? Oh, not much. I'm going to see the Cayugas beat the Wanderers, that's all; an' Abe Mackinnon's mother said he could ask me to come back to tea with them. Can I, mother?"

"There's no objection that I know of," said Mrs. Murchison,

shaking her apron free of stray potato-parings, "but you won't get money for the lacrosse match or anything else from your father to-day, *I* can assure you. They didn't do five dollars' worth of business at the store all day yesterday, and he's as cross as two sticks."

"Oh, that's all right." Lorne jingled his pocket and Oliver took a fascinated step toward him. "I made thirty cents this morning, delivering papers for Fisher. His boy's sick. I did the North Ward—took me over'n hour. Guess I can go all right, can't I?"

"Why, yes, I suppose you can," said his mother. The others were dumb. Oliver hunched his shoulders and kicked at the nearest thing that had paint on it. Abby clung to the pump handle and sobbed aloud. Lorne looked gloomily about him and went out. Making once more for the back fence, he encountered Alexander in the recognized family retreat. "Oh, my goodness!" he said, and stopped. In a very few minutes he was back in the kitchen, followed sheepishly by Alexander, whose grimy face expressed the hope that beat behind his little waistcoat.

"Say, you kids," he announced, "Alec's got four cents, an' he says he'll join up. This family's going to celebrate all right. Come on down town."

No one could say that the Murchisons were demonstrative. They said nothing, but they got their hats. Mrs. Murchison looked up from her occupation.

"Alec," she said, "out of this house you don't go till you've washed your face. Lorne, come here," she added in a lower voice, producing a bunch of keys. "If you look in the right-hand corner of the top small drawer in my bureau you'll find about twenty cents. Say nothing about it, and mind you don't meddle with anything else. I guess the Queen isn't going to owe it all to you."

Chapter II

"We've seen changes, Mr. Murchison. Aye. We've seen changes."

Dr. Drummond[1] and Mr. Murchison stood together in the store door, over which the sign, "John Murchison: Hardware," had explained thirty years of varying commercial fortune. They had pretty well begun life together in Elgin. John Murchison was one of those who had listened to Mr. Drummond's trial sermon, and had given his vote to "call" him to the charge. Since then there had been few Sundays when, morning and evening, Mr. Murchison had not been in his place at the top of his pew, where his dignified and intelligent head appeared with the isolated significance of a strong individuality. People looked twice at John Murchison in a crowd; so did his own children at home. Hearing some discussion of the selection of a Premier, Alec, looking earnestly at him once said, "Why don't they tell Father to be it?" The young minister looked twice at him that morning of the trial sermon, and asked afterward who he was. A Scotchman, Mr. Drummond was told, not very long from the old country,[2] who had bought the Playfair business on Main Street, and settled in the "Plummer Place," which already had a quarter of a century's standing in the annals of the town. The Playfair business was a respectable business to buy; the Plummer Place, though it stood in an unfashionable outskirt, was a respectable place to settle in; and the minister, in casting his lot in Elgin, envisaged John Murchison as part of it, thought of him confidently as a "dependence," saw him among the future elders and office-bearers of the congregation, a man who would be punctual with his pew-rent, sage in his judgments, and whose views upon church attendance would be extended to his family.

So the two came, contemporaries, to add their labour and their lives to the building of this little outpost of Empire. It was the frankest transfer, without thought of return; they were there to spend and be spent within the circumference of the spot they had chosen, with no ambition beyond. In the course of nature, even their bones and their memories would enter into the fabric. The new country filled their eyes; the new town was their opportunity, its destiny their fate. They were altogether occupied with its affairs, and the affairs of the growing Dominion, yet obscure in the heart of each of them ran the undercurrent of the old allegiance. They had gone the length of their tether, but the tether was always there. Thus, before a congregation that always stood in the early days, had the minister every Sunday morning for thirty years besought the Almighty, with ardour and humility, on behalf of the Royal Family. It came in the long prayer, about the middle. Not in the perfunctory words of a ritual, but in the language of his choice, which varied according to what he believed to be the spiritual needs of the reigning House, and was at one period, touching certain of its members, though respectful, extremely candid.[3] The General Assembly of the Church of Scotland, "now in session," also—was it ever forgotten once? And even the Prime Minister, "and those who sit in council with him," with just a hint of extra commendation if it happened to be Mr. Gladstone.[4] The minister of Knox Church, Elgin, Ontario, Canada, kept his eye on them all. Remote as he was, and concerned with affairs of which they could know little, his sphere of duty could never revolve too far westward to embrace them, nor could his influence, under any circumstances, cease to be at their disposal. It was noted by some that after Mr. Drummond had got his "D.D." from an American University[5] he also prayed occasionally for the President of the neighbouring Republic; but this was rebutted by others, who pointed out that it happened only on the occurrence of assassinations, and held it reasonable enough. The cavillers mostly belonged to the congregation of St. Andrew's, "Established"[6]—a glum, old-fashioned lot indeed, who now and then dropped in of a Sunday evening to hear Mr. Drummond preach. (There wasn't much to be said for the preaching at St Andrew's.) The Established folk went on calling the minister of Knox Church "Mr." Drummond long after he was "Doctor" to his own congregation, on account of what they chose to consider the dubious source of the dignity; but the Knox Church people had their own theory to explain this hypercriticism, and would promptly turn the conversation to the merits of the sermon.

Twenty-five years it was, in point, this Monday morning when the Doctor—not being Established we need not hesitate, besides by this time nobody did—stood with Mr. Murchison in the store door and talked about having seen changes. He had preached his anniversary sermon the night before to a full church, when, laying his hand upon his people's heart, he had himself to repress tears. He was aware of another strand completed in their mutual bond: the sermon had been a moral, an emotional, and an oratorical success; and in the expansion of the following morning Dr. Drummond had remembered that he had promised his housekeeper a new gas cooking-range, and that it was high time he should drop into Murchison's to inquire about it. Mrs. Forsyth had mentioned at breakfast that they had ranges with exactly the improvement she wanted at Thompson's, but the minister was deaf to the hint. Thompson was a Congregationalist, and, improvement or no improvement, it wasn't likely that Dr. Drummond was going "outside the congregation" for anything he required. It would have been on a par with a wandering tendency in his flock, upon which he systematically frowned. He was as great an autocrat in this as the rector of any country parish in England undermined by Dissent; but his sense of obligation worked unfailingly both ways.

John Murchison had not said much about the sermon; it wasn't his way, and Dr. Drummond knew it. "You gave us a good sermon last night, Doctor;" not much more than that, "and I noticed the Milburns there; we don't often get Episcopalians;" and again, "The Wilcoxes"—Thomas Wilcox, wholesale grocer, was the chief prop of St. Andrew's—"were sitting just in front of us. We overtook them going home, and Wilcox explained how much they liked the music. 'Glad to see you,' I said. 'Glad to see you for any reason,' " Mr. Murchison's eye twinkled. "But they had a great deal to say about 'the music.' " It was not an effusive form of felicitation; the minister would have liked it less if it had been, felt less justified, perhaps, in remembering about the range on that particular morning. As it was, he was able to take it with perfect dignity and good humour, and to enjoy the point against the Wilcoxes with that laugh of his that did everybody good to hear; so hearty it was, so rich in the grain of the voice, so full of the zest and flavour of the joke. The range had been selected, and their talk of changes had begun with it, Mr. Murchison pointing out the new idea in the boiler, and Dr. Drummond remembering his first kitchen stove that burned wood and stood on its four legs, with nothing behind but the stove pipe, and if you wanted a boiler you took off the front lids and put it on, and how remarkable even that had seemed to his eyes, fresh from the conservative kitchen notions of the old country. He had come, unhappily, a widower to the domestic improvements on the other side of the Atlantic. "Often I used to think," he said to Mr. Murchison, "if my poor wife could have seen that stove how delighted she would have been! But I doubt this would have been too much for her altogether!"

"That stove!" answered Mr. Murchison. "Well I remember it. I sold it myself to your predecessor, Mr. Wishart, for thirty dollars—the last purchase he ever made, poor man. It was great business for me—I had only two others in the store like it. One of them old Milburn bought—the father of this man, d'ye mind him?—the other stayed by me a matter of seven years. I carried a light stock in those days."

It was no longer a light stock. The two men involuntarily glanced round them for the satisfaction of the contrast Murchison evoked, though neither of them, from motives of vague delicacy, felt inclined to dwell upon it. John Murchison had the shyness of an artist in his commercial success, and the minister possibly felt that his relation toward the prosperity of a member had in some degree the embarrassment of a tax-gatherer's. The stock was indeed heavy now. You had to go upstairs to see the ranges, where they stood in rows, and every one of them bore somewhere upon it, in raised black letters, John Murchison's name. Through the windows came the iterating ring on the iron from the foundry in Chestnut Street which fed the shop, with an overflow that found its way from one end of the country to the other. Finicking visitors to Elgin found this wearing, but to John Murchison it was the music that honours the conqueror of circumstances. The ground floor was given up to the small wares of the business, chiefly imported; two or three young men, steady and knowledgeable-looking, moved about in their shirt sleeves among shelves and packing cases. One of them was our friend Alec; our other friend Oliver looked after the books at the foundry. Their father did everything deliberately; but presently, in his own good time, his commercial letter paper would be headed, with regard to these two, "John Murchison and Sons." It had long announced that the business was "Wholesale and Retail."

Dr. Drummond and Mr. Murchison, considering the changes

in Elgin from the store door, did it at their leisure, the merchant with his thumbs thrust comfortably in the armholes of his waist-coat, the minister, with that familiar trick of his, balancing on one foot and suddenly throwing his slight weight forward on the other. "A bundle of nerves" people called the Doctor: to stand still would have been a penance to him; even as he swayed backward and forward in talking his hand must be busy at the seals on his watch chain and his shrewd glance travelling over a dozen things you would never dream so clever a man would take notice of. It was a prospect of moderate commercial activity they looked out upon, a street of mellow shop-fronts, on both sides, of varying height and importance, wearing that air of marking a period, a definite stop in growth, that so often co-exists with quite a reasonable degree of activity and independence in colonial towns.[7] One could almost say, standing there in the door at Murchison's, where the line of legitimate enterprise had been over-passed and where its intention had been none too sanguine—on the one hand in the faded and pretentious red brick building with the false third story, occupied by Cleary, which must have been let at a loss to dry-goods or anything else; on the other hand in the solid "Gregory block," opposite the market, where rents were as certain as the dividends of the Bank of British North America.

Main Street expressed the idea that, for the purpose of growing and doing business, it had always found the days long enough. Drays passed through it to the Grand Trunk station, but they passed one at a time; a certain number of people went up and down about their affairs, but they were never in a hurry; a street car jogged by every ten minutes or so, but nobody ran after it. There was a decent procedure; and it was felt that Bofield—he was dry-goods, too—in putting in an elevator was just a little unneces-sarily in advance of the times. Bofield had only two stories, like everybody else, and a very easy staircase, up which people often declared they preferred to walk rather than wait in the elevator for a young man to finish serving and work it. These, of course, were the sophisticated people of Elgin; country folk, on a market day, would wait a quarter of an hour for the young man, and think nothing of it; and I imagine Bofield found his account in the eleva-tor, though he did complain sometimes that such persons went up and down on frivolous pretexts or to amuse the baby. As a matter of fact, Elgin had begun as the centre of "trading" for the farmers of Fox County, and had soon over-supplied that limit in demand; so that when other interests added themselves to the activity of the town there was still plenty of room for the business they brought. Main Street was really, therefore, not a fair index; nobody in Elgin would have admitted it. Its appearance and demeanour would never have suggested that it was now the chief artery of a thriving manufacturing town, with a collegiate institute, eleven churches, two newspapers, and an asylum for the deaf and dumb, to say nothing of a fire department unsurpassed for organization and achievement in the Province of Ontario.[8] Only at twelve noon it might be partly realized, when the prolonged "toots" of seven factory whistles at once let off, so to speak, the hour. Elgin liked the demonstration; it was held to be cheerful and unmistakable, an indication of "go-ahead" proclivities which spoke for itself. It occurred while yet Dr. Drummond and Mr. Murchison stood together in the store door.

"I must be getting on," said the minister, looking at his watch. "And what news have you of Lorne?"

"Well, he seems to have got through all right."

"What—you've heard already, then?"

"He telegraphed from Toronto on Saturday night." Mr. Murchison stroked his chin, the better to retain his satisfaction. "Waste of money—the post would have brought it this morning—but it pleased his mother. Yes, he's through his Law Schools examination, and at the top, too, as far as I can make out."

"Dear me, and you never mentioned it!" Dr. Drummond spoke with the resigned impatience of a familiar grievance. It was certainly a trying characteristic of John Murchison that he never cared about communicating anything that might seem to ask for congratulation. "Well, well! I'm very glad to hear it."

"It slipped my mind," said Mr. Murchison. "Yes, he's full-fledged 'barrister and solicitor' now; he can plead your case or draw you up a deed with the best of them. Lorne's made a fair record, so far. We've no reason to be ashamed of him."

"That you have not." Personal sentiments between these two Scotchmen were rather indicated than indulged. "He's going in with Fulke and Warner, I suppose—you've got that fixed up?"

"Pretty well. Old man Warner was in this morning to talk it over. He says they look to Lorne to bring them in touch with the new generation. It's a pity he lost that son of his."

"Oh, a great pity. But since they had to go outside the firm they couldn't have done better; they couldn't have done better. I hope Lorne will bring them a bit of Knox Church business too; there's no reason why Bob Mackintosh should have it all. They'll be glad to see him back at the Hampden Debating Society. He's a great light there, is Lorne; and the Young Liberals, I hear, are wanting him for chairman this year."

"There's some talk of it. But time enough—time enough for that! He'll do first-rate if he gets the law to practise, let alone the making of it."

"Maybe so; he's young yet. Well, good-morning to you. I'll just step over the way to the *Express* office[9] and get a proof out of them of that sermon of mine. I noticed their reporter fellow— what's his name?—Rawlins with his pencil out last night, and I've no faith in Rawlins."

"Better cast an eye over it," responded Mr. Murchison, cordi- ally, and stood for a moment or two longer in the door watching the crisp, significant little figure of the minister as he stepped briskly over the crossing to the newspaper office. There Dr. Drummond sat down, before he explained his errand, and wrote a paragraph.

"We are pleased to learn," it ran, "that Mr. Lorne Murchison, eldest son of Mr. John Murchison, of this town, has passed at the capital of the Province his final examination in Law, distinguish- ing himself by coming out at the top of the list. It will be remem- bered that Mr. Murchison, upon entering the Law Schools, also carried off a valuable scholarship. We are glad to be able to announce that Mr. Murchison, junior, will embark upon his pro- fession in his native town, where he will enter the well-known firm of Fulke and Warner."

The editor, Mr. Horace Williams, had gone to dinner, and Rawlins was out, so Dr. Drummond had to leave it with the press foreman. Mr. Williams read it appreciatively on his return, and sent it down with the following addition —

"This is doing it as well as it can be done. Elgin congratulates Mr. L. Murchison upon having produced these results, and herself upon having produced Mr. L. Murchison."

Chapter III

From the day she stepped into it Mrs. Murchison knew that the Plummer Place[1] was going to be the bane of her existence. This may have been partly because Mr. Murchison had bought it, since a circumstance welded like that into one's life is very apt to assume the character of a bane, unless one's temperament leads one to philosophy, which Mrs. Murchison's didn't. But there were other reasons more difficult to traverse: it was plainly true that the place did require a tremendous amount of "looking after," as such things were measured in Elgin, far more looking after than the Murchisons could afford to give it. They could never have afforded, in the beginning, to possess it, had it not been sold, under mortgage, at a dramatic sacrifice. The house was a dignified old affair, built of wood and painted white, with wide green verandahs compassing the four sides of it, as they often did in days when the builder had only to turn his hand to the forest. It stood on the very edge of the town; wheatfields in the summer billowed up to its fences, and cornstacks in the autumn camped around it like a besieging army. The plank sidewalk finished there; after that you took the road, or, if you were so inclined, the river, into which you could throw a stone from the orchard of the Plummer Place. The house stood roomily and shadily in ornamental grounds, with a lawn in front of it and a shrubbery at each side, an orchard behind, and a vegetable garden, the whole intersected by winding gravel walks, of which Mrs. Murchison was wont to say that a man might do nothing but weed them and have his hands full. In the middle of the lawn was a fountain, an empty basin with a plaster Triton,[2] most difficult to keep looking respectable and pathetic in his frayed air of exile from some garden of Italy sloping to the sea. There was also a barn with stabling, a loft, and big carriage doors opening on a lane to the street. The originating Plummer, Mrs. Murchison often said, must have been a person of large ideas, and she hoped he had the money to live up to them. The Murchisons at one time kept a cow in the barn, till a succession of "girls" left on account of the milking, and the lane was useful as an approach to the back yard by the teams that brought the cordwood in the winter. It was trying enough for a person with the instinct of order to find herself surrounded by out-of-door circumstances which she simply could not control, but Mrs. Murchison often declared that she could put up with the grounds if it had stopped there. It did not stop there. Though I was compelled to introduce Mrs. Murchison in the kitchen, she had a drawing-room in which she might have received the Lieutenant Governor, with French windows and a cut-glass chandelier, and a library with an Italian marble mantelpiece. She had an ice-house and wine cellar, and a string of bells in the kitchen that connected with every room in the house; it was a negligible misfortune that not one of them was in order. She had far too much, as she declared, for any one pair of hands and a growing family, and if the ceiling was not dropping in the drawing-room, the cornice was cracked in the library, or the gas was leaking in the dining-room, or the verandah wanted re-flooring if any one coming to the house was not to put his foot through it; and as to the barn, if it was dropping to pieces it would just have to drop. The barn was definitely outside the radius of possible amelioration—it passed gradually, visibly, into decrepitude, and Mrs. Murchison often wished she could afford to pull it down.

It may be realized that in spite of its air of being impossible to "overtake"—I must, in this connection, continue to quote its mistress—there was an attractiveness about the dwelling of the Murchisons, the attractiveness of the large ideas upon which it had been built and designed, no doubt by one of those gentlefolk of reduced income who wander out to the colonies with a nebulous view to economy and occupation, to perish of the readjustment. The case of such persons, when they' arrive, is at once felt to be pathetic; there is a tacit local understanding that they have made a mistake. They may be entitled to respect, but nothing can save them from the isolation of their difference and their misapprehension. It was like that with the house. The house was admired—without enthusiasm—but it was not copied. It was felt to be outside the general need, misjudged, adventitious; and it wore its superiority in the popular view like a folly. It was in Elgin, but not of it; it represented a different tradition; and Elgin made the same allowance for its bedroom bells and its old-fashioned dignities as was conceded to its original master's habit of a six o'clock dinner, with wine.

The architectural expression of the town was on a different scale, beginning with "frame," rising through the semi-detached, culminating expensively in Mansard roofs, cupolas and modern conveniences, and blossoming, in extreme instances, into Moorish fretwork and silk *portières*[3] for interior decoration. The Murchison house gained by force of contrast: one felt, stepping into it, under influences of less expediency and more dignity, wider scope and more leisured intention; its shabby spaces had a redundancy the pleasanter and its yellow plaster cornices a charm the greater for the numerous close-set examples of contemporary taste in red brick[4] which made, surrounded by geranium beds, so creditable an appearance in the West Ward. John Murchison in taking possession of the house had felt in it these satisfactions, had been definitely penetrated and soothed by them, the more perhaps because he brought to them a capacity for feeling the worthier things of life which circumstances had not previously developed. He seized the place with a sense of opportunity leaping sharp and conscious out of early years in the grey "wynds"[5] of a northern Scottish town; and its personality sustained him, very privately but none the less effectively, through the worry and expense of it for years. He would take his pipe and walk silently for long together about the untidy shrubberies in the evening for the acute pleasure of seeing the big horse-chestnuts in flower; and he never opened the hall door without a feeling of gratification in its weight as it swung under his hand. In so far as he could, he supplemented the idiosyncrasies he found. The drawing-room walls, though mostly bare in their old fashioned French paper—lavender and gilt, a grape-vine pattern—held a few good engravings; the library was reduced to contain a single bookcase, but it was filled with English classics. John Murchison had been made a careful man, not by nature, by the discipline of circumstances; but he would buy books. He bought them between long periods of abstinence, during which he would scout the expenditure of an unnecessary dollar, coming home with a parcel under his arm for which he vouchsafed no explanation, and which would disclose itself to be Lockhart, or Sterne, or Borrow, or Defoe. Mrs. Murchison kept a discouraging eye upon such purchases; and when her husband brought home Chambers' *Dictionary of English Literature*, after shortly and definitely repulsing her demand that he should get himself a new winter overcoat, she declared that it was beyond all endurance. Mrs. Murchison was surrounded, indeed, by more of "that sort of thing" than she could find use or excuse for; since, though books made but a sporadic appearance, current literature, daily, weekly, and monthly, was perpetually under her feet. The Toronto paper came as a matter of course, as the London daily takes its morning flight into the provinces, the local organ as simply indispensable, the *Westminster* as the corollary of church membership and for Sunday reading. These were constant, but there were also mutables —*Once a Week, Good Words for the Young, Blackwood's* and the *Cornhill*, they used to be; years of back numbers Mrs. Murchison had packed away in the attic, where Advena on rainy days came into the inheritance of them, and made an early acquaintance of fiction in *Ready Money Mortiboy* and *Verner's Pride*, while Lorne, flat on his stomach beside her, had glorious hours on *The Back of the North Wind*.[6] Their father considered such publications and their successors essential, like tobacco and tea. He was also an easy prey to the subscription agent, for works published in parts and paid for in instalments, a custom which Mrs. Murchison regarded with abhorrence. So much so that when John put his name down for *Masterpieces of the World's Art* which was to cost twenty dollars by the time it was complete, he thought it advisable to let the numbers accumulate at the store.

Whatever the place represented to their parents, it was pure joy to the young Murchisons. It offered a margin and a mystery to life. They saw it far larger than it was; they invested it, arguing purely by its difference from other habitations, with a romantic past. "I guess when the Prince of Wales came to Elgin, mother, he stayed here,"[7] Lorne remarked, as a little boy. Secretly he and Advena took up boards in more than one unused room, and rapped on more than one thick wall to find a hollow chamber; the house revealed so much that was interesting, it was apparent to the meanest understanding that it must hide even more. It was never half lighted, and there was a passage in which fear dwelt—wild were the gallopades from attic to cellar in the early nightfall, when every young Murchison tore after every other, possessed, like cats, by a demoniac ecstasy of the gloaming. And the garden, with the autumn moon coming over the apple trees and the neglected asparagus thick for ambush, and a casual untrimmed boy or two with the delicious recommendation of being utterly without credentials, to join in the rout and be trusted to make for the back fence without further hint at the voice of Mrs. Murchison—these were joys of the very fibre, things to push ideas and envisage life with an attraction that made it worth while to grow up.

And they had all achieved it—all six. They had grown up sturdily, emerging into sobriety and decorum by much the same degrees as the old house, under John Murchison's improving fortunes, grew cared for and presentable. The new roof went on, slate replacing shingles, the year Abby put her hair up; the bathroom was contemporary with Oliver's leaving school; the electric light was actually turned on for the first time in honour of Lorne's return from Toronto, a barrister and solicitor; several rooms had been done up for Abby's wedding. Abby had married, early and satisfactorily, Dr. Harry Johnson, who had placidly settled down to await the gradual succession of his father's practice; "Dr. Harry and Dr. Henry" they were called. Dr. Harry lived next door to Dr. Henry, and had a good deal of the old man's popular manner. It was an unacknowledged partnership, which often provided two opinions for the same price; the town prophesied well of it. That left only five at home, but they always had Abby over in the West Ward, where Abby's housekeeping made an interest and Abby's baby a point of pilgrimage. These considerations almost consoled Mrs. Murchison, declaring, as she did, that all of them might have gone but Abby, who alone knew how to be "any comfort or any dependence" in the house; who could be left with a day's preserving; and I tell you that to be left by Mrs. Murchison with a day's preserving, be it cherries or strawberries, damsons or pears, was a mark of confidence not easy to obtain. Advena never had it; Advena, indeed, might have married and removed no prop of the family economy. Mrs. Murchison would have been "sorry for the man"—she maintained a candour toward and about those belonging to her that permitted no illusions—but she would have stood cheerfully out of the way on her own account. When you have seen your daughter reach and pass the age of twenty-five without having learned properly to make her own bed, you know, without being told, that she will never be fit for the management of a house—don't you? Very well then. And for ever and for ever, no matter what there was to do, with a book in her hand—Mrs. Murchison would put an emphasis on the "book" which scarcely concealed a contempt for such absorption. And if, at the end of your patience, you told her for any sake to put it down and attend to matters, obeying in a kind of dream that generally drove you to take the thing out of her hands and do it yourself, rather than jump out of your skin watching her.

Sincerely Mrs. Murchison would have been sorry for the man if he had arrived, but he had not arrived. Advena justified her existence by taking the university course for women at Toronto, and afterward teaching the English branches to the junior forms in the Collegiate Institute, which placed her arbitrarily outside the sphere of domestic criticism.[8] Mrs. Murchison was thankful to have her there—outside—where little more could reasonably be expected of her than that she should be down in time for breakfast. It is so irritating to be justified in expecting more than seems likely to come. Mrs. Murchison's ideas circulated strictly in the orbit of equity and reason; she expected nothing from anybody that she did not expect from herself; indeed, she would spare others in far larger proportion. But the sense of obligation which led her to offer herself up to the last volt of her energy made her miserable when she considered that she was not fairly done by in return. Pressed down and running over were the services she offered to the general good, and it was on the ground of the merest justice that she required from her daughters "some sort of interest" in domestic affairs. From her eldest she got no sort of interest, and it was like the removal of a grievance from the hearth when Advena took up employment which ranged her definitely beyond the necessity of being of any earthly use in the house. Advena's occupation to some extent absorbed her shortcomings, which was much better than having to attribute them to her being naturally "through-other,"[9] or naturally clever, according to the bias of the moment. Mrs. Murchison no longer excused or complained of her daughter; but she still pitied the man.

"The boys," of course, were too young to think of matrimony. They were still the boys, the Murchison boys; they would be the boys at forty if they remained under their father's roof. In the mother country, men in short jackets and round collars emerge from the preparatory schools; in the daughter lands boys in tail coats conduct serious affairs. Alec and Oliver, in the business, were frivolous enough as to the feminine interest. For all Dr. Drummond's expressed and widely-known views upon the subject, it was a common thing for one or both of these young men to stray from the family pew on Sunday evenings to the services of other communions, thereafter to walk home in the dusk under the maples with some attractive young person, and be sedately invited to finish the evening on her father's verandah. Neither of them was guiltless of silk ties knitted or handkerchiefs initialled by certain fingers; without repeating scandal, one might say by various fingers. For while the ultimate import of these matters was not denied in Elgin, there was a general feeling against giving too much meaning to them, probably originating in a reluctance among heads of families to add to their responsibilities. These early spring indications were belittled and laughed at; so much so that the young people themselves hardly took them seriously, but regarded them as a form of amusement almost conventional. Nothing would have surprised or embarrassed them more than to learn that their predilections had an imperative corollary, that anything should, of necessity, "come of it." Something, of course, occasionally did come of it; and, usually after years of "attention," a young man of Elgin found himself mated to a young woman, but never under circumstances that could be called precipitate or rash. The cautious blood and far sight of the early settlers, who had much to reckon with, were still preponderant social characteristics of the town they cleared the site for. Meanwhile, however, flowers were gathered, and all sorts of evanescent idylls came and went in the relations of young men and maidens. Alec and Oliver Murchison were already in the full tide of them.

From this point of view they did not know what to make of Lorne. It was not as if their brother were in any way ill calculated to attract that interest which gave to youthful existence in Elgin almost the only flavour that it had. Looks are looks, and Lorne had plenty of them; taller by an inch than Alec, broader by two than Oliver, with a fine square head and blue eyes in it, and features which conveyed purpose and humour, lighted by a certain simplicity of soul that pleased even when it was not understood. "Open," people said he was, and "frank"—so he was, frank and open, with horizons and intentions; you could see them in his face. Perhaps it was more conscious of them than he was. Ambition, definitely shining goals, adorn the perspectives of young men in new countries less often than is commonly supposed. Lorne meant to be a good lawyer, squarely proposed to himself that the country should hold no better; and as to more selective usefulness, he hoped to do a little stumping for the right side when Frank Jennings ran for the Ontario House in the fall. It wouldn't be his first electioneering: from the day he became chairman of the Young Liberals the party had an eye on him, and when occasion arose, winter or summer, by bobsleigh or buggy, weatherbeaten local bosses would convey him to country school-houses for miles about to keep a district sound on railway policy, or education, or tariff reform. He came home smiling with the triumphs of these occasions, and offered them, with the slow, good-humoured, capable drawl that inspired such confidence in him, to his family at breakfast, who said "Great!" or "Good for you, Lorne!" John Murchison oftenest said nothing, but would glance significantly at his wife, frowning and pursing his lips when she, who had most spirit of them all, would exclaim, "You'll be Premier yet, Lorne!" It was no part of the Murchison policy to draw against future balances: they might believe everything, they would express nothing; and I doubt whether Lorne himself had any map of the country he meant to travel over in that vague future, already defining in local approbation, and law business coming freely in with a special eye on the junior partner. But the tract was there, sub-conscious, plain in the wider glance, the alerter manner; plain even in the grasp and stride which marked him in a crowd; plain, too, in the preoccupation with other issues, were it only turning over a leader in the morning's *Dominion*, that carried him along indifferent to the allurements I have described. The family had a bond of union in their respect for Lorne, and this absence of nugatory inclinations in him was among its elements. Even Stella, who, being just fourteen, was the natural mouthpiece of family sentiment, would declare that Lorne had something better to do than go hanging about after girls, and for her part she thought all the more of him for it.

Chapter IV

"I am requested to announce," said Dr. Drummond after the singing of the last hymn, "the death, yesterday morning, of James Archibald Ramsay, for fifteen years an adherent and for twenty-five years a member of this church. The funeral will take place from the residence of the deceased, on Court House Street, to- morrow afternoon at four o'clock. Friends and acquaintances are respectfully—invited—to attend."

The minister's voice changed with the character of its affairs. Still vibrating with the delivery of his sermon, it was now charged with the official business of the interment. In its inflections it expressed both elegy and eulogy; and in the brief pause before and after "invited" and the fall of "attend" there was the last word of comment upon the mortal term. A crispation of interest passed over the congregation; every chin was raised. Dr. Drummond's voice had a wonderful claiming power, but he often said he wished his congregation would pay as undivided attention to the sermon as they did to the announcements.

"The usual weekly prayer meeting will be held in the basement of the church on Wednesday evening." Then almost in a tone of colloquy, and with just a hint of satire about his long upper lip —

"I should be glad to see a better attendance of the young people at these gatherings. Time was when the prayer meeting counted among our young men and women as an occasion not to be lightly passed over. In these days it would seem that there is too much business to be done, or too much pleasure to be enjoyed, for the oncoming generation to remember their weekly engagement with the Lord. This is not as it should be; and I rely upon the fathers and mothers of this congregation, who brought these children in their arms to the baptismal font, there to be admitted to the good hopes and great privileges of the Church of God—I rely upon them to see that there shall be no departure from the good old rule, and that time is found for the weekly prayer meeting."

Mrs. Murchison nudged Stella, who returned the attention, looking elaborately uninterested, with her foot. Alec and Oliver smiled consciously; their father, with an expression of severe gravity, backed up the minister, who, after an instant's pause, continued—

"On Tuesday afternoon next, God willing, I shall visit the following families in the East Ward—Mr. Peterson, Mr. Macormack, Mrs. Samuel Smith, and Mr. John Flint. On Thursday afternoon in the South Ward, Mrs. Reid, Mr. P.C. Cameron, and Mr. Murchison. We will close by singing the Third Doxology:

> "Blessed, blessed be Jehovah,
> Israel's God to all eternity —"

The congregation trooped out; the Murchisons walked home in a clan, Mr. and Mrs. Murchison, with Stella skirting the edge of the side-walk beside them, the two young men behind. Abby, when she married Harry, had "gone over" to the Church of England. The wife must worship with the husband; even Dr. Drummond recognised the necessity, though he professed small opinion of the sway of the spouse who, with Presbyterian traditions behind her, could not achieve union the other way about; and Abby's sanctioned defection was a matter of rather shamefaced reference by her family. Advena and Lorne had fallen into the degenerate modern habit of preferring the evening service.

"So we're to have the Doctor on Thursday," said Mrs. Murchison, plainly not displeased. "Well, I hope the dining-room carpet will be down."

"I expect he'll be wanting his tea," replied Mr. Murchison. "He's got you in the right place on the list for that, mother—as usual."

"I'd just like to see him go anywhere else for his tea the day he was coming to our house," declared Stella. "But he *generally* has too much sense."

"You boys," said Mrs. Murchison, turning back to her sons, "will see that you're on hand that evening. And I hope the Doctor will rub it in about the prayer meeting." Mrs. Murchison chuckled. "I saw it went home to both of you, and well it might. Yes; I think I may as well expect him to tea. He enjoys my scalloped oysters, if I do say it myself."

"We'll get Abby over," said Mr. Murchison. "That'll please the Doctor."

"I must say," remarked Stella, "he seems to think a lot more of Abby now that she's Mrs. Episcopal Johnson."

"Yes, Abby and Harry must come," said Mrs. Murchison, "and I was thinking of inviting Mr. and Mrs. Horace Williams. We've been there till I'm ashamed to look them in the face. And I've pretty well decided," she added autocratically, "to have chicken salad. So if Dr. Drummond has made up his mouth for scalloped oysters he'll be disappointed."

"Mother," announced Stella, "I'm perfectly certain you'll have both."

"I'll consider it," replied her mother. "Meanwhile we would be better employed in thinking of what we have been hearing. That's the third sermon from the Book of Job in six weeks. I must say, with the whole of the two Testaments to select from, I don't see why the Doctor should be so taken up with Job."

Stella was vindicated; Mrs. Murchison did have both. The chicken salad gleamed at one end of the table and the scalloped oysters smoked delicious at the other. Lorne had charge of the cold tongue and Advena was entrusted with the pickled pears. The rest of the family were expected to think about the tea biscuits and the cake, for Lobelia had never yet had a successor that was any hand with company. Mrs. Murchison had enough to do to pour out the tea. It was a table to do anybody credit, with its glossy damask and the old-fashioned silver and best china that Mrs. Murchison had brought as a bride to her housekeeping—for, thank goodness, her mother had known what was what in such matters—a generous attractive table that you took some satisfaction in looking at. Mrs. Murchison came of a family of noted housekeepers; where she got her charm I don't know. Six o'clock tea, and that the last meal in the day, was the rule in Elgin, and a good enough rule for Mrs. Murchison, who had no patience with the innovation of a late dinner recently adopted by some people who could keep neither their servants nor their digestions in consequence. It had been a crisp October day; as Mr. Murchison remarked, the fall evenings were beginning to draw in early; everybody was glad of the fire in the grate and the closed curtains. Dr. Drummond had come about five, and the inquiries and comments upon family matters that the occasion made incumbent had been briskly exchanged, with just the word that marked the pastoral visit and the practical interest that relieved it. And he had thought, on the whole, that he might manage to stay to tea, at which Mrs. Murchison's eyes twinkled as she said affectionately—

"Now, Doctor, you know we could never let you off."

Then Abby had arrived and her husband, and finally Mr. and Mrs. Williams, just a trifle late for etiquette, but well knowing that it mustn't be enough to spoil the biscuits. Dr. Drummond, in the place of honour, had asked the blessing, and that brief reminder of the semi-official character of the occasion having been delivered, was in the best of humours. The Murchisons were not far wrong in the happy divination that he liked coming to their house. Its atmosphere appealed to him; he expanded in its humour, its irregularity, its sense of temperament. They were doubtful allurements, from the point of view of a minister of the Gospel, but it would not occur to Dr. Drummond to analyse them. So far as he was aware, John Murchison was just a decent, prosperous Christian man, on whose word and will you might depend, and Mrs. Murchison a stirring, independent little woman, who could be very good company when she felt inclined. As to their sons and daughters, in so far as they were a credit, he was as proud of them as their parents could possibly be, regarding himself as in a much higher degree responsible for the formation of their characters and the promise of their talents. And indeed, since every one of them had "sat under" Dr. Drummond from the day he or she was capable of sitting under anybody, Mr. and Mrs. Murchison would have been the last to dispute this. It was not one of those houses where a pastor could always be sure of leaving some spiritual benefit behind; but then he came away himself with a pleasant sense of nervous stimulus which was apt to take his mind off the matter. It is not given to all of us to receive or to extend the communion of the saints; Mr. and Mrs. Murchison were indubitably of the elect, but he was singularly close-mouthed about it, and she had an extraordinary way of seeing the humorous side—altogether it was paralysing, and the conversation would wonderfully soon slip round to some robust secular subject, public or domestic. I have mentioned Dr. Drummond's long upper lip; all sorts of racial virtues resided there, but his mouth was also wide and much frequented by a critical, humorous, philosophical smile which revealed a view of life at once kindly and trenchant. His shrewd grey eyes were encased in wrinkles, and when he laughed his hearty laugh they almost disappeared in a merry line. He had a fund of Scotch stories, and one or two he was very fond of, at the expense of the

Methodists, that were known up and down the Dominion, and nobody enjoyed them more than he did himself. He had once worn his hair in a high curl on his scholarly forehead, and a silvering tuft remained brushed upright; he took the old-fashioned precaution of putting cotton wool in his ears, which gave him more than ever the look of something highly-concentrated and conserved but in no way detracted from his dignity. St. Andrew's folk accused him of vanity because of the diamond he wore on his little finger. He was by no means handsome, but he was intensely individual; perhaps he had vanity; his people would have forgiven him worse things. And at Mrs. Murchison's tea party he was certainly, as John Murchison afterwards said, "in fine feather."

An absorbing topic held them, a local topic, a topic involving loss and crime and reprisals. The Federal Bank had sustained a robbery of five thousand dollars, and in the course of a few days had placed their cashier under arrest for suspected complicity. Their cashier was Walter Ormiston, the only son of old Squire Ormiston, of Moneida Reservation, ten miles out of Elgin, who had administered the affairs of the Indians there for more years than the Federal Bank had existed.[1] Mr. Williams brought the latest news, as was to be expected; news flowed in rivulets to Mr. Williams all day long; he paid for it, dealt in it, could spread or suppress it.

"They've admitted the bail," Mr. Williams announced, with an air of self-surveillance. Rawlins had brought the intelligence in too late for the current issue, and Mr. Williams was divided between his human desire to communicate and his journalistic sense that the item would be the main feature of the next afternoon's *Express*.

"I'm glad of that. I'm glad of that," repeated Dr. Drummond. "Thank you, Mrs. Murchison, I'll send my cup. And did you learn, Williams, for what amount?"

Mr. Williams ran his hand through his hair in the effort to remember, and decided that he might as well let it all go. The *Mercury* couldn't fail to get it by to-morrow anyhow.

"Three thousand," he said; "Milburn and Dr. Henry Johnson."

"I thought Father was bound to be in it," remarked Dr. Harry.

"Half and half?" asked John Murchison.

"No," contributed Mrs. Williams. "Mr. Milburn two and Dr.

Henry one. Mr. Milburn is Walter's uncle, you know."

Mr. Williams fastened an outraged glance on his wife, who looked another way. Whatever he thought proper to do, it was absolutely understood that she was to reveal nothing of what "came in," and was even carefully to conserve anything she heard outside with a view to bringing it in. Mrs. Williams was too prone to indiscretion in the matter of letting news slip prematurely; and as to its capture, her husband would often confess, with private humour, that Minnie wasn't much of a mouser.

"Well, that's something to be thankful for," said Mrs. Murchison. "I lay awake for two hours last night thinking of that boy in jail, and his poor old father, seventy-nine years of age, and such a fine old man, so thoroughly respected."

"I don't know the young fellow," said Dr. Drummond, "but they say he's of good character, not over-solid, but bears a clean reputation. They're all Tories together, of course, the Ormistons."

"It's an old U.E. Loyalist family," remarked Advena. "Mr. Ormiston has one or two rather interesting Revolutionary trophies at his house out there."

"None the worse for that. None the worse for that," said Dr. Drummond.

"Old Ormiston's father," contributed the editor of the *Express*, "had a Crown grant of the whole of Moncida Reservation at one time. Government actually bought it back from him to settle the Indians there. He was a well-known Family Compact man, and fought tooth and nail for the Clergy Reserves in 'fifty."[2]

"Well, well," said Dr. Drummond, with a twinkle. "We'll hope young Ormiston is innocent, nevertheless."

"Nasty business for the Federal Bank if he is," Mr. Williams went on. "They're a pretty unpopular bunch as it is."

"Of course he's innocent," contributed Stella, with indignant eyes; "and when they prove it, what can he do to the bank for taking him up? That's what I want to know."

Her elders smiled indulgently. "A lot you know about it, kiddiè," said Oliver. It was the only remark he made during the meal. Alec passed the butter assiduously, but said nothing at all. Adolescence was inarticulate in Elgin on occasions of ceremony.

"I hear they've piled up some big evidence," said Mr. Williams. "Young Ormiston's been fool enough to do some race-betting lately. Minnie, I wish you'd get Mrs. Murchison to show you how to pickle pears. Of course," he added, "they're keeping it up their sleeve."

"It's a hard place to keep evidence," said Lorne Murchison at last, with a smile which seemed to throw light on the matter. They had all been waiting, more or less consciously, for what Lorne would have to say.

"Lorne, you've got it!" divined his mother instantly.

"Got what, Mother?"

"The case! I've suspected it from the minute the subject was mentioned! That case came in to-day!"

"And you sitting there like a bump on a log, and never telling us!" exclaimed Stella, with reproach.

"Stella, you have a great deal too much to say," replied her brother. "Suppose you try sitting like a bump on a log. We won't complain. Yes, the Squire seems to have made up his mind about the defence, and my seniors haven't done much else to-day."

"Rawlins saw him hitched up in front of your place for about two hours this morning," said Mr. Williams. "I told him I thought that was good enough, but we didn't say anything, Rawlins having heard it was to be Flynn from Toronto. And I hadn't forgotten the Grand Trunk case we put down to you last week without exactly askin'. Your old man was as mad as a hornet—wanted to stop his subscription; Rawlins had no end of a time to get round him. Little things like that will creep in when you've got to trust to one man to run the whole local show. But I didn't want the *Mercury* to have another horse on us."

"Do you think you'll get a look in, Lorne?" asked Dr. Harry.

"Oh, not a chance of it. The old man's as keen as a razor on the case, and you'd think Warner never had one before! If I get a bit of grubbing to do, under supervision, they'll consider I ought to be pleased." It was the sunniest possible tone of grumbling; it enlisted your sympathy by its very acknowledgement that it had not a leg to stand on.

"They're pretty wild about it out Moneida way," said Dr. Harry. "My father says the township would put down the bail three times over."

"They swear by the Squire out there," said Mr. Horace Williams, liberally applying his napkin to his moustache. "He treated some of them more than square when the fall wheat failed three years running, about ten years back; do you remember, Mr. Murchison? Lent them money at about half the bank rate, and wasn't in an awful sweat about getting it in at that either."

"And wasn't there something about his rebuilding the school-house at his own expense not so long ago?" asked Dr. Drummond.

"Just what he did. I wanted to send Rawlins out and make a story of it—we'd have given it a column, with full heads; but the old man didn't like it. It's hard to know what some people will like. But it was my own foolishness for asking. A thing like that is public property."

"There's a good deal of feeling," said Lorne. "So much that I understand the bank is moving for change of venue."

"I hope they won't get it," said Dr. Drummond sharply. "A strong local feeling is valuable evidence in a case like this. I don't half approve this notion that a community can't manage its own justice when it happens to take an interest in the case. I've no more acquaintance with the Squire than 'How d'ye do?' and I don't know his son from Adam; but I'd serve on the jury to-morrow if the Crown asked it, and there's many more like me."

Mr. Williams, who had made a brief note on his shirt cuff, restored his pencil to his waistcoat pocket. "I shall oppose a change of venue," said he.

Chapter V

It was confidently expected by the Murchison family that when Stella was old enough she would be a good deal in society. Stella, without doubt, was well equipped for society; she had exactly those qualities which appealed to it in Elgin, among which I will mention two—the quality of being able to suggest that she was quite as good as anybody without saying so, and the even more important quality of not being any better. Other things being equal—those common worldly standards that prevailed in Elgin as well as anywhere else in their degree—other things being equal, this second simple quality was perhaps the most important of all. Mr. and Mrs. Murchison made no claim and small attempt upon society. One doubts whether, with children coming fast and hard times long at the door, they gave the subject much consideration; but if they did, it is highly unlikely to have occurred to them that they were too good for their environment. Yet in a manner they were. It was a matter of quality, of spiritual and mental fabric; they were hardly aware that they had it, but it marked them with a difference, and a difference is the one thing a small community, accustomed comfortably to scan its own intelligible averages, will not tolerate. The unusual may take on an exaggeration of these; an excess of money, an excess of piety, is understood; but idiosyncrasy susceptible to no common translation is regarded with the hostility earned by the white crow, modified, among law-abiding humans, into tacit repudiation. It is a sound enough social principle to distrust that which is not understood, like the strain of temperament inarticulate but vaguely manifest in the Murchisons. Such a strain may any day produce an eccentric or a genius, emancipated from the common interests, possibly inimical to the general good; and when, later on, your genius takes flight or your eccentric sells all that he has and gives it to the poor, his fellow townsmen exchange shrewd nods before the vindicating fact.

Nobody knew it at all in Elgin, but this was the Murchisons' case. They had produced nothing abnormal, but they had to prove that they weren't going to, and Stella was the last and most convincing demonstration. Advena, bookish and unconventional, was regarded with dubiety. She was out of the type; she had queer satisfactions and enthusiasms. Once as a little girl she had taken a papoose from a drunken squaw and brought it home for her mother to adopt. Mrs. Murchison's reception of the suggested duty may be imagined, also the comments of acquaintances—a trick like that! The inevitable hour arrived when she should be instructed on the piano, and the second time the music teacher came her pupil was discovered on the roof of the house, with the ladder drawn up after her. She did not wish to learn the piano, and from that point of vantage informed her family that it was a waste of money. She would hide in the hayloft with a novel; she would be off by herself in a canoe at six o'clock in the morning; she would go for walks in the rain of windy October twilights and be met kicking the wet leaves along in front of her "in a dream." No one could dream with impunity in Elgin, except in bed. Mothers of daughters sympathized in good set terms with Mrs. Murchison. "If that girl were mine—" they would say, and leave you with a stimulated notion of the value of corporal punishment. When she took to passing examinations and teaching, Elgin considered that her parents ought to be thankful in the probability that she had escaped some dramatic end. But her occupation further removed her from intercourse with the town's more exclusive circles: she had taken a definite line, and she pursued it, preoccupied. If she was a brand snatched from the burning, she sent up a little curl of reflection in a safe place, where she was not further interrupted.

Abby, inheriting all these prejudices, had nevertheless not done so badly; she had taken no time at all to establish herself; she had almost immediately married. In the social estimates of Elgin the Johnsons were "nice people," Dr. Henry was a fine old figure in the town, and Abby's chances were good enough. At all events, when she opened her doors as a bride, receiving for three afternoons in her wedding dress, everybody had "called." It was very distinctly understood, of course, that this was a civility that need not lead to anything whatever, a kind of bowing recognition, to be formally returned and quite possibly to end there. With Abby, in a good many cases, it hadn't ended there; she was doing very well, and as she often said with private satisfaction, if she went out anywhere she was just as likely as not to meet her brothers. Elgin society, shaping itself, I suppose, to ultimate increase and prosperity, had this peculiarity, that the females of a family, in general acceptance, were apt to lag far behind the males. Alec and Oliver enjoyed a good deal of popularity, and it was Stella's boast that if Lorne didn't go out much it needn't be supposed he wasn't asked. It was an accepted state of things in Elgin that young men might be invited without their sisters, implying an imperturbability greater than London's, since London may not be aware of the existence of sisters, while Elgin knew all sorts of more interesting things about them. The young men were more desirable than the young women; they forged ahead, carrying the family fortunes, and the "nicest" of them were the young men in the banks. Others might be more substantial, but there was an allure about a young man in a bank as difficult to define as to resist. To say of a certain party-giver that she had "about every bank clerk in town" was to announce the success of her entertainment in ultimate terms. These things are not always penetrable, but no doubt his gentlemanly form of labour and its abridgment in the afternoons, when other young men toiled on till the stroke of six, had something to do with this apotheosis of the bank clerk, as well as his invariable taste in tailoring, and the fact that some local family influence was probably represented in his appointment. Privilege has always its last little stronghold, and it still operates to admiration on the office stools of minor finance in towns like Elgin. At all events, the sprouting tellers and cashiers held unquestioned sway—young doctors and lawyers simply didn't think of competing; and since this sort of thing carries its own penalty, the designation which they shared with so many distinguished persons in history became a byword on the lips of envious persons and small boys, by which they wished to express effeminacy and the substantive of "stuck-up." "D'ye take me fur a bank clurk?" was a form of repudiation among corner loafers as forcible as it was unjustifiable.

I seem to have embarked, by way of getting to the Milburns' party—there is a party at the Milburns and some of us are going—upon an analysis of social principles in Elgin, an adventure of difficulty, as I have once or twice hinted, but one from which I cannot well extricate myself without at least leaving a clue or two more for the use of the curious. No doubt these rules had their nucleus in the half-dozen families, among whom we may count the shadowy Plummers, who took upon themselves for Fox County, by the King's pleasure, the administration of justice, the practice of medicine and of the law, and the performance of the charges of the Church of England a long time ago. Such persons would bring their lines of demarcation with them, and in their new *milieu* of backwoods settlers and small traders would find no difficulty in drawing them again. But it was a very long time ago. The little knot of gentry-folk soon found the limitations of their new conditions; years went by in decades, aggrandizing none of them. They took, perforce, to the ways of the country, and soon nobody kept a groom but the doctor, and nobody dined late but the Judge. There came a time when the Sheriff's whist club and the Archdeacon's port became a tradition to the oldest inhabitant. Trade flourished, education improved, politics changed. Her Majesty removed her troops—the Dominion wouldn't pay, a poor-spirited business[1]—and a bulwark went with the regiment. The original dignified group broke, dissolved, scattered. Prosperous traders foreclosed them, the spirit of the times defeated them, young Liberals succeeded them in office. Their grandsons married the daughters of well-to-do persons who came from the north of Ireland, the east of Scotland, and the Lord knows where. It was a sorry tale of disintegration with a cheerful sequel of rebuilding, leading to a little unavoidable confusion as the edifice went up. Any process of blending implies confusion to begin with; we are here at the making of a nation.[2]

This large consideration must dispose of small anomalies, such as the acceptance, without cant, of certain forms of the shop, euphemized as the store, but containing the same old vertebral counter. Not all forms. Dry goods were held in respect and chemists in comparative esteem; house furnishings and hardware made an appreciable claim, and quite a leading family was occupied with seed grains. Groceries, on the other hand, were harder to swallow, possibly on account of the apron, though the grocer's apron, being of linen, had several degrees more consideration than the shoemaker's, which was of leather; smaller trades made smaller pretensions; Mrs. Milburn could tell you where to draw the line. They were all hard-working folk together, but they had their little prejudices: the dentist was known as "Doc," but he was not considered quite on a medical level; it was doubtful whether you bowed to the piano-tuner, and quite a curious and unreasonable contempt was bound up in the word "veterinary." Anything "wholesale" or manufacturing stood, of course, on its own feet; there was nothing ridiculous in molasses, nothing objectionable in

a tannery, nothing amusing in soap. Such airs and graces were far
from Elgin, too fundamentally occupied with the amount of capital
invested, and too profoundly aware how hard it was to come by.
The valuable part of it all was a certain bright freedom, and this
was of the essence. Trade was a decent communal way of making
a living, rooted in independence and the general need; it had none
of the meaner aspects. Your bow was negligible to the piano-tuner,
and everything veterinary held up its head. And all this again
qualified, as everywhere, by the presence or absence of the social
faculty, that magnetic capacity for coming, as Mrs. Murchison
would say, "to the fore," which makes little of disadvantages that
might seem insuperable, and, in default, renders null and void the
most unquestionable claims. Any one would think of the Delarues.
Mr. Delarue had in the dim past married his milliner, yet the
Delarues were now very much indeed to the fore. And, on the
other hand, the Leverets of the saw mills, rich and benevolent; the
Leverets were not in society simply, if you analysed it, because
they did not appear to expect to be in it. Certainly it was well not
to be too modest; assuredly, as Mrs. Murchison said, you put your
own ticket on, though that dear soul never marked herself in very
plain figures; not knowing, perhaps, for one thing, quite how much
she was worth. On the other hand, "Scarce of company, welcome
trumpery," Mrs. Murchison always emphatically declared to be no
part of her social philosophy. The upshot was that the Murchisons
were confined to a few old friends and looked, as we know, half
humorously, half ironically, for more brilliant excursions, to Stella
and "the boys."

It was only, however, the pleasure of Mr. Lorne Murchison's
company that was requested at the Milburns' dance. Almost alone
among those who had slipped into wider and more promiscuous
circles with the widening of the stream, the Milburns had made
something like an effort to hold out. The resisting power was not
thought to reside in Mr. Milburn, who was personally aware of no
special ground for it, but in Mrs. Milburn and her sister, Miss
Filkin, who seemed to have inherited the strongest ideas, in the
phrase of the place, about keeping themselves *to* themselves. A
strain of this kind is sometimes constant, even so far from the
fountain head, with its pleasing proof that such views were once
the most general and the most sacred defence of middle-class

firesides, and that Thackeray had, after all, a good deal to excuse him. Crossing the Atlantic they doubtless suffered some dilution; but all that was possible to conserve them under very adverse conditions Mrs. Milburn and Miss Filkin made it their duty to do. Nor were these ideas opposed, contested, or much traversed in Elgin. It was recognized that there was "something about" Mrs. Milburn and her sister—vaguely felt that you did not come upon that thinness of nostril, and slope of shoulder, and set of elbow at every corner. They must have got it somewhere. A Filkin tradition prevailed, said to have originated in Nova Scotia: the Filkins never had been accessible, but if they wanted to keep to themselves, let them. In this respect Dora Milburn, the only child, was said to be her mother's own daughter. The shoulders, at all events, testified to it; and the young lady had been taught to speak, like Mrs. Milburn, with what was known as an "English accent." The accent in general use in Elgin was borrowed—let us hope temporarily—from the other side of the line. It suffered local modifications and exaggerations, but it was clearly an American product. The English accent was thought affected, especially the broad "a." The time may come when Elgin will be at considerable pains to teach itself the broad "a," but that is in the embroidery of the future, and in no way modifies the criticism of Dora Milburn.

Lorne Murchison, however, was invited to the dance. The invitation reached him through the post: coming home from office early on Saturday he produced it from his pocket. Mrs. Murchison and Abby sat on the verandah enjoying the Indian summer afternoon; the horse-chestnuts dropped crashing among the fallen leaves, the roadside maples blazed, the quiet streets ran into smoky purple, and one belated robin hopped about the lawn. Mrs. Murchison had just remarked that she didn't know why, at this time of year, you always felt as if you were waiting for something.

"Well, I hope you feel honoured," remarked Abby. Not one of them would have thought that Lorne should feel especially honoured; but the insincerity was so obvious that it didn't matter. Mrs. Murchison, cocking her head to read the card, tried hard not to look pleased.

"*Mrs. Milburn. At Home,*" she read. "*Dancing.*" Well, she might *be* at home dancing, for all me! Why couldn't she just write you a little friendly note, or let Dora do it? It's that Ormiston case," she went on shrewdly. "They know you're taking a lot of trouble about it. And the least they could do, too."

Lorne sat down on the edge of the verandah with his hands in his trousers pockets, and stuck his long legs out in front of him. "Oh, I don't know," he said. "They have the name of being nifty, but I haven't got anything against the Milburns."

"Name!" ejaculated Mrs. Murchison. "How long ago was it the Episcopalians began that sewing circle business for the destitute clergy of Saskatchewan?"

"Mother!" put in Abby, with deprecation.

"Well, I won't be certain about the clergy, but I tell you it had to do with Saskatchewan, for that I remember! And anyhow, the first meeting was held at the Milburns'—members lent their drawing-rooms. Well, Mrs. Leveret and Mrs. Delarue went to the meeting—they were very thick just then, the Leverets and the Delarues. They were so pleased to be going that they got there about five minutes too soon, and they were the first to come. Well, they rang the bell and in they went. The girl showed them into the front drawing-room and asked them to sit down. And there in the back drawing-room sat Mrs. Milburn and Miss Filkin, *and never spoke to them!* Their own denomination, mind you, too! And there they might have been sitting still if Mrs. Leveret hadn't had the spirit to get up and march out. No, thank you. No Milburns for me."

Lorne watched his mother with twinkling eyes till she finished.

"Well, mother, after that, if it was going to be a sewing circle I think I'd send an excuse," he said, "but maybe they won't be so mean at a dance."

Chapter VI

Octavius Milburn would not, I think, have objected to being considered, with relation to his own line in life, a representative man.[1] He would have been wary to claim it, but if the stranger had arrived unaided at this view of him, he would have been inclined to think well of the stranger's power of induction. That is what he was—a man of averages, balances, the safe level, no more disposed to an extravagant opinion than to wear one side whisker longer than the other. You would take him any day, especially on Sunday in a silk hat, for the correct medium: by his careful walk with the spring in it, his shrewd glance with the caution in it, his look of being prepared to account for himself, categorically, from head to foot. He was fond of explaining, in connection with an offer once made him to embark his capital in Chicago, that he preferred a fair living under his own flag to a fortune under the Stars and Stripes. There we have the turn of his mind, convertible into the language of book-keeping, a balance struck, with a profit on the side of the flag, the patriotic equivalent in good sound terms of dollars and cents. With this position understood, he was prepared to take you up on any point of comparison between the status and privileges of a subject and a citizen—the political *morale* of a monarchy and a republic—the advantage of life on this and the other side of the line. There was nothing he liked better to expatiate upon, with that valuable proof of his own sincerity always at hand for reference and illustration. His ideal was life in a practical, go-ahead, self-governing colony, far enough from England actually to be disabused of her inherited anachronisms and make your own tariff, near enough politically to keep your securities up by virtue of her protection. He was extremely satisfied with his own country; one saw in his talk the phenomenon of patriotism in double bloom, flower within flower. I have mentioned his side whiskers: he preserved that facial decoration of the Prince Consort; and the large steel engraving that represents Queen Victoria in a flowing habit and the Prince in a double-breasted frock coat and a stock, on horseback, hung over the mantlepiece in his drawing-room. If the outer patriotism was a little vague, the inner had vigour enough. Canada was a great place. Mr.

Milburn had been born in the country, and had never "gone over" to England; Canada was good enough for him. He was born, one might say, in the manufacturing interest, and inherited the complacent and Conservative political views of a tenderly-nourished industry. Mr. Milburn was of those who were building up the country; with sufficient protection he was prepared to go on doing it long and loyally; meanwhile he admired the structure from all points of view. As President of the Elgin Chamber of Commerce, he was enabled once a year to produce no end of gratifying figures; he was fond of wearing on such occasions the national emblem in a little enamelled maple leaf; and his portrait and biography occupied a full page in a sumptuous work entitled *Canadians of To-Day*, sold by subscription, wherein he was described as "the Father of the Elgin Boiler."

Mr. and Mrs. Milburn were in the drawing-room to receive their young guests, a circumstance which alone imparted a distinction to the entertainment. At such parties the appearance of the heads of the house was by no means invariable; frequently they went to bed. The simple explanation was that the young people could stand late hours and be none the worse next day; their elders had to be more careful if they wanted to get down to business. Moreover, as in all new societies, between the older and the younger generation there was a great gulf fixed, across which intercourse was difficult. The sons and daughters, born to different circumstances, evolved their own conventions, the old people used the ways and manners of narrower days; one paralysed the other. It might be gathered from the slight tone of patronage in the address of youth to age that the advantage lay with the former; but polite conversation, at best, was sustained with discomfort. Such considerations, however, were far from operating with the Milburns. Mrs. Milburn would have said that they were characteristic of quite a different class of people; and so they were.

No one would have supposed, from the way in which the family disposed itself in the drawing-room, that Miss Filkin had only just finished making the claret-cup, or that Dora had been cutting sandwiches till the last minute, or that Mrs. Milburn had been obliged to have a distinct understanding with the maid—Mrs. Milburn's servants were all "maids," even the charwoman, who had buried three husbands—on the subject of wearing a cap when she answered the door. Mrs. Milburn sat on a chair she had worked herself, occupied with something in the new stitch; Dora performed lightly at the piano; Miss Filkin dipped into *Selections from the Poets of the Century*, placed as remotely as possible from the others; Mr. Milburn, with his legs crossed, turned and folded a Toronto evening paper. Mrs. Milburn had somewhat objected to the evening paper in the drawing-room. "Won't you look at a magazine, Octavius?" she said; but Mr. Milburn advanced the argument that it removed "any appearance of stiffness," and prevailed. It was impossible to imagine a group more disengaged from the absurd fuss that precedes a party among some classes of people; indeed, when Mr. Lorne Murchison arrived—like the unfortunate Mrs. Leveret and Mrs. Delarue, he was the first—they looked almost surprised to see him.

Lorne told his mother afterwards that he thought, in that embarrassing circumstance, of Mrs. Leveret and Mrs. Delarue, and they laughed consumedly together over his discomfiture; but what he felt at the moment was not the humour of the situation. To be the very first and solitary arrival is nowhere esteemed the happiest fortune, but in Elgin a kind of ridiculous humiliation attached to it, a greed for the entertainment, a painful unsophistication. A young man of Elgin would walk up and down in the snow for a quarter of an hour with the thermometer at zero to escape the ignominy of it; Lorne Murchison would have so walked. Our young man was potentially capable of not minding, by next morning he didn't mind; but immediately he was fast tied in the cobwebs of the common prescription, and he made his way to each of the points of the compass of the Milburns' drawing-room to shake hands, burning to the ears. Before he subsided into a chair near Mr. Milburn he grasped the collar of his dress coat on each side and drew it forward, a trick he had with his gown in court, a nervous and mechanical action. Dora, who continued to play, watched him over the piano with an amusement not untinged with malice. She was a tall fair girl, with several kinds of cleverness. She did her hair quite beautifully, and she had a remarkable, effective, useful reticence. Her father declared that Dora took in a great deal more than she ever gave out—an accomplishment, in Mr. Milburn's eyes, on the soundest basis. She looked remarkably pretty and had remarkably good style, and as she proceeded with her mazurka she was thinking, "He has never been asked here before: how perfectly silly he must feel coming so early!" Presently as Lorne grew absorbed in talk and forgot his unhappy chance, she further reflected, "I don't think I've ever seen him till now in evening dress; it does make him a good figure." This

went on behind a faultless coiffure and an expression almost classical in its detachment; but if Miss Milburn could have thought on a
level with her looks, I, for one, would hesitate to take any liberty
with her meditations.

However, the bell began to ring with the briefest intermissions,
the maid in the cap to make constant journeys. She opened the door
with a welcoming smile, having practically no deportment to go
with the cap: human nature does not freeze readily anywhere. Dora
had to leave the piano; Miss Filkin decided that when fifteen had
come she would change her chair. Fifteen soon came, the young
ladies mostly in light silks or muslins cut square, not low, in the
neck, with half sleeves. This moderation was prescribed in Elgin,
where evening dress was more a matter of material than of cut, a
thing in itself symbolical if it were desirable to consider social
evolution here. For middle-aged ladies high necks and long sleeves
were usual; and Mrs. Milburn might almost have been expected to
appear thus, in a nicely-made black *broché*,[2] perhaps. It was recognized as like Mrs. Milburn, in keeping with her unbending ideas, to
wear a dress cut as square as any young lady's, with just a little lace
let in, of a lavender stripe. The young men were nearly all in the
tailor's convention for their sex the world over, with here and there
a short coat that also went to church; but there were some departures
from orthodoxy in the matter of collars and ties, and where white
bows were achieved, I fear none of the wearers would have dreamed
of defending them from the charge of being ready-made.

It was a clear, cold January night, and everybody, as usual,
walked to the party; the snow creaked and ground underfoot, one
could hear the arriving steps in the drawing-room. They stamped
and scraped to get rid of it in the porch, and hurried through the hall,
muffled figures in overshoes, to emerge from an upstairs bedroom
radiant, putting a last touch to hair or button hole, smelling of the
fresh winter air. Such gatherings usually consisted entirely of
bachelors and maidens, with one or two exceptions so recently
yoked together that they had not yet changed the plane of existence;
married people, by general consent, left these amusements to the
unculled. They had, as I have hinted, more serious pre-occupations,
"something else to do"; nobody thought of inviting them. Nobody,
that is, but Mrs. Milburn and a few others of her way of thinking,
who saw more elegance and more propriety in a mixture. On this
occasion she had asked her own clergyman, the pleasant-faced

rector of St. Stephen's, and Mrs. Emmett, who wore that pathetic expression of fragile wives and mothers who have also a congregation at their skirts. Walter Winter[3] was there, too. Mr. Winter had the distinction of having contested South Fox in the Conservative interest three times unsuccessfully. Undeterred, he went on contesting things: invariably beaten, he invariably came up smiling and ready to try again. His imperturbability was a valuable asset; he never lost heart or dreamed of retiring from the arena, nor did he ever cease to impress his party as being their most useful and acceptable representative. His business history was chequered and his exact financial equivalent uncertain, but he had tremendously the air of a man of affairs; as the phrase went, he was full of politics, the plain repository of deep things. He had a shrewd eye, a double chin, and a bluff, crisp, jovial manner of talking as he lay back in an arm-chair with his legs crossed and played with his watch chain, an important way of nodding assent, a weighty shake of denial. Voting on purely party lines, the town had lately rewarded his invincible expectation by electing him Mayor, and then provided itself with unlimited entertainment by putting in a Liberal majority on his council, the reports of the weekly sittings being constantly considered as good as a cake-walk.[4] South Fox, as people said, was not a healthy locality for Conservatives. Yet Walter Winter wore a look of remarkable hardiness. He had also tremendously the air of a dark horse, the result both of natural selection and careful cultivation. Even his political enemies took it kindly when he "got in" for Mayor, and offered him amused congratulations. He made a personal claim on their cordiality, which was not the least of his political resources. Nature had fitted him to public uses; the impression overflowed the ranks of his own supporters and softened asperity among his opponents. Illustration lies, at this moment, close to us. They had not been in the same room a quarter of an hour before he was in deep and affectionate converse with Lorne Murchison, whose party we know, and whose political weight was increasing, as this influence often does, with a rapidity out of proportion with his professional and general significance.

"It's a pity now," said Mr. Winter, with genial interest, "you can't get that Ormiston defence into your own hands. Very useful thing for you."

The younger man shifted a little uncomfortably in his seat. It is one thing to entertain a private vision and another to see it materialized on other lips.

"Oh, I'd like it well enough," he said, "but it's out of the question, of course. I'm too small potatoes."

"There's a lot of feeling for old Ormiston. Folks out there on the Reserve don't know how to show it enough."

"They've shown it a great deal too much. We don't want to win on 'feeling,' or have it said either. And we were as near as possible having to take the case to the Hamilton Assizes."

"I guess you were—I guess you were." Mr. Winter's suddenly increased gravity expressed his appreciation of the danger. "I saw Lister of the Bank the day they heard from Toronto—rule refused. Never saw a man more put out. Seems they considered the thing as good as settled. General opinion was it would go to Hamilton, sure. Well, I don't know how you pulled it off, but it was a smart piece of work, sir."

Lorne encountered Mr. Winter's frank smile with an expression of crude and rather stolid discomfort. It had a base of indignation, corrected by a concession to the common idea that most events, with an issue pendent, were the result of a smart piece of work: a kind of awkward shrug was in it. He had no desire to be unpleasant to Walter Winter—on the contrary. Nevertheless, an uncompromising line came on each side of his mouth with his reply.

"As far as I know," he said, "the application was dismissed on its demerits."

"Of course it was," said Mr. Winter good-humouredly. "You don't need to tell me that. Well, now, this looks like dancing. Miss Filkin, I see, is going to oblige on the piano. Now I wonder whether I'm going to get Miss Dora to give me a waltz or not."

Chairs and tables were in effect being pushed back, and folding doors opened which disclosed another room prepared for this relaxation. Miss Filkin began to oblige vigorously on the piano, Miss Dora granted Mr. Winter's request, which he made with elaborate humour as an impudent old bachelor whom "the boys" would presently take outside and kill. Lorne watched him make it, envying him his assurance; and Miss Milburn was aware that he watched and aware that he envied. The room filled with gaiety and movement: Mr. Milburn, sidling dramatically along the wall to escape the rotatory couples, admonished Mr. Murchison to get a partner. He withdrew himself from the observation of Miss Dora and Mr. Winter, and approached a young lady on a sofa, who said "With very great pleasure." When the dance was over he re-established the young lady on the sofa, and fanned her with energy. Looking across the room, he saw that Walter Winter, seated beside Dora, was fanning himself. He thought it disgusting and, for some reason which he did not pause to explore, exactly like Winter. He had met Miss Milburn once or twice before without seeing her in any special way: here, at home, the centre of the little conventions that at once protected and revealed her, conventions bound up in the impressive figures of her mother and her aunt, she had a new interest, and all the attraction of that which is not easily come by. It is also possible that although Lorne had met her before, she had not met him; she was meeting him now for the first time, as she sat directly opposite and talked very gracefully to Walter Winter. Addressing Walter Winter, Lorne was the object of her pretty remarks. While Mr. Winter had her superficial attention, he was the bland medium which handed her on. Her consciousness was fixed on young Mr. Murchison, quite occupied with him: she could not imagine why they had not asked him long ago; he wasn't exactly "swell," but you could see he was somebody. So already she figured the potential distinction in the set of his shoulders and the carriage of his head. It might have been translated in simple terms of integrity and force by any one who looked for those things. Miss Milburn was incapable of such detail, but she saw truly enough in the mass.

Lorne, on the opposite sofa, looked at her across all the town's traditions of Milburn exclusiveness. Oddly enough, at this moment, when he might have considered that he had overcome them, they seemed to gather force, exactly in his line of vision. He had never before been so near Dora Milburn, and he had never before perceived her so remote. He had a sense of her distance beyond those few yards of carpet quite incompatible with the fact. It weighed upon him, but until she sent him a sudden unexpected smile he did not know how heavily. It was a dissipating smile; nothing remained before it. Lorne carefully restored his partner's fan, bowed before her, and went straight across the room.

Chapter VII

It is determined with something like humour that communities very young should occupy themselves almost altogether with matters of grave and serious import. The vision of life at that period is no doubt unimpeded and clear; its conditions offer themselves with a certain nakedness and force, both as to this world and to that which is to come. The town of Elgin thus knew two controlling interests—the interest of politics and the interest of religion. Both are terms we must nevertheless circumscribe. Politics wore a complexion strictly local, provincial, or Dominion. The last step of France in Siam, the disputed influence of Germany in the Persian Gulf, the struggle of the Powers in China were not matters greatly talked over in Elgin; the theatre of European diplomacy had no absorbed spectators here. Nor can I claim that interest in the affairs of Great Britain was in any way extravagant.

A sentiment of affection for the reigning house certainly prevailed. It was arbitrary, rococo, unrelated to current conditions as a tradition sung down in a ballad, an anachronism of the heart, cherished through long rude lifetimes for the beauty and poetry of it—when you consider, beauty and poetry can be thought of in this. Here was no Court aiding the transmutation of the middle class, no King spending money; here were no picturesque contacts of Royalty and the people, no pageantry, no blazonry of the past, nothing to lift the heart but an occasional telegram from the monarch expressing, upon an event of public importance, a suitable emotion.[1] Yet the common love for the throne amounted to a half-ashamed enthusiasm that burned with something like a sacred flame, and was among the things not ordinarily alluded to, because of the shyness that attaches to all feeling that cannot be justified in plain terms.[2] A sentiment of affection for the reigning house certainly prevailed; but it was a thing by itself. The fall of a British Government would hardly fail to excite comment, and the retirement of a Prime Minister would induce both the *Mercury* and the *Express* to publish a biographical sketch of him, considerably shorter than the leader embodying the editor's views as to who should get the electric light contract. But the Government might become the sole employer of labour in those islands, Church and school might part company for ever, landlords might be deprived of all but compassionate allowances, and, except for the degree of extravagance involved in these propositions, they would hardly be current in Elgin. The complications of England's foreign policy were less significant still. It was recognized dimly that England had a foreign policy, more or less had to have it, as they would have said in Elgin; it was part of the huge unnecessary scheme of things for which she was responsible—unnecessary from Elgin's point of view as a father's financial obligations might be to a child he had parted with at birth. It all lay outside the facts of life, far beyond the actual horizon, like the affairs of a distant relation from whom one has nothing to hope, not even personal contact, and of whose wealth and greatness one does not boast much, because of the irony involved. Information upon all these matters was duly put before Elgin every morning in the telegrams of the Toronto papers; the information came, until the other day, over cables to New York and was disseminated by American news agencies. It was, therefore, not devoid of bias; but if this was perceived it was by no means thought a matter for protesting measures, especially as they would be bound to involve expense. The injury was too vague, too remote, to be more than sturdily discounted by a mental attitude. Belief in England was in the blood, it would not yield to the temporary distortion of facts in the newspapers—at all events, it would not yield with a rush. Whether there was any chance of insidious sapping was precisely what the country was too indifferent to discover. Indifferent, apathetic, self-centred—until whenever, down the wind, across the Atlantic, came the faint far music of the call to arms. Then the old dog of war that has his kennel in every man rose and shook himself, and presently there would be a baying! The sense of kinship, lying too deep for the touch of ordinary circumstance, quickened to that; and in a moment "we" were fighting, "we" had lost or won.[3]

Apart, however, from the extraordinary, the politics of Elgin's daily absorption were those of the town, the Province, the Dominion. Centres of small circumference yield a quick swing; the concern of the average intelligent Englishman as to the consolidation of his country's interests in the Yangtse Valley would be a languid manifestation beside that of an Elgin elector in the chances of an appropriation for a new court house. The single mind is the most fervid: Elgin had few distractions from the question of the

court house or the branch line to Clayfield. The arts conspired to
be absent; letters resided at the nearest university city; science was
imported as required, in practical improvements. There was
nothing, indeed, to interfere with Elgin's attention to the immediate, the vital, the municipal: one might almost read this concentration of interest in the white dust of the rambling streets, and the
shutters closed against it. Like other movements of the single
mind, it had something of the ferocious, of the inflexible, of the
unintelligent; but it proudly wore the character of the go-ahead,
and, as Walter Winter would have pointed out to you, it had
granted eleven bonuses to "capture" sound commercial concerns
in six years.

In wholesome fear of mistake, one would hesitate to put church
matters either before or after politics among the preoccupations of
Elgin. It would be safer and more indisputable to say that nothing
compared with religion but politics, and nothing compared with
politics but religion. In offering this proposition also we must
think of our dimensions. There is a religious fervour in Oxford, in
Mecca, in Benares, and the sign for these ideas is the same; we
have to apply ourselves to the interpretation. In Elgin religious
fervour was not beautiful, or dramatic, or self-immolating; it was
reasonable. You were perhaps your own first creditor; after that
your debt was to your Maker. You discharged this obligation in a
spirit of sturdy equity: if the children didn't go to Sunday school
you knew the reason why. The habit of church attendance was not
only a basis of respectability, but practically the only one: a person
who was "never known to put his head inside a church door" could
not be more severely reprobated, by Mrs. Murchison at all events.
It was the normal thing, the thing which formed the backbone of
life, sustaining to the serious, impressive to the light, indispensable
to the rest, and the thing that was more than any of these, which
you can only know when you stand in the churches among the
congregations. Within its prescribed limitations it was for many
the intellectual exercise, for more the emotional lift, and for all the
unfailing distraction of the week. The repressed magnetic excitement in gatherings of familiar faces, fellow beings bound by the
same convention to the same kind of behaviour, is precious in
communities where the human interest is still thin and sparse. It is
valuable in itself, and it produces an occasional detached sensa-

tion. There was the case, in Dr. Drummond's church, of placid-faced, saintly old Sandy MacQuhot, the epileptic. It used to be a common regret with Lorne Murchison that as sure as he was allowed to stay away from church Sandy would have a fit. That was his little boy's honesty; the elders enjoyed the fit and depre-cated the disturbance.

There was a simple and definite family feeling within commu-nions. "They come to our church" was the argument of first force whether for calling or for charity. It was impossible to feel toward a Congregationalist or an Episcopalian as you felt toward one who sang the same hymns and sat under the same admonition week by week, year in and year out, as yourself. "Wesleyans, are they?" a lady of Knox Church would remark of the newly arrived, in whom her interest was suggested. "Then let the Wesleyans look after them." A pew-holder had a distinct status; an "adherent" enjoyed friendly consideration, especially if he adhered faithfully; and stray attendants from other congregations were treated with punctilious hospitality, places being found for them in the Old Testament, as if they could hardly be expected to discover such things for themselves. The religious interest had also the strongest domestic character in quite another sense from that of the family prayers which Dr. Drummond was always enjoining. "Set your own house in order and then your own church" was a wordless working precept in Elgin. Threadbare carpet in the aisles was almost as personal a reproach as a hole under the dining-room table; and self-respect was barely possible to a congregation that sat in faded pews. The minister's gown even was the subject of scrutiny as the years went on. It was an expensive thing to buy, but an oyster supper would do it and leave something over for the organ. Which brings us to the very core and centre of these activities, their pivot, their focus, and, in a human sense, their inspiration—the minister himself.

The minister was curiously special among a people so general; he was in a manner raised in life on week-days as he was in the pulpit on Sundays. He had what one might call prestige; some form of authority still survived in his person, to which the spiritual democracy he presided over gave a humorous, voluntary assent. He was supposed to be a person of undetermined leisure—what was writing two sermons a week to earn your living by?—and he was probably the more reverend, or the more revered, from the fact that he was in the house all day. A particular importance attached to everything he said and did; he was a person whose life answered different springs, and was sustained on quite another principle than that of supply and demand. The province of public criticism was his; but his people made up for the meekness with which they sat under it by a generous use of the corresponding privilege in private. Comments upon the minister partook of hardiness; it was as if the members were determined to live up to the fact that the office-bearers could reduce his salary if they liked. Needless to say, they never did like. Congregations stood loyally by their pastors, and discussion was strictly intramural. If the Methodists handed theirs on at the end of three years with a breath of relief, they exhaled it among themselves; after all, for them it was a matter of luck. The Presbyterians, as in the case of old Mr. Jamieson of St. Andrew's, held on till death, pulling a long upper lip: election was not a thing to be trifled with in heaven or upon earth.

It will be imagined whether Dr. Drummond did not see in these conditions his natural and wholesome element, whether he did not fit exactly in. The God he loved to worship as Jehovah had made him a beneficent despot, and given him, as it were, a commission. If the temporal power had charged him to rule an eastern province, he would have brought much the same qualities to the task. Knox Church, Elgin, was his dominion, its moral and material affairs his jealous interest, and its legitimate expansion his chief pride. In "anniversary" sermons, which he always announced the Sunday before, he seldom refrained from contrasting the number on the roll of church membership then and now, with the particular increase in the year just closed. If the increase was satisfactory, he made little comment beyond the duty of thanksgiving—figures spoke for themselves. If it was otherwise Dr. Drummond's displeasure was not a thing he would conceal. He would wing it eloquently on the shaft of his grief that the harvest had been so light; but he would more than hint the possibility that the labourers had been few. Most important among his statistics was the number of young communicants. Wanderers from other folds he admitted, with a not wholly satisfied eye upon their early theological training, and to persons duly accredited from Presbyterian churches elsewhere he gave the right hand of fellowship; but the young people of his own congregation were his chief concern always, and if a gratifying number of these had failed to "come forward" during the year, the responsibility must lie somewhere. Dr. Drummond was willing to take his own share; "the ministrations of this pulpit" would be more than suspected of having come short, and the admission would enable him to tax the rest upon parents and Bible-class teachers with searching effect. The congregation would go gloomily home to dinner, and old Sandy MacQuhot would remark to his wife, "It's hard to say why will the Doctor get himself in sic a state aboot mere numbers. We're told 'where two or three are gathered together.' But the Doctor's all for a grand congregation."

Knox Church, under such auspices, could hardly fail to enlarge her borders; but Elgin enlarged hers faster.[4] Almost before you knew where you were there spread out the district of East Elgin, all stacks of tall chimneys and rows of little houses. East Elgin was not an attractive locality; it suffered from inundation sometimes, when the river was in spring flood; it gave unresentful room to a tannery. It was the home of dubious practices at the polls, and the invariable hunting ground for domestic servants. Nevertheless, in the view of Knox Church, it could not bear a character wholly degraded; too many Presbyterians, Scotch foremen and others, had their respectable residence there. For these it was a far cry to Dr. Drummond in bad weather, and there began to be talk of hiring the East Elgin schoolhouse for Sunday exercises if suitable persons could be got to come over from Knox Church and lead them. I do not know who was found to broach the matter to Dr. Drummond; report says his relative and housekeeper, Mrs. Forsyth, who perhaps might do it under circumstances of strategical advantage. Mrs. Forsyth, or whoever it was, had her reply in the hidden terms of an equation—was it any farther for the people of East Elgin to walk to hear him preach than for him to walk to minister to the people of East Elgin, which he did quite once a week, and if so, how much? Mrs. Forsyth, or whoever it was, might eliminate the unknown quantity. It cannot be said that Dr. Drummond discouraged the project; he simply did not mention it, and as it was known to have been communicated to him, this represented effectively the policy of the closed door. He found himself even oftener in East Elgin, walking about on his pastoral errands with a fierce briskness of aspect and a sharp inquiring eye, before which one might say

the proposition slunk away. Meanwhile, the Methodists, who, it
seemed, could tolerate decentralization, or anything short of round
dances, opened a chapel with a cheerful sociable, and popularized
the practice of backsliding among those for whom the position was
theologically impossible. Good Presbyterians in East Elgin began
to turn into makeshift Methodists. The Doctor missed certain
occupants of the gallery seats and felt the logic of circumstances.
Here we must all yield, and the minister concealed his discomfiture in a masterly initiative. The matter came up again at a meeting
of the church managers, brought up by Dr. Drummond, who had
the satisfaction of hearing that a thing put into the Doctor's hands
was already half done. In a very few weeks it was entirely done.
The use of the school-house was granted, through Dr. Drummond's influence with the Board, free of charge; and to understand the triumph of this it should be taken into account that three
of the trustees were Wesleyans. Services were held regularly,
certain of Dr. Drummond's elders officiating; and the conventicle
in the school-house speedily became known as Knox Church
Mission. It grew and prospered. The first night "I to the hills will
lift mine eyes" went up from East Elgin on the uplifting tune that
belongs to it, the strayed came flocking back.

This kind never go forth again; once they re-find the ark of the
covenant there they abide. In the course of time it became a
question of a better one, and money was raised locally to build it.
Dr. Drummond pronounced the first benediction in Knox Mission
Church, and waited, well knowing human nature in its Presbyterian aspect, for the next development. It came, and not later than
he anticipated, in the form of a prayer to Knox Church for help to
obtain the services of a regularly ordained minister. Dr. Drummond had his guns ready: he opposed the application; where a
regularly ordained minister was already at the disposal of those
who chose to walk a mile and a half to hear him, the luxury of
more locally consecrated services should be at the charge of the
locality. He himself was willing to spend and be spent in the
spiritual interests of East Elgin; that was abundantly proven; what
he could not comfortably tolerate was the deviation of congrega-
tional funds, the very blood of the body of belief, into other than
legitimate channels. He fought for his view with all his tactician's
resources, putting up one office-bearer after another to endorse it,

but the matter was decided at the general yearly meeting of the congregation; and the occasion showed Knox Church in singular sympathy with its struggling offspring. Dr. Drummond, for the first time in his ministry, was defeated by his people. It was less a defeat than a defence, an unexpected rally round the corporate right to direct corporate activities; and the congregation was so anxious to wound the minister's feelings as little as possible that the grant in aid of the East Elgin Mission was embodied in a motion to increase Dr. Drummond's salary by two hundred and fifty dollars a year. The Doctor, with a wry joke, swallowed his gilded pill, but no coating could dissimulate its bitterness, and his chagrin was plain for long. The issue with which we are immediately concerned is that three months later Knox Church Mission called to minister to it the Reverend Hugh Finlay, a young man from Dumfriesshire and not long out. Dr. Drummond had known beforehand what their choice would be. He had brought Mr. Finlay to occupy Knox Church pulpit during his last July and August vacation, and Mrs. Forsyth had reported that such midsummer congregations she had simply never worshipped with. Mrs. Forsyth was an excellent hand at pressed tongue and a wonder at knitted counterpanes, but she had not acquired tact and never would.

Chapter VIII

The suggestion that the Reverend Hugh Finlay preached from the pulpit of Knox Church "better sermons" than its permanent occupant, would have been justly considered absurd, and nobody pronounced it. The church was full, as Mrs. Forsyth observed, on these occasions; but there were many other ways of accounting for that. The Murchisons, as a family, would have been the last to make such an admission. The regular attendance might have been, as much as anything, out of deference to the wishes of the Doctor himself, who invariably and sternly hoped, in his last sermon, that no stranger occupying his place would have to preach to empty pews. He was thinking, of course, of old Mr. Jamieson, with whom he occasionally exchanged, and whose effect on the attendance had not failed to reach him. With regard to Mr. Jamieson he was compelled, in the end, to resort to tactics: he omitted to announce the Sunday before that his venerable neighbour would preach, and the congregation, outwitted, had no resource but to sustain the beard-wagging old gentleman through seventhly[1] to the finish. There came a time when the dear human Doctor also omitted to announce that Mr. Finlay would preach, but for other reasons. Meanwhile, as Mrs. Forsyth said, he had no difficulty in conjuring a vacation congregation for his young substitute. They came trooping, old and young. Mr. and Mrs. Murchison would survey their creditable family rank with a secret compunction, remembering its invariable gaps at other times, and then resolutely turn to the praise of God with the reflection that one means to righteousness was as blessed as another. They themselves never missed a Sunday, and as seldom failed to remark on the way back that it was all very interesting, but Mr. Finlay couldn't drive it home like the Doctor. There were times, sparse and special occasions, when the Doctor himself made one of the congregation. Then he would lean back luxuriously in the corner of his own pew, his wiry little form half lost in the upholstery, his arms folded, his knees crossed, his face all humorous indulgence; yes, humorous. At the announcement of the text a twinkle would lodge in the shrewd grey eyes and a smile but half suppressed would settle about the corners of the flexible mouth: he knew what the young

fellow there would be at.[2] And as the young fellow proceeded, his
points would be weighed to the accompaniment of the Doctor's
pendent foot, which moved perpetually, judiciously; while the
smile sometimes deepened, sometimes lapsed, since there were
moments when any young fellow had to be taken seriously. It was
an attitude which only the Doctor was privileged to adopt thus
outwardly; but in private it was imitated all up and down the
aisles, where responsible heads of families sat considering the
quality of the manna that was offered them. When it fell from the
lips of Mr. Finlay the verdict was, upon the whole, very favourable, as long as there was no question of comparison with the
Doctor.

There could be, indeed, very little question of such comparison. There was a generation between them and a school, and to
that you had to add every set and cast of mind and body that can
make men different. Dr. Drummond, in faith and practice, moved
with precision along formal and implicit lines; his orbit was established, and his operation within it as unquestionable as the simplest exhibit of nature. He took in a wonderful degree the stamp of
the teaching of his adolescent period; not a line was missing nor
a precept; nor was the mould defaced by a single wavering tendency of later date.[3] Religious doctrine was to him a thing for ever
accomplished, to be accepted or rejected as a whole. He taught
eternal punishment and retribution, reconciling both with Divine
love and mercy; he liked to defeat the infidel with the crashing
question, "Who then was the architect of the Universe?" The
celebrated among such persons he pursued to their death-beds;
Voltaire and Rousseau owed their reputation, with many persons
in Knox Church, to their last moments and to Dr. Drummond. He
had a triumphant invective which drew the mind from chasms in
logic, and a tender sense of poetic beauty which drew it, when he
quoted great lines, from everything else. He loved the euphony of
the Old Testament; his sonorous delivery would lift a chapter from
Isaiah to the height of ritual, and every Psalm he read was a
Magnificat whether he would or no. The warrior in him was happy
among the Princes of Issachar; and the parallels he would find for
modern events in the annals of Judah and of Israel were astound-
ing. Yet he kept a sharp eye upon the daily paper, and his reference to current events would often give his listeners an audacious
sense of up-to-dateness which might have been easily discounted

by the argument they illustrated. The survivors of a convulsion of
nature, for instance, might have learned from his lips the cause and
kind of their disaster traced back forcibly to local acquiescence in
iniquity, and drawn unflinchingly from the text, "Vengeance is
mine; I will repay, saith the Lord." The militant history of his
Church was a passion with him; if ever he had to countenance
canonization he would have led off with Jenny Geddes.[4] "A
tremendous Presbyterian" they called him in the town. To hear
him give out a single psalm, and sing it with his people, would
convince anybody of that. There was a choir, of course, but to the
front pews, at all events, Dr. Drummond's leading was more
important than the choir's. It was a note of dauntless vigour, and
it was plain by the regular forward jerk of his surpliced shoulder
that his foot was keeping time:

> "Where the assemblies of the just
> And congregations are."[5]

You could not help admiring, and you could not help respect-
ing; you were compelled by his natural force and his unqualified
conviction, his tireless energy and his sterling sort.

It is possible to understand, however, that after sitting for
twenty-five years under direction so unfailing and so uncompromising, the congregation of Knox Church might turn with a
moderate curiosity to the spiritual indications of the Reverend
Hugh Finlay. He was a passionate romantic, and his body had shot
up into a fitting temple for such an inhabitant as his soul. He was
a great long fellow, with a shock of black hair and deep dreams in
his eyes; his head was what people called a type, a type I suppose
of the simple motive and the noble intention, the detached point of
view and the somewhat indifferent attitude to material things, as
it may be humanly featured anywhere. His face bore a confusion
of ideals; he had the brow of a Covenanter and the mouth of Adonais,[6] the flame of religious ardour in his eyes and the composure
of perceived philosophy on his lips. He was fettered by an
impenetrable shyness; it was in the pulpit alone that he could expand, and then only upon written lines, with hardly a gesture, and
the most perfunctory glances, at conscientious intervals, towards
his hearers. A poor creature, indeed, in this respect, Dr. Drum-

mond thought him—Dr. Drummond, who wore an untrammeled surplice which filled like an agitated sail in his quick tacks from right to left. "The man loses half his points," said Dr. Drummond. I doubt whether he did, people followed so closely, though Sandy MacQuhot was of the general opinion when he said that it would do nobody any harm if Mr. Finlay would lift his head oftener from the book.

Advena Murchison thought him the probable antitype of an Oxford don. She had never seen an Oxford don, but Mr. Finlay wore the characteristics these schoolmen were dressed in by novelists; and Advena noted with delight the ingenuity of fate in casting such a person into the pulpit of the Presbyterian Church in a young country. She had her perception of comedy in life; till Finlay came she had found nothing so interesting. With his arrival, however, other preoccupations fell into their proper places.

Finlay, indeed, it may be confessed at once, he, and not his message, was her engrossment from the beginning. The message she took with reverent gentleness; but her passionate interest was for the nature upon which it travelled, and never for the briefest instant did she confuse these emotions. Those who write, we are told, transcribe themselves in spite of themselves; it is more true of those who preach, for they are also candid by profession, and when they are not there is the eye and the voice to help to betray them. Hugh Finlay, in the pulpit, made himself manifest in all the things that matter to Advena Murchison in the pew; and from the pew to the pulpit her love went back with certainty, clear in its authority and worshipping the ground of its justification. When she bowed her head it was he whom she heard in the language of his invocations; his doctrine rode, for her, on a spirit of wide and sweet philosophy; in his contemplation of the Deity she saw the man. He had those lips at once mobile, governed and patient, upon which genius chooses oftenest to rest. As to this, Advena's convictions were so private as to be hidden from herself; she never admitted that she thought Finlay had it, and in the supreme difficulty of proving anything else we may wisely accept her view. But he had something, the subtle Celt; he had horizons, lifted lines beyond the common vision, and an eye rapt and a heart intrepid; and though for a long time he was unconscious of it, he must have adventured there with a happier confidence because of her companionship.

From the first Advena knew no faltering or fluttering, none of the baser nervous betrayals. It was all one great delight to her, her discovery and her knowledge and her love of him. It came to her almost in a logical development; it found her grave, calm, and receptive. She had even a private formula of gratitude that the thing which happened to everybody, and happened to so many people irrelevantly, should arrive with her in such a glorious, defensible, demonstrable sequence. Toward him it gave her a kind of glad secret advantage; he was loved and he was unaware. She watched his academic awkwardness in church with the inward tender smile of the eternal habile feminine, and when they met she could have laughed and wept over his straitened sentences and his difficult manner, knowing how little significant they were. With his eyes upon her and his words offered to her intelligence, she found herself treating his shy formality as the convention it was, a kind of make-believe which she would politely and kindly play up to until he should happily forget it and they could enter upon simpler relations. She had to play up to it for a long time, but her love made her wonderfully clever and patient; and of course the day came when she had her reward. Knowing him as she did, she remembered the day and the difference it made.

It was toward the end of an afternoon in early April; the discoloured snow still lay huddled in the bleaker fence corners. Wide puddles stood along the roadsides, reflecting the twigs and branches of the naked maples; last year's leaves were thick and wet underfoot, and a soft damp wind was blowing. Advena was on her way home and Finlay overtook her. He passed her at first, with a hurried silent lifting of his hat; then perhaps the deserted street gave a suggestion of unfriendliness to his act, or some freshness in her voice stayed him. At all events, he waited and joined her, with a word or two about their going in the same direction; and they walked along together. He offered her his companionship, but he had nothing to say; the silence in which they pursued their way was no doubt to him just the embarrassing condition he usually had to contend with. To her it seemed pregnant, auspicious; it drew something from the low grey lights of the wet spring afternoon and the unbound heart-lifting wind; she had a passionate prevision that the steps they took together would lead somehow to freedom. They went on in that strange bound way, and the day drew away from them till they turned a sudden corner, when it lay all along the yellow sky across the river, behind a fringe of winter woods, stayed in the moment of its retreat on the edge of the unvexed landscape. They stopped involuntarily to look, and she saw a smile come up from some depth in him.

"Ah, well," he said, as if to himself, "it's something to be in a country where the sun still goes down with a thought of the primeval."

"I think I prefer the sophistication of chimney-pots," she replied. "I've always longed to see a sunset in London, with the fog breaking over Westminster."

"Then you don't care about them for themselves, sunsets?" he asked, with the simplest absence of mind.

"I never yet could see the sun go down,
But I was angry in my heart."

she said, and this time he looked at her.

"How does it go on?" he said.

"Oh, I don't know. Only those two lines stay with me. I feel it that way, too. It's the seal upon an act of violence, isn't it, a sunset? Something taken from us against our will. It's a hateful reminder, in the midst of our delightful volitions, of how arbitrary every condition of life is."

"The conditions of business are always arbitrary. Life is a business—we have to work at ourselves till it is over. So much cut off and ended it is," he said, glancing at the sky again. "If space is the area of life and time is its opportunity, there goes a measure of opportunity."

"I wonder," said Advena, "where it goes?"

"Into the void behind time?" he suggested, smiling straight at her.

"Into the texture of the future," she answered, smiling back.

"We might bring it to bear very intelligently on the future, at any rate," he returned. "The world is wrapped in destiny, and but revolves to roll it out."

"I don't remember that," she said curiously.

"No, you couldn't," he laughed outright. "I haven't thought it good enough to publish."

"And it isn't the sort of thing," she ventured gaily, "you could put in a sermon."

"No, it isn't." They came to a corner of the street which led to Mr. Finlay's boarding-house. It stretched narrowly to the north and there was a good deal more snow on each side of it. They lingered together for a moment talking, seizing the new joy in it, which was simply the joy of his sudden liberation with her, consciously pushing away the moment of parting; and Finlay's eyes rested once again on the evening sky beyond the river.

"I believe you are right, and I am a moralizer," he said. "There *is* pain over there. One thinks a sunset beautiful and impressive, but one doesn't look at it long."

Then they separated, and he took the road to the north, which was still snowbound, while she went on into the chilly yellow west, with the odd sweet illusion that a summer day was dawning.

Chapter IX

The office of Messrs. Fulke, Warner, & Murchison was in Market Street, exactly over Scott's drug store. Scott, with his globular blue and red and green vessels in the window and his soda-water fountain inside, was on the ground floor; the passage leading upstairs separated him from Mickie, boots and shoes; and beyond Mickie, Elgin's leading tobacconist shared his place of business with a barber. The last two contributed most to the gaiety of Market Street: the barber with the ribanded pole, which stuck out at an angle; the tobacconist with a nobly-featured squaw in chocolate effigy, who held her draperies under her chin with one hand and outstretched a packet of cigars with the other.

The passage staircase between Scott's and Mickie's had a hardened look, and bore witness to the habit of expectoration; ladies, going up to Dr. Simmons, held their skirts up and the corners of their mouths down. Dr. Simmons was the dentist: you turned to the right. The passage itself turned to the left, and after passing two doors bearing the law firm's designation in black letters on ground glass, it conducted you with abruptness to the office of a bicycle agent, and left you there. For greater emphasis the name of the firm of Messrs. Fulke, Warner, & Murchison was painted on the windows also; it could be seen from any part of the market square, which lay, with the town hall in the middle, immediately below. During four days in the week the market square was empty. Odds and ends of straw and paper blew about it; an occasional pedestrian crossed it diagonally for the short cut to the post-office; the town hall rose in the middle, and defied you to take your mind off the ugliness of municipal institutions. On the other days it was a scene of activity. Farmers' wagons, with the shafts turned in, were ranged round three sides of it; on a big day they would form into parallel lanes and cut the square into sections as well. The produce of all Fox County filled the wagons, varying agreeably as the year went round. Bags of potatoes leaned against the side-walk, apples brimmed in bushel measures, ducks dropped their twisted necks over the cart wheels; the town hall, in this play of colour, stood redeemed. The produce was mostly left to the women to sell. On the fourth side of the square loads of hay and cordwood demanded the master mind, but small matters of fruit, vegetables, and poultry submitted to feminine judgment. The men "unhitched," and went away on their own business; it was the wives you accosted, as they sat in the middle, with their knees drawn up and their skirts tucked close, vigilant in rusty bonnets, if you wished to buy. Among them circulated the housewives of Elgin, pricing and comparing and acquiring; you could see it all from Dr. Simmons' window, sitting in his chair that screwed up and down. There was a little difficulty always about getting things home; only very ordinary people carried their own marketing. Trifling articles, like eggs or radishes, might be smuggled into a brown wicker basket with covers, but it did not consort with elegance to "trapse" home with anything that looked inconvenient or had legs sticking out of it. So that arrangements of mutual obligation had to be made: the good woman from whom Mrs. Jones had bought her tomatoes would take charge of the spring chickens Mrs. Jones had bought from another good woman just as soon as not, and deliver them at Mrs. Jones's residence, as under any circumstances she was "going round that way."

It was a scene of activity but not of excitement, or in any sense of joy. The matter was of too hard an importance; it made too much difference on both sides whether potatoes were twelve or fifteen cents a peck. The dealers were laconic and the buyers anxious; country neighbours exchanged the time of day, but under the pressure of affairs. Now and then a lady of Elgin stopped to gossip with another; the countrywomen looked on, curious, grim, and a little contemptuous of so much demonstration and so many words. Life on an Elgin market day was a serious presentment even when the sun shone, and at times when it rained or snowed the aesthetic seemed a wholly unjustifiable point of view. It was not misery, it was even a difficult kind of prosperity, but the margin was small and the struggle plain. Plain, too, it was that here was no enterprise of yesterday, no fresh broken ground of dramatic promise, but a narrow inheritance of the opportunity to live which generations had grasped before. There were bones in the village graveyards of Fox County to father all these sharp features; Elgin market square, indeed, was the biography of Fox County, and, in little, the history of the whole Province. The heart of it was there, the enduring heart of the new country already old in acquiescence. It was the deep root of the race in the land, twisted and unlovely, but holding the promise of all. Something like that Lorne Murchison felt about it as he stood for a moment in the passage I have mentioned and looked across the road. The spectacle never failed to cheer him; he was uniformly in gayer spirits, better satisfied with life and more consciously equal to what he had to do, on days when the square was full than on days when it was empty. This morning he had an elation of his own; it touched everything with more vivid reality. The familiar picture stirred a joy in him in tune with his private happiness; its under-note came to him with a pang as keen. The sense of kinship surged in his heart; these were his people, this his lot as well as theirs. For the first time he saw it in detachment. Till now he had regarded it with the friendly eyes of a participator who looked no further. To-day he did look further: the whole world invited his eyes, offering him a great piece of luck to look through. The opportunity was in his hand, which, if he could seize and hold, would lift and carry him on. He was as much aware of its potential significance as any one could be, and what leapt in his veins till he could have laughed aloud was the splendid conviction of resource. Already in the door of the passage he had achieved; and from that point he looked at the scene before him with an impulse of loyalty and devotion. A tenderness seized him for the farmers of Fox County, a throb of enthusiasm for the idea they represented, which had become for him suddenly moving and pictorial. At that moment his country came subjectively into his possession; great and helpless it came into his inheritance as it comes into the inheritance of every man who can take it, by deed of imagination and energy and love. He held this microcosm of it, as one might say, in his hand and looked at it ardently; then he took his way across the road.

A tall thickly-built young fellow detached himself from a group, smiling broadly at the sight of Murchison, and started to meet him.

"Hello, Lorne," he said. He had smiled all the way, anticipating the encounter. He was obviously in clothes which he did not put on every day, but the seriousness of this was counteracted by his hard felt hat, which he wore at an angle that disregarded convention.

"Hello, Elmore! You back?"

"That's about it."

"You don't say! Back to stay?"

"Far's I can see. Young Alf's made up his mind to learn the dentist business, and the old folks are backin' him; so I don't see but I've got to stop on and run the show. Father's gettin' up in years now."

"Why, yes. I suppose he must be. It's a good while since you went West. Well, what sort of a country have they got out Swan River way? Booming right along?"

"Boom nothing. I don't mean to say there's anything the matter with the country; there ain't; but you've got to get up just as early in the mornings out there as y'do anywhere, far's I noticed. An' it's a lonesome life. Now I *am* back I don't know but little old Ontario's good enough for me. 'N I hear you've taken up the law, Lorne. Y'always had a partiality for it, d'y' remember, up there to the Collegiate? I used to think it'd be fine to travel with samples, those days. But you were dead gone on the law. 'N by all reports it pans out pretty well, don't it?"

The young men had taken their way among the shifting crowd together. Lorne Murchison, although there was something too large about him for the town's essential stamp, made by contrast as he threaded the desultory groups of country people, a type of the conventional and the formed; his companion glanced at him now and then with admiration. The values of carriage and of clothes are relative: in Fifth Avenue Lorne would have looked countrified, in Piccadilly colonial. Districts are imaginable, perhaps not in this world, where the frequenters of even those fashionable thoroughfares would attract glances of curiosity by their failure to achieve the common standard in such things. Lorne Murchison, to dismiss the matter, was well up to the standard of Elgin, though he wore his straw hat quite on the back of his head and buried both hands in his trouser pockets. His eye was full of pleasant easy familiarity with the things he saw, and ready to see larger things; it had that beam of active inquiry, curious but never amazed, that marks the man likely to expand his horizons. Meanwhile he was on capital terms with his little world, which seemed to take pleasure in hailing him by his Christian name; even morose Jim Webster, who had failed three times in groceries, said "Morning, Lorne," with a look of toleration. He moved alertly, the poise of his head was sanguine; the sun shone on him, the timidest soul came nearer to him. He and Elmore Crow, who walked beside him, had gone through the lower forms of the Elgin Collegiate Institute together, that really "public"[1] kind of school which has so much to do with reassorting the classes of a new country. The Collegiate Institute took in raw material and turned out teachers, more teachers than anything. The teachers taught, chiefly in rural districts where they could save money, and with the money they saved changed themselves into doctors, Fellows of the University, mining engineers. The Collegiate Institute was a potential melting-pot: you went in as your simple opportunities had made you; how you shaped coming out depended upon what was hidden in the core of you. You could not in any case be the same as your father before you; education in a new country is too powerful a stimulant for that, working upon material too plastic and too hypothetical; it is not yet a normal force, with an operation to be reckoned on with confidence. It is indeed the touchstone for character in a new people, for character acquired as apart from that inherited; it some-times reveals surprises. Neither Lorne Murchison nor Elmore Crow illustrate this point very nearly. Lorne would have gone into the law in any case, since his father was able to send him, and Elmore would inevitably have gone back to the crops since he was early defeated by any other possibility. Nevertheless, as they walk together in my mind along the Elgin market square, the Elgin Collegiate Institute rises infallibly behind them, a directing influ-ence and a responsible parent. Lorne was telling his great news.

"You don't say!" remarked Elmore in response to it. "Lum-bago is it? Pa's subject to that too; gets an attack most springs. Mr. Fulke'll have to lay right up—it's the only thing."

"I'm afraid he will. And Warner never appeared in court in his life."

"What d'ye keep Warner for, then?"

"Oh, he does the conveyancing.[2] He's a good conveyancer, but he isn't any pleader and doesn't pretend to be. And it's too late to transfer the case; nobody could get to the bottom of it as we have in the time. So it falls on me."

"Caesar, his ghost! How d'ye feel about it, Lorne? I'd be scared green. Y'don't *talk* nervous. Now I bet you get there with both feet."

"I hope to get there," the young lawyer answered; and as he spoke a concentration came into his face which drove the elation and everything else that was boyish out of it. "It's bigger business than I could have expected for another five years. I'm sorry for the old man, though—*he's* nervous, if you like. They can hardly keep him in bed. Isn't that somebody beckoning to you?"

Elmore looked everywhere except in the right direction among the carts. If you had been "to the Collegiate," relatives among the carts selling squashes were embarrassing.

"There," his companion indicated.

"It's mother," replied Mr. Crow, with elaborate unconcern; "but I don't suppose she's in anything of a hurry. I'll just go along with you far's the post-office." He kept his glance carefully from the spot at which he was signalled, and a hint of copper colour crawled up the back of his neck.

"Oh, but she is. Come along, Elmore; I can go that way."

"It'll be longer for you."

"Not a bit." Lorne cast a shrewd glance at his companion. "And as we're passing you might just introduce me to your mother, see?"

"She won't expect it, Lorne."

"That's all right, my son. She won't refuse to meet a friend of yours." He led the way as he spoke to the point of vantage occupied by Mrs. Crow, followed, with plain reluctance, by her son. She was a frail-looking old woman, with a knitted shawl pinned tightly across her chest, and her bonnet, in the course of commercial activity, pushed so far back as to be almost falling off.

"You might smarten yourself with that change, Elmore," she addressed him, ignoring his companion. "There's folks coming back for it. Two-dollar bill, wa'n't it? Fifty cents—seventy-five—dollar'n a half. That's a Yankee dime, an' you kin march straight back with it. They don't pass but for nine cents, as you're old enough to know. Keep twenty-five cents for your dinner—you'll get most for the money at the Barker House[3]—an' bring me back another quarter. Better go an' get your victuals now—it's gone twelve—while they're hot."

Elmore took his instructions without visible demur; and then, as Lorne had not seen fit to detach himself, performed the ceremony of introduction. As he performed it he drew one foot back and bowed himself, which seemed obscurely to facilitate it. The suspicion faded out of Mrs. Crow's tired old sharp eyes under the formula, and she said she was pleased to make our friend's acquaintance.

"Mr. Murchison's changed some since the old days at the Collegiate," Elmore explained, "but he ain't any different under his coat. He's practisin' the law."

"Lawyers," Mrs. Crow observed, "are folks I like to keep away from."

"Quite right, too," responded Lorne, unabashed. "And so you've got my friend here back on the farm, Mrs. Crow?"

"Well, yes, he's back on the farm, an' when he's wore out his Winnipeg clothes and his big ideas, we're lookin' to make him some use." Mrs. Crow's intention, though barbed, was humorous, and her son grinned broadly.

"There's more money in the law," he remarked, "once you get a start. Here's Mr. Murchison goin' to run the Ormiston case; his old man's down sick, an' I guess it depends on Lorne now whether Ormiston gets off or goes to penitentiary."

Mrs. Crow's face tied itself up into criticism as she looked our young man up and down. "Depends upon you, does it?" she commented. "Well, all I've got to say is it's a mighty young dependence. Coming on next week, ain't it? You won't be much older by then. Yes'm," she turned to business, "I don't say but what it's high for rhubarb, but there ain't another bunch in the market, and won't be for a week yet."

Under cover of this discussion Lorne bade the Crows good morning, retreating in the rear of the lady who found the rhubarb high. Mrs. Crow's drop of acid combined with his saving sense of the humour of it to adjust all his courage and his confidence, and with a braver face than ever he involuntarily hastened his steps to keep pace with his happy chance.

Chapter X

In the wide stretches of a new country there is nothing to bound a local excitement, or to impede its transmission at full value. Elgin was a manufacturing town in southern Ontario, but they would have known every development of the Federal Bank case at the North Pole if there had been anybody there to learn. In Halifax they did know it, and in Vancouver, B.C., while every hundred miles nearer it warmed as a topic in proportion. In Montreal the papers gave it headlines; from Toronto they sent special reporters. Of course, it was most of all the opportunity of Mr. Horace Williams, of the *Elgin Express*, and of Rawlins, who held all the cards in their hands, and played them, it must be said, admirably, reducing the *Mercury* to all sorts of futile expedients to score, which the *Express* would invariably explode with a guffaw of contradiction the following day. It was to the *Express* that the Toronto reporters came for details and local colour; and Mr. Williams gave them just as much as he thought they ought to have and no more. It was the *Express* that managed, while elaborately abstaining from improper comment upon a matter sub judice, to feed and support the general conviction of young Ormiston's innocence, and thereby win for itself, though a "Grit" paper, wide reading in that hotbed of Toryism, Moneida Reservation, while the Conservative *Mercury*, with its reckless sympathy for an old party name, made itself criminally liable by reviewing cases of hard dealing by the bank among the farmers, and only escaped prosecution by the amplest retraction and the most contrite apology. As Mr. Williams remarked, there was no use in dwelling on the unpopularity of the bank, *that* didn't need pointing out; folks down Moneida way could put any newspaper wise on the number of mortgages foreclosed and the rate for secondary loans exacted by the bank in those parts. That consideration, no doubt, human nature being what it is, contributed the active principle to the feeling so widely aroused by the case. We are not very readily the prey to emotions of faith in our fellows, especially, perhaps, if we live under conditions somewhat hard and narrow; the greater animosity behind is, at all events, valuable to give force and relief and staying power to a sentiment of generous conviction. But however we may depreciate its origin, the conviction was there, widespread in the townships; young Ormiston would "get clear"; the case for the defence might be heard over every bushel of oats in Elgin market-place.

In Elgin itself opinion was more reserved. There was a general view that these bank clerks were fast fellows, and a tendency to contrast the habits and the pay of such dashing young men; an exercise which ended in a not unnatural query. As to the irritating caste feeling maintained among them, young Ormiston perhaps gave himself as few airs as any. He was generally conceded indeed by the judging sex to be "nice to everybody"; but was not that exactly the nature for which temptations were most easily spread? The town, moreover, had a sapience of its own. Was it likely that the bank would bring a case so publicly involving its character and management without knowing pretty well what it was about? The town would not be committed beyond the circle of young Ormiston's intimate friends, which was naturally small if you compared it with the public; the town wasn't going to be surprised at anything that might be proved. On the other hand, the town was much more vividly touched than the country by the accident which had made Lorne Murchison practically sole counsel for the defence, announced as it was by the *Express* with every appreciation of its dramatic value. Among what the *Express* called "the farming community" this, in so far as it had penetrated, was regarded as a simple misfortune, a dull blow to expectancy, which expectancy had some work to survive. Elgin, with its finer palate for sensation, saw in it heightened chances, both for Lorne and for the case; and if any ratepayer within its limits had remained indifferent to the suit, the fact that one side of it had been confided to so young and so "smart" a fellow townsman would have been bound to draw him into the circle of speculation. Youth in a young country is a symbol wearing all its value. It stands not only for what it is. The trick of augury invests it, at a glance, with the sum of its possibilities, the augurs all sincere, confident, and exulting. They have been justified so often; they know, in their wide fair fields of opportunity, just what qualities will produce what results. There is thus a complacence among adolescent peoples which is vaguely irritating to their elders; but the greybeards need not be over-captious; it is only a question of time, pathetically shortlived in the history of the race. Sanguine persons in Elgin were freely disposed to "bet on" Lorne Murchison, and there were none so despondent as to take the view that he would not come out of it, somehow, with an added personal significance. To make a spoon is a laudable achievement, but it may be no mean business to spoil a horn.

As the *Express* put it, there was as little standing room for ladies and gentlemen in the courthouse the first day of the Spring Assizes as there was for horses in the Court House Square. The County Crown Attorney was unusually, oddly, reinforced by Cruickshank, of Toronto—the great Cruickshank, K.C., probably the most distinguished criminal lawyer in the Province. There were those who considered that Cruickshank should not have been brought down, that it argued undue influence on the part of the bank, and his retainer was a fierce fan to the feeling in Moneida; but there is no doubt that his appearance added all that was possible to the universal interest in the case. Henry Cruickshank was an able man, and, what was rarer, a fastidious politician. He had held office in the Dominion Cabinet, and had resigned it because of a difference with his colleagues in the application of a principle; they called him, after a British politician of lofty but abortive views, the Canadian Renfaire.[1] He had that independence of personality, that intellectual candour, and that touch of magnetism which combine to make a man interesting in his public relations. Cruickshank's name alone would have filled the courthouse, and people would have gone away quoting him.

From the first word of the case for the prosecution there was that in the leading counsel's manner—a gravity, a kindness, an inclination to neglect the commoner methods of scoring—that suggested, with the sudden chill of unexpectedly bad news, a foregone conclusion. The reality of his feeling reference to the painful position of the defendant's father, the sincerity of his regret, on behalf of the bank, for the deplorable exigency under which proceedings had been instituted, spread a kind of blankness through the court; men frowned thoughtfully, and one or two ladies shed furtive tears. Even the counsel for the defence, it was afterward remembered, looked grave, sympathetic, and concerned, in response to the brief but significant and moving sentences with which his eminent opponent opened the case. It is not my duty to report the trial for any newspaper; I will therefore spare myself more than the most general references; but the facts undoubtedly were that a safe in the strong room of the bank had been opened between certain hours on a certain night and its contents abstracted; that young Ormiston, cashier of the bank, was sleeping, or supposed to be sleeping, upon the premises at this time, during the illness of the junior whose usual duty it was; and that the Crown was in possession of certain evidence which would be brought forward to prove collusion with the burglary on the part of the defendant, collusion to cover deficits for which he could be held responsible. In a strain almost apologetic, Mr. Cruickshank explained to the jury the circumstances which led the directors to the suspicion which they now believed only too regrettably well founded. These consisted in the fact that the young man was known to be living beyond his means, and so to be constantly visited by the temptation to such a crime; the special facilities which he controlled for its commission, and, in particular, the ease and confidence with which the actual operation had been carried out, arguing no fear of detection on the part of the burglars, no danger of interference from one who should have stood ready to defend with his life the property in his charge, but who would shortly be seen to have been toward it, first, a plunderer in his own person, and afterward the accomplice of plunderers to conceal his guilt. Examination showed the safe to have been opened with the dexterity that demands both time and coolness; and the ash from a pipe knocked out against the wall at the side of the passage offered ironical testimony to the comfort in which the business had been done.

The lawyer gave these considerations their full weight, and it was in dramatic contrast with the last of them that he produced the first significant fragment of evidence against Ormiston. There had been after all some hurry of departure. It was shown by a sheet of paper bearing the mark of a dirty thumb and a hasty boot-heel, bearing also the combination formula for opening the safe.[2]

The public was familiar with that piece of evidence, it had gone through every kind of mill of opinion; it made no special sensation. The evidence of the caretaker who found the formula and of the witnesses who established it to be in young Ormiston's handwriting, produced little interest. Mr. Cruickshank in elaborating his theory as to why, with the formula in their hands, the depredators still found it necessary to pick the lock, offered nothing to speculations already current—the duplicate key with which they had doubtless been enabled to supply themselves was a clumsy copy and had failed them; that conclusion had been drawn commonly enough. The next scrap of paper produced by the prosecution was another matter. It was the mere torn end of a greasy sheet; upon it was written "Not less than 3,000 net," and it had been found in the turning out of Ormiston's dressing-table. It might have been anything—a number of people pursed their lips contemptuously—or it might have been, without doubt, the fragment of a disreputable transaction that the prosecuting counsel endeavoured to show it. Here, no doubt, was one of the pieces of evidence the prosecution was understood to have up its sleeve, and that portion of the prosecuting counsel's garment was watched with feverish interest for further disclosures. They came rapidly enough, but we must hurry them even more. The name of Miss Florence Belton, when it rose to the surface of the evidence, riveted every eye and ear. Miss Belton was one of those ambiguous ladies who sometimes drift out from the metropolitan vortex and circle restfully in backwaters for varying periods, appearing and disappearing irrelevantly. They dress beautifully; they are known to "paint" and thought to dye their hair. They establish no relations, being much too preoccupied, making exceptions only, as a rule, in favour of one or two young men, to whom they extend amenities based—it is the common talk—upon late hours and whisky-and-soda. They seem superior to the little prevailing conventions; they excite an unlawful interest; though nobody knows them black, nobody imagines them white; and when they appear upon Main Street in search of shoelaces or elastic, heads are turned and nods, possibly nudges, exchanged. Miss Belton had come from New York to the Barker House, Elgin, and young Ormiston's intimacy with her was one of the things that counted against him in the general view. It was to so count more seriously in the particular instance. Witnesses were called to prove that he had spent the evening of the burglary with Miss Belton at her hotel, that he had remained with her until one o'clock, that he was in the habit of spending his evenings with Miss Belton.

Rawlins of the *Express* did not overdo the sensation which was caused in the court-room when the name of this lady herself was called to summon her to the witness-box. It was indeed the despair of his whole career. He thought despondingly ever after of the thrill, to which he himself was not superior, and which, if he had only been able to handle it adequately, might have led him straight up the ladder to a night editorship. Miss Belton appeared from some unsuspected seat near the door, throwing back a heavy veil, and walking as austerely as she could, considering the colour of her hair. She took her place without emotion, and there she corroborated the evidence of the servants of the hotel. To the grave questions of the prosecution she fluently replied that the distraction of these evenings had been cards—cards played, certainly, for money, and that she, certainly, had won very considerable sums from the defendant from time to time. In Elgin the very mention of cards played for money will cause a hush of something deeper than disapproval; there was silence in the court at this. In producing several banknotes for Miss Belton's identification Mr. Cruickshank seemed to profit by the silence. Miss Belton identified them without hesitation, as she might easily, since they had been traced to her possession. Asked to account for them, she stated, without winking, that they had been paid to her by Mr. Walter Ormiston at various times during the fortnight preceding the burglary, in satisfaction of debts at cards. She, Miss Belton, had left Elgin for Chicago the day after the burglary. Mr. Ormiston knew that she was going. He had paid her the four fifty-dollar notes actually traced, the night before she left, and said, "You won't need to break these here, will you?" He seemed anxious that she should not, but it was the merest accident that she hadn't. In all, she had received from Mr. Ormiston four hundred and fifty dollars. No, she had no suspicion that the young man might not be in a position to make such payments. She understood that Mr. Ormiston's family was wealthy, and never thought twice about it.

She spoke with a hard dignity, the lady, and a great effect of doing business, a kind of assertion of the legitimate. The farmers of Fox County told each other in chapfallen appreciation that she was about as level-headed as they make them. Lawyer Cruickshank, as they called him, brought forth from her detail after detail, and every detail fitted damningly with the last. The effect upon young Ormiston was so painful that many looked another way. His jaw was set and his features contorted to hold himself from the disgrace of tears. He was generally acknowledged to be overwhelmed by the unexpected demonstration of his guilt, but distress was so plain in him that there was not a soul in the place that was not sorry for him. In one or two resolute faces hope still glimmered, but it hardly survived the cross-examination of the Crown's chief witness by the counsel for the defence, which, as far as it went, had a perfunctory air and contributed little to the evidence before the Court. It did not go all the way, however. The case having opened late, the defence was reserved till the following day, when proceedings would be resumed with the further cross-examination of Miss Belton.

As the defendant's counsel went down the courthouse steps Rawlins came up to him to take note of his demeanour and anything else that might be going.

"Pretty stiff row to hoe you've got there, Lorne," he said.

"Pretty stiff," responded Lorne.

Chapter XI

Imagination, one gathers, is a quality dispensed with of necessity in the practice of most professions, being that of which nature is, for some reason, most niggardly. There is no such thing as passing in imagination for any department of public usefulness, even the government of Oriental races;[1] the list of the known qualified would be exhausted, perhaps, in getting the papers set. Yet neither poet nor philosopher enjoys it in monopoly; the chemist may have it, and the inventor must; it has been proved the mainspring of the mathematician, and I have hinted it the property of at least two of the Murchisons. Lorne was indebted to it certainly for his constructive view of his client's situation, the view which came to him and stayed with him like a chapter in a novel, from the hour in which Ormiston had reluctantly accounted for himself upon the night of the burglary. It was a brilliant view, that perceived the young clerk the victim of the conspiracy he was charged with furthering; its justification lay back, dimly, among the intuitions about human nature which are part of the attribute I have quoted. I may shortly say that it was justified; another day's attendance at the Elgin Courthouse shall not be compulsory here, whatever it may have been there. Young Ormiston's commercial probity is really no special concern of ours; the thing which does matter, and considerably, is the special quality which Lorne Murchison brought to the task of its vindication, the quality that made new and striking appeal, through every channel of the great occasion, to those who heard him. It was that which reinforced and comforted every friend Ormiston had in the court-room, before Lorne proceeded either to deal with the evidence of the other side, or to produce any jot or tittle of his own; and it was that which affected his distinguished opponent to the special interest which afterwards showed itself so pleasantly superior to the sting of defeat. The fact that the defence was quite as extraordinarily indebted to circumstantial evidence as the prosecution in no way detracted from the character of Lorne's personal triumph; rather, indeed, in the popular view and Rawlins's, enhanced it. There was in it the primitive joy of seeing a ruffian knocked down with his own illegitimate weapons, from the moment the dropped formula

was proved to be an old superseded one, and unexpected indication was produced that Ormiston's room, as well as the bank vault,
had been entered the night of the robbery, to the more glorious
excitement of establishing Miss Belton's connection—not to be
quoted—with a cracksman[2] at that moment being diligently inquired for by the New York police with reference to a dramatically
bigger matter. You saw the plot at once as he constructed it; the
pipe ash became explicable in the seduction of Miss Belton's
charms. The cunning net unwove itself, delicately and deliberately,
to tangle round the lady. There was in it that superiority in the art
of legerdemain, of mere calm, astonishing manipulation, so applauded in regions where romance has not yet been quite trampled
down by reason. Lorne scored; he scored in face of probability,
expectation, fact; it was the very climax and coruscation of score.
He scored not only by the cards he held but by the beautiful way
he played them, if one may say so. His nature came into this, his
gravity and gentleness, his sympathy, his young angry irony. To
mention just one thing, there was the way he held Miss Belton up,
after the exposure of her arts, as the lady for whom his client had
so chivalric a regard that he had for some time refused to state his
whereabouts at the hour the bank was entered in the fear of compromising her. For this, no doubt, his client could have strangled
him, but it operated, of course, to raise the poor fellow in the
estimation of everybody, with the possible exception of his employers. When, after the unmistakable summing-up, the foreman
returned in a quarter of an hour with the verdict of "Not guilty,"
people noticed that the young man walked out of court behind his
father with as drooping a head as if he had gone under sentence;
so much so that by common consent he was allowed to slip quietly
away. Miss Belton departed, followed by the detective, whose
services were promptly transferred to the prosecution, and by a
proportion of those who scented further entertainment in her per-
fumed, perjured wake. But the majority hung back, leaving their
places slowly; it was Lorne the crowd wanted to shake hands with,
to say just a word of congratulation to, Lorne's triumph that they
desired to enhance by a hearty sentence, or at least an admiring
glance. Walter Winter was among the most genial.

"Young man," he said, "what did I tell you? Didn't I tell you
you ought to take this case?" Mr. Winter, with his chest thrust out,

plumed and strutted in justifiable pride of prophecy. "Now, I'll tell
you another thing: to-day's event will do more for you than it has
for Ormiston. Mark my words!"

They were all of that opinion, all the fine foretellers of the
profit Lorne should draw from his spirited and conspicuous
success; they stood about in knots discussing it; to some extent it
eclipsed the main interest and issue of the day, at that moment
driving out, free and disconsolate, between the snake-fences of the
South Riding to Moneida Reservation. The quick and friendly
sense of opportunity was abroad on Lorne Murchison's behalf;
friends and neighbours and Dr. Drummond, and people who
hardly knew the fellow, exchanged wise words about what his
chance would do for him. What it would immediately do was
present to nobody so clearly, however, as to Mr. Henry Cruickshank, who decided that he would, after all, accept Dr. Drummond's invitation to spend the night with him, and find out the
little he didn't know already about this young man.

That evening the Murchisons' doorbell rang twice. The first
time it was to admit the Rev. Hugh Finlay, who had come to return
Sordello,³ which he had borrowed from Advena, and to find out
whether she thought with him about the interpretation of certain
passages, and if not—there was always the possibility—wherein
their divergence lay. The second time the door opened to Dr.
Drummond and Mr. Cruickshank; and the electric light had to be
turned on in the drawing-room, since the library was already
occupied by Mr. Finlay and Advena, Mr. and Mrs. Murchison
never having got over their early habit of sitting in the dining-
room after tea. Even then Mrs. Murchison had to put away her
work-basket, and John Murchison to knock the ashes out of his
pipe, looking at one another with surprised inquiry when Eliza
informed them of their visitors. Luckily, Mr. Lorne was also in,
and Eliza was sent to tell him, and Mr. Lorne came down the stairs
two at a time to join the party in the drawing-room, which was
presently supplied by Eliza with a dignified service of cake and
wine. The hall divided that room from the library, and both doors
were shut. We cannot hesitate about which to open; we have only,
indeed, to follow the recognized tradition of Elgin, which would
never have entered the library. No vivid conclusion should be
drawn, no serious situation may even be indicated. It would simply

have been considered, in Elgin, stupid to go into the library.

"It isn't a case for the High Commissioner for Canada," Mr. Cruickshank was saying. "It's a case for direct representation of the interests concerned, and their view of the effect upon trade. That's the only voice to speak with if you want to get anything done. Conviction carries conviction. The High Commissioner is a very useful fellow to live in London and look after the ornamental, the sentimental, and immigration—nobody could do it better than Selkirk. And in England, of course, they like that kind of agency. It's the good old dignified way; but it won't do for everything. You don't find our friend Morgan[4] operating through the American equivalent of a High Commissioner."

"No, you don't," said John Murchison.

"He goes over there as a principal, and the British Government, if he wants to deal with it, is only another principal. That's the way our deputation will go. We're practically all shippers, though of course the matter of tenders will come later. There is big business for them here, national business, and we propose to show it. The subsidy we want will come back to the country four times over in two years. Freights from Boston alone —"

"It's the patriotic, imperial argument you'll have to press, I doubt," said John Murchison. "They're not business people over there—the men in office are not. How should they be? the system draws them from the wrong class. They're gentlemen—noblemen, maybe—first, and they've no practical education. There's only one way of getting it, and that's to make your own living. How many of them have ever made tuppence? There's where the Americans beat them so badly—they've got the sixth sense, the business sense. No; you'll not find them responding greatly to what there is in it for trade—they'd like to well enough, but they just won't see it; and, by George! what a fine suspicion they'll have of ye! As to freights from Boston," he continued, as they all laughed, "I'm of opinion you'd better not mention them. What! steal the trade of a friendly Power! Tut, tut!"

It was a long speech for John Murchison, but they were all excited to a pitch beyond the usual. Henry Cruickshank had brought with him an event of extraordinary importance. It seemed to sit there with him, significant and propitious, in the middle of the sofa; they all looked at it in the pauses. Dr. Drummond, lost in an armchair, alternately contemplated it and remembered to assert himself part of it. As head of a deputation from the United Chambers of Commerce of Canada shortly to wait on the British Government to press for the encouragement of improved communications within the Empire, Cruickshank had been asked to select a secretary. The appointment, in view of the desirability, for political reasons, of giving the widest publicity to the hopes and motives of the deputation, was an important one. The action of the Canadian Government, in extending conditional promises of support, had to be justified to the Canadian taxpayer; and that shy and weary person whose shoulders uphold the greatness of Britain, had also to receive such conciliation and reassurance as it was possible to administer to him, by way of nerving the administrative arm over there to an act of enterprise. Mr. Cruickshank had had two or three young fellows, mostly newspaper men, in his mind's eye; but when Lorne came into his literal range of vision, the others had promptly been retired in our friend's favour. Young Mr. Murchison, he had concluded, was the man they wanted; and if his office could spare him, it would probably do young Mr. Murchison no harm in any sort of way to accompany the deputation to London and throw himself into the matter the deputation had at heart.

"But it's the Empire!" said Lorne, with a sort of shy fire, when Mr. Cruickshank enunciated this.

We need not, perhaps, dwell upon the significance of his agreement. It was then not long since the maple leaf had been stained brighter than ever, not without honour, to maintain the word that fell from him.[5] The three older men looked at him kindly; John Murchison, rubbing his chin as he considered the situation, slightly shook his head. One took it that in his view the Empire was not so readily envisaged.

"That has a strong bearing," Mr. Cruickshank assented.

"It's the whole case—it seems to me," repeated young Murchison.

"It should help to knit us up," said Dr. Drummond. "I'll put my name down on the first passenger list, if Knox Church will let me off. See that you have special rates," he added, with a twinkle, "for ministers and missionaries."

"And only ten days to get him ready in," said Mrs. Murchison. "It will take some seeing to, I assure you; and I don't know how it's to be done in the time. For once, Lorne, I'll have to order you ready-made shirts, and you'll just have to put up with it. Nothing else could possibly get back from the wash."

"I'll put up with it, mother."

They went into other details of Lorne's equipment while Mrs. Murchison's eye still wandered over the necessities of his wardrobe. They arranged the date on which he was to meet the members of the deputation in Montreal, and Mr. Cruickshank promised to send him all available documents, and such presentation of the project as had been made in the newspapers.

"You shall be put in immediate possession of the bones of the thing," he said, "but what really matters," he added, pleasantly, "I think you've got already."

It took, of course, some discussion, and it was quite ten o'clock before everything was gone into, and the prospect was clear to them all. As they emerged into the hall together, the door of the room opposite also opened, and the Rev. Hugh Finlay found himself added to their group. They all made the best of the unexpected encounter. It was rather an elaborate best, very polite and entirely grave, except in the instance of Dr. Drummond, who met his subaltern with a smile in which cordiality struggled in vain to overcome the delighted humour.

Chapter XII

It was the talk of the town, the pride of the market-place, Lorne Murchison's having been selected to accompany what was known as the Cruickshank deputation to England. The general spirit of congratulation was corrected by a tendency to assert it another proof of sagacity on the chairman's part; Elgin wouldn't be too flattered; Lawyer Cruickshank couldn't have done better. You may be sure the *Express* was well ahead with it. "Honour to Our Young Fellow Townsman. A Well-Merited Compliment," and Rawlins was round promptly next morning to glean further particulars. He found only Mrs. Murchison, on a step-ladder tying up the clematis that climbed about the verandah, and she told him a little about clematis and a good deal about the inconvenience of having to abandon superintending the spring cleaning in order to get Lorne ready to go to the old country at such short notice, but nothing he could put in the paper. Lorne, sought at the office, was hardly more communicative. Mr. Williams himself dropped in there. He said the *Express* would now have a personal interest in the object of the deputation, and proposed to strike out a broad line, a broader line than ever.

"We've got into the way of taking it for granted," said Mr. Williams, "that the subsidy idea is a kind of mediæval idea. Raise a big enough shout and you get things taken for granted in economics for a long while. Conditions keep changing, right along, all the time, and presently you've got to reconsider. There ain't any sort of ultimate truth in the finest economic position, my son; not any at all."

"We'll subsidize over here, right enough," said Lorne.

"That's the idea—that's the prevailing idea, just now. But lots of people think different—more than you'd imagine. I was talking to old man Milburn just now—he's dead against it. 'Government has no business,' he said, 'to apply the taxes in the interests of any company. It oughtn't to know how to spell "subsidy." If the trade was there it would get itself carried,' he said."

"Well, that surprises me," said Lorne.

"Surprised me, too. But I was on the spot with him; just thought of it in time. 'Well, now, Mr. Milburn,' I said, 'you've changed your mind. Thought that was a thing you Conservatives never did,' I said. 'We don't—I haven't,' he said. 'What d'ye mean?' 'Twenty-five years ago,' I said, 'when you were considering whether you'd start the Milburn Boiler Works here or in Hamilton, Hamilton offered you a free site, and Elgin offered you a free site and a dam for your water power. You took the biggest subsidy an' came here,' I said."

Lorne laughed: "What did he say to that?"

"Hadn't a word. 'I guess it's up to me,' he said. Then he turned round and came back. 'Hold on, Williams,' he said. 'You know so much already about my boiler works, it wouldn't be much trouble for you to write out an account of them from the beginning, would it? Working in the last quarter of a century of the town's progress, you know, and all that. Come round to the office to-morrow, and I'll give you some pointers.' And he fixed up a two-column ad. right away. He was afraid I'd round on him, I suppose, if I caught him saying anything more about the immorality of subsidies."

"He won't say anything more."

"Probably not. Milburn hasn't got much of a political conscience, but he's got a sense of what's silly. Well, now, I expect you want all the time there is."

Mr. Williams removed himself from the edge of the table, which was strewn with maps and bluebooks, printed official, and typewritten demi-official papers.

"Give 'em a notion of those Assiniboian wheat acres, my boy, and the ranch country we've got; tell 'em about the future of quick passage and cold storage. Get 'em a little ashamed to have made so many fortunes for Yankee beef combines; persuade 'em the cheapest market has a funny way of getting the dearest price in the end. Give it 'em, Lorne, hot and cold and fricasseed. The *Express* will back you up."

He slapped his young friend's shoulder, who seemed occupied with matters that prevented his at once feeling the value of this assurance. "Bye-bye," said Mr. Williams. "See you again before you start."

"Oh, of course!" Lorne replied. "I'll—I'll come round. By the way, Williams, Mr. Milburn didn't say anything—anything about me in connection with this business? Didn't mention, I suppose, what he thought about my going."

"Not a word, my boy! He was away up in abstract principles; he generally is. Bye-bye."

"It's gone to his head a little bit—only natural," Horace reflected as he went down the stairs. "He's probably just feeding on what folks think of it. As if it mattered a pin's head what Octavius Milburn thinks or don't think!"

Lorne, however, left alone with his customs returns and his immigration reports, sat still, attaching a weight quite out of comparison with a pin's head to Mr. Milburn's opinion. He turned it over and over, instead of the tabulated figures that were his business: he had to show himself his way to the conclusion that such a thing could not matter seriously in the end, since Milburn hadn't a dollar involved—it would be different if he were a shareholder in the Maple Line. He wished heartily, nevertheless, that he could demonstrate a special advantage to boiler-makers in competitive freights with New York. What did they import, confound them! Pig-iron? Plates and rivets? Fortunately he was in a position to get at the facts, and he got at them with an interest of even greater intensity than he had shown to the whole question since ten that morning. Even now, the unprejudiced observer, turning up the literature connected with the Cruickshank deputation, may notice a stress laid upon the advantages to Canadian importers of ore in certain stages of manufacture which may strike him as slightly, very slightly, special. Of course there are a good many of them in the country. So that Mr. Horace Williams was justified to some extent in his kindly observation upon the excusable egotism of youth. Two or three letters, however, came in while Lorne was considering the relation of plates and rivets to the objects of his deputation. They were all congratulatory; one was from the chairman of the Liberal Association at its headquarters in Toronto. Lorne glanced at them and stowed them away in his pocket. He would read them when he got home, when it would be a pleasure to hand them over to his mother. She was making a collection of them.

He had a happy perception that same evening that Mr. Milburn's position was not, after all, finally and invincibly taken against the deputation and everything—everybody—concerned with it. He met that gentleman at his own garden gate. Octavius paused in his exit, to hold it open for young Murchison, thus even assisting the act of entry, a thing which thrilled Lorne sweetly

enough when he had time to ponder its possible significance. Alas!
the significance that lovers find! Lorne read a world in the behaviour of Dora's father in holding the gate open. He saw political
principle put aside in his favour, and social position forgotten in
kindness to him. He saw the gravest, sincerest appreciation of his
recent success, which he took as humbly as a dog will take a bone;
he read a fatherly thought at which his pulses bounded in an arro-
gance of triumph, and his heart rose to ask its trust. And Octavius
Milburn had held the gate open because it was more convenient to
hold it open than to leave it open. He had not a political view in
the world that was calculated to affect his attitude toward a practical matter; and his opinion of Lorne was quite uncomplicated: he
thought him a very likely young fellow. Milburn himself, in the
Elgin way, preferred to see no great significance of this sort anywhere. Young people were young people; it was natural enough
that they should like each other's society. They, the Milburns,
were very glad to see Mr. Murchison, very glad indeed. It was
frequent matter for veiled humorous reference at the table that he
had been to call again, at which Dora would look very stiff and
dignified, and have to be coaxed back into the conversation. As to
anything serious, there was no hurry; plenty of time to think of
that. Such matters dwelt under the horizon; there was no need to
scan them closely; and Mr. Milburn went his way, conscious of
nothing more than a comfortable gratification that Dora, so far as
the young men were concerned, seemed as popular as other girls.

Dora was not in the drawing-room. Young ladies in Elgin had
always to be summoned from somewhere. For all the Filkin
instinct for the conservation of polite tradition, Dora was probably
reading the Toronto society weekly—illustrated, with correspondents all over the Province—on the back verandah, and, but for the
irruption of a visitor, would probably not have entered the formal
apartment of the house at all that evening. Drawing-rooms in Elgin
had their prescribed uses—to receive in, to practise in, and for the
last sad entertainment of the dead, when the furniture was dis-
arranged to accommodate the trestles; but the common business of
life went on outside them, even among prosperous people, the
survival, perhaps, of a habit based upon thrift. The shutters were
opened when Lorne entered, to let in the spring twilight, and the
servant pulled a chair into its proper relation with the room as she

went out.

Mrs. Milburn and Miss Filkin both came in before Dora did. Lorne found their conversation enchanting, though it was mostly about the difficulty of keeping the lawn tidy; they had had so much rain. Mrs. Milburn assured him kindly that there was not such another lawn as his father's in Elgin. How Mr. Murchison managed to have it looking so nice always she could not think. Only yesterday she and Mr. Milburn had stopped to admire it as they passed.

"Spring is always a beautiful time in Elgin," she remarked. "There are so many pretty houses here, each standing in its own grounds. Nothing very grand, as I tell my friend, Miss Cham, from Buffalo, where the residences are, of course, on quite a different scale; but grandeur isn't everything, is it?"

"No, indeed," said Lorne.

"But you will be leaving for Great Britain very soon now, Mr. Murchison," said Miss Filkin. "Leaving Elgin and all its beauties! And I dare say you won't think of them once again till you get back!"

"I hope I shall not be so busy as that, Miss Filkin."

"Oh, no, I'm sure Mr. Murchison won't forget his native town altogether," said Mrs. Milburn, "though perhaps he won't like it so well after seeing dear old England!"

"I expect," said Lorne simply, "to like it better."

"Well, of course, we shall all be pleased if you say that, Mr. Murchison," Mrs. Milburn replied graciously. "We shall feel quite complimented. But I'm afraid you will find a great deal to criticize when you come back—that is, if you go at all into society over there. I always say there can be nothing like good English society."

"I want to attend a sitting of the House," Lorne said. "I hope I shall have time for that. I want to see those fellows handling their public business. I don't believe I shall find our men so far behind, for point of view and grasp and dispatch. Of course there's always Wallingham[1] to make a standard for us all. But they haven't got so many Wallinghams."

"Wasn't it Wallingham, Louisa, that Mr. Milburn was saying at breakfast was such a dangerous man? So able, he said, but dangerous. Something to do with the tariff."

"Oh?" said Lorne, and he said no more, for at that moment

Dora came in. She came in looking very straight and graceful and composed. Her personal note was carried out in her pretty clothes, which hung and sat upon her like the rhythm of verses; they could fall no other way. She had in every movement the definite accent of young ladyhood; she was very much aware of herself, of the situation, and of her value in it, a setting for herself she saw it, and saw it truly. No one, from the moment she entered the room, looked at anything else.

"Oh, Mr. Murchison," she said. "How do you do? Mother, do you mind if I open the window? It's quite warm out of doors— regular summer."

Lorne sprang to open the window, while Miss Filkin, murmuring that it had been a beautiful day, moved a little farther from it.

"Oh, please don't trouble, Mr. Murchison; thank you very much!" Miss Milburn continued, and subsided on a sofa. "Have you been playing tennis this week?"

Mr. Murchison said that he had been able to get down to the club only once.

"The courts aren't a bit in good order. They want about a week's rolling. The balls get up anywhere," said Dora.

"Lawn tennis," Mrs. Milburn asserted herself, "is a delightful exercise. I hope it will never go out of fashion; but that is what we used to say of croquet, and it has gone out and come in again."

Lorne listened to this with deference; there was a hint of patience in the regard Dora turned upon her mother. Mrs. Milburn continued to dilate upon lawn tennis, dealt lightly with badminton, and brought the conversation round with a graceful sweep to canoeing. Dora's attitude before she had done became slightly permissive, but Mrs. Milburn held on till she had accomplished her conception of conduct for the occasion; then she remembered a meeting in the schoolhouse.

"We are to have an address by an Indian bishop," she told them. "He is on his way to England by China and Japan, and is staying with our dear rector, Mr. Murchison. Such a treat I expect it will be."

"What I am dying to know," said Miss Filkin, in a sprightly way, "is whether he is black or white!"

Mrs. Milburn then left the room, and shortly afterward Miss Filkin thought she could not miss the bishop either, conveying the feeling that a bishop was a bishop, of whatever colour. She stayed three minutes longer than Mrs. Milburn, but she went. The Filkin tradition, though strong, could not hold out entirely against the unwritten laws, the silently claimed privileges, of youth in Elgin. It made its pretence and vanished.

Even as the door closed the two that were left looked at one another with a new significance. A simpler relation established itself between them and controlled all that surrounded them; the very twilight seemed conscious with it; the chairs and tables stood in attentive harmony.

"You know," said Dora, "I hate your going, Lorne!"

She did indeed seem moved, about the mouth, to discontent. There was some little injury in the way she swung her foot.

"I was hoping Mr. Fulke wouldn't get better in time; I was truly!"

The gratitude in young Murchison's eyes should have been dear to her. I don't know whether she saw it; but she must have been aware that she was saying what touched him, making her point.

"Oh, it's a good thing to go, Dora."

"A good thing for you! And the regatta coming off the first week in June, and a whole crowd coming from Toronto for it. There isn't another person in town I care to canoe with, Lorne, you know perfectly well!"

"I'm awfully sorry!" said Lorne. "I wish —"

"Oh, I'm *going*, I believe. Stephen Stuart has written from Toronto, and asked me to sail with him. I haven't told mother, but he's my second cousin, so I suppose she won't make a fuss."

The young man's face clouded; seeing which she relented. "Oh, of course, I'm glad you're going, really," she assured him. "And we'll all be proud to be acquainted with such a distinguished gentleman when you get back. Do you think you'll see the King? You might, you know, in London."

"I'll see him if he's visible," laughed Lorne. "That would be something to tell your mother, wouldn't it? But I'm afraid we won't be doing business with his Majesty."

"I expect you'll have the loveliest time you ever had in all your life. Do you think you'll be asked out much, Lorne?"

"I can't imagine who would ask me. We'll get off easy if the street boys don't shout: 'What price Canucks?' at us! But I'll see

England, Dora; I'll feel England, eat and drink and sleep and live
in England, for a little while. Isn't the very name great? I'll be a
better man for going, till I die. We're all right out here, but we're
young and thin and weedy. They didn't grow so fast in England,
to begin with, and now they're rich with character and strong with
conduct and hoary with ideals. I've been reading up the history of
our political relations with England. It's astonishing what we've
stuck to her through, but you can't help seeing why—it's for the
moral advantage. Way down at the bottom, that's what it is. We
have the sense to want all we can get of that sort of thing. They've
developed the finest human product there is, the cleanest, the most
disinterested, and we want to keep up the relationship—it's important. Their talk about the value of their protection doesn't take
in the situation as it is now. Who would touch us if we were running our own show?"

"I don't believe they are a bit better than we are," replied Miss
Milburn. "I'm sure I haven't much opinion of the Englishmen that
come out here. They don't think anything of getting into debt, and
as often as not they drink, and they never know enough to—to
come in out of the rain. But, Lorne —"

"Yes, but we're very apt to get the failures. The fellows their
folks give five or six hundred pounds to and tell them they're not
expected back till they're making a living.[2] The best men find their
level somewhere else, along recognized channels. Lord knows we
don't want them—this country's for immigrants. We're manufacturing our own gentlemen quite fast enough for the demand."

"I should think we were! Why, Lorne, Canadians—nice Canadians—are just as gentlemanly as they can be! They'll compare
with anybody. Perhaps Americans have got more style:" she
weighed the matter; "but Canadians are much better form, I think.
But, Lorne, how perfectly dear of you to send me those roses. I
wore them, and nobody there had such beauties. All the girls
wanted to know where I got them, but I only told Lily, just to
make her feel a pig for not having asked you—my very greatest
friend! She just about apologized—told me she wanted to ask
about twenty more people, but her mother wouldn't let her.
They've lost an uncle or something lately, and if it hadn't been for
Clara Sims staying with them they wouldn't have been giving
anything."

"I'll try to survive not having been asked. But I'm glad you wore the roses, Dora."

"I dropped one, and Phil Carter wanted to keep it. He's so silly!"

"Did you—did you let him keep it?"

"Lorne Murchison! Do you think I'd let any man keep a rose I'd been wearing?"

He looked at her, suddenly emboldened.

"I don't know about roses, Dora, but pansies—those are awfully nice ones in your dress. I'm very fond of pansies; couldn't you spare me one? I wouldn't ask for a rose, but a pansy—"

His eyes were more ardent than what he found to say. Beneath them Dora grew delicately pink. The pansies drooped a little; she put her slender fingers under one, and lifted its petals.

"It's too faded for your buttonhole," she said.

"It needn't stay in my buttonhole. I know lots of other places!" he begged.

Dora considered the pansy again, then she pulled it slowly out, and the young man got up and went over to her, proffering the lapel of his coat.

"It spoils the bunch," she said prettily. "If I give you this you will have to give me something to take its place."

"I will," said Lorne.

"I know it will be something better," said Dora, and there was a little effort in her composure. "You send people such beautiful flowers, Lorne."

She rose beside him as she spoke, graceful and fair, to fasten it in; and it was his hand that shook.

"Then may I choose it?" said Lorne. "And will you wear it?"

"I suppose you may. Why are you—why do you—Oh, Lorne, stand still!"

"I'll give you, you sweet girl, my whole heart!" he said, in the vague tender knowledge that he offered her a garden, where she had but to walk, and smile, to bring about her unimaginable blooms.

Chapter XIII

They sat talking on the verandah in the close of the May evening, Mr. and Mrs. Murchison. The Plummer Place was the Murchison Place in the town's mouth now, and that was only fair; the Murchisons had overstamped the Plummers. It lay about them like a map of their lives: the big horse-chestnut stood again in flower to lighten the spring dusk for them, as it had done faithfully for thirty years. John was no longer in his shirt-sleeves; the growing authority of his family had long prescribed a black alpaca coat. He smoked his meerschaum with the same old deliberation, however, holding it by the bowl as considerately as he held its original, which lasted him fifteen years. A great deal of John Murchison's character was there, in the way he held his pipe, his gentleness and patience, even the justice and repose and quiet strength of his nature. He smoked and read the paper, the unfailing double solace of his evenings. I should have said that it was Mrs. Murchison who talked. She had the advantage of a free mind, only subconsciously occupied with her white wool and agile needles; and John had frequently to choose between her observations and the politics of the day.

"You saw Lorne's letter this morning, father?"

John took his pipe out of his mouth.

"Yes," he said.

"He seems tremendously taken up with Wallingham. It was all Wallingham, from one end to the other."

"It's not remarkable," said John Murchison, patiently.

"You'd think he had nothing else to write about. There was that reception at Lord What-you-may-call-him's, the Canadian Commissioner's, when the Prince and Princess of Wales came, and brought their family. I'd like to have heard something more about that than just that he was there. He might have noticed what the children had on. Now that Abby's family is coming about her I seem to have my hands as full of children's clothes as ever I had. Abby seems to think there's nothing like my old patterns; I'm sure I'm sick of the sight of them!"

Mr. Murchison refolded his newspaper, took his pipe once more from his mouth, and said nothing.

"John, put down that paper! I declare it's enough to drive anybody crazy! Now look at that boy walking across the lawn. He does it every night, delivering the *Express*, and you take no more notice! He's wearing a regular path!"

"Sonny," said Mr. Murchison, as the urchin approached, "you mustn't walk across the grass."

"Much good that will do!" remarked Mrs. Murchison. "I'd teach him to walk across the grass, if—if it were my business. Boy—isn't your name Willie Parker? Then it was your mother I promised the coat and the other things to, and you'll find them ready there, just inside the hall door. They'll make down very well for you, but you can tell her from me that she'd better double-seam them, for the stuff's apt to ravel. And attend to what Mr. Murchison says; go out by the gravel—what do you suppose it's there for?"

Mrs. Murchison readjusted her glasses, and turned another row of the tiny sock. "I must say it's a pleasure to have the lawn neat and green," she said, with a sigh. "Never did I expect to see the day it would be anything but chickweed and dandelions. We've a great deal to be thankful for, and all our children spared to us, too. John," she continued, casting a shrewd glance over her needles at nothing in particular; "do you suppose anything was settled between Lorne and Dora Milburn before he started?"

"He said nothing to me about it."

"Oh, well, very likely he wouldn't Young people keep such a tremendous lot to themselves nowadays. But it's my belief they've come to an understanding."

"Dora might do worse," said John Murchison, judicially.

"I should think Dora might do worse! I don't know where she's going to do better! The most promising young man in Elgin, well brought up, well educated, well started in a profession! There's not a young fellow in this town to compare with Lorne, and perfectly well you know it, John. Might do worse! But that's you all over. Belittle your own belongings!"

Mr. Murchison smiled in amused tolerance.

"They've always got you to blow their trumpet, mother," he replied.

"And more than me. You ought to hear Dr. Drummond about Lorne! He says that if the English Government starts that line of boats to Halifax the country will owe it to him, much more than to

Cruickshank, or anybody else."

"Lorne's keeping his end up all right," remarked Stella, jumping off her bicycle in time to hear what her mother said. "It's great, that old Wallingham asking him to dinner. And haven't I just been spreading it!"

"Where have you been, Stella?" asked Mrs. Murchison.

"Oh, only over to the Milburns'. Dora asked me to come and show her the new flower-stitch for table-centres. Dora's suddenly taken to fancy work. She's started a lot—a lot too much!" Stella added gloomily.

"If Dora likes to do fancy work I don't see why anybody should want to stop her," remarked Mrs. Murchison, with a meaning glance at her husband.

"I suppose she thinks she's going to get Lorne," said Stella. Her resentment was only half serious, but the note was there.

"What put that into your head?" asked her mother.

"Oh, well, anybody can see that he's devoted to her, and has been for ages, and it isn't as if Lorne was one to *have* girl friends; she's absolutely the only thing he's ever looked at twice. She hasn't got a ring, that's true, but it would be just like her to want him to get it in England. And I know they correspond. She doesn't make any secret of it."

"Oh, I dare say! Other people have eyes in their head as well as you, Stella," said Mrs. Murchison, stooping for her ball. "But there's no need to take things for granted at such a rate. And, above all, you're not to go *talking*, remember!"

"Well, if you think Dora Milburn's good enough," returned Lorne's youngest sister in threatening accents, "it's more than I do, that's all. Hello, Miss Murchison!" she continued, as Advena appeared. "You're looking 'xtremely dinky-dink. Expecting his reverence?"

Advena made no further reply than a look of scornful amusement, which Stella, bicycling forth again, received in the back of her head.

"Father," said Mrs. Murchison, "if you had taken any share in the bringing up of this family, Stella ought to have her ears boxed this minute!"

"We'll have to box them," said Mr. Murchison, "when she comes back." Advena had retreated into the house. "Is she expecting his reverence?" asked her father with a twinkle.

"Don't ask me! I'm sure it's more than I can tell you. It's a mystery to me, that matter, altogether. I've known him come three evenings in a week and not again for a month of Sundays. And when he does come there they sit, talking about their books and their authors; you'd think the world had nothing else in it! I know, for I've heard them, hard at it, there in the library. Books and authors won't keep their house or look after their family for them, I can tell them that, if it does come to anything, which I hope it won't."

"Finlay's fine in the pulpit," said John Murchison cautiously.

"Oh, the man's well enough; it's him I'm sorry for. I don't call Advena fitted to be a wife, and last of all a minister's. Abby was a treasure for any man to get, and Stella won't turn out at all badly; she's taking hold very well for her age. But Advena simply hasn't got it in her, and that's all there is to say about it." Mrs. Murchison pulled her needles out right side out with finality. "I don't deny the girl's talented in her own way, but it's no way to marry on. She'd much better make up her mind just to be a happy independent old maid; any woman might do worse. And take no responsibilities."

"There would always be you, mother, for them to fall back on." It was as near as John Murchison ever got to flattery.

"No thank you, then! I've brought up six of my own, as well as I was able, which isn't saying much, and a hard life, I've had of it. Now I'm done with it; they'll have to find somebody else to fall back on. If they get themselves into such a mess"—Mrs. Murchison stopped to laugh with sincere enjoyment—"they needn't look to me to get them out."

"I guess you'd have a hand, mother."

"Not I. But the man isn't thinking of any such folly. What do you suppose his salary is?"

"Eight hundred and fifty dollars a year. They raised it last month."

"And how far would Advena be able to make that go, with servants getting the money they do and expecting the washing put out as a matter of course? Do you remember Eliza, John, that we had when we were first married? Seven dollars a month she got; she would split wood at a pinch, and I've never had one since that could do up shirts like her. Three years and a half she was with me, and did everything, everything I didn't do. But that was management, and Advena's no manager. It would be me that would tell him, if I had the chance. Then he couldn't say he hadn't been warned. But I don't think he has any such idea."

"Advena," pronounced Mr. Murchison, "might do worse."

"Well, I don't know whether she might. The creature is well enough to preach before a congregation. But what she can see in him out of the pulpit is more than I know. A great gawk of a fellow, with eyes that always look as if he were in the middle of next week! He may be able to talk to Advena, but he's no hand at general conversation; I know he finds precious little to say to me. But he's got no such notion. He comes here because, being human, he's got to open his mouth some time or other, I suppose; but it's my opinion he has neither Advena nor anybody else in his mind's eye at present. He doesn't go the right way about it."

"H'm!" said John Murchison.

"He brought her a book the last time he came—what do you think the name of it was? The something or other of Plato! Do you call that a natural thing from a young man who is thinking seriously of a girl? Besides, if I know anything about Plato he was a Greek heathen, and no writer for a Presbyterian minister to go lending around. I'd Plato him to the rightabout¹ if it was me!"

"She might read worse than Plato," remarked John.

"Oh, well, she read it fast enough. She's your own daughter for outlandish books. Mercy on us, here comes the man! We'll just say 'How d'ye do?' to him, and then start for Abby's, John. I'm not easy in my mind about the baby, and I haven't been over since the morning. Harry says it's nothing but stomach, but I think I know whooping-cough when I hear it. And if it is whooping-cough the boy will have to come here and rampage, I suppose, till they're clear of it. There's some use in grandmothers, if I do say it myself!"

Chapter XIV

If any one had told Mr. Hugh Finlay, while he was pursuing his rigorous path to the ideals of the University of Edinburgh, that the first notable interest of his life in the calling and the country to which even then he had given his future would lie in his relations with any woman, he would have treated the prediction as mere folly. To go far enough back in accounting for this, one would arrive at the female sort, sterling and arid, that had presided over his childhood and represented the sex to his youth, the Aunt Lizzie, widowed and frugal and spare, who had brought him up; the Janet Wilson, who had washed and mended him from babyhood, good gaunt creature, half servant and half friend—the mature respectable women and impossible blowsy girls of the Dumfriesshire village whence he came. With such as these, relations, actual or imagined, could only be of the most practical kind, matters to be arranged on grounds of expediency, and certainly not of the first importance. The things of first importance—what you could do with your energy and your brains to beat out some microscopic good for the world, and what you could see and feel and realize in it of value to yourself—left little room for the feminine consideration in Finlay's eyes; it was not a thing, simply, that existed there with any significance. Woman, in her more attractive presentment, was a daughter of the poets, with an esoteric, or perhaps only a symbolic, or perhaps a merely decorative function; in any case, a creature that required an initiation to perceive her—a process to which Finlay would have been as unwilling as he was unlikely to submit. Not that he was destitute of ideals about women—they would have formed in that case a strange exception to his general outlook—but he saw them on a plane detached and impersonal, concerned with the preservation of society, the maintenance of the home, the noble devotions of motherhood. Women had been known, historically, to be capable of lofty sentiments and fine actions: he would have been the last to withhold their due from women. But they were removed from the scope of his imagination, partly by the accidents I have mentioned, and partly, no doubt, by a simple lack in him of the inclination to seek and to know them.

So that Christie Cameron, when she came to stay with his aunt in Bross during the few weeks after his ordination and before his departure for Canada, found a fair light for judgment and more than a reasonable disposition to acquiesce in the scale of her merits, as a woman, on the part of Hugh Finlay. He was familiar with the scale of her merits before she came; his Aunt Lizzie did little but run them up and down. When she arrived she answered to every item: she was a good height, but not too tall; a nice figure of a woman, but not what you would call stout; a fresh-faced body whose excellent principles were written in every feature she had. She was five years older than Hugh, but even that he came to accept in Aunt Lizzie's skilful exhibition as something to the total of her advantages. A pleasant independent creature with a hundred a year of her own, sensible and vigorous and good-tempered, belonging as well to the pre-eminently right denomination, she had virtues that might have figured handsomely in an advertisement had Aunt Lizzie, in the plenitude of her good-will, thought fit to take that measure on Christie's behalf. But nothing was farther from Aunt Lizzie's mind. We must, in fairness, add Christie Cameron to the sum of Finlay's acquaintance with the sex; but even then the total is slender, little to go upon.

Yet the fact which Mr. Finlay would in those days have considered so unimaginable remained; it had come into being and it remained. The chief interest of his life, the chief human interest, did lie in his relations with Advena Murchison. He might challenge it, but he could not move it; he might explain, but he could not alter it. And there had come no point at which it would have occurred to him to do either. When at last he had seen how simple and possible it was to enjoy Miss Murchison's companionship upon unoccupied evenings he had begun to do it with eagerness and zest, the greater because Elgin offered him practically no other. Dr. Drummond lived, for purposes of intellectual contact, at the other end of the century, the other clergy and professional men of the town were separated from Finlay by all the mental predispositions that rose from the virgin soil. He was, as Mrs. Murchison said, a great gawk of a fellow; he had little adaptability; he was not of those who spend a year or two in the New World and go back with a trans-Atlantic accent, either of tongue or of mind. Where he saw a lack of dignity, of consideration, or of

restraint, he did not insensibly become less dignified or considerate or restrained to smooth out perceptible differences; nor was he
constituted to absorb the qualities of those defects, and enrich his
nature by the geniality, the shrewdness, the quick mental movement that stood on the other side of the account. He cherished in
secret an admiration for the young men of Elgin, with their unap-
peasable energy and their indomitable optimism, but he could not
translate it in any language of sympathy; and but for Advena his
soul would have gone uncomforted and alone.

Advena, as we know, was his companion. Seeing herself just
that, constantly content to be just that, she walked beside him
closer than he knew. She had her woman's prescience and trusted
it. Her own heart, all sweetly alive, counselled her to patience; her
instincts laid her in bonds to concealment. She knew, she was sure;
so sure that she could play sometimes, smiling, with her living
heart—

> "The nightingale was not yet heard
> For the rose was not yet blown,"

she could say of his; and what was that but play, and tender
laughter, at the expense of her own? And then, perhaps, looking
up from the same book, she would whisper, alone in her room—

> "Oh, speed the day, thou dear, dear May."[1]

and gaze humbly through tears at her own face in the glass, loving
it on his behalf. She took her passion with the weight of a thing
ordained; she had come upon it where it waited for her, and they
had gone on together, carrying the secret. There might be farther
to go, but the way could never be long.

Finlay said when he came in that the heat for May was extraordinary; and Advena reminded him that he was in a country
where everything was accomplished quickly, even summer.

"Except perhaps civilization," she added. They were both
young enough to be pleased with cleverness for its specious self.

"Oh, that is slow everywhere," he observed; "but how you can
say so, with every modern improvement staring you in the face
—"

"Electric cars and telephones! Oh, I didn't say we hadn't the products," and she laughed. "But the thing itself, the precious thing, that never comes just by wishing, does it? The art of indifference, the art of choice —"

"If you had refinements in the beginning what would the end be?" he demanded. "Anaemia."

"Oh, I don't quarrel with the logic of it. I only point out the fact. To do that is to acquiesce, really. I acquiesce; I have to. But one may long for the more delicate appreciations that seem to flower where life has gone on longer."

"I imagine," Finlay said, "that to wish truly and ardently for such things is to possess them. If you didn't possess them you wouldn't desire them! As they say, as they say —"

"As they say?"

"About love. Some novelist does. To be conscious in any way toward it is to be fatally infected."

"What novelist?" Advena asked, with shining interest.

"Some novelist. I—I can't have invented it," he replied, somewhat confounded. He got up and walked to the window, where it stood open upon the verandah. "I don't write novels," he said.

"Perhaps you live them," suggested Advena. "I mean, of course," she added, laughing, "the highest class of fiction."

"Heaven forbid!"

"Why Heaven forbid? You are sensitive to life, and a great deal of it comes into your scope. You can't see a thing truly without feeling it; you can't feel it without living it. I don't write novels either, but I experience—whole publishers' lists."

"That means," he said, smiling, "that your vision is up to date. You see the things, the kind of things that you read of next day. The modern moral sophistications—?"

"Don't make me out boastful," she replied; "I often do."

"Mine would be old-fashioned, I am afraid. Old stories of pain"—he looked out upon the lawn, white where the chestnut blossoms were dropping, and his eyes were just wistful enough to stir her adoration—"and of heroism that is quite dateless in the history of the human heart. At least one likes to hope so."

"I somehow think," she ventured timidly, "that yours would be classic."

Finlay withdrew his glance abruptly from the falling blossoms as if they had tempted him to an expansion he could not justify. He was impatient always of the personal note, and in his intercourse with Miss Murchison he seemed of late to be constantly sounding it.

"Oh, I don't know," he said, almost irritably. "I only meant that I see the obvious things, while you seem to have an eye for the subtle. There's reward, I suppose, in seeing anything. But about those more delicate appreciations of societies longer evolved, I sometimes think that you don't half realize, in a country like this, how much there is to make up."

"Is there anything really to make up?" she asked.

"Oh, so much! Freedom from old habits, inherited problems: look at the absurd difficulty they have in England in handling such a matter as education![2] Here you can't even conceive it—the schools have been on logical lines from the beginning, or almost. Political activity over there is half strangled at this moment by the secular arm of religion; here it doesn't even impede the circulation! Conceive any Church, or the united Churches, for the matter of that, asking a place in the conduct of the common schools of Ontario! How would the people take it? With anger, or with laughter, but certainly with sense. 'By all means let the ministers serve education on the School Boards,' they would say, 'by election like other people'—an opportunity, by the way, which has just been offered to me. I'm nominated for East Elgin in place of Leveret, the tanner, who is leaving the town. I shall do my best to get in, too; there are several matters that want seeing to over there. The girls' playground, for one thing, is practically under water in the spring."

"You should get in without the least difficulty. Oh, yes, there is something in a fresh start: we're on the straight road as a nation, in most respects; we haven't any picturesque old prescribed lanes to travel. So you think that makes up?"

"It's one thing. You might put down space—elbow-room."

"An empty horizon," Advena murmured.

"For faith and the future. An empty horizon is better than none. England has filled hers up. She has now—these," and he nodded at a window open to the yellow west. Advena looked with him.

"Oh, if you have a creative imagination," she said, "like Wallingham's. But even then your visions must be only political, economic, material. You can't conceive the—flowers—that will come out of all that. And if you could, it wouldn't be like having them."

"And the scope of the individual, his chance of self-respect, unhampered by the traditions of class, which either deaden it or irritate it in England! His chance of significance and success! And the splendid, buoyant, unused air to breath, and the simplicity of life, and the plenty of things!"

"I am to be consoled because apples are cheap."

"You are to be consoled for a hundred reasons. Doesn't it console you to feel under your very feet the forces that are working to the immense amelioration of a not altogether undeserving people?"

"No," said Advena, rebelliously; and indeed he had been a trifle didactic to her grievance. They laughed together, and then with a look at her in which observation seemed suddenly to awake, Finlay said—

"And those things aren't all, or nearly all. I sometimes think that the human spirit, as it is set free in these wide unblemished spaces, may be something more pure and sensitive, more sincerely curious about what is good and beautiful—"

He broke off, still gazing at her, as if she had been an idea and no more. How much more she was she showed him by a vivid and beautiful blush.

"I am glad you are so well satisfied," she said, and then, as if her words had carried beyond their intention, she blushed again.

Upon which Hugh Finlay saw his idea incarnate.

Chapter XV

If it were fair or adequate to so quote, I should be very much tempted to draw the history of Lorne Murchison's sojourn in England from his letters home. He put his whole heart into these, his discoveries and his recognitions and his young enthusiasm, all his claimed inheritance, all that he found to criticize and to love. His mother said, half jealously when she read them, that he seemed tremendously taken up with the old country; and of course she expressed the thing exactly, as she always did: he was tremendously taken up with it. The old country fell into the lines of his imagination, from the towers of Westminster to the shops in the Strand; from the Right Hon. Fawcett Wallingham, who laid great issues before the public, to the man who sang melancholy hymns to the same public up and down the benevolent streets. It was naturally London that filled his view; his business was in London and his time was short; the country he saw from the train, whence it made a low cloudy frame for London, with decorations of hedges and sheep. How he saw London, how he carried away all he did in the time and under the circumstances, may be thought a mystery; there are doubtless people who would consider his opportunities too limited to gather anything essential. Cruickshank was the only one of the deputation who had been "over" before; and they all followed him unquestioningly to the temperance hotel of his preference in Bloomsbury, where bedrooms were three and six and tea was understood as a solid meal and the last in the day. Bates would have voted for the Metropole, and McGill had been advised that you saw a good deal of life at the Cecil, but they bowed to Cruickshank's experience. None of them were total abstainers, but neither had any of them the wine habit; they were not inconvenienced, therefore, in taking advantage of the cheapness with which total abstinence made itself attractive, and they took it, though they were substantial men. As one of them put it, they weren't over there to make a splash, a thing that was pretty hard to do in London, anyhow; and home comforts came before anything. The conviction about the splash was perhaps a little the teaching of circumstances. They were influential fellows at home, who had lived for years in the atmosphere of appreciation that surrounds success; their movements were observed in the newspapers; their names stood for wide interests, big concerns. They had known the satisfaction of a positive importance, not only in their community but in their country; and they had come to England invested as well with the weight that is attached to a public mission. It may very well be that they looked for some echo of what they were accustomed to, and were a little dashed not to find it—to find the merest published announcement of their arrival, and their introduction by Lord Selkirk to the Colonial Secretary; and no heads turned in the temperance hotel when they came into the dining-room. It may very well be. It is even more certain, however, that they took the lesson as they found it, with the quick eye for things as they are which seems to come of looking at things as they will be, and with just that humorous comment about the splash. It would be misleading to say that they were humbled; I doubt whether they even felt their relativity, whether they ever dropped consciously, there in the Bloomsbury hotel, into their places in the great scale of London. Observing the scale, recognizing it, they held themselves unaffected by it; they kept, in a curious, positive way, the integrity of what they were and what they had come for; they maintained their point of view. So much must be conceded. The Empire produces a family resemblance, but here and there, when oceans intervene, a different mould of the spirit.

Wallingham certainly invited them to dinner one Sunday, in a body, an occasion which gave one or two of them some anxiety until they found that it was not to be adorned by the ladies of the family. Tricorne was there, President of the Board of Trade, and Fleming, who held the purse-strings of the United Kingdom, two Ministers whom Wallingham had asked because they were supposed to have open minds—open, that is to say, for purposes of assimilation. Wallingham considered, and rightly, that he had done very well for the deputation in getting these two. There were other "colleagues" whose attendance he would have liked to compel; but one of them, deep in the country, was devoting his weekends to his new French motor, and the other to the proofs of a book upon Neglected Periods of Mahomedan History, and both were at the breaking strain with overwork. Wallingham asked the deputation to dinner. Lord Selkirk, who took them to Wallingham, dined them too, and invited them to one of those garden parties for the sumptuous scale of which he was so justly famed; the occasion we have already heard about, upon which royalty was present in two generations. They travelled to it by special train, a circumstance which made them grave, receptive, and even slightly ceremonious with one another. Lord Selkirk, with royalty on his hands, naturally could not give them much of his time, and they moved about in a cluster, avoiding the ladies' trains and advising one another that it was a good thing the High Commissioner was a man of large private means; it wasn't everybody that could afford to take the job. Yet they were not wholly detached from the occasion; they looked at it, after they had taken it in, with an air half amused, half proprietary. All this had, in a manner, come out of Canada, and Canada was theirs. One of them—Bates it was—responding to a lady who was effusive about the strawberries, even took the modestly depreciatory attitude of the host. "They're a fair size for this country, ma'am, but if you want berries with a flavour we'll do better for you in the Niagara district."

It must be added that Cruickshank lunched with Wallingham at his club, and with Tricorne at his; and on both occasions the quiet and attentive young secretary went with him, for purposes of reference, his pocket bulging with memoranda. The young secretary felt a little embarrassed to justify his presence at Tricorne's lunch, as the Right Honourable gentleman seemed to have forgotten what his guests had come for beyond it, and talked exclusively and exhaustively about the new possibilities for fruit-farming in England. Cruickshank fairly shook himself into his overcoat with irritation afterwards. "It's the sort of thing we must expect," he said, as they merged upon Pall Mall. It was not the sort of thing Lorne expected; but we know him unsophisticated and a stranger to the heart of the Empire, which beats through such impediment of accumulated tissue. Nor was it the sort of thing they got from Wallingham, the keen-eyed and probing, whose skill in adjusting conflicting interests could astonish even their expectation, and whose vision of the essentials of the future could lift even their enthusiasm. One would like to linger over their touch with Wallingham, that fusion of energy with energy, that straight, satisfying, accomplishing dart. There is more drama here, no doubt, than in all the pages that are to come. But I am explaining now how little, not how much, the Cruickshank deputation, and especially

Lorne Murchison, had the opportunity of feeling and learning in London, in order to show how wonderful it was that Lorne felt and learned so widely. That, what he absorbed and took back with him is, after all, what we have to do with; his actual adventures are of no great importance.

The deputation to urge improved communications within the Empire had few points of contact with the great world, but its members were drawn into engagements of their own, more, indeed, than some of them could conveniently overtake. Mr. Bates never saw his niece in the post-office, and regrets it to this day. The engagements arose partly out of business relations. Poulton, who was a dyspeptic, complained that nothing could be got through in London without eating and drinking; for his part he would concede a point any time not to eat and drink, but you could not do it; you just had to suffer. Poulton was a principal in one of the railway companies that were competing to open up the country south of Hudson's Bay to the Pacific, but having dealt with that circumstance in the course of the day he desired only to be allowed to go to bed on bread and butter and a little stewed fruit. Bates, whose name was a nightmare to every other dry-goods man in Toronto, naturally had to see a good many of the wholesale people; he, too, complained of the number of courses and the variety of the wines, but only to disguise his gratification. McGill, of the Great Bear Line, had big proposals to make in connection with southern railway freights from Liverpool; and Cameron, for private reasons of magnitude, proposed to ascertain the real probability of a duty to foreigners on certain forms of manufac-tured leather—he turned out in Toronto a very good class of suit-case. Cruickshank had private connections to which they were all respectful. Nobody but Cruickshank found it expedient to look up the lost leader of the Canadian House of Commons, contributed to a cause still more completely lost in home politics;[1] nobody but Cruickshank was likely to be asked to dine by a former Gover-nor-General of the Dominion, an invitation which nobody but Cruickshank would be likely to refuse.

"It used to be a 'command' in Ottawa," said Cruickshank, who had got on badly with his sovereign's representative there, "but here it's only a privilege. There's no business in it, and I haven't time for pleasure."

The nobleman in question had, in effect, dropped back into the Lords. So far as the Empire was concerned, he was in the impressive rearguard, and this was a little company of fighting men.

The entertainments arising out of business were usually on a scale more or less sumptuous. They took place in big, well-known restaurants, and included a look at many of the people who seem to lend themselves so willingly to the great buzzing show that anybody can pay for in London, their names in the paper in the morning, their faces at Prince's in the evening, their personalities no doubt advantageously exposed in various places during the day. But there were others, humbler ones in Earl's Court Road or Maida Vale,² where the members of the deputation had relatives whom it was natural to hunt up. Long years and many billows had rolled between, and more effective separations had arisen in the whole difference of life; still, it was natural to hunt them up, to seek in their eyes and their hands the old subtle bond of kin, and perhaps—such is our vanity in the new lands— to show them what the stock had come to overseas. They tended to be depressing, these visits: the married sister was living in a small way; the first cousin seemed to have got into a rut; the uncle and aunt were failing, with a stooping, trembling, old-fashioned kind of decrepitude, a rigidity of body and mind, which somehow one didn't see much over home.

"England," said Poulton, the Canadian born, "is a dangerous country to live in; you run such risks of growing old." They agreed, I fear, for more reasons than this that England was a good country to leave early; and you cannot blame them—there was not one of them who did not offer in his actual person proof of what he said. Their own dividing chance grew dramatic in their eyes.

"I was offered a clerkship with the Cunards the day before I sailed," said McGill. "Great Scott, if I'd taken that clerkship!" He saw all his glorious past, I suppose, in a suburban aspect.

"I was kicked out," said Cameron, "and it was the kindest attention my father ever paid me;" and Bates remarked that it was worth coming out second-class, as he did, to go back in the best cabin in the ship.

The appearance and opinions of those they had left behind them prompted them to this kind of congratulation, with just a thought of compunction at the back of it for their own better fortunes. In the further spectacle of England most of them saw the repository of singularly old-fashioned ideas, the storehouse of a good deal of money, and the market for unlimited produce. They looked cautiously at imperial sentiment; they were full of the terms of their bargain, and had, as they would have said, little use for schemes that did not commend themselves on a basis of common profit. Cruickshank was the biggest and the best of them; but even Cruickshank submitted the common formulas; submitted them and submitted to them.

Only Lorne Murchison among them looked higher and further; only he was alive to the inrush of the essential; he only lifted up his heart.

Chapter XVI

L orne was thus an atom in the surge of London. The members of the deputation, as their business progressed, began to feel less like atoms and more like a body exerting an influence, however obscurely hid in a temperance hotel, upon the tide of international affairs; but their secretary had naturally no initiative that appeared, no importance that was taken account of. In these respects, no less than in the others, he justified Mr. Cruickshank's selection. He did his work as unobtrusively as he did it admirably well; and for the rest he was just washed about, carried hither and thither, generally on the tops of omnibuses, receptive, absorbent, mostly silent. He did try once or twice to talk to the 'bus drivers —he had been told it was a thing to do if you wanted to get hold of the point of view of a particular class; but the thick London idiom defeated him, and he found they grew surly when he asked them too often to repeat their replies. He felt a little surly himself after a while, when they asked him, as they nearly always did, if he wasn't an American. "Yes," he would say in the end, "but not the United States kind," resenting the necessity of explaining to the Briton beside him that there were other kinds. The imperial idea goes so quickly from the heart to the head. He felt compelled, nevertheless, to mitigate his denial to the 'bus drivers.

"I expect it's the next best thing," he would say, "but it's only the next best."

It was as if he felt charged to vindicate the race, the whole of Anglo-Saxondom, there in his supreme moment, his splendid position, on the top of an omnibus lumbering west out of Trafalgar Square.

One introduction of his own he had. Mrs. Milburn had got it for him from the rector, Mr. Emmett, to his wife's brother, Mr. Charles Chafe, who had interests in Chiswick and a house in Warwick Gardens. Lorne put off presenting the letter—did not know, indeed, quite how to present it, till his stay in London was half over. Finally he presented himself with it, as the quickest way, at the office of Mr. Chafe's works at Chiswick. He was cordially received, both there and in Warwick Gardens, where he met Mr. Alfred Hesketh. Lorne went several times to the house in Warwick

Gardens, and Hesketh—a nephew—was there on the very first occasion. It was an encounter interesting on both sides. He—Hesketh—was a young man with a good public school and a university behind him, where his very moderate degree, however, failed to represent the activity of his mind or the capacity of his energy. He had a little money of his own, and no present occupation; he belonged to the surplus. He was not content to belong to it; he cast about him a good deal for something to do. There was always the Bar, but only the best fellows get on there, and he was not quite one of the best fellows; he knew that. He had not money enough for politics or interest enough for the higher departments of the public service, nor had he those ready arts of expression that lead naturally into journalism. Anything involving further examinations he rejected on that account; and the future of glassware, in view of what they were doing in Germany, did not entice him to join his uncle in Chiswick. Still he was aware of enterprise, convinced that he had loafed long enough.

Lorne Murchison had never met any one of Hesketh's age in Hesketh's condition before. Affluence and age he knew, in honourable retirement; poverty and youth he knew, embarked in the struggle; indolence and youth he also knew, as it cumbered the ground; but youth and a competence, equipped with education, industry, and vigour, searching vainly in fields empty of opportunity, was to him a new spectacle. He himself had intended to be a lawyer since he was fourteen. There never had been any impediment to his intention, any qualification to his desire. He was still under his father's roof, but that was for the general happiness; any time within the last eighteen months, if he had chosen to hurry fate, he might have selected another. He was younger than Hesketh by a year, yet we may say that he had arrived, while Hesketh was still fidgeting at the starting-point.

"Why don't you farm?" he asked once.

"Farming in England may pay in a quarter of a century, not before. I can't wait for it. Besides, why should I farm? Why didn't you?"

"Well," said Lorne, "in your case it seems about the only thing left. I? Oh, it doesn't attract us over there. We're getting away from it—leaving it to the new-comers from this side. Curious circle, that. I wonder, when our place gets overcrowded, where we shall go to plough?"

Hesketh's situation occupied them a good deal; but their great topic had a wider drift, embracing nothing less than the Empire, pausing nowhere short of the flag. The imperial idea was very much at the moment in the public mind;[1] it hung heavily, like a banner, in every newspaper, it was filtering through the slow British consciousness, solidifying as it travelled. In the end it might be expected to arrive at a shape in which the British consciousness must either assimilate it or cast it forth. They were saying in the suburbs that they wanted it explained; at Hatfield[2] they were saying, some of them, with folded arms, that it was self-evident; other members of that great house, swinging their arms, called it blackness of darkness and ruin, so had a prophet divided it against itself. Wallingham, still in the Cabinet,[3] was going up and down the country trying not to explain too much. There was division in the Cabinet, sore travail among private members. The conception being ministerial, the Opposition applied itself to the task of abortion, fearing the worst if it should be presented to the country fully formed and featured, the smiling offspring of progress and imagination. Travellers to Greater Britain[4] returned waving joyous torches in the insular fog; they shed a brilliance and an infectious enthusiasm, but there were not enough to do more than make the fog visible. Many persons found such torches irritating. They pointed out that as England had groped to her present greatness she might be trusted to feel her way further. "Free trade," they said, "has made us what we are. Put out these lights!"[5]

Mr. Chafe was one of these. He was a cautious, heavy fellow, full of Burgundy and distrust. The basis of the imperial idea inspired him with suspicion and hostility. He could accept the American tariff on English manufactures; that was a plain position, simple damage, a blow full in the face, not to be dodged. But the offer of better business in the English colonies in exchange for a duty on the corn and meat of foreign countries—he could see too deep for that. The colonials might or might not be good customers; he knew how many decanters he sold in the United States, in spite of the tariff. He saw that the tax on food-stuffs was being commended to the working man with the argument of higher wages. Higher wages, with the competition of foreign labour, spelt only one word to English manufacturers, and that was ruin. The bugbear of higher wages, immediate, threatening, near, the terror of the last thirty years, closed the prospect for Charles Chafe; he could see nothing beyond. He did not say so, but to him the prosperity of the British manufacturer was bound up in the indigence of the operative. Thriving workmen, doing well, and looking to do better, rose before him in terms of menace, though their prosperity might be rooted in his own. "Give them cheap food and keep them poor," was the sum of his advice. His opinions had the emphasis of the unexpected, the unnatural: he was one of the people whom Wallingham's scheme in its legitimate development of a tariff on foreign manufactures might be expected to enrich. This fact, which he constantly insisted on, did give them weight; it made him look like a cunning fellow not to be caught with chaff. He and his business had survived free trade—though he would not say this either—and he preferred to go on surviving it rather than take the chances of any zollverein.[6] The name of the thing was enough for him, a word made in Germany, thick and mucky, like their tumblers. As to the colonies—Mr. Chafe had been told of a certain spider who devoured her young ones. He reversed the figure, and it stood, in the imperial connection, for all the argument he wanted.

Alfred Hesketh had lived always in the hearing of such doctrine; it had stood to him for political gospel by mere force of repetition. But he was young, with the curiosity and enterprise and impatience of dogma of youth; he belonged by temperament and situation to those plastic thousands in whom Wallingham hoped to find the leaven that should leaven the whole lump. His own blood stirred with the desire to accomplish, to carry further; and as the scope of the philanthropist did not attract him, he was vaguely conscious of having been born too late in England. The new political appeal of the colonies, clashing suddenly upon old insular harmonies, brought him a sense of wider fields and chances; his own case he freely translated into his country's, and offered an open mind to politics that would help either of them. He looked at the new countries with interest, an interest evoked by their sudden dramatic leap into the forefront of public concern. He looked at them with what nature intended to be the eye of a practical business man. He looked at Lorne Murchison, too, and listened to him, with steady, critical attention. Lorne seemed in a way to sum it all up in his person, all the better opportunity a man had out there; and he handled large matters of the future with a confidence and a grip that quickened the circulation. Hesketh's open mind gradually became filled with the imperial view as he had the capacity to take it; and we need not be surprised if Lorne Murchison, gazing in the same direction, supposed that they saw the same thing.

Hesketh confessed, declared, that Murchison had brought him round; and Lorne surveyed this achievement with a thrill of the happiest triumph. Hesketh stood, to him, a product of that best which he was so occupied in admiring and pursuing. Perhaps he more properly represented the second best; but we must allow something for the confusion of early impressions. Hesketh had lived always in the presence of ideals disengaged in England as nowhere else in the world; in Oxford, Lorne knew, they clustered thick. There is no doubt that his manners were good, and his ideas unimpeachable in the letter; the young Canadian read the rest into him and loved him for what he might have been.

"As an Englishman," said Hesketh one evening as they walked together back from the Chafes' along Knightsbridge, talking of the policy urged by the Colonial representatives at the last Conference,[7] "I could wish the idea were more our own—that we were pressing it on the colonies instead of the colonies pressing it on us."

"Doesn't there come a time in the history of most families," Lorne replied, "when the old folks look to the sons and daughters to keep them in touch with the times? Why shouldn't a vigorous policy of Empire be conceived by its younger nations—who have the ultimate resources to carry it out? We've got them and we know it—the iron and the coal and the gold, and the wheat-bearing areas. I dare say it makes us seem cheeky, but I tell you the last argument lies in the soil and what you can get out of it. What has this country got in comparison? A market of forty million people, whom she can't feed, and is less and less able to find work for. Do you call that a resource? I call it an impediment—a penalty. It's something to exploit, for the immediate profit in it, something to bargain with; but even as a market it can't preponderate always, and I can't see why it should make such tremendous claims."

"England isn't superannuated yet, Murchison."

"Not yet. Please God she never will be. But she isn't as young as she was, and it does seem to me —"

"What seems to you?"

"Well, I'm no economist, and I don't know how far to trust my impressions, and you needn't tell me I'm a rank outsider, for I know that; but coming here as an outsider, it does seem to me that it's from the outside that any sort of helpful change in the conditions of this country has got to come. England still has military initiative, though it's hard to see how she's going to keep that un less she does something to stop the degeneration of the class she draws her army from;[8] but what other kind do we hear about? Company promoting, bee-keeping, asparagus growing, poultry farming for ladies, the opening of a new Oriental Tea-Pot in Regent Street, with samisen-players between four and six, and Japanese attendants, who take the change on their hands and knees. London's one great stomach—how many eating places have we passed in the last ten minutes? The place seems all taken up with inventing new ways of making rich people more comfortable and better amused—I'm fed up with the sight of shiny carriages with cockaded flunkeys on 'em, wooden smart, rolling about with an elderly woman and a parasol and a dog.[9] England seems to have fallen back on itself, got content to spend the money there is in the country already; and about the only line of commercial activity the stranger sees is the onslaught on that accumulation. London isn't the headquarters for big new developing enterprises any more. If you take out Westminster and Wallingham, London is a collection of traditions and great houses, and newspaper offices, and shops. That sort of thing can't go on for ever. Already capital is drawing away to conditions it can find a profit in—steel works in Canada, woollen factories in Australia, jute mills in India. Do you know where the boots came from that shod the troops in South Africa? Cawnpore.[10] The money will go, you know, and that's a fact; the money will go, and the people will go, anyhow. It's only a case of whether England sends them with blessing and profit and greater glory, or whether she lets them slip away in spite of her."

"I dare say it will," replied Hesketh; "I've got precious little, but what there is I'd take out fast enough, if I saw a decent chance of investing it. I sometimes think of trying my luck in the States.

Two or three fellows in my year went over there and aren't making half a bad thing of it."

"Oh, come," said Lorne, half swinging round upon the other, with his hands in his pockets, "it isn't exactly the time, is it, to talk about chucking the Empire?"

"Well, no, it isn't," Hesketh admitted. "One might do better to wait, I dare say. At all events, till we see what the country says to Wallingham."

They walked on for a moment or two in silence; then Lorne broke out again.

"I suppose it's unreasonable, but there's nothing I hate so much as to hear Englishmen talk of settling in the United States."

"It's risky, I admit. And I've never heard anybody yet say it was comfortable."

"In a few years, fifty maybe, it won't matter. Things will have taken their direction by then; but now it's a question of the lead. The Americans think they've got it, and unless we get imperial federation of course they have. It's their plain intention to capture England commercially."

"We're a long way from that," said Hesketh.

"Yes, but it's in the line of fate. Industrial energy is deserting this country; and you have no large movement, no counter-advance, to make against the increasing forces that are driving this way from over there—nothing to oppose to assault. England is in a state of siege, and doesn't seem to know it. She's so great—Hesketh, it's pathetic!—she offers an undefended shore to attack, and a stupid confidence, a kindly blindness, above all to Americans, whom she patronizes in the gate."

"I believe we do patronize them," said Hesketh. "It's rotten bad form."

"Oh, form! I may be mad, but one seems to see in politics over here a lack of definition and purpose, a tendency to cling to the abstract and to precedent—'the mainstay of the mandarin' one of the papers calls it; that's a good word—that give one the feeling that this kingdom is beginning to be aware of some influence stronger than its own. It lies, of course, in the great West, where the corn and the cattle grow; and between Winnipeg and Chicago choose quickly, England!"

His companion laughed. "Oh, I'm with you," he said, "but you take a pessimistic view of this country, Murchison."

"It depends on what you call pessimism," Lorne rejoined. "I
see England down the future the heart of the Empire, the conscience of the world, and the Mecca of the race."

Chapter XVII

The Cruickshank deputation returned across that North Atlantic which it was their desire to see so much more than ever the track of the flag, toward the middle of July. The shiny carriages were still rolling about in great numbers when they left; London's air of luxury had thickened with the advancing season and hung heavily in the streets; people had begun to picnic in the Park on Sundays. They had been from the beginning a source of wonder and of depression to Lorne Murchison, the people in the Park, those, I mean, who walked and sat and stood there for the refreshment of their lives, for whom the place has a lyrical value as real as it is unconscious. He noted them ranged on formal benches, quiet, respectable, absorptive, or gathered heavily, shoulder to shoulder, docile under the tutelage of policemen, listening to any one who would lift a voice to speak to them.[1] London, beating on all borders, hemmed them in; England outside seemed hardly to contain for them a wider space. Lorne, with his soul full of free airs and forest depths, never failed to respond to a note in the Park that left him heavy-hearted, longing for an automatic distributing system for the Empire. When he saw them bring their spirit-lamps and kettles and sit down in little companies on four square yards of turf, under the blackened branches, in the roar of the traffic, he went back to Bloomsbury to pack his trunk, glad that it was not his lot to live with that enduring spectacle.

They were all glad, every one of them, to turn their faces to the West again. The unready conception of things, the political concentration upon parish affairs, the cumbrous social machinery, oppressed them with its dull anachronism in a marching world; the problems of sluggish over-population clouded their eager outlook. These conditions might have been their inheritance. Perhaps Lorne Murchison was the only one who thanked Heaven consciously that it was not so; but there was no man among them whose pulse did not mark a heart rejoiced as he paced the deck of the Allan liner the first morning out of Liverpool, because he had leave to refuse them. None dreamed of staying, of settling, though such a course was practicable to any of them except Lorne. They were all rich enough to take the advantages that money brings in England, the comfort, the importance, the state; they had only to add their wealth to the sumptuous side of the dramatic contrast. I doubt whether the idea even presented itself. It is the American who takes up his appreciative residence in England. He comes as a foreigner, observant, amused, having disclaimed responsibility for a hundred years. His detachment is as complete as it would be in Italy, with the added pleasure of easy comprehension. But home-comers from Greater Britain have never been cut off, still feel their uneasy share in all that is, and draw a long breath of relief as they turn again to their life in the lands where they found wider scope and different opportunities, and that new quality in the blood which made them different men.

The deputation had accomplished a good deal; less, Cruickshank said, than he had hoped, but more than he had expected. They had obtained the promise of concessions for Atlantic services, both mail and certain classes of freight, by being able to demonstrate a generous policy on their own side. Pacific communications the home Government were more chary of, there were matters to be fought out with Australia. The Pacific was further away, as Cruickshank said, and you naturally can't get fellows who have never been there to see the country under the Selkirks and south of the Bay—any of them except Wallingham, who had never been there either, but whose imagination took views of the falcon. They were reinforced by news of a shipping combination in Montreal to lower freights to South Africa against the Americans; it wasn't news to them, some of them were in it; but it was to the public, and it helped the sentiment of their aim, the feather on the arrow. They had secured something, both financially and morally; what best pleased them, perhaps, was the extent to which they got their scheme discussed. Here Lorne had been invaluable; Murchison had done more with the newspapers, they agreed, than any of them with Cabinet Ministers. The journalist everywhere is perhaps more accessible to ideas, more susceptible to enthusiasm, than his fellows, and Lorne was charged with the object of his deputation in its most communicable, most captivating form. At all events, he came to excellent understanding, whether of agreement or opposition, with the newspaper men he met—Cruickshank knew a good many of them, and these occasions were more fruitful than the official ones—and there is no doubt that the guarded approval of certain leading columns had fewer ifs and buts and other qualifications in consequence, while the disapproval of others was marked by a kind of unwilling sympathy and a freely accorded respect. Lorne found London editors surprisingly unbiassed, London newspapers surprisingly untrammelled. They seemed to him to suffer from no dictated views, no interests in the background or special local circumstances. They had open minds, most of them, and when a cloud appeared it was seldom more than a prejudice. It was only his impression, and perhaps it would not stand cynical inquiry; but he had a grateful conviction that the English Press occupied in the main a lofty and impartial ground of opinion, from which it desired only a view of the facts in their proportion. On his return he confided it to Horace Williams, who scoffed, and ran the national politics of the *Express* in the local interests of Fox County as hard as ever; but it had fallen in with Lorne's beautiful beliefs about England, and he clung to it for years.

The Williamses had come over the second evening following Lorne's arrival, after tea. Rawlins had gone to the station, just to see that the *Express* would make no mistake in announcing that Mr. L. Murchison had "Returned to the Paternal Roof," and the *Express* had announced it, with due congratulation. Family feeling demanded that for the first twenty-four hours he should be left to his immediate circle, but people had been dropping in all the next day at the office, and now came the Williamses, "trapesing," as Mrs. Murchison said, across the grass, though she was too content to make it more than a private grievance, to where they all sat on the verandah.

"What I don't understand," Horace Williams said to Mr. Murchison, "was why you didn't give him a blow on the whistle. You and Milburn and a few others might have got up quite a toot. You don't get the secretary to a deputation for tying up the Empire home every day."

"You did that for him in the *Express*," said John Murchison, smiling as he pressed down, with an accustomed thumb, the tobacco into his pipe.

"Oh, we said nothing at all! Wait till he's returned for South Fox," Williams responded jocularly.

"Why not the Imperial Council—of the future—at Westminster, while you're about it?" remarked Lorne, flipping a pebble back on the gravel path.

"That will keep, my son. But one of these days, mark my words, Mr. L. Murchison will travel to Elgin Station with flags on his engine, and he'll be very much surprised to find the band there, and a large number of his fellow citizens, all able-bodied shouting men, and every factory whistle in Elgin let off at once, to say nothing of kids with tin ones. And if the Murchison Stove and Furnace Works siren stands out of that occasion I'll break in and pull it myself."

"It won't stand out," Stella assured him. "I'll attend to it. Don't you worry."

"I suppose you had a lovely time, Mr. Murchison?" said Mrs. Williams, gently tilting to and fro in a rocking chair, with her pretty feet in their American shoes well in evidence. It is a fact, or perhaps a parable, that should be interesting to political economists, the adaptability of Canadian feet to American shoes; but fortunately it is not our present business. Though I must add that the "rocker" was also American, and the hammock in which Stella reposed came from New York, and upon John Murchison's knee, with the local journal, lay a pink evening paper published in Buffalo.[2]

"Better than I can tell you, Mrs. Williams, in all sorts of ways. But it's good to be back, too. Very good!" Lorne threw up his head and drew in the pleasant evening air of midsummer with infinite relish, while his eye travelled contentedly past the chestnuts on the lawn, down the vista of the quiet tree-bordered street. It lay empty in the solace of the evening, a blue hill crossed it in the distance, and gave it an unfettered look, the wind stirred in the maples. A pair of schoolgirls strolled up and down bareheaded; now and then a buggy passed.

"There's room here," he said.

"Find it kind of crowded up over there?" asked Mr. Williams. "Worse than New York?"

"Oh, yes. Crowded in a patient sort of way—it's enough to break your heart—that you don't see in New York! The poor of New York—well, they've got the idea of not being poor. In England they're resigned, they've got callous.[3] My goodness! the fellows out of work over there—you can *see* they're used to it, see it in the way they slope along and the look in their eyes, poor dumb dogs. They don't understand it, but they've just got to take it! Crowded? Rather!"

"We don't say, 'rather' in this country, mister," observed Stella.

"Well, you can say it now, kiddie."

They laughed at the little passage—the traveller's importation of one or two Briticisms had been the subject of skirmish before —but silence fell among them for a moment afterward. They all had in the blood the remembrance of what Lorne had seen.

"Well, you've been doing big business," said Horace Williams. Lorne shook his head. "We haven't done any harm," he said, "but our scheme's away out of sight now. At least it ought to be." "Lost in the bigger issue," said Williams, and Lorne nodded.

The bigger issue had indeed in the meantime obscured the political horizon, and was widely spreading. A mere colonial project might well disappear in it. England was absorbed in a single contemplation. Wallingham, though he still supported the disabilities of a right honourable evangelist with a gospel of his own,[4] was making astonishing conversions; the edifice of the national economic creed seemed coming over at the top. It was a question of the resistance of the base, and the world was watching.

"Cruickshank says if the main question had been sprung a month ago we wouldn't have gone over. As it is, on several points we've got to wait. If they reject the preferential trade idea over there we shall have done a little good, for any government would be disposed to try to patch up something to take the place of imperial union in that case; and a few thousands more for shipping subsidies and cheap cablegrams would have a great look of strengthening the ties with the colonies. But if they commit themselves to a zollverein with us and the rest of the family you won't hear much more about the need to foster communications. Communications will foster themselves."

"Just so," remarked John Murchison. "They'll save their money."

"I wouldn't think so before—I couldn't," Lorne went on, "but I'm afraid it's rather futile, the kind of thing we've been trying to do. It's fiddling at a superstructure without a foundation. What we want is the common interest. Common interest, common taxation for defence, common representation, domestic management of domestic affairs, and you've got a working Empire."[5]

"Just as easy as slippin' off a log," remarked Horace Williams.

"Common interest, yes," said his father; "common taxation, no, for defence or any other purpose. The colonies will never send money to be squandered by the London War Office. We'll defend ourselves, as soon as we can manage it, and buy our own guns and our own cruisers. We're better business people than they are, and we know it."

"I guess that's right, Mr. Murchison," said Horace Williams. "Our own army and navy—in the sweet bye and bye. And let 'em understand they'll be welcome to the use of it, but quite in a family way—no sort of compulsion."

"Well," said Lorne, "that's compatible enough."

"And your domestic affairs must include the tariff," Mr. Murchison went on. "There's no such possibility as a tariff that will go round. And tariffs are kittle⁶ cattle to shoo behind."

"Has anybody got a Scotch dictionary?" inquired Stella. "This conversation is making me tired."

"Suppose you run away and play with your hoop," suggested her brother. "I can't see that as an insuperable difficulty, father. Tariffs could be made adaptable, relative to the common interest as well as to the individual one. We could do it if we liked."

"Your adaptability might easily lead to other things. What's to prevent retaliation among ourselves? There's a slump in textiles, and the home Government is forced to let in foreign wool cheaper. Up goes the Australian tax on the output of every mill in Lancashire. The last state of the Empire might be worse than the first."

"It wouldn't be serious. If I pinched Stella's leg as I'm going to in a minute, she will no doubt kick me; and her instincts are such that she will probably kick me with the leg I pinched, but that won't prevent our going to the football match together tomorrow and presenting a united front to the world."

They all laughed, and Stella pulled down her lengthening petticoats with an air of great offence, but John Murchison shook his head. "If they manage it, they will be clever," he said.

"Talking of Lancashire," said Williams, "there are some funny fellows over there writing in the Press against a tax on foreign cotton because it's going to ruin Lancashire. And at this very minute thousands of looms are shut down in Lancashire because of the high price of cotton produced by an American combine—and worse coming, sevenpence a pound I hear they're going to have it, against the fourpence ha'penny they've got it up to already. That's the sort of thing they're afraid to discourage by a duty."

"Would a duty discourage it?" asked John Murchison.

"Why not—if they let British-grown cotton in free? They won't discourage the combine much—that form of enterprise has got to be tackled where it grows; but the Yankee isn't the only person in the world that can get to understand it. What's to prevent preferential conditions creating British combines, to compete with the American article, and what's to prevent Lancashire getting cheaper cotton in consequence? Two combines are better than one monopoly any day."

"Maybe so. It would want looking into. We won't see a duty on cotton though, or wool either for that matter. The manufacturers would be pleased enough to get it on the stuff they make, but there would be a fine outcry against taxing the stuff they use."

"Did you see much of the aristocracy, Mr. Murchison?" asked Mrs. Williams.

"No," replied Lorne, "but I saw Wallingham."

"You saw the whole House of Lords," interposed Stella, "and you were introduced to three."

"Well, yes, that's so. Fine-looking set of old chaps they are, too. We're a little too funny over here about the Lords—we haven't had to make any."

"What were they doing the day you were there, Lorne?" asked Williams.

"Motor-car legislation," replied Lorne. "Considerably excited about it, too. One of them had had three dogs killed on his estate. I saw his letter about it in the *Times*."[7]

"I don't see anything to laugh at in that," declared Stella. "Dogs are dogs."

"They are, sister, especially in England."

"Laundresses aren't washerwomen there," observed Mrs. Murchison. "I'd like you to see the colour of the things he's brought home with him, Mrs. Williams. Clean or dirty, to the laundry they go—weeks it will take to get them right again—ingrained London smut, and nothing else."

"In this preference business they've got to lead the way," Williams reverted. "We're not so grown up but what grandma's got to march in front. Now, from your exhaustive observation of

Great Britain, extending over a period of six weeks, is she going to?"

"My exhaustive observation," said Lorne, smiling, "enables me to tell you one thing with absolute accuracy; and that is that nobody knows.[8] They adore Wallingham over there—he's pretty nearly a god[9]—and they'd like to do as he tells them, and they're dead sick of theoretic politics; but they're afraid—oh, they're afraid!"

"They'll do well to ca' canny," said John Murchison.

"There's two things in the way, at a glance," Lorne went on. "The conservatism of the people—it isn't a name, it's a fact—the hostility and suspicion; natural enough: they know they're stupid, and they half suspect they're fair game. I suppose the Americans have taught them that. Slow—oh, slow! More interested in the back- garden fence than anything else. Pick up a paper, at the moment when things are being done, mind, all over the world, done against them—when their shipping is being captured, and their industries destroyed, and their goods undersold beneath their very noses—and the thing they want to know is—'Why Are the Swallows Late?' I read it myself, in a ha'penny morning paper, too, that they think rather dangerously go-ahead—a whole column, leaded, to inquire what's the matter with the swallows. The *Times* the same week had a useful leader on Alterations in the Church Service,[10] and a special contribution on Prayers for the Dead. Lord, they need 'em! Those are the things they *think* about! The session's nearly over, and there's two Church Discipline Bills, and five Church Bills—bishoprics and benefices, and Lord knows what—still to get through. Lot of anxiety about 'em, apparently! As to a business view of politics, I expect the climate's against it. They'll see over a thing—they're fond of doing that—or under it, or round one side of it, but they don't seem to have any way of seeing *through* it. What they just love is a good round catchword; they've only got to hear themselves say it often enough, and they'll take it for gospel. They're convinced out of their own mouths. There was the driver of a 'bus I used to ride on pretty often, and if he felt like talking, he'd always begin, 'As I was a-sayin' of yesterday —' Well, that's the general idea—to repeat what they were a-sayin' of yesterday; and it doesn't matter two cents that the rest of the world has changed the subject. They've been a-sayin' a long time that they object to import duties of any sort or kind, and you won't get them to *see* the business in changing. If they do this it won't be because they want to, it will be because Wallingham wants them to."

"I guess that's so," said Williams. "And if Wallingham gets them to he ought to have a statue in every capital in the Empire. He will, too. Good cigar this, Lorne! Where'd you get it?"

"They are Indian cheroots—'Planters' they call 'em—made in Madras. I got some through a man named Hesketh, who has friends out there, at a price you wouldn't believe for as decent a smoke. You can't buy 'em in London; but you will all right, and here, too, as soon as we've got the sense to favour British-grown tobacco."

"Lorne appreciates his family better than he did before," remarked his youngest sister, "because we're British grown."

"You were saying you noticed two things specially in the way?" said his father.

"Oh, the other's of course the awful poverty—the twelve millions that haven't got enough to do with.[11] I expect it's an outside figure and it covers all sorts of qualifying circumstances; but it's the one the Free Fooders[12] quote, and it's the one Wallingham will have to handle. They've muddled along until they've *got* twelve million people in that condition, and now they have to carry on with the handicap. We ask them to put a tax on foreign food to develop our wheat areas and cattle ranges. We say, 'Give us a chance and we'll feed you and take your surplus population.' What is to be done with the twelve million while we are growing the wheat? The colonies offer to create prosperity for everybody concerned at a certain outlay—we've got the raw materials—and they can't afford the investment because of the twelve millions, and what may happen meanwhile. They can't face the meanwhile—that's what it comes to—."

"Fine old crop of catchwords in that situation," Mr. Williams remarked; and his eye had the spark of the practical politician. "Can't you hear 'em at it, eh?"

"It scares them out of everything but hand-to-mouth politics. Any other remedy is too heroic. They go on pointing out and contemplating and grieving, with their percentages of misery and degeneration; and they go on poulticing the cancer with benevolence—there are people over there who want the State to feed the school children! Oh, they're kind, good, big-hearted people; and they've got the idea that if they can only give enough away everything will come right. I was talking with a man one day, and I asked him whether the existence of any class justified governing a great country on the principle of an almshouse. He asked me who the almsgivers ought to be, in any country. Of course it was tampering with my figure—in an almshouse there aren't any; but that's the way it presents itself to the best of them. Another fellow was frantic at the idea of a tax on foreign food—he nearly cried—but would be very glad to see Government do more to assist emigration to the colonies. I tried to show him it would be better to make it profitable to emigrate first, but I couldn't make him see it.

"Oh, and there's the old thing against them, of course—the handling of imperial and local affairs by one body. Anybody's good enough to attend to the Baghdad Railway, and nobody's too good to attend to the town pump. Is it any wonder the Germans beat them in their own shops and Russia walks into Thibet?[13] The eternal marvel is that they stand where they do."

"At the top," said Mr. Williams.

"Oh—at the top! Think of what you mean when you say 'England.' "

"I see that the demand for a tariff on manufactured goods is growing," Williams remarked, "even the anti-food-tax organs are beginning to shout for that."

"If they had put it on twenty years ago," said Lorne, "there would be no twelve million people making a problem for want of work, and it would be a good deal easier to do imperial business to-day."

"You'll find," said John Murchison, removing his pipe, "that protection'll have to come first over there. They'll put up a fence and save their trade—in their own good time, not next week or next year—and when they've done that they'll talk to us about our big ideas—not before. And if Wallingham hadn't frightened them with the imperial job, he never would have got them to take up the other. It's just his way of getting both done."[14]

"I hope you're right, father," said Lorne, with a covert glance at his watch. "Horace—Mrs. Williams—I'll have to get you to excuse me. I have an engagement at eight."

He left them with a happy spring in his step, left them looking after him, talking of him, with pride and congratulation. Only Stella, with a severe lip and a disapproving eye, noted the direction he took as he left the house.

Chapter XVIII

Peter Macfarlane had carried the big Bible up the pulpit
steps of Knox Church, and arranged the glass of water and
the notices to be given out beside it, twice every Sunday for twenty years. He was a small spare man, with thin grey hair that fell
back from the narrow dome of his forehead to his coat collar,
decent and severe. He ascended the pulpit exactly three minutes
before the minister did; and the dignity with which he put one foot
before the other made his appearance a ceremonious feature of the
service and a thing quoted. "I was there before Peter" was a triumphant evidence of punctuality. Dr. Drummond would have liked
to make it a test. It seemed to him no great thing to expect the
people of Knox Church to be there before Peter.

Macfarlane was also in attendance in the vestry to help the
minister off with his gown and hang it up. Dr. Drummond's gown
needed neither helping nor hanging; the Doctor was deftness and
neatness and impatience itself, and would have it on the hook with
his own hands, and never a fold crooked. After Mr. Finlay, on the
contrary, Peter would have to pick up and smooth out—ten to one
the garment would be flung on a chair. Still, he was invariably
standing by to see it flung, and to hand Mr. Finlay his hat and
stick. He was surprised and put about to find himself one Sunday
evening too late for this attendance. The vestry was empty, the
gown was on the floor. Peter gathered it up with as perturbed an
air as if Mr. Finlay had omitted a point of church observance. "I
doubt they get into slack ways in these missions," said Peter. He
had been unable, with Dr. Drummond, to see the necessity for
such extensions.

Meanwhile Hugh Finlay, in secular attire, had left the church
by the vestry door, and was rapidly overtaking groups of his
hearers as they walked homeward. He was unusually aware of his
change of dress because of a letter in the inside pocket of his coat.
The letter, in that intimate place, spread a region of consciousness
round it which hastened his blood and his step. There was purpose
in his whole bearing; Advena Murchison, looking back at some
suggestion of Lorne's, caught it, and lost for a moment the

meaning of what she said. When he overtook them, with plain intention, she walked beside the two men, withdrawn and silent, like a child. It was unexpected and overwhelming, his joining them after the service, accompanying them, as it were, in the flesh after having led them so far in the spirit; he had never done it before. She felt her heart confronted with a new, an immediate issue, and suddenly afraid. It shrank from the charge for which it longed, and would have fled; yet, paralysed with delight, it kept time with her sauntering feet.

They talked of the sermon, which had been strongly tinged with the issue of the day. Dreamer as he was by temperament, Finlay held to the wisdom of informing great public questions with the religious idea, vigorously disclaimed that it was anywhere inadmissible.

"You'll have to settle with the Doctor, Mr. Finlay," Lorne warned him gaily, "if you talk politics in Knox Church. He thinks he never does."

"Do you think," said Finlay, "that he would object to—to one's going as far afield as I did to-night?"

"He oughtn't to," said Lorne. "You should have heard him when old Sir John Macdonald gerrymandered the electoral districts and gave votes to the Moneida Indians.[1] The way he put it, the Tories in the congregation couldn't say a word, but it was a treat for his fellow Grits."

Finlay smiled gravely. "Political convictions are a man's birthright," he said. "Any man or any minister is a poor creature without them. But of course there are limits beyond which pulpit influence should not go, and I am sure Dr. Drummond has the clearest perception of them. He seems to have been a wonderful fellow, Macdonald, a man with extraordinary power of imagination enterprise. I wonder whether he would have seen his way to linking up the Empire as he linked up your Provinces here?"

"He'd have hated uncommonly to be in opposition, but I don't see how he could have helped it," Lorne said. "He was the godfather of Canadian manufactures, you know—the Tories have always been the industrial party.[2] He couldn't have gone for letting English stuff in free, or cheap; and yet he was genuinely loyal and attached to England.[3] He would discriminate against Manchester with tears in his eyes! Imperialist in his time spelled Conservative, now it spells Liberal. The Conservatives have always talked the loudest about the British bond, but when it lately came to doing we're on record on the right side, and they're on record on the wrong.[4] But it must make the old man's ghost sick to see—"

"To see his court suit stolen," Advena finished for him. "As Disraeli[5] said—wasn't it Disraeli?" She heard, and hated the note of constraint in her voice. "Am I reduced," she thought, indignantly, "to falsetto?" and chose, since she must choose, the betrayal of silence.

"It did one good to hear the question discussed on the higher level," said Lorne. "You would think, to read the papers, that all its merits could be put into dollars and cents."

"I've noticed some of them in terms of sentiment—affection for the mother country—"

"Yes, that's lugged in. But it doesn't cover the moral aspect," Lorne returned. "It's too easy and obvious, as well; it gives the enemy cause to offend."

"Well, there's a tremendous moral aspect," Finlay said, "tremendous moral potentialities hidden in the issue. England has more to lose than she dreams."

"That's just where I felt, as a practical politician, a little restless while you were preaching," said Lorne, laughing. "You seemed to think the advantage of imperialism was all with England. You mustn't press that view on us, you know. We shall get harder to bargain with. Besides, from the point of your sermon, it's all the other way."

"Oh, I don't agree! The younger nations can work out their own salvation unaided; but can England alone? Isn't she too heavily weighted?"

"Oh, materially, very likely! But morally, no," said Lorne, stoutly. "There, if you like, she has accumulations that won't depreciate. Money isn't the only capital the colonies offer investment for."

"I'm afraid I see it in the shadow of the degeneration of age and poverty," said Finlay, smiling— "or age and wealth, if you prefer it."

"And we in the disadvantage of youth and easy success," Lorne retorted. "We're all very well, but we're not the men our fathers were: we need a lot of licking into shape. Look at that disgraceful business of ours in the Ontario legislature the other day, and look at that fellow of yours walking out of office at Westminster last session because of a disastrous business connection which he was morally as clear of as you or I! I tell you we've got to hang on to the things that make us ashamed; and I guess we've got sense enough to know it. But this is my corner. I am going to look in at the Milburns', Advena. Good-night, Mr. Finlay."

Advena, walking on with Finlay, became suddenly aware that he had not once addressed her. She had the quick impression that Lorne left him bereft of a refuge; his plight heartened her.

"If the politicians on both sides were only as mutually appreciative," she said, "the Empire would soon be knit."

For a moment he did not answer. "I am afraid the economic situation is not quite analogous," he said, stiffly and absently, when the moment had passed. "Why does your brother always call me 'Mr.' Finlay?" he demanded presently. "It isn't friendly."

The note of irritation in his voice puzzled her. "I think the form is commoner with us," she said, "even among men who know each other fairly well." Her secret glance flashed over the gulf that nevertheless divided Finlay and her brother, that would always divide them. She saw it with something like pain, which struggled through her pride in both. "And then, you know—your calling—"

"I suppose it is that," he replied, ill content.

"I've noticed Dr. Drummond's way," she told him, with rising spirits. "It's delightful. He drops the 'Mr.' with fellow ministers of his own denomination only—never with Wesleyans or Baptists, for a moment. He always comes back very genial from the General Assembly, and full of stories. 'I said to Grant,' or 'Macdonald said to me'—and he always calls you 'Finlay,'" she added shyly. "By the way, I suppose you know he's to be the new Moderator?"[6]

"Is he, indeed? Yes—yes, of course, I knew! We couldn't have a better."

They walked on through the early autumn night. It was just not raining. The damp air was cool and pungent with the smell of fallen leaves, which lay thick under their feet. Advena speared the dropped horse-chestnut husks with the point of her umbrella as they went along. She had picked up half a dozen when he spoke again. "I want to tell you—I have to tell you—something—about myself, Miss Murchison."

"I should like," said Advena steadily, "to hear."

"It is a matter that has, I am ashamed to confess, curiously gone out of my mind of late—I should say until lately. There was little until lately—I am so poor a letter writer—to remind me of it. I am engaged to be married!"

"But how interesting!" exclaimed Advena.

He looked at her, taken aback. His own mood was heavy; it failed to answer this lightness from her. It is hard to know what he expected, what his unconscious blood expected for him; but it was not this. If he had little wisdom about the hearts of women, he had less about their behaviour. She said nothing more, but inclined her head in an angle of deference and expectation toward what he should further communicate.

"I don't know that I have ever told you much about my life in Scotland," he went on. "It has always seemed to me so remote and—disconnected with everything here. I could not suppose it would interest any one. I was cared for and educated by my father's only sister, a good woman. It was as if she had whole charge of the part of my life that was not absorbed in work. I don't know that I can make you understand. She was identified with all the rest—I left it to her. Shortly before I sailed for Canada she spoke to me of marriage in connection with my work and— welfare, and with—a niece of her husband's who was staying with us at the time, a person suitable in every way. Apart from my aunt, I do not know—However, I owed everything to her, and I—took her advice in the matter. I left it to her. She is a managing woman; but she can nearly always prove herself right. Her mind ran a great deal, a little too much perhaps, upon creature comforts, and I suppose she thought that in emigrating a man might do well to companion himself."

"That was prudent of her," said Advena.

He turned a look upon her. "You are not—making a mock of it?" he said.

"I am not making a mock of it."

"My aunt now writes to me that Miss Christie's home has been broken up by the death of her mother, and that if it can be arranged she is willing to come to me here. My aunt talks of bringing her. I am to write."

He said the last words slowly, as if he weighed them. They had passed the turning to the Murchisons', walking on with the single consciousness of a path under them, and space before them. Once or twice before that had happened, but Advena had always been aware. This time she did not know.

"You are to write," she said. She sought in vain for more words; he also, throwing back his head, appeared to search the firmament for phrases without result. Silence seemed enforced between them, and walked with them, on into the murky landscape, over the fallen leaves. Passing a street-lamp, they quickened their steps, looking furtively at the light, which seemed leagued against them with silence.

"It seems so extraordinarily—far away," said Hugh Finlay, of Bross, Dumfries, at length.

"But it will come near," Advena replied.

"I don't think it ever can."

She looked at him with a sudden leap of the heart, a wild, sweet dismay.

"They, of course, will come. But the life of which they are a part, and the man whom I remember to have been me—there is a gulf fixed—"

"It is only the Atlantic," Advena said. She had recovered her vision; in spite of the stone in her breast she could look. The weight and the hurt she would reckon with later. What was there, after all, to do? Meanwhile she could look, and already she saw with passion what had only begun to form itself in his consciousness, his strange, ironical, pitiful plight.

He shook his head. "It is not marked in any geography," he said, and gave her a troubled smile. "How can I make it clear to you? I have come here into a new world, of interests unknown and scope unguessed before. I know what you would say, but you have no way of learning the beauty and charm of mere vitality—you have always been so alive. One finds a physical freedom in which one's very soul seems to expand; one hears the happiest calls of fancy. And the most wonderful, most delightful thing of all is to discover that one is oneself, strangely enough, able to respond—"

The words reached the woman beside him like some cool dropping balm, healing, inconceivably precious. She knew her share in all this that he recounted. He might not dream of it, might well confound her with the general pulse; but she knew the sweet and separate subcurrent that her life had been in his, felt herself underlying all these new joys of his, could tell him how dear she was.

But it seemed that he must not guess.

It came to her with force that his dim perception of his case was grotesque, that it humiliated him. She had a quick desire that he should at least know that civilized, sentient beings did not lend themselves to such outrageous comedies as this which he had confessed; it had somehow the air of a confession. She could not let him fall so lamentably short of man's dignity, of man's estate, for his own sake.

"It is a curious history," she said. "You are right in thinking I should not find it quite easy to understand. We make those—arrangements—so much more for ourselves over here. Perhaps we think them more important than they are."

"But they are of the highest importance." He stopped short, confounded.

"I shall try to consecrate my marriage," he said presently, more to himself than to Advena.

Her thought told him bitterly: "I am afraid it is the only thing you can do with it," but something else came to her lips.

"I have not congratulated you. I am not sure," she went on, with astonishing candour, "whether I can. But I wish you happiness with all my heart. Are you happy now?"

He turned his great dark eyes on her.

"I am as happy, I dare say, as I have any need to be."

"But you are happier since your letter came?"

"No," he said. The simple word fell on her heart, and she forebore.

They went on again in silence until they arrived at a place from which they saw the gleam of the river and the line of the hills beyond. Advena stopped.

"We came here once before together—in the spring. Do you remember?" she asked.

"I remember very well." She had turned, and he with her. They stood together with darkness about them, through which they could just see each other's faces.

"It was spring, then, and I went back alone. You are still living up that street? Good-night, then, please. I wish again—to go back—alone."

He looked at her for an instant in dumb bewilderment, though her words were simple enough. Then as she made a step away from him he caught her hand.

"Advena," he faltered, "what has happened to us? This time I cannot let you."

Chapter XIX

"**L**orne," said Dora Milburn, in her most animated manner, "who do you think is coming to Elgin? Your London friend, Mr. Hesketh! He's going to stay with the Emmetts, and Mrs. Emmett is perfectly distracted; she says he's accustomed to so much, she doesn't know how he will put up with their plain way of living. Though what she means by that, with late dinner and afternoon tea every day of her life, is more than I know."

"Why, that's splendid!" replied Lorne. "Good old Hesketh! I knew he thought of coming across this fall, but the brute hasn't written to me. We'll have to get him over to our place. When he gets tired of the Emmetts' plain ways he can try ours—they're plainer. You'll like Hesketh; he's a good fellow, and more go-ahead than most of them."

"I don't think I should ask him to stay if I were you, Lorne. Your mother will never consent to change her hours for meals. I wouldn't dream of asking an Englishman to stay if I couldn't give him late dinner; they think so much of it. It's the trial of mother's life that father will not submit to it. As a girl she was used to nothing else. Afternoon tea we do have, he can't prevent that,[1] but father kicks at anything but one o'clock dinner and meat tea at six, and I suppose he always will."

"Doesn't one tea spoil the other?" Lorne inquired. "I find it does when I go to your minister's and peck at a cress sandwich at five. You haven't any appetite for a reasonable meal at six. But I guess it won't matter to Hesketh; he's got a lot of sense about things of that sort. Why he served out in South Africa—volunteered. Mrs. Emmett needn't worry. And if we find him pining for afternoon tea we can send him over here."

"Well, if he's nice. But I suppose he's pretty sure to be nice. Any friend of the Emmetts—What is he like, Lorne?"

"Oh, he's just a young man with a moustache! You seem to see a good many over there. They're all alike while they're at school in round coats, and after they leave school they get moustaches, and then they're all alike again."

"I wish you wouldn't tease. How tall is he? Is he fair or dark? What colour are his eyes?"

Lorne buried his head in his hands in a pretended agony of recollection. "So far as I remember, not exactly tall, but you wouldn't call him short. Complexion—well, don't you know?—that kind of middling complexion. Colour of his eyes—does anybody ever notice a thing like that? You needn't take my word for it, but I should say they were a kind of average coloured eyes."

"Lorne! You *are*—I suppose I'll just have to wait till I see him. But the girls are wild to know, and I said I'd ask you. He'll be here in about two weeks anyhow, and I dare say we won't find him so much to make a fuss about. The best sort of Englishmen don't come over such a very great deal, as you say. I expect they have a better time at home."

"Hesketh's a very good sort of Englishman," said Lorne.

"He's awfully well off, isn't he?"

"According to our ideas I suppose he is," said Lorne. "Not according to English ideas."

"Still less according to New York ones, then," asserted Dora. "They wouldn't think much of it there even if he passed for rich in England." It was a little as if she resented Lorne's comparison of standards, and claimed the American one as at least cis-Atlantic.

"He has a settled income," said Lorne, "and he's never had to work for it, whatever luck there is in that. That's all I know. Dora —"

"Now, Lorne, you're not to be troublesome."

"Your mother hasn't come in at all this evening. Don't you think it's a good sign?"

"She isn't quite so silly as she was," remarked Dora. "Why I should not have the same freedom as other girls in entertaining my gentleman friends I never could quite see."

"I believe if we told her we had made up our minds it would be all right," he pleaded.

"I'm not so sure, Lorne. Mother's so deep. You can't always tell just by what she *does*. She thinks Stephen Stuart likes me—it's too perfectly idiotic; we are the merest friends—and when it's any question of you and Stephen—well, she doesn't say anything, but she lets me see! She thinks such a lot of the Stuarts because Stephen's father was Ontario Premier once, and got knighted."

"I might try for that myself if you think it would please her," said the lover.

"Please her! And I should be Lady Murchison!" she let fall

upon his ravished ears. "Why, Lorne, she'd just worship us both! But you'll never do it."

"Why not?"

Dora looked at him with pretty speculation. She had reasons for supposing that she did admire the young man.

"You're too nice," she said.

"That isn't good enough," he responded, and drew her nearer.

"Then why did you ask me?—No, Lorne, you are not to. Suppose father came in?"

"I shouldn't mind—father's on my side, I think."

"Father isn't on anybody's side," said his daughter, wisely.

"Dora, let me speak to him!"

Miss Milburn gave a clever imitation of a little scream of horror.

"*Indeed* I won't! Lorne, you are never, *never* to do that! As if we were in a ridiculous English novel!"

"That's the part of an English novel I always like," said Lorne. "The going and asking. It must about scare the hero out of a year's growth; but it's a glorious thing to do—it would be next day, anyhow."

"It's just the sort of thing to please mother," Dora meditated, "but she can't be indulged all the time. No, Lorne, you'll have to leave it to me—when there's anything to tell."

"There's everything to tell now," said he, who had indeed nothing to keep back.

"But you know what mother is, Lorne. Suppose they hadn't any objection, she would never keep it to herself! She'd want to go announcing it all over the place; she'd think it was the proper thing to do."

"But, Dora, why not? If you knew how I want to announce it! I should like to publish it in the sunrise—and the wind—so that I couldn't go out of doors without seeing it myself."

"I shouldn't mind having it in *Toronto Society*, when the time comes. But not yet, Lorne—not for ages. I'm only twenty-two— nobody thinks of settling down nowadays before she's twenty-five at the very earliest. I don't know a single girl in this town that has—among my friends, anyway. That's three years off, and you *can't* expect me to be engaged for three years."

"No," said Lorne, "engaged six months, married the rest of the time. Or the periods might run concurrently if you preferred—I shouldn't mind."

"An engaged girl has the very worst time. She gets hardly any attention, and as to dances—well, it's a good thing for her if the person she's engaged to *can* dance," she added, teasingly.

Lorne coloured. "You said I was improving, Dora," he said, and then laughed at the childish claim. "But that isn't really a thing that counts, is it? If our lives only keep step it won't matter much about the 'Washington Post.'[2] And so far as attention goes, you'll get it as long as you live, you little princess. Besides, isn't it better to wear the love of one man than the admiration of half a dozen?"

"And be teased and worried half out of your life by everybody you meet? Now, Lorne, you're getting serious and sentimental, and you know I hate that. It isn't any good either—mother always used to say it made me more stubborn to appeal to me. Horrid nature to have, isn't it?"

Lorne's hand went to his waistcoat pocket and came back with a tiny packet. "It's come, Dora—by this morning's English mail."

Her eyes sparkled, and then rested with guarded excitement upon the little case. "Oh, Lorne!"

She said nothing more, but watched intently while he found the spring, and disclosed the ring within. Then she drew a long breath. "Lorne Murchison, what a lovely one!"

"Doesn't it look," said he, "just a little serious and sentimental?"

"But *such* good style, too," she declared, bending over it. "And quite new—I haven't seen anything a bit like it. I do love a design when it's graceful. Solitaires are so old-fashioned."

He kept his eyes upon her face, feeding upon the delight in it. Exultation rose up in him: he knew the primitive guile of man, indifferent to such things, alluring with them the other creature. He did not stop to condone her weakness; rather he seized it in ecstasy; it was all part of the glad scheme to help the lover. He turned the diamonds so that they flashed and flashed again before her. Then, trusting his happy instinct, he sought for her hand. But she held that back. "I want to *see* it," she declared, and he was obliged to let her take the ring in her own way and examine it, and place it in every light, and compare it with others worn by her friends, and make little tentative charges of extravagance in his purchase of it, while he sat elated and adoring, the simple fellow.

Reluctantly at last she gave up her hand.

"But it's only trying on—not putting on," she told him. He said nothing till it flashed upon her finger, and in her eyes he saw a spark from below of that instinctive cupidity toward jewels that man can never recognize as it deserves in woman, because of his desire to gratify it.

"You'll wear it, Dora?" he pleaded.

"Lorne, you are the dearest fellow! But how could I? Everybody would guess!"

Her gaze, nevertheless, rested fascinated on the ring, which she posed as it pleased her.

"Let them guess! I'd rather they knew, but—it does look well on your finger, dear."

She held it up once more to the light, then slipped it decisively off and gave it back to him. "I can't, you know, Lorne. I didn't really say you might get it; and now you'll have to keep it till—till the time comes. But this much I will say—it's the sweetest thing, and you've shown the loveliest taste, and if it weren't such a dreadful give-away I'd like to wear it awfully."

They discussed it with argument, with endearment, with humour, and reproach, but her inflexible basis soon showed through their talk: she would not wear the ring. So far he prevailed, that it was she, not he, who kept it. Her insistence that he should take it back brought something like anger out of him; and in the surprise of this she yielded so much. She did it unwillingly at the time, but afterward, when she tried on the thing again in the privacy of her own room, she was rather satisfied to have it, safe under lock and key, a flashing, smiling mystery to visit when she liked and reveal when she would.

"Lorne could never get me such a beauty again if he lost it," she advised herself, "and he's awfully careless. And I'm not sure that I won't tell Eva Delarue, just to show it to her. She's as close as wax."

One feels a certain sorrow for the lover on his homeward way, squaring his shoulders against the foolish perversity of the feminine mind, resolutely guarding his heart from any hint of real reprobation. Through the sweetness of her lips and the affection of her pretty eyes, through all his half-possession of all her charms and graces, must have come dully the sense of his great occasion *manqué*, that dear day of love when it leaves the mark of its claim. And in one's regret there is perhaps some alloy of pity, that less respectful thing. We know him elsewhere capable of essaying heights, yet we seem to look down upon the drama of his heart. It may be well to remember that the level is not everything in love. He who carefully adjusts an intellectual machine may descry a higher mark; he can construct nothing in a mistress; he is, therefore, able to see the facts and to discriminate the desirable. But Lorne loved with all his imagination. This way dares the imitation of the gods, by which it improves the quality of the passion, so that such a love stands by itself to be considered, apart from the object, one may say. A strong and beautiful wave lifted Lorne Murchison along to his destiny, since it was the pulse of his own life, though Dora Milburn played moon to it.

Chapter XX

Alfred Hesketh had, after all, written to young Murchison about his immediate intention of sailing for Canada and visiting Elgin; the letter arrived a day or two later. It was brief and business-like, but it gave Lorne to understand that since his departure the imperial idea had been steadily fermenting, not only in the national mind, but particularly in Hesketh's; that it produced in his case a condition only to be properly treated by personal experience. Hesketh was coming over to prove whatever advantage there was in seeing for yourself. That he was coming with the right bias Lorne might infer, he said, from the fact that he had waited a fortnight to get his passage by the only big line to New York that stood out for our mercantile supremacy against American combination.

"He needn't bother to bring any bias," Lorne remarked when he had read this, "but he'll have to pay a lot of extra luggage on the one he takes back with him."

He felt a little irritation at being offered the testimony of the Cunard ticket. Back on his native soil, its independence ran again like sap in him: nobody wanted a present of good-will; the matter stood on its merits.

He was glad, nevertheless, that Hesketh was coming, gratified that it would now be his turn to show prospects, and turn figures into facts, and make plain the imperial profit from the further side. Hesketh was such an intelligent fellow, there would be the keenest sort of pleasure in demonstrating things, big things, to him, little things, too, ways of living, differences of habit. Already in the happy exercise of his hospitable instinct he saw how Hesketh would get on with his mother, with Stella, with Dr. Drummond. He saw Hesketh interested, domiciled, remaining—the ranch life this side of the Rockies, Lorne thought, would tempt him, or something new and sound in Winnipeg. He kept his eye open for chances, and noted one or two likely things. "We want labour mostly," he said to Advena, "but nobody is refused leave to land because he has a little money."

"I should think not, indeed," remarked Mrs. Murchison, who was present. "I often wish your father and I had had a little more when we began. That whole Gregory block was going for three thousand dollars then. I wonder what it's worth now?"

"Yes, but you and father are worth more, too," remarked Stella acutely.

"In fact, all the elder members of the family have approximated in value, Stella," said her brother, "and you may too, in time."

"I'll take my chance with the country," she retorted. They were all permeated with the question of the day; even Stella, after holding haughtily aloof for some time, had been obliged to get into step, as she described it, with the silly old Empire. Whatever it was in England, here it was a family affair; I mean in the town of Elgin, in the shops and the offices, up and down the tree-bordered streets as men went to and from their business, atomic creatures building the reef of the future, but conscious, and wanting to know what they were about. Political parties had long declared themselves, the Hampden Debating Society had had several grand field nights. Prospective lifelong friendships, male and female, in every form of "the Collegiate," had been put to this touchstone, sometimes with shattering effect. If you would not serve with Wallingham the greatness of Britain you were held to favour going over to the United States; there was no middle course. It became a personal matter in the ward schools, and small boys pursued small boys with hateful cries of "Annexationist!" The subject even trickled about the apple-barrels and potato-bags of the market square. Here it should have raged, pregnant as it was with bucolic blessing; but our agricultural friends expect nothing readily except adverse weather, least of all a measure of economic benefit to themselves. Those of Fox County thought it looked very well, but it was pretty sure to work out some other way. Elmore Crow failed heavily to catch a light even from Lorne Murchison.

"You keep your hair on, Lorne," he advised. "We ain't going to get such big changes yet. An' if we do the blooming syndicates'll spoil 'em for us."

There were even dissentients among the farmers. The voice of one was raised who had lived laborious years, and many of them, in the hope of seeing his butter and cheese go unimpeded across the American line. It must be said, however, that still less attention was paid to him, and it was generally conceded that he would die without the sight.

It was the great topic. The day Wallingham went his defiant

furthest in the House and every colonial newspaper set it up in acclaiming headlines, Horace Williams, enterprising fellow, remembered that Lorne had seen the great man under circumstances that would probably pan out, and sent round Rawlins. Rawlins was to get something that would do to call "Wallingham in the Bosom of his Family," and as much as Lorne cared to pour into him about his own view of the probable issue. Rawlins failed to get the interview, came back to say that Lorne didn't seem to think himself a big enough boy for that, but he did not return empty handed. Mr. Murchison sent Mr. Williams the promise of some contributions upon the question of the hour which he had no objection to sign, and which Horace should have for the good of the cause. Horace duly had them, the *Express* duly published them, and they were copied in full by the *Dominion* and several other leading journals, with an amount of comment which every one but Mrs. Murchison thought remarkable.

"I don't pretend to understand it," she said, "but anybody can see that he knows what he's talking about." John Murchison read them with a critical eye and a pursed-out lip.

"He takes too much for granted."

"What does he take for granted?" asked Mrs. Murchison.

"Other folks being like himself," said the father.

That, no doubt, was succinct and true; nevertheless, the articles had competence as well as confidence. The writer treated facts with restraint and conditions with sympathy. He summoned ideas from the obscurity of men's minds, and marshalled them in the light, so that many recognized what they had been trying to think. He wrote with homeliness as well as force, wishing much more to make the issue recognizable than to create fine phrases, with the result that one or two of his sentences passed into the language of the discussion, which, as any of its standard-bearers would have told you, had little use for rhetoric. The articles were competent: if you listened to Horace Williams you would have been obliged to accept them as the last, or latest, word of economic truth, though it must be left to history to endorse Mr. Williams. It was their enthusiasm, however, that gave them the wing on which they travelled. People naturally took different views, even of this quality. "Young Murchison's working the imperial idea for all it's worth," was Walter Winter's; and Octavius Milburn humorously summed up the series as "tall talk."

Alfred Hesketh came, it was felt, rather opportunely into the midst of this. Plenty of people, the whole of Market Square and East Elgin, a good part, too, probably, of the Town Ward, were unaware of his arrival; but for the little world he penetrated he was clothed with all the interest of the great contingency. His decorous head in the Emmetts' pew on Sunday morning stood for a symbol as well as for a stranger. The nation was on the eve of a great far-reaching transaction with the mother country, and thrilling with the terms of the bargain. Hesketh was regarded by people in Elgin who knew who he was with the mingled cordiality and distrust that might have met a principal. They did not perhaps say it, but it was in their minds. "There's one of them," was what they thought when they met him in the street. At any other time he would have been just an Englishman; now he was invested with the very romance of destiny. The perception was obscure, but it was there. Hesketh, on the other hand, found these good people a very well-dressed, well-conditioned, decent lot, rather sallower than he expected, perhaps, who seemed to live in a fair-sized town in a great deal of comfort, and was wholly unconscious of anything special in his relation to them or theirs to him.

He met Lorne just outside the office of Warner, Fulke, and Murchison the following day. They greeted heartily. "Now this *is* good!" said Lorne, and he thought so. Hesketh confided his first impression. "It's not unlike an English country town," he said, "only the streets are wider, and the people don't look so much in earnest."

"Oh, they're just as much in earnest some of the time," Lorne laughed, "but maybe not all the time!"

The sun shone crisply round them; there was a brisk October market; on the other side of the road Elmore Crow dangled his long legs over a cart flap and chewed a cheroot. Elgin was abroad, doing business on its wide margin of opportunity. Lorne cast a backward glance at conditions he had seen.

"I know what you mean," he said. "Sharp of you to spot it so soon, old chap! You're staying with the English Church minister, aren't you—Mr. Emmett? Some connection of yours, aren't they?"

"Mrs. Emmett is Chafe's sister—Mrs. Chafe, you know, is my aunt," Hesketh reminded him. "I say, Murchison, I left old Chafe wilder than ever. Wallingham's committee keep sending him leaflets and things. They take it for granted he's on the right side, since his interests are. The other day they asked him for a subscription! The old boy sent his reply to the *Daily News* and carried it about for a week. I think that gave him real satisfaction; but he hates the things by post."

Lorne laughed delightedly. "I expect he's snowed under with them. I sent him my own valuable views last week."

"I'm afraid they'll only stiffen him. That got to be his great argument after you left, the fact that you fellows over here want it. He doesn't approve of a bargain if the other side see a profit. Curiously enough, his foremen and people out in Chiswick are all for it. I was talking to one of them just before I left—'Stands to reason, sir,' he said, 'we don't want to pay more for a loaf than we do now. But we'll do it, sir, if it means downing them Germans,' he said."

Lorne's eyebrows half perceptibly twitched. "They do 'sir' you a lot over there, don't they?" he said. "It was as much as I could do to get at what a fellow of that sort meant, tumbling over the 'sirs' he propped it up with. Well, all kinds of people, all kinds of argument, I suppose, when it comes to trying to get 'em solid! But I was going to say we are all hoping you'll give us a part of your time while you're in Elgin. My family are looking forward to meeting you. Come along and let me introduce you to my father now—he's only round the corner."

"By all means!" said Hesketh, and they fell into step together. As Lorne said, it was only a short distance, but far enough to communicate a briskness, an alertness, from the step of one young man to that of the other.

"I wish it were five miles," Hesketh said, all his stall-fed muscles responding to the new call of his heart and lungs. "Any good walks about here? I asked Emmett, but he didn't know—supposed you could walk to Clayfield if you didn't take the car. He seems to have lost his legs. I suppose parsons do."

"Not all of them," said Lorne. "There's a fellow that has a church over in East Elgin, Finlay his name is, that beats the record of anything around here. He just about ranges the county in the course of a week."

"The place is too big for one parish, no doubt," Hesketh remarked.

"Oh, he's a Presbyterian! The Episcopalians haven't got any hold to speak of over there. Here we are," said Lorne, and turned in at the door. The old wooden sign was long gone. "John Murchison and Sons" glittered instead in the plate-glass windows, but Hesketh did not see it.

"Why do you think he'll be in here?" he asked, on young Murchison's heels.

"Because he always is when he isn't over at the shop," replied Lorne. "It's his place of business—his store, you know. There he is! Hard luck—he's got a customer. We'll have to wait."

He went on ahead with his impetuous step; he did not perceive the instant's paralysis that seemed to overtake Hesketh's, whose foot dragged, however, no longer than that. It was an initiation; he had been told he might expect some. He checked his impulse to be amused, and guarded his look round, not to show unseemly curiosity. His face, when he was introduced to Alec, who was sorting some odd dozens of tablespoons, was neutral and pleasant. He reflected afterward that he had been quite equal to the occasion. He thought, too, that he had shown some adaptability. Alec was not a person of fluent discourse, and when he had inquired whether Hesketh was going to make a long stay, the conversation might have languished but for this.

"Is that Birmingham?" he asked, nodding kindly at the spoons.

"Came to us through a house in Liverpool," Alec responded.

"I expect you had a stormy crossing, Mr. Hesketh."

"It was a bit choppy. We had the fiddles on most of the time," Hesketh replied. "Most of the time. Now, how do you find the bicycle trade over here? Languishing, as it is with us?"

"Oh, it keeps up pretty well," said Alec, "but we sell more spoons. N' what do you think of this country, far as you've seen it?"

"Oh, come now, it's a little soon to ask, isn't it? Yes—I suppose bicycles go out of fashion, and spoons never do. I was thinking," added Hesketh, casting his eyes over a serried rank, "of buying a bicycle."

Alec had turned to put the spoons in their place on the shelves. "Better take your friend across to Cox's," he advised Lorne over his shoulder. "He'll be able to get a motorbike there," a suggestion which gave Mr. Hesketh to reflect later that if that was the general idea of doing business it must be an easy country to make money in.

The customer was satisfied at last, and Mr. Murchison walked sociably to the door with him; it was the secretary of the local Oddfellows' Lodge, who had come in about a furnace.

"Now's our chance," said Lorne. "Father, this is Mr. Hesketh, from London—my father, Hesketh. He can tell you all you want to know about Canada—this part of it, anyway. Over thirty years, isn't it, father, since you came out?"

"Glad to meet you," said John Murchison, "glad to meet you, Mr. Hesketh. We've heard much about you."

"You must have been quite among the pioneers of Elgin, Mr. Murchison," said Hesketh as they shook hands. Alec hadn't seemed to think of that; Hesketh put it down to the counter.

"Not quite," said John. "We'll say among the early arrivals."

"Have you ever been back in your native Scotland?" asked Hesketh.

"Aye, twice."

"But you prefer the land of your adoption?"

"I do. But I think by now it'll be kin," said Mr. Murchison. "It was good to see the heather again, but a man lives best where he's taken root."

"Yes, yes. You seem to do a large business here, Mr. Murchison."

"Pretty well for the size of the place. You must get Lorne here to take you over Elgin. It's a fair sample of our rising manufacturing towns."

"I hope he will. I understand you manufacture to some extent yourself?"

"We make our own stoves and a few odd things."

"You don't send any across the Atlantic yet?" queried Hesketh jocularly.

"Not yet. No, sir!"

Then did Mr. Hesketh show himself in true sympathy with the novel and independent conditions of the commonwealth he found himself in.

"I beg you won't use that form with me," he said, "I know it isn't the custom of the country, and I am a friend of your son's, you see."

The iron merchant looked at him, just an instant's regard, in which astonishment struggled with the usual deliberation. Then his considering hand went to his chin.

"I see. I must remember," he said.

The son, Lorne, glanced in the pause beyond John Murchison's broad shoulders, through the store door and out into the moderate commerce of Main Street, which had carried the significance and the success of his father's life. His eye came back and moved over the contents of the place, taking stock of it, one might say, and adjusting the balance with pride. He had said very little since they had been in the store. Now he turned to Hesketh quietly.

"I wouldn't bother about that if I were you," he said. "My father spoke quite—colloquially."

"Oh!" said Hesketh.

They parted on the pavement outside. "I hope you understand," said Lorne, with an effort at heartiness, "how glad my parents will be to have you if you find yourself able to spare us any of your time?"

"Thanks very much," said Hesketh; "I shall certainly give myself the pleasure of calling as soon as possible."

Chapter XXI

"Dear me!" said Dr. Drummond. "Dear me! Well! And what does Advena Murchison say to all this?"

He and Hugh Finlay were sitting in the Doctor's study, the pleasantest room in the house. It was lined with standard religious philosophy, standard poets, standard fiction, all that was standard, and nothing that was not; and the shelves included several volumes of the Doctor's own sermons, published in black morocco through a local firm that did business by the subscription method, with Drummond in gold letters on the back.[1] There were more copies of these, perhaps, than it would be quite thoughtful to count, though a good many were annually disposed of at the church bazaar, where the Doctor presented them with a generous hand. A sumptuous desk, and luxurious leather-covered armchairs furnished the room; a beautiful little Parian copy of a famous Cupid and Psyche decorated the mantelpiece, and betrayed the touch of pagan in the Presbyterian. A bright fire burned in the grate, and there was not a speck of dust anywhere.

Dr. Drummond, lost in his chair, with one knee dropped on the other, joined his fingers at the tips, and drew his forehead into a web of wrinkles. Over it his militant grey crest curled up; under it his eyes darted two shrewd points of interrogation.

"What does Miss Murchison say to it?" he repeated with craft and courage, as Finlay's eyes dropped and his face slowly flushed under the question. It was in this room that Dr. Drummond examined intending communicants and cases likely to come before the Session; he never shirked a leading question.

"Miss Murchison," said Finlay, after a moment, "was good enough to say that she thought her father's house would be open to Miss—to my friends when they arrived; but I thought it would be more suitable to ask your hospitality, sir."

"Did she so?" asked Dr. Drummond gravely. It was more a comment than an inquiry. "Did she so?" Infinite kindness was in it.

The young man assented with an awkward gesture, half bend, half nod, and neither for a moment spoke again. It was one of those silences with a character, conscious, tentative. Half veiled, disavowed thoughts rose up in it, awakened by Advena's name, turning away their heads. The ticking of the Doctor's old-fashioned watch came through it from his waistcoat pocket. It was he who spoke first.

"I christened Advena Murchison," he said. "Her father was one of those who called me, as a young man, to this ministry. The names of both her parents are on my first communion roll. Aye!"

The fire snapped and the watch went on ticking.

"So Advena thought well of it all. Did she so?"

The young man raised his heavy eyes and looked unflinchingly at Dr. Drummond.

"Miss Murchison," he said, "is the only other person to whom I have confided the matter. I have written, fixing that date, with her approval—at her desire. Not immediately. I took time to— think it over. Then it seemed better to arrange for the ladies' reception first, so before posting I have come to you."

"Then the letter has not gone?"

"It is in my pocket."

"Finlay, you will have a cigar? I don't smoke myself; my throat won't stand it; but I understand these are passable. Grant left them here. He's a chimney, that man Grant. At it day and night."

This was a sacrifice. Dr. Drummond hated tobacco, the smell of it, the ash of it, the time consumed in it. There was no need at all to offer Finlay one of the Reverend Grant's cigars. Propitiation must indeed be desired when the incense is abhorred. But Finlay declined to smoke. The Doctor, with his hands buried deep in his trousers pockets, where something metallic clinked in them, began to pace and turn. His mouth had the set it wore when he handled a difficult motion in the General Assembly.

"I'm surprised to hear that, Finlay; though it may be well not to be surprised at what a woman will say—or won't say."

"Surprised?" said the younger man confusedly. "Why should any one be surprised?"

"I know her well. I've watched her grow up. I remember her mother's trouble because she would scratch the paint on the pew in front of her with the nails in her little boots. John Murchison sang in the choir in those days. He had a fine bass voice; he has it still. And Mrs. Murchison had to keep the family in order by herself. It was sometimes as much as she could do, poor woman. They sat near the front, and many a good hard look I used to give them while I was preaching. Knox Church was a different place then. The choir sat in the back gallery, and we had a precentor, a fine fellow—he lost an arm at Ridgway in the Fenian raid.[2] Well I mind him and the frown he would put on when he took up the fork. But, for that matter, every man Jack in the choir had a frown on in the singing, though the bass fellows would be the fiercest. We've been twice enlarged since, and the organist has long been a salaried professional. But I doubt whether the praise of God is any heartier than it was when it followed Peter Craig's tuning-fork. Aye. You'd always hear John Murchison's note in the finish."

Finlay was listening with the look of a charmed animal. Dr. Drummond's voice was never more vibrant, more moving, more compelling than when he called up the past; and here to Finlay the past was itself enchanted.

"She always had those wonderful dark eyes. She's pale enough now, but as a child she was rosy. Taking her place of a winter evening, with the snow on her fur cap and her hair, I often thought her a picture. I liked to have her attention while I was preaching, even as a child; and when she was absent I missed her. It was through my ministrations that she saw her way to professing the Church of Christ, and under my heartfelt benediction that she first broke bread in her Father's house. I hold the girl in great affection, Finlay; and I grieve to hear this."

The other drew a long breath, and his hand tightened on the arm of his chair. He was, as we know, blind to many of the world's aspects, even to those in which he himself figured; and Dr. Drummond's plain hypothesis of his relations with Advena came before him in forced illumination, flash by tragic flash. This kind of revelation is more discomforting than darkness, since it carries the surprise of assault, and Finlay groped in it, helpless and silent.

"You are grieved, sir?" he said mechanically.

"Man, she loves you!" exclaimed the Doctor, in a tone that would no longer forbear.

Hugh Finlay seemed to take the words just where they were levelled, in his breast. He half leaped from his chair; the lower part of his face had the rigidity of iron.

"I am not obliged to discuss such a matter as that," he said hoarsely, "with you or with any man."

He looked confusedly about him for his hat, which he had left in the hall; and Dr. Drummond profited by the instant. He stepped across and laid a hand on the younger man's shoulder. Had they both been standing the gesture would have been impossible to Dr. Drummond with dignity; as it was, it had not only that, but benignance, a kind of tender good-will, rare in expression with the minister, rare, for that matter, in feeling with him too, though the chord was always there to be sounded.

"Finlay," he said; "Finlay!"

Between two such temperaments the touch and the tone together made an extraordinary demonstration. Finlay, with an obvious effort, let it lie upon him. The tension of his body relaxed, that of his soul he covered, leaning forward and burying his head in his hands.

"Will you say I have no claim to speak?" asked Dr. Drummond, and met silence. "It is upon my lips to beg you not to send that letter, Finlay." He took his hand from the young man's shoulder, inserted a thumb in each of his waistcoat pockets, and resumed his walk.

"On my own account I must send it," said Finlay. "On Miss Murchison's—she bids me to. We have gone into the matter together."

"I can imagine what you made of it together. There's a good deal of her father in Advena. He would be the last man to say a word for himself. You told her this tale you have told me, and she told you to get Miss Christie out and marry her without delay, eh? And what would you expect her to tell you—a girl of that spirit?"

"I cannot see why pride should influence her."

"Then you know little about women. It was pride, pure and simple, Finlay, that made her tell you that—and she'll be a sorry woman if you act on it."

"No," said Finlay, suddenly looking up, "I may know little about women, but I know more about Advena Murchison than that. She advised me in the sense she thought right and honourable, and her advice was sincere. And, Dr. Drummond, deeply as I feel the bearing of Miss Murchison's view of the matter, I could not, in any case, allow my decision to rest upon it. It must stand by itself."

"You mean that your decision to marry to oblige your aunt should not be influenced by the fact that it means the wrecking of your own happiness and that of another person. I can't agree, Finlay. I spoke first of Advena Murchison because her part and lot in it are most upon my heart. I feel, too, that some one should put her case. Her own father would never open his lips. If you're to be hauled over the coals about this I'm the only man to do it. And I'm going to."

A look of sharp determination came into the minister's eyes; he had the momentary air of a small Scotch terrier with a bidding. Finlay looked at him in startled recognition of another possible phase of his dilemma; he thought he knew it in every wretched aspect. It was a bold reference of Dr. Drummond's; it threw down the last possibility of withdrawal for Finlay; they must have it out now, man to man, with a little, perhaps, even in that unlikely place, of penitent to confessor. It was an exigency, it helped Finlay to pull himself together, and there was something in his voice, when he spoke, like the vibration of relief.

"I am pained and distressed more than I have any way of telling you, sir," he said, "that—the state of feeling—between Miss Murchison and myself should have been so plain to you. It is incomprehensible to me that it should be so, since it is only very lately that I have understood it truly myself. I hope you will believe that it was the strangest, most unexpected, most sudden revelation."

He paused and looked timidly at the Doctor; he, the great fellow, in straining bondage to his heart, leaning forward with embarrassed tension in every muscle, Dr. Drummond alert, poised, critical, balancing his little figure on the hearthrug.

"I preach faith in miracles," he said. "I dare say between you and her it would be just that."

"I have been deeply culpable. Common sense, common knowledge of men and women should have warned me that there might be danger. But I looked upon the matter as our own—as between us only. I confess that I have not till now thought of that part of it, but surely—You cannot mean to tell me that what I have always supposed my sincere and devoted friendship for Miss Murchison has been in any way prejudicial —"

"To her in the ordinary sense? To her prospects of marriage and her standing in the eyes of the community? No, Finlay. No. I have not heard the matter much referred to. You seem to have taken none of the ordinary means—you have not distinguished her in the eye of gossip. If you had it would be by no means the gravest thing to consider. Such tokens are quickly forgotten, especially here, where attentions of the kind often, I've noticed, lead to nothing. It is the fact, and not the appearance of it, that I speak of—that I am concerned with."

"The fact is beyond mending," said Finlay, dully.

"Aye, the fact is beyond mending. It is beyond mending that Advena Murchison belongs to you and you to her in no common sense. It's beyond mending that you cannot now be separated without such injury to you both as I would not like to look upon. It's beyond mending, Finlay, because it is one of those things that God has made. But it is not beyond marring, and I charge you to look well what you are about in connection with it."

A flash of happiness, of simple delight, lit the young man's sombre eyes as the phrases fell. To the minister they were mere forcible words; to Finlay they were soft rain in a famished land. Then he looked again heavily at the pattern of the carpet.

"Would you have me marry Advena Murchison?" he said, with a kind of shamed yielding to the words.

"I would—and no other. Man, I saw it from the beginning!" exclaimed the Doctor. "I don't say it isn't an awkward business. But at least there'll be no heartbreak in Scotland. I gather you never said a word to the Bross lady on the subject, and very few on any other. You tell me you left it all with that good woman, your aunt, to arrange after you left. Do you think a creature of any sentiment would have accepted you on those terms? Not she. So far as I can make out, Miss Cameron is just a sensible, wise woman that would be the first to see the folly in this business if she knew the rights of it. Come, Finlay, you're not such a great man with the ladies—you can't pretend she has any affection for you."

The note of raillery in the Doctor's voice drew Finlay's brows together.

"I don't know," he said, "whether I have to think of her affections, but I do know I have to think of her dignity, her confidence, and her belief in the honourable dealing of a man whom she met under the sanction of a trusted roof. The matter may look light here; it is serious there. She has her circle of friends; they are acquainted with her engagement. She has made all her arrangements to carry it out; she has disposed of her life. I cannot ask her to reconsider her lot because I have found a happier adjustment for mine."

"Finlay," said Dr. Drummond, "you will not be known in Bross or anywhere else as a man who has jilted a woman. Is that it?"

"I will not be a man who has jilted a woman."

"There is no sophist like pride. Look at the case on its merits. On the one side a disappointment for Miss Cameron. I don't doubt she's counting on coming, but at worst a worldly disappointment. And the very grievous humiliation for you of writing to tell her that you have made a mistake. You deserve that, Finlay. If you wouldn't be a man who has jilted a woman you have no business to lend yourself to such matters with the capacity of a blind kitten. That is the damage on the one side. On the other —"

"I know all that there is to be said," interrupted Finlay, "on the other."

"Then face it, man. Go home and write the whole truth to Bross. I'll do it for you—no, I won't, either. Stand up to it yourself. You must hurt one of two women; choose the one that will suffer only in her vanity. I tell you that Scotch entanglement of yours is pure cardboard farce—it won't stand examination. It's appalling to think that out of an extravagant, hypersensitive conception of honour, egged on by that poor girl, you could be capable of turning it into the reality of your life."

"I've taken all these points of view, sir, and I can't throw the woman over. The objection to it isn't in reason—it's somehow in the past and the blood. It would mean the sacrifice of all that I hold most valuable in myself. I should expect myself after that to stick at nothing—why should I?"

"There is one point of view that perhaps you have not taken," said Dr. Drummond, in his gravest manner. "You are settled here in your charge. In all human probability you will remain here in East Elgin, as I have remained here, building and fortifying the place you have won for the Lord in the hearts of the people. Advena Murchison's life will also go on here—there is nothing to take it away. You have both strong natures. Are you prepared for that?"

"We are both prepared for it. We shall both be equal to it. I count upon her, and she counts upon me, to furnish in our friend-

ship the greater part of whatever happiness life may have in store
for us."

"Then you must be a pair of born lunatics!" said Dr. Drummond, his jaw grim, his eyes snapping. "What you propose is little
less than a crime, Finlay. It can come to nothing but grief, if no
worse. And your wife, poor woman, whatever she deserves, it is
better than that! My word, if she could choose her prospect, think
you she would hesitate? Finlay, I entreat you as a matter of
ordinary prudence, go home and break it off. Leave Advena out of
it—you have no business to make this marriage whether or no.
Leave other considerations to God and to the future. I beseech
you, bring it to an end!"

Finlay got up and held out his hand. "I tell you from my heart
it is impossible," he said.

"I can't move you?" said Mr. Drummond. "Then let us see if
the Lord can. You will not object, Finlay, to bring the matter
before Him, here and now, in a few words of prayer? I should find
it hard to let you go without them."

They went down upon their knees where they stood; and Dr.
Drummond did little less than order Divine interference; but the
prayer that was inaudible was to the opposite purpose.

Ten minutes later the minister himself opened the door to let
Finlay out into the night. "You will remember," he said as they
shook hands, "that what I think of your position in this matter
makes no difference whatever to the question of your aunt's
coming here with Miss Cameron when they arrive. You will bring
them to this house as a matter of course. I wish you could be
guided to a different conclusion, but, after all, it is your own
conscience that must be satisfied. They will be better here than at
the Murchisons'," he added with a last shaft of reproach, "and they
will be very welcome."

It said much for Dr. Drummond that Finlay was able to fall in
with the arrangement. He went back to his boarding-house, and
added a postscript embodying it to his letter to Bross. Then he
walked out upon the midnight two feverish miles to the town, and
posted the letter. The way back was longer and colder.

Chapter XXII

"Well, Winter," said Octavius Milburn, "I expect there's business in this for you."

Mr. Milburn and Mr. Winter had met in the act of unlocking their boxes at the post-office. Elgin had enjoyed postal delivery for several years, but not so much as to induce men of business to abandon the post-office box that had been the great convenience succeeding window inquiry. In time the boxes would go, but the habit of dropping in for your own noonday mail on the way home to dinner was deep-rooted, and undoubtedly you got it earlier. Moreover, it takes time to engender confidence in a postman when he is drawn from your midst, and when you know perfectly well that he would otherwise be driving the mere watering-cart, or delivering the mere ice, as he was last year.

"Looks like it," responded Mr. Winter, cheerfully. "The boys have been round as usual. I told them they'd better try another shop this time, but they seemed to think the old reliable was good enough to go on with."

This exchange, to any one in Elgin, would have been patently simple. On that day there was only one serious topic in Elgin, and there could have been only one reference to business for Walter Winter. The *Dominion* had come up the day before with the announcement that Mr. Robert Farquharson,[1] who, for an aggregate of eleven years, had represented the Liberals of South Fox in the Canadian House of Commons, had been compelled under medical advice to withdraw from public life. The news was unexpected, and there was rather a feeling among Mr. Farquharson's local support in Elgin that it shouldn't have come from Toronto. It will be gathered that Horace Williams, as he himself acknowledged, was wild. The general feeling, and to some extent Mr. Williams's, was appeased by the further information that Mr. Farquharson had been obliged to go to Toronto to see a specialist, whose report he had naturally enough taken to party headquarters, whence the *Dominion* would get it, as Mr. Williams said, by telephone or any quicker way there was. Williams, it should be added, was well ahead with the details, as considerate as was consistent with public enterprise, of the retiring member's malady, its duration, the date

of the earliest symptoms, and the growth of anxiety in Mrs.
Farquharson, who had finally insisted—and how right she was!—
on the visit to the specialist, upon which she had accompanied Mr.
Farquharson. He sent round Rawlins. So that Elgin was in possession of all the facts, and Walter Winter, who had every pretension to contest the seat again, and every satisfaction that it
wouldn't be against Farquharson, might naturally be expected to
be taken up with them sufficiently to understand a man who
slapped him on the shoulder in the post-office with the remark I
have quoted.

"I guess they know what they're about," returned Mr. Milburn.
"It's a bad knock for the Grits, old Farquharson having to drop
out. He's getting up in years, but he's got a great hold here. He'll
be a dead loss in votes to his party. I always said our side wouldn't
have a chance till the old man was out of the way."

Mr. Winter twisted the watch-chain across his protuberant waistcoat, and his chin sank in reflective folds above his necktie. Above
that again his nose drooped over his moustache, and his eyelids over
his eyes, which sought the floor. Altogether he looked sunk, like an
overfed bird, in deferential contemplation of what Mr. Milburn was
saying.

"They've nobody to touch him, certainly, in either ability or
experience," he replied, looking up to do it, with a handsome air
of concession. "Now that Martin's dead, and Jim Fawkes come
that howler over Pink River, they'll have their work cut out for
them to find a man. I hear Fawkes takes it hard, after all he's done
for 'em, not to get the nomination, but they won't hear of it. Quite
right, too; he's let too many people in over that concession of his
to be popular, even among his friends."

"I suppose he has. Dropped anything there yourself?—No? Nor
I. When a thing gets to the boom stage I say let it alone, even if
there's gold in it and you've got a School of Mines man to tell you
so. Fawkes came out of it at the small end himself, I expect, but
that doesn't help him any in the eyes of business men."

"I hear," said Walter Winter, stroking his nose, "that old man
Parsons has come right over since the bosses at Ottawa have put
so much money on preference trade with the old country. He says
he was a Liberal once, and may be a Liberal again, but he doesn't
see his way to voting to give his customers blankets cheaper than
he can make them, and he'll wait till the clouds roll by."

"He won't be the only one, either," said Milburn. "Take my word for it, they'll be dead sick and sorry over this imperial craze in a year's time, every Government that's taken it up. The people won't have it. The Empire looks nice on the map, but when it comes to practical politics their bread and butter's in the home industries. There's a great principle at stake, Winter; I must say I envy you standing up for it under such favourable conditions. Liberals like Young and Windle may talk big, but when it comes to the ballot-box you'll have the whole manufacturing interest of the place behind you, and nobody the wiser. It's a great thing to carry the standard on an issue above and beyond party politics—it's a purer air, my boy."

Walter Winter's nod confirmed the sagacity of this, and appreciated the highmindedness. It was a parting nod; Mr. Winter had too much on hand that morning to waste time upon Octavius Milburn; but it was full of the qualities that ensure the success of a man's relation with his fellows. Consideration was in it, and understanding, and that kind of geniality that offers itself on a plain business footing, a commercial heartiness that has no nonsense about it. He had half a dozen casual chats like this with Mr. Milburn on his way up Main Street, and his manner expanded in cordiality and respect with each, as if his growing confidence in himself increased his confidence in his fellow men. The same assurance greeted him several times over. Every friend wanted to remind him of the enemy's exigency, and to assure him that the enemy's new policy was enough by itself to bring him romping in at last; and to every assurance he presented the same acceptable attitude of desiring for particular reasons to take special note of such valuable views. At the end he had neither elicited nor imparted a single opinion of any importance; nevertheless, he was quite entitled to his glow of satisfaction.

Among Mr. Winter's qualifications for political life was his capacity to arrive at an estimate of the position of the enemy. He was never persuaded to his own advantage; he never stepped ahead of the facts. It was one of the things that made him popular with the other side, his readiness to do justice to their equipment, to acknowledge their chances. There is gratification of a special sort in hearing your points of vantage confessed by the foe; the vanity is soothed by his open admission that you are worthy of his steel. It makes you a little less keen, somehow, about defeating him. It may be that Mr. Winter had an instinct for this, or perhaps he thought such discourse more profitable, if less pleasant, than derisive talk in the opposite sense. At all events, he gained something and lost nothing by it, even in his own camp, where swagger might be expected to breed admiration. He was thought a level-headed fellow who didn't expect miracles; his forecast in most matters was quoted, and his defeats at the polls had been to some extent neutralized by his sagacity in computing the returns in advance.

So that we may safely follow Mr. Winter to the conclusion that the Liberals of South Fox were somewhat put to it to select a successor to Robert Farquharson who could be depended upon to keep the party credit exactly where he found it. The need was unexpected, and the two men who would have stepped most naturally into Farquharson's shoes were disqualified as Winter described. The retirement came at a calculating moment. South Fox still declared itself with pride an unhealthy division for Conservatives; but new considerations had thrust themselves among Liberal counsels, and nobody yet knew what the country would say to them. The place was a "Grit" stronghold, but its steady growth as an industrial centre would give a new significance to the figures of the next returns. The Conservative was the manufacturers' party, and had been ever since the veteran Sir John Macdonald declared for a protective "National Policy," and placed the plain issue before the country which divided the industrial and the agricultural interests. A certain number of millowners—Mr. Milburn mentioned Young and Windle—belonged to the Liberals, as if to illustrate the fact that you inherit your party in Canada as you inherit your "denomination," or your nose; it accompanies you, simply, to the grave.[2] But they were exceptions, and there was no doubt that the other side had been considerably strengthened by the addition of two or three thriving and highly capitalized concerns during the past five years. Upon the top of this had come the possibility of a great and dramatic change of trade relations with Great Britain, which the Liberal Government at Ottawa had given every sign of willingness to adopt—had, indeed, initiated, and were bound by word and letter to follow up.[3] Though the moment had not yet come, might never come, for its acceptance or rejection by the country as a whole, there could be no doubt that every bye-election would be concerned with the policy involved, and that every Liberal candidate must be prepared to stand by it in so far as the leaders had conceived and pushed it. Party feeling was by no means unanimous in favour of the change; many Liberals saw commercial salvation closer in improved trade relations with the United States.[4] On the other hand, the new policy, clothed as it was in the attractive sentiment of loyalty, and making for the solidarity of the British race, might be depended upon to capture votes which had been hitherto Conservative mainly because these professions were supposed to be an indissoluble part of Conservatism. It was a thing to split the vote sufficiently to bring an unusual amount of anxiety and calculation into Liberal counsels. The other side were in no doubt or difficulty: Walter Winter was good enough for them, and it was their cheerful conviction that Walter Winter would put a large number of people wise on the subject of preference trade bye-and-bye who at present only knew enough to vote for it.

The great question was the practicability of the new idea, and how much further it could safely be carried in a loyal Dominion which was just getting on its industrial legs. It was debated with anxiety at Ottawa, and made the subject of special instruction to South Fox, where the bye-election would have all the importance of an early test. "It's a clear issue," wrote an influential person at Ottawa to the local party leaders at Elgin, "we don't want any tendency to hedge or double. It's straight business with us, the thing we want, and it will be till Wallingham either gets it through over there, or finds he can't deal with us. Meanwhile it might be as well to ascertain just how much there is in it for platform purposes in a safe spot like South Fox, and how much the fresh opposition will cost us where we can afford it. We can't lose the seat, and the returns will be worth anything in their bearing on the General Election next year. The objection to Carter is that he's only half convinced; he couldn't talk straight if he wanted to, and that lecture tour of his in the United States ten years ago pushing reciprocity with the Americans would make awkward literature."

The rejection of Carter practically exhausted the list of men available whose standing in the town and experience of its suffrages brought them naturally into the field of selection; and at this point Cruickshank wrote to Farquharson suggesting the dramatic departure involved in the name of Lorne Murchison. Cruickshank wrote judiciously, leaving the main arguments in Lorne's favour to form themselves in Farquharson's mind, but countering the objections that would rise there by the suggestion that after a long period of confidence and steady going, in fact of the orthodox and expected, the party should profit by the swing of the pendulum toward novelty and tentative, rather than bring forward a candidate who would represent, possibly misrepresent, the same beliefs and intentions on a lower personal level. As there was no first-rate man of the same sort to succeed Farquharson, Cruickshank suggested the undesirability of a second-rate man; and he did it so adroitly that the old fellow found himself in a good deal of sympathy with the idea. He had small opinion of the lot that was left for selection, and smaller relish for the prospect of turning his honourable activity over to any one of them. Force of habit and training made him smile at Cruickshank's proposition as impracticable, but he felt its attraction, even while he dismissed it to an inside pocket. Young Murchison's name would be so unlooked-for that if he, Farquharson, could succeed in imposing it upon the party it would be almost like making a personal choice of his successor, a grateful idea in abdication. Farquharson wished regretfully that Lorne had another five years to his credit in the Liberal record of South Fox. By the time the young fellow had earned them, he, the retiring member, would be quite on the shelf, if in no completer oblivion; he could not expect much of a voice in any nomination five years hence. He sighed to think of it.

It was at that point of his meditations that Mr. Farquharson met Squire Ormiston on the steps of the Bank of British North America, an old-fashioned building with an appearance of dignity and probity, a look of having been founded long ago upon principles which raised it above fluctuation, exactly the place in which Mr. Farquharson and Squire Ormiston might be expected to meet. The two men, though politically opposed, were excellent friends; they greeted cordially.

"So you're ordered out of politics, Farquharson?" said the squire. "We're all sorry for that, you know."

"I'm afraid so; I'm afraid so. Thanks for your letter—very friendly of you, squire. I don't like it—no use pretending I do—but it seems I've got to take a rest if I want to be known as a going concern."

"A fellow with so much influence in committee ought to have more control of his nerve centres," Ormiston told him. The squire belonged to that order of elderly gentlemen who will have their little joke. "Well, have you and Bingham and Horace Williams made up your minds who's to have the seat?"

Farquharson shook his head. "I only know what I see in the papers," he said. "The *Dominion* is away out with Fawkes, and the *Express* is about as lukewarm with Carter as he is with federated trade."

"Your Government won't be obliged to you for Carter," said Mr. Ormiston; "a more slack-kneed, double-jointed scoundrel was never offered a commission in a respectable cause. He'll be the first to rat if things begin to look queer for this new policy of yours and Wallingham's."

"He hasn't got it yet," Farquharson admitted, "and he won't with my good-will. So you're with us for preference trade, Ormiston?"

"It's a thing I'd like to see. It's a thing I'm sorry we're not in a position to take up practically ourselves. But you won't get it, you know. You'll be defeated by the senior partner. It's too much of a doctrine for the people of England. They're listening to Wallingham just now because they admire him, but they won't listen to you. I doubt whether it will ever come to an issue over there. This time next year Wallingham will be sucking his thumbs and thinking of something else. No, it's not a thing to worry about politically, for it won't come through."

The squire's words suggested so much relief in that conviction that Farquharson, sharp on the flair of the experienced nose for waverers, looked at him observantly.

"I'm not so sure. It's a doctrine with a fine practical application for them as well as for us, if they can be got to see it, and they're bound to see it in time. It's a thing I never expected to live to believe, never thought would be practicable until lately, but now I think there's a very good chance of it. And, hang it all," he added, "it may be unreasonable, but the more I notice the Yankees making propositions to get us away from it, the more I want to see it come through."

"I have very much the same feeling," the squire acknowledged. "I've been turning the matter over a good deal since that last

Conference showed which way the wind was blowing. And the fellows in your Government gave them a fine lead. But such a proposition was bound to come from your side. The whole political history of the country shows it. We're pledged to take care of the damned industries."[5]

Farquharson smiled at the note of depression. "Well, we want a bigger market somewhere," he said with detachment, "and it looks as if we could get it now Uncle Sam has had a fright. If the question comes to be fought out at the polls, I don't see how your party could do better than go in for a wide scheme of reciprocity with the Americans—in raw products, of course, with a tariff to match theirs on manufactured goods. That would shut a pretty tight door on British connection though."

"They'll not get my vote if they do," said the squire, thrusting his hands fiercely into his breeches pockets.

"As you say, it's most important to put up a man who will show the constituency all the credit and benefit there is in it, anyhow," Farquharson observed. "I've had a letter this morning," he added, laughing, "from a fellow—one of the bosses, too—who wants us to nominate young Murchison."

"The lawyer?"

"That's the man. He's too young, of course—not thirty. But he's well known in the country districts; I don't know a man of his age with a more useful service record. He's got a lot of friends, and he's come a good deal to the front lately through that inter-imperial communications business—we might do worse. And upon my word, we're in such a hole —"

"Farquharson," said old Squire Ormiston, the red creeping over features that had not lost in three generations the lines of the old breed, "I've voted in the Conservative interest for forty years, and my father before me. We were Whigs[6] when we settled in Massachusetts, and Whigs when we pulled up stakes and came North rather than take up arms against the King; but it seemed decent to support the Government that gave us a chance again under the flag, and my grandfather changed his politics. Now, confound it! the flag seems to be with the Whigs again, for fighting purposes, anyhow; and I don't seem to have any choice. I've been debating the thing for some time now, and your talk of making that fine young fellow your candidate settles it. If you can get your committee to accept young Murchison, you can count on my vote, and

I don't want to brag, but I think you can count on Moneida too, though it's never sent in a Grit majority yet."

The men were standing on the steps of the bank, and the crisp air of autumn brought them both an agreeable tingle of enterprise. Farquharson's buggy was tied to the nearest maple.

"I'm going over to East Elgin to look at my brick-kilns," he said. "Get in with me; will you?"

As they drove up Main Street they encountered Walter Winter, who looked after them with a deeply considering eye.

"Old Ormiston always had the Imperial bee in his bonnet," said he.

Chapter XXIII

Alfred Hesketh was among the first to hear of Lorne's nomination to represent the constituency of South Fox in the Dominion Parliament. The Milburns told him; it was Dora who actually made the communication. The occasion was high tea; Miss Milburn's apprehension about Englishmen and late dinner had been dissipated in great amusement. Mr. Hesketh liked nothing better than high tea, liked nothing so much. He came often to the Milburns' after Mrs. Milburn said she hoped he would, and pleased her extremely by the alacrity with which he accepted her first invitation to stay to what she described as their very simple and unconventional meal. Later he won her approval entirely by saying boldly that he hoped he was going to be allowed to stay. It was only in good English society, Mrs. Milburn declared, that you found such freedom and confidence; it reminded her of Mrs. Emmett's saying that her sister-in-law in London was always at home to lunch. Mrs. Milburn considered a vague project of informing a select number of her acquaintances that she was always at home to high tea, but on reflection dismissed it, in case an inconvenient number should come at once. She would never have gone into detail, but since a tin of sardines will only hold so many, I may say for her that it was the part of wisdom.

Mr. Hesketh, however, wore the safe and attractive aspect of a single exceptional instance; there were always sardines enough for him. It will be imagined what pleasure Mrs. Milburn and Miss Filkin took in his visits, how he propped up their standard of behaviour in all things unessential, which was too likely to be growing limp, so far from approved examples. I think it was a real aesthetic satisfaction; I know they would talk of it afterward for hours, with sighing comparisons of the "form" of the young men of Elgin, which they called beside Hesketh's quite *outré*. It was a favourite word with Mrs. Milburn—*outré*.[1] She used it like a lorgnette, and felt her familiarity with it a differentiating mark. Mr. Milburn, never so susceptible to delicate distinctions, looked upon the young Englishman with benevolent neutrality. Dora wished it to be understood that she reserved her opinion. He might be all that he seemed, and again he might not. Englishmen were so deep.

They might have nice manners, but they didn't always act up to them, so far as she had noticed. There was that Honourable Somebody, who was in jail even then for trying to borrow money under false pretences from the Governor-General. Lorne, when she expressed these views to him, reassured her, but she continued to maintain a guarded attitude upon Mr. Hesketh, to everybody except Mr. Hesketh himself.

It was Dora, as I have said, who imparted the news. Lorne had come over with it in the afternoon, still a little dazed and unbeliev- ing in the face of his tremendous luck, helped by finding her so readily credulous to thinking it reasonably possible himself. He could not have done better than come to Dora for a correction of any undue exaltation that he might have felt, however. She sup- plied it in ten minutes by reminding him of their wisdom in keep- ing the secret of their relations. His engagement to the daughter of a prominent Conservative would not indeed have told in his favour with his party, to say nothing of the anomaly of Mr. Milburn's unyielding opposition to the new policy. "I never knew father so nearly bitter about anything," Dora said, a statement which left her lover thoughtful, but undaunted.

"We'll bring him round," said Lorne, "when he sees that the British manufacturer can't possibly get the better of men on the spot, who know to a nut the local requirements."

To which she had responded, "Oh, Lorne, don't begin *that* again," and he had gone away hot-foot for the first step of preparation.

"It's exactly what I should have expected," said Hesketh, when she told him. "Murchison is the very man they want. He's cut out for a political success. I saw that when he was in England."

"You haven't been very long in the country, Mr. Hesketh, or we shouldn't hear you saying that," said Mr. Milburn, amicably. "It's a very remarkable thing with us, a political party putting forward so young a man. Now with you I expect a young fellow might get it on his rank or his wealth—your principle of non- payment of members confines your selection more or less. I don't say you're not right, but over here we do pay, you see, and it makes a lot of difference in the competition. It isn't a greater honour, but it's more sought for. I expect there'll be a good many sore heads over this business."

"It's all the more creditable to Murchison," said Hesketh.

"Of course it is—a great feather in his cap. Oh, I don't say young Murchison isn't a rising fellow, but it's foolishness for his party—I can't think who is responsible for it. However, they've got a pretty foolish platform just now—they couldn't win this seat on it with any man. A lesson will be good for them."

"Father, don't you think Lorne will get in?" asked Dora, in a tone of injury and slight resentment.

"Not by a handful," said her father. "Mr. Walter Winter will represent South Fox in the next session of Parliament, if you ask my opinion."

"But, father," returned his daughter, with an outraged inflection, "you'll vote for Lorne?"

A smile went round the table, discreetest in Mrs. Milburn.

"I'm afraid not," said Mr. Milburn, "I'm afraid not. Sorry to disoblige, but principles are principles."

Dora perceptibly pouted. Mrs. Milburn created a diversion with green-gage preserves. Under cover of it Hesketh asked, "Is he a great friend of yours?"

"One of my very greatest," Dora replied. "I know he'll expect father to vote for him. It makes it awfully embarrassing for me."

"Oh, I fancy he'll understand!" said Hesketh, easily. "Political convictions are serious things, you know. Friendship isn't supposed to interfere with them. I wonder," he went on, meditatively, "whether I could be of any use to Murchison. Now that I've made up my mind to stop till after Christmas I'll be on hand for the fight. I've had some experience. I used to canvass now and then from Oxford; it was always a tremendous lark."

"Oh, Mr. Hesketh, *do*! Really and truly he is one of my oldest friends, and I should love to see him get in. I know his sister, too. They're a very clever family. Quite self-made, you know, but highly respected. Promise me you will."

"I promise with pleasure. And I wish it were something it would give me more trouble to perform. I like Murchison," said Hesketh.

All this transpiring while they were supposed to be eating green-gage preserves, and Mrs. Milburn and Miss Filkin endeavoured to engage the head of the house in the kind of easy allusion to affairs of the moment to which Mr. Hesketh would be accustomed as a form of conversation—the accident to the German

Empress, the marriage of one of the Rothschilds. The ladies were compelled to supply most of the facts and all of the interest, but they kept up a gallant line of attack; and the young man, taking gratified possession of Dora's eyes, was extremely obliged to them.

Hesketh lost no time in communicating his willingness to be of use to Murchison, and Lorne felt all his old friendliness rise up in him as he cordially accepted the offer. It was made with British heartiness, it was thoroughly meant. Lorne was half ashamed in his recognition of its quality. A certain aloofness had grown in him against his will since Hesketh had prolonged his stay in the town, difficult to justify, impossible to define. Hesketh as Hesketh was worthily admirable as ever, wholesome and agreeable, as well turned out by his conscience as he was by his tailor; it was Hesketh in his relation to his new environment that seemed vaguely to come short. This in spite of an enthusiasm which was genuine enough; he found plenty of things to like about the country. It was perhaps in some manifestation of sensitiveness that he failed; he had the adaptability of the pioneer among rugged conditions, but he could not mingle quite immediately with the essence of them; he did not perceive the *genius loci*.[2] Lorne had been conscious of this as a kind of undefined grievance; now he specified it and put it down to Hesketh's isolation among ways that were different from the ways he knew. You were bound to notice that Hesketh as a stranger had his own point of view, his own training to retreat upon.

"I certainly liked him better over there," Lorne told Advena, "but then he was a part of it—he wasn't separated out as he is here. He was just one sort of fellow that you admired, and there were lots of sorts that you admired more. Over here you seem to see round him somehow."

"I shouldn't have thought it difficult," said his sister.

"Besides," Lorne confessed, "I expect it was easier to like him when you were inclined to like everybody. A person feels more critical of a visitor, especially when he's had advantages," he added, honestly. "I expect we don't care about having to acknowledge 'em so very much—that's what it comes to."

"I don't see them," said Advena. "Mr. Hesketh seems well enough in his way, fairly intelligent and anxious to be pleasant.

But I can't say I find him a specially interesting or valuable type."

"Interesting, you wouldn't. But valuable—well, you see, you haven't been in England—you haven't seen them over there, crowds of 'em, piling up the national character. Hesketh's an average, and for an average he's high. Oh, he's a good sort—and he just *smells* of England."

"He seems all right in his politics," said John Murchison, filling his pipe from the tobacco-jar on the mantelpiece. "But I doubt whether you'll find him much assistance the way he talks of. Folks over here know their own business—they've had to learn it. I doubt if they'll take showing from Hesketh."

"They might be a good deal worse advised."

"That may be," said Mr. Murchison, and settled down in his armchair behind the *Dominion*.

"I agree with father," said Advena. "He won't be any good, Lorne."

"Advena prefers Scotch," remarked Stella.

"I don't know. He's full of the subject," said Lorne. "He can present it from the other side."

"The side of the British exporter?" inquired his father, looking over the top of the *Dominion* with unexpected humour.

"No, sir. Though there are places where we might talk cheap overcoats and tablecloths and a few odds and ends like that. The side of the all-British loaf and the lot of people there are to eat it," said Lorne. "That ought to make a friendly feeling. And if there's anything in the sentiment of the scheme," he added, "it shouldn't do any harm to have a good specimen of the English people advocating it. Hesketh ought to be an object-lesson."

"I wouldn't put too much faith in the object-lesson," said John Murchison.

"Neither would I," said Stella emphatically. "Mister Alfred Hesketh may pass in an English crowd, but over here he's just an ignorant young man, and you'd better not have him talking with his mouth at any of your meetings. Tell him to go and play with Walter Winter."

"I heard he was asking at Volunteer Headquarters the other night," remarked Alec, "how long it would be before a man like himself, if he threw in his lot with the country, could expect to get nominated for a provincial seat."

"What did they tell him?" asked Mr. Murchison, when they had finished their laugh.

"I heard they said it would depend a good deal on the size of the lot."

"And a little on the size of the man," remarked Advena.

"He said he would be willing to take a seat in a Legislature and work up," Alec went on. "Ontario for choice, because he thought the people of this Province more advanced."

"There's a representative committee being formed to give the inhabitants of the poor-house a turkey dinner on Thanksgiving Day," said Advena. "He might begin with that."

"I dare say he would if anybody told him. He's just dying to be taken into the public service," Alec said. "He's in dead earnest about it. He thinks this country's a great place because it gives a man the chance of a public career."

"Why is it," asked Advena, "that when people have no capacity for private usefulness they should be so anxious to serve the public?"

"Oh, come," said Lorne, "Hesketh has an income of his own. Why should he sweat for his living? We needn't pride ourselves on being so taken up with getting ours. A man like that is in a position to do some good, and I hope Hesketh will get a chance if he stays over here. We'll soon see how he speaks. He's going to follow Farquharson at Jordanville on Thursday week."

"I wonder at Farquharson," said his father.

By this time the candidature of Mr. Lorne Murchison was well in the public eye. The *Express* announced it in a burst of beaming headlines, with a biographical sketch and a "cut" of its young fellow townsman. Horace Williams, whose hand was plain in every line, apologized for the brevity of the biography—quality rather than quantity, he said; it was all good, and time would make it better. This did not prevent the *Mercury* observing, the next evening, that the Liberal organ had omitted to state the age at which the new candidate was weaned. The Toronto papers commented according to their party bias, but so far as the candidate was concerned there was lack of the material of criticism. If he had achieved little for praise he had achieved nothing for detraction. There was no inconsistent public utterance, no doubtful transaction, no scandalous paper to bring forward to his detriment. When the fact that he was but twenty-eight years of age had been exhausted in elaborate ridicule, little more was available. The policy he championed, however, lent itself to the widest discussion, and it was instructive to note how the Opposition press, while continuing to approve the great principle involved, found material for gravest criticism in the Government's projected application of it. Interest increased in the South Fox bye-election as its first touchstone, and gathered almost romantically about Lorne Murchison as its spirited advocate. It was commonly said that whether he was returned or not on this occasion, his political future was assured; and his name was carried up and down the Dominion with every new wind of imperial doctrine that blew across the Atlantic. He himself felt splendidly that he rode upon the crest of a wave of history. However the event appeared which was hidden beyond the horizon, the great luck of that buoyant emotion, of that thrilling suspense, would be his in a very special way. He was exhilarated by the sense of crisis, and among all the conferences and calculations that armed him for his personal struggle, he would now and then breathe in his private soul, "Choose quickly, England," like a prayer.

Elgin rose to its liking for the fellow, and even his political enemies felt a half-humorous pride that the town had produced a candidate whose natural parts were held to eclipse the age and experience of party hacks. Plenty of them were found to declare that Lorne Murchison would poll more votes for the Grits than any other man they could lay their hands on, with the saving clause that neither he nor any other man could poll quite enough this time. They professed to be content to let the issue have it; meanwhile they congratulated Lorne on his chance, telling him that a knock or two wouldn't do him any harm at his age. Walter Winter, who hadn't been on speaking terms with Farquharson, made a point of shaking hands with Murchison in the publicity of the post-office, and assuring him that he, Winter, never went into a contest more confident of the straight thing on the part of the other side. Such cavilling as there was came from the organized support of his own party, and had little importance because it did. The grumblers fell into line almost as soon as Horace Williams said they would; a little oil, one small appointment wrung from the Ontario Government—Fawkes, I believe, got it—and the machine was again in good working order. Lorne even profited, in the opinion of many, by the fact of his youth, with its promise of energy and initiative, since Mr. Farquharson had lately been showing the defects as well as the qualities of age and experience, and the charge of servile timidity was already in the mouths of his critics.

The agricultural community took it, as usual, with phlegm; but there was a distinct tendency in the bar at Barker's, on market-days, to lay money on the colt.

Chapter XXIV

M r. Farquharson was to retain his seat until the early spring, for the double purpose of maintaining his influence upon an important commission of which he was chairman until the work should be done, and of giving the imperial departure championed by his successor as good a chance as possible of becoming understood in the constituency. It was understood that the new writ would issue for a date in March; Elgin referred all interest to that point, and prophesied for itself a lively winter. Another event, of importance less general, was arranged for the end of February—he arrival of Miss Cameron and Mrs. Kilbannon from Scotland. Finlay had proposed an earlier date, but matters of business connected with her mother's estate would delay Miss Cameron's departure. Her arrival would be the decisive point of another campaign. He and Advena faced it without misgiving, but there were moments when Finlay greatly wished the moment past. Their intimacy had never been conspicuous, and their determination to make no change in it could be carried out without attracting attention. It was very dear to them, that determination. They saw it as a test, as an ideal. Last of all, perhaps, as an alleviation. They were both too much encumbered with ideas to move simply, quickly, on the impulse of passion. They looked at it through the wrong end of the glass, and thought they put it farther away. They believed that their relation comprised, would always comprise, the best of life. It was matter for discussion singularly attractive; they allowed themselves upon it wide scope in theory. They could speak of it in the heroic temper, without sadness or bitterness; the thing was to tear away the veil and look fate in the face. The great thing, perhaps, was to speak of it while still they could give themselves leave; a day would arrive, they acknowledged with averted eyes, when dumbness would be more becoming. Meanwhile, Mrs. Murchison would have found it hard to sustain her charge against them that they talked of nothing but books and authors; the philosophy of life, as they were intensely creating it, was more entrancing than any book or any author. Simply and definitely, and to their own satisfaction, they had abandoned the natural demands of their state; they lived in its exaltation and were far from accidents. Deep in both of them was a kind of protective nobility; I will not say it cost them nothing, but it turned the scenes between them into comedy of the better sort, the kind that deserves the relief of stone or bronze. Advena, had she heard it, would have repelled Dr. Drummond's warning with indignation. If it were so possible to keep their friendship on an unfaltering level then, with the latitude they had, what danger could attend them later, when the social law would support them, divide them, protect them? Dr. Drummond, suspecting all, looked grimly on, and from November to March found no need to invite Mr. Finlay to occupy the pulpit of Knox Church.

They had come to full knowledge that night of their long walk in the dark together; but even then, in the rush and shock and glory of it, they had held apart; and their broken avowals had crossed with difficulty from one to the other. The whole fabric of circumstance was between them, to realize and to explore; later surveys, as we know, had not reduced it. They gave it great credit as a barrier; I suppose because it kept them out of each other's arms. It had done that.

It was Advena, I fear, who insisted most that they should continue upon terms of happy debt to one another, the balance always changing, the account never closed and rendered. She no doubt felt that she might impose the terms; she had unconsciously the sense of greater sacrifice, and knew that she had been mistress of the situation long before he was aware of it. He agreed with joy and with misgiving; he saw with enthusiasm her high conception of their alliance, but sometimes wondered, poor fellow, whether he was right in letting it cover him. He came to the house as he had done before, as often as he could, and reproached himself that he could not, after all, come very often.

That they should discuss their relation as candidly as they sustained it was perhaps a little peculiar to them, so I have laid stress on it; but it was not by any means their sole preoccupation. They talked like tried friends of their every-day affairs. Indeed, after the trouble and intoxication of their great understanding had spent itself, it was the small practical interests of life that seemed to hold them most. One might think that Nature, having made them her invitation upon the higher plane, abandoned them in the very scorn of her success to the warm human commonplaces that do her work well enough with the common type. Mrs. Murchison would have thought better of them if she had chanced again to overhear.

"I wouldn't advise you to have it lined with fur," Advena was saying. The winter had sharply announced itself, and Finlay, to her reproach about his light overcoat, had declared his intention of ordering a buffalo-skin the following day. "And the buffaloes are all gone, you know—thirty years ago," she laughed. "You really are not modern in practical matters. Does it ever surprise you that you get no pemmican for dinner, and hardly ever meet an Indian in his feathers?"

He looked at her with delight in his sombre eyes. It was a new discovery, her capacity for happily chaffing him, only revealed since she had come out of her bonds to love; it was hard to say which of them took the greater pleasure in it.

"What is the use of living in Canada if you can't have fur on your clothes?" he demanded.

"You may have a little—astrakhan, I would—on the collar and cuffs," she said. "A fur lining is too hot if there happens to be a thaw, and then you would leave it off and take cold. You have all the look," she added, with a gravely considering glance at him, "of a person who ought to take care of his chest."

He withdrew his eyes hurriedly, and fixed them instead on his pipe. He always brought it with him, by her order, and Advena usually sewed. He thought as he watched her that it made the silences enjoyable.

"And expensive, I dare say, too," he said.

"Yes, more or less. Alec paid fifty dollars for his, and never liked it."

"Fifty dollars—ten pounds! No vair[1] for me!" he declared. "By the way, Mrs. Firmin is threatening to turn me out of house and home. A married daughter is coming to live with her, and she wants my rooms."

"When does she come—the married daughter?"

"Oh, not till the early spring! There's no immediate despair," said Finlay, "but it is dislocating. My books and I had just succeeded in making room for one another."

"But you will have to move, in any case, in the early spring."

"I suppose I will. I had—I might have remembered that."

"Have you found a house yet?" Advena asked him.

"No."

"Have you been looking?" It was a gentle, sensible reminder.

"I'm afraid I haven't." He moved in his chair as if in physical discomfort. "Do you think I ought—so soon? There are always plenty of—houses, aren't there?"

"Not plenty of desirable ones. Do you think you must live in East Elgin?"

"It would be rather more convenient."

"Because there are two semi-detached in River Street, just finished, that look very pretty and roomy. I thought when I saw them that one of them might be what you would like."

"Thank you," he said, and tried not to say it curtly.

"They belong to White, the grocer. River Street isn't East Elgin, but it is that way, and it would be a great deal pleasanter for—for her."

"I must consider that, of course. You haven't been in them? I should hope for a bright sitting-room, and a very private study."

If Advena was aware of any unconscious implication, the pair of eyes she turned upon him showed no trace of satisfaction in it.

"No, I haven't. But if I could be of any use I should be very glad to go over them with you, and—"

She stopped involuntarily, checked by the embarrassment in his face, though she had to wait for his words to explain it.

"I should be most grateful. But—but might it not be misunderstood?"

She bent her head over her work, and one of those instants passed between them which he had learned to dread. They were so completely the human pair as they sat together, withdrawn in comfort and shelter, absorbed in homely matters and in each other; it was easy to forget that they were only a picture, a sham, and that the reality lay farther on, in the early spring. It must have been hard for him to hear without resentment that she was ready to help him to make a home for that reality. He was fast growing instructed in women, although by a post-graduate course.

Advena looked up. "Possibly," she said, calmly, and their agitation lay still between them. He was silently angry; the thing that stirred without their leave had been sweet.

"No," said Advena, "I can't go, I suppose. I'm sorry. I should have liked so much to be of use." She looked up at him appeal-ingly, and sudden tears came and stood in her eyes, and would perhaps have undone his hurt but that he was staring into the fire.

"How can you be of use," he said, almost irritably, "in such ways as those? They are not important, and I am not sure that for us they are legitimate. If you were about to be—married"—he seemed to plunge at the word—"I should not wish either to hasten you or to house you. I should turn my back on it all. You should have nothing from me," he went on, with a forced smile, "but my blessing, delivered over my shoulder."

"I am sure they are not important," she said humbly—privately all unwilling to give up her martyrdom, "but surely they are legitimate. I would like to help you in every little way I can. Don't you like me in your life? You have said that I may stay."

"I believe you think that by taking strong measures one can exorcise things," he said. "That if we could only write out this history of ours in our hearts' blood it would somehow vanish."

"No," she said, "but I should like to do it all the same."

"You must bear with me if I refuse the heroic in little. It is even harder than the other." He broke off, leaning back and looking at her from under his shading hand as if that might protect him from too complete a vision. The firelight was warm on her cheek and hair, her needle once again completed the dear delusion: she sat there his wife. This was an aspect he forbade, but it would return; here it was again.

"It is good to have you in my life," he said. "It is also good to recognize one's possibilities."

"How can you definitely lose me?" she asked, and he shook his head.

"I don't know. Now that I have found you it is as if you and I had been rocked together on the tide of that inconceivable ocean that casts us half awake upon life," he said dreamily. "It isn't a friendship of ideas, it's a friendship of spirit. Indeed, I hope and pray never wholly to lose that."

"You never will," she told him. "How many worlds one lives in as the day goes by with the different people one cares for—one beyond the other, concentric, ringing from the heart! Yours comprises all the others; it lies the farthest out—and alas! at present, the closest in," she added irresistibly to the asking of his eyes.

"But," she hurried on, taking high ground to remedy her

indiscretion, "I look forward to the time when this—other feeling of ours will become just an idea, as it is now just an emotion, at which we should try to smile. It is the attitude of the gods."

"And therefore not becoming to men. Why should we, not being gods, borrow their attitude?" said Finlay.

"I could never kill it," she put her work in her lap to say, "by any sudden act of violence. It would seem a kind of suicide. While it rules it is like one's life—absolute. But to isolate it—to place it beyond the currents from the heart—to look at it, and realize it, and conquer it for what it is—I don't think it need take so very long. And then our friendship will be beautiful without reproach."

"I sometimes fear there may not be time enough in life," he said. "And if I find that I must simply go—to British Columbia, I think—those mining missions would give a man his chance against himself. There is splendid work to be done there, of a rough-and-ready kind that would make it puerile to spend time in self-questioning."

She smiled as if at a violent boy. "We can do it. We can do it here," she said. "May I quote another religion to you? 'From purification there arises in the Yogi a thorough discernment of the cause and nature of the body, whereupon he loses that regard which others have for the bodily form.' Then, if he loves, he loves in spirit and in truth. I look forward to the time," she went on calmly, "when the best that I can give you or you can give me will ride upon a glance."

"I used to feel more drawn to the ascetic achievement and its rewards," he remarked thoughtfully, "than I do now."

"If I were not a Presbyterian in Canada," she told him, "I would be a Buddhist in Burma. But I have inherited the Shorter Catechism; I must remain without the Law."

Finlay smiled. "They are the simple," he said. "Our Law makes wise the simple."

Advena looked for a moment into the fire. She was listening, with admiration, to her heart; she would not be led to consider esoteric contrasts of East and West.

"Isn't there something that appeals to you," she said, "in the thought of just leaving it, all unsaid and all undone, a dear and tender projection upon the future that faded—a lovely thing we turned away from, until one day it was no longer there?"

"Charming," he said, averting his eyes so that she should not see the hunger in them. "Charming—literature!"

She smiled and sighed, and he wrenched his mind to the consideration of the Buddhism of Browning. She followed him obediently, but the lines they wanted did not come easily; they were compelled to search and verify. Something lately seemed lost to them of that kind of glad activity; he was more aware of it than she, since he was less occupied in the aesthetic ecstasy of self-torture. In the old time before the sun rose they had been so conscious of realms of idea lying just beyond the achievement of thought, approachable, visible by phrases, brokenly, realms which they could see closer when they essayed together. He constantly struggled to reach those enchanted areas again, but they seemed to have gone down behind the horizon; and the only inspiration that carried them far drew its impetus from the poetry of their plight. They looked for verses to prove that Browning's imagination carried him bravely through lives and lives to come, and found them to speculate whether in such chances they might hope to meet again.[2]

And the talk came back to his difficulties with his Board of Management, and to her choice of a frame for the etching he had given her, by his friend the Glasgow impressionist, and to their opinion of a common acquaintance, and to Lorne and his prospects. He told her how little she resembled her brother, and where they diverged, and how; and she listened with submission and delight, enchanted to feel his hand upon her intimate nature. She lingered in the hall while he got into his overcoat, and saw that a glove was the worse for wear. "Would it be the heroic-in-little," she begged, "to let me mend that?"

As he went out alone into the winter streets he too drew upon a pagan for his admonition. "'What then art thou doing here, O imagination?'" he groaned in his private heart. "'Go away, I entreat thee by the gods, for I want thee not. But thou art come again according to thy old fashion. I am not angry with thee, only go away!'"

Chapter XXV

Miss Milburn pressed her contention that the suspicion of his desire would be bad for her lover's political prospects till she made him feel his honest passion almost a form of treachery to his party. She also hinted that, for the time being, it did not make particularly for her own comfort in the family circle, Mr. Milburn having grown by this time quite bitter. She herself drew the excitement of intrigue from the situation, which she hid behind her pretty, pale, decorous features, and never betrayed by the least of her graceful gestures. She told herself that she had never been so right about anything as about that affair of the ring—imagine, for an instant, if she had been wearing it now! She would have banished Lorne altogether if she could. As he insisted on an occasional meeting, she clothed it in mystery, appointing it for an evening when her mother and aunt were out, and answering his ring at the door herself. To her family she remarked with detachment that you saw hardly anything of Lorne Murchison now, he was so taken up with his old election; and to Hesketh she confided her fear that politics did interfere with friendship, whatever he might say. He said a good deal, he cited lofty examples; but the only agreement he could get from her was the hope that the estrangement wouldn't be permanent

"But you are going to say something, Lorne," she insisted, talking of the Jordanville meeting.

"Not much," he told her. "It's the safest district we've got, and they adore old Farquharson. He'll do most of the talking—they wouldn't thank me for taking up the time. Farquharson is going to tell them I'm a first-class man, and they couldn't do better, and I'm practically only to show my face and tell them I think so too."

"But Mr. Hesketh will speak?"

"Yes; we thought it would be a good chance of testing him. He may interest them, and he can't do much harm, anyhow."

"Lorne, I should simply love to go. It's your first meeting."

"I'll take you."

"Mr. Murchison, *have* you taken leave of your senses? Really, you are—"

"All right, I'll send you. Farquharson and I are going out to the

Crow place to supper, but Hesketh is driving straight there. He'll be delighted to bring you—who wouldn't?"

"I shouldn't be allowed to go with him alone," said Dora, thoughtfully.

"Well, no. I don't know that I'd approve of that myself," laughed the confident young man. "Hesketh is driving Mrs. Farquharson, and the cutter will easily hold three. Isn't it lucky there's sleighing?"

"Mother couldn't object to that," said Dora. "Lorne, I always said you were the dearest fellow! I'll wear a thick veil, and not a soul will know me."

"Not a soul would in any case," said Lorne. "It'll be a Jordanville crowd, you know—nobody from Elgin."

"We don't visit much in Jordanville, certainly. Well, mother mayn't object. She has a great idea of Mrs. Farquharson, because she has attended eleven Drawing-Rooms at Ottawa, and one of them was given—held, I should say—by the Princess Louise."[1]

"I won't promise you eleven," said Lorne, "but there seems to be a pretty fair chance of one or two."

At this she had a tale for him which charmed his ears. "I didn't know where to look," she said. "Aunt Emmie, you know, has a very bad trick of coming into my room without knocking. Well, in she walked last night, and found me before the glass *practising my curtsey*! I could have killed her. Pretended she thought I was out."

"Dora, would you like *me* to promise something?" he asked, with a mischievous look.

"Of course, I would. I don't care how much *you* promise. What?"

But already he repented of his daring, and sat beside her suddenly conscious and abashed. Nor could any teasing prevail to draw from him what had been on his audacious lips to say.[2]

Social precedents are easily established in the country. The accident that sent the first Liberal canvasser for Jordanville votes to the Crow place for his supper would be hard to discover now; the fact remains that he has been going there ever since. It made a greater occasion than Mrs. Crow would ever have dreamed of acknowledging. She saw to it that they had a good meal of victuals, and affected indifference to the rest; they must say their say, she supposed. If the occasion had one satisfaction which she came nearer to confessing than another, it was that the two or three substantial neighbours who usually came to meet the politicians left their wives at home, and that she herself, to avoid giving any offence on this score, never sat down with the men. Quite enough to do it was, she would explain later, for her and the hired girl to wait on them and to clear up after them. She and Bella had their bite afterward when the men had hitched up, and when they could exchange comments of proud congratulation upon the inroads on the johnny-cake or the pies. So there was no ill feeling, and Mrs. Crow, having vindicated her dignity by shaking hands with the guests of the evening in the parlour, solaced it further by maintaining the masculine state of the occasion, in spite of protests or entreaties. To sit down opposite Mr. Crow would have made it ordinary "company"; she passed the plates and turned it into a function.

She was waiting for them on the parlour sofa when Crow brought them in out of the nipping early dark of December, Elmore staying behind in the yard with the horses. She sat on the sofa in her best black dress with the bead trimming on the neck and sleeves, a good deal pushed up and wrinkled across the bosom, which had done all that would ever be required of it when it gave Elmore and Abe their start in life. Her wiry hands were crossed in her lap in the moment of waiting: you could tell by the look of them that they were not often crossed there. They were strenuous hands; the whole worn figure was strenuous, and the narrow set mouth, and the eyes which had looked after so many matters for so long, and even the way the hair was drawn back into a knot in a fashion that would have given a phrenologist his opportunity. It was a different Mrs. Crow from the one that sat in the midst of her poultry and garden-stuff in the Elgin market square; but it was even more the same Mrs. Crow, the sum of a certain measure of opportunity and service, an imperial figure in her bead trimming, if the truth were known.

The room was heated to express the geniality that was harder to put in words. The window was shut; there was a smell of varnish and whatever was inside the "suite" of which Mrs. Crow occupied the sofa. Enlarged photographs—very much enlarged— of Mr. and Mrs. Crow hung upon the walls, and one other of a young girl done in that process which tells you at once that she was an only daughter and that she is dead. There had been other bereavements; they were written upon the silver coffin-plates which, framed and glazed, also contributed to the decoration of the room; but you would have had to look close, and you might feel a delicacy.

Mrs. Crow made her greetings with precision, and sat down again upon the sofa for a few minutes' conversation.

"I'm telling them," said her husband, "that the sleighin's just held out for them. If it 'ud been to-morrow they'd have had to come on wheels. Pretty soft travellin' as it was, some places, I guess."

"Snow's come early this year," said Mrs. Crow. "It was an open fall, too."

"It has certainly," Mr. Farquharson backed her up. "About as early as I remember it. I don't know how much you got out here; we had a good foot in Elgin."

" 'Bout the same, 'bout the same," Mr. Crow deliberated, "but it's been layin' light all along over Clayfield way—ain't had a pair of runners out, them folks."

"Makes a more cheerful winter, Mrs. Crow, don't you think, when it comes early?" remarked Lorne. "Or would you rather not get it till after Christmas?"

"I don't know as it matters much, out here in the country. We don't get a great many folks passin', best of times. An' it's more of a job to take care of the stock."

"That's so," Mr. Crow told them. "Chores come heavier when there's snow on the ground, a great sight, especially if there's drifts."

And for an instant, with his knotted hands hanging between his knees, he pondered this unvarying aspect of his yearly experience. They all pondered it, sympathetic.

"Well, now, Mr. Farquharson," Mrs. Crow turned to him. "An' how reely *be* ye? We've heard better, an' worse, an' middlin'— there's ben such contradictory reports."

"Oh, very well, Mrs. Crow! Never better. I'm going to give a lot more trouble yet. I can't do it in politics, that's the worst of it. But here's the man that's going to do it for me. Here's the man!"

The Crows looked at the pretendant, as in duty bound, but not any longer than they could help.

"Why, I guess you were at school with Elmore?" said Crow, as if the idea had just struck him.

"He may be right peart,[3] for all that," said Elmore's mother, and Elmore, himself, entering with two leading Liberals of Jordanville, effected a diversion, under cover of which Mrs. Crow escaped, to superintend, with Bella, the last touches to the supper in the kitchen.

Politics in and about Jordanville were accepted as a purely masculine interest. If you had asked Mrs. Crow to take a hand in them she would have thanked you with sarcasm, and said she thought she had about enough to do as it was. The schoolhouse, on the night of such a meeting as this, was recognized to be no place for ladies. It was a man's affair, left to the men, and the appearance there of the other sex would have been greeted with remark and levity. Elgin, as we know, was more sophisticated in every way, plenty of ladies attended political meetings in the Drill Shed, where seats as likely as not would be reserved for them; plenty of handkerchiefs waved there for the encouragement of the hero of the evening. They did not kiss him; British phlegm, so far, had stayed that demonstration at the southern border.

The ladies of Elgin, however, drew the line somewhere, drew it at country meetings. Mrs. Farquharson went with her husband because, since his state of health had handed him over to her more than ever, she saw it a part of her wifely duty. His retirement had been decided upon for the spring, but she would be on hand to retire him at any earlier moment should the necessity arise. "We'll be the only female creatures there, my dear," she had said to Dora on the way out, and Hesketh had praised them both for public spirit. He didn't know, he said, how anybody would get elected in England without the ladies, especially in the villages, where the people were obliged to listen respectfully.

"I wonder you can afford to throw away all the influence you get in the rural districts with soup and blankets," he said; "but this is an extravagant country in many ways." Dora kept silence, not being sure of the social prestige bound up with the distribution of soup and blankets, but Mrs. Farquharson set him sharply right.

"I guess we'd rather do without our influence if it came to that," she said.

Hesketh listened with deference to her account of the rural district which had as yet produced no Ladies Bountiful, made mental notes of several points, and placed her privately as a woman of more than ordinary intelligence. I have always claimed for Hesketh an open mind; he was filling it now, to its capacity, with care and satisfaction.

The schoolroom was full and waiting when they arrived. Jordanville had been well billed, and the posters held, in addition to the conspicuous names of Farquharson and Murchison, that of Mr. Alfred Hesketh (of London, England). There was a "send-off" to give to the retiring member, there was a critical inspection to make of the new candidate, and there was Mr. Alfred Hesketh, of London, England, and whatever he might signify. They were big, quiet, expectant fellows, with less sophistication and polemic than their American counterparts, less stolid aggressiveness than their parallels in England, if they have parallels there. They stood, indeed, for the development between the two; they came of the new country but not of the new light; they were democrats who had never thrown off the monarch—what harm did he do there overseas? They had the air of being prosperous, but not prosperous enough for theories and doctrines. The Liberal vote of South Fox had yet to be split by Socialism or Labour. Life was a decent rough business that required all their attention; there was time enough for sleep but not much for speculation. They sat leaning forward with their hats dropped between their knees, more with the air of big schoolboys expecting an entertainment than responsible electors come together to approve their party's choice. They had the uncomplaining bucolic look, but they wore it with a difference; the difference, by this time, was enough to mark them of another nation. Most of them had driven to the meeting; it was not an adjournment from the public-house. Nor did the air hold any hint of beer. Where it had an alcoholic drift the flavour was of whisky; but the stimulant of the occasion had been tea or cider, and the room was full of patient good-will.

The preliminaries were gone through with promptness; the Chair had supped with the speakers, and Mr. Crow had given him a friendly hint that the boys wouldn't be expecting much in the way of trimmings from *him*. Stamping and clapping from the back benches greeted Mr. Farquharson. It diminished, grew more subdued, as it reached the front. The young fellows were mostly at the back, and the power of demonstration had somehow ebbed in the old ones. The retiring member addressed his constituents for half an hour. He was standing before them as their representative for the last time, and it was natural to look back and note the milestones behind, the changes for the better with which he could fairly claim association. They were matters of Federal business chiefly, beyond the immediate horizon of Jordanville, but Farquharson made them a personal interest for that hour at all events, and there were one or two points of educational policy which he could illustrate by their own schoolhouse. He approached them, as he had always done, on the level of mutual friendly interest, and in the hope of doing mutual friendly business. "You know and I know," he said more than once; they and he knew a number of things together.

He was afraid, he said, that if the doctors hadn't chased him out of politics, he never would have gone. Now, however, that they gave him no choice, he was glad to think that though times had been pretty good for the farmers of South Fox all through the eleven years of his appearance in the political arena, he was leaving it at a moment when they promised to be better still. Already, he was sure, they were familiar with the main heads of that attractive prospect, and, agreeable as the subject, great as the policy was to him, he would leave it to be further unfolded by the gentleman whom they all hoped to enlist in the cause, as his successor for this constituency, Mr. Lorne Murchison, and by his friend from the old country, Mr. Alfred Hesketh. He, Farquharson, would not take the words out of the mouth of these gentlemen, much as he envied them the opportunity of uttering them. The French Academy, he told them, that illustrious body of literary and scientific men, had a custom, on the death of a member and the selection of his successor, of appointing one of their number to eulogize the newcomer. The person upon whom the task would most appropriately fall, did circumstances permit, would be the departing academician. In this case, he was happy to say, circumstances did permit— his political funeral was still far enough off to enable him to express his profound confidence in and his hearty admiration of the young and vigorous political heir whom the Liberals of South Fox had selected to stand in his shoes. Mr. Farquharson proceeded to give his grounds for this confidence and admiration, reminding the Jordanville electors that they had met Mr. Murchison as a Liberal standard-bearer in the last general election, when he, Farquharson, had to acknowledge very valuable services on Mr. Murchison's

part. The retiring member then thanked his audience for the kind
attention and support they had given him for so many years, made
a final cheerful joke about a Pagan divinity known as Anno Dom-
ini, and took his seat.

They applauded him, and it was plain that they regretted him,
the tried friend, the man there was never any doubt about, whose
convictions they had repeated, and whose speeches in Parliament
they had read with a kind of proprietorship for so long. The Chair
had to wait, before introducing Mr. Alfred Hesketh, until the back
benchers had got through with a double rendering of "For He's a
Jolly Good Fellow," which bolder spirits, from the anteroom
where the little girls kept their hats and comforters, interspersed
with whoops. Hesketh, it had been arranged, should speak next,
and Lorne last.

Mr. Hesketh left his wooden chair with smiling ease, the ease
which is intended to level distinctions and put everybody concerned on the best of terms. He said that though he was no stranger
to the work of political campaigns, this was the first time that he
had had the privilege of addressing a colonial audience. "I consider," said he handsomely, "that it is a privilege." He clasped his
hands behind his back and threw out his chest.

"Opinions have differed in England as to the value of the colonies, and the consequence of colonials. I say here with pride that
I have ever been among those who insist that the value is very
high and the consequence very great. The fault is common to
humanity, but we are, I fear, in England, too prone to be led away
by appearances, and to forget that under a rough unpolished
exterior may beat virtues which are the brightest ornaments of
civilization, that in the virgin fields of the possessions which the
good swords of our ancestors wrung for us from the Algonquins
and the—and the other savages—may be hidden the most glorious
period of the British race."

Mr. Hesketh paused and coughed. His audience neglected the
opportunity for applause, but he had their undivided attention.
They were looking at him and listening to him, these Canadian
farmers, with curious interest in his attitude, his appearance, his
inflection, his whole personality as it offered itself to them—it was
a thing new and strange. Far out in the North-West, where the
emigrant trains had been unloading all the summer, Hesketh's
would have been a voice from home; but here, in long-settled

Ontario, men had forgotten the sound of it, with many other things. They listened in silence, weighing with folded arms, appraising with chin in hand; they were slow, equitable men.

"If we in England," Hesketh proceeded, "required a lesson—as perhaps we did—in the importance of the colonies, we had it, need I remind you? in the course of the late protracted campaign in South Africa. Then did the mother country indeed prove the loyalty and devotion of her colonial sons. Then were envious nations compelled to see the spectacle of Canadians and Australians rallying about the common flag, eager to attest their affection for it with their life-blood, and to demonstrate that they, too, were worthy to add deeds to British traditions and victories to the British cause."

Still no mark of appreciation. Hesketh began to think them an unhandsome lot. He stood bravely, however, by the note he had sounded. He dilated on the pleasure and satisfaction it had been to the people of England to receive this mark of attachment from far-away dominions and dependencies, on the cementing of the bonds of brotherhood by the blood of the fallen, on the impossibility that the mother country should ever forget such voluntary sacrifices for her sake, when, unexpectedly and irrelevantly, from the direction of the cloak-room, came the expressive comment—"Yah!"

Though brief, nothing could have been more to the purpose, and Hesketh sacrificed several effective points to hurry to the quotation—

> What should they know of England
> Who only England know?[4]

which he could not, perhaps, have been expected to forbear. His audience, however, were plainly not in the vein for compliment. The same voice from the ante-room inquired ironically, "That so?" and the speaker felt advised to turn to more immediate considerations.

He said he had had the great pleasure on his arrival in this country to find a political party, the party in power, their Canadian Liberal party, taking initiative in a cause which he was sure they all had at heart—the strengthening of the bonds between the colonies and the mother country. He congratulated the Liberal party warmly upon having shown themselves capable of this great function—a point at which he was again interrupted; and he recapitulated some of the familiar arguments about the desirability of closer union from the point of view of the army, of the Admiralty, and from one which would come home, he knew, to all of them, the necessity of a dependable food supply for the mother country in time of war. Here he quoted a noble lord. He said that he believed no definite proposals had been made, and he did not understand how any definite proposals could be made; for his part, if the new arrangement was to be in the nature of a bargain, he would prefer to have nothing to do with it.[5]

"England," he said, loftily, "has no wish to buy the loyalty of her colonies, nor, I hope, has any colony the desire to offer her allegiance at the price of preference in British markets. Even proposals for mutual commercial benefit may be underpinned, I am glad to say, by loftier principles than those of the market-place and the counting-house."

At this one of his hearers, unacquainted with the higher commercial plane, exclaimed, "How be ye goin' to get 'em kept to, then?"

Hesketh took up the question. He said a friend in the audience asked how they were to ensure that such arrangements would be adhered to. His answer was in the words of the Duke of Dartmoor, "By the mutual esteem, the inherent integrity, and the willing compromise of the British race."

Here someone on the back benches, impatient, doubtless, at his own incapacity to follow this high doctrine, exclaimed intemperately, "Oh, shut up!" and the gathering, remembering that this, after all, was not what it had come for, began to hint that it had had enough in intermittent stamps and uncompromising shouts for "Murchison!"

Hesketh kept on his legs, however, a few minutes longer. He had a trenchant sentence to repeat to them which he thought they would take as a direct message from the distinguished nobleman who had uttered it. The Marquis of Aldeburgh was the father of the pithy thing, which he had presented, as it happened, to Hesketh himself. The audience received it with respect—Hesketh's own respect was so marked—but with misapprehension; there had been too many allusions to the nobility for a community so far removed from its soothing influence.

"Had ye no friends among the commoners?" suddenly spoke up a dry old fellow, stroking a long white beard; and the roar that greeted this showed the sense of the meeting. Hesketh closed with assurances of the admiration and confidence he felt towards the candidate proposed to their suffrages by the Liberal party that were quite inaudible, and sought his yellow pinewood schoolroom chair with rather a forced smile. It had been used once before that day to isolate conspicuous stupidity.

They were at bottom a good-natured and a loyal crowd, and they had not, after all, come there to make trouble, or Mr. Alfred Hesketh might have carried away a worse opinion of them. As it was, young Murchison, whose address occupied the rest of the evening, succeeded in making an impression upon them distinct enough, happily for his personal influence, to efface that of his friend. He did it by the simple expedient of talking business, and as high prices for produce and low ones for agricultural implements would be more interesting there than here, I will not report him. He and Mr. Farquharson waited, after the meeting, for a personal word with a good many of those present, but it was suggested to Hesketh that the ladies might be tired, and that he had better get them home without unnecessary delay. Mrs. Farquharson had less comment to offer during the drive home than Hesketh thought might be expected from a woman of her intelligence, but Miss Milburn was very enthusiastic. She said he had made a lovely speech, and she wished her father could have heard it.

A personal impression, during a time of political excitement, travels unexpectedly far. A week later Mr. Hesketh was concernedly accosted in Main Street by a boy on a bicycle.

"Say, mister, how's the dook?"

"What duke?" asked Hesketh, puzzled.

"Oh, any dook," responded the boy, and bicycled cheerfully away.

Chapter XXVI

Christmas came and went. Dr. Drummond had long accepted the innovation of a service on Christmas Day, as
he agreed to the anthem while the collection was being taken up,
to flowers about the pulpit, and to the habit of sitting at prayer. He
was a progressive by his business instinct, in everything but theology, where perhaps his business instinct also operated the other
way, in favour of the sure thing. The Christmas Day service soon
became one of those "special" occasions so dear to his heart,
which made a demand upon him out of the ordinary way. He rose
to these on the wing of the eagle, and his congregation never
lacked the lesson that could be most dramatically drawn from
them. His Christmas Day discourse gathered everything into it that
could emphasize the anniversary, including a vigorous attack upon
the saints' days and ceremonies of the Church of England calculated to correct the concession of the service, and pull up sharply
any who thought that Presbyterianism was giving way to the
spurious attractions of sentimentality or ritual. The special Easter
service, with every appropriate feature of hymn and invocation,
was apt to be marked by an unsparing denunciation of the pag-
eants and practices of the Church of Rome. Balance was thus preserved, and principle relentlessly indicated. Dr. Drummond loved,
as I have said, all that asked for notable comment; the poet and the
tragedian in him caught at the opportunity, and revelled in it.
Public events carried him far, especially if they were disastrous,
but what he most profited by was the dealing of Providence with
members of his own congregation. Of all the occasions that inspired him, the funeral sermon was his happiest opportunity, nor
was it, in his hands, by any means unstinted eulogy. Candid was
his summing-up, behind the decent veil, the accepted apology of
death; he was not afraid to refer to the follies of youth or the weaknesses of age in terms as unmistakable as they were kindly.

"Grace," he said once, of an estimable plain spinster who had
passed away, "did more for her than ever nature had done." He
repeated it, too. "She was far more indebted, I say, to grace, than
to nature," and before his sharp earnestness none were seen to
smile. Nor could you forget the note in his voice when the loss he

deplored was that of a youth of virtue and promise, or that of a personal friend. His very text would be a blow upon the heart; the eyes filled from the beginning. People would often say that they were "sorry for the family," sitting through Dr. Drummond's celebration of their bereavement; and the sympathy was probably well founded. But how fine he was when he paid the last tribute to that upright man, his elder and office-bearer, David Davidson! How his words marched, sorrowing to the close! "Much I have said of him, and more than he would have had me say." Will it not stay with those who heard it till the very end, the trenchant, mournful fall of that "more than he would have had me say?"

It was a thing that Hugh Finlay could not abide in Dr. Drummond.

As the winter passed, the little Doctor was hard put to it to keep his hands off the great political issue of the year, bound up as it was in the tenets of his own politics, which he held only less uncompromisingly than those of the Shorter Catechism. It was, unfortunately for him, a gradual and peaceful progress of opinion, marked by no dramatic incidents; and analogy was hard to find in either Testament for a change of fiscal policy based on imperial advantage. Dr. Drummond liked a pretty definite parallel; he had small opinion of the practice of drawing a pint out of a thimble, as he considered Finlay must have done when he preached the gospel of imperialism from Deuteronomy xxx. 14. "For the word is very nigh unto thee, in thy mouth and in thy heart, that thou mayest do it." Moreover, to preach politics in Knox Church was a liberty in Finlay.

The fact that Finlay had been beforehand with him operated perhaps to reconcile the Doctor to his difficulty; and the candidature of one of his own members in what was practically the imperial interest no doubt increased his embarrassment. Nevertheless, he would not lose sight of the matter for more than two or three weeks together. Many an odd blow he delivered for its furtherance by way of illustrating higher things, and he kept it always, so to speak, in the practical politics of the long prayer.

It was Sunday evening, and Abby and her husband, as usual, had come to tea. The family was complete with the exception of Lorne, who had driven out to Clayfield with Horace Williams, to talk over some urgent matters with persons whom he would meet at supper at the Metropole Hotel at Clayfield. It was a thing Mrs. Murchison thought little short of scandalous—supper to talk business on the Sabbath day, and in an hotel, a place of which the smell about the door was enough to knock you down, even on a weekday. Mrs. Murchison considered, and did not scruple to say so, that politics should be let alone on Sundays. Clayfield votes might be very important, but there were such things as commandments, she supposed. "It'll bring no blessing," she declared severely, eyeing Lorne's empty place.

The talk about the lamplit table was, nevertheless, all of the election, blessed or unblessed. It was not in human nature that it shouldn't be, as Mrs. Murchison would have very quickly told you if you had found her inconsistent. There was reason in all things, as she frequently said.

"I hear," Alec had told them, "that Octavius Milburn is going around bragging he's got the Elgin Chamber of Commerce consolidated this time."

"Against us?" exclaimed Stella; and her brother said, "Of course!"

"Those Milburns," remarked Mrs. Murchison, "are enough to make one's blood boil. I met Mrs. Milburn in the market yesterday; she'd been pricing Mrs. Crow's ducks, and they were just five cents too dear for her, and she stopped—wonderful thing for her—and had *such* an amount to say about Lorne, and the honour it was, and the dear only knows what! Butter wouldn't melt in her mouth—and Octavius Milburn doing all he knew against him the whole time! That's the Milburns! I cut her remarkably short," Mrs. Murchison added, with satisfaction, "and when she'd made up her mind she'd have to give that extra five cents for the ducks because there weren't any others to be had, she went back and found I'd bought them."

"Well done, mother!" said Alec, and Oliver remarked that if those were to-day's ducks they were too good for the Milburn crowd, a lot.

"I expect she wanted them, too," remarked Stella. "They've got the only Mr. Hesketh staying with them now. Miss Filkin's in a great state of excitement."

"I guess we can spare them Hesketh," said John Murchison.

"He's a lobster," said Stella with fervour.

"He seems to bring a frost where he goes," continued Abby's

husband, "in politics, anyhow. I hear Lorne wants to make a present of him to the other side, for use wherever they'll let him speak longest. Is it true he began his speech out at Jordanville— 'Gentlemen—and those of you who are not gentlemen'?"

"Could he have meant Mrs. Farquharson and Miss Milburn?" asked Mr. Murchison quietly, when the derision subsided; and they laughed again.

"He told me," said Advena, "that he proposed to convert Mr. Milburn to the imperial policy."

"He'll have his job cut out for him," said her father.

"For my part," Abby told them, "I think the Milburns are beneath contempt. You don't know exactly what it is, but there's something *about* them—not that we ever come in contact with them," she continued with dignity. "I believe they used to be patients of Dr. Henry's till he got up in years, but they don't call in Harry."

"Maybe that's what there is about them," said Mr. Murchison, innocently.

"Father's made up his mind," announced Dr. Harry, and they waited breathless. There could be only one point upon which Dr. Henry could be dubitating at that moment.

"He's going to vote for Lorne."

"He's a lovely old darling!" cried Stella. "Good for Dr. Henry Johnson! I knew he would."

The rest were silent with independence and gratification. Dr. Henry's Conservatism had been supposed to be invincible. Dr. Harry they thought a fair prey to Murchison influence, and he had capitulated early, but he had never promised to answer for his father.

"Yes, he's taken his time about it, and he's consulted about all the known authorities," said his son, humorously. "Went right back to the Manchester school to begin with—sat out on the verandah reading Cobden and Bright¹ the whole summer; if anybody came for advice sent 'em in to me. I did a trade, I tell you! He thought they talked an awful lot of sense, those fellows—from the English point of view. 'D'ye mean to tell me,' he'd say, 'that a generation born and bred in political doctrine of that sort is going to hold on to the colonies at a sacrifice? They'd rather let 'em go at a sacrifice!' Well, then he got to reading the other side of the

question, and old Ormiston lent him Parkin,[2] and he lent old
Ormiston Goldwin Smith,[3] and then he subscribed to the *Times* for
six months—the bill must have nearly bust him; and then the
squire went over without waiting for him and without any assistance from the *Times* either; and finally—well, he says that if it's
good enough business for the people of England it's good enough
business for him. Only he keeps on worrying about the people of
England, and whether they'll make enough by it to keep them
contented, till he can't half enjoy his meals. And though he's
going to vote for Lorne next month all right, he wants it to be
distinctly understood that family connection has nothing to do
with it."

"Of course it hasn't," Advena said.

"But we're just as much obliged," remarked Stella.

"A lot of our church people[4] are going to stay at home election
day," declared Abby; "they won't vote for Lorne, and they won't
vote against imperialism, so they'll just sulk. Silly, I call it."

"Good enough business for us," said Alec.

"Well, what I want to know is," said Mrs. Murchison, "whether
you are coming to the church you were born and brought up in,
Abby, or not, to-night? There's the first bell."

"I'm not going to any church," said Abby. "I went this morning. I'm going home to my baby."

"Your father and mother," said Mrs. Murchison, "can go twice
a day, and be none the worse for it. By the way, father, did you
know old Mrs. Parr was dead? Died this morning at four o'clock.
They telephoned for Dr. Drummond, and I think they had little to
do, for he had been up with her half the night already, Mrs.
Forsyth told me."

"Did he go?" asked Mr. Murchison.

"He did not, for the very good reason that he knew nothing
about it. Mrs. Forsyth answered the telephone, and told them he
hadn't been two hours in his bed, and she wouldn't get him out
again for an unconscious deathbed, and him with bronchitis on
him and two sermons to preach to-day."

"I'll warrant Mrs. Forsyth caught it in the morning," said John
Murchison.

"That she did. The doctor was as cross as two sticks that she
hadn't had him out to answer the 'phone. 'I just spoke up,' she
said, 'and told him I didn't see how he was going to do any good

to the poor soul over a telephone wire.' 'It isn't that,' he said, 'but I might have put them on to Peter Fratch for the funeral. We've never had an undertaker in the church before,' he said; 'he's just come, and he ought to be supported. Now I expect it's too late, they'll have gone to Liscombe.' He rang them up right away, but they had."

"Dr. Drummond can't stand Liscombe," said Alec, as they all laughed a little at the Doctor's foible, all except Advena, who laughed a great deal. She laughed wildly, then weakly. "I wouldn't—think it a pleasure—to be buried by Liscombe myself!" she cried hysterically, and then laughed again until the tears ran down her face, and she lay back in her chair and moaned, still laughing.

Mr. and Mrs. Murchison, Alec, Stella, and Advena made up the family party; Oliver, for reasons of his own, would attend the River Avenue Methodist Church that evening. They slipped out presently into the crisp white winter night. The snow was banked on both sides of the street. Spreading garden fir-trees huddled together weighted down with it; ragged icicles hung from the eaves or lay in long broken fingers on the trodden paths. The snow snapped and tore under their feet; there was a glorious moon that observed every tattered weed sticking up through the whiteness, and etched it with its shadow. The town lay under the moon almost dramatic, almost mysterious, so withdrawn it was out of the cold, so turned in upon its own soul of the fireplace. It might have stood, in the snow and the silence, for a shell and a symbol of the humanity within, for angels or other strangers to mark with curiosity. Mr. and Mrs. Murchison were neither angels nor strangers; they looked at it and saw that the Peterson place was still standing empty, and that old Mr. Fisher hadn't finished his new porch before zero weather came to stop him.

The young people were well ahead; Mrs. Murchison, on her husband's arm, stepped along with the spring of an impetus undisclosed.

"Is it to be the Doctor to-night?" asked John Murchison. "He was so hoarse this morning I wouldn't be surprised to see Finlay in the pulpit. They're getting only morning services in East Elgin just now, while they're changing the lighting arrangements."

"Are they, indeed? Well, I hope they'll change them and be

done with it, for I can't say I'm anxious for too much of their Mr. Finlay in Knox Church."

"Oh you like the man well enough for a change, mother!" John assured her.

"I've nothing to say against his preaching. It's the fellow himself. And I hope we won't get him to-night, for, the way I feel now, if I see him gawking up the pulpit steps it'll be as much as I can do to keep in my seat, and so I just tell you, John."

"You're a little out of patience with him, I see," said Mr. Murchison.

"And it would be a good thing if more than me were out of patience with him. There's such a thing as too much patience, I've noticed."

"I dare say," replied her husband, cheerfully.

"If Advena were any daughter of mine she'd have less patience with him."

"She's not much like you," assented the father.

"I must say I like a girl to have a little spirit if a man has none. And before I'd have him coming to the house week after week the way he has, I'd see him far enough."

"He might as well come there as anywhere," Mr. Murchison replied, ambiguously. "I suppose he has now and then time on his hands?"

"Well, he won't have it on his hands much longer."

"He won't, eh?"

"No, he won't," Mrs. Murchison almost shook the arm she was attached to. "John, I think you might show a little interest! The man's going to be married."

"You don't say that?" John Murchison's tone expressed not only astonishment but concern. Mrs. Murchison was almost mollified.

"But I do say it. His future wife is coming here to Elgin next month, she and her aunt, or her grandmother, or somebody, and they're to stay at Dr. Drummond's and be married as soon as possible."

"Nonsense," said Mr. Murchison, which was his way of expressing simple astonishment.

"There's no nonsense about it. Advena told me herself this afternoon."

"Did she seem put out about it?"

"She's not a girl to show it," Mrs. Murchison hedged, "if she was. I just looked at her. 'Well,' I said, 'that's a piece of news. When did you hear it?' I said. 'Oh, I've known it all the winter!' says my lady. What I wanted to say was that for an engaged man he had been pretty liberal with his visits, but she had such a queer look in her eyes I couldn't express myself, somehow."

"It was just as well left unsaid," her husband told her, thoughtfully.

"I'm not so sure," Mrs. Murchison retorted. "You're a great man, John, for letting everything alone. When he's been coming here regularly for more than a year, putting ideas into the girl's head —"

"He seems to have told her how things were."

"That's all very well—if he had kept himself to himself at the same time."

"Well, mother, you know you never thought much of the prospect."

"No, I didn't," Mrs. Murchison said. "It wouldn't be me that would be married to him, and I've always said so. But I'd got more or less used to it," she confessed. "The man's well enough in some ways. Dear knows there would be a pair of them—one's as much of a muddler as the other! And anybody can see with half an eye that Advena likes him. It hasn't turned out as I expected, that's a fact, John, and I'm just very much annoyed."

"I'm not best pleased about it myself," said John Murchison, expressing, as usual, a very small proportion of the regret that he felt, "but I suppose they know their own business."

Thus, in their different ways, did these elder ones also acknowledge their helplessness before the advancing event. They could talk of it in private and express their dissatisfaction with it, and that was all they could do. It would not be a matter much further turned over between them at best. They would be shy of any affair of sentiment in terms of speech, and from one that affected a member of the family, self-respect would help to pull them the other way. Mrs. Murchison might remember it in the list of things which roused her vain indignation; John Murchison would put it away in the limbo of irremediables that were better forgotten. For the present they had reached the church door. Mrs. Murchison saw with relief that Dr. Drummond occupied his own pulpit, but if her glance had gone the length of three pews behind her she would have discovered that Hugh Finlay made one of the congregation. Fortunately, perhaps, for her enjoyment of the service, she did not look round. Dr. Drummond was more observing, but his was a position of advantage. In the accustomed sea of faces two, heavy shadowed and obstinately facing fate, swam together before Dr. Drummond, and after he had lifted his hands and closed his eyes for the long prayer he saw them still. So that these words occurred, near the end, in the long prayer—

"O Thou Searcher of hearts, who hast known man from the beginning, to whom his highest desires and his loftiest intentions are but as the desires and intentions of a little child, look with Thine own compassion, we beseech Thee, upon souls before Thee in any peculiar difficulty. Our mortal life is full of sin, it is also full of the misconception of virtue. Do Thou clear the understanding, O Lord, of such as would interpret Thy will to their own undoing; do Thou teach them that as happiness may reside in chastening, so chastening may reside in happiness. And though such stand fast to their hurt, do Thou grant to them in Thine own way, which may not be our way, a safe issue out of the dangers that beset them."

Dr. Drummond had his own method of reconciling foreordination and free will. To Advena his supplication came with that mysterious double emphasis of chance words that fit. Her thought played upon them all through the sermon, rejecting and rejecting again their application and their argument and the spring of hope in them. She, too, knew that Finlay was in church, and, half timidly, she looked back for him, as the congregation filed out again into the winter streets. But he, furious, and more resolved than ever, had gone home by another way.

Chapter XXVII

Octavius Milburn was not far beyond the facts when he said that the Elgin Chamber of Commerce was practically solid this time against the Liberal platform, though to what extent this state of things was due to his personal influence might be a matter of opinion. Mr. Milburn was President of the Chamber of Commerce, and his name stood for one of the most thriving of Elgin's industries, but he was not a person of influence except as it might be represented in a draft on the Bank of British North America. He had never converted anybody to anything, and never would, possibly because the governing principle of his life was the terror of being converted to anything himself. If an important nonentity is an imaginable thing, perhaps it would stand for Mr. Milburn; and he found it a more valuable combination than it may appear, since his importance gave him position and opportunity, and his nonentity saved him from their risks. Certainly he had not imposed his view upon his fellow members—they would have blown it off like a feather—yet they found themselves much of his mind. Most of them were manufacturing men of the Conservative party, whose factories had been nursed by high duties upon the goods of outsiders, and few even of the Liberals among them felt inclined to abandon this immediate safeguard for a benefit more or less remote, and more or less disputable. John Murchison thought otherwise, and put it in few words as usual. He said he was more concerned to see big prices in British markets for Canadian crops than he was to put big prices on ironware he couldn't sell. He was more afraid of hard times among the farmers of Canada than he was of competition by the manufacturers of England. That is what he said when he was asked if it didn't go against the grain a little to have to support a son who advocated low duties on British ranges; and when he was not asked he said nothing, disliking the discount that was naturally put upon his opinion. Parsons, of the Blanket Mills, bolted at the first hint of the new policy and justified it by reminding people that he always said he would if it ever looked like business.

"We give their woollen goods a pull of a third[1] as it is," he said, "which is just a third more than I approve of. I don't propose to vote to make it any bigger—can't afford it."

He had some followers, but there were also some, like Young, of the Plough Works, and Windle, who made bicycles, who announced that there was no need to change their politics to defeat a measure that had no existence, and never would have. What sickened them, they declared, was to see young Murchison allowed to give it so much prominence as Liberal doctrine. The party had been strong enough to hold South Fox for the best part of the last twenty years on the old principles, and this British boot-licking feature wasn't going to do it any good. It was fool politics in the opinion of Mr. Young and Mr. Windle.

Then remained the retail trades, the professions, and the farmers.[2] Both sides could leave out of their counsels the interests of the leisured class, since the leisured class in Elgin consisted almost entirely of persons who were too old to work, and therefore not influential. The landed proprietors were the farmers, when they weren't, alas! the banks. As to the retail men, the prosperity of the stores of Main Street and Market Street was bound up about equally with that of Fox County and the Elgin factories. The lawyers and doctors, the odd surveyors and engineers, were inclined, by their greater detachment, to theories and prejudices, delightful luxuries where a certain rigidity of opinion is dictated by considerations of bread and butter. They made a factor debatable, but small. The farmers had everything to win, nothing to lose. The prospect offered them more for what they had to sell, and less for what they had to buy, and most of them were Liberals already; but the rest had to be convinced, and a political change of heart in a bosom of South Fox was as difficult as any other. Industrial, commercial, professional, agricultural, Lorne Murchison scanned them all hopefully, but Walter Winter felt them his garnered sheaves.

It will be imagined how Mr. Winter, as a practical politician, rejoiced in the aspect of things. The fundamental change, with its incalculable chances to play upon, the opening of the gate to admit plain detriment in the first instance for the sake of benefit, easily beclouded, in the second, the effective arm, in the hands of a satirist, of sentiment in politics—and if there was a weapon Mr. Winter owned a weakness for it was satire—the whole situation, as he often confessed, suited him down to the ground. He professed himself, though no optimist under any circumstances, very well pleased. Only in one other place, he declared, would he have preferred to conduct a campaign at the present moment on the issue involved, though he would have to change his politics to do it there,[3] and that place was England. He cast an envious eye across the ocean at the trenchant argument of the dear loaf;[4] he had no such straight road to the public stomach and grand arbitrator of the fate of empires. If the Liberals in England failed to turn out the Government over this business, they would lose in his eyes all the respect he ever had for them, which wasn't much, he acknowledged. When his opponents twitted him with discrepancy here, since a bargain so bad for one side could hardly fail to favour the other, he poured all his contempt on the scheme as concocted by damned enthusiasts for the ruin of business men of both countries. Such persons, Mr. Winter said, if they could have their way, would be happy and satisfied; but in his opinion neither England nor the colonies could afford to please them as much as that. He professed loud contempt for the opinions of the Conservative party organs at Toronto, and stood boldly for his own views. That was what would happen, he declared, in every manufacturing division in the country, if the issue came to be fought in a general election. He was against the scheme, root and branch.

Mr. Winter was skilled, practised, and indefatigable. We need not follow him in all his ways and works; a good many of his arguments, I fear, must also escape us. The Elgin *Mercury*, if consulted, would produce them in daily disclosure; so would the Clayfield *Standard*. One of these offered a good deal of sympathy to Mayor Winter, the veteran of so many good fights, in being asked to contest South Fox with an opponent who had not so much as a village reeveship to his public credit. If the Conservative candidate felt the damage to his dignity, however, he concealed it.

In Elgin and Clayfield, where factory chimneys had also begun to point the way to enterprise, Winter had a clear field. Official reports gave him figures to prove the great and increasing prosperity of the country, astonishing figures of capital coming in, of emigrants landing, of new lands broken, new mineral regions exploited, new railways projected, of stocks and shares normal, safe, assured. He could ask the manufacturers of Elgin to look no farther than themselves, which they were quite willing to do, for illustration of the plenty and the promise which reigned in the land from one end to the other.[5] He could tell them that in their own

Province more than one hundred new industries had been established in the last year. He could ask them, and he did ask them,
whether this was a state of things to disturb with an inrush from
British looms and rolling mills, and they told him with applause
that it was not.

Country audiences were not open to arguments like these; they
were slow in the country, as the *Mercury* complained, to understand that agricultural prospects were bound up with the prosperity
of the towns and cities; they had been especially slow in the country in England, as the *Express* ironically pointed out, to understand
it. So Winter and his supporters asked the farmers of South Fox if
they were prepared to believe all they heard of the good-will of
England to the colonies, with the flattering assumption that they
were by no means prepared to believe it. Was it a likely thing, Mr.
Winter inquired, that the people of Great Britain were going to pay
more for their flour and their bacon, their butter and their cheese, '
than they had any need to do, simply out of a desire to benefit
countries which most of them had never seen, and never would
see? No, said Mr. Winter, they might take it from him, that was
not the idea. But Mr. Winter thought there was an idea, and that
they and he together would not have much trouble in deciphering
it. He did not claim to be longer-sighted in politics than any other
man, but he thought the present British idea was pretty plain. It
was, in two words, to secure the Canadian market for British
goods, and a handsome contribution from the Canadian taxpayer
toward the expense of the British army and navy, in return for the
offer of favours to food supplies from Canada. But this, as they all
knew, was not the first time favours had been offered by the
British Government to food supplies from Canada. Just sixty years
ago the British Government had felt one of these spasms of
benevolence to Canada, and there were men sitting before him
who could remember the good-will and the gratitude, the hope and
the confidence, that greeted Stanley's bill[6] of that year, which
admitted Canadian wheat and flour at a nominal duty. Some could
remember, and those who could not remember could read, how the
farmers and the millers of Ontario took heart and laid out capital,
and how money was easy and enterprise was everywhere, and how
agricultural towns such as Elgin was at that time sent up streets of
shops to accommodate the trade that was to pour in under the new
and generous "preference" granted to the Dominion by the mother

country. And how long, Mr. Winter demanded, swinging round in that pivotal manner which seems assisted by thumbs in the arm-holes of the waistcoat, how long did the golden illusion last? Precisely three years. In precisely three years the British nation compelled the British Government to adopt the Free Trade Act of '46. The wheat of the world flowed into every port in England, and the hopes of Canada, especially the hopes of Ontario, based then, as now, on preferential treatment, were blasted to the root. Enterprise was laid flat, mortgages were foreclosed, shops were left empty, the milling and forwarding interests were temporarily ruined, and the Governor-General actually wrote to the Secretary of State in England that things were so bad that not a shilling could be raised on the credit of the Province.

Now Mr. Winter did not blame the people of England for insisting on free food. It was the policy that suited their interests, and they had just as good a right to look after their interests, he conceded handsomely, as anybody else. But he did blame the British Government for holding out hopes, for making definite pledges, to a young and struggling nation, which they must have known they would not be able to redeem. He blamed their action then, and he would blame it now, if the opportunity were given to them to repeat it, for the opportunity would pass and the pledge would pass into the happy hunting ground of unrealizable politics, but not—and Mr. Winter asked his listeners to mark this very carefully—not until Canada was committed to such relations of trade and taxes with the Imperial Government as would require the most heroic efforts—it might run to a war—to extricate herself from. In plain words, Mr. Winter assured his country audiences, Great Britain had sold them before, and she would sell them again. He stood there before them as loyal to British connection as any man. He addressed a public as loyal to British connection as any public. *But*—once bitten twice shy.

Horace Williams might riddle such arguments from end to end in the next day's *Express*, but if there is a thing that we enjoy in the country, it is having the dodges of Government shown up with ignominy, and Mr. Winter found his account in this historic parallel.

Nothing could have been more serious in public than his line of defence against the danger that menaced, but in friendly ears

Mr. Winter derided it as a practical possibility, like the Liberals, Young and Windle.

"It seems to me," he said, talking to Octavius Milburn, "that the important thing at present is the party attitude to the disposition of Crown lands and to Government-made railways. As for this racket of Wallingham's, it has about as much in it as an empty bun-bag. He's running round taking a lot of satisfaction blowing it out just now, and the swells over there are clapping like anything, but the first knock will show that it's just a bun-bag, with a hole in it."

"Folks in the old country are solid on the buns, though," said Milburn as they parted, and Alfred Hesketh, who was walking with his host, said—"It's bound in the end to get down to that, isn't it?"

Presently Hesketh came back to it.

"Quaint idea, that—describing Wallingham's policy as a bun-bag," he said, and laughed. "Winter is an amusing fellow."

"Wallingham's policy won't even be a bun-bag much longer," said Milburn. "It won't be anything at all. Imperial union is very nice to talk about, but when you come down to hard fact it's Australia for the Australians, Canada for the Canadians, Africa for the Africans, every time."

"Each for himself, and devil take the hindmost," said Hesketh; "and when the hindmost is England, as our friend Murchison declares it will be —"

"So much the worse for England," said Milburn, amiably. "But we should all be sorry to see it, and, for my part, I don't believe such a thing is at all likely. And you may be certain of one thing," he continued, impressively: "No flag but the Union Jack will ever wave over Canada."

"Oh, I'm sure of that!" Hesketh responded. "Since I have heard more of your side of the question I am quite convinced that loyalty to England and complete commercial independence—I might say even commercial antagonism—may exist together in the colonies. It seems paradoxical, but it is true."

Mr. Hesketh had naturally been hearing a good deal more of Mr. Milburn's side of the question, staying as he was under Mr. Milburn's hospitable roof. It had taken the least persuasion in the world to induce him to make the Milburns a visit. He found them delightful people. He described them in his letters home as the most typically Canadian family he had met, quite simple and unconventional, but thoroughly warm-hearted, and touchingly devoted to far-away England. Politically he could not see eye to eye with Mr. Milburn, but he could quite perceive Mr. Milburn's grounds for the view he held. One thing, he explained to his correspondents, you learned at once by visiting the colonies, and that was to make allowance for local conditions, both social and economic.

He and Mr. Milburn had long serious discussions, staying behind in the dining-room to have them after tea, when the ladies took their fancy work into the drawing-room, and Dora's light touch was heard upon the piano. It may be supposed that Hesketh brought every argument forward in favour of the great departure that had been conceived in England; he certainly succeeded in interesting his host very deeply in the English point of view. He had, however, to encounter one that was made in Canada—it resided in Mr. Milburn as a stone might reside in a bag of wool. Mr. Milburn wouldn't say that this preference trade idea, if practicable, might not work out for the benefit of the Empire as a whole. That was a thing he didn't pretend to know. But it wouldn't work out for his benefit—that was a thing he did know. When a man was confronted with a big political change the question he naturally asked himself was, "Is it going to be worth my while?" and he acted on the answer to that question. He was able to explain to Hesketh, by a variety of facts and figures, of fascinating interest to the inquiring mind, just how and where such a concern as the Milburn Boiler Company would be "hit" by the new policy, after which he asked his guest fairly, "Now, if you were in my shoes, would you see your way to voting for any such thing?"

"If I were in your shoes," said Hesketh, thoughtfully, "I can't say I would."

On grounds of sentiment, Octavius assured him, they were absolutely at one, but in practical matters a man had to proceed on business principles. He went about at this time expressing great esteem for Hesketh's capacity to assimilate facts. His opportunity to assimilate them was not curtailed by any further demand for his services in the South Fox campaign. He was as willing as ever, he told Lorne Murchison, to enlist under the flag, and not for the first time; but Murchison and Farquharson, and that lot, while grateful for the offer, seemed never quite able to avail themselves of it: the fact was all the dates were pretty well taken up. No doubt, Hesketh acknowledged, the work could be done best by men familiar with the local conditions, but he could not avoid the conviction that this attitude toward proffered help was very like dangerous trifling. Possibly these circumstances gave him an added impartiality for Mr. Milburn's facts. As the winter advanced his enthusiasm for the country increased with his intelligent appreciation of the possibilities of the Elgin boiler. The Elgin boiler was his object-lesson in the development of the colonies; he paid several visits to the works to study it, and several times he thanked Mr. Milburn for the opportunity of familiarizing himself with such an important and promising branch of Canadian industry.

"It looks," said Octavius one evening in early February, "as if the Grits were getting a little anxious about South Fox—high time, too. I see Cruickshank is down to speak at Clayfield on the seventh, and Tellier is to be here for the big meeting at the opera-house on the eleventh."

"Tellier is Minister of Public Works, isn't he?" asked Hesketh.

"Yes—and Cruickshank is an ex-Minister," replied Mr. Milburn. "Looks pretty shaky when they've got to take men like that away from their work in the middle of the session."

"I shall be glad," remarked his daughter Dora, "when this horrid election is over. It spoils everything."

She spoke a little fretfully. The election and the matters it involved did interfere a good deal with her interest in life. As an occupation it absorbed Lorne Murchison even more completely than she occasionally desired; and as a topic it took up a larger share of the attention of Mr. Alfred Hesketh than she thought either reasonable or pleasing. Between politics and boilers Miss Milburn almost felt at times that the world held a second place for her.

Chapter XXVIII

The progress of Mrs. Kilbannon and Miss Christie Cameron up the river to Montreal, and so west to Elgin, was one series of surprises, most of them pleasant and instructive to such a pair of intelligent Scotch-women, if we leave out the number of Roman Catholic churches that lift their special symbol along the banks of the St. Lawrence and the fact that Hugh Finlay was not in Elgin to meet them upon their arrival. Dr. Drummond, of course, was there at the station to explain. Finlay had been obliged to leave for Winnipeg only the day before, to attend a mission conference in place of a delegate who had been suddenly laid aside by serious illness. Finlay, he said, had been very loth to go, but there were many reasons why it was imperative that he should; Dr. Drummond explained them all. "I insisted on it," he assured them, frankly. "I told him I would take the responsibility."

He seemed very capable of taking it, both the ladies must have thought, with his quick orders about the luggage and his waiting cab. Mrs. Kilbannon said so. "I'm sure," she told him, "we are better off with you than with Hugh. He was always a daft dependence at a railway station."

They both—Mrs. Kilbannon and Dr. Drummond—looked out of the corners of their eyes, so to speak, at Christie, the only one who might be expected to show any sensitiveness; but Miss Cameron accepted the explanation with readiness. Indeed, she said, she would have been real vexed if Mr. Finlay had stayed behind on her account—she showed herself well aware of the importance of a nomination, and the desirability of responding to it.

"It will just give me an opportunity of seeing the town," she said, looking at it through the cab windows as they drove; and Dr. Drummond had to admit that she seemed a sensible creature. Other things being equal, Finlay might be doing very well for himself. As they talked of Scotland—it transpired that Dr. Drummond knew all the braes¹ about Bross as a boy—he found himself more than ever annoyed with Finlay about the inequality of other things; and when they passed Knox Church and Miss Cameron told him she hadn't realized it was so imposing an edifice, he felt downright sorry for the woman.

Dr. Drummond had persuaded Finlay to go to Winnipeg with a vague hope that something, in the fortnight's grace thus provided, might be induced to happen. The form it oftenest took to his imagination was Miss Christie's announcement, when she set foot upon the station platform, that she had become engaged, on the way over, to somebody else—some fellow-traveller. Such things, Dr. Drummond knew, did come about, usually bringing distress and discomfiture in their train. Why, then, should they not happen when all the consequences would be rejoiceful?

It was plain enough, however, that nothing of the kind had come to pass. Miss Christie had arrived in Elgin, bringing her affections intact; they might have been in any one of her portmanteaux. She had come with definite calm intention, precisely in the guise in which she should have been expected. At the very hour, in the very clothes, she was there. Robust and pleasant, with a practical eye on her promising future, she had arrived, the fulfilment of despair. Dr. Drummond looked at her with acquiescence, half cowed, half comic, wondering at his own folly in dreaming of anything else. Miss Cameron brought the situation, as it were, with her; it had to be faced, and Dr. Drummond faced it like a philosopher. She was the material necessity, the fact in the case, the substantiation of her own legend; and Dr. Drummond promptly gave her all the consideration she demanded in this aspect. Already he heard himself pronouncing a blessing over the pair—and they would make the best of it. With characteristic dispatch he decided that the marriage should take place the first Monday after Finlay's return. That would give them time to take a day or two in Toronto, perhaps, and get back for Finlay's Wednesday prayer meeting. "Or I could take if off his hands," said Dr. Drummond to himself. "That would free them till the end of the week." Solicitude increased in him that the best should be made of it; after all, for a long time they had been making the worst. Mrs. Forsyth, whom it had been necessary to inform when Mrs. Kilbannon and Miss Cameron became actually imminent, saw plainly that the future Mrs. Finlay had made a very good impression on the Doctor; and as nature, in Mrs. Forsyth's case, was more powerful than grace, she became critical accordingly. Still, she was an honest soul: she found more fault with what she called Miss Cameron's "shirt-waists" than with Miss Cameron herself,

whom she didn't doubt to be a good woman though she would
never see thirty-five again. Time and observation would no doubt
mend or remodel the shirt-waists; and meanwhile both they and
Miss Cameron would do very well for East Elgin, Mrs. Forsyth
avowed. Mrs. Kilbannon, definitely given over to caps and curls
as they still wear them in Bross, Mrs. Forsyth at once formed a
great opinion of. She might be something, Mrs. Forsyth thought,
out of a novel by Mr. Crockett,[2] and made you long to go to
Scotland, where presumably every one was like her. On the whole
the ladies from Bross profited rather than lost by the new frame
they stepped into in the house of Dr. Drummond, of Elgin,
Ontario. Their special virtues, of dignity and solidity and frugality,
stood out saliently against the ease and unconstraint about them;
in the profusion of the table it was little less than edifying to hear
Mrs. Kilbannon, invited to preserves, say, "Thank you, I have
butter." It was the pleasantest spectacle, happily common enough,
of the world's greatest inheritance. We see it in immigrants of all
degrees, and we may perceive it in Miss Cameron and Mrs. Kilbannon. They come in couples and in companies from those little
imperial islands, bringing the crusted qualities of the old blood
bottled there so long, and sink with grateful absorption into the
wide bountiful stretches of the further countries. They have much
to take, but they give themselves; and so it comes about that the
Empire is summed up in the race, and the flag flies for its ideals.

Mrs. Forsyth had been told of the approaching event; but
neither Dr. Drummond, who was not fond of making communications he did not approve of, nor the Murchisons, who were shy of
the matter as a queer business which Advena seemed too much
mixed up with, had mentioned it to any one else. Finlay himself
had no intimates, and moved into his new house in River Street
under little comment. His doings excited small surprise, because
the town knew too little about him to expect him to do one thing
more than another. He was very significant among his people, very
important in their lives, but not, somehow, at any expense to his
private self. He knew them, but they did not know him; and it is
high praise of him that this was no grievance among them. They
would tell you without resentment that the minister was a "very
reserved" man; there might be even a touch of proper pride in it.
The worshippers of Knox Church mission were rather a reserved

lot themselves. It was different with the Methodists; plenty of expansion there.

Elgin, therefore, knew nothing, beyond the fact that Dr. Drummond had two ladies from the old country staying with him, about whom particular curiosity would hardly be expected outside of Knox Church. In view of Finlay's absence, Dr. Drummond, consulting with Mrs. Kilbannon, decided that for the present Elgin need not be further informed. There was no need, they agreed, to give people occasion to talk; and it would just be a nuisance to have to make so many explanations. Both Mrs. Kilbannon and her niece belonged to the race that takes great satisfaction in keeping its own counsel. Their situation gained for them the further interest that nothing need be said about it; and the added importance of caution was plainly to be discerned in their bearing, even toward one another. It was a portentous business, this of marrying a minister, under the most ordinary circumstances, not to be lightly dealt with, and even more of an undertaking in a far new country where the very wind blew differently, and the extraordinary freedom of conversation made it more than ever necessary to take heed to what you were saying. So far as Miss Cameron and Mrs. Kilbannon were aware, the matter had not been "spoken of" elsewhere at all. Dr. Drummond, remembering Advena Murchison's acquaintance with it, had felt the weight of a complication, and had discreetly held his tongue. Mrs. Kilbannon approved her nephew in this connection. "Hugh," she said, "was never one to let on more than necessary." It was a fine secret between Hugh, in Winnipeg, whence he had written all that was lawful or desirable, and themselves at Dr. Drummond's. Miss Cameron said it would give her more freedom to look about her.

In the midst of all this security, and on the very first day after their arrival, it was disconcerting to be told that a lady, whose name they had never heard before, had called to see Miss Cameron and Mrs. Kilbannon. They had not even appeared at church, as they told one another with dubious glances. They had no reason whatever to expect visitors. Dr. Drummond was in the cemetery burying a member; Mrs. Forsyth was also abroad. "Now who in the world," asked Mrs. Kilbannon of Miss Cameron, "is Miss Murchison?"

"They come to our church," said Sarah, in the door. "They've got the foundry. It's the oldest one. She teaches."

Sarah in the door was even more disconcerting than an unexpected visitor. Sarah invariably took them off their guard, in the door or anywhere. She freely invited their criticism, but they would not have known how to mend her. They looked at her now helplessly, and Mrs. Kilbannon said, "Very well. We will be down directly."

"It may be just some friendly body," she said, as they descended the stairs together, "or it may be common curiosity. In that case we'll disappoint it."

Whatever they expected, therefore, it was not Advena. It was not a tall young woman with expressive eyes, a manner which was at once abrupt and easy, and rather a lounging way of occupying the corner of a sofa. "When she sat down," as Mrs. Kilbannon said afterward, "she seemed to untie and fling herself as you might a parcel." Neither Mrs. Kilbannon nor Christie Cameron could possibly be untied or flung, so perhaps they gave this capacity in Advena more importance than it had. But it was only a part of what was to them a new human demonstration, something to inspect very carefully and accept very cautiously—the product, like themselves, yet so suspiciously different, of these free airs and these astonishingly large ideas. In some ways, as she sat there in her graceful dress and careless attitude, asking them direct smiling questions about their voyage, she imposed herself as of the class whom both these ladies of Bross would acknowledge unquestioningly to be "above" them; in others she seemed to be of no class at all; so far she came short of small standards of speech and behaviour. The ladies from Bross, more and more confused, grew more and more reticent, when suddenly, out of a simple remark of Miss Cameron's about missing in the train the hot-water cans they gave you "to your feet" in Scotland, reticence descended upon Miss Murchison also. She sat in an odd silence, looking at Miss Cameron, absorbed apparently in the need of looking at her, finding nothing to say, her flow of pleasant inquiry dried up, and all her soul at work, instead, to perceive the woman. Mrs. Kilbannon was beginning to think better of her—it was so much more natural to be a little backward with strangers—when the moment passed. Their visitor drew herself out of it with almost a perceptible effort, and seemed to glance consideringly at them in their aloofness, their incommunicativeness, their plain odds with her. I don't know what she expected; but we may assume that she was there simply to offer herself up, and the impulse of sacrifice seldom considers whether or not it may be understood. It was to her a normal, natural thing that a friend of Hugh Finlay's should bring an early welcome to his bride; and to do the normal, natural thing at keen personal cost was to sound that depth, or rise to that height of the spirit where pain sustains. We know of Advena that she was prone to this form of exaltation. Those who feel themselves capable may pronounce whether she would have been better at home crying in her bedroom.

She decided badly—how could she decide well?—on what she would say to explain herself.

"I am so sorry," she told them, "that Mr. Finlay is obliged to be away."

It was quite wrong; it assumed too much, her knowledge and their confidence, and the propriety of discussing Mr. Finlay's absence. There was even an unconscious hint of another kind of assumption in it—a suggestion of apology for Mr. Finlay. Advena was aware of it even as it left her lips, and the perception covered her with a damning blush. She had a sudden terrified misgiving that her *rôle* was too high for her, that she had already cracked her mask. But she looked quietly at Miss Cameron and smiled across the tide that surged in her as she added, "He was very distressed at having to go."

They looked at her in an instant's blank astonishment. Miss Cameron opened her lips and closed them again, glancing at Mrs. Kilbannon. They fell back together, but not in disorder. This was something much more formidable than common curiosity. Just what it was they would consider later; meanwhile Mrs. Kilbannon responded with what she would have called cool civility.

"Perhaps you have heard that Mr. Finlay is my nephew?" she said.

"Indeed I have. Mr. Finlay has told me a great deal about you, Mrs. Kilbannon, and about his life at Bross," Advena replied. "And he has told me about you, too," she went on, turning to Christie Cameron.

"Indeed?" said she.

"Oh, a long time ago. He has been looking forward to your arrival for some months, hasn't he?"

"We took our passages in December," said Miss Cameron.

"And you are to be married almost immediately, are you not?" Miss Murchison continued, pleasantly.

Mrs. Kilbannon had an inspiration. "Could he by any means have had the banns[3] cried?" she demanded of Christie, who looked piercingly at their visitor for the answer.

"Oh, no," Advena laughed softly. "Presbyterians haven't that custom over here—does it still exist anywhere? Mr. Finlay told me himself."

"Has he informed all his acquaintances?" asked Mrs. Kilbannon. "We thought maybe his elders would be expecting to hear, or his Board of Management. Or he might have just dropped a word to his Sessions Clerk. But —"

Advena shook her head. "I think it unlikely," she said.

"Then why would he be telling you?" inquired the elder lady, bluntly.

"He told me, I suppose, because I have the honour to be a friend of his," Advena said, smiling. "But he is not a man, is he? who makes many friends. It is possible, I dare say, that he has mentioned it to no one else."

Poor Advena! She had indeed uttered her ideal to unsympathetic ears—brought her pig, as her father would have said, to the wrong market. She sat before the ladies from Bross, Hugh Finlay's only confidante. She sat handsome and upheld and not altogether penetrable, a kind of gipsy to their understanding, though indeed the Romany strain in her was beyond any divining of theirs. They, on their part, reposed in their clothes with all their bristles out— what else could have been expected of them?—convinced in their own minds that they had come not only to a growing but to a forward country.

Mrs. Kilbannon was perhaps a little severe. "I wonder that we have not heard of you, Miss Murchison," said she, "but we are happy to make the acquaintance of any of my nephew's friends. You will have heard him preach, perhaps?"

"Often," said Advena, rising. "We have no one here who can compare with him in preaching. There was very little reason why you should have heard of me. I am of no importance." She hesitated and fought for an instant with a trembling of the lip. "But now that you have been persuaded to be a part of our life here," she said to Christie, "I thought I would like to come and offer you my friendship because it is his already. I hope—so much—that you will be happy here. It is a nice little place. And I want you to let me help you—about your house, and in every way that is possible. I am sure I can be of use." She paused and looked at their still half-hostile faces. "I hope," she faltered, "you don't mind my—having come?"

"Not at all," said Christie, and Mrs. Kilbannon added, "I'm sure you mean it very kindly."

A flash of the comedy of it shot up in Advena's eyes. "Yes," she said, "I do. Good-bye."

If they had followed her departure they would have been further confounded to see her walk not quite steadily away, shaken with fantastic laughter. They looked instead at one another, as if to find the solution of the mystery where indeed it lay, in themselves.

"She doesn't even belong to his congregation," said Christie. "Just a friend, she said."

"I expect the friendship's mostly upon her side," remarked Mrs. Kilbannon. "She seemed frank enough about it. But I would see no necessity for encouraging her friendship on my own account, if I were in your place, Christie."

"I think I'll manage without it," said Christie.

Chapter XXIX

The South Fox fight was almost over. Three days only remained before the polling booths would be open, and the voters of the towns of Elgin and Clayfield and the surrounding townships would once again be invited to make their choice between a Liberal and a Conservative representative of the district in the Dominion House of Commons. The ground had never been more completely covered, every inch of advantage more stubbornly held, by either side, in the political history of the riding. There was no doubt of the hope that sat behind the deprecation in Walter Winter's eye, nor of the anxiety that showed through the confidence freely expressed by the Liberal leaders. The issue would be no foregone conclusion, as it had been practically any time within the last eleven years; and as Horace Williams remarked to the select lot that met pretty frequently at the *Express* office for consultation and rally, they had "no use for any sort of carelessness."

It was undeniably felt that the new idea, the great idea whose putative fatherhood in Canada certainly lay at the door of the Liberal party, had drawn in fewer supporters than might have been expected. In England Wallingham, wearing it like a medal, seemed to be courting political excommunication with it, except that Wallingham was so hard to effectively curse. The ex-Minister deserved, clearly, any ban that could be put upon him. No sort of remonstrance could hold him from going about openly and persistently exhorting people to "think imperially," a liberty which, as is well known, the Holy Cobdenite Church, supreme in those islands, expressly forbids.[1] Wallingham appeared to think that by teaching and explaining he could help his fellow islanders to see further than the length of their fists, and exorcise from them the spirit, only a century and a quarter older and a trifle more sophisticated, that lost them the American colonies. But so far little had transpired to show that Wallingham was stronger than nature and destiny. There had been Wallingham meetings of remarkable enthusiasm; his supporters called them epoch-making, as if epochs were made of cheers. But the working man of Great Britain was declaring stolidly in the bye-elections against any favour to colo-

nial produce at his expense, thereby showing himself one of those
humble instruments that Providence uses for the downfall of arro-
gant empires. It will be thus, no doubt, that the working man will
explain in the future his eminent usefulness to the government of
his country, and it will be in these terms that the cost of educating
him by means of the ballot will be demonstrated. Meanwhile we
may look on and cultivate philosophy; or we may make war upon
the gods with Mr. Wallingham, which is, perhaps, the better part.

That, to turn from recrimination, was what they saw in Canada
looking across;—the queerest thing of all was the recalcitrance of
the farm labourer; they could only stare at that—and it may be that
the spectacle was depressing to hopeful initiative. At all events, it
was plain that the new policy was suffering from a certain flatness
on the further side.² As a *ballon d'essai* it lacked buoyancy; and no
doubt Mr. Farquharson was right in declaring that above all things
it lacked actuality, business—the proposition, in good set terms,
for men to turn over, to accept or reject. Nothing could be done
with it, Mr. Farquharson averred, as a mere prospect; it was useful
only to its enemies. We of the young countries must be invited to
deeds, not theories, of which we have a restless impatience; and
this particular theory, though of golden promise, was beginning to
recoil to some extent, upon the cause which had been confident
enough to adopt it before it could be translated into action and its
hard equivalent. The Elgin *Mercury* probably overstated the matter
when it said that the Grits were dead sick of the preference they
would never get;³ but Horace Williams was quite within the mark
when he advised Lorne to stick to old Reform principles—clean
administration, generous railway policy, sympathetic labour legislation, and freeze himself a little on imperial love and attachment.

"They're not so sweet on it in Ottawa as they were, by a long
chalk," he said. "Look at the Premier's speech to the Chambers of
Commerce in Montreal.⁴ Pretty plain statement that, of a few
things the British Government needn't expect."

"Oh, I don't know," said Lorne. "He was talking to manufacturers, you know, a pretty skittish lot anywhere. It sounded independent, but if you look into it you won't find it gave the cause
away any."

"The old man's got to think of Quebec, where his fat little
majority lives," remarked Bingham, chairman of the most difficult
subdivision in the town. "The Premier of this country drives a

team, you know."

"Yes," said Lorne, "but he drives it tandem, and Johnny François is the second horse."[5]

"Maybe so," returned Mr. Williams, "but the organ's singing pretty small, too. Look at this." He picked up the *Dominion* from the office table and read aloud: " 'If Great Britain wishes to do a deal with the colonies she will find them willing to meet her in a spirit of fairness and enthusiasm. But it is for her to decide, and Canada would be the last to force her bread down the throat of the British labourer at a higher price than he can afford to pay for it.'[6] What's that, my boy? Is it high-mindedness? No, sir, it's luke-warmness."

"The *Dominion* makes me sick," said young Murchison. "It's so scared of the Tory source of the scheme in England that it's handing the whole boom of the biggest chance this country ever had over to the Tories here. If anything will help us to lose it that will. No Conservative Government in Canada can put through a cent of preference on English goods when it comes to the touch, and they know it. They're full of loyalty just now—baying the moon—but if anybody opens a window they'll turn tail fast enough."

"I guess the *Dominion* knows it, too," said Mr. Williams. "When Great Britain is quite sure she's ready to do business on preference lines it's the Liberal party on this side she'll have to talk to. No use showing ourselves too anxious, you know. Besides, it might do harm over there. We're all right; we're on record. Wallingham knows as well as we do the lines we're open on—he's heard them from Canadian Liberals more than once. When they get good and ready they can let us know."

"Jolly them up with it at your meetings by all means," advised Bingham, "but use it as a kind of superfluous taffy; don't make it your main lay-out."

The Reform Association of South Fox had no more energetic officer than Bingham, though as he sat on the edge of the editorial table chewing portions of the margin of that afternoon's *Express*, and drawling out maxims to the Liberal candidate, you might not have thought so. He was explaining that he had been in this business for years, and had never had a job that gave him so much trouble.

"We'll win out," he said, "but the canvass isn't any Christmas joy—not this time. There's Jim Whelan," he told them. "We all know what Jim is—a Tory from way back, where they make 'em so they last, and a soaker from way back, too, one day on his job and two days sleepin' off his whisky. Now we don't need Jim Whelan's vote, never did need it, but the boys have generally been able to see that one of those two days was election day. There's no necessity for Jim's putting in his paper—a character like that—no necessity at all—he'd much better be comfortable in bed. This time, I'm darned if the old boozer hasn't sworn off! Tells the boys he's on to their game, and there's no liquor in this town that's good enough to get him to lose his vote—wouldn't get drunk on champagne. He's held out for ten days already, and it looks like Winter'd take his cross all right on Thursday."

"I guess I'd let him have it, Bingham," said Lorne Murchison with a kind of tolerant deprecation, void of offence, the only manner in which he knew how to convey disapproval to the older man. "The boys in your division are a pretty tough lot, anyhow. We don't want the other side getting hold of any monkey tricks."

"It's necessary to win this election, young man," said Bingham, "lawfully. You won't have any trouble with my bunch."

It was not, as will be imagined, the first discussion, so late in the day, of the value of the preference trade argument to the Liberal campaign. They had all realized, after the first few weeks, that their young candidate was a trifle overbitten with it, though remonstrance had been a good deal curbed by Murchison's treatment of it. When he had brought it forward at the late fall fairs and in the lonely country schoolhouses, his talk had been so trenchant, so vivid and pictorial, that the gathered farmers listened with open mouths, like children, pathetically used with life, to a grown-up fairy tale. As Horace Williams said, if a dead horse could be made to go this one would have brought Murchison romping in. And Lorne had taken heed to the counsel of his party leaders. At joint meetings, which offered the enemy his best opportunity for travesty and derision, he had left it in the background of debate, devoting himself to arguments of more immediate utility. In the literature of the campaign it glowed with prospective benefit, but vaguely, like a halo of Liberal conception and possible achievement, waiting for the word from overseas. The *Express* still approved it, but not in headlines, and wished the fact to be widely understood that while the imperial idea was a very big idea, the Liberals of South Fox were going to win this election without any assistance from it.

Lorne submitted. After all, victory was the thing. There could be no conquest for the idea without the party triumph first. He submitted, but his heart rebelled. He looked over the subdivisional reports with Williams and Farquharson, and gave ear to their warning interpretations; but his heart was an optimist, and turned always to the splendid projection upon the future that was so incomparably the title to success of those who would unite to further it. His mind accepted the old working formulas for dealing with an average electorate, but to his eager apprehending heart it seemed unbelievable that the great imperial possibility, the dramatic chance for the race that hung even now, in the history of the world, between the rising and the setting of the sun, should fail to be perceived and acknowledged as the paramount issue, the contingency which made the bye-election of South Fox an extraordinary and momentous affair. He believed in the Idea; he saw it, with Wallingham, not only a glorious prospect, but an educative force; and never had he a moment of such despondency that it confounded him upon his horizon in the faded colours of some old Elizabethan mirage.

The opera-house, the night of Mr. Murchison's final address to the electors of South Fox, was packed from floor to ceiling, and a large and patient overflow made the best of the hearing accommodation of the corridors and the foyer. A Minister was to speak, Sir Matthew Tellier, who held the portfolio of Public Works; and for drawing a crowd in Elgin there was nothing to compare with a member of the Government.[7] He was the sum of all ambition and the centre of all importance; he was held to have achieved in the loftiest sense, and probably because he deserved to; a kind of afflatus sat upon him. They paid him real deference and they flocked to hear him. Cruickshank was a second attraction; and Lorne himself, even at this stage of the proceedings, "drew" without abatement. They knew young Murchison well enough; he had gone in and out among them all his life; yet since he had come before them in this new capacity a curious interest had gathered about him. People looked at him as if he had developed something they did not understand, and perhaps he had; he was in touch with the Idea. They listened with an intense personal interest in him which, no doubt, went to obscure what he said: perhaps a less absorbing personality would have carried the Idea further. However, they did look and listen—that was the main point, and on their last opportunity they were in the opera-house in great numbers.

Lorne faced them with an enviable security; the friendliness of the meeting was in the air. The gathering was almost entirely of one political complexion: the Conservatives of the town would have been glad enough to turn out to hear Minister Tellier; but the Liberals were of no mind to gratify them at the cost of having to stand themselves, and were on hand early to assert a prior moral claim to chairs. In the seated throng Lorne could pick out the fine head of his father, and his mother's face, bright with anticipation, beside. Advena was there, too, and Stella; and the boys would have a perch, not too conspicuous, somewhere in the gallery. Dr. Drummond was in the second row, and a couple of strange ladies with him: he was chuckling with uncommon humour at some remark of the younger one when Lorne noted him. Old Sandy MacQuhot was in a good place; had been since six o'clock, and Peter Macfarlane, too, for that matter, though Peter sat away back as beseemed a modest functionary whose business was with the book and the bell. Altogether, as Horace Williams leaned over to tell him, it was like a Knox Church sociable—he could feel completely at home; and though the audience was by no means confined to Knox Church, Lorne did feel at home. Dora Milburn's countenance he might perhaps have missed, but Dora was absent by arrangement. Mr. Milburn, as the fight went on, had shown himself so increasingly bitter, to the point of writing letters in the *Mercury* attacking Wallingham and the Liberal leaders of South Fox, that his daughter felt an insurmountable delicacy in attending even Lorne's "big meeting." Alfred Hesketh meant to have gone, but it was ten by the Milburns' drawing-room clock before he remembered. Miss Filkin actually did go, and brought home a great report of it. Miss Filkin would no more have missed a Minister than she would a bishop; but she was the only one.

Lorne had prepared for this occasion for a long time. It was certain to come, the day of the supreme effort, when he should make his final appeal under the most favourable circumstances that could be devised, when the harassing work of the campaign would be behind him, and nothing would remain but the luxury of one last strenuous call to arms. The glory of that anticipation had been with him from the beginning; and in the beginning he saw his great moment only in one character. For weeks, while he plodded through the details of the benefits South Fox had received and might expect to receive at the hands of the Liberal party, he privately stored argument on argument, piled phrase on phrase, still further to advance and defend the imperial unity of his vision on this certain and special opportunity. His jehad[8] it would be, for the faith and purpose of his race; so he scanned it and heard it, with conviction hot in him, and impulse strong, and intention noble. Then uneasiness had arisen, as we know; and under steady pressure he had daily drawn himself from these high intentions, persuaded by Bingham and the rest that they were not yet "in shape" to talk about. So that his address on this memorable evening would have a different stamp from the one he designed in the early burning hours of his candidature. He had postponed those matters, under advice, to the hour of practical dealing, when a Government which it would be his privilege to support would consider and carry them. He put the notes of his original speech away in his office desk with solicitude—it was indeed very thorough, a grand marshalling of the facts and review of the principles involved—and pigeonholed it in the chambers of his mind, with the good hope to bring it forth another day. Then he devoted his attention to the history of Liberalism in Fox County—both ridings were solid—and it was upon the history of Liberalism in Fox County, its triumphs and its fruits, that he embarked so easily and so assuredly, when he opened his address in the opera-house that Tuesday night.

Who knows at what suggestion, or even precisely at what moment, the fabric of his sincere intention fell away? Bingham does not; Mr. Farquharson has the vaguest idea; Dr. Drummond declares that he expected it from the beginning, but is totally unable to say why. I can get nothing more out of them, though they were all there, though they all saw him, indeed a dramatic figure, standing for the youth and energy of the old blood, and heard him, as he slipped away into his great preoccupation, as he made what Bingham called his "bad break." His very confidence may have accounted for it; he was off guard against the enemy, and the more completely off guard against himself. The history of Liberalism in Fox County offered, no doubt, some inlet to the rush of the Idea; for suddenly, Mr. Farquharson says, he was "off." Mr. Farquharson was on the platform, and "I can tell you," said he, "I pricked up my ears." They all did; the Idea came in upon such a personal note.

"I claim it my great good fortune," the young man was suddenly telling them, in a note of curious gravity and concentration, "and however the fight goes, I shall always claim it my great good fortune to have been identified, at a critical moment, with the political principles that are ennobled in this country by the imperialistic aim. An intention, a great purpose in the endless construction and reconstruction of the world, will choose its own agency; and the imperial design in Canada has chosen the Liberal party, because the Liberal party in this country is the party of the soil, the land, the nation as it springs from that which makes it a nation; and imperialism is intensely and supremely a national affair. Ours is the policy of the fields. We stand for the wheat-belt and the stock-yard, the forest and the mine, as the basic interests of the country. We stand for the principles that make for nation-building by the slow sweet processes of the earth, cultivating the individual rooted man who draws his essence and his tissues from the soil, and so, by unhurried, natural, healthy growth, labour sweating his vices out of him, forms the character of the commonwealth, the foundation of the State.[9] So the imperial idea seeks its Canadian home in Liberal councils. The imperial idea is far-sighted. England has outlived her own body. Apart from her heart and her history, England is an area where certain trades are carried on—still carried on. In the scrolls of the future it is already written that the centre of the Empire must shift—and where, if not to Canada?"[10]

There was a half-comprehending[11] burst of applause, Dr. Drummond's the first clap. It was a curious change from the simple colloquial manner in which young Murchison had begun and to which the audience were accustomed; and on this account probably they stamped the harder. They applauded Lorne himself; something from him infected them; they applauded being made to feel like that. They would clap first and consider afterwards. John Murchison smiled with pleasure, but shook his head. Bingham, doubled up and clapping like a repeating rifle, groaned aloud under cover of it to Horace Williams: "Oh, the darned kid!"

"A certain Liberal peer of blessed political memory," Lorne continued, with a humorous twist of his mouth, "on one of those graceful, elegant, academic occasions which offer political peers such happy opportunities of getting in their work over there, had lately a vision, which he described to his university audience, of what might have happened if the American colonies had remained faithful to Great Britain—a vision of monarch and Ministers, Government and Parliament, departing solemnly for the other hemisphere. They did not so remain; so the noble peer may conjure up his vision or dismiss his nightmare as he chooses; and it is safe to prophesy that no port of the United States will see that entry. But, remembering that the greater half of the continent did remain faithful, the northern and strenuous half, destined to move with sure steps and steady mind to greater growth and higher place among the nations than any of us can now imagine—would it be as safe to prophesy that such a momentous sailing-day will never be more than the after-dinner fantasy of aristocratic rhetoric? Is it not at least as easy to imagine that even now, while the people of England send their viceroys to the ends of the earth, and vote careless millions for a reconstructed army, and sit in the wrecks of Cabinets disputing whether they will eat our bread or the stranger's, the sails may be filling, in the far harbour of time, which will bear their descendants to a representative share of the duties and responsibilities of Empire in the capital of the Dominion of Canada?"[12]

It was the boldest proposition, and the Liberal voters of the town of Elgin blinked a little, looking at it. Still they applauded, hurriedly, to get it over and hear what more might be coming. Bingham, on the platform, laughed heartily and conspicuously, as if anybody could see that it was all an excellent joke. Lorne half turned to him with a gesture of protest. Then he went on—

"If that transport ever left the shores of England we would go far, some of us, to meet it; but for all the purposes that matter most it sailed long ago. British statesmen could bring us nothing better than the ideals of British government; and those we have had since we levied our first tax and made our first law. That precious cargo was our heritage, and we never threw it overboard, but chose rather to render what impost it brought; and there are those who say that the impost has been heavy, though never a dollar was paid."

He paused for an instant and seemed to review and take account of what he had said. He was hopelessly adrift from the subject he had proposed to himself, launched for better or for worse upon the theme that was subliminal in him and had flowed up, on which he was launched, and almost rudderless, without construction and without control. The speech of his first intention, orderly, developed, was as far from him as the history of Liberalism in Fox County. For an instant he hesitated; and then, under the suggestion, no doubt, of that ancient misbehaviour in Boston Harbour at which he had hinted, he took up another argument. I will quote him a little.

"Let us hold," he said simply, "to the Empire. Let us keep this patrimony that has been ours for three hundred years. Let us not forget the flag. We believe ourselves, at this moment, in no danger of forgetting it. The day after Paardeburg,[13] that still winter day, did not our hearts rise within us to see it shaken out with its message everywhere, shaken out against the snow? How it spoke to us, and lifted us, the silent flag in the new fallen snow! Theirs— and ours .... That was but a little while ago, and there is not a man here who will not bear me out in saying that we were never more loyal, in word and deed, than we are now. And that very state of things has created for us an undermining alternative ....

"So long as no force appeared to improve the trade relations between England and this country Canada sought in vain to make commercial bargains with the United States. They would have none of us or our produce; they kept their wall just as high against us as against the rest of the world: not a pine plank or a bushel of barley could we get over under a reciprocal arrangement. But the imperial trade idea has changed the attitude of our friends to the south. They have small liking for any scheme which will improve trade between Great Britain and Canada, because trade between Great Britain and Canada must be improved at their expense. And now you cannot take up an American paper without finding the report of some commercial association demanding closer trade relations with Canada, or an American magazine in which some far-sighted economist is not urging the same thing. They see us thinking about keeping the business in the family; with that hard American common sense that has made them what they are, they accept the situation; and at this moment they are ready to offer us better terms to keep our trade."[14]

Bingham, Horace Williams, and Mr. Farquharson applauded loudly. Their young man frowned a little and squared his chin. He was past hints of that kind.

"And that," he went on to say, "is, on the surface, a very satisfactory state of things. No doubt a bargain between the Americans and ourselves could be devised which would be a very good bargain on both sides. In the absence of certain pressing family affairs, it might be as well worth our consideration as we used to think it before we were invited to the family council. But if any one imagines that any degree of reciprocity with the United States could be entered upon without killing the idea of British preference trade for all time, let him consider what Canada's attitude toward that idea would be to-day if the Americans had consented to our proposals twenty-five years ago,[15] and we were invited to make an imperial sacrifice of the American trade that had prospered, as it would have prospered, for a quarter of a century! I doubt whether the proposition would even be made to us ....

"But the alternative before Canada is not a mere choice of markets; we are confronted with a much graver issue. In this matter of dealing with our neighbour our very existence is involved. If we would preserve ourselves as a nation, it has become our business, not only to reject American overtures in favour of the overtures of our own great England, but to keenly watch and actively resist American influence, as it already threatens us through the common channels of life and energy. We often say that we fear no invasion from the south, but the armies of the south have already crossed the border. American enterprise, American capital, is taking rapid possession of our mines and our water-power, our oil areas and our timber limits. In to-day's *Dominion*, one paper alone, you may read of charters granted to five industrial concerns with headquarters in the United States. The trades unions of the two countries are already international. American settlers are pouring into the wheat-belt of the Northwest, and when the Dominion of Canada has paid the hundred million dollars she has just voted for a railway to open up the great lone northern lands between Quebec and the Pacific, it will be the American farmer and the American capitalist who will reap the benefit. They approach us to-day with all the arts of peace, commercial missionaries to the ungathered harvests of neglected territories; but the day may come when they will menace our coasts to protect their markets—unless, by firm, resolved, whole- earted action now, we keep our opportunities for our own people."

They cheered him promptly, and a gathered intensity came into his face at the note of praise.

"Nothing on earth can hold him now," said Bingham, as he crossed his arms upon a breast seething with practical politics, and waited for the worst.

"The question of the hour for us," said Lorne Murchison to his fellow townsmen, curbing the strenuous note in his voice, "is deeper than any balance of trade can indicate, wider than any department of statistics can prove. We cannot calculate it in terms of pig-iron, or reduce it to any formula of consumption. The question that underlies this decision for Canada is that of the whole stamp and character of her future existence. Is that stamp and character to be impressed by the American Republic effacing—he smiled a little—the old Queen's head and the new King's oath?[16] Or is it to be our own stamp and character, acquired in the rugged discipline of our colonial youth, and developed in the national usage of the British Empire? ....

Dr. Drummond clapped alone; everybody else was listening.

"It is ours," he told them, "in this greater half of the continent, to evolve a nobler ideal. The Americans from the beginning went in a spirit of revolt; the seed of disaffection was in every Puritan bosom. We from the beginning went in a spirit of amity, forgetting nothing, disavowing nothing, to plant the flag with our fortunes. We took our very Constitution, our very chart of national life, from England—her laws, her liberty, her equity were good enough for us. We have lived by them, some of us have died by them ... and, thank God, we were long poor ....

"And this Republic," he went on hotly, "this Republic that menaces our national life with commercial extinction, what past has she that is comparable? The daughter who left the old stock to be the light woman among nations, welcoming all comers, mingling her pure blood, polluting her lofty ideals until it is hard indeed to recognize the features and the aims of her honourable youth ..."[17]

Allowance will be made for the intemperance of his figure. He believed himself, you see, at the bar for the life of a nation.

" ... Let us not hesitate to announce ourselves for the Empire, to throw all we are and all we have into the balance for that great decision. The seers of political economy tell us that if the stars continue to be propitious, it is certain that a day will come which will usher in a union of the Anglo-Saxon nations of the world.[18] As between England and the United States the predominant partner in that firm will be the one that brings Canada. So that the imperial movement of the hour may mean even more than the future of the mother land, may reach even further than the boundaries of Greater Britain ...."

Again he paused, and his eye ranged over their listening faces. He had them all with him, his words were vivid in their minds; the truth of them stood about him like an atmosphere. Even Bingham looked at him without reproach. But he had done.

"Ladies and gentlemen," he said, his voice dropping, with a hint of tiredness, to another level, "I have the honour to stand for your suffrages as candidate in the Liberal interest for the riding of South Fox in the Dominion House of Commons the day after to-morrow. I solicit your support, and I hereby pledge myself to justify it by every means in my power. But it would be idle to disguise from you that while I attach all importance to the immediate interests in charge of the Liberal party, and if elected shall use my best efforts to further them, the great task before that party, in my opinion, the overshadowing task to which, I shall hope, in my place and degree to stand committed from the beginning, is the one which I have endeavoured to bring before your consideration this evening."

They gave him a great appreciation, and Mr. Cruickshank, following, spoke in complimentary terms of the eloquent appeal made by the "young and vigorous protagonist" of the imperial cause, but proceeded to a number of quite other and apparently more important grounds why he should be elected. The Hon. Mr. Tellier's speech—the Minister was always kept to the last—was a defence of the recent dramatic development of the Government's railway policy,[19] and a reminder of the generous treatment Elgin was receiving in the Estimates for the following year—thirty thousand dollars for a new Drill Hall, and fifteen thousand for improvements to the post-office. It was a telling speech, with the chink of hard cash in every sentence, a kind of audit by a chartered accountant of the Liberal books of South Fox, showing good sound reason why the Liberal candidate should be returned on Thursday, if only to keep the balance right. The audience listened with practical satisfaction. "That's Tellier all over," they said to one another ....

The effect in committee of what, in spite of the Hon. Mr. Tellier's participation, I must continue to call the speech of the evening, may be gathered from a brief colloquy between Mr. Bingham and Mr. Williams, in the act of separating at the door of the opera-house.

"I don't know what it was worth to preference trade," said Bingham, "but it wasn't worth a hill o'beans to his own election."

"He had as soft a snap,"[20] returned Horace Williams, on the brink of tears—"as soft a snap as anybody ever had in this town. And he's monkeyed it all away. All away."

Both the local papers published the speech in full the following day. "If there's anything in Manchester or Birmingham that Mr. Lorne Murchison would like" commented the *Mercury* editorially, "we understand he has only to call for it."

Chapter XXX

The Milburns' door-bell rang very early the morning of the election. The family and Alfred Hesketh were just sitting down to breakfast. Mr. Hesketh was again the guest of the house. He had taken a run out to Vancouver with Mr. Milburn's partner, who had gone to settle a point or two in connection with the establishment of a branch there. The points had been settled, and Hesketh, having learned more than ever, had returned to Elgin.

The maid came back into the room with a conscious air, and said something in a low voice to Dora, who flushed and frowned a little, and asked to be excused. As she left the room a glance of intelligence passed between her and her mother. While Miss Milburn was generally thought to be "most like" her father both in appearance and disposition, there were points upon which she could count on an excellent understanding with her other parent.

"Oh, Lorne," she said, having carefully closed the drawing-room door, "what in the world have you come here for? To-day of all days! Did anybody see you?"

The young man, standing tall and broad-shouldered before the mantelpiece, had yet a look of expecting reproach.

"I don't know," he said humbly.

"I don't think father would like it," Dora told him, "if he knew you were here. Why, we're having an early breakfast on purpose to let him get out and work for Winter. I never saw him so excited over an election. To think of your coming to-day!"

He made a step toward her. "I came because it is to-day," he said. "Only for a minute, dear. It's a great day for me, you know—whether we win or lose. I wanted you to be in it. I wanted you to wish me good luck."

"But you know I always do," she objected.

"Yes, I know. But a fellow likes to hear it, Dora—on the day, you know. And I've seen so little of you lately."

She looked at him measuringly. "You're looking awfully thin," she exclaimed, with sudden compunction. "I wish you had never gone into this horrid campaign. I wish they had nominated some-body else."

Lorne smiled half bitterly. "I shouldn't wonder if a few other people wished the same thing," he said. "But I'm afraid they'll have to make the best of it now."

Dora had not sanctioned his visit by sitting down; and as he came nearer to her she drew a step away, moving by instinct from the capture of the lover. But he had made little of that, and almost as he spoke was at her side. She had to yield her hands to him.

"Well, you'll win it for them if anybody could," she assured him.

"Say 'win it for us,' dear."

She shook her head. "I'm not a Liberal—yet," she said, laughing.

"It's only a question of time."

"I'll never be converted to Grit politics."

"No, but you'll be converted to me," he told her, and drew her nearer. "I'm going now, Dora. I dare say I shouldn't have come. Every minute counts to-day. Good-bye."

She could not withhold her face from his asking lips, and he had bent to take his privilege when a step in the hall threatened and divided them.

"It's only Mr. Hesketh going upstairs," said Dora, with relief. "I thought it was father. Oh, Lorne—fly!"

"Hesketh!" Young Murchison's face clouded. "Is he working for Winter, too?"

"Lorne! What a thing to ask when you know he believes in your ideas. But he's a Conservative at home, you see, so he says he's in an awkward position, and he has been taking perfectly neutral ground lately. He hasn't a vote, anyway."

"No," said Lorne. "He's of no consequence." The familiar easy step in the house of his beloved, the house he was being entreated to leave with all speed, struck upon his heart and his nerves. She, with her dull surface to the more delicate vibrations of things, failed to perceive this, or perhaps she would have thought it worth while to find some word to bring back his peace. She disliked seeing people unhappy. When she was five years old and her kitten broke its leg, she had given it to a servant to drown.

He took his hat, making no further attempt to caress her, and opened the door. "I hope you *will* win, Lorne," she said, half resentfully, and he, with forced cheerfulness, replied, "Oh, we'll have a shot at it." Then with a little silent nod at her, which, notwithstanding her provocations, conveyed his love and trust, he went out into the struggle of the day.

In spite of Squire Ormiston's confident prediction, it was known that the fight would be hottest, among the townships, in Moneida Reservation. Elgin itself, of course, would lead the van for excitement, would be the real theatre for the arts of practical politics; but things would be pretty warm in Moneida, too. It was for that reason that Bingham and the rest strongly advised Lorne not to spend too much of the day in the town, but to get out to Moneida early, and drive around with Ormiston—stick to him like a fly to poison-paper.

"You leave Elgin to your friends," said Bingham. "Just show your face here and there wearing a smile of triumph, to encourage the crowd; but don't worry about the details—we'll attend to them."

"We can't have him upsettin' his own election by any interference with the boys," said Bingham to Horace Williams. "He's got too long a nose for all kinds of things to be comfortable in town to-day. He'll do a great deal less harm trotting round the Reserve braced up against old Ormiston."

So Elgin was left to the capable hands of the boys, for the furtherance of the Liberal interest and the sacred cause of imperialism. Mr. Farquharson, whose experience was longer and whose nose presumably shorter than the candidate's, never abandoned the Town Ward. Bingham skirmished between the polling-booths and the committee-room. Horace Williams was out all day—Rawlins edited the paper. The returns wouldn't be ready in time for anything but an extra anyhow, and the "Stand to Arms, South Fox," leader[1] had been written two days ago. The rest was millinery, or might be for all anybody would read it. The other side had a better idea of the value of their candidate than to send him into the country. Walter Winter remained where he was most effective and most at home. He had a neat little livery outfit, and he seemed to spend the whole day in it accompanied by intimate personal friends who had never spoken to him, much less driven with him, before. Two or three strangers arrived the previous night at the leading hotels. Their business was various, but they had one point in common: they were very solicitous about their personal luggage.[2] I should be sorry to assign their politics, and none of them seemed to know much about the merits of the candidates, so they are not perhaps very pertinent, except for the curiosity shown by the public at the spectacle of gentlemen carrying their own bags when there were porters to do it.

It was a day long remembered and long quoted. The weather was spring-like, sun after a week's thaw; it was pleasant to be abroad in the relaxed air and the drying streets, that here and there sent up threads of steam after the winter house-cleaning of their wooden sidewalks. Voting was a privilege never unappreciated in Elgin; and today the weather brought out every soul to the polls; the ladies of his family waiting, in many instances, on the veran-dah, with shawls over their heads, to hear the report of how the fight was going. Abby saw Dr. Harry back in his consulting-room, and Dr. Henry safely off to vote, and then took the two children and went over to her father's house because she simply could not endure the suspense anywhere else. The adventurous Stella pick-eted herself at a corner near the empty grocery which served as a polling-booth for Subdivision Eleven, one of the most doubtful, but was forced to retire at the sight of the first carryall full of men from the Milburn Boiler Company flaunting a banner inscribed "We are Solid for W.W." Met in the hall by her sister, she pro-tested that she hadn't cried till she got inside the gate, anyhow. Abby lectured her soundly on her want of proper pride: she was much too big a girl to be "seen around" on a day when her brother was "running," if it were only for school trustee. The other ladies of the family, having acquired proper pride, kept in the back of the house so as not to be tempted to look out of the front windows. Mrs. Murchison assumed a stoical demeanour and made a pud-ding; though there was no reason to help Eliza, who was suffi-ciently lacking in proper pride to ask the milkman whether Mr. Lorne wasn't sure to be elected down there now. The milkman said he guessed the best man 'ud get in, but in a manner which roused general suspicion as to which he had himself favoured.

"We'll finish the month," said Mrs. Murchison, "and then not another quart do we take from *him*—a gentleman that's so uncer-tain when he's asked a simple question."

The butcher came, and brought a jovial report without being asked for it; said he was the first man to hand in a paper at his place, but they were piling up there in great shape for Mr. Mur-chison when he left.

"If he gets in, he gets in," said Mrs. Murchison. "And if he doesn't it won't be because of not deserving to. Those were real nice cutlets yesterday, Mr. Price, and you had better send us a sirloin for to-morrow, about six pounds; but it doesn't matter to an ounce. And you can save us sweetbreads for Sunday; I like yours better than Luff's."

John Murchison, Alec, and Oliver came shortly up to dinner, bringing stirring tales from the field. There was the personator in Subdivision Six of a dead man—a dead Grit—wanted by the bloodhounds of the other side and tracked to the Reform committee-room, where he was ostensibly and publicly taking refuge.

"Why did he go there?" asked Stella, breathlessly.

"Why, to make it look like a put-up job of ours, of course," said her brother. "And it was a put-up job, a good old Tory fake. But they didn't calculate on Bingham and Bingham's memory. Bingham happened to be in the committee-room, and he recognized this fellow for a regular political tough from up Muskoka way, where they get six for a bottle of Canadian and ten if it's Scotch. 'Why, good morning,' says Bingham, 'thought you were in jail,' and just then he catches sight of a couple of trailers of Winter's from the window. Well, Bingham isn't just lightning smart, but then he isn't *slow*, you know. 'Well,' he says, 'you can't stop here,' and in another second he was throwing the fellow out. Threw him out pretty hard, too, I guess; right down the stairs, and Bingham on top. Met Winter's men at the door. 'The next time you want information from the headquarters of this association, gentlemen,' Bingham said, 'send somebody respectable.' Bingham thought the man was just any kind of low spy at first, but when they claimed him for personation, Bingham just laughed. 'Don't be so hard on your friends,' he said. I don't think we'll hear much more about that little racket."

"Can't anything be done to any of them?" asked Stella. "Not to-day, of course, but when there's time."

"We'll have to see about it, Stella," said Alec. "When there's time."

"Talking about Bingham," Oliver told them; "you know Bingham's story about Jim Whelan keeping sober for two weeks, for the first time in twenty years, to vote for Winter? Wouldn't touch a thing—no, he was going to do it this time, if he died for it; it was disagreeable to refuse drinks, but it was going to be worth his

while. Been boasting about the post-office janitorship Winter was
to give him if he got in. Well, in he came to Number Eleven this
morning all dressed up, with a clean collar, looking thirstier than
any man you ever saw, and gets his paper. Young Charlie Bingham is deputy-returning officer at Number Eleven. In a second
back comes Whelan. 'This ballot's marked,' he says; 'you don't
fool me.' 'Is it?' says Charlie, taking it out of his hand. 'That's
very wrong, Jim; you shouldn't have marked it,' and drops it into
the ballot-box. Oh, Jim was wild! The paper had gone in blank,
you see, and he'd lost all those good drunks and his vote too! He
was going to have Charlie's blood right away. But there it
was—done. He'd handed in his ballot—he couldn't have another."

They all laughed, I fear, at the unfortunate plight of the too
suspicious Whelan. "Why did he think the ballot was marked?"
asked Advena.

"Oh, there was a little smudge on it—a fly-spot or something,
Charlie says. But you couldn't fool Whelan."

"I hope," said Stella meditatively, "that Lorne will get in by
more than one. He wouldn't like to owe his election to a low-down
trick like that."

"Don't you be at all alarmed, you little girlish thing," replied
her brother. "Lorne will get in by five hundred."

John Murchison had listened to their excited talk, mostly in
silence, going on with his dinner as if that and nothing else were
the important matter of the moment. Mrs. Murchison had had this
idiosyncrasy of his "to put up with" for over thirty years. She bore
it now as long as she could.

"*Father!*" she exploded at last. "Do you think Lorne will get in
by five hundred? Mr. Murchison shook his head, and bestowed his
whole attention upon the paring of an apple. If he kept his hopes
to himself, he also kept his doubts.

"That remains to be seen," he said.

"Well, considering it's your own son, I think you might show
a little more confidence," said Mrs. Murchison. "No thank you; no
dessert for me. With a member of the family being elected—or
not—for a seat in Parliament, I'm not the one to want dessert."

Between Mr. Murchison and the milkman that morning, Mrs.
Murchison felt almost too much tried by the superior capacity for
reticence.

It was seven in the evening before the ballot-boxes were all in

the hands of the sheriff, and nine before that officer found it necessary to let the town know that it had piled up a majority of three
hundred for Walter Winter. He was not a supporter of Walter
Winter, and he preferred to wait until the returns began to come in
from Clayfield and the townships, in the hope that they would make
the serious difference that was required of them. The results were
flashed one after the other to the total from the windows of the
Express and the *Mercury* upon the cheering crowd that gathered in
Market Square. There were moments of wild elation, moments of
deep suspense upon both sides, but when the final addition and
subtraction was made the enthusiastic voters of South Fox, including Jim Whelan, who had neglected no further opportunity, read,
with yells and groans, hurrahs and catcalls, that they had elected Mr.
Lorne Murchison to the Dominion House of Commons by a majority of seventy.

Then the band began to play and all the tin whistles to rejoice.
Young and Windle had the grace to blow their sirens, and across the
excited darkness of the town came the long familiar boom of the
Murchison Stove Works. Every Liberal in Elgin who had any means
of making a noise made it. From the window of the Association
committee-room their young fellow-townsman thanked them for the
honour they had done him, while his mother sat in the cab he had
brought her down in and applauded vigorously between tears, and
his father took congratulations from a hundred friendly hands. They
all went home in a torchlight procession, the band always playing,
the tin whistles always performing; and it was two in the morning
before the occasion could in any sense be said to be over.

Lights burned quite as late, however, in the Conservative committee room, where matters were being arranged to bark threaten-
ingly at the heels of victory next day. Victory looked like something
that might be made to turn and parley. A majority of seventy was
too small for finality. Her attention was called without twenty- four
hours' delay to a paragraph in the Elgin *Mercury*, plainly authoritative, to the effect that the election of Mr. Murchison would be
immediately challenged, on the ground of the infringement in the
electoral district of Moneida of certain provisions of the Ontario
Elections Act with the knowledge and consent of the candidate,
whose claim to the contested seat, it was confidently expected,
would be rendered within a very short time null and void.

Chapter XXXI

"**Y**ou can never trust an Indian,"[1] said Mrs. Murchison at the anxious family council. "Well do I remember them when you were a little thing, Advena, hanging round the town on a market-day; and the squaws coming to the back door with their tin pails of raspberries to sell, and just knowing English enough to ask a big price for them. But it was on the squaws we depended in those days, or go without raspberry preserves for the winter. Slovenly-looking things they were with their three or four coloured petticoats and their papooses on their backs. And for dirt—! But I thought they were all gone long ago."

"There are enough of them left to make trouble all right," said Alec. "They don't dress up like they used to, and I guess they send the papooses to kindergarten now; but you'll find plenty of them lying around any time there's nothing to do but vote and get drunk."

Allowing for the natural exaggeration of partisanship, the facts about the remaining red man of Moneida were much as Alec described them. On market-days he slid easily, unless you looked twice, into what the *Express* continues to call the farming community. Invariably, if you did look twice, you would note that his stiff felt hat was an inch taller in the crown than those worn generally by the farming community, the pathetic assertion, perhaps, of an old sovereignty; invariably, too, his coat and trousers betrayed a form within, which, in the effort at adaptation, had become high-shouldered and lank of leg. And the brown skin was there to be noticed, though you might pass it by, and the high cheek-bones and the liquidly muddy eye. He had taken on the sign of civilization at the level which he occupied; the farming community had lent him its look of shrewdness in small bargains and its rakish sophistication in garments, nor could you always assume with certainty, except at Fox County fairs and elections, that he was intoxicated. So much Government had done for him in Fox County, where the "Reservation," nursing the dying fragment of his race,[2] testified that there is such a thing as political compunction. Out in the wide spaces of the West he still protects his savagery; they know an Indian there to-day as far as they can see him, without a second glance.

And in Moneida, upon polling-days, he still, as Alec said, "made trouble." Perhaps it would be more to the fact to say that he presented the elements of which trouble is made. Civilization had given him a vote, not with his coat and trousers, but shortly after; and he had not yet learned to keep it anywhere but in his pocket, whence the transfer was easy, and could be made in different ways. The law contemplated only one, the straight drop into the ballot-box; but the "boys" had other views. The law represented one level of political sentiment, the boys represented another; both parties represented the law, both parties were represented by the boys; and on the occasion of the South Fox election the boys had been active in Moneida. There are, as we know, two kinds of activity on these occasions, one being set to observe the other; and Walter Winter's boys, while presumably neglecting no legitimate opportunity of their own, claimed to have been highly successful in detecting the methods of the other side.

The Indians owed their holdings, their allowances, their school, and their protecting superintendent, Squire Ormiston, to a Conservative Government. It made a grateful bond of which a later Conservative Government was not, perhaps, unaware, when it added the ballot to its previous benefits. The Indians, therefore, on election-days, were supposed to "go solid" for the candidate in whom they had been taught to see good-will. If they did not go quite solid, the other side might point to the evolution of the political idea in every dissentient—a gladdening spectacle, indeed, on which, however, the other side seldom showed any desire to dwell.

Hitherto the desires and intentions of the "Reserve" had been exemplified in its superintendent. Squire Ormiston had never led his wards to the polls—there were strong reasons against that. But the squire made no secret of his politics, either before or, unluckily, after he changed them. The Indians had always known that they were voting on the same side as "de boss." They were likely, the friends of Mr. Winter thought, to know now that they were voting on a different side. This was the secret of Mr. Winter's friends' unusual diligence on voting-day in Moneida. The mere indication of a wish on the part of the superintendent would constitute undue influence in the eye of the law. The squire was not

the most discreet of men—often before it had been the joke of
Conservative councils how near the old man had come to making
a case for the Grits in connection with this chief or that. I will not
say that he was acquainted with the famous letter from Queen
Victoria, affectionately bidding her Indian children to vote for the
Conservative candidate. But perhaps he had not adhered to the
strictest interpretation of the law which gave him fatherly influence in everything pertaining to his red-skinned charges' interests,
temporal and spiritual, excepting only their sacred privilege of the
ballot. He may even have held it in some genial derision, their
sacred privilege; it would be natural, he had been there among
them in unquestioned authority so long. Now it had assumed an
importance. The squire looked at it with the ardour of a converted
eye. When he told Mr. Farquharson that he could bring Moneida
with him to a Liberal victory, he thought and spoke of the farmers
of the township, not of his wards of the Reserve. Yet as the day
approached these would infallibly become voters in his eyes, to
swell or to diminish the sum of Moneida's loyalty to the Empire.
They remembered all this in the committee-room of his old party.
"The squire," they said to one another, "will give himself away
this time if ever he did." Then young Murchison hadn't known
any better than to spend the best part of the day out there, and
there were a dozen witnesses to swear that old Ormiston introduced him to three or four of the chiefs. That was basis enough for
the boys detailed to watch Moneida, basis enough in the end for a
petition constructed to travel to the High Court at Toronto for the
purpose of rendering null and void the election of Mr. Lorne Murchison, and transferring the South Fox seat to the candidate of the
opposite party.

That possibility had been promptly frustrated by a cross petition. There was enough evidence in Subdivision Eleven, according
to Bingham, to void the Tory returns on six different counts; but
the house-cat sold by Peter Finnigan to Mr. Winter for five dollars
would answer all practical purposes. It was a first-rate mouser,
Bingham said, and it would settle Winter. They would have plenty
of other charges "good and ready" if Finnigan's cat should fail
them, but Bingham didn't think the court would get to anything
else; he had great confidence in the cat.

The petitions had been lodged with promptness. "Evidence,"
as Mr. Winter remarked, "is like a good many other things—better

when it's hot, especially the kind you get on the Reserve." To
which, when he heard it, Bingham observed sarcastically that the
cat would keep. The necessary thousand dollars were ready on
each side the day after the election, lodged in court the next.
Counsel were as promptly engaged—the Liberals selected Cruickshank—and the suit against the elected candidate, beginning with
charges against his agents in the town, was shortly in full hearing
before the judges sent from Toronto to try it. Meanwhile the Elgin
Mercury had shown enterprise in getting hold of Moneida evidence, and foolhardiness, as the *Express* pointed out, in publishing
it before the matter was reached in court. There was no foolhardiness in printing what the *Express* knew about Finnigan's cat; it
was just a common cat, and Walter Winter paid five dollars for it,
Finnigan declaring that if Mr. Winter hadn't filled him up with bad
whisky before the bargain, he wouldn't have let her go under ten,
he was that fond of the creature. The *Express* pointed out that this
was grasping of Finnigan, as the cat had never left him, and Mr.
Winter showed no intention of taking her away; but there was
nothing *sub judice* about the cat. Finnigan, before he sobered up,
had let her completely out of the bag. It was otherwise with the
charges that were to be made, according to the *Mercury,* on the
evidence of Chief Joseph Fry and another member of his tribe, to
the effect that he and his Conservative friends had been instructed
by Squire Ormiston and Mr. Murchison to vote on this occasion
for both the candidates, thereby producing, when the box was
opened, eleven ballot-papers inscribed with two crosses instead of
one, and valueless. Here, should the charges against a distinguished and highly respected Government official fail, as in the
opinion of the *Express* they undoubtedly would fail, of substantiation, was a big libel case all dressed and ready and looking for the
Mercury office. "Foolish—foolish," wrote Mr. Williams at the
close of his editorial comments. "Very ill-advised."

"They've made no case so far," Mr. Murchison assured the
family. "I saw Williams on my way up, and he says the evidence
of that corner grocery fellow—what's his name?—went all to
pieces this morning. Oliver was in court. He says one of the
judges—Hooke—lost his patience altogether."

"They won't do anything with the town charges," Alec said,
"and they know it. They're saving themselves for Moneida and old

man Ormiston."

"Well, I heartily wish," said Mrs. Murchison, in a tone of grievance with the world at large, and if you were not responsible you might keep out of the way—"I heartily wish that Lorne had stayed at home that day and not got mixed up with old man Ormiston."

"They'll find it pretty hard to fix anything on Lorne," said Alec. "But I guess the squire did go off his head a little."

"Have they anything more than Indian evidence?" asked Advena.

"We don't know what they've got," said her brother darkly, "and we won't till Wednesday, when they expect to get round to it."

"Indian evidence will be a poor dependence in Cruickshank's hands," Mr. Murchison told them, with a chuckle. "They say this Chief Joseph Fry is going about complaining that he always got three dollars for one vote before, and this time he expected six for two, and got nothing!"

"Chief Joseph Fry!" exclaimed Alec. "They make me tired with their Chief Josephs and Chief Henrys! White Clam Shell— that wasn't the name he got when he was christened."

"That's the name," remarked Advena, "that he probably votes under."

"Well," said Mrs. Murchison, "it was very kind of Squire Ormiston to give Lorne his support, but it seems to me that as far as Moneida is concerned he would have done better alone."

"No, I guess he wouldn't, mother," said Alec. "Moneida came right round with the squire, outside the Reserve. If it hadn't been for the majority there we would have lost the election. The old man worked hard, and Lorne is grateful to him, and so he ought to be."

"If they carry the case against Lorne," said Stella, "he'll be disqualified for seven years."

"Only if they prove him personally mixed up in it," said the father. "And that," he added, with a concentration of family sentiment in the emphasis of it, "they'll not do."

Chapter XXXII

It was late afternoon when the train from the West deposited Hugh Finlay upon the Elgin platform, the close of one of those wide, wet, uncertain February days when the call of spring is on the wind though spring is weeks away. The lights of the town flashed and glimmered down the streets under the bare swaying maple branches. The early evening was full of soft bluster; the air was conscious with an appeal of nature, vague yet poignant. The young man caught at the strange sympathy that seemed to be abroad for his spirit. He walked to his house, courting it, troubled by it. They were expecting him that evening at Dr. Drummond's, and there it was his intention to go. But on his way he would call for a moment to see Advena Murchison. He had something to tell her. It would be news of interest at Dr. Drummond's also; but it was of no consequence, within an hour or so, when they should receive it there, while it was of great consequence that Advena should hear it at the earliest opportunity, and from him. There is no weighing or analyzing the burden of such a necessity as this. It simply is important: it makes its own weight; and those whom it concerns must put aside other matters until it has been accomplished. He would tell her: they would accept it for a moment together, a moment during which he would also ascertain whether she was well and strong, with a good chance of happiness—God protect her—in the future that he should not know. Then he would go on to Dr. Drummond's.

The wind had risen when he went out again; it blew a longer blast, and the trees made a steady sonorous rhythm in it. The sky was full of clouds that dashed upon the track of a failing moon; there was portent everywhere, and a hint of tumult at the end of the street. No two ways led from Finlay's house to his first destination. River Street made an angle with that on which the Murchisons lived—half a mile to the corner, and three-quarters the other way. Drops drove in his face as he strode along against the wind, stilling his unquiet heart, that leaped before him to that brief interview. As he took the single turning he came into the full blast of the veering, irresolute storm. The street was solitary and full of the sound of the blown trees, wild and uplifting. Far down the

figure of a woman wavered before the wind across the zone of a
blurred lamp-post. She was coming toward him. He bent his head
and lowered his umbrella and lost sight of her as they approached,
she with the storm behind her, driven with hardly more resistance
than the last year's blackened leaves that blew with her, he
assailed by it and making the best way he could. Certainly the
wind was taking her part and his, when in another moment her
skirt whipped against him and he saw her face glimmer out. A
mere wreck of lines and shadows it seemed in the livid light, with
suddenly perceiving eyes and lips that cried his name. She had on
a hat and a cloak, but carried no umbrella, and her hands were bare
and wet. Pitifully the storm blew her into his arms, a tossed and
straying thing that could not speak for sobs; pitifully and with a
rough incoherent sound he gathered and held her in that refuge. A
rising fear and a great solicitude laid a finger upon his craving
embrace of her; he had a sense of something strangely different in
her, of the unknown irremediable. Yet she was there, in his arms,
as she had never been before; her plight but made her in a manner
sweeter; the storm that brought her barricaded them in the empty
spaces of the street with a divinely entreating solitude. He had
been prepared to meet her in the lighted decorum of her father's
house and he knew what he should say. He was not prepared to
take her out of the tempest, helpless and weeping and lost for the
harbour of his heart, and nothing could he say. He locked his lips
against all that came murmuring to them. But his arms tightened
about her and he drew her into the shelter of a wall that jutted out
in the irregular street; and there they stood and clung together in
a long, close, broken silence that covered the downfall of her
spirit. It was the moment of their great experience of one another;
never again, in whatever crisis, could either know so deep, so
wonderful a fathoming of the other soul. Once as it passed,
Advena put up her hand and touched his cheek. There were tears
on it, and she trembled, and wound her arm about his neck, and
held up her face to his. "No," he muttered, and crushed it against
his breast. There without complaint she let it lie; she was all
submission to him: his blood leaped and his spirit groaned with the
knowledge of it.

"Why did you come out? Why did you come, dear?" he said at
last.

"I don't know. There was such a wind. I could not stay in the house."

She spoke timidly, in a voice that should have been new to him, but that it was, above all, her voice.

"I was on my way to you."

"I know. I thought you might perhaps come. If you had not—I think I was on my way to you."

It seemed not unnatural.

"Did you find—any message from me when you came?" she asked presently, in a quieted, almost a contented tone.

It shot—the message—before his eyes, though he had seen it no message in the preoccupation of his arrival.

"I found a rose on my dressing-table," he told her; and the rose stood for him in a wonder of tenderness, looking back.

"I smuggled it in," she confessed, "I knew your old servant—she used to be with us. The others—from Dr. Drummond's— have been there all day making it warm and comfortable for you. I had no right to do anything like that, but I had the right, hadn't I, to bring the rose?"

"I don't know," he answered her, hard pressed, "how we are to bear this."

She shrank away from him a little, as if at a glimpse of a surgeon's knife.

"We are not to bear it," she said eagerly. "The rose is to tell you that. I didn't mean it, when I left it, to be anything more— more than a rose; but now I do. I didn't even know when I came out to-night. But now I do. We aren't to bear it, Hugh.[1] I don't want it so—now. I can't— can't have it so."

She came nearer to him again and caught with her two hands the lapels of his coat. He closed his own over them and looked down at her in that half detachment, which still claimed and held her.

"Advena," he whispered, out of the sudden clamour in his mind, "she can't be—she isn't—nothing has happened to her?"

She smiled faintly, but her eyes were again full of fear at his implication of the only way.

"Oh, no!" she said. "But you have been away, and she has come. I have seen her; and oh! she won't care, Hugh—she won't care."

Her asking, straining face seemed to gather and reflect all the light there was in the shifting night about them. The rain had stopped, but the wind still hurtled past, whirling the leaves from one darkness to another. They were as isolated, as outlawed there in the wild wet wind as they were in the confusion of their own souls.

"We must care," he said helplessly, clinging to the sound and form of the words.

"Oh, no!" she cried. "No, no! Indeed I know now what is possible and what is not!"

For an instant her eyes searched the rigid lines of his face in astonishment. In their struggle to establish the impossible she had been so far ahead, so greatly the more confident and daring, had tempted him to such heights, scorning every dizzy verge, that now, when she turned quite back from their adventure, humbly confessing it too hard, she could not understand how he should continue to set himself doggedly toward it. Perhaps, too, she trusted unconsciously in her prerogative. He loved her, and she him: before she would not, now she would. Before she had preferred an ideal to the desire of her heart; now it lay about her; her strenuous heart had pulled it down to foolish ruin, and how should she lie abased with it and see him still erect and full of the deed they had to do?

"Come," he said, "let me take you home, dear," and at that and some accent in it that struck again at hope, she sank at his feet in a torrent of weeping, clasping them and entreating him, "Oh send her away! Send her away!"

He lifted her, and was obliged literally to support her. Her hat had fallen off; he stroked her hair and murmured such comfort to her as we have for children in their extremity, of which the burden is chiefly love and "Don't cry." She grew gradually quieter, drawing one knows not what restitution from the intrinsic in him; but there was no pride in her, and when she said "Let me go home now," it was the broken word of hapless defeat. They struggled together out into the boisterous street, and once or twice she failed and had to stop and turn. Then she would cling to a wall or a tree, putting his help aside with a gesture in which there was again some pitiful trace of renunciation. They went almost without a word, each treading upon the heart of the other toward the gulf that was to come. They reached it at the Murchisons' gate, and there they paused, as briefly as possible, since pause was torture, and he told her what he could not tell her before.

"I have accepted the charge of the White Water Mission Station in Alberta," he said. "I, too, learned very soon after I left you what was possible and what was not. I go as soon as—things can be set in order here. Good-bye, my dear love, and may God help us both."

She looked at him with a pitiful effort at a steady lip. "I must try to believe it," she said. "And afterward, when it comes true for you, remember this—I was ashamed."

Then he saw her pass into her father's house, and he took the road to his duty and Dr. Drummond's.

His extremity was very great. Through it lines came to him from the beautiful archaic inheritance of his Church. He strode along hearing them again and again in the dying storm.

> "So, I do stretch my hands
> To Thee my help alone
> Thou only understands
> All my complaint and moan."

He listened to the prayer on the wind, which seemed to offer it for him, listened and was gravely touched. But he himself was far from the throes of supplication. He was looking for the forces of his soul; and by the time he reached Dr. Drummond's door we may suppose that he had found them.[2]

Sarah, who let him in, cried, "How wet you are, Mr. Finlay!" and took his overcoat to dry in the kitchen. The Scotch ladies, she told him, and Mrs. Forsyth, had gone out to tea, but they would be back right away, and meanwhile "the Doctor" was expecting him in the study—he knew the way.

Finlay did know the way, but, as a matter of fact, there had been time for him to forget it; he had not crossed Dr. Drummond's threshold since the night on which the Doctor had done all, as he would have said, that was humanly possible to bring him, Finlay, to reason upon the matter of his incredible entanglement in Bross. The door at the end of the passage was ajar, however, as if impatient; and Dr. Drummond himself, standing in it, heightened that appearance, with his "Come you in, Finlay. Come you in!"

The Doctor looked at the young man in a manner even more acute, more shrewd, and more kindly than was his wont. His eye searched Finlay thoroughly, and his smile seemed to broaden as his glance travelled.

"Man," he said, "you're shivering," and rolled him an armchair near the fire. ("The fellow came into the room," he would say, when he told the story afterward to the person most concerned, "as if he were going to the stake!") "This is extraordinary weather we are having, but I think the storm is passing over."

"I hope," said Finlay, "that my aunt and Miss Cameron are well. I understand they are out."

"Oh, very well—finely. They're out at present, but you'll see them bye-and-bye. An excellent voyage over they had—just the eight days. But we'll be doing it in less than that when the new fast line is running to Halifax. But four days of actual ocean travelling they say now it will take. Four days from imperial shore to shore! That should incorporate us—that should bring them out and take us home."

The Doctor had not taken a seat himself, but was pacing the study, his thumbs in his waistcoat pockets; and a touch of embarrassment seemed added to the inveterate habit.

"I hear the ladies had pleasant weather," Finlay remarked.

"Capital—capital! You won't smoke? I know nothing about these cigars; they're some Grant left behind him—a chimney, that man Grant. Well, Finlay"—he threw himself into the armchair on the other side of the hearth—"I don't know what to say to you."

"Surely," said Finlay restively, "it has all been said, sir."

"No, it has not all been said," Dr. Drummond retorted. "No, it has not. There's more to be said, and you must hear it, Finlay, with such patience as you have. But I speak the truth when I say that I don't know how to begin."

The young man gave him opportunity, gazing silently into the fire. He was hardly aware that Dr. Drummond had again left his seat when he started violently at a clap on the shoulder.

"Finlay!" exclaimed the Doctor. "You won't be offended? No—you couldn't be offended!"

It was half jocular, half anxious, wholly inexplicable.

"At what," asked Hugh Finlay, "should I be offended?"

Again, with a deep sigh, the Doctor dropped into his chair. "I see I must begin at the beginning," he said. But Finlay, with sudden intuition, had risen and stood before him trembling, with a hand against the mantelpiece.

"No," he said, "if you have anything to tell me of importance, for God's sake begin at the end."

Some vibration in his voice went straight to the heart of the Doctor, banishing as it travelled, every irrelevant thing that it encountered.

"Then the end is this, Finlay," he said. "The young woman, Miss Christie Cameron, whom you were so wilfully bound and determined to marry, has thrown you over—that is, if you will give her back her word—has jilted you—that is, if you'll let her away. Has thought entirely better of the matter."

("He stared out of his great sockets of eyes as if the sky had fallen," Dr. Drummond would say, recounting it.)

"For—for what reason?" asked Finlay, hardly yet able to distinguish between the sound of disaster and the sense that lay beneath.

"May I begin at the beginning?" asked the Doctor, and Hugh silently nodded.

("He sat there and never took his eyes off me, twisting his fingers. I might have been in a confession-box," Dr. Drummond would explain to her.)

"She came here, Miss Cameron, with that good woman, Mrs. Kilbannon, it will be three weeks next Monday," he said, with all the air of beginning a story that would be well worth hearing. "And I wasn't very well pleased to see her, for reasons that you know. However, that's neither here nor there. I met them both at the station, and I own to you that I thought when I made Miss Cameron's acquaintance that you were getting better than you deserved in the circumstances. You were a thousand miles away—now that was a fortunate thing!—and she and Mrs. Kilbannon just stayed here and made themselves as comfortable as they could. And that was so comfortable that any one could see with half an eye—" the Doctor's own eye twinkled—"so far as Miss Cameron was concerned, that she wasn't pining in any sense of the word. But I wasn't sorry for you, Finlay, on that account." He stopped to laugh enjoyingly, and Finlay blushed like a girl.

"I just let matters bide and went about my own business. Though after poor Mrs. Forsyth here—a good woman enough, but the brains of a rabbit—it was pleasant to find these intelligent ladies at every meal, and wonderful how quick they were at picking up the differences between points of Church administration here and at home. That was a thing I noticed particularly in Miss Cameron.

"Matters went smoothly enough—smoothly enough—till one afternoon that foolish creature Advena Murchison"[3]—Finlay started—"came here to pay a call on Miss Cameron and Mrs. Kilbannon. It was well and kindly meant, but it was not a wiselike thing to do. I didn't exactly make it out, but it seems that she came all because of you and on account of you; and the ladies didn't understand it, and Mrs. Kilbannon came to me. My word, but there was a woman to deal with! Who was this young lady, and what was she to you that she should go anywhere or do anything in your name? Without doubt"—he put up a staying hand—"it was foolish of Advena. And what sort of freedom, and how far, and why, and what way, and I tell you it was no easy matter, to quiet her. 'Is Miss Cameron distressed about it?' said I. 'Not a bit,' said she, 'but I am, and I must have the rights of this matter,' said she, 'if I have to put it to my nephew himself.'

"It was at that point, Finlay, that the idea—just then that the thought came into my mind—well I won't say absolutely, but practically for the first time—'Why can't this matter be arranged on a basis to suit all parties?' So I said to her, 'Mrs. Kilbannon,' I said, 'if you had reasonable grounds for it, do you think you could persuade your niece not to marry Hugh Finlay?' Wait—patience!" He held up his hand, and Finlay gripped the arm of his chair again.

"She just stared at me. 'Are you gone clean daft, Dr. Drummond?' she said. 'There could be no grounds serious enough for that. I will not believe that Hugh Finlay has compromised himself in any way.' I had to stop her; I was obliged to tell her there was nothing of the kind—nothing of the kind; and later on I'll have to settle with my conscience about that. 'I meant,' I said, 'the reasonable grounds of an alternative.' 'An alternative?' said she. To cut a long story short," continued the Doctor, leaning forward, always with the finger in his waistcoat pocket to emphasize what he said, "I represented to Mrs. Kilbannon that Miss Cameron was not in sentimental relations toward you, that she had some reason to suspect you of having placed your affections elsewhere, and that I myself was very much taken up with what I had seen of Miss Cameron. In brief, I said to Mrs. Kilbannon that if Miss Cameron saw no objection to altering the arrangements to admit of it, I should be pleased to marry her myself. The thing was much more suitable in every way. I was fifty-three years of age last week, I told her, 'but,' I said, 'Miss Cameron is thirty-six or seven, if she's a day, and Finlay there would be like nothing but a grown-up son to her. I can offer her a good home and the minister's pew in a church that any woman might be proud of—and though far be it from me,' I said, 'to depreciate mission work, either home or foreign, Miss Cameron in that field would be little less than thrown away. Think it over,' I said.

"Well, she was pleased, I could see that. But she didn't half like the idea of changing the original notion. It was leaving you to your own devices that weighed most with her against it; she'd set her heart on seeing you married with her approval. So I said to her, to make an end of it, 'Well, Mrs. Kilbannon,' I said, 'suppose we say no more about it for the present. I think I see the finger of Providence in this matter; but you'll talk it over with Miss Cameron, and we'll all just make it, for the next few days, the subject of quiet and sober reflection. Maybe at the end of that time I'll think better of it myself, though that is not my expectation.'

" 'I think,' she said, 'we'll just leave it to Christie.' "

As the Doctor went on with his tale, relaxation had stolen dumbly about Finlay's brow and lips. He dropped from the plane of his own absorption to the humorous common sense of the recital: it claimed and held him with infinite solace. His eyes had something like the light of laughter in them, flashing behind a cloud, as he fixed them on Dr. Drummond, and said, "And did you?"

"We did," said Dr. Drummond, getting up once more from his chair, and playing complacently with his watch-charms as he took another turn about the study. "We left it to Miss Cameron, and the result is"—the Doctor stopped sharply and wheeled round upon Finlay—"the result is—why, the upshot seems to be that I've cut you out, man!"

Finlay measured the little Doctor standing there twisting his watch-chain, beaming with achieved satisfaction, in a consuming desire to know how far chance had been kind to him, and how far he had to be simply, unspeakably grateful. He stared in silence, occupied with his great debt; it was like him that that, and not his liberty, should be first in his mind. We who have not his opportunity may find it more difficult to decide; but from our private knowledge of Dr. Drummond we may remember what poor Finlay probably forgot at the moment, that even when pitted against Providence, the Doctor was a man of great determination. The young fellow got up, still speechless, and confronted Dr. Drummond. He was troubled for something to say; the chambers of his brain seemed empty or reiterating foolish sounds. He pressed the hand the minister offered him and his lips quivered. Then a light came into his face, and he picked up his hat.

"And I'll say this for myself," chuckled Dr. Drummond. "It was no hard matter."

Finlay looked at him and smiled. "It would not be, sir," he said lamely. Dr. Drummond cast a shrewd glance at him and dropped the tone of banter.

"Aye—I know! It's no joking matter," he said, and with a hand behind the young man's elbow, he half pushed him to the door and took out his watch. He must always be starting somebody, something, in the right direction, the Doctor. "It's not much after half-past nine, Finlay," he said. "I notice the stars are out."

It had the feeling of a colloquial benediction, and Finlay carried it with him all the way.

It was nevertheless nearly ten when he reached her father's house, so late that the family had dispersed for the night. Yet he had the hardihood to ring, and the hour blessed them both, for Advena on the stair, catching who knows what of presage out of the sound, turned, and found him at the threshold herself.

Chapter XXXIII

"I understand how you must feel in the matter, Murchison," said Henry Cruickshank. "It's the most natural thing in the world that you should want to clear yourself definitely, especially, as you say, since the charges have been given such wide publicity. On the other hand, I think it quite possible that you exaggerate the inference that will be drawn from our consenting to saw off with the other side on the two principal counts."

"The inference will be," said Lorne, "that there's not a pin to choose between Winter's political honesty and my own. I'm no Pharisee, but I don't think I can sit down under that. I can't impair my possible usefulness by accepting a slur upon my reputation at the very beginning."

"Politics are very impersonal. It wouldn't be remembered a year."

"Winter, of course," said young Murchison moodily, "doesn't want to take any chances. He knows he's done for if we go on. Seven years for him would put him pretty well out of politics. And it would suit him down to the ground to fight it over again. There's nothing he would like better to see than another writ for South Fox."

"That's all right," the lawyer responded, "but Moneida doesn't look altogether pleasant, you know. We may have good grounds for supposing that the court will find you clear of that business; but Ormiston, so far as I can make out, was playing the fool down there for a week before polling-day, and there are three or four Yellow Dogs and Red Feathers only too anxious to pay back a grudge on him. We'll have to fight again, there's no doubt about that. The only question is whether we'll ruin Ormiston first or not. Have you seen Bingham?"

"I know what Bingham thinks," said Lorne, impatiently. "The squire's position is a different consideration. I don't see how I can—However, I'll go across to the committee-room now and talk it over."

It is doubtful whether young Murchison knew all that Bingham thought; Bingham so seldom told it all. There were matters in the back of Bingham's mind that prompted him to urge the course that

Cruickshank had been empowered by the opposing counsel to suggest—party considerations that it would serve no useful purpose
to talk over with Murchison. Bingham put it darkly when he said
he had quite as much hay on his fork as he cared to tackle already,
implying that the defence of indiscretions in Moneida was quite an
unnecessary addition. Contingencies seemed probable, arising out
of the Moneida charges, that might affect the central organization
of the party in South Fox to an extent wholly out of proportion
with the mere necessity of a second election. Bingham talked it
over with Horace Williams, and both of them with Farquharson;
they were all there to urge the desirability of sawing off upon
Lorne when he found them at headquarters. Their most potent
argument was, of course, the squire and the immediate dismissal
that awaited him under the law if undue influence were proved
against him. Other considerations found the newly elected member
for South Fox obstinate and troublesome, but to that he was bound
to listen, and before that he finally withdrew his objections. The
election would come on again, as happened commonly enough.
Bingham could point to the opening, in a few days, of a big flour
milling industry across the river, which would help; operations on
the Drill Hall and the Post Office would be hurried on at once, and
the local party organization would be thoroughly overhauled.
Bingham had good reason for believing that they could entirely
regain their lost ground, and at the same time dissipate the dangerous impression that South Fox was being undermined. Their
candidate gave a reluctant ear to it all, and in the end agreed to
everything.

So that Chief Joseph Fry—the White Clam Shell of his own
lost fires—was never allowed the chance of making good the election losses of that year, as he had confidently expected to do when
the charge came on; nor was it given to any of the Yellow Dogs
and Red Feathers of Mr. Cruickshank's citation to boast at the
tribal dog-feasts of the future, of the occasion on which they had
bested "de boss." Neither was any further part in public affairs,
except by way of jocular reference, assigned to Finnigan's cat. The
proceedings of the court abruptly terminated, the judges reported
the desirability of a second contest, and the public accepted with
a wink. The wink in any form was hateful to Lorne Murchison, but
he had not to encounter it long.

The young man had changed in none of the aspects he presented to his fellow citizens since the beginning of the campaign. In the public eye he wore the same virtues as he wore the same clothes; he summed up even a greater measure of success; his popularity was unimpaired. He went as keenly about the business of life, handling its details with the same capable old drawl. Only his mother, with the divination of mothers, declared that since the night of the opera-house meeting Lorne had been all worked up. She watched him with furtive anxious looks, was solicitous about his food, expressed relief when she knew him to be safely in bed and asleep. He himself observed himself with discontent, unable to fathom his extraordinary lapse from self-control on the night of his final address. He charged it to the strain of unavoidable office work on top of the business of the campaign, abused his nerves, talked of a few days' rest when they had settled Winter. He could think of nothing but the points he had forgotten when he had his great chance. "The flag should have come in at the end," he would say to himself, trying vainly to remember where it did come in. He was ill-pleased with the issue of that occasion; and it was small compensation to be told by Stella that his speech gave her shivers up and down her back.

Meanwhile the theory of Empire coursed in his blood, fed by the revelation of the future of his country in every newspaper, by the calculated prophecies of American onlookers, and by the telegrams which repeated the trumpet notes of Wallingham's war upon the mandarinate of Great Britain. It occupied him so that he began to measure and limit what he had to say about it, and to probe the casual eye for sympathy before he would give an inch of rope to his enthusiasm. He found it as hard as ever to understand that the public interest should be otherwise preoccupied, as it plainly was, that the party organ, terrified of Quebec, should shuffle away from the subject with perfunctory and non-committal reference, that among the men he met in the street, nobody's blood seemed stirred, whatever the day's news was from England. He subscribed to the Toronto *Post*, the leading organ of the Tories,[1] because of its fuller reports and more sympathetic treatment of the Idea, due to the fact that the Idea originated in a brain temporarily affiliated to the Conservative party. If the departure to imperial preference had any damage in it for Canadian interests, it would be for those which the *Post* made its special care; but the spirit of party draws the breath of expediency, and the *Post* flaunting the Union Jack every other day, put secondary manufactures aside for future discussion, and tickled the wheat-growers with the two-shilling advantage they were coming into at the hands of the English Conservatives, until Liberal leaders began to be a little anxious about a possible loss of wheat-growing votes. It was, as John Murchison said, a queer position for everybody concerned; queer enough, no doubt, to admit a Tory journal into the house on sufferance and as a special matter; but he had a disapproving look for it as it lay on the hall floor, and seldom was the first to open it.

Nevertheless Lorne found more satisfaction in talking imperialism with his father than with any one else. While the practical half of John Murchison was characteristically alive to the difficulties involved, the sentimental half of him was ready at any time to give out cautious sparks of sympathy with the splendour of Wallingham's scheme; and he liked the feeling that a son of his should hark back in his allegiance to the old land. There was a kind of chivalry in the placing of certain forms of beauty—political honour and public devotion, which blossomed best, it seemed, over there—above the material ease and margin of the new country, and even above the grand chance it offered for a man to make his mark. Mr. Murchison was susceptible to this in any one, and responsive to it in his son.

As to the local party leaders, they had little more than a shrug for the subject. So far as they were concerned, there was no Empire and no Idea; Wallingham might as well not have been born. It seemed to Lorne that they maintained toward him personally a special reticence about it. Reticence indeed characterized their behaviour generally during the period between the abandonment of the suits and the arrangement of the second Liberal convention. They had little advice for him about his political attitude, little advice about anything. He noticed that his presence on one or two occasions seemed to embarrass them, and that his arrival would sometimes have a disintegrating effect upon a group in the post-office or at a street corner. He added it, without thinking, to his general heaviness; they held it a good deal against him, he supposed, to have reduced their proud standing majority to a beggarly two figures; he didn't blame them.

I cannot think that the sum of these depressions alone would have been enough to overshadow so buoyant a soul as Lorne

Murchison's. The characteristics of him I have tried to convey were grafted on an excellent fund of common sense. He was well aware of the proportions of things; he had no despair of the Idea, nor would he despair should the Idea etherealize and fly away. Neither had he, for his personal honour, any morbid desires toward White Clam Shell or Finnigan's cat. His luck had been a good deal better than it might have been; he recognized that as fully as any sensible young man could, and as for the Great Chance, and the queer grip it had on him, he would have argued that too if any one had approached him curiously about it. There I think we might doubt his conclusions. There is nothing subtler, more elusive to trace than the intercurrents of the emotions. Politics and love are thought of at opposite poles, and Wallingham perhaps would have laughed to know that he owed an exalted allegiance in part to a half-broken heart. Yet the impulse that is beyond our calculation, the thing we know potential in the blood but not to be summoned or conditioned, lies always in the shadow of the ideal; and who can analyze that, and say, "Of this class is the will to believe in the integrity of the beloved and false; of that is the desire to lift a nation to the level of its mountain-ranges?" Both dispositions have a tendency to overwork the heart; and it is easy to imagine that they might interact. Lorne Murchison's wish, which was indeed a burning longing and necessity, to believe in the Dora Milburn of his passion, had been under a strain since the night on which he brought her the pledge which she refused to wear. He had hardly been conscious of it in the beginning, but by constant suggestion it had grown into his knowledge, and for weeks he had taken poignant account of it. His election had brought him no nearer a settlement with her objection to letting the world know of their relations. The immediate announcement that it was to be disputed gave Dora another chance, and once again postponed the assurance that he longed for with a fever which was his own condemnation of her, if he could have read that sign. For months he had seen so little of her, had so altered his constant habit of going to the Milburns', that his family talked of it, wondering among themselves; and Stella indulged in hopeful speculations. They did not wonder or speculate at the Milburns'. It was an axiom there that it is well to do nothing rashly.

Lorne, in the office on Market Street, had been replying to Mr.

Fulke to the effect that the convention could hardly be much longer postponed, but that as yet he had no word of the date of it, when
the telephone bell rang and Mr. Farquharson's voice at the other
end asked him to come over to the committee-room. "They've
decided about it now, I imagine," he told his senior, putting on his
hat; and something of the wonted fighting elation came upon him
as he went down the stairs. He was right in his supposition. They
had decided about it, and they were waiting, in a group that made
every effort to look casual, to tell him when he arrived.

They had delegated what Horace Williams called "the job" to
Mr. Farquharson, and he was actually struggling with the preliminaries of it, when Bingham, uncomfortable under the curious
quietude of the young fellow's attention, burst out with the whole
thing.

"The fact is, Murchison, you can't poll the vote. There's no
man in the Riding we'd be better pleased to send to the House; but
we've got to win this election, and we can't win it with you."

"You think you can't?" said Lorne.

"You see, old man," Horace Williams put in, "you didn't get
rid of that save-the-Empire-or-die scheme of yours soon enough.
People got to think you meant something by it."

"I shall never get rid of it," Lorne returned simply, and the
others looked at one another.

"The popular idea seems to be," said Mr. Farquharson judicially, "that you would not hesitate to put Canada to some material
loss, or at least to postpone her development in various important
directions, for the sake of the imperial connection."

"Wasn't that," Lorne asked him, "what, six months ago, you
were all prepared to do?"

"Oh, no," said Bingham, with the air of repudiating for everybody concerned. "Not for a cent. We were willing at one time to
work it for what it was worth, but it never was worth that, and if
you'd had a little more experience, Murchison, you'd have
realized it."

"That's right, Lorne," contributed Horace Williams. "Experience—that's all you want. You've got everything else, and a
darned sight more. We'll get you there, all in good time. But this
time—"

"You want me to step down and out," said Lorne.

"That's for you to say," Bingham told him. "We can nominate

you again all right, but we're afraid we can't get you the convention. Young and Windle have been working like moles for the past ten days—"

"For Carter?" interrupted Lorne. "Carter, of course."

They nodded. Carter stood the admitted fact.

"I'm sorry it's Carter," said Lorne thoughtfully. "However—" And he dropped, staring before him, into silence. The others eyed him from serious, underhung faces. Horace Williams, with an obvious effort, got up and clapped him on the shoulder.

"Brace up, old chap," he said. "You made a blame good fight for us, and we'll do the same for you another day."

"However, gentlemen," the young man gathered himself up to say, "I believe I understand the situation. You are my friends and this is your advice. We must save the seat. I'll see Carter. If I can get anything out of him to make me think he'll go straight on the scheme to save the Empire"—he smiled faintly—"when it comes to a vote, I'll withdraw in his favour at the convention. Horace here will think up something for me—any old lie will do, I suppose? In any case, of course, I withdraw."

He took his hat, and they all got up, startled a little at the quick and simple close of the difficult scene they had anticipated. Horace Williams offered his hand.

"Shake, Lorne," he said, and the other two, coming nearer, followed his example.

"Why, yes," said Lorne.

He left them with a brief excuse, and they stood together in a moment's silence, three practical politicians who had delivered themselves from a dangerous network involving higher things.

"Dash these heart-to-heart talks," said Bingham irritably, "it's the only thing to do, but why the devil didn't he want something out of it? I had that Registrarship in my inside pocket."

"If anybody likes to kick me round the room," remarked Horace Williams with depression, "I have no very strong objection."

"And now," Mr. Farquharson said with a sigh, "we understand it's got to be Carter. I suppose I'm too old a man to do jockey for a three-year-old, but I own I've enjoyed the ride."

Lorne Murchison went out into the companionship of Main Street, the new check in his fortunes hanging before him. We may imagine that it hung heavily; we may suppose that it cut off the view. As Bingham would have said, he was up against it, and that, when one is confidently treading the straight path to accomplishment, is a dazing experience. He was up against it, yet already he had recoiled far enough to consider it; already he was adapting his heart, his nerves, and his future to it. His heart took it greatly, told him he had not yet force enough for the business he had aspired to, but gave him a secret assurance. Another time he would find more strength and show more cunning; he would not disdain the tools of diplomacy and desirability, he would dream no more of short cuts in great political departures. His heart bowed to its sorry education and took counsel with him, bidding him be of good courage and push on. He was up against it, but he would get round it, and there on the other side lay the same wide prospect, with the Idea shining high. At one point he faltered, but that was a matter of expediency rather than of courage. He searched and selected, as he went along the street, among phrases that would convey his disaster to Dora Milburn.

Just at that point, the turning to his own office, he felt it hard luck that Alfred Hesketh should meet and want a word with him. Hesketh had become tolerable only when other things were equal. Lorne had not seen him since the night of his election, when his felicitations had seemed to stand for very little one way or another. His manner now was more important, charged with other considerations. Lorne waited on the word, uncomfortably putting off the necessity of coming out with his misfortune.

"I haven't come across you, Murchison, but you've had my sympathy, I needn't say, all this time. A man can't go into politics with gloves on, there's no doubt about that. Though, mind you, I never for a moment believed that you let yourself in personally. I mean, I've held you all through, above the faintest suspicion."

"Have you?" said Lorne. "Well, I suppose I ought to be grateful."

"Oh, I have—I assure you! But give me a disputed election for the revelation of a rotten state of things—eh?"

"It does show up pretty low, doesn't it?"

"However, upon my word, I don't know whether it's any better in England. At bottom we've got a lower class to deal with, you know. I'm beginning to have a great respect for the electorate of this country, Murchison—not necessarily the methods, but the rank and file of the people. They know what they want, and they're going to have it."

"Yes," said Lorne, "I guess they are."

"And that brings me to my news, old man. I've given the matter a lot of time and a lot of consideration, and I've decided that I can't do better than drive in a stake for myself in this new country of yours."

"It isn't so very new," Lorne told him, in rather dull response, "but I expect that's a pretty good line to take. Why, yes—first rate."

"As to the line," Hesketh went on, weightily, leading the way through an encumbering group of farmers at a corner, "I've selected that, too. Traction-engines. Milburn has never built them yet, but he says the opportunity is ripe—"

"Milburn!" Lorne wheeled sharply.

"My future partner. He was planning extensions just as I came along, a fortunate moment, I hope it will prove, for us both. I'd like to go into it with you, some time when you have leisure—it's a scheme of extraordinary promise. By the way, there's an idea in it that ought to appeal to you—driving the force that's to subdue this wilderness of yours."

"When you've lived here for a while," said Lorne, painfully preoccupied, "you'll think it quite civilized. So you're going in with Milburn?"

"Oh, I'm proud of it already! I shall make a good Canadian, I trust. And as good an imperialist," he added, "as is consistent with the claims of my adopted country."

"That seems to be the popular view," said Lorne.

"And a very reasonable view, too. But I'm not going to embark on that with you, old fellow—you shan't draw me in. I know where you are on that subject."

"So do I—I'm stranded. But it's all right—the subject isn't," Lorne said quietly; and Hesketh's exclamations and inquiries brought out the morning's reverse. The young Englishman was cordially sorry, full of concern and personal disappointment, abandoning his own absorbing affairs, and devoting his whole attention to the unfortunate exigency which Lorne dragged out of his breast, in pure manfulness, to lay before him.

However, they came to the end of it, arriving at the same time at the door which led up the stairs to the office of Fulke, Warner, and Murchison.

"Thank you," said Lorne. "Thank you. Oh, I dare say it will come all right in the course of time. You return to England, I suppose—or do you?—before you go in with Milburn?"

"I sail next week," said Hesketh, and a great relief shot into the face of his companion. "I have a good deal to see to over there. I shan't get back much before June, I fancy. And—I must tell you—I am doing the thing very thoroughly. This business of naturalizing myself, I mean. I am going to marry that very charming girl—a great friend of yours, by the way, I know her to be—Miss Milburn."

For accepting the strokes of fate we have curiously trivial demonstrations. Lorne met Hesketh's eye with the steadiness of a lion's in his own; the unusual thing he did was to take his hands out of his pockets and let his arms hang loosely by his side. It was as tragic a gesture of helplessness as if he had flung them above his head.

"Dora is going to marry you?"

"I believe she will do me that honour. And I consider it an honour. Miss Milburn will compare with any English girl I ever met. But I half expected you to congratulate me. I know she wrote to you this morning—you were one of the first."

"I shall probably find the letter," said Lorne mechanically, "when I go home."

He still eyed Hesketh narrowly, as if he had somewhere concealed about him the explanation of this final bitter circumstance. He had a desire not to leave him, to stand and parley—to go upstairs to the office would be to plunge into the gulf. He held back from that and leaned against the door frame, crossing his arms and looking over into the marketplace for subjects to postpone Hesketh's departure. They talked of various matters in sight, Hesketh showing the zest of his newly-determined citizenship in every observation—the extension of the electric tramway, the pulling down of the old Fire Hall. In one consciousness Lorne made concise and relevant remarks; in another he sat in a spinning dark world and waited for the crash.

It seemed to come when Hesketh said, preparing to go, "I'll tell Miss Milburn I saw you. I suppose this change in your political prospects won't affect your professional plans in any way—you'll stick on here, at the Bar?"

It was the very shock of calamity, and for the instant he could see nothing in the night of it but one far avenue of escape, a possibility he had never thought of seriously until that moment. The conception seemed to form itself on his lips, to be involuntary.

"I don't know. A college friend has been pressing me for some time to join him in Milwaukee. He offers me plenty of work, and I am thinking seriously of closing with him."

"Go over to the United States? You can't mean that!"

"Oh yes—it's the next best thing!"

Hesketh's face assumed a gravity, a look of feeling and of remonstrance. He came a step nearer and put a hand on his companion's arm.

"Come now, Murchison," he said, "I ask you—is this a time to be thinking of chucking the Empire?"

Lorne moved further into the passage with an abruptness which left his interlocutor staring. He stood there for a moment in silence, and then turned to mount the stair with a reply which a passing dray happily prevented from reaching Hesketh's ears.

"No, damn you," he said. "It's not!"

I cannot let him finish on that uncontrolled phrase, though it will be acknowledged that his provocation was great. Nor must we leave him in heavy captivity to the thought of oblivion in the unregarding welter of the near republic, of plunging into more strenuous activities and abandoning his ideal, in queer inverted analogy to the refuging of weak women in a convent. We know that his ideal was strong enough to reassert itself, under a keen irony of suggestion, in the very depth of his overwhelming: and the thing that could rise in him at that black moment may be trusted, perhaps, to reclaim his fortitude and reconsecrate his energy when these things come again into the full current of his life. The illness that, after two or three lagging days, brought him its merciful physical distraction was laid in the general understanding at the door of his political disappointment; and, among a crowd of sympathizers confined to no party, Horace Williams, as his wife expressed it, was pretty nearly wild during its progress. The power of the press is regrettably small in such emergencies, but what restoration it had Horace anxiously administered; the

Express published a daily bulletin. The second election passed only half noticed by the Murchison family; Carter very nearly re-established the Liberal majority. The *Dominion* dwelt upon this repeated demonstration of the strength of Reform principles in South Fox, and Mrs. Murchison said they were welcome to Carter. Many will sympathize with Mrs. Murchison at this point, I hope, and regret to abandon her in such equivocal approval of the circumstances which have arisen round her. Too anxiously occupied at home to take her share in the general pleasant sensation of Dr. Drummond's marriage, she was compelled to give it a hurried consideration and a sanction which was practically wrested from her. She could not be clear as to the course of events that led to it, nor entirely satisfied, as she said, about the ins and outs of that affair; this although she felt she could be clearer, and possibly had better grounds for being satisfied, than other people. As to Advena's simple statement that Miss Cameron had made a second choice of the Doctor, changing her mind, as far as Mrs. Murchison could see, without rhyme or reason, that Mrs. Murchison took leave to find a very poor explanation. Advena's own behaviour toward the rejection is one of the things which her mother declares, probably truly, that she never will understand. To pick up a man in the actual fling of being thrown over, will never, in Mrs. Murchison's eyes, constitute a decorous proceeding. I suppose she thinks the creature might have been made to wait at least until he had found his feet. She professes to cherish no antagonism to her future son-in-law on this account, although, as she says, it's a queer way to come into a family; and she makes no secret of her belief that Miss Cameron showed excellent judgment in doing as she did, however that far-seeing woman came to have the opportunity.

Hesketh had sailed before Lorne left his room, to return in June to those privileges and prospects of citizenship which he so eminently deserves to enjoy. When her brother's convalescence and departure for Florida had untied her tongue, Stella widely proclaimed her opinion that Mr. Hesketh's engagement to Miss Milburn was the most suitable thing that could be imagined or desired. We know the youngest Miss Murchison to be inclined to impulsive views; but it would be safe, I think, to follow her here. Now that the question no longer circles in the actual vortex of Elgin politics Mr. Octavius Milburn's attitude toward the conditions of imperial connection has become almost as mellow as ever. Circumstances may arise any day, however, to stir up that latent bitterness which is so potential in him: and then I fear there will be no restraining him from again attacking Wallingham in the papers.

Henry Cruickshank, growing old in his eminence and less secure, perhaps, in the increasing conflict of loud voices, of his own grasp of the ultimate best, fearing too, no doubt, the approach of that cynicism which, moral or immoral, is the real hoar of age, wrote to young Murchison while he was still examining the problems of the United States with the half heart of the alien, and offered him a partnership. The terms were so simple and advantageous as only to be explicable on the grounds I have mentioned, though no phrase suggested them in the brief formulas of the letter, in which one is tempted to find the individual parallel of certain propositions of a great government also growing old. The offer was accepted, not without emotion, and there, too, it would be good to trace the parallel, were we permitted; but for that it is too soon, or perhaps it is too late. Here, for Lorne and for his country, we lose the thread of destiny. The shuttles fly, weaving the will of the nations, with a skein for ever dipped again; and he goes forth to his share in the task among those by whose hand and direction the pattern and the colours will be made.

Textual Appendix

The following list records all the substantive variants between the first version of Duncan's text, as a serialization in *The Queen*, and the final version, the English edition. Page and line numbers refer to the present text. The wording of the English edition, which is the basis of the present text, is given first. In the infrequent cases in which the serialization contains a passage dropped from the English edition, the last word the two versions have in common is given first, along with the page and line numbers of the present text, for ease of reference. In all but the most minor instances, the relationship of the intermediate American edition (A) to the serialization (Q) and the English edition (E) is indicated. This appendix may therefore be used as a means of observing in the greatest detail the evolution of Duncan's text in an important paragraph, scene or chapter. Long passages in the English edition are represented by the first and last words separated by ellipses in order to conserve.

1. 17	**rarer** less common
2. 16	**so intelligent a meliorist** so true a democrat *A as in E.*
2. 17	**heart for the work** just and indignant soul *A as in E.*
2. 20	**this chapter about Elgin;** this brief chapter;
2. 23	**Nobody in Elgin can possibly have forgotten it.** *Not in Q.*
3. 7	**such persons** they
3. 18	**half the farmers** the whole rural population
3. 25	**public appetite** public stomach
3. 33	**five-cent quantities** five-cent ones
3. 34	**and for very small boys one dish and the requisite number of spoons** *Not in Q; A as in E.*
4. 17	**at the first street corner** at any street corner
4. 24	**the Milburn Boiler Company** Milburn's engine-works
4. 30	**easily appreciated** easy of exact appreciation
4. 38	**hold up** point to
4. 39	**There was recently to be pointed out in England** I once met, casually, *A as in E.*
5. 4	**at present little more than** have only
5. 8	**vinegar** vinegar, composed and conspicuous,
5. 16	**like the young Flannigans and Finnigans,** *Not in Q; A as in E.*
5. 18	**quarter.** quarter, and were reluctantly compelled to admit that there was no necessity for their attendance; *A as in E.*
5. 22	**running shoes** moccasins

5. 23   **The Birthday** The day
5. 30   **Everybody was subject .... in the kitchen.** *Not in Q; A as in E.*
6. 20   **pan** dish pan
6. 22   **I call it downright deceit!** The deceit of her!
6. 29   **spare room,** dining-room,
6. 30   **Dear me!" .... that performance!** *Not in Q; A as in E.*
6. 34   **their mother,** Mrs. Murchison,
6. 38   **an old colonial economy she hated to resign —** *Not in Q.*
7. 13   **Mrs. Murchison** Mrs. Murchison I have always understood
7. 20   **the whole of Knox Church** Mrs. Murchison *A as in E.*
7. 25   **willingly acknowledged** truly said
7. 39   **Abby** Abigail
8. 13   **a-row in the family pew,** *Not in Q.*
8. 25   **pond** little pond
8. 31   **in the flickering May shadows** on the kitchen stoop, *A as in E.*
10. 3   *I* **can assure you. They didn't do five dollars worth of business** *I* warn you. They didn't take two dollars
11. 5   **thirty years** twenty-five years *A as in Q.*
11. 12   **John Murchison** J. Murchison
11. 13   **so did his own children. .... to be it?** *Not in Q; A as in E.*
11. 18   **Playfair business** Bennett business *A as in E.*
11. 27   **sage in his judgments,** *Not in Q or A.*
12. 1   **altogether occupied** wholly preoccupied
12. 5   **a congregation that always stood in the old days** a standing congregation
12. 6   **thirty years** twenty-five years *A as in Q.*
12. 11   **touching certain of its members,** touching the Heir Apparent *A as in E.*
13. 18   **but his sense of obligation worked unfailingly both ways.** *Not in Q; A as in E.*
13. 23   **"The Wilcoxes"** "The Weymses" *A as in E.*
14. 26   **with an overflow ... to the other.** *Not in Q; A as in E.*
15. 4   **slight weight** weight
15. 5   **the Doctor** the little Doctor
15. 20   **"Gregory block,"** "Plummer block," *A as in E.*
16. 11   **seven** four
16. 24   **Law Schools examination,** his examination
16. 36   **indulged** described
17. 26   **It will be remembered .... to announce that** *Not in Q; A as in E.*
18. 12   **The house was a dignified old affair .... The house stood roomily and shadily in ornamental grounds,** The house stood roomily in two acres of land *A as in E until* "the Plummer Place" *(22, 19), then omits next two sentences.*
18. 27   **pathetic in his frayed air of exile from some garden of Italy**

sloping to the sea the drive to the door was flanked by a lamp-post on either side, exactly like those at the street corners. If ever they were of use it was not in the Murchisons' time, who finally, for the sake of appearances, thought it better to take the glass out entirely.

20. 8 **red brick** white brick

20. 16 **early years in the "wynds" of a northern Scottish town** bleak early years on the East Coast *A as in Q.*

20. 19 **for long together** *Not in Q.*

20. 38 **beyond all endurance.** more than flesh and blood could bear. *A as in E.*

21. 8 ***Blackwood's),* and the *Cornhill)* they used to be** *Appleton's Journal) A as in Q.*

21. 20 **it was complete,** you got it all, *A as in E.*

22. 11 **early and satisfactorily** at twenty-two *A as in Q.*

22. 31 **have seen** see

22. 32 **reach and pass the age of twenty-five** has reached the age of twenty-six *A as in E.*

22. 38 **for such absorption.** for all literature. *A as in E.*

23. 6 **taking the university course for women at Toronto, and afterward teaching** by teaching *A as in E.*

23. 12 **more than seems likely to come** more than you get.

24. 3 **was guiltless** were guiltless

24. 6 **was not denied** was recognized

24. 34 **face** upper lip

25. 1 **Frank Jennings** Alf Jennings

25. 9 **with the slow ... in him** humorously *A as in E, except omits* slow.

25. 12 **and pursing his lips** terribly *A as in E.*

25. 18 **already defining** now defining

25. 19 **coming freely in** incoming in

27. 4 **Mr John Flint** Mr. John Finlay

27. 5 **South Ward** Town Ward

27. 6 **the Third Doxology: "Blessed, blessed be Jehovah, Israel's God to all eternity—"** the First Doxology: "Praise God from Whom all blessings flow—" *A as in E.*

27. 20 **the Doctor** the Little Doctor

28. 2 **Horace Williams** Williams

28. 9 **"I'll consider it .... taken up with Job"** *Not in Q; A as in E.*

28. 14 **Stella** And Stella

28. 24 **in such matters** *Not in Q.*

28. 25 **Mrs. Murchison ... I don't know** *Not in Q; A as in E, but adds:* charm as she sat there in her black silk and old lace and fresh colors.

28. 30 **recently adopted** adopted

29. 39   **He had a fund ... did himself.** *Not in Q; A as in E.*
30. 4   **he took ... his dignity** he put cotton wool in his ears, which in no way detracted from his dignity. *A as in E.*
31. 8   **with private humour,** to himself
31. 29   **"Nasty business .... as it is."** *Not in Q; A as in E, except:* already *instead of* as it is
32. 4   **which seemed to throw light on the matter.** to the general relief.
34. 2   **a good deal in society.** "in society."
34. 8   **—those common worldly standards that prevailed in Elgin as well as anywhere else in their degree—** I mean keeping a "girl" and making the butcher go to the back door, living in a two-storey brick (though with the usual social paradox, there were aristocrats who lived in a one-storey frame) and turning out creditably on Sundays— *A as in E.*
34. 33   **prove that they weren't going to,** prove it,
34. 36   **with dubiety.** with suspicion. *A as in E.*
34. 36   **She was out .... in the morning;** Things were said about her, about her untidiness, and how she had been found doing her Latin grammar on the roof to escape the children, and how *A as in E.*
35. 15   **daughters** daughters, when Advena was undergoing the penible process of growing up—she whistled, and wrote poetry in the local newspaper— *A as in Q.*
35. 25   **had nevertheless .... were "nice people,"** would nevertheless not have done so badly, but she had taken no time to establish herself; she had almost immediately married. Hence it was quite as likely that she would draw Dr. Harry down, if we may speak of depth in Elgin, as that he would buoy her up. Still, the Johnsons were certainly "nice people," *A as in E.*
35. 29   **chances** chances, but for an obstinate affection for her old friends, *A as in E.*
35. 33   **bowing recognition** social prospectus *A as in E.*
36. 31   **there is a party ... going** *Not in Q; A as in E.*
37. 32   **smaller trades .... draw the line** saddlers and furriers made a poor pretension, and a tailor could hardly expect recognition outside of his own denomination. *A as in E.*
38. 4   **The valuable part .... up its head.** *Not in Q; A as in E.*
41. 2   **to his own line in life,** to his own Dominion, *A as in Q.*
41. 33   **double-breasted frock coat and** *Not in Q; A as in E.*
42. 34   **claret-cup** lemonade
43. 35   **remarkably pretty and had remarkably good style,** remarkably pure and remarkably good style, *A has:* remarkably pretty and remarkably good style,
44. 38   **a few others** one or two others

45. 11	**uncertain** dubious
45. 21	**cake-walk.** circus.
45. 27	**resources.** assets.
47 .6	**without seeing her in any special way;** without being specially aware of it;
47. 23	**she saw truly enough in the mass.** she generalized with remarkable accuracy. *A as in Q.*
48. 1	**It is determined with something like humour** It is humorously determined by the law of evolution *A as in E.*
48. 9	**local, provincial, or Dominion.** local or at most Dominion
48. 20	**this.** this attitude.
48. 21	**no King** here was no King
48. 21	**here were no picturesque** no picturesque
48. 28	**in plain terms.** in terms of arithmetic. *A as in E.*
48. 29	**British Government** Government, coinciding with the strenuous speech of a member fond of initiative, *A as in E.*
48. 34	**Government** British Government
49. 7	**said in Elgin** put it in Elgin
49. 8	**Elgin's point of view** Elgin's comfortable point of view
49. 16	**until the other day,** *Not in Q.*
49. 25	**the country** Elgin
49. 36	**the average intelligent English man** a member of the House of Lords *A as in E.*
49. 39	**appropriation** provincial appropriation
50. 7	**against it** against them to keep out fantasies *A as in E.*
50. 18	**think of** lower
50. 29	**the backbone of life,** the vertebral arrangement of life,
50. 31	**and the thing ... the congregations.** *Not in Q; A as in E.*
50. 34	**for more the emotional lift,** *Not in Q or A.*
51. 12	**a lady of Knox Church** Mrs. Murchison *A as in E.*
52. 5	**his people** his charge
53. 28	**his relative and housekeeper,** his excellent housekeeper *A has:* his talkative housekeeper
53. 30	**her reply** his reply
54. 19	**The first night ... came flocking back.** the strayed came flocking back with a renewed sense of the discomfort of more emotional forms, the first night "I to the hills will lift mine eyes" swung out upon East Elgin, led by an improvised precentor with a fork to the uplifting tune that belongs to it. *A as in E.*
55. 7	**anxious** sensitively anxious
55. 14	**Hugh Finlay** James Finlay *So throughout; A as in E.*
55. 15	**Dumfriesshire** Aberdeenshire
56. 7	**The regular** Their regular
58. 5	**The militant history ... Jenny Geddes.** *In Q, this sentence*

precedes the sentence at 62. 37: Yet he kept .... *A as in E.*

58. 7   **"A tremendous Presbyterian .... congregations are."** *Not in Q; A as in E.*

58. 26   **deep dreams** Celtic dreams

58. 30   **His face bore .... an impenetrable shyness;** He had a slight stoop and an impenetrable shyness; *A as in E.*

59. 11   **noted with delight the ingenuity of fate** appreciated the humorous ingenuity of fate *A as in E, except* humorous *omitted.*

59. 13   **her perception** that perception

59. 30   **in his contemplation of the Deity she saw the man.** and she was not ashamed to detect artistic curiosity in his contemplation of the Deity. *A as in Q.*

60. 16   **politely,** quite politely

62. 5   **seizing the new joy ... moment of parting;** without a reason, without a pretext; *A as in Q.*

65. 1   **It was the deep root ... promise of all.** *Not in Q or A.*

65. 15   **the whole world ... look through.** *Not in Q; A has:* the whole world had an aspect of opportunity;

65. 16   **The opportunity was in his hand,** the happy chance had come *A as in Q.*

65. 18   **He was as much aware of its potential significance as any one could be,** *Not in Q or A.*

66. 28   **common standard in such things.** common standard of tournure.

67. 22   **early defeated** defeated

67. 37   **I'd be scared green.** *Not in Q; A as in E.*

68. 17   **Not a bit.** "That's all right." *A as in E.*

70. 23   **reckless** bungling

70. 25   **contrite** grovelling

71. 2   **Young Ormiston would "get clear";** *Not in Q; A as in E.*

71. 7   **pay** emoluments

71. 28   **its limits** municipal limits

71. 30   **been bound** infallibly

72. 10   **Cruickshank, K.C., probably the most distinguished criminal lawyer in the Province.** Cruickshank, Q.C., Standing Counsel for the provincial government. *A as in E.*

72. 20   **after a British politician of lofty but abortive views, the Canadian Renfaire.** the Canadian Rosebery, and they meant to indicate more than a frivolous attitude towards responsibility. *A as in E.*

72. 23   **interesting** interesting to the last degree

73. 6   **the Crown** the bank

73. 8   **the defendant** their clerk

73. 10   **to the jury** *Not in Q.*

73. 32   **for opening the safe.** for opening the safe. Young Ormiston,

who came at this point under examination, promptly acknowledged the formula to be in his handwriting. How it had come
into the vault-passage he could not say; no, he himself could
not have dropped it there; to the best of his knowledge it had
been, up to the day of the burglary, in a pocket-book with some
private papers in his bedroom; after that, as his effects had been
seized, he could say nothing. He looked without special interest
at the paper, and remained, as Rawlins put it, "unmoved." *Not
in A or E.*

73. 35   **The evidence ... little interest.** *Not in Q; A as in E.*

74. 6   **It might have ... to show it.** It was generally felt to be foolish
and undesirable that the young man should know nothing about
this, should be unable to connect it with any communication,
should never have seen it before. There might have been so
many ways of explaining it, and simple astonishment did not
somehow fit in; there was no way of explaining that. *A as in E.*

74. 19   **beautifully;** quite beautifully;

74. 32   **Witnesses were called to prove** Cross-examination elicited
from Ormiston *A as in E.*

74. 35   **Belton.** Belton, that he had played bridge with her, had lost
money to her. Questioned as to the amount of his losses,
Ormiston said it was three hundred dollars. He had not paid
Miss Belton, but—here the defendant blushed deeply—he
intended to do so.

"You have paid Miss Belton nothing at all?" asked the
counsel.

"Nothing at all," Ormiston replied, and winced visibly.

The slight pause which the lawyer permitted himself at this
point accentuated the young man's reply, made it heavily significant. Then, turning to the Court, Mr. Cruickshank imparted
the information that the efforts of the Crown towards obtaining
unmistakable justification for its present action had been
crowned with unusually immediate success. A proportion of the
missing notes had been traced and were now in the Crown's
possession. In this connection he would call but one witness,
whose evidence, he ventured to think, would be found conclu-
sive. *Not in A or E.*

74. 36   **of the *Express*.** *Not in Q.*

75. 2   **him straight up the ladder to a night editorship** to anything
in the nature of a metropolitan engagement. *A as in E.*

75. 6   **without emotion, and there ....** "without winking, that they"
without emotion in the witness box, and there she testified that
the notes for which she had been asked to account *A as in E.*

75. 40   **distress was so plain in him** his face held such feeling

76. 1   **In one or two .... all the way, however.** Mr. Cruickshank

brought the prosecution to an impressive close. *A as in E.*
76. 5   **The case .... Miss Belton.** The defence was reserved till the following day, the case having opened late. *A as in E.*
77. 14   **brilliant view** penetrating view
79. 30   **Eliza** Jennie *So throughout.*
80. 8   **nobody could do it better than Selkirk.** *Not in Q or A.*
80. 17   **big business** good business
80. 18   **national business,** *Not in Q.*
80. 19   **we want** we want for the Halifax line
80. 31   **by George!** my goodness
81. 2   **As head of a deputation from the United Chambers of Commerce of Canada** As chairman of a deputation of Members of the Canadian Parliament *A as in E.*
81. 5   **within the Empire** with the Colonies
81. 26   **It was then ... fell from him** *Not in Q or A.*
81. 33   **"It's the whole case ... Murchison.** *Not in Q or A.*
83. 13   **superintending** *Not in Q.*
83. 14   **to go to the old country at such short notice,** for what she mentioned as his "trip," *A as in Q.*
90. 10   **They've developed ... it's important.** *Not in Q or A.*
90. 13   **doesn't take in the situation as it is now.** is all bunkum. *A has:* is all buncombe.
90. 38   **Clara Sims** Clara Jones
91. 6   **any man** any boy
91. 32   **in the vague ... blooms.** *Not in Q or A.*
92. 7   **shirt-sleeves;** shirt-sleeves; it is possible he would have preferred them, but *A as in E.*
92. 30   **the children** the Wales children
93. 13   **attend to** mind you
93. 26   **tremendous lot** mighty lot
94. 8   **table-centres.** d'oyleys.
94. 30   **'xtremely dinky-dink.** very dinky-dink.
95. 17   **her needles out** the sock
95. 31   **isn't thinking of any such folly.** won't be such a fool. *A as in Q.*
95. 39   **she would split wood at a pinch,** *Not in Q or A.*
96. 6   **The creature** The man's
96. 10   **he's** the man's
96. 31   **if I do say it myself!"** thanks be!"
97. 10   **Janet Wilson** Janet Macbeth
97. 13   **Dumfriesshire** Aberdeenshire
99. 20   **looking up** *Not in Q; A as in E.*
99. 26   **the secret.** their secret.
99. 28   **Finlay said** He said
103. 22   **and they all .... Cruickshank's experience.** and though

Poulton would have preferred the Cecil and McGill the Metropole, they all followed him unquestioningly to the temperance hotel in Bloomsbury where bedrooms were three and six and tea was understood as a solid meal and the last in the day. *A as in E, except omits final sentence.*

104. 8 **and their introduction by Lord Selkirk to the Colonial Secretary;** *Not in Q or A.*

104. 39 **Lord Selkirk ... dined them too, and** and Lord Selkirk not only dined them but *A as in E.*

105. 4 **They travelled ... with one another.** *Not in Q or A.*

105. 8 **cluster, avoiding** cluster, humorously acquiescent in all they saw, avoiding *A as in E.*

105. 12 **after they ... proprietary** with half a proprietory air.

106. 15 **a principal in** President of

106. 27 **of a duty to foreigners on certain forms of manufactured leather—he turned out in Toronto a very good class of suitcase.** of a preferential duty on certain raw materials, with special reference to its amount and date of incidence. *A as in E.*

106. 35 **would be likely to refuse.** would have been likely to refuse.

107. 1 **dropped back** dropped

107. 27 **to leave early;** to get out of;

107. 35 **second-class** steerage

108. 3 **they were full of the terms of their bargain** *Not in Q or A.*

108. 9 **among them looked higher and further; only he ... his heart.** whose soul was alive to the inrush of the essential, lifted up his heart. *A as in E, except omits* looked higher and further; only he

109. 17 **Yes, ... other kinds.** *Not in Q or A.*

110. 36 **in your case** *Not in Q.*

111. 10 **at Hatfield they were saying, some of them.** in Hatfield they were saying *A as in E.*

111. 12 **other members ... against itself.** *Not in Q; A as in E.*

111. 14 **still in the Cabinet** *Not in Q or A.*

111. 29 **The basis** the fiscal basis

111. 33 **better business** free business

111. 34 **corn and meat** corn and meat and wool

111. 37 **food-stuffs** bread

112. 15 **take the chances of any zollverein.** take any chances. *A as in Q.*

113. 17 **the young Canadian** Lorne

113. 20 **talking of the policy urged by the Colonial representatives at the last Conference,** *Not in Q or A.*

114. 12 **asparagus growing,** *Not in Q.*

114. 27 **and great houses,** *Not in Q.*

114. 30 **jute mills** cotton mills

117. 32 **a heart rejoiced** a lifted heart
118. 15 **the promise of concessions** ready concessions
118. 22 **south of the Bay—** south of the Yukon,
118. 25 **against the Americans;** *Not in Q.*
118. 28 **arrow.** arrow. Inter-Imperial cables were postponed by the Marconigraph, but
121. 14 **The bigger issue .... world was watching.** *Not in Q or A.*
121. 28 **cablegrams** telegrams
122. 2 **Common interest .... that's compatible enough.** *Not in Q; A as in E to*: we know it; *next two paragraphs not included.*
122. 20 **adaptable** adaptive
122. 34 **"If they manage it, they will be clever," he said.** *Not in Q; A as in E.*
122. 36 **cotton** cotton and wool
123. 13 **"Maybe so .... they use."** "H'm," said John Murchison. *A has:* "Maybe so. It would want looking into."
123. 32 **sister** kiddie
123. 35 **to the laundry** to the wash
123. 38 **"In this preference business** *Not in Q or A.*
125. 5 **And if Wallingham .... He will, too.** *Not in Q or A.*
125. 21 **the Free Fooders** they *A as in Q.*
126. 9 **—he nearly cried—** *Not in Q or A.*
126. 14 **"Oh, and there's .... when you say 'England.'** *Not in Q; A as in E to*: walks into Thibet?; *next four lines not included.*
126. 32 **—in their own good time, not next week or next year—** *Not in Q or A.*
129. 12 **informing** infusing
129. 13 **vigorously disclaimed** passionately and disclaimed
129. 18 **said Finlay,** said Finlay anxiously,
129. 29 **clearest** nicest
129. 37 **he was genuinely loyal and attached to England.** the loyal card was always one of his trumps. *A as in Q.*
129. 38 **He would discriminate against Manchester with tears in his eyes!** *Not in Q or A.*
129. 40 **The Conservatives ... on the wrong.** *Not in Q; A as in E.*
130. 5 **"As Disraeli said—wasn't it Disraeli?"** *Not in Q; A as in E.*
130. 38 **"We're all very well .... to know it."** *Not in Q; A as in E.*
132. 5 **exclaimed Advena.** Advena exclaimed.
132. 7 **answer** comprehend
132. 19 **that** if
132. 31 **He turned a look upon her.** He turned upon her pale with anger. *A has:* He turned upon her with a look that was almost angry.
133. 12 **Dumfries** Aberdeenshire
133. 35 **the woman** the girl

134. 3   **quick desire** fierce desire
136. 12   **good fellow** nice fellow
136. 26   **Why** Good gracious,
137. 1   **pretended** mock
139. 33   **to help the lover.** of creation.
141. 2   **regret** sorrow
141. 6   **He who carefully adjusts an intellectual machine** The intel-
          lectual machine   *A as in Q.*
141. 12   **strong** mighty
142. 17   **He felt** Murchison felt
143. 1   **Gregory** Jackson
143. 12   **tree-bordered** maple-bordered
144. 19   **critical eye** proud eye *A as in Q.*
145. 32   **a cheroot** a straw
148. 20   **the heather again** the heather again over yon
148. 39   **The iron merchant** John
150. 34   **half bend** half bow
151. 8   **The fire snapped and the watch went on ticking.** *Not in Q*
          or A.
151. 21   **that man Grant.** *Not in Q; A has:* that man
151. 26   **The Doctor** the little Doctor
151. 28   **His mouth** His upper lip
152. 3   **Well I mind him .... the fiercest.** *Not in Q; A as in E.*
152. 29   **in forced illumination** like forced illumination
152. 30   **discomforting** discomfiting
152. 33   **The Doctor,** the little Doctor,
153. 12   **lie upon him** let it play upon him.
153. 27   **that spirit?** any spirit? *A as in Q.*
158. 12   **the mere watering-cart, or delivering the mere ice,** the
          watering-cart, or delivering ice, *A as in E.*
158. 21   **the day before** *Not in Q.*
158. 26   **local support** loyal supporters
159. 5   **who had every pretension ... against Farquaharson,** who
          had succeeded in lowering the sitting member's majority by
          nearly two hundred at the last general election, *A as in Q,*
          except: by over one hundred
159. 8   **taken up with them** occupied with them
160. 28   **to take special note of such valuable views.** to get at your
          views. *A has:* to get at such valuable views.
160. 39   **worthy** so worthy
161. 17   **calculating moment.** awkward moment.
161. 19   **but new considerations .... next returns.** but indications
          were not lacking that its sanitary record might shortly tell a
          different story. For years the Conservatives had held a small
          majority in the town vote, which the last general election had

heavily increased. Unpopular temperance legislation accounted
for some of it, but the steady growth of the place as an industrial centre accounted for more;   *A as in Q.*

161. 28   **as if to illustrate .... were exceptions, and**   but   *A as in Q.*

161. 35   **the possibility of a great and dramatic change**   the great and
dramatic possibility of change   *A has:* the great and dramatic
change

161. 37   **—had indeed, initiated ... follow up.**   *A as in E.*

162. 1   **concerned**   influenced   *A as in E.*

162. 2   **to stand by it ... and pushed it.**   to take into his scheme of
action.   *A as in E.*

162. 18   **The great question .... anxiety at Ottawa.**   The great exigency was the explanation and defence of the new idea; that
was impressed upon every Liberal caucus throughout the length
and breadth of the Dominion,   *A as in E.*

162. 23   **an influential person at Ottawa**   the secretary of the committee at Ottawa   *A as in E.*

162. 27   **Meanwhile .... next year.**   *Not in Q; first sentence only in A.*

162. 33   **he couldn't talk straight if he wanted to,**   *Not in Q; A as in
E.*

162. 34   **that lecture tour of his in the United States**   those speeches
of his   *A as in Q.*

163. 22   **record**   book-keeping

164. 13   **this new policy of yours and Wallingham's."**   for your new
policy."   *A as in Q.*

164. 19   **practically**   *Not in Q; A as in E.*

164. 29   **waverers**   opinion.   *A as in Q.*

164. 31   **and they're bound to see it in time.**   *Not in Q or A.*

164. 39   **that last Conference**   that last Colonial Conference   *A as in E.*

165. 1   **And the fellows ... fine lead.**   *Not in Q; A as in E, except:*
such a fine lead.

165. 7   **with detachment,**   *Not in Q or A.*

165. 11   **with a tariff .... though."**   *Not in Q; A as in E.*

165. 19   **a fellow**   a man

165. 36   **for fighting purposes, anyhow;**   *Not in Q or A.*

168. 13   **that he might have felt, however.**   that might have been his.

169. 28   **always a tremendous lark."**   tremendous larks."

169. 36   **transpiring**   transpired

169. 37   **and ... to engage**   Mrs. Milburn and Miss Filkin, elaborately
inattentive, endeavoured to engage.   *A as in E.*

170. 4   **gratified**   delighted

170. 11   **prolonged**   taken up

170. 24   **Hesketh as a stranger**   he

170. 34   **inclined to like everybody.**   on the like.

170. 35   **visitor**   stranger

171. 23 **overcoats ... like that.** threshing-machines. *A as in E.*
172. 2 **"I heard** "I believe
172. 9 **the poor-house** the Elgin poor-house
172. 20 **with getting ours.** with ours.
172. 38 **no scandalous paper** no damaging private paper *A as in E.*
173. 1 **The policy ... application of it.** Attack and defence settled upon the new policy, however; *A as in Q.*
173. 37 **one small appointment ... got it—** *Not in Q or A.*
175. 1 **the early spring,** the spring,
175. 4 **the work** its work
175. 6 **It was understood that the new writ would issue** The election was fixed *A as in E.*
175. 13 **decisive point** culminating decisive point
175. 19 **They were both .... farther away.** *Not in Q or A.*
175. 28 **could give themselves leave; a day would arrive,** still they could; a day was coming, *A as in Q, except:* a day would come,
175. 35 **natural demands** natural impulses *A as in Q.*
176. 16 **to realize and to explore;** unrealized, unexplored; *A as in Q.*
177. 10 **pemmican** venison
177. 40 **asked him.** asked him steadily.
178. 4 **Do you think** Have you decided
179. 2 **undone his hurt** undone everything *A as in Q.*
179. 19 **the other." He broke off,** the other. There are certain aspects"—he broke off, *A as in Q.*
179. 26 **possibilities."** limitations." *A as in E.*
179. 30 **on the tide of** on the shoreward waves of *A as in E.*
179. 32 **friendship of spirit.** fellowship of spirit. *A as in Q.*
179. 34 **told him.** assured him. *A as in Q.*
179. 36 **Yours ... farthest out** Yours lies the furthest out; it comprises all the others—
180. 8 **absolute.** indistinguishable.
180. 13 **to British Columbia, I think—those mining missions** to the North-West I think—those Assiniboian missions *A as in E.*
180. 22 **Then, if he loves .... upon a glance."** *Not in Q or A.*
181. 31 **admonition.** comfort.
181. 32 **he groaned in his private heart.** he demanded, heavily. *A has:* he demanded.
183. 25 **"Dora, would you like me to promise something?"** "Dora, would you like to promise me something?"
183. 29 **But already .... lips to say.** Never to come into your room without knocking.

"Lorne Murchison!" she exclaimed with outraged propriety, but perhaps more outrage than propriety. And we aren't even engaged! *A as in Q, except that Lorne's speech ends at* come— *and* stopped him *is substituted for* exclaimed.

183. 39   **one satisfaction**   a satisfaction
184. 1   **substantial**   leading
184. 5   **Bella**   Eliza
184. 31   **imperial**   Imperial
184. 33   **harder**   so much harder
184. 34   **there was a smell of varnish**   it smelled of varnish
185. 29   **unvarying aspect**   familiar phenomenon
185. 39   **were**   was
186. 14   **Drill Shed**   Drill Hall or the Opera House
187. 3   **with care and satisfaction.**   with rapidity and enjoyment.   *A as in E.*
187. 26   **was enough to mark them of another nation.**   was just race.   *A as in E.*
187. 30   **tea or cider,**   chiefly tea or cider,
188. 19   **was**   were
188. 21   **in the cause**   in its defence   *A has neither version.*
189. 30   **the Algonquins and the—and the other savages—**
          the Hurons and the Iroquois   *A as in E.*
190. 22   **expressive**   feeling
190. 27   **should they know**   can they know   *A has:* Little they know.
          The E. version is correctly quoted.
190. 29   **which he could .... The same voice**   whereupon the same
          voice   *A as in Q.*
190. 32   **and the speaker felt advised to turn to**   with which he turned
          to   *A as in E.*
191. 2   **shown themselves capable of this great function**   been
          chosen by destiny to carry out this high purpose   *A as in E.*
191. 19   **At this**   At which
191. 27   **Here**   Whereupon
191. 31   **intermittent stamps and uncompromising shouts**   loud and
          repeated demands   *A has:* uncompromising shouts
192. 5   **the admiration and confidence he felt**   his admiration for and
          confidence in
192. 23   **the drive home**   the drive
193. 4   **about the pulpit,**   upon the communion table,   *A as in E.*
194. 7   **David Davidson!**   John Macfarlane
194. 26   **Moreover ... in Finlay.**   *Not in Q; A has:* which was a liberty
          in Finlay. *A, but not Q, omits Deuteronomy reference and text.*
194. 29   **to his difficulty**   to the difficulty of finding a text to sanction
          very straight hitting;   *A as in E.*
195. 21   **make one's blood boil.**   turn one's stomach.   *A as in E.*
195. 27   **remarkably**   mighty
195. 39   **"He's a lobster," said Stella with fervour.**   *Not in Q; A as in
          E.*
196. 3   **Is it true .... laughed again.**   *Not in Q or A.*

196. 17   **said Mr. Murchison, innocently**   said her father slyly, and
they all laughed. *A as in Q.*
197. 28   **Mrs. Forsyth** Mrs. Forbes   *A as in Q.*
198. 30   **old Mr. Fisher**   Jim Fisher
199. 30   **Mrs. Murchison**   his wife
200. 5   **liberal**   free
200. 6   **express myself,**   get it out,
200. 20   **more or less**   kind of
200. 21   **would be**   was   *A has:* there's
200. 21   **one's as much of a muddler as the other!**   one's as through-
other as the other! *A as in E.*
200. 23   **Advena**   the girl
200. 24   **just very much annoyed."**   just good and mad."   *A as in E.*
202. 2   **that the Elgin ... was practically solid**   that he had the Elgin
... practically solid
202. 25   **ironware**   stores [stoves?]   *A as in E.*
202. 35   **a pull of a third**   a preference of a third
204. 12   **damned enthusiasts**   enthusiasts   *A as in E.*
204. 15   **He professed .... root and branch.**   *Not in Q or A.*
204. 25   **Clayfield *Standard*.**   Clayfield *Standard,* and now and then
general principles for his support and comfort, as apart from
special canons for local application, could be found in the party
organs of Toronto. *A as in Q.*
205. 4   **rolling mills**   melting vats
205. 38   **at that time**   then
206. 23   **happy hunting ground**   limbo
206. 30   **He stood there .... But**   *Not in Q or A.*
207. 13   **It's bound ... isn't it?"**   It does begin to look like that, doesn't
it?" *A as in E, except:* to come back to that
208. 35   **His opportunity**   The young Englishman's opportunity
208. 37   **South Fox campaign**   Liberal or Imperial cause. *A as in E.*
210. 34   **other things**   things
211. 7   **some fellow-traveller.**   *Not in Q.*
212. 17   **immigrants**   emigrants
212. 24   **ideals.**   ideal.
212. 39   **The worshippers**   The long-lipped worshippers
213. 11   **great satisfaction**   profound satisfaction   *A as in E.*
213. 12   **Their situation**   Their interesting situation
213. 13   **added**   additional
214. 2   **in the door or anywhere.**   *Not in Q or A.*
215. 38   **looking forward to**   looking forward"—oh, Advena!—"to   *A
as in E.*
215. 40   **passages**   passage
216. 6   **"Presbyterians**   "We
216. 26   **in their clothes**   *Not in Q; A has:* in their chairs

218. 19　**fewer supporters**　fewer fresh supporters
218. 21　**excommunication**　burial　*A as in Q.*
218. 22　**effectively curse**　bury　*A as in Q.*
228. 22　**the ex-Minister deserved** .... **expressly forbids**　*Not in Q or A.*
218. 31　**little had transpired**　there had been little to show　*A as in E.*
218. 34　**as if epochs were made of cheers.**　*Not in Q; A as in E.*
219. 10　**the queerest thing ... stare at that—**　*Not in Q or A.*
219. 14　**on the further side.**　*Not in Q or A.*
219. 17　**Nothing could be ... its enemies.**　*Not in Q or A.*
219. 38　**"The old man's ... second horse.**　*Not in Q; A as in E.*
220. 4　**so,**　not,
220. 16　**lose it.**　use it
220. 17　**No conservative .... fast enough."**　They're buying [baying?] the moon with their loyalty now, but, when it comes to the touch, no Conservative Government in Canada could put through a cent of preference on English goods—and they know it."　*A as in E.*
220. 25　**Besides .... let us know."**　*Not in Q; A as in E, except omits third sentence:* Wallingham knows
220. 31　**Bingham,**　Bingham, chairman of the most difficult subdivision in the town,
220. 38　**had**　he had
221. 1　**"We'll win ... this time**　*Not in Q or A.*
221. 2　**he told them.**　he said.
221. 21　**my bunch."**　my crowd."
221. 39　**waiting for the word from overseas.**　*Not in Q or A.*
223. 11　**Liberals**　Reformers
223. 29　**in**　to
224. 13　**intentions**　initiatives
224. 16　**designed**　had designed
224. 20　**consider**　judge
224. 28　**so assuredly, when**　so assuredly, and with such happy charm, when　*A as in E.*
225. 7　**was suddenly ... concentration,**　told them,　*A as in E, except:* on a note
225. 31　**half-comprehending burst**　fine burst　*A as in Q.*
225. 36　**something from him**　his ardour　*A as in E.*
225. 37　**They would clap first and consider afterwards**　*Not in Q or A.*
226. 11　**port of the United States**　American port
227. 8　**developed, was as far**　developed, enforcing the last economic word for preference trade, was as far　*A as in Q.*
227. 16　**The day after Paardeburg .... in saying that**　*Not in Q; A as in E, except omits:* Theirs—and ours.

227. 21   **more loyal** more enthusiastically loyal *A as in E.*
227. 28   **a pine plank or a bushel of barley** an ounce of butter or an egg. *A as in Q.*
228. 5   **on the surface.** *Not in Q.*
228. 12   **British** inter-Imperial
228. 18   **ever** ever *A as in Q.*
228. 32   **The trades unions .... international.** *Not in Q or A.*
229. 5   **promptly** then *A as in E.*
229. 5   **gathered intensity** white intensity *A as in Q.*
229. 12   **any** a
229. 19   **our own stamp** the old stamp *A as in Q.*
229. 31   **and thank God, we were long poor.** *Not in Q; A as in E.*
229. 32   **he went on hotly,** *Not in Q; A as in E.*
230. 1   **announce ourselves** decide *A as in E.*
230. 13   **his words ... like an atmosphere.** his hand was upon their hearts; *A as in Q.*
230. 28   **They gave him a great appreciation, and** *Not in Q; A as in E.*
230. 29   **spoke in complimentary terms** made a complimentary reference *A as in E.*
231. 16   **Both the local papers .... call for it."** *Not in Q or A.*
233. 35   **a servant** the servant
235. 11   **the report** his report
236. 4   **sweetbreads** some sweetbreads
236. 7   **personator** impersonator *A as in E.*
238. 6   **The results** So that the results
238. 11   **enthusiastic voters** voters
238. 11   **including** excluding
238. 19   **Every Liberal ... made it.** Stella had attended to it. *A as in Q.*
238. 31   **A majority of seventy was too small for finality.** *Not in Q or A.*
238. 32   **called without twenty-four hours delay** promptly called *A as in Q.*
238. 36   **Ontario Elections Act** The Act for the Preventation of Corrupt Practices *A as in E.*
240. 16   **highly successful** conspicuously successful
240. 19   **superintendent, Squire** superintendent, then Squire
241. 3   **I will not say ... candidate. But** *Not in Q or A.*
241. 6   **the strictest interpretation of the law** the very letter of the law *A as in Q.*
241. 7   **fatherly influence in** fatherly control of
241. 32   **to void the Tory returns** to upset six elections *A as in E.*
242. 7   **was shortly in** had been in
242. 32   **comments** remarks
243. 34   **the father** her father

244. 35   **and full ... a woman wavered** but for the figure of a woman wavering
245. 2   **She was coming towards him** *Not in Q.*
245. 9   **with suddenly perceiving eyes and** *Not in Q or A.*
245. 14   **rough** strange *A as in Q.*
245. 15   **rising fear** great fear *A as in Q.*
245. 16   **strangely different** broken *A as in Q.*
245. 25   **to them.** up *A as in Q.*
246. 9   **in a quieted, almost a contented tone.** *Not in Q or A.*
246. 19   **hard pressed,** in agony, *A as in Q.*
246. 23   **is** was *A as in Q.*
246. 24   **I didn't mean it .... bear it, Hugh.** *Not in Q or A.*
246. 33   **nothing has happened to her?** dead? *A as in Q.*
247. 30   **restitution from the intrinsic in him;** helpful restitution out of his silence; *A as in Q.*
247. 34   **Then she would ... renunciation.** clinging to him, for respite. *A as in Q.*
247. 40   **could not** could not in his love and suffering, *A as in E.*
248. 11   **His extremity was very great .... he had found them.** *Not in Q; A as in E, until:* and moan.; *next three sentences only in E.*
248. 36   **The Doctor** The little doctor
249. 5   **to the person most concerned,** to the lady privileged to hear it, *A has:* to the lady concerned,
249. 13   **But four days .... take us home."** *Not in Q or A.*
249. 39   **trembling,** pale and trembling, *A as in E.*
250. 20   **to her.)** *Not in Q.*
250. 24   **very well pleased** well pleased
252. 36   **consuming desire** great desire
252. 38   **He stared ... first in his mind.** *Not in Q or A.*
253. 21   **It had the feeling ... all the way** *Not in Q or A.*
255. 3   **Bingham put it darkly ... unnecessary addition.** *Not in Q or A.*
255. 8   **wholly** quite
255. 17   **before that ... his objections.** to that he finally succumbed. *A as in Q.*
255. 17   **The election .... agreed to everything.** *Not in Q or A.*
256. 14   **He could think of nothing .... down her back.** *Not in Q; A contains only the third sentence.*
256. 30   **party organ, terrified of Quebec,** *Dominion A has:* party organ
256. 34   **to the Toronto *Post*** for the Toronto *Standard* So throughout; *A as in E.*
256. 36   **Idea** idea *A as in E.*
257. 1   **draws the breath of expediency,** inspires much inconsistency, *A as in Q.*

257. 4   **at the hands of the English Conservatives,**   *Not in Q or A.*
257. 19 **blossomed best**   best blossomed
257. 20 **margin**   luxury
257. 29 **period**   fortnight
257. 31 **They had ... about anything.**   *Not in Q or A.*
257. 39 **I cannot think that**   I doubt whether   *A as in Q.*
257. 39 **alone**   *Not in Q or A.*
258. 4   **etherealize**   evaporate   *A as in E.*
258. 9   **argued ... about it.**   philosophised upon that too if anyone had propounded it to him.   *A as in Q.*
258. 14 **exalted**   etherealised
258. 39 **in the office ... Mr. Fulke**   had been replying to Mr. Fulke in the office   *A as in Q.*
259. 5   **he told his senior,**   he said,   *A as in Q.*
259. 7   **He was right in his supposition.**   *Not in Q or A.*
259. 19 **put in,**   put in, with an effort of consoling explanation,   *A as in Q.*
259. 39 **out,"**   out?"   *A as in E.*
260. 29 **"—these heart-to-heart .... strong objection."**   "It's the only thing to do," said Bingham irritably, "but I'd have been better satisfied if he'd wanted to argue about it."
         "He didn't make," remarked Horace Williams with depression, "a single darned objection."   *A as in Q.*
261. 9   **not disdain**   work with   *A as in Q.*
261. 15 **of expediency rather than of courage.**   of nerves   *A as in E.*
261. 38 **At bottom,**   *Not in Q or A.*
264. 3   **a possibility ... until that moment.**   *Not in Q or A.*
264. 6   **"I don't know."**   "I don't quite know."   *A as in E.*
264. 7   **Milwaukee.**   Chicago.   *A as in Q.*
264. 8   **I am thinking seriously of closing with him."**   I have pretty well decided to close with him."   *A as in Q.*
264. 12 **his companion's arm**   young Murchison's arm.   *A as in E.*
264. 20 **damn you**   darn you   *A as in E.*
264. 31 **things**   components   *A as in Q.*
265. 11 **which was practically wrested from her.**   which were by no means adequate.   *A as in Q.*
265. 27 **she makes no secret of**   there is no doubt about   *A as in E.*
265. 33 **her brother's**   Lorne's
265. 38 **views;**   judgments;
266. 8   **moral or immoral,**   *Not in Q or A.*
266. 15 **also growing old.**   *Not in Q or A.*

Explanatory Notes

The notes are designed not only to provide specific information but also to document Duncan's intimate knowledge of the political and social realities of Brantford life, and of the debate about imperialism as it was being played out in England and Canada.

CHAPTER I

1. Like many characters in *The Imperialist*, Mother Beggarlegs evidently had a counterpart in reality. A letter from H.E. Millard, dated 21 July 1932 and held by the Brant County Museum, states:

> In the 70s I was a boy living in your city ... my mind lingers along the Old Market place on Dalhousie St. especially on Market day. I still can see that dear old Black mammy, with her basket of Gingerbread covered with little caraway seeds & sugar.

2. In the years from 1875 to 1885, the *Brantford Expositor* descriptions reveal some variation in the degree of enthusiasm with which the holiday was celebrated. In every other respect, Duncan's account is a faithful reflection of the atmosphere and entertainments she would have observed in her early years.

3. "The young people as usual began, continued and ended the day with that instrument of torture, the 'fire-cracker.' " *Expositor*, 25 May 1875.

4. "At one o'clock, the Foresters formed in procession on Market street in front of their hall ... preceded by a number of uniformed Foresters, who looked exceedingly imposing in their green velvet coats and plumed hats." *Expositor*, 26 May 1875.

5. The lacrosse match was an annual feature of the holiday. In 1884, the *Expositor* reported: "The attendance at Recreation Park was representative of the *elite* of the city. There was ... an air of respectability which one scarcely expects on a holiday."

6. Cf. a column Duncan wrote on the servant problem (*The Globe* 4 Nov. 1886): "The most intelligent and self-respectful of the girls that are compelled to earn their own living by their hands, prefer to earn it in a shop or a factory." Servants are much on the minds of the central characters in many of Duncan's novels.

7. Sir John Campbell, Marquis of Lorne (afterwards Duke of Argyll), Governor-General of Canada from 1878 to 1883. *The Dictionary of National Biography 1912-1921* comments rather unenthusiastically that "The Duke of Argyll's interests were less of a political than of a dilettante literary character" and Sandra Gwyn describes him as "The Gay

Governor-General" (Gwyn 179-90; 205-14). The Marquis of Lorne visited Brantford on 16 Sept. 1879 (when Duncan was seventeen) and formally opened a bridge named in his honour.

8. Liberal Prime Minister of Canada, 1873 to 1878.

9. Liberal Premier of Ontario, 1872 to 1896. Duncan had a brother whose Christian name, Blake, presumably was bestowed in honour of Edward Blake, the leader of the federal Liberals from 1880 to 1887. Charles Duncan, the novelist's father, was a speaker at the Reform [i.e. Liberal] Association of Brantford annual meeting on 6 October 1899.

CHAPTER II

1. Based on Dr. William Cochrane, minister of Zion Presbyterian Church, Brantford, from 1862 to 1898. Cf. Duncan's letter to Mac-Mechan, reprinted in full in the appendix to this volume:

> I rejoice that you enjoyed Dr. Drummond. The dear original was Dr.W. Cochrane of Brantford who christened most of the Presbyterians now there. He has been dead these five or six years—or I would never have dared!

In his diary entry for the week of 24 August 1890, Dr. Cochrane wrote: "Miss Sarah Duncan (Garth Grafton) in the evening, after her 2 years stay in Europe and her literary triumph." Dr. Cochrane was a Liberal, and admired both Mackenzie and Mowat (R.N. Grant, *Life of Rev. William Cochrane, D. D.* 154).

2. Charles Duncan, to whom the novel is dedicated, and on whom the character of John Murchison is based, came to Canada in 1851, and to Brantford in 1855.

3. In the initial publication of the novel (as a serial in *The Queen* magazine), this phrase appears as "touching the Heir Apparent," i.e. the playboy Prince of Wales, later Edward VII.

4. Liberal Prime Minister of England, 1868-74, 1880-85, 1886 and 1892-94.

5. Dr. Cochrane received an honorary Doctor of Divinity degree in 1875 from his undergraduate alma mater, Hanover College, Hanover, Indiana.

6. Members of the Church of England are called "Established" or "Episcopalians" in the novel, rather than the more familiar "Anglicans."

7. Duncan's observation goes back to the atmosphere of her youth, when Canada suffered a prolonged economic depression. In political terms, the novel is set in 1903, a year that marked the culmination of several years of extraordinary prosperity.

8. A generally accurate summary of Brantford institutions. In addition to the Collegiate Institute, Brantford had a Young Ladies' College (which Duncan attended and Dr. Cochrane helped to found). Rather than

"an asylum for the deaf and dumb," Brantford had a School for the Blind, built in 1872.

9. *The Express* is based on *The Expositor*, the Liberal newspaper. *The Mercury* is based on *The Courier*, the Conservative paper. Horace Williams, the editor of *The Express* in the novel shares with T.H. Preston, the proprietor of *The Expositor*, a partisan dedication to politics. Preston was the M.P.P. for South Brant from 1899 to 1908.

CHAPTER III

1. In character and distinction, if not in architectural details, the Plummer Place is clearly modelled on the Duncan house at 96 West Street.

2. Triton: "the merman of Greek, or rather pre-Greek mythology" (*Oxford Classical Dictionary*).

3. "portière": "a curtain hung over a door or doorway to prevent draught, to serve as a screen, or for ornament" (*Oxford English Dictionary*).

4. In *The Queen* serialization, "white brick"—a more appropriate description.

5. "wynds" (Scottish): "a narrow street or passage turning off from a main thoroughfare" (O.E.D.).

6. For an interpretation of the significance of *Ready-Money Mortiboy* and *Verner's Pride* in relation to Advena's character, see the essay by Elisabeth Köster in the Criticism section of this edition. *The Back of the North Wind*: a children's novel by George Macdonald (1871).

7. The Prince of Wales visited Brantford on 14 September 1860. The luncheon in his honour included fifty-two separate dishes.

8. Duncan herself attended the Toronto Normal School, but did not go to university. In her journalism, however, she speaks admiringly of pioneering women university students. Like Advena, Duncan apparently did some teaching in Brantford.

9. "Through-other": "disorderly; wild, reckless; disordered" (O.E.D.)

CHAPTER IV

1. The Six Nations reserve is located near Brantford; the site of Brantford itself was purchased from the Indians. The Superintendent of the reserve from 1862 to 1891 was Jasper Gilkinson.

2. In 1850, a motion in the Parliament of United Canada that the clergy reserves (land set aside to support the Anglican church) be abolished failed to carry by a narrow margin.

CHAPTER V

1. The British government decided in December 1868, soon after Confederation, to withdraw its troops from Canada. Desmond Morton suggests (*A Military History of Canada* 91) that Canadian politicians were powerless to alter the British resolve: "they were witnesses to an imperial revolution."

2. Charles Duncan was born in Cupar, Fifeshire, in the east of Scotland. Marian Fowler describes his wife, Jane Bell, as "an Ulster [i.e. in Duncan's terms from "the north of Ireland"] lass" (Fowler 16). The social analysis of this paragraph may be compared with a passage from J. Castell Hopkins's *Progress of Canada in the Nineteenth Century* (1900; quoted in Carl Berger, *The Sense of Power* 88):

> In English-speaking centres the old-time Loyalist clan with its official connections, hereditary sentiment and sympathetic touch with English social tradition, has largely passed away or else has experienced the loss of position which so often follows the loss of property or means. Successful merchants, well-to-do manufacturers and prosperous professional men have succeeded to its social place and traditions ...

CHAPTER VI

1. It has been suggested that the Milburn family is based on the Waterous family of Brantford. Yet, as Marian Fowler has remarked, this would be curious bravado on Duncan's part, since her sister Ruby had married a Waterous. If political allegiances are to be taken into account, a more likely candidate for the dubious honour of being the model for Milburn is W.F. Cockshutt, another Brantford industrialist. C.H. Waterous was approached to run for the Liberal nomination in South Brant in the 1899 bye-election, according to the Conservative candidate (*Expositor*, 17 Nov. 1899); Waterous was the chairman at both the Liberal nomination meeting and the first Liberal rally of that campaign. Cockshutt, on the other hand, ran as a Conservative candidate in 1887 and was elected as a Conservative several times beginning in 1904. Like Milburn, Cockshutt was an ardent and consistent protectionist and like Milburn, Cockshutt was president of the local Chamber of Commerce (F. Douglas Reville, *History of the County of Brant*, 374-75).

2. "broché": "(Of fabrics, especially silk) embossed, woven with a pattern on the surface; (noun) such fabric" (*Oxford Concise Dictionary*).

3. The model for Walter Winter is likely Robert Henry, a Conservative who was elected Mayor of Brantford in 1878 and 1879 and finally won a federal seat in 1896 (for a year) after several unsuccessful tries—for Duncan's use of the 1896 election, see "The Writing of *The Imperial-*

ist" elsewhere in this volume. Henry was "for many years. ... the recognized local head of the Conservative party" (Reville 372).

4. "good as a cake-walk": "1: An American Negro entertainment having a cake as prize for the most accomplished steps and figures in walking ... 3: a one-sided contest" (*Webster's New Collegiate Dictionary*). For the Great Southern Fair of 1896, Brantford engaged "the Pickanniny band, consisting of twelve little darkey boys from Hamilton" to assist in a cake-walk (*Expositor* 17 Sept. 1896).

CHAPTER VII

1. Duncan seems to be alluding here to Henry James's famous list of "absent things in American life" in his study of Hawthorne: "No sovereign, no court, no personal loyalty, no aristocracy, no church, no army, no diplomatic service, no country gentlemen; no palaces, no castles, nor manors, nor old country houses, nor parsonages, nor thatched cottages, nor ivied ruins."

2. A feeling Duncan both shared personally, and also attributed to the Canadian people at large. Cf. "Our Latent Loyalty," *The Week*, 26 May 1887: "Sentiment is difficult of analysis, and the sentiment of the flag of the most difficult sort .... We love our Queen: for the span of a long lifetime she has been to us the embodiment of all the tender virtues of a woman, all the noble graces of a queen."

3. An allusion to the feelings aroused by the Boer War. See note 5 to Chapter XI.

4. During the period of Dr. Cochrane's ministry, the membership of Zion Church grew from 150 to 830 (Grant, *Cochrane*, p. 77). During the same period, the population of Brantford grew from 6,000 to 18,000. The proportion of Presbyterians in Brantford rose from 15% in 1852 to 20% in 1881 (Burley, *A Particular Condition in Life* 74).

CHAPTER VIII

1. "Seventhly": in the seventh place "with reference to the heads of a sermon" (O.E.D.).

2. "Like most Scotchmen ... he enjoyed ecclesiastical discussion. Seldom did he look happier than when he took his favourite position in the corner of a pew at a meeting of Presbytery or Assembly ... and listened with a smile as the brethren thrashed out some difficult question" (Grant, *Cochrane* 142).

3. "Dr. Cochrane was in the highest sense of the term an evangelical preacher .... The old theology, as he heard it in Paisley and was taught it in Princeton, he preached to the end of his days in Zion Church" (Grant, *Cochrane* 90).

4. "His old lecture on the 'Hero Martyrs of Scotland' stirred the blood, and stiffened the back, and moistened the eyes of many a Presbyterian" (Grant, *Cochrane* 79). Jenny Geddes: a poor Scotswoman who is said to have expressed her displeasure at King Charles I's efforts to impose a new liturgy on the Scottish church by hurling her stool at the minister in St. Giles' Cathedral (23 July 1637).

5. Cf. Psalm 1: "Nor in the assembly of the just/ Shall wicked men appear." *The Book of Praise: Approved and Commended by the General Assembly of the Presbyterian Church in Canada* (Oxford: Oxford UP, 1897), p. 1.

6. "Covenanter": The Covenanters were Scottish Presbyterians of the 17th century who joined together to resist the imposition of the episcopal system. Adonais: the name given by Shelley to the central figure of his elegy on Keats.

CHAPTER IX

1. "public": as opposed to British public schools, which are private and reinforce the class system.

2. "Conveyancing" from "conveyance": "the transference of property (especially real property) from one person to another by any lawful act (in modern use only by deed or writing between living persons)" (O.E.D.).

3. Until recently, the Kerby House, built in 1854, occupied the corner of George and Colborne streets in Brantford. Damaged by fire in 1976, it was subsequently demolished.

CHAPTER X

1. *The Queen* serialization reads "the Canadian Rosebery." The Earl of Rosebery was Gladstone's successor as Prime Minister (1894-95), but resigned as Liberal party leader (1896) as the result of a dispute with his colleagues. Within Canadian politics, the description of Cruickshank might be said to fit Edward Blake, who was a distinguished lawyer and a fastidious politician. In 1874, Blake resigned his post as Minister Without Portfolio in Mackenzie's government. As already noted, Duncan had a brother named after him.

2. *The Queen* serialization continues with three more sentences not in the final version, beginning "Young Ormiston, who came at this point under examination, promptly acknowledged the formula to be in his handwriting ..." In her letter of 24 November 1903 to John Willison, who subsequently serialized the novel in his Toronto *Daily News*, Duncan wrote: "The case in court, as it appeared in *the Queen* is laughable. Please be sure to get these slips substituted for the corresponding matter you

have in hand." The account in the Toronto *Daily News* is nearly identical to the final version. Presumably, an objection to *The Queen* account is that Ormiston testifies as a witness for the Crown. It must be said that even in the final version the trial scene is not a model of clarity.

CHAPTER XI

1. The Indian Civil Service Examination was instituted in 1855.
2. "cracksman": "a house-breaker" (Eric Partridge, *A Dictionary of Slang and Unconventional English, 5th ed.*).
3. *Sordello*: a long poem (1840) by Robert Browning. William C. DeVane, author of *A Browning Handbook*, describes it as "a bewildering potpourri of poetry, psychology, love, romance, humanitarianism, philosophy, fiction and history": the kind of work that would appeal to Advena and Finlay.
4. J. Pierpont Morgan, the American multi-millionaire. In 1902, he did negotiate with the British government after the North Atlantic Shipping Combine he had formed seemed to threaten British interests.
5. Three soldiers from Brantford were among the 224 Canadians who died in the Boer War (1899-1902), fought to impose British control on South Africa. A monument in honour of the Boer War soldiers was unveiled in Brantford's Jubilee Park on 25 May 1903. A good indication of the boost the Boer War gave to the Imperial cause is provided by *The Expositor*'s account (24 Oct. 1899) of the departure of the first Brantford soldiers for the war:

> From the moment the men left the armory, the scene was one of the wildest enthusiasm, and one never to be forgotten by those who were present. The men themselves were proud of the send-off, although they were unable to understand it. A small boy ventured to ask [Private] Sherritt what he thought of it, and Sherritt made the characteristic reply, "Search me!"

The sentence alluding to the Boer War does not appear in the American edition.

CHAPTER XII

1. Wallingham: A character clearly based on Joseph Chamberlain. As Colonial Secretary, Chamberlain made a series of daring proposals designed to promote the unity of the Empire.
2. Such persons were often called "remittance men" at the time: "a term once widely used, especially in the West before World War I, for an immigrant living in Canada on funds remitted by his family in England, usually to ensure that he would not return home and be a source of embarrassment" (John Robert Colombo, *Canadian Encyclopedia*).

CHAPTER XIII

1. "[send] to the rightabout": "to cause to turn and retreat or flee, to send packing; to dismiss or turn away unceremoniously" (O.E.D.)

CHAPTER XIV

1. These two passages of poetry are not by either Tennyson or Browning, and have resisted identification. I am grateful to my colleague, Donald S. Hair, an authority on Victorian poetry, for his efforts to trace these lines.

2. In 1902 and 1903, England was immersed in violent controversy over the Government's Education Bill which gave public support to Church of England schools. Finlay's view is in agreement with an editorial, which Duncan no doubt read, in *The Times* of 5 June 1903. The writer deplores "the greater slowness of education development in England, as compared with countries whose education systems have been ... developed in an atmosphere of freedom from old traditions and ... of comparative immunity from the paralysing influences of religious controversy."

CHAPTER XV

1. In 1892, Edward Blake moved to England where he became an M.P. devoted to the cause of Irish nationalism.

2. Prince's Sporting Club in Knightsbridge "acquired a considerable reputation for snobbishness" (Ben Weinreb and Christopher Hibbert eds., *The London Encyclopedia*). Earl's Court and Maida Vale: modest residential areas of London extensively developed in the late Victorian period.

CHAPTER XVI

1. On 15 May 1903, in Birmingham, Joseph Chamberlain made a speech calling for Britain to abandon free trade and adopt a system of tariffs giving preference to the Empire. In the words of his biographer, Julian Amery, "no one speech in British history has ever caused such a sensation ... or led on to such momentous consequences" (*Chamberlain* V, 192). This proposal was the central political issue of the next several months; the split in Conservative ranks it produced led to a Liberal landslide victory in the election of 1906.

2. Hatfield House, Hertfordshire (near London), is the ancestral home of the Cecils, the dominant political family of this period. Lord Salisbury, Prime Minister from 1885 to 1892 and again from 1895 to 1902, died on 22 August 1903 without expressing himself publicly on

Chamberlain's proposal. His son, Hugh Cecil, was opposed to it. Salisbury's nephew, Arthur Balfour, succeeded him as Prime Minister, and vacillated on the issue in an effort, ultimately unsuccessful, to keep his Cabinet together. Gerald Balfour, President of the Board of Trade, was loyal to his brother.

3. Chamberlain resigned on 16 Sept. 1903 in order to speak out more freely about his proposal. At the same time, three ministers in favour of Free Trade also resigned.

4. Greater Britain: a term used by Imperialists to designate the Empire.

5. "Inseparable from these real advantages of the Free Trade system was the strength of the Free Trade 'mythos.' .... whatever the historic reality, public opinion—even among many fiscal reformers—was convinced that our unexampled prosperity had been due to Free Trade" (Avery, *Chamberlain* V, 220).

6. Zollverein: in 19th century German history, a customs union among the German states, accompanied by a tariff barrier against other countries. Chamberlain had proposed a Zollverein for the Empire in 1896; his new proposal called for preferential trade rather than free trade within the Empire.

7. At the Colonial Conference of 1902, Laurier had promised to make tariff concessions to Britain if the mother country were willing to favour Canada in duties on wheat. Chamberlain could not accept the offer at that time.

8. In 1902, an army general alleged that sixty per cent of Englishmen were unfit for military service. The formation of the Boy Scout movement was a direct response to this claim and its aftermath in public debate. See Samuel Hynes, *The Edwardian Turn of Mind* 22 ff.

9. Cf. C.F.G. Masterman, *The Condition of England* (1909): "The whole standard of life has been sensibly raised, not so much in comfort as in ostentation .... Where one house sufficed, now two are demanded; where a dinner of a certain quality, now a dinner of a superior quality; where clothes or dresses or flowers, now more clothes, more dresses, more flowers." (1960 Metheun edition 20-21). Colonel Denison, a leading Canadian imperialist, wrote a friend in 1899: "I can see that the day is fast approaching when the selfishness, luxury, and worship of gold above everything else in England is going to destroy the British race unless the new blood in the Colonies, will leaven the mass." (Quoted in Carl Berger, *The Sense of Power* 181.)

10. Cawnpore: A major city in north central India, known for its leather goods.

CHAPTER XVII

1. The famous Speakers' Corner, open to anyone with a message of any sort, was established after the right of public assembly in Hyde Park was granted in 1872 (*London Encyclopedia*).

2. Cf. a column Duncan had written sixteen years before on "American Influence on Canadian Thought" (*The Week* 7 July 1887): "Any bookseller in the city will tell us that for one reader of Blackmore or Meredith he finds ten of Howells or James ... any newsdealer will give us startling facts as to the comparative circulation of the American and the English magazines, and if he be a Toronto newsdealer may add a significant word or two about the large sale in this city of the Buffalo *Sunday Express.*"

3. Cf. Masterman, *Condition of England*, on "the invincible patience of the English workman. He will endure almost anything—in silence—until it becomes unendurable" (16).

4. An elaborate way of saying that Chamberlain was hampered by remaining in the Cabinet while favouring a policy of his own. Between June and September, Chamberlain made no major speeches, in accordance with a Cabinet agreement to minimize internal differences. This paragraph does not appear in the American edition.

5. Lorne advocates economic, military and political Imperialism.

6. "kittle": "difficult to deal with, requiring great caution or skill; unsafe to meddle with" (O.E.D.).

7. For weeks, in May and June of 1903, *The Times* printed letters on The Motor Problem. On 9 June, one writer complained that "no one dare take his dog for a walk without running the great risk of seeing it reduced to a mess of blood and bones."

8. The success or failure of Chamberlain's initiative remained unclear for several months. Cf. the Toronto *Globe*'s comment on 9 June: "The safest generalization in the anomalous political situation is that the British people are preserving an open mind to the questions raised by Mr. Chamberlain ... the country awaits with cautious, sluggish conservatism full explanations from the shrewdest and cleverest of statesmen."

9. On Chamberlain's popularity, we have the word of his biographer (Amery, vol. V, p. 311): "Had the Press of those days run public opinion polls as they do today, there is little doubt that Chamberlain would have topped the poll."

10. An editorial on this subject appeared in *The Times* of 1 June 1903.

11. Cf. a June, 1903 speech by Chamberlain (Amery, *Chamberlain*, V, p. 267): "Is it the fact, as we are told on the high authority of Sir Henry Campbell-Bannerman [Liberal leader], is it the fact that 12,000,000 of our people, more than one fourth of our whole population, are always

on the verge of starvation? Is that a proof of the blessings of free imports?"

12. Supporters of free trade founded the Free Food League on 13 July 1903 (Amery, V, 304). "Free" food meant food imported into the country without tax. Chamberlain acknowledged that his plan would entail more expensive food; this admission weighed heavily against him.

13. Imperialists and others had been concerned about German competition for years. Fear of Russian expansion was a leading motive of British policy in India; the year after the novel was written, the British sent a military expedition to Tibet.

14. Cf. the commentary of Chamberlain's biographer (Amery, V, 356): "The Protectionist and Retaliationist parts of his programme, which to him were largely incidental, were what appealed most to his supporters. The Preferential part which he cared about most appealed to a limited section of opinion and aroused passionate resistance on the score of 'dear food.' "

CHAPTER XVIII

1. Cf. Reville, *History of the County of Brant*, p. 358: "During the period named, Mr. Paterson and his friends made the objection that two deliberate attempts had been made to knife him by means of the so-called gerrymander and the enfranchisement of the Indians."

The gerrymanders ("a method of arranging election districts so that the political party making the arrangement will be enabled to elect a greater number of representatives than they could on a fair system," [O.E.D.]) were attempted throughout Ontario in 1882 and 1892. For the enfranchisement of the Indians, see "The Writing of *The Imperialist.*"

2. Duncan refers to Macdonald's National Policy of erecting tariff barriers to foster Canadian industry. In an article written in 1896, entitled "Imperial Sentiment in Canada," Duncan had said that "the Conservatives' very being lay in the hands of the manufacturers." Interestingly, David G. Burley, in his analysis of 1878 voting patterns concludes that "the successful businessmen of Brantford found less of self-interest in tariff protection than did the economically marginal and those depending on wage labour," and so they voted Liberal (*A Particular Condition of Life* 232).

3. In *The Queen* serialization and the American edition, Duncan had written, more cynically, "yet the loyal card was always one of his trumps."

4. Cf. a speech by William Paterson, Liberal M.P. for South Brant, as reported by The *Expositor* (15 Nov. 1899): "They talked their loyalty to the old land; we acted it; that was the difference (Loud cheers)."

5. Conservative Prime Minister of England, 1868, 1874-80.

6. Dr. Cochrane was elected Moderator of the Presbyterian Church in 1882. The allusion to Grant (also mentioned in Chapter XXI) is sly, since R. N. Grant was Cochrane's biographer.

CHAPTER XIX

1. Duncan had defended the custom of afternoon tea against masculine attack in a column written for the Montreal *Star* (21 November 1887). A regular column Duncan wrote for *The Week* was entitled "Afternoon Tea."

2. Duncan's private joke: she had worked for the Washington *Post* in 1885-86.

CHAPTER XXI

1. Dr. Cochrane's sermons were published in this way.

2. Fenian raid: Irish-Americans attempting an invasion of Canada fought a Canadian militia contingent at Ridgway on 2 June 1866.

CHAPTER XXII

1. Two veteran Liberal politicians might have contributed to the character of Farquharson. William Paterson, M.P. for South Brant (1872-99) and North Brant (1900-11) was Minister of Customs in Laurier's government at the time the novel was written. A. S. Hardy, M.P.P. for South Brant (1873-99) was Ontario Premier from 1896 to 1899. Like Farquharson, he retired from politics because of ill health. Reville (363) says of Hardy that for many years he secured the votes of many of the Conservatives of the South Brant riding on personal grounds.

2. This penetrating observation, linking politics and religion as in Chapter VII, appears only in the English and Canadian editions.

3. The reference is to the Liberal initiative at the Colonial Conference of 1902 (see "The Writing of *The Imperialist* essay in this volume for a discussion of the political background of the novel). Chamberlain certainly felt that the Canadian Liberals should "follow up": he wrote Lord Minto, the Governor-General on 31 July 1903: "I am not by any means entirely satisfied with the action of the Canadian ministers. Seeing that, in all their conversations they pressed for the adoption of the policy I am now advocating, I certainly hoped for a warmer and a more indisputable welcome" (qtd Avery, V, 346).

4. Out of the need to find an alternative to Macdonald's "National Policy" of protection, the Liberals under their new leader Laurier adopted reciprocity with the United States as their policy in March 1888. It was to become party policy again: Laurier fought the 1911 election on a platform

of reciprocity with the United States.

5. Duncan puts in the Squire's mouth the theory about the Conservative party that she assigned to Lorne in Chapter XVIII (see note 2 to that chapter) and that she herself stated directly in her "Imperial Sentiment in Canada" newspaper article of 1896. The Squire's comment a few lines earlier that imperialism "won't come through" because of "the senior partner" is prophetic.

6. "Whigs": the name of the political party opposed to the Tories in eighteenth century England. In the nineteenth century, they became part of the Liberal party. The Whigs were also to be found in the United States, but "As a party it did not exist before 1834" (*Columbia Encyclopedia*). So the Squire may be getting his family history wrong, but essentially he is seeking a rationalization for his changed allegiance.

CHAPTER XXIII

1. "outré" (Fr.): "beyond the bounds of what is usual or considered correct and proper; unusual, eccentric, out-of-the-way; exaggerated" (O.E.D.).

2. "genius loci" (Latin): "the presiding deity or spirit" of the place; often used in the sense of "the body of associations connected with or inspirations that may be derived" from a place (O.E.D.).

CHAPTER XXIV

1. "vair: "A fur obtained from a variety of squirrel with grey back and white belly, much used in the 13th or 14th centuries as a trimming or lining for garments" (O.E.D.). Perhaps Finlay is rejecting the idea of a fur lining in any form.

2. In looking to Browning for spiritual comfort, Advena and Finlay were engaged in a fashionable pursuit. *The Imperialist* is contemporary with such works as *Browning as a Philosophical and Religious Thinker* (1902); *Guidance from Robert Browning in Matters of Faith* (1903); *Sermons from Browning* (1905).

CHAPTER XXV

1. Princess Louise (1848-1939), sixth child of Queen Victoria, was married to the Marquis of Lorne, after whom Lorne Murchison is said to be named. She was in Ottawa during some of his term as Governor-General (1878-83), but stayed away for long periods. Sandra Gwyn says that she "had inherited her mother's highly sexed nature" (184). Drawing-Room: a formal reception held by the monarch or (as in this case) her representative.

2. This rather cryptic paragraph is not present in *The Queen* serialization. Instead, after Dora asks "What?" the dialogue continues:

> "Never to come into your room without knocking."
>
> "Lorne Murchison! she exclaimed with outraged propriety, but perhaps more outrage than propriety. "And we aren't even engaged!"

3. "peart": "clever, intelligent, sharp" (O.E.D.).

4. Rudyard Kipling, "The English Flag."

5. Imperialists of every stripe were wont to disclaim interest in bargaining. Cf. a letter by Chamberlain (2 April 1903) to W.S. Fielding, the Canadian Minister of Finance:

> If we are to have an Empire at all in which our Colonies are to share, we must all be prepared to turn to make sacrifices to maintain it, and we must not look too closely into the proportion of charge as if it were merely a money bargain (Amery, V, 166).

Yet Chamberlain wrote Lord Minto, the Governor-General, with perhaps more candour: "The change will be carried, if at all, by mixed considerations of sentiment and interest" (Amery, V, 346).

CHAPTER XXVI

1. Richard Cobden and John Bright were founders of the Anti-Corn Law League (1839) and leaders of the Manchester School of economics. Their influence led to the adoption of Free Trade by Britain; their disparagement of the value of colonies also had a considerable effect on British policy (and an adverse effect on Canada).

2. Sir George Parkin, leading Canadian advocate of imperialism, and author of *Imperial Federation: the Problem of National Unity* (1892).

3. Goldwin Smith, an Oxford intellectual who lived in Toronto for many years. In *Canada and the Canadian Question* (1891), Smith argued that Canada should join the United States. He was the owner and editor of *The Week*, among other journals, and Duncan, who was a regular contributor to *The Week*, knew him personally.

4. "church people": i.e., Anglicans, who would not want to vote for a Presbyterian. Cf. the narrator's comments on denominational loyalties in Chapter VII.

CHAPTER XXVII

1. The Laurier government had given British imports a tariff reduction of twenty-five per cent in 1897, and increased the reduction to one-third in 1900.

2. Duncan appropriately leaves women out of her categories of

voters; women were not allowed to vote in federal elections until 1917 (selectively) or 1918 (universally). The omission of the workers of East Elgin is more puzzling; see the essay by Teresa Hubel in this volume on Duncan's view of the working class.

3. To oppose Imperial Preference in England, Winter would have to campaign as a Liberal.

4. "Dear" loaf in the sense of expensive—bread would cost more in England if a tariff were imposed on the rest of the world to give an advantage to Canadian grain. See note 12 to Chap. XVII.

5. The *Expositor* of 28 August 1903 proudly proclaimed: "Brantford's army of industrial workers is growing, and growing fast ... The merchants have participated in the general good of this growing time, and are busy as they never were before." For the reason Winter would have a "clear field" with the manufacturers, see note 4 to Chap. XXIX.

6. Edward Geoffrey, Baron Stanley was Colonial Secretary in the Conservative government of Robert Peel which, in 1843, won Parliamentary approval for the Canada Corn Act. This bill, accurately described by Duncan, was overturned by the Repeal of the Corn Laws (1846), with the disastrous consequences for Canada that Duncan indicates.

CHAPTER XXVIII

1. "brae": "the steep bank bounding a river valley" (O.E.D.).

2. S.N. Crockett was one of what was then called the "Kailyard School" of Scottish novelists. His *The Stickit Minister* (1893) is an imitation of J.M. Barrie's *The Little Minister* (1891). In her article "Canadian Cabbage, Canadian Rose," Elizabeth Waterston says that in *The Imperialist* Duncan "used the very essence of kailyard in her pungent reporting of speech patterns, social nuances and sectarian biases" (131).

3. "banns": "proclamation or public notice given in church of an intended marriage, in order that those who know of any impediment thereto may have opportunity of lodging objections" (O.E.D.). Anglicans still retain "that custom."

CHAPTER XXIX

1. An ironic allusion to Richard Cobden and the Manchester School.

2. Elie Halévy says (*Imperialism and the Rise of Labour* 357) that "at the end of 1903 the bye-elections were still so indecisive that it was possible to believe that the country was accepting the compromise arranged between the two leaders [Chamberlain and Balfour]. But with the opening of the New Year the rout began. Even the agricultural districts refused to accept Chamberlain's bait of higher prices for their pro-

duce." "Ballon d'essai" (Fr.): trial balloon.

3. Cf. a speech by the Hon. Mr. Tisdale (Conservative) in the House of Commons (*Expositor*, 12 Sept. 1903):

> They harness the city of Brantford up, because even the strong Liberal workers there are becoming a little uneasy about the trade question, and the people are becoming more inclined to give the Liberal candidate a hotter time than he has lately had. They are in fact, becoming suspicious that they may not be able to carry the seat.

The Liberals did lose South Brant in 1904, and in two out of the three subsequent elections (to W.F. Cockshutt).

4. In mid-August of 1903, Laurier addressed the Congress of Chambers of Commerce of the Empire in Montreal. He said:

> So far as Canada is concerned I may say to our friends from the Motherland that we are intensely desirous of having a preferential market for our food products in Great Britain, but we think the first step would better come from Britain than from ourselves, and we do not want to force our view on our brothers. If such an arrangement would not be satisfactory to them, for my part I do not want to have such an arrangement. (qtd Amery V, 349).

Horace Williams seems a more astute analyst of this speech than Lorne, though Lorne is right to point out the hostility with which manufacturers regarded Imperial preference. In private, Laurier told Lord Minto on August 31st that "when the time comes for action he will have the whole manufacturing interest of Canada opposed to him, and he considers it entirely unadvisable to make any move here at present until H.M. [His Majesty's] Government is in a position to make a concrete offer to Canada" (qtd. Amery V, 350). Willison had written Lord Minto on 14 July 1903: "Both parties here fear the manufacturers and properly so, for they have been the controlling factor in every election since 1878" (qtd. Amery V, 342).

5. "Tandem": "an arrangement of people or things one behind another" (O.E.D.). "Johnny François": name for French Canadians collectively. Imperialists sometimes resented, and, sometimes minimized, French Canadian opposition to their schemes. See Berger, *Sense of Power* 134-47.

6. Cf. *The Globe* (the Liberal "organ" in reality): "We have no idea of suggesting any course of action to the British people" (10 June 1903).

7. The Brantford opera house was the location chosen for large rallies. Cf. the *Expositor* account of the first rally of the 1896 campaign: "Before 8 o'clock not a single seat was visible in the house and already many were taking up positions in the rear of the building. A political team of the calibre of Messrs. Paterson and Hardy [see note 1 to Chap. XXII]

would be a drawing card anywhere, and under any circumstances. But at this time, when the sound of battle is in the air and all classes and conditions of men were talking politics their names are a perfect magnet" (*Expositor* 13 May 1896).

8. "Jehad": a religious war of Muslims against unbelievers.

9. "One of the fundamental features of Canadian imperialist social thought was an idealized conception of agriculture and a tendency to regard it as the most healthy foundation of national life." Berger, *Sense of Power* 177.

10. Cf. Stephen Leacock, "Greater Canada: An Appeal" (1907): "What say you, little puffing steam-fed industry of England, to the industry of Coming Canada. Think you, you can heave your coal hard enough, sweating and grunting with your shovel to keep pace with the snow-fed cataracts of the north?"

11. As Darlene Kelly has pointed out, "the fine burst of applause" of the first three versions of the text has been replaced by a "half-comprehending" burst of applause.

12. Lorne's vision is of an Imperial Parliament meeting in Ottawa.

13. Paardeburg: Site of a surrender by Boer troops, February 1900. "In the week-long battle of Paardeberg February 18-27, the Canadians performed well under fire .... A night attack on February 26 collapsed in confusion, with most Canadians racing back to their trenches, but a handful held their ground and at dawn they overlooked the Boer positions. By coincidence it was the very moment which Piet Cronje had already chosen to surrender. Journalists gave the Canadians the credit .... The notion that gallant colonials had avenged Britain's humiliation was irresistible to Imperial orators." Desmond Morton, *A Military History of Canada*, p. 116.

The reference to the Boer War does not appear in either *The Queen* serialization or the American edition.

14. Cf. the Toronto *Daily News*, 8 Oct. 1903:

> The Movement in the United States towards reciprocity with Canada deserves watching. New England for some time has favored the change. Now the Iowa Republicans are turning their eyes in that direction .... The movement for a relaxation of the tariff may become so strong as to induce the Republicans to adopt reciprocity with Canada as a chief feature of their policy.

15. Various Canadian governments made several unsuccessful attempts in the last quarter of the 19th century to negotiate a reciprocity treaty with the United States. Thirty years before the time of the novel, Macdonald made efforts to have a reciprocity provision included in the Treaty of Washington (1871) and George Brown, acting for the Mackenzie Liberal government, failed to obtain a reciprocity treaty in 1874.

16. On coins that have been "stamped." In the *The Queen* serialization, the next sentence begins, "Or is it to be the old stamp and character ..."—a very significant difference. Imperialists argued, as the final version implies, that a distinctive Canadian identity could be fostered by means of Imperial ties.

17. Imperialists favoured British immigration, and criticized the United States for welcoming others. Cf. Col. Denison, quoted in Berger, *Sense of Power* 164: "Since the revolution it has been the dumping ground of Europe, and they are forming a community there entirely different in its characteristics from ours."

18. The Canadian imperialist G.N. Grant looked to "a moral re-union of the English-speaking race" (qtd. Berger, *Sense of Power* 171) and Duncan's friend J.S. Willison told the Canadian Club of Boston in 1905 that "we shall stand together for the spread of Anglo-Saxon civilization" (qtd. Berger, *Sense of Power* 173).

19. The reference is to the Grand Trunk Pacific Railway, a project Lorne had mentioned more skeptically in his speech.

20. "as soft a snap": "an easy matter, business, project" (Partridge).

CHAPTER XXX

1. Cf. "Liberals, Forward," an editorial in the Brantford *Expositor* the day before the 1896 election: "The day of battle is at hand. The forces of coercion and corruption are in their last ditch. Tomorrow the bugle sounds for the fight. Let no Liberal be recreant in his duty."

2. The luggage presumably carried money for votes.

CHAPTER XXXI

1. For a discussion of the ways in which Duncan treated the Indian aspect of the election, see "The Writing of *The Imperialist.*"

2. Duncan shared with many of her contemporaries the view that Indians were doomed to extinction. She attended the unveiling of a statue to Joseph Brant (still to be found dominating Brantford's Victoria Park) and wrote: "One thought instinctively of the time which cannot be many centuries away, when these people shall have vanished as a dark, impotently-forbidding shadow on this continent." *The Week*, 21 Oct. 1886.

CHAPTER XXXII

1. This sentence, and the three preceding sentences, which clarify Advena's crucial change of heart, occur only in the English and Canadian editions.

2. This paragraph attributing a new resolution to Finlay, appears

only in the English and Canadian editions.

    3. There seems to be a discrepancy between the passage of time noted by Dr. Drummond and the suggestion, in Chap. XXVIII, that Advena paid her ill-advised visit to the Scottish ladies "the very first day after their arrival."

CHAPTER XXXIII

    1. In reality, the Toronto *Mail and Empire*.

Backgrounds and Contexts

Sara Jeannette Duncan's Letters
about *The Imperialist*

In recent years, several illuminating letters Duncan wrote about *The Imperialist* have been discovered. Most of them are addressed to John Willison, editor-in-chief of the Toronto *Globe* and subsequently managing director of the Toronto *News*. Duncan's other letters were written to R.W. Gilder, editor of the American *Century* magazine, to Lord Lansdowne, Governor-General of Canada (1883-88), Viceroy of India (1888-94) and Foreign Secretary in the governments of Salisbury and Balfour (1900-05), and to Archibald MacMechan, Professor of English Language and Literature at Dalhousie University (1889-1931).

The existence of Duncan's letters to Willison was first mentioned in print by Clara Thomas. I am very grateful to Marian Fowler for providing me with copies of this correspondence before she published the texts in her Duncan biography. The originals are in the Willison Papers, National Archives of Canada. Dr. Fowler discovered the MacMechan letter, which is in the MacMechan Papers, Dalhousie University. The letter to R.W. Gilder is in the Century Collection of the New York Public Library, and was drawn to my attention by Professor James Doyle of Wilfrid Laurier University. The letter to Lord Lansdowne is in a presentation copy of *The Imperialist*, now owned by the Toronto Public Library. The text of the letter was first given in Rae Goodwin's thesis, "The Early Journalism of Sara Jeannette Duncan" (University of Toronto M.A., 1964).

The complete texts of these letters follow, in chronological order. Their significance in terms of Duncan's composition of the novel is discussed in the "The Writing of *The Imperialist*" essay in the "Backgrounds" section of the volume.

Holcombe, Simla
Sept. 18th [1902]

Dear Mr. Willison,
    I have taken upon myself to write a Canadian novel, with a political *motif*, and I am rather anxious that none of you shall be

ashamed of it. I feel a little helpless so far from my material and I write to ask if you will very kindly send me a little. I want a week's issues of the *Globe* preferably numbers dealing editorially with the question of *Imperial federation*, and I want, if they are to be had in pamphlet form, all *Sir W. Laurier's speeches* on the subject, or any others that may be useful. It is asking a good deal of a busy man to look up this sort of thing, I know, but I trust to your interest in the result to excuse me. I am trying very hard to make it my best book, and the ground is practically unbroken. I have Holland's "Imperium et Libertas" which strikes me, admirable as it is, as a little like whipping a dead horse. If you know of anything more closely occupied with the practical intricacies of the question, will you send it to me, and I will pay up by return. Some Canadian must have published a view. I am sending per money order only one miserable dollar to pay for the papers etc but I should be only too glad to afford anything that would be helpful.

I wonder if you have seen "Those Delightful Americans." I have given up as hopeless any attempt to get my books on the market of my own country. They always seem to fall between the two stools of the London & New York publishers. However, I have had the luck lately to place stories with Scribner & The Century, and a couple of Burmese sketches with Harpers, so should not complain. I am going to England after the big Durbar in January—anybody coming out to represent the *Globe*? All press correspondents to be well taken care of by the hospitable Govt. of India. You ought to come. The *Times* is sending a man, also Daily Mail and Morning Post, and Reuter is to have 3,000 words a day!—and expect to be in Canada in June. It will be a pleasure to see you all again in Toronto.

> With kind regards
> & many apologies
> Yours very sincerely
> Sara Jeannette Cotes.

> Holcombe
> Simla
> Oct. 22nd [1902].

Dear Mr. Gilder,

Can you tell me if you are likely to use "The Pool in the Desert" by March? It is to form part of my next book which I want to bring out in the spring if possible, and an approximate date from you, if you can give it to me, would help me to arrange.

I would like to tell you about the serial I am at present at work upon—in confidence, please, as the matter and especially the title is in the air and I hold my breath over every batch of reviews. It will deal with Canadian life of the present (as typically colonial) in relation to Great Britain and the Imperial idea and from the point of view of a small manufacturing town—intimate—homely. To be called "The Imperialist" after the hero. To involve political and social relations with England, an ideal, broken of course, on the wheel of economic fact, a love interest, and to show, I hope, the real Imperial situation as it works out in colonial lives. It should have a keen interest for Americans as it traces the contrasting political fate involved in the parting of the ways in '76, and will be full of a sense of difference. Please let me know if it in any way appeals to you, and whether you would like a sketch of the plot & a look at the opening chapters. I could send you ten by the time I hear from you. It is untouched material and if I can only treat it as I imagine it, should work up well.

Yours sincerely,
Sara Jeannette Cotes

96 West St.
Brantford
Nov. 20th [1903]

Dear Mr. Willison,

Herewith by registered parcel *The Imperialist*. The proofs I send are in a rough state and want a lot of work, which I should like to give them before the story appears, if you care about having it. The law case especially wants attention, and the political situation. Please send me back the proofs as soon as you have looked them over, as they form my only complete set at present and I would like to work on them. The novel finishes in the *Queen* by the 1st of January and will be published as a book probably about the end of that month in England, though we could delay the Canadian edition if it suited you better. If you care to make a feature of it in The News I will accept whatever you think it is worth to the paper, as I should be particularly gratified to have the story identified with a journal based on the higher polity—for which by the way, I hope you will find it not unsuited. With these lofty sentiments and best wishes, and many thanks for your kindness in wanting to see the thing.

Believe me

Yours sincerely

Sara Jeannette Cotes.

96 West St.

Brantford

Nov. 24 [1903]

Dear Mr. Willison,

The very attractive looking pair of volumes that form your *Laurier* reached me this afternoon. They will travel across the Atlantic with me, and I expect to know a good deal more about Canadian Liberalism—and Laurier—when I arrive at Liverpool than I did when I left that port. Please accept my very best thanks. I will take the books to Simla and teach the wider Imperialism out of them there. I am glad my story commends itself to you. Please let me know when you intend to begin and tell them to post the paper to me while it is running. If proofs arrive in time from New York I will send them on to you, if not I suppose the copy you have must do. I send you herewith a few slips containing important and necessary corrections. The case in court, as it appeared in the *Queen* is laughable. Please be sure to get these slips substituted for the corresponding matter you have in hand. I hope you found Chap. XXVII later. I am almost certain I sent a complete set. If it is still missing let me know and I will see that you get it in good time. If you publish a chapter a day you will finish about coterminously with the *Queen* which would be desirable. It appears that I am again to visit Toronto at the benevolent bidding of the Authors' Society—when I come we will meet.

With kind regards

Yours very sincerely

Sara Jeannette Cotes.

96 West St
Brantford
Dec. 20th [1903]

Dear Mr. Willison,

I was so sorry not to have a spare minute as I rushed through Toronto last week to say a final goodbye in. It would be difficult however, in view of my constant conversations with you in the News, which now by the way arrives in the mornings. Well, fight the good fight—there is nobody but you. What Foster said was true you know, about those silent ministers. I saw Sir Wilfrid. He paid me the honour of a visit. He may be a politician and Frenchman, but he is a nice thing.

I am off on Xmas Day. May I have my cheque from the News in time to cash?

It is quite abominable to have to go. Is it any wonder that my sentiments are Imperial, with a husband in India, and a family in Canada and everybody else in England!

Remember me cordially please to Mrs. Willison
and believe me
Always yours sincerely
Sara Jeannette Cotes.

The Ladies' Empire Club
69, Grosvenor Street.W.
[Feb. 24, 1904]

Dear Mr. Willison,

Your most kind letter has just reached me. I am sorry to say that it is too late now for any alterations in the first edition, which should be on the book-stalls in a few days; but I shall gladly keep your hints for a reference, and if there is an opportunity later will see to the ballot announcement mistake. The Indian anachronism I considered upon, but it is only a matter of a few years, and I was in the difficulty of either having to sacrifice the whole Imperial situation—as it is now—or my "Indian interest" neither of which I could make up my mind to do. So I left it. If you like to make a little note of this explanation and publish it when the book appears, it would discount criticism of that point perhaps, and I hope the reviewers won't be as well up as you are in practical politics! I am *very* glad you like the story. I now think of a novel bringing Lorne Murchison over here and giving the critical colonial view of London society, marrying him eventually. Would you like to have it for the News? I propose to do it this coming summer. Dear old Jimmy Johnson lunched with me here yesterday, and Baroness Macdonald joined us afterward. It was quite an Ottawa reunion. I wish you could have made another. I am off to Holcombe, Simla, on the 17th of next month. My husband has not yet proceeded against me for desertion but I don't know what he may have in mind. By the way I particularly want you to read his article on "The situation in the Persian Gulf" in the Contemporary probably for April. Don't forget.

Always cordially yours

S.J.Cotes

The Ladies' Empire Club

69 Grosvenor Street.W

Jan. 8th [1905]

Dear Lord Lansdowne,

I wonder if I may count upon your affection for Canada and the kind interest you expressed in the beginnings of my literary work there, far enough to send you my Canadian novel *The Imperialist*? The book was published a few months ago, but I was in India at the time, and felt too far out upon the periphery of the Empire to take a very active share in its distribution from the centre. It seemed to me that among the assumptions and disputes over here as to what the "colonial view" really is, it might be worth while to present the situation as it appears to the average Canadian of the average small town, inarticulate except at election times, but whose view in the end counts for more than that of those pictorial people whose speeches at Toronto banquets go so far to over-colour the British imagination about Canadian sentiment. I thought it might be useful to bring this practical person forward and let him be seen. I hope I have not made him too prominent, but he is there.

My book offers only a picture of life and opinion, and attempts no argument. I have on this account the better courage in sending it. I should be very happy indeed if it might claim some stray half hour of your leisure time.

and I am

dear Lord Lansdowne

Yours sincerely

Sara Jeannette Cotes

Red Roof
Simla S.W.
May 4th, [1905]

Dear Dr. MacMechan,

   Your two most kind letters and the delightful article in the Halifax Herald have at last found me here. I hope, if it has occurred to you to wonder at my tardy acknowledgement of them, that you have remembered how near I live to the Roof of the World, to which the mails climb slowly. I need not say that I have taken the greatest pleasure in your generous expression of liking for *The Imperialist*. I confess I *had* wondered, a little here on my remote hill top, whether anybody had listened to me in Canada and had come rather to the conclusion that I had been too far away to be well heard, or perhaps I had forgotten my country's note. But that anyone should write like this reassures me quite, and that you alone should feel the book as you do justifies me very happily in having written it. I share with you the conviction of the individuality of the Canadian type. The spirit of place always seems to me strong in the land. I want to come back and work at it from closer range, and soon I think this will be possible. I am especially curious about your Eastern past. My mother is a New Brunswicker—Shediac and all that country has the charm for me of nursery description. I am sure it is as different from Ontario as Massachusetts is from Illinois. We feel that we have been almost long enough in India and I hope to sail through the "Ditch" for the last time, westward bound, in November, and be in Canada next summer. The Empire is a big place and interesting everywhere, but ours is by far the best part of it, and the most full of the future. I rejoice that you enjoyed Dr. Drummond. The dear original was Dr. Wm. Cochrane of Brantford who christened most of the Presbyterians now there. He has been dead these five or six years—or I would never have dared!

Please accept my best and warmest thanks
and believe me
Yours very sincerely
Sara Jeannette Cotes

The College Magazine has not reached me. If you have another copy might I receive it direct? I should like so much to keep it.
S.J.C.

Reviews

The reviews of *The Imperialist* are discussed on pp. 470-72 and 477 of this edition.

"The attitude of the ladies of Elgin toward the town, the world, and the proprieties is a thing which the reader can feel fairly bristling from the pages which have to deal with them."

Mrs. Cotes's new book, which is certainly clever, gives the effect of a sort of Canadian "Cranford," [novel by the British writer Mrs. Gaskell—Ed.] with projections into the field of English imperial politics. The picture of society in the small Canadian town of Elgin, and in the still narrower field of the Knox Presbyterian Church of that town, is not presented at large, rather in bits and suggestions, but it is presented effectively none the less. The attitude of the ladies of Elgin toward the town, the world, and the proprieties is a thing which the reader can feel fairly bristling from the pages which have to deal with them. Mrs. Cotes, who is Canadian herself, has a humorous eye for provincial marks, and a pleasing fashion of comment on the side ....

As for the other side of the book, that which relates to politics, one is eager to suspect that it is designed to be an elaborate satire on the Imperial Zollverein and all that. Yet one cannot be sure how much real enthusiasm for the English imperial idea is hidden in the appearance of satire. One cannot quite be sure even that Mrs. Cotes herself knows at times whether she is preaching Mr. Joseph Chamberlain's doctrine, or laughing at it.

It is evident anyhow that Mrs. Cotes has the knack of characterization .... she draws better women and parsons than she does men.

Barring the politics, which is interesting, but only so-so, as might be expected, it is a story very far above the average of stories—perhaps the most worthwhile which has come out here in some time.

New York *Times*, 5 March 1904

" ... the material is much too good to be used as a vehicle for a fiscal sermon"

... The Imperialist himself at the first introduction seemed an adequate crusader and of the right quality; no Union Jackass, blunt and heavy, but a good example of the Canadian—"straight," after the favourite Canadian superlative of praise, and simple. But he proved no Lothair [hero of a novel by Disraeli—Ed.], capable of carrying a great political or religious theme; and even Mr. Chamberlain would hardly wish Mrs. Cotes to quash her habile capacity for the small humours of life under a load of political essay-writing. Politics are not merely an atmosphere, an environment, an accident of life. A particular Bill, and nothing but the Bill, is discussed, and it would be unfair to review the work except as a preferential pamphlet. It is not a bad pamphlet; but one may hope that the moral, which is made very distinct, is not true—that patriotism is not yet enough advanced in England or Canada to carry through an imperial scheme. Even the young lady is symbolic, and throws over the Imperialist at the very moment when his party does the same. Until the Imperialism dominated it, the theme promised well. The setting demands a good romance. Those good Scotch settlers, many of them staunch Presbyterians, who form so large a part of some of the townships in Ontario, and the U.E. Loyalists, still very "stark to traitors" to the imperial sentiment; the busy jealousy of the United States and the strengthened pride in the superiority of Canadian liberty; the keenness, even the corruption, of the elections are new and good material ready to the hand of any novelist of knowledge. Certainly the material is much too good to be used as a vehicle for a fiscal sermon, and to be left behind as soon as the hero is well set on his hobby-horse ....

Times Literary Supplement, 22 April 1904

The average reader about half-way through *The Imperialist* will experience all the indignant feelings of the child who finds a powder concealed in a proffered spoonful of jam. Under the disguise of an innocent and lively modern novel, Mrs. Cotes has actually had the perfidy to entice her readers into perusing a fiscal pamphlet. Pages of what is called "the Imperial argument" for the widest development of Mr. Chamberlain's scheme will be found in her story; and the weary political economist who has taken it up for a little rest and oblivion from the problem which is constantly in his mind will find himself most treacherously betrayed. The book gives otherwise an interesting picture of life in modern Canada, though Mrs. Cotes is rather a long time getting her story under way. For about the first hundred pages the reader feels that each new chapter breaks fresh ground, and the result is a little fatiguing. But until the fiscal chapters are reached Mrs. Cotes's charm of writing triumphs over the rather wearisome nature of her materials, and the reader is upheld by the hope of better things later in the book. How that hope is belied has been indicated above.

The Spectator, 23 April 1904

Mrs. Everard Cotes has departed from her familiar fields and given, in the study of a Canadian town, a ponderous political novel. Elgin is pictured in its prosaic life with realistic fidelity, but neither strength of characterization nor the story of four lovers can save the book from dullness. With discussions of imperial federation and pre-ferential tariffs, "The Imperialist" is as dreary reading as the campaign documents of a contested election.

The Academy, 23 April 1904

Adopting the principle of Mark Twain's famous tonic with a broad whisky basis, Mrs. Everard Cotes (Sara Jeannette Duncan) gives her readers a somewhat strong dose of Imperialism rendered palatable by a sweetening admixture of romance. The result, however, does not strike us as particularly satisfactory. Political novels are not, as a rule, a success, even when the acknowledged masters of fiction have attempted them, and Mrs. Cotes's essay in the same field is not one of those brilliant exceptions that disprove the rule. The bulk of novel-readers will resent the introduction of Preferential tariffs and Imperialist theories, and the serious student of politics will regard the very commonplace love stories of some very commonplace persons in a remote Canadian townlet as an unworthy setting for a topic involving such grave and far-reaching issues....

The London *Daily Telegraph*, 4 May 1904

" *...can so much jealousy and ill-will exist where nothing but good-humor and toleration are returned?* "

Mrs. Everard Cotes's new story, "The Imperialist," concerns itself with the growing sense of a united British Empire, in the Young Canadian party. According to her, they see a great menace in the commercial inroads of the United States, and attribute to us a more far-sighted and crafty policy towards our neighbor than many of our citizens are themselves conscious of. It is a pity for her clever and forceful book that Mrs. Cotes permits herself such arguments as these: "And this republic, that menaces our national life with commercial extinction, what past has she that is comparable. The daughter who left the old stock to be the light woman among nations ..."

It would be interesting to those who have any curiosity at all on the subject, to know if these are the sentiments of Canadians toward us; can so much jealousy and ill-will exist where nothing but good-humor and toleration are returned? And a disparaging comparison of our past with that of Canada is so novel a point of view that it is only interesting to find that any one can hold it.

However, this is not the great issue of the book, which is the idea of union in the British Empire. The book is closely and skilfully written, and contains 476 pages. Details are dwelt upon with the minuteness of Tolstoi or George Eliot, and without perhaps the "portrait-eating, portrait-painting eyes" that light up the details of either of these geniuses. The love story, or love stories, for there are two, are full of humor and of human nature.

The Critic (New York), May 1904

" ...*much enlightenment as to political economy, but no illumination of romance*"

The author, whose experiments in literary methods are as startling as clever, gave us in her last volume of Indian stories, psychological subtleties worthy of Henry James himself, and now confronts us with a neighbourhood chronicle of homely realism, which recalls the later work of Howells. "The Imperialist" is a study of a small Canadian town, Elgin, and gives us the Murchison household in outdoor activities, in indoor domesticities, in "Knox Church" connections, in social relations, and in politics. There is comfortable middle-class prosperity in Elgin, the record of which makes very dull reading ....There are studies of phases of opinion in England and the colony, debates, discussions, and campaign speeches—much enlightenment as to political economy, but no illumination of romance.... The only happy human interest in the book is the love of the erratic Advena Murchison for Hugh Finlay, the Mission preacher. The coming out of his Scotch betrothed, a sensible spinster, and Dr. Drummond's appropriation of the superfluous lady, is a delightful bit of comedy amid the arid wastes of leading articles and electioneering pamphlets.

The Outlook, 4 June 1904.

"*One of the prettiest, most humorous and touching things that have been written for our own country*"

... Nowhere else but in Canada can the book be entirely understood; and anyone who goes without reading it will miss a part of present Canadian life which in its own way is as useful as it is inspiring. Few political novels have been as much in earnest, or as generous and enthusiastic as "The Imperialist."

Putting the question of Canadian love for English principles and the fiscal problem—which is a great part of "The Imperialist"—to one side, there is still much left in the book to be considered only as imaginative writing. There are many Canadians, of course, who will feel that they have not been brought up precisely in the same way as the Murchisons. But how charming to everyone are the early chapters, written with the unhasting geniality of one who remembers very well. The Queen's Birthday—the Twenty-fourth of May—in Elgin is one of the prettiest, most humorous and touching things that have been written for our own country. For Mr. and Mrs. Murchison—Lorne's father and mother—Mrs. Cotes has not before ever done quite such good work as this. If she will consent to write another Canadian novel, and has the opportunity to make it purely a domestic one, her audience will be fortunate. The enthusiasm and intensity of "The Imperialist," however, comes from the development of the problem in its name; and there can be little doubt that her countrymen will be the better Canadians for having known Lorne Murchison. Advena is another variation of the same elevated type, a very admirable and lovable one. Lorne's lady-love, who adores England after her own fashion, is a type too; and indeed, most of the characters in "The Imperialist" can stand for representatives of real people, individuals, or by classes. It is a book, after all, to be read and not analyzed, since those who know best whether it is a true presentation cannot have at the same time the advantage of an outsider's point of view.

Toronto *Daily News*, 4 June 1904

"We owe a debt to Mrs. Everard Cotes, who has told our story"

It cannot be said that Mrs. Everard Cotes has been without honor among her own people. Her "Globe" articles, signed "Garth Grafton," excited general interest, and when, as Sara Jeannette Duncan, she gave us "A Social Departure," Canadians felt proud of "a Brantford girl" who had written a book. Since those days she has travelled far, has seen many parts of the Empire, and now regards India as her home. But she will probably be known to the end of the chapter among her Canadian friends as a Brantford girl, and no doubt will be content with the description, since she has not forgotten her Ontario home, and Brantford is no mean city.

.... Bound in bright red, with the Canadian coat-of-arms patriotically adorning the cover, "The Imperialist," with its 472 pages of comfortable, large type, is not a book to be taken in hand lightly or undiscerningly. The English critic or the United States reviewer may say what he likes about the book, but we know, before we have finished the first chapter, that it is the very life of our people. It is not "about" or "concerning" us, but here is an Ontario town, with its every-day trials and triumphs, its local ambitions, and its national significance. Elgin, the town described, is said to be Brantford, but it might be Guelph or Stratford or Goderich. We all know the Murchisons, the family circle into which Mrs. Cotes so warmly welcomes us; in fact, I know I have had tea at the Murchisons where "the chicken salad gleamed at one end of the table and the scalloped oysters smoked delicious at the other. Lorne had charge of the cold tongue and Advena was entrusted with the pickled pears."

"The Imperialist" is not a book to be read in a hammock on a summer afternoon, for it is to be taken seriously, although the charge of dullness may not for a moment be preferred against it. The first chapter introduces us to the town of Elgin and the Murchison household on the twenty-fourth of May, and there isn't a "grown-up" in the Province of Ontario whose heart will not recognize the scene.

.... The place of Canada in the British fabric puzzles both English and United States visitors when, from season to season, they condescendingly drop in upon us and make remarks concerning our climate and our politics. Mrs. Cotes has most clearly and even humorously set forth our sentiments without distracting from the individual interests in the novel. The title leads one to expect a political atmosphere, but how could a novel of Ontario affairs be written without hauling in politics? We are a people given to such mild dissipation as is occasioned by a provincial election or a party picnic, and Elgin is not behind the rest of the country in its political ardor.

.... "The Imperialist," although rather long and somewhat given to politics, is a thoroughly readable and stimulating book. It is photographic in its fidelity to local conditions and types, while its subtle humor and literary finish set it far above the average novel. Anyone may read it with interest and satisfaction. But to the Canadian, to the Ontarian especially, it means more than any other Canadian story, for it gives with truth and with art a depiction of our own community as it appears in the "pattern and the colors" [a quotation from the last sentence of the novel—Ed.] of the Empire. There is much that is trivial, much that is amusing, and a great deal to be proud of in the Elgins of Ontario—and as Canadians and Imperialists, in the best sense of that abused word, we owe a debt to Mrs. Everard Cotes, who has told our story.

"J.G.," *Saturday Night*, 4 June 1904

"That half of the population which is disenfranchised takes but little interest in politics"

A story with contemporary Canadian life for its materials by Mrs. Everard Cotes is something in which the Canadian reader will undisguisedly be interested. It was natural, therefore, to turn to "The Imperialist" with high expectations which in most cases, it may be surmised, will be unrealized. Mrs. Cotes has won recognition in more than one branch of literature, but she has essayed in this book one of the hardest tasks a novelist could undertake. The genius of Jane Austen is manifested in her power to reflect for us in the pages of a book, as in a mirror, the very essence and spirit of the life by which she was surrounded. The judgment of her contemporaries was that she effected this feat with wonderful fidelity and verisimilitude. Nothing short of genius could have acquitted itself so perfectly. Mrs. Cotes has set herself the same elusive task; and it is sound praise to say that there are glimpses here and there of a high range of accomplishment. The possibility of success is unquestionably lessened, however, by the attempt to weave a political theme into the simplicity and common-places of the ordinary life of a country town. That half of the popu-lation which is disenfranchised takes but little interest in politics, and it is a rule to which there are few exceptions that even when our sis-ters and wives make a conscious effort to compass the mystery their success is but partial. That is about all that could be said of the poli-tical passages of *The Imperialist.*

Toronto *Globe*, 13 August 1904

"Perhaps the book was too true"

... She has written only one story which deals with Canadian life, *The Imperialist* (1904), which first ran in *The Globe* [actually the Toronto *Daily News*—Ed.] as a serial; but that story stands out from the vast desert of well-intentioned mediocrity known as Canadian fiction. Its distinction lies in its choice of theme and its truth of obser-vation. It does not deal with the romantic periods of our history, nor of the Acadian French, nor of the adventurous west, but of plain, *bourgeois*, money-getting Ontario and the humdrum activities of a little town which grows slowly in wealth and population, and in which the greatest excitements are a tea-meeting or a Dominion election. The characters are all carefully drawn. The Murchisons are a typical "com-mon Canadian" family. Hesketh, the patronizing "Englishman in

Canada" is not a caricature. In the English-speaking parts of Canada there is a real homogeneity, no matter how widely they are scattered; and the types of *The Imperialist* are to be found both east and west. True as the novel is, it was not a popular success. The appearance in *The Globe* of a tale preaching that salvation for the Empire could only come by Joseph Chamberlain was something of a joke; and perhaps Mrs. Cotes had been too long out of Canada. Perhaps the book was too true.

Archibald MacMechan,
Headwaters of Canadian Literature (1924)

Canadian Imperialism and Why It Failed*

Carl Berger

.... This sense of Canadian nationalism and the commitment to conservatism which shaped it was the essence of Canadian imperialism as these men [G.M. Grant and George Parkin] understood it. Tariff preferences, improved communications, and defence agreements were its instruments and servants, not its substance.

When Canadian imperialism is defined in this way, the limitations of its appeal are obvious and its failure almost self-explanatory. It demanded too much of human nature and its conception of national interest was too far out of reach. The imperialists' antipathy to business and their conviction that moral ideals and values must transcend material considerations certainly placed them in opposition to some of the most powerful forces in the Canada of their time. When Denison campaigned against unrestricted reciprocity with the United States he was not primarily interested in safeguarding Canadian industries. He thought that commercial policy undesirable because he felt that any arrangements with the United States would only complicate and possibly delay the coming of intra-imperial free trade. Ironically, he inadvertently worked to protect the very interests which made the realization of imperial unity impossible. Canadian business enterprise was no more willing to remove tariff protection against British manufacturers than against American ones. G.M. Grant realized that Canadian manufacturers were "the most formidable opponents" of imperial free trade: they have, he truly stated, "no intention of sharing their home market, with their British competitors."[1]

Critics of imperial preference correctly saw that it would stultify Canadian industrial growth and prevent a diversification of her economy. "A country would not be great which has only one large rural district, and whose inhabitants were cut off from great intellectual centres," said Adam Shortt in 1903. "Therefore, we could not meet the request that we should curtail our normal development and devote ourselves to supplying food or other raw materials and limit our manufacturing to primary industries" (Shortt 20). While there is little reason to doubt that Denison welcomed the very prospect that Shortt feared, other imperialists who did not go this far still justified imperial unity by arguments that recognized economic considerations but did not accord priority to them. In a course of extension lectures delivered at Ottawa in 1906, Leacock stressed the "claim of Imperial Unity over purely commercial considerations" (Leacock n.p.), and in 1911 Parkin contemptuously repudiated "the idea that any mere trade relation is going to change our national feeling."[2] They made extensive use of economic arguments but were not themselves driven by economic motives.

However much this emphasis testified to their rectitude, it did little to broaden the support for their cause. In a review of Parkin's *Imperial Federation*, a Winnipeg paper judged that imperialism "is simply an appeal to sacrifice practical advantages in order to gratify a sentiment which does not exist except in the case of a few individuals here and there."[3] A press report described those attending a meeting sponsored by the Imperial Federation League as composed mainly of members of the "comfortable, prosperous classes," as distinct from those "to whom life is an arena of perpetual struggle and toil for the where-withal to supply the daily wants, and who may therefore be pardoned if they are disposed to take a more intensely practical view of such questions ..."[4] And in Miss Duncan's novel, when Lorne is rejected by his party he is told: "You didn't get rid of that save- the-Empire-or-die scheme of yours soon enough. People got to think you meant something by it." Word got about that "you would not hesitate to put Canada to some material loss, or at least to postpone her development in various important directions, for the sake of the imperial connection."

The very nature of the imperialist ideology ensured that those who accepted it as totally and as seriously as did G.M. Grant and Parkin would always remain a very small number. Many invoked the slogans of imperial unity, but for few did these have such an intense personal meaning. A determined mental effort was required to grasp the inter-relationships and see the geographical reality of the Empire as Parkin did. "I sometimes think that only those who have seen can understand," he admitted, "but to see one must sail on every ocean and traverse every continent."[5] Their European education and world travels made Parkin, Grant and Macphail very exceptional Canadians and it was with some justice that John Ewart asked, "How can Canadians love the British Empire which they have not seen, when they do not love their own country which they have seen?" (Ewart 17).

Endnotes

1 Sir J.S. Willison Papers, Grant to Willison 9 April 1896; G.M. Grant, "Current Events," *Queens Quarterly* 3 (1895): 156.
2 G.M. Wrong Papers, Fisher Library, University of Toronto, Parkin to Wrong, 10 March 1911.
3 Sir George R. Parkin Papers, National Archives of Canada, vol. 80, clipping from the Winnipeg *Tribune*, 12 Nov. 1892.
4 Parkin Papers, vol. 83, clipping from *The Week*, n.d.
5 Parkin Papers, vol. 69, ms. "The Church in the Empire," n.d.

* Source: Carl Berger, *The Sense of Power: Studies in the Ideas of Canadian Imperialism 1867-1914*. Toronto: U of Toronto P, 1970. 262-64. Reprinted by kind permission of the University of Toronto Press.

Canada's Most Articulate Advocate of Realism in Fiction*

Carole Gerson

.... Duncan's occasional liberties and disagreements with the masters of American realism merely enhanced her frequent iterations of their principles. She did her best to cultivate their personal acquaintance, from her 1886 interview with Howells' boots[1] to her request for Henry James's opinion of *His Honour and a Lady* (1896).[2] Throughout her brief career as a Canadian literary journalist she referred to the work of James and Howells whenever she applauded the way in which "Fiction seems determined to broaden its scope in all directions" ("Saunterings," *The Week* 2 August 1888). And she usually gave short shrift to writing shaped by "the old fashioned method in fiction by which the heroine was brought safely and comfortably out of her woes and the reader was left in the agreeable certainty that only the unnecessary people had died, the evil disposed fallen into their own pit, and the truly deserving married and lived happily ever afterward." Duncan endorsed the advancements being made in progressive literary circles, where "modern tendencies in fiction" were fast gaining hold: "The idea seems to be gaining ground that life should be represented as it is and not as we should like it to be, regardless of probabilities. And in life as it is the traditions of the novelist are very often reversed. There is always consolation for the disconsolate, though, on the top shelves of the circulating libraries and in the old numbers of *The Young Ladies' Journal* and similar publications" ("Bric A Brac," Montreal *Daily Star* 17 Jan. 1888).

Herself eminently a New Woman (albeit not a suffragette), Duncan acclaimed the modern heroine as one of the major achievements of the new realism:

> The woman of to-day is no longer an exceptional being surrounded by exceptional circumstances. She bears a translatable relation to the world; and the novelists who translate it correctly have ceased to mark it by unduly exalting one woman by virtue of her sex to a position of interest in their books which dwarfs all the other characters ... The woman of today understands herself, and is understood in her present and possible worth. The novel of today is a reflection of our present social state. The women who enter into its composition are but intelligent agents in this reflection, and show themselves as they are, not as a false ideal would have them. ("Saunterings," *The Week* 28 Oct. 1886)

Nonetheless she applied clear boundaries to acceptable subjects for literature, conceding that "The modern school of fiction, if it is fairly subject to reproach, may bear the blame of dealing too exclusively in the corporealities of human life, to the utter and scornful neglect of its idealities" (*The Week* 15 July 1886). Duncan's sense of propriety emerged again in her 1887 defence of female hack novelists. Bad novels were produced by men just as often as by women, she declared, and women, at least, "have no part in contributing the depraved element of fiction which drags the average down. The work of women in fiction does not increase the statistics of crime. In being denied such contact with the world as might serve to make their books stronger and more realistic they are also deprived of the temptation of making them the dangerous social force that cheap sensational literature represents" ("Bric A Brac," Montreal *Daily Star* 31 Dec. 1887).

In a *Globe* column ostensibly describing the literary tastes of women in general, Duncan defined the qualified realism she favoured: "The ordinary detail of humdrum life and circumstance, pen-painted by an artist with sympathies keen enough to detect the mysterious throbbing of the life that is inner and under, fascinates us like our own photographs. As a rule we dislike strong situation, and sanguinary scenes are the exception in recent novels of the better class. Coarseness we cannot tolerate, even with that saving sauce in the eyes of men—humour" ("Other People and I," Toronto *Globe* 17 June 1885).

Her own preferences thus clearly articulated, Duncan understood that the major achievement of the realistic school was not to change the novel so much as to expand it: "The novel of to-day may be written to show the cumulative action of a passion, to work out an ethical problem of everyday occurrence, to give body and form to a sensation of the finest or of the coarsest kind, for almost any reason which can be shown to have a connection with the course of human life, and development of human character ... Fiction has become a law unto itself, and its field has broadened with the assumption" ("Outworn Literary Methods," *The Week* 9 June 1887). The flexibility implied by this acknowledgment of the breadth of the genre was borne out by her glowing, almost sentimental appreciation of *A Christmas Carol* (*The Week* 23 Dec. 1886), her report of Tennyson's admiration of Kirby's *The Golden Dog* with minimal irony (*The Week* 3 Feb. 1887), and her occasional scepticism regarding proponents of realism who autocratically "announce to their scribbling emulators the only proper and acceptable form of the modern novel, announce it imperiously, and note departures from it with wrath" ("Saunterings," *The Week* 13 Jan. 1887).

.... It is not surprising that Canada's most articulate advocate of realism in fiction should also prove its most accomplished practitioner. Duncan's version of reality is, of course, carefully laundered, a celebration of Elgin's strengths as much as an inventory of its limitations. Elgin is untroubled by labour unrest, significant poverty, or serious sexual scandal. What the novel best represents is a marriage of form and content almost unique in Canadian fiction until the modern era. The gentle irony of its narrative voice matches its dissection of small town values and manners, and the plot and characters complement each other with minimal external intervention.

Endnotes

1 "W.D. Howells at Washington," *The Week*, 22 April 1886. The chief evidence of continuing personal contact between the two writers is a letter from Duncan to Howells held by the Houghton Library and reprinted by Thomas Tausky, *Journal of Canadian Fiction* 13 (1975), 148.

2 Evidence of this interchange is James' reply, dated 26 Jan. 1900, in Leon Edel, ed. *Henry James Letters* 4 (Cambridge: Harvard UP, 1984): 131-32.

* Source: Carole Gerson, *A Purer Taste: The Writing and Reading of Fiction in English in Nineteenth Century Canada.* Toronto: U of Toronto P, 1989. 59-61; 150-51 (final paragraph). Reprinted by kind permission of the University of Toronto Press.

The Writing of *The Imperialist*

Thomas E. Tausky

In September, 1902, Sara Jeannette Duncan, of Holcombe, Simla, India was three months short of her forty-first birthday. Having been a pioneering woman journalist in Canada, she now was a novelist with twelve books to her credit. All of her work had been published by major English and American firms, and most of it had been highly praised. She lived in a charming home in which, a later owner was to say, "the drawing-room is like a room in some old country house" (Macleod 322). After several years in the appalling climate of cholera-ridden Calcutta, she had escaped to Simla, a small community largely peopled by bureaucrats (it was the summer capital of British India) with a dazzling setting in the Himalayas. She had ample opportunity to write, since the army of servants a well-to-do memsahib could afford did all the menial tasks. She had a kindly husband, a journalist with whom she shared an interest in politics.

So much for the pleasant aspects of her existence. There was also a dark side. The turn of the century had brought a serious case of tuberculosis and a child who died a few days after birth (Fowler 239). There are indications that her marriage suffered from the union of opposed temperaments. It is evident from her fiction that Duncan was not comfortable in the Philistine world of Indian officialdom. She was a world away from her family and home town of Brantford, Ontario.

None of Duncan's previous books had taken her Canadian experience as its central subject. India was close at hand, and of greater interest to English readers. Nevertheless, Canada was not absent from her thoughts. In *On the Other Side of the Latch* (1901), an account of a summer spent in Simla battling her tuberculosis, she looks back nostalgically to her most recent glimpse of Brantford:

> As we went along the country roads I saw again, in the light of a long absence, the quiet of the fields and the broad pebbled stretches of the river, and the bronze and purple of the untrimmed woods that had always been for me the margin of the thought of home.

On 18 September 1902, Duncan wrote to John Willison, a man she had first met when they were both Parliamentary correspondents in Ottawa, fifteen years before (Fowler 129). Willison by now was editor of the Toronto *Globe*, and soon was to become managing director of the Toronto *News*. To him, Duncan confided her new ambition:

> I have taken upon myself to write a Canadian novel, with a
> political *motif,* and I am rather anxious that none of you shall
> be ashamed of it .... I am trying very hard to make it my best
> book.

In this very early statement, Duncan unites two of the central
elements of her novel in the making. It became a Canadian novel,
not just because it was set in Canada, but also because it sought,
with brilliant success, to capture the flavour of life in a representative Canadian community. In asking Willison for a week's copies
of the *Globe,* and for Laurier's speeches (the full text of the letter
is given elsewhere in this volume), Duncan gives an indication of
the extent to which she intended to base her novel on the leading
political issue of the moment. Imperialism, in its then current
meaning, was the movement advocating closer ties—economic,
military or political—within the Empire. Economic imperialism
(efforts to abolish or reduce tariff barriers previously erected by
countries of the Empire against one another, and to form a common economic front against the rest of the world) was the most
pragmatic and least radical of the three broad forms of imperialism. Canada furthered the cause of economic imperialism by
making tariff concessions to England in 1897 and 1900.

Just before Duncan wrote to Willison, Canada took another
initiative in imperial politics. At the Colonial Conference held in
the summer of 1902, Canada offered to extend the tariff preference
already granted to England, in exchange for an exemption from
English duties on grain. Though the Canadian Prime Minister,
Laurier, at the same time flatly rejected proposals for closer military cooperation made by Joseph Chamberlain, the British Colonial Secretary, it was widely reported that Canada had again taken
the lead in furthering imperialism.

The timing of Duncan's letter makes one suspect that the
Canadian move had much to do with her decision to undertake her
new novel. She might well have been proud of Brantford's role at
the Conference: an important member of the Canadian delegation
was William Paterson, the Minister of Customs and veteran member for South Brant and then North Brant.

It is tempting to believe that some of the seeds that ultimately
led to the writing of *The Imperialist* were first planted in Duncan's

imagination several years before, as a result of political events that occurred in 1896.

In the spring of that year, an election campaign was fought in Canada, resulting on June 23rd in the defeat of a Conservative government for the first time in nearly twenty years, and in the formation of a Liberal government headed by Wilfrid Laurier. In the riding of South Brant, however, William Paterson, who had held the seat for the Liberals in every election since 1872 was not so lucky; he was defeated by 86 votes (Brantford *Expositor* 24 June 1896). While working as a Parliamentary correspondent, Duncan had spoken warmly of Paterson as "respected and liked on his merits on both sides of the House" and as a person inclined to "make unstatistical jokes in your neighborhood" on a social occasion ("Bric-à-Brac," Montreal *Star* 19 April 1888).

Just as in *The Imperialist*, after Lorne wins a majority of 70 the Conservative Elgin *Mercury* announces "that the election of Mr. Murchison would be immediately challenged," so too the Liberal *Expositor*, the day after Robert Henry's narrow victory, hinted darkly that "it is possible that other more sinister influences may have been at work." Both the fictional election and the real one were ultimately set aside.

In both cases, Indian votes, allegedly gained through irregularities, were said to be responsible for the victories. In all the other polling stations the contest between Henry and Paterson was extremely close, but in the two largely Indian polling districts of Onondaga and Tuscurora Henry won by 71 and 66 votes respectively.

Duncan captured the fierce, often unscrupulous partisanship and the excitement of an election campaign in that era with remarkable accuracy—her book is "photographic in its fidelity to local conditions," as *Saturday Night* put it in its insightful review. Yet her "Indian interest," as she chose to call it, may be regarded, not only as regretably racist from a present-day perspective, but also as selective in its attempt to depict the realities of Indian voting patterns.

In one of her letters to Willison, Duncan apologizes for a factual error of considerable significance in the political dimension of the novel:

> The Indian anachronism I considered upon, but it is only
> a matter of a few years, and I was in the difficulty of either
> having to sacrifice the whole Imperial situation—as it is now—
> or my "Indian interest" neither of which I could make up my
> mind to do. So I left it.

Malcolm Montgomery's fascinating article about changes in
Indian voting status in the late nineteenth century provides the
information we need to interpret this statement. Indians were
granted the vote in Sir John A. Macdonald's Electoral Franchise
Act of 1885, which was intemperately opposed by the Liberals.
Once in power, the Liberals, in 1898, proceeded to take away the
Indian franchise—hence Duncan's need to apologize. In the 1896
campaign, Henry unscrupulously but shrewdly capitalized on
Liberal bigotry by reproducing, not always in context, the racist
statements Liberals had made and distributing them on the reserve.
This action must have turned some Indians against the Liberal
party, but after the election the Liberals had a strategy of their
own. John Charlton, a Liberal M.P., wrote Paterson that the loss
was "attributable I suppose ... to the free use of boodle which
proved especially efficacious among the Indians." A. S. Hardy, a
Brantford politician who rose to be Liberal Premier of Ontario in
1896, wrote Paterson that Henry must be unseated: "Lou Heyd is
a tremendous man at getting up evidence in such cases .... He goes
down amongst the Indians himself and he has several of them sort
of in his pay who can hunt up evidence" (Montgomery 23-24).

The exact process by which the election was nullified has
striking parallels with the aftermath of the election in *The Imperialist.* Henry had to face a preliminary examination on which the
Expositor commented in its headline, "Mr. Henry Has a Very
Feeble Memory—He Forgets a Lot of Things that Most Men
Would Remember" (31 Oct. 1896). Then, on December 3rd, the
day the examination of witnesses before two judges took place,
another drama was going on elsewhere in the courthouse:

> Henry's lawyer, Mr. Nesbitt, ... offered to vacate the seat be-
> fore the trial commenced at all. Mr. Henry's friends were satis-
> fied that he would be unseated and so they offered to vacate the
> seat on condition that each side paid its own costs, and that no
> charge of personal bribery be brought against Mr. Henry. When
> the offer was made, the Protest committee of the Liberal Party

was called together, and the proposition laid before them. Mr. Osler was called in. He said that while ready to go on, he thought time and money would be saved by agreeing to drop the charges against Mr. Henry and accept the offer of his vacating the seat.

This was agreed to.

The case of the Indian, Wm. Sugar, who was bribed with $4 to vote for Mr. Henry by Peter Aikens, chairman of Sub-Division No. 28, was put up as a "sample brick," and to occupy the trial while the Grit committee, sitting in the library, were considering whether they should accept Mr. Henry's offer or not ... (*Expositor*, 4 Dec. 1896).

The fact that a case of bribery involving an Indian had been chosen was not lost on the Conservative *Courier*, which seized upon this aspect of the compromise. "Mr. Henry Unseated/On the Testimony of a Pagan Indian/Who Would Not Take the Oath, but Affirmed that he was Paid Money" was their headline (qtd *Expositor* 4 Dec. 1896). The *Expositor* replied: "If Mr. Henry's seat was only endangered because of the affirmation of 'one Pagan Indian,' as the *Courier* would have us believe, why were such determined efforts made to secure a 'saw-off'? R.S.V.P."

" ...Our consenting to sawoff with the other side"—the same expression is used in *The Imperialist* to describe the agreement Lorne is unwillingly persuaded to accept by which his election is nullified. The speaker in the novel is a prominent Liberal criminal lawyer, Henry Cruickshank; when the 1896 deal is struck it is on the advice of "Mr. Osler," who had been identified for the *Expositor*'s readers the previous day: "to the surprise of the entire court in walked Mr. B.B. Osler, the great criminal lawyer." And of course bribery of Indians (which had been hinted at in the preliminary examination of Henry as well as chosen to be the sole case against him) is in the forefront of both the real and the fictional episode. The eventual outcome is also the same—in the bye-election, the Liberals choose another candidate and won. In 1897, Lou Heyd, the man who was entrusted with finding evidence on the reservation and then acted as the lawyer in the examination of Henry, was the victor, defeating Henry. The Rev. William Cochrane, "Dr. Drummond" of *The Imperialist*, wrote in his diary: "great excitement in the city, ending in the election of Mr. Heyd by 381. While the result was expected, not such a majority seemed possible."

Duncan in her novel creates a situation that has close parallels with the allegations and outcome of the 1896 campaign. Yet we can see Duncan as a loyal Liberal and friend of Paterson creating a fictional episode which presents Indian corruptibility in the darkest terms while conveniently ignoring the motive the Indian voters might have had for feeling ill-treated by the Liberals, as well as Liberal participation in bribery attempts. In the novel, Squire Ormiston, converted to Lorne's cause, acts innocently if imprudently on his behalf, and Duncan also echoes the rationalization Liberals created for denying the vote to the Indians. The narrator of *The Imperialist* comments:

> The Indians owed their holdings, their allowances, their school, and their protecting superintendent, Squire Ormiston, to a Conservative Government. It made a grateful bond of which a later Conservative Government was not, perhaps, unaware, when it added the ballot to its previous benefits. The Indians, therefore, on election-days, were supposed to "go solid" for the candidate in whom they had been taught to see good-will.

As Montgomery reports, the Liberals argued vehemently in the 1885 debate that Indians were completely under the political control of the official who, through a patronage appointment, was to secure their votes. Paterson himself, addressing an 1897 election rally, echoed this argument while maintaining that the strategy backfired: "In 1882 they tore up the riding to politically kill him. These men who prated of pure life and honesty? Next year they enfranchised the Indians, but the intelligent Indians rallied to his [side] and he won the election" (*Expositor* 7 Jan. 1897). In that same election, the Liberals carried the reservation: their ally in the Indian leadership, David Hill, "took the platform" at the victory rally "with becoming modesty and in terse and felicitous terms passed the credit of redeeming the Reserve to Mr. F.L. Heyd." (*Expositor* 5 Feb. 1897).

It can be conjectured that Duncan, who in a 1886 column for *The Week* had already portrayed Indians as a "stolid" and doomed race ("Saunterings" 21 Oct. 1886), was aware of their important role in the 1896 election and, out of sympathy to Paterson, may have been impelled to portray them in a particularly unflattering light.

Both nationally and in Brantford, the 1896 election had as its principal issues allegations of Conservative corruption and incompetence, and the Manitoba schools question. Trade policy, a central matter in the elections of 1887 and 1891, was secondary in this one, and Paterson, unlike Lorne Murchison, confined himself to evasive denials of the accusation that he was a closet Free Trader. Less than a month after the election, however, the *Expositor* observed shrewdly if disapprovingly that "Just now some people in Britain and some in Canada are taking up what they call 'preferential trade' " (*Expositor* 10 July 1896). Among those pushing this initiative, the editorial sourly noted, were "Mr. Chamberlain [the model for "Wallingham" in the novel] and his jingoistic touters." W.H. Cockshutt, likely the model for Octavius Milburn in the novel and a pillar of the local Conservative party, returned home from a London meeting of the Chambers of Commerce of the Empire that Chamberlain had addressed and told the *Expositor* that "Chamberlain's idea of a zollverein [customs union] did not seem to many Canadians to be just the thing" (*Expositor* 28 July 1896).

The speech that Cockshutt heard with such skepticism was a crucial moment in Chamberlain's conversion from his former position as a Free Trader to his subsequent passionate crusade in favour of preferential trade within the Empire (Marsh 392, 422). At her Calcutta listening-post, Duncan noted both Chamberlain's change of heart and, at a time when it was barely evident, Laurier's potential willingness to respond "with favour upon designs for Imperial Federation based on a preferential tariff for the goods of Great Britain and her colonies." This policy change was only made possible, Duncan claimed, because "especially during the past year, the political outlook of the Dominion has been affected by the growth of the Imperial sentiment" (*Indian Daily News* 7 Oct. 1896; *Selected Journalism* 61). Not only a political and economic opportunity but also, for Duncan, a fictional opportunity was created by these developments both in Canada and in England. In Brantford, by the time of the 1897 bye-election, trade policy had become, along with political morality, a major issue of the campaign, with the Liberals anxious to assure both manufacturers and workingmen that Laurier's still unannounced tariff reductions would not harm them.

Duncan was not in Brantford when the 1896 and 1897 elections took place, but she was back there in July 1898 (Fowler 235-36). Returning to a passionately Liberal household—her father, Alderman Charles Duncan, had been selected to be a member of the "reception committee" which escorted Paterson and Hardy from Hamilton to Brantford the night they were publicly honoured in a civic parade attended by "thousands" (*Expositor* 17 July 1896)—Duncan could not have failed to absorb the details, including the "Indian interest," of the defeat Paterson had suffered.

In his diary entry of July 3 to 10th 1898, Dr. Cochrane notes, "Thursday to Mr. Duncan's." The purpose of this visit may have been to meet Mr. Duncan's daughter, who gives "Brantford" as her address in her July 4, 1898 letter to Willison (Fowler 236). Possibly on that occasion, certainly during her stay, Duncan would have heard about the furor in Zion Church when Dr. Cochrane attempted to fight off efforts to appoint a minister to serve the working-class district of Brantford. Duncan's treatment of the incident in Chapter VII may be compared with Dr. Cochrane's entry in his diary (week of Feb. 7-13 1898):

> The Annual meeting was a crowded one, and towards the last a rather stormy one, between Robert Henry [the Henry who was the Conservative candidate in 1896 - Ed.] and George Watt. The latter wanted the church to increase my salary by $600 and after that consider the question of the minister for the Mission stations. The former, as the spokesman for the Missions, wanted the two things *coupled* [Dr. Cochrane's emphasis], evidently afraid that unless they were so I would have the preference. Both were carried together, but I declined under the circumstances to take anything more. Mr. Henry did not at all raise himself in the estimation of the good people of the church. The crafty politician more than the candid Christian was evident in all his bearing and speech.
>
> I greatly regretted the occurrence. For 36 years not such a meeting—indeed the most perfect harmony has characterised Zion Church—of course it will be so still, so far as I am concerned for in the little left of my life, I shall keep more than ever away from the "Maddening strife" of such as care more for victory in debate than truth and justice.

In the novel, Dr. Drummond's defeat leads to the importation of Hugh Finlay and consequently to the entire Finlay-Advena sub-

plot. Dr. Cochrane died in 1898, apparently before a second minister was found, so the development of this element in the story is
purely imaginative, but the precipitating incident is firmly rooted
in the realities of Brantford church politics.

In 1902, just at the time the letter to Willison indicates that
Duncan was starting her novel in earnest, an international incident
occurred which is mentioned in *The Imperialist* and might have
contributed to its genesis. The American financier J. Pierpont Morgan bought up shipping companies and "by 7 April 1902 ... had
gained control of all our best Atlantic shipping excepting only the
Cunard and Allan lines .... Something like a panic ensued"
(Amery, V, 21). The *National Review* of June 1902 called the
formation of the North Atlantic Shipping Combine "a national
humiliation" which made "Great Britain a mere annex of the
United States" (Amery 21). The British government's response,
which involved a subsidy of £150,000 to the rival Cunard Line,
was publicly announced on 30 September (Hyde 146; see Hyde
137-47 for a very detailed account of the crisis).

In essence, this episode contributed to the heightening of
imperialist fears and hopes that took place in 1902 and 1903.
Joseph Chamberlain was actively involved in the negotiations with
Cunard. The situation also had its Canadian side. The Cunard line,
though British-owned, had originally been founded and named
after a Nova Scotian; the Allan line was Canadian and at one stage
a proposal was abandoned because one of the participants "insisted
that the Canadian part of the scheme involving the Beaver line
must be kept separate from the rest of the merger" (Hyde 145).

The subsidy to Cunard was not an isolated decision in that
shipping subsidies had been a part of the national policy of many
countries throughout much of the nineteenth century. In 1902
"there was already in being a revived Parliamentary committee on
existing steamships subsidies" (Hyde 140). In *The Imperialist*,
Duncan sends Lorne to England as secretary of a delegation the
members of which were "practically all shippers," though their
professed aim is to promote "the encouragement of improved
communications within the Empire"; his role is not only crucial to
his career, but the galvanizing event for the political dimension of
the novel as a whole. Though the delegation's purpose may seem
obscure to the present-day reader, its importance would have been
readily understood at the time it was written, as a natural out-

growth of the awakened interest in imperialism, and as a corollary
to the Morgan-Cunard crisis of 1902.

Duncan was evidently still at an early stage of composition
when she wrote Willison in September 1902 and the American
magazine editor R.W. Gilder a month later. She took the manuscript with her to England in May of 1903 (Fowler 262) and to
Canada in the fall of that year. Meanwhile, an electrifying event
had occurred which was to have a marked effect on the novel. On
15 May 1903, Joseph Chamberlain made a dramatic speech reaffirming the principle of preferential trade despite the fact that such
a position was not the official policy of the Cabinet in which he
was a member. In his words we can find a foreshadowing of the
bitter debate that was to ensue between the supporters of his position and the advocates of the firmly entrenched British doctrine of
Free Trade:

> But the Ministers of Canada, when they were over here last
> year, made me a further definite offer ... which we had to
> refuse .... I am obliged to say that it [the Canadian offer] is
> contrary to the established fiscal policy of this country; that we
> hold ourselves bound to keep open market for all the world,
> even if they close their markets to us.

Numbered among Chamberlain's opponents were the Chancellor
of the Exchequor and several other members of the Government.
Arriving in London at a crucial moment, Duncan was well placed
to observe and adapt for her purposes the major political debate of
the Edwardian era. By September, both Chamberlain and his
ideological enemies resigned from the cabinet; eventually nobody
won and the Conservative party lost, resoundingly, in the next
election, but for months Chamberlain's vision of a united Empire
looked like a potential reality rather than a mirage. His campaign
is explicitly described in Chapter XVI of *The Imperialist*, and the
development of the controversy certainly affected the novel as a
whole.

While the battle raged in England, the response to Chamberlain's step was much more muted in Canada. Duncan was probably not pleased to find that the Liberals, having provided an
incentive for the Chamberlain speech, were content to watch pass-
ively to see which side in England was going to prevail. Cham-

berlain desperately wanted assurances of Canadian support, but a prominent Liberal minister, Sir Clifford Sifton, said "the next word does not require to come from Canada (qtd *Globe* 9 June 1903), and the following day *The Globe* in its editorial pages obediently followed his lead: "We do not desire unduly to intrude our opinions upon the domestic concerns of Great Britain." Two months later, Laurier told a Montreal business convention that "we think the first step would better come from Britain than from ourselves" (qtd Amery V, 349). In the opening pages of Chapter XXIX, just before Lorne's defiantly imperialist speech, we can see caution about this issue descending upon both national politicians ("They're not so sweet on it in Ottawa as they were") and local hacks ("don't make it your main lay-out"). Presumably, Duncan read these signs upon her arrival in Canada and adjusted her plot accordingly—she was in Canada, an advertisement in the English edition of the novel was later to state, "for the purpose of getting in touch with the latest development of Canadian opinion on the project for closer relations with the Mother Country"— though it seems from her letter to Gilder as if she had already anticipated in 1902 that the imperial "ideal" would be "broken, of course."

On 3 October 1903, while the fate of Chamberlain's plan remained very much in doubt, *The Imperialist* began its first form of publication, as a weekly serial in a British periodical called *The Queen* (sub-titled *The Lady's Newspaper*). By 20 November, Duncan was sending a set of proofs (which she modestly described as being "in a rough state") to Willison to see if he would consider running the novel in the Toronto *News*. He evidently accepted very quickly, for by 24 November she was writing him her thanks and making detailed arrangements.

By Christmas, Duncan was on her way back to England and India —after having been paid the honour of a visit by Laurier himself, whom she calls "a Nice Thing" (letter of 20 December). She wrote Willison yet again from London on 24 February 1904, with another project for his consideration: "I now think of a novel bringing Lorne Murchison over here and giving the critical colonial view of London society." Duncan proposes to write her new novel "this coming summer." This idea was clearly the germ of *Cousin Cinderella*, but that novel was not published until 1908, and though it did contain the promised critical view of London, its protagonist was no longer named Lorne Murchison. It may be, sadly, that the largely hostile British reviews of *The Imperialist* diminished Duncan's enthusiasm for writing an immediate sequel. The serialization in *The Queen* concluded, after thirteen weekly parts, on 26 December 1903. The serialization in the Toronto *News* began on 28 November 1903, and ran daily until 17 February 1904. The American edition of *The Imperialist*, published by D. Appleton (Duncan's customary American publisher) appeared in February, 1904, according to a statement on the copyright page. The British edition, published by Constable (the first time Duncan had written for this firm) seems to have appeared in April, 1904. The first British reviews came out in a cluster on 22 and 23 April, and the novel is listed in the May issue of *The Bookman*, a British trade journal. The Canadian edition, published by Copp Clark, was printed in England and, apart from the imprint, is identical to the British edition. The book was distributed in Canada in early June, a few weeks after its publication in England.

Duncan's correspondence complicates this orderly progression to some degree. In her letter of 20 November to Willison, she says: "Please send me back the proofs as soon as you have looked them over, as they form my only complete set at present and I would like to work on them." Presumably, these are proofs from *The Queen*, but by this time she had already sent a manuscript to her American publisher, for she writes Willison only four days later:

> If proofs arrive in time from New York I will send them on to you, if not I suppose the copy you have must do. I send you herewith a few slips containing important and necessary corrections. The case in court, as it appeared in *The Queen* is laughable. Please be sure to get these slips substituted for the corresponding matter you have in hand.

As it turned out, Willison used the proofs from *The Queen*. The change in the court case made possible by Duncan's slips (for the precise nature of the revision, see note 2 to Chapter X) constitutes one of the very few differences between the version in *The Queen* and the Toronto *News* version. The *News* must have been an important outlet from Duncan's point of view since it had considerable prestige as a newspaper, and also, with a circulation of over 20,000, provided a larger audience in her homeland than Duncan could hope to achieve through book sales.

Duncan evidently felt that the text she had prepared for the American edition was markedly superior to the text of the serialization in *The Queen*. It seems likely that she made most of the revisions that appear in the American edition before that version was typeset (and some time before 24 November, since she considers it possible that Willison may receive proofs from New York before his serialization begins).

The oddest aspect of the novel's publication history is the considerable delay in the appearance of the English edition. Duncan writes Willison on 20 November that "the novel ... will be published as a book probably about the end of that month [January] in England." As we have seen, the edition did not appear until April. Authors can be overly optimistic about the speed of the publication process, but it must be remembered that books could be produced very quickly in that era. On 24 February, Duncan tells Willison that "it is too late now for any alterations in the first edition, which should be on the book-stalls in a few days."

When it finally appeared, the British edition contained over 130 changes from the American edition. Valuable time had slipped away, however; some of the timeliness which must have seemed crucial in the short run had been lost. It was now more apparent than it would have been in January that Chamberlain's campaign was not going to succeed. Reviewers who had any pre-established prejudice against either imperialism or women novelists could now feel free to scoff at the book's treatment of politics.

It is the British edition, which incorporates Duncan's final revisions, which has been chosen as the text for the present reprint.

Though *The Imperialist* has now gained a more respectful audience, in Canada at least, Duncan's treatment of imperial politics remains controversial in another sense—critics are quite divided about whether the narrator identifies completely with Lorne's political views or not. A look at Duncan's letters may not resolve this problem definitively, but it at least provides some clues as to her conscious intentions.

At first sight all we seem to have is a contradiction. To Willison, Duncan writes as if she intended her novel to argue directly in favour of imperialism:

> I should be particularly gratified to have the story identified
> with a journal based on the higher polity—for which by the
> way, I hope you will find it not unsuited. (Letter of 20 Nov.
> 1903)

Writing to Lord Lansdowne, a man she had known both when he
was Governor-General of Canada and when he was Viceroy of
India, Duncan disclaims any didactic intention: "My book offers
only a picture of life and opinion, and attempts no argument."
Duncan seems to be writing what she thinks might appeal to
her correspondents. She evidently believed Willison to be an apos-
tle of imperialism. She may have misjudged him, for the *News* on
two occasions rivalled the *Globe* in expressing caution: "prudence
seems to suggest that it would be better for Canada to adopt a
waiting attitude" (8 Oct. 1903); "our policy still must be to watch
for developments" (18 Dec. 1903). Willison may have simply
fallen in step with Liberal caution, however; Berger describes him
as a liberal imperialist (*Sense of Power* 173), and as a friend of the
leading imperialists Denison and Parkin (20, 41). What matters, in
any event, is Duncan's evaluation of him.
Lord Lansdowne was Foreign Secretary in the government
Chamberlain split apart. Despite his service in the Empire, Lansdowne was known to be very lukewarm at best towards Chamberlain's initiative (Marsh 607, 635). Duncan would have "the better
courage in sending it [*The Imperialist*]" if she could assure Lansdowne that he was not about to read a plea for an argument he did
not much favour. It is a law of human nature that potential publishers and Viceroys usually are told what they like to be told.
The most reliable expression of Duncan's attitude towards the
question of imperialism appears in the advertisement at the back
of the English edition. This statement could be in Duncan's own
words, and in any event would have been approved by her:

> Mrs. Everard Cotes' (Sara Jeannette Duncan's) new novel, *The
> Imperialist*, though strongly tinged with the Author's sympathy
> with British ties of sentiment and business with Canada, is by
> no means a contribution to the propaganda of either side in the
> fiscal struggle. It is rather a picture of the political situation in
> Canada, and the views that currently obtain there.

This passage seems to reconcile the positions adopted in the letters to Willison and Lord Lansdowne. The author is said to have allowed her sympathy for Imperial ties to appear in the novel, yet she does not make the mistake of arguing a case. This statement may be seen as consistent with Duncan's comment to Gilder when the novel was barely begun: an aim of the book, she wrote, was "to show, I hope, the real Imperial situation as it works out in colonial lives."

Lorne Murchison, as Duncan says in the same letter, is "the hero" of the novel, but she also writes of colonial "lives" in the plural. Lorne's brand of imperialism is not the only version of that very complex political doctrine to be stated in the novel. Lorne's father takes issue with him in a crucial scene:

> Lorne went on .... "What we want is the common interest. Common interest, common taxation for defence, common representation, domestic management of domestic affairs, and you've got a working Empire."
>
> "Common interest, yes," said his father; "common taxation, no, for defence or any other purpose. The colonies will never send money to be squandered by the London War Office."

The disagreement presented here is profound. John Murchison goes on to scoff at the possibility of a common tariff policy, and in this conversation seems hardly an imperialist at all, apart from vague feelings of loyalty; later in the novel, it is reported that "the sentimental half of him was ready at any time to give out cautious sparks of sympathy with the splendour of Wallingham's scheme." Lorne, on the other hand, in one sentence expresses full approval for both military imperialism and political imperialism ("common representation" refers to the idea of an Imperial Parliament which would direct policy for the Empire as a whole). It is evident that adoption of Lorne's ideas would entail a considerable loss in Canadian sovereignty, in exchange for greater participation in the affairs of the Empire.

Was Sara Jeannette Duncan a cautious imperialist like John Murchison or a radical imperialist like Lorne? Her "sentiments are Imperial," she told Willison (letter of 20 December) and it seems likely that she shared Lorne's views to some extent. Yet, unlike her hero, she did not allow herself to become carried away by the

Imperial cause. Another passage from the letter to Lord Lansdowne shows that Duncan was well aware that the imperial fire
did not blaze in every provincial heart:

> It seemed to me that ... it might be worth while to present the
> situation as it appears to the average Canadian of the average
> small town, inarticulate except at election times, but whose
> view in the end counts for more than that of those pictorial
> people whose speeches at Toronto banquets go so far to over-
> colour the British imagination about Canadian sentiment. I
> thought it might be useful to bring this practical person forward
> and let him be seen.

Duncan was right to suggest that in Canada imperialism was
an elitist movement with limited popular appeal. As its distinguished historian, Carl Berger, has said, it "demanded too much of
human nature" (*Sense of Power* 262). The "practical person" that
Duncan brings forward is Octavius Milburn, that "important nonentity" who "inherited the complacent and Conservative political
views of a tenderly nourished industry." Resistance to Lorne's
schemes is not, however, the exclusive property of ideological
adversaries like Milburn. By allotting Lorne's *coup de grace* to his
own friends and political advisers, Duncan shows her shrewd
understanding of the tendency in small towns to run away from
what is perceived as unrealistic or fanciful.

The turning point in Lorne's political fortunes is the speech he
delivers at his final election rally. As I have tried to show in the
explanatory notes, this address synthesizes many of the principal
ideas of the Imperialist movement as a whole. The episode also
illustrates the emotional power and clear-sighted insight Duncan
can bring to this issue. As an imperialist herself, she can present
for the reader's admiration "a dramatic figure, standing for the
youth and energy of the old blood." She can invest his speech with
remarkable eloquence and passion. At the same time, however, she
shows an embryonic politician discarding the prudence that is
essential in a closely-fought election and delivering an extremely
idealistic appeal to a pragmatic audience. When Lorne goes so far
as to say "Thank God, we were long poor!" he is indeed "almost
rudderless, without construction and without control." The narrator's guiding comment occurs just before Lorne undertakes "ano-

ther argument," the self-destructive proposition that though free trade with the United States might be "a very good bargain on both sides," it must be rejected because "our very existence is involved." It is Duncan's triumph that she shows the reader both sides of Lorne's noble and rash act.

Duncan tended to expand rather than condense in her revisions: the English text is slightly longer than any other version. In general, her changes fall into three categories: political updating, stylistic improvements, and clarification of character. The presentation of the political situation is perhaps not as extensively modified as one might expect. The wording of Lorne's speech is slightly altered in several places, but only three changes are significant: the substitution of "our own stamp and character" for "the old stamp and character"; the addition of a reference to the Boer War as a catalyst for Canadian imperial sentiment, and the addition of Lorne's ill-advised exclamation, "Thank God we were long poor!". The two changes last mentioned were made by the time of the American edition. The account of Chamberlain's campaign in Chapter XVI is virtually the same in all versions, though much later in the text, just before Lorne's speech, Duncan added a sentence ironically censuring Chamberlain for daring to attack "The Holy Cobdenite Church."

The political passage that is most extensively altered is Lorne's argument with his father about imperialism (Chapter XVII). In the *Queen* serialization, John Murchison's repudiation of military imperialism is not present, though his arguments against economic imperialism are given. In the American edition, the paragraph beginning "Common interest, yes ..." is added, but it is not until the English edition that Horace Williams' speech seconding the elder Murchison's comments makes its first appearance.

The narrator's view of the change in Liberal policy and its impact on South Fox (Chap. XXII) contains some interesting revisions. One passage reads as follows in the first version:

> Upon the top of this had come the great and dramatic possibility of change in trade relations with Great Britain which the Liberal Government at Ottawa had given every sign of willingness to adopt. Though the moment had not yet come, might

never come, for its acceptance or rejection by the country as a
whole, there could be no doubt that every bye-election would
be influenced by the policy involved, and that *every Liberal
candidate must be prepared to take it into his scheme of action.*
[Emphasis mine.]

In the American and English editions, the first sentence ends with
an even more emphatic assertion of Liberal responsibility for the
new imperial trade policy: after "to adopt," the sentence now goes
on "—had indeed, initiated, and were bound by word and letter to
follow up." The end of the second sentence in the final version
again emphasizes the party leadership's enthusiasm for imperialism: "every Liberal candidate must be prepared to stand by it in
so far as the leaders had conceived and pushed it." At the same
time, the limiting phrase "in so far as" is a preparation for the
scene in which the local party become aware of the cooling of
imperial ardour among the national Liberals (Chap. XXIX). As
Lorne soon finds out, his duty is not to be right, but to be in step.

Most of Duncan's revisions have nothing to do with politics;
she simply alters a word or phrase to achieve greater stylistic
grace. Both the narration and the dialogue are revised in this way,
but the re-writing never extends to whole paragraphs, and there
does not appear to be any consistent pattern (such as an effort to
achieve greater dignity, or more informality) behind the changes.

Smaller in number but more important in overall effect are the
revisions which define a character in new ways. Several such passages concern Lorne and Advena Murchison. The description of
Advena's nature (Chap. V) is considerably expanded in the American edition; the process of revision is initiated in the *News* version, in one of its few departures from the text of the *Queen* serialization. When Advena's relationship with Finlay runs into difficulties, the English edition adds to the analysis given by the narrator in Chap. XXIV that "They were both too much encumbered
with ideas to move simply, quickly, on the impulse of passion."
Lorne's emotional identification with his country in the Elgin
market-place undergoes successive slight expansions in the American and English editions. His exclamation, in conversation with
Dora, that "the English have developed the finest human product
there is, the cleanest, the most disinterested" is a tribute that
appears only in the English edition (and was singled out for praise

by an English reviewer).

A few touches are added to finish the portrait of Hugh Finlay. In the first serialization, he is "James" Finlay, and the initial description he is accorded (Chap. VIII) does not contain the sentence defining his "confusion of ideals." The two well-written paragraphs describing his efforts to look for "the forces of his soul" as he despairingly leaves Advena at the end of the novel do not appear in the *Queen* version; only the first paragraph is given in the American edition.

In summary, a study of the four versions does not reveal a writer dramatically changing her mind about character or theme. Rather than being repaired or rebuilt, the basic structure of the novel is left intact. Duncan has chosen instead to use her craftsman's touch to polish the text with hundreds of small strokes in order to give it a high gloss.

So at least I believe. In a worthwhile and stimulating article, Darlene Kelly, conducting independent research into Duncan's revisions, reaches much the same conclusions in matters of fact, but makes somewhat greater claims as to the significance of Duncan's changes. Attributing to Duncan the motive of elevating the social status and propriety of the Murchison family in her revisions, Kelly says that these changes "collectively improve the image of Lorne Murchison ... and that of his family" (26). She points out that Lorne's "idealism" is strengthened in the British edition in several small ways (32) and regards John Murchison's increasingly emphasized disapproval of his son's opinions in the scene from Chapter XVII I have just discussed as a means by which Duncan reveals "the flaws in his [Lorne's] approach to imperial questions" (33).

Opinions may well differ about the significance of the documents that serve to trace Duncan's progress in writing *The Imperialist*. It is surely a remarkable stroke of good fortune, however, that so much factual evidence has survived that we can watch over her shoulder as she worked on her masterpiece.

Critical Interpretations

Humour and balance in *The Imperialist*: Sara Jeannette Duncan's "Instinct of Presentation"*

Michael Peterman

Early in the 1960s, while preparing his contributions to the *Literary History of Canada*, Professor Gordon Roper was surprised to discover a letter from Sara Jeannette Duncan to her old friend Lord Lansdowne, tucked away inside the cover of the Toronto Public Library's copy of *The Imperialist*. The text of the letter may be found on p. 310 of this edition.

Two aspects of this letter are particularly intriguing. The first is Duncan's statement that "My book offers only a picture of life and opinion, and attempts no argument." Though, like Stephen Leacock, she was herself an ardent imperialist, it was her design in *The Imperialist* to present the political issue in a balanced way. Balance, in fact, is the ordering principle of the novel; it extends beyond the political question to the presentation of the town itself and, in the degree that Elgin (Brantford, Ontario) is a microcosm of the country, to the presentation of Canada as a whole. A brief piece of dialogue between the restless Advena Murchison and her romantic interest, Hugh Finlay, catches the novel's sprightly sense of balance in a representative way:

> Finlay said when he came in that the heat for May was extraordinary; and Advena reminded him that he was in a country where everything was accomplished quickly, even summer.
> "Except perhaps civilization," she added. They were both young enough to be pleased with cleverness for its specious self. (99)

* First published in *Journal of Canadian Studies* 11.2 (1976): 56-64. Slightly condensed, with some quotations omitted. Minor revisions by the author. Reprinted by kind permission of *Journal of Canadian Studies*.

Such a passage reminds the reader of the sustained humour, charm and amiability of Duncan's writing. She is adept at developing the comedy of contrasting points of view and at making both the humour and the contrast serve her larger thematic interests. Indeed her sense of humour, a careful and deft balancing of wry sympathy and probing satire, pervades the novel, providing its buoyancy of tone and, more importantly, an intelligent perspective in which to view the complexities of the political and social analysis on the one hand and the excessive self-seriousness of certain of her characters on the other. Certainly, no other Canadian novel of Duncan's time achieved such a convincing picture of social life or such an effective sense of balanced presentation. In *The Imperialist*, Canada is both "elbow-room" and "an empty horizon"; it is a place where there is "scope" for the individual, a "chance of self-respect, ... of significance and success," a place distinguished by "the plenty of things" while at the same time it is a place where the force of traditional culture is absent, a place where, as Advena puts it, one is "to be consoled because apples are cheap" (101-102).

The second intriguing aspect is Duncan's phrase "my Canadian novel." As she implies in the letter, *The Imperialist* was something of a departure for her. It was an undertaking stirred by a clear sense of purpose, so much so that one wonders if she would ever have chosen to write seriously about Canada had not the problem of Imperialism appealed so strongly to her. It seems likely that, as a professional writer always aware of her audience, she would have continued to focus her attention on the possibilities of the international theme using America, England, India and, to a lesser extent, France, as her sources. *The Imperialist*, after all, was her twelfth book and, in the nearly fifteen years since *A Social Departure* (1890), she had shown little inclination "to be tethered in native pastures" (Lewis 126).

It took a definite stimulus—the idea of Imperialism as she judged it might affect "the average Canadian of the average small town"—to lead Duncan to consider the possibility of realistic fiction in a Canadian setting. Even with that emphasis, however, she did most of her immediate research for the novel by carefully following the attitudes to Imperialism expressed in English political campaigning ("M.E.R." 16). The book, in fact, has an English audience clearly in mind. It seems likely that she placed her hope for its sales not so much in the authenticity of the "picture of

[Canadian] life and opinion" as in the topicality of the political issue and in her proven ability to work humorously with the clash of cultural assumptions and values. The attempt to treat Canada realistically in a novel was, then, something of a gamble and an indulgence for Duncan. Except as a romantic setting for travel or adventure, Canada was unimportant to the turn-of-the-century reader of novels, popular or otherwise. Duncan was well aware that she could not expect an enthusiastic Canadian response. Her experiences as a journalist in Toronto and Montreal had given her ample proof of the difficulties faced by serious Canadian writers within Canada. The mood of 1904 was little different from the mood of 1889. As it was matter-of-factly reported in *The Canadian Magazine* in the year *The Imperialist* appeared, "So far as Canada is concerned, there are few novels published, except those written in other countries." Accordingly, she aimed her book at the wider and more urbane audiences of England particularly, and of America; she realized that publishing success was best generated from "the centre" of the Empire and she deemed it important to dramatize for that English audience, so easily misled in its opinions about Canada, the realities of the quiet but complex Canadian reaction to imperialism and to England. She was correct, as it turned out, in her sense of the Canadian market. *The Imperialist* "was not a popular success" (MacMechan 139) either in its serialization in the *Toronto Daily News* or as a novel.

The roundabout way in which Duncan came to write her "Canadian novel" is not to be ignored in any attempt to understand *The Imperialist* or her curious literary career as a whole. Much of the instability of her reputation today grows out of the fact that, because of her flexibility and cosmopolitan ease, she seemed in her time a homeless writer, one who could write trenchantly of India's political difficulties, of life in Parisian garrets, of social comedy in London and New York, but one who never closely identified herself with a national literary tradition. Though she enjoyed an international reputation in her day, the openness of her interests and themes, and the "delightful" manner in which she made use of the international theme had the effect of denationalizing her. Readers had to be reminded that she was in fact a Canadian. Not surprisingly, after her death in 1922, she remained a homeless writer, and was soon forgotten both in England and in America. Even today very few American book-sellers list her titles (under either of her writing names), though, when *The Imperialist* appeared in 1904 a reviewer for *The New York Times Book Review* astutely suggested that "it is a story very far above the average of stories—perhaps the most worthwhile book which has come out here in some time."

Only in Canada is Sara Jeannette Duncan remembered, and too often in merely a chauvinistic or patronizing way. *The Imperialist*, however, is a highly important work. The fact that it is being used increasingly on university courses in Canadian history and politics attests to the exactness of its detail and its ability to capture the mood of the time. It integrates Duncan's shrewd political awareness (Moss [53] says "she displays one of the most acute political minds that Canadian literature has yet allowed to flourish in its midst"), her capability as a novelist of manners, her "knack of characterization" (*New York Times* review) and the balancing power of her lively sense of humour. More significantly still, it taps the rich store of memories of her own childhood, adolescence and early adulthood in Brantford, Ontario. She wrote *The Imperialist* with a naturalness that grew out of the formative experiences of her own imagination, out of her own sense of roots and place. At the same time, however, she wrote from a distance in space and time, with a mature and complex awareness, both appreciative and critical, of the world out of which she had come. *The Imperialist* was the longest of her novels precisely because she had so much to say about the shape and texture of life in such a thriving community. The novel's title, aimed to attract the contemporary reader, belies its range, density, humour and tenderness.

The qualities that distinguish *The Imperialist* are its balance and its understated, but nevertheless conscious Canadianness. Its buoyancy of narrative tone and its humour help to disguise and lighten its complexity of view. On the one hand there is an affectionate feeling for the value and significance of growing up in "the sunny little town" (3) of Elgin. The experience had about it "a certain bright freedom" (38) not in conflict with the solid commercial realities of a market town in the midst of its own growth. Openness and opportunity were indeed available there, especially for the young:

> The Collegiate Institute was a potential melting-pot: you went
> in as your simple opportunities had made you; how you shaped

> coming out depended upon what was hidden in the core of you.
> You could not in any case be the same as your father before
> you; education is too powerful a stimulus for that .... it is
> indeed the touchstone for character in a new people. (67)

The opportunities were not, however, of a rags-to-riches nature.
One grew up not so much to pursue money and the myth of
success as to cultivate "that beam of active inquiry, curious but
never amazed." "Ambition," Duncan suggests, "definitely shining
goals, adorn the perspectives of young men in new countries less
often than is commonly supposed" (24). On the other hand, Duncan presents a firm and vivid sense of Elgin's limits. The imaginative and intelligent youth must feel the need, however much he is
attracted to the place, to move beyond its dull and restrictive pall.
Religion and politics were the town's "two controlling interests."
"The arts conspired to be absent." At its worst, Elgin concentrated
solely upon its local concerns to the exclusion of all else. "Like
other movements of the single mind, it had something of the ferocious, of the inflexible, of the unintelligent" (50) about it.

Throughout the first chapter, the reader is allowed to see Elgin
at its best. A holiday mood prevails. "I will say at once," remarks
Duncan's narrator, "for the reminder of persons living in England,
that the twenty-fourth of May was the Queen's Birthday." In
Elgin, where "the common love for the throne amounted to a half-
ashamed enthusiasm that burned with something like a sacred
flame," Victoria's birthday was "a real holiday," "a day with an
essence of it" (2). In England, we are reminded, such enthusiasm
is reserved exclusively for Bank holidays.

The light-hearted attention to the holiday is by no means an
irrelevant starting-point. From a point of view which is at once
that of a cosmopolitan and a perceptive insider, the reader is presented with one of the curious but basic elements in the Canadian
relation to England. He is allowed to see what really matters in
Canada even as he is alerted to differing English (and where
applicable, American) views and standards. Simultaneously, Duncan offers a loving attention to the details of Elgin life and a
carefully controlled application of irony to those details. The narrative voice of the novel is relaxed and informal, yet capable of
supplying a larger perspective which is consistently purposeful.

Nowhere is this more evident than in the description of the

eccentric market-place figure, Mother Beggarlegs. "A venerable stooping hawk" who sells gingerbread and taffy, the old woman is a member of "the group of odd characters, rarer now than they used to be, etched upon the vague consciousness of small towns as in a way mysterious and uncanny." Though Mother Beggarlegs has but a brief appearance in the novel, she indicates certain basic qualities of Elgin. More than a curious figure of picturesque and dramatic interest, she is used to suggest, though the inference is softened by the humour, a number of negative aspects of Elgin— its worship of conformity, its insistence upon orderliness, its penchant for rumour, and its power to isolate the unusual. Lorne demonstrates his freedom from such qualities and his own latent "beam of active inquiry" in politely addressing her on that holiday. His friendly action and the question he asks prefigures his future tendency to idealism, to think both imaginatively and rather excessively.

> he asked her sociably ... why the gilt was generally off her gingerbread. He had been looking long, as a matter of fact, for gingerbread with the gilt on it, being accustomed to the phrase on the lips of his father in connection with small profits.

When abstracted from the leisurely flow of the first chapter, the question assumes its importance. Lorne will not find gilt on Elgin's gingerbread, despite his idealistic efforts. Perhaps he will not find such gingerbread anywhere, but by nature he will at least continue to look for it. That the question grows out of his youthful experience in Elgin and the language of his father makes the event both natural and realistic, as well as symbolic.

The purpose of the first chapter is to introduce and give substance to the town, the representative classes of people within the community and, in particular, the independent and imaginative Murchison family. In characterizing the Murchisons, Duncan showed her familiarity with the important realists of the day. As Henry James did in *The Portrait of a Lady* and *The Bostonians* and as William Dean Howells did in *The Rise of Silas Lapham*, Duncan uses the family home as a symbol for the moral principles, social standing, tastes and vision of its inhabitants. In her description, she writes in a considered and grateful manner about her own experiences in the old Duncan family home at 96 West Street in

Brantford. There, the eldest daughter and second of eleven children, she had enjoyed a conjunction of influences which gave her a very sure sense of her own identity and worth. From that home, she had emerged optimistic and capable, independent and open-minded, enterprising and lively, a Canadianized version of James's "heiress of all the ages," albeit without monetary inheritance.

Duncan describes "the Plummer Place" at considerable length in the third chapter of *The Imperialist*. The symbolic aspects of the house are developed throughout the novel; it lies about the Murchisons "like a map of their lives" (92) and signifies their special quality. Conservative, unadventurous and dull, Elgin is incapable of appreciating its differences and its "large ideas" (19). It is, in fact, essential to the novel's design and to Duncan's use of humour that the Murchisons, like their chosen home, be "in Elgin but not of it" (19). The personality of the place sustains their sense of quiet independence, their dignity and, as in the case of the father, "the undercurrent of the old allegiance" (12) to England and to things larger than Elgin. Doubtless, the young Sara Duncan learned from her own father a similar "capacity for feeling the worthier things of life which circumstances had not previously developed" (20).

Duncan's characterizations of the Murchisons are not, however, exercises in excessive praise. To the degree that their approach to life exemplifies the best of Elgin they are indeed valued and admired, in contrast especially to the Milburns. Octavius Milburn, the self-satisfied "Father of the Elgin Boiler" (42) is a man of balances in the worst sense. Seeking always "the safe level," his approach is utilitarian and without vision. Typically, England is of value to him only as a protection for his own securities and as a boast, in the person of Alfred Hesketh, to his family's pretensions. But, while satirizing the Milburns ("Mrs. Milburn's servants were all 'maids,' even the charwoman"), Duncan readily acknowledges the force they represent in Elgin. By contrast, in her presentation of Lorne and Advena Murchison, she balances her praise by suggesting the degree to which they are fundamentally at odds with their town. Both Lorne and Advena are independent, imaginative and open-minded, but they are at the same time vulnerable to the folly of over-reaction, to the tendency to be blinded by their enthusiasms and passions. Lorne's childhood interest in the gingerbread foreshadows his inclination, as a

fortunate young lawyer and politician, to let the soarings of his
heart and imagination outstrip the realities of Elgin and its citizens.
To this end, Duncan parallels his infatuation for Dora Milburn
with his commitment to Imperialism. In Dora's case, he mistakes
her beauty and charm for a deeper beauty of personality, failing to
see in her a pervasive superficiality, a lady-like maliciousness and
an insensitivity "to the more delicate vibrations of things" (233).
In the case of Imperialism, he allows the appeal of the idea to
cloud his sense of its applicability to Elgin. The "moral advantage"
(90) he sees in Imperial union is not shared by the people who
count in Elgin, be they the realistic back-room politicians, businessmen like Milburn, or the practical Fox County farmers.

Lorne pays a severe price for loving "with all his imagination"
(141). Still, his very lapses from a perspective of common sense
are what distinguish him most. As the narrator phrases it, "There
was something too large about him for the town's essential
stamp." But, though his capacity for vision and "large ideas"
separates him from the town and leads him into difficulties, it does
not prevent him from understanding Elgin and identifying with it:

> The spectacle [of the Elgin market square] never failed to cheer
> him; .... these were his people, this his lot as well as theirs. For
> the first time he saw it in detachment. Till now he had regarded
> it with the friendly eyes of a participator who looked no further.
> To-day he did look further .... At that moment his country
> came subjectively into his possession; great and helpless it
> came into his inheritance as it comes into the inheritance of
> every man who can take it, by deed of imagination and energy
> and love. He held this microcosm of it, as one might say, in his
> hand and looked at it ardently; then he took his way across the
> road. (65)

Lorne's vision of Elgin is at the core of the novel. It blends
imagination with fact, subjectivity with objectivity, an aesthetic
sense with the reality of plain struggle and small margin. For the
moment he sees things in balance. His enthusiasms, however, lead
him into excesses as the action further unfolds. Hence, the fault for
his later frustrations lies both in his failure to maintain a realistic
perspective and in the town's inability to be anything more than it
is.

In considering the treatment of Lorne, it is a matter of some importance to remember that Duncan, like Howells, was a realist. In general, she chose to focus upon "the smiling aspects of life," realizing that, by the phrase, Howells meant that life, for the average person, must be viewed as an on-going comedy of ordinary experience, not as a tragedy. The moral norm for such a fiction is perhaps best described as an ordered and reasonable approach to personal and social problems. In this sense, the realistic novel depends upon the dramatic unfolding of the problems for its force and tension; it then seeks, in the language of reason and of everyday experience, to offer a realistic solution, at once soundly moral, pragmatic, and sensitive to the needs of others.

Such is Duncan's approach in *The Imperialist.* The failure of Lorne's simultaneous enthusiasms are treated by Duncan as a learning experience. Though he is for a time laid low emotionally, his inner resources are of such a quality that they allow him to recover and go on. In the end he is still a young man on the verge of larger things, less the fool of his imagination, and certainly, by experience less a provincial. The emphasis upon youth and elasticity in both Lorne and his sister suggests a further dimension to the novel's symbolic treatment of Canada.

While Duncan's use of humour to maintain balance plays a part in her treatment of Lorne, it is more evident in the presentation of Advena's enthusiasms. "Bookish and unconventional" (34) in a town where "no one could dream with impunity ... except in bed" (35), Advena is isolated in Elgin until the arrival of the new Presbyterian minister, Hugh Finlay. Thereafter, under the guise of intellectual discussion, they play out a sort of comic love-dance, half-conscious and half-unconscious, a tango of conventional restraint and indirect passion, one of the highlights of which is their mutual passion for Browning's *Sordello.* Finlay is a wonderfully protean character, a heavy-handed intellectual to Dr. Drummond, a great gawk to Mrs. Murchison, a "subtle Celt" (59) to the winking narrator and, of course, a genius to Advena. His excessive feelings for Canada, his blindness to his own emotions and his ponderous sense of duty are counterbalanced by Advena's sharp wit, her frankness and her indulgent sense of "the aesthetic ecstasy of self-torture" (181). Like many of Howells' female characters, Advena is guilty of too readily seeking out an opportunity for passionate self-sacrifice and martyrdom, of finding "exaltation" in striving to attain "that height of the spirit where pain sustains"

(215). The humour created at her expense and sustained for much of the novel is again a means of suggesting the need for more reason and less excess in the characters' emotional lives. Browning, it is implied, is more hindrance than help in such cases of heightened feeling.

The balancing effect of Duncan's humour is not confined to the treatment of places and characters. Of a pervasive quality and belonging to the very spirit of presentation, much of it can only with difficulty be removed from the larger context. However, certain incidents directly related to the novel's political concerns are worth noting, both because they can be enjoyed in isolation and because they demonstrate Duncan's concentration upon balanced effects. There is, for instance, the occasion of Lorne's return from the Cruickshank deputation's visit to England. With the attention so attuned at that point to all things English, Duncan's narrator wryly reminds the reader that,

> "Mrs. Williams [was] gently tilting to and fro in a rocking chair, with her pretty feet in their American shoes well in evidence. It is a fact, or perhaps a parable, that should be interesting to political economists, the adaptability of Canadian feet to American shoes; but fortunately it is not our present business. Though I must add that the "rocker" was also American, and the hammock in which Stella reposed came from New York, and upon John Murchison's knee, with the local journal, lay a pink evening paper published in Buffalo. (120)

There is also the occasion of the speech made by Alfred Hesketh to the sober, down-to-earth farmers of Fox County. Hesketh, a rather pretentious Englishman totally unaware of the kind of group he is addressing, begins on a calculated note of "smiling ease," remarking that "this was the first time that he had had the privilege of addressing a colonial audience" (189). It is, in short, one of the most ill-judged speeches imaginable, and it is not long before only slightly muffled remarks like "Oh, shut up!" and "Had ye no friends among the commoners?" begin to punctuate his "pithy" remarks. Duncan ends the incident on a broadly humorous note designed to accentuate her depiction of the political and social identity of "the average Canadian of the average small town." That "practical person" has no time to waste nor illusions to project on the Heskeths of the world. As the narrator reports,

> A personal impression, during a time of political excitement,
> travels unexpectedly far. A week later Mr. Hesketh was con-
> cernedly accosted in Main Street by a boy on a bicycle.
> "Say, mister, how's the dook?"
> "What duke?" asked Hesketh, puzzled.
> "Oh, any dook," responded the boy, and bicycled cheerful-
> ly away. (192)

The achievement of Duncan's *The Imperialist* lies in the fact
that she was writing for the first time about what she knew best
and in a manner that drew upon all her resources as a writer. She
knew what living was like "in communities where the human
interest is still sparse," but she also knew how to make such
thinness a matter of interest. Knowing such a life, having valued
it for what it gave her and finally having moved beyond it, she
could approach the world of her early years with a double view, a
view at once *within* and *without* her representative town. The
accomplished, controlled humour of the novel depends in large
part upon Duncan's doubleness of vision, upon the charming and
buoyant way in which she allows her narrator to share in the experiences of Elgin while at the same time casting the more exact-
ing scrutiny of a thoroughly cosmopolitan mind upon them.

The Imperialist succeeds in doing the sorts of things which
Lionel Trilling claimed a novel should do. In presenting the typical Canadian experience, it "tells us about the look and feel of
things, how things are done and what they are worth and what they
cost and what the odds are." It recognizes that "manners indicate
the largest intentions of men's souls as well as the smallest" and
that, to catch the meaning of even a sparse cultural experience, the
writer must be attuned "to catch the meaning of every dim implicit
hint" (Trilling 205). The humour which animates Duncan's prose
is never gratuitous in this regard. She would have agreed with
Trollope that it is the first necessity of the novelist's position to
make himself pleasant. At the same time, however, she realized
that the real value of humour lies in its potential for delineating
contrasts, for implying distinctions and for suggesting the need for
more sensible behaviour in ordinary life; in short, for creating
perspectives and a sense of balance. She must have realized that

it functioned also as a means of balancing her own enthusiasms for the Murchison way, the cause of Imperialism and the value of the English connection.

The Imperialist is Duncan's most Jamesian novel in the sense that she turned all her attention, not to playing cleverly and delightfully with the international theme, but to using it as a means to draw a comprehensive portrait of what was most essential to her own roots and identity, the generic Canadian character. As James was always at heart most interested in "the American," Duncan took a chance in *The Imperialist* on the very thing that was basic to her, even as she was sure that it would be of little interest as such to audiences, Canadian or otherwise. It must have cheered her immensely and perhaps even helped her in her planning to write her "Canadian novel" to have received in late January, 1900, a letter from "the Master" himself. He had read *His Honour, and a Lady* (1896) and wrote her one of those wonderfully self-abasing, slightly malicious tributes which were no doubt a stock-in-trade response, at that time in his career, to the fluttering attentions of women writers in search of "real" recognition. Though he had several criticisms to offer, he generously praised her intelligence, delicacy and cleverness, as well as their shared awareness that "a work of art must make some small effort to *be* one." "Go on and go on—," he advised her in conclusion, "you are full of talent; of the sense of life and the instinct of presentation; of wit and perception and resource. Voilà" (131-32). What Henry James saw in Sara Jeannette Duncan is still very much worth our attention today.

Canadian Social Mythologies in
The Imperialist *

Clara Thomas

.... From Simla, Duncan looked back at the Ontario town as she remembered it. Elgin certainly has some of the lineaments of Brantford, her home town, and the Murchison family may well have their roots in Duncan's own family. But her creation of town and people transcends particularity to move into the area of social mythology, those beliefs and legends which cohere in the history of a place and a people to establish what Northrop Frye calls "the area of serious belief ... . essentially a statement of a desire to attach oneself to, or live in or among, a specific kind of community" (170). The basic fabric of *The Imperialist* is an interweaving of two of our powerful and pervasive mythologies—"the Small Town" and "The Hero and Nation-Builder (Scotch)."

Duncan's distance and detachment from Canada must certainly have given point and wit to *The Imperialist*'s best passages. Likewise its best and one of its few external and climactic descriptions may well have originated in a cooling memory of Ontario from a Simla veranda in the hills, with the Indian plains shimmering in a heat-haze below:

> They slipped out presently into the crisp white winter night. The snow was banked on both sides of the street. Spreading garden fir-trees huddled together weighted down with it; ragged icicles hung from the eaves or lay in long broken fingers on the trodden paths. The snow snapped and tore under their feet; there was a glorious moon that observed every tattered weed sticking up through the whiteness, and etched it with its shadow. The town lay under the moon almost dramatic, almost mysterious, so withdrawn it was out of the cold, so turned in upon its own soul of the fireplace. It might have stood, in the snow and the silence, for a shell and a symbol of the humanity

---

*First published in *Journal of Canadian Studies* 12.2 (1977): 38-49. Somewhat condensed, with some lengthy quotations omitted. Reprinted by kind permission of *Journal of Canadian Studies*.

within, for angels or other strangers to mark with curiosity. Mr.
and Mrs. Murchison were neither angels nor strangers; they
looked at it and saw that the Peterson place was still standing
empty, and that old Mr. Fisher hadn't finished his new porch
before zero weather came to stop him. (198)

The duality that passage expresses, between the town, "almost dramatic, almost mysterious," and Mr. and Mrs. Murchison, "neither
angels nor strangers," but eminently reasonable and practical
townspeople, contains the duality of Sara Duncan's point of view
as well. Her picture of Elgin is, on balance, warm with remembered affection and romantic with its potential to individuals for
challenge and growth. Her narrator's voice, however, moves easily
and often into the ironic range, interrupting the action of the novel
to instruct the reader on Elgin's past and present, its social hierarchy, opportunities and constraints. She constantly and success-
fully invites us to a double-focus vision of Elgin, sometimes pointing out areas of positive value and potential that its people are not
aware of, at other times deflating individual or corporate areas of
pretension or meagreness of spirit. Her narrator's voice, all-wise
and insistently instructive, is sometimes condescending to her
reader and sometimes, also, to the town and the people of Elgin.

With a precision of detail that often seems documentary, and
that can even be mistaken for totality of detail, Duncan records a
town in southern Ontario in the last quarter of the nineteenth century. Her detail is, of course, highly selective, but for all that she
takes great trouble to show us how complex, not how simple, a
society her town represents. Her straight focus shows us Elgin as
the kind of town that hard-working, gradually prospering and
God-fearing Protestant Canadians liked to think they lived in and
were building. The corporate personality of a small town became
very strong, as scores of works in our literature attest, and it was
strong precisely because the controlling townspeople were disposed to believe in and perpetuate the kind of structure that Duncan particularizes so minutely. Her ironic focus is a corrective to
the idealized, or sentimentalized, vision of the small town, but the
two views together do not subtract from the quality of the picture.
They add detail, depth, movement and the possibilities of laughter
to it.

The town of Elgin is no simple static setting for the action of

The Imperialist, but a dynamic element in the action, established from the beginning of the book when Duncan set up its time continuum and establishes its past. She may have been conscious, as Henry James was, of difficulties in writing the romance of a new land where the monuments of the past, its glamorous ruins, were not readily visible and available to the writer (James's essay on Hawthorne). Certainly in India the sense of layer upon layer of history could hardly have failed to touch and modify her imagination. In any case she makes it clear from the beginning that Elgin is no frontier town perched in a new continent at the beginning of its history. Elgin already has its own past, partly known through its institutions, and partly mysterious. Old Mother Beggarlegs, the gingerbread woman of the introduction, is a living relic of the past and a piece of its folklore. She presides "like a venerable stooping hawk, over a stall in the covered part of the Elgin market-place, where she sold gingerbread horses and large round gingerbread cookies, and brown sticky squares of what was known in all circles in Elgin as taffy." Magic stories were told about her, that she was a witch, coming with the dawn and vanishing with the night:

> She belonged to the group of odd characters, rarer now than they used to be, etched upon the vague consciousness of small towns as in a way mysterious and uncanny; some said that Mother Beggarlegs was connected with the aristocracy and some that she had been "let off" being hanged.

In her presence and in her functions, Mother Beggarlegs' influence is benign. For the children, who will bring the future to Elgin, she conjures up a glamorous and scarifying past, stretching their imaginations beyond the town's boundaries, as her gingerbread and taffy are provisions outside the boundary of their mothers' kitchens.

Neither the history of Elgin as a matter of dates and records, nor its topographical and geographical locations concern Duncan very much, though she gives us a short, concrete outline. It is a manufacturing town in Southern Ontario on the Grand Trunk Railway. It is the centre of an agricultural district and the Moneida Indian Reservation is within its periphery. The town has a "right" and a "wrong" side of the tracks, the wrong being the East Ward where streets of small houses have sprung up, and the Methodists (Weslayans) are a challenge to Presbyterian strength. Elements of its social history, however, are introduced repeatedly. Five pages of what she calls "an analysis of social principles in Elgin, an adventure of some difficulty," are inserted to introduce a dancing party. This long passage incorporates a short history of the social leaders of the town, "who took upon themselves for Fox County, by the King's pleasure, the administration of justice, the practice of medicine and of the law, and the performances of the charges of the Church of England a long time ago." The decline of these people she calls "a sorry tale of disintegration with the cheerful sequel of rebuilding, leading to a little unavoidable confusion as the edifice went up ... we are here at the making of a nation" (37). Realities, traditions, prejudices and achievements of the past are all shown as active elements of the present: racial attitudes—Mrs. Murchison's "you can never trust an Indian ... I thought they were all gone long ago" (239); religious segregation—" 'Wesleyan are they?' a lady of Knox Church would remark of the newly arrived, in whom her interest was suggested, 'then let the Wesleyans look after them' " (51); and the historically based lines of party adherence.

.... The movement of past into present and its dynamic for action in the future are recapitulated and climaxed in Duncan's description of an Elgin market-place and Lorne Murchison's recognition of belonging, responsibility, and opportunity ... As Lorne looked at the market scene, "the sense of kinship surged in his heart; these were his people, this his lot as well as theirs." Lorne's recognition involves his commitment to his place and people; it also contains a sudden revelation of his own opportunity: ".... At that moment his country came subjectively into his inheritance as it comes into the inheritance of every man who can take it, by deed of imagination and energy and love" (65).

Dynamic energy, able to effect the forward movement of progress, is especially personalized in Lorne, the hero. But the sense of a social order already in the process of change from dreams of privilege for a few to reality of opportunity for the many is first established in the book through Lorne's father John Murchison, and Duncan's description, in Chapter III, of the Murchison family home.

.... The house is unique among houses in Elgin and it is a very real symbol of John Murchison's place in his own concept of Canada, and even more so, of his idea of the future progress of his family in Canada. The house is a fitting shelter for his family, a setting for their growth and a launching-point for their future. By so far had John Murchison come from his origin in Scotland to become a leading citizen of Elgin, by so much the farther did he have every reason to believe that his children would progress in prosperity and in influence from Elgin, their centre, to all Canada beyond.

.... Prudence and thrift, added to natural ability and taste, have assured John Murchison's steady progress in business prosperity. His children are first-generation Scotch-Canadian— they are to become the agents for Canada's future growth. The old colonial order, represented by those who built the house, has crumbled. The present pretension, time-serving and prejudice of such neo-colonialists as the Englishman, Octavius Milburn, "the father of the Elgin Boiler" (42), are clearly to be vanquished by the rising generation. Hesketh, the young emigrant Englishman, set up as a foil to Lorne Murchison, is shown up to be quite ridiculously unaware of the temper of the past and present of Canada—and by Canadians' standards, a snob to boot. But, in a cautionary lesson to Canadians, Duncan also shows him to be adaptive. He does not have to learn the hard lessons Lorne must learn in order to temper his idealism to the realities of Fox County, or Canada.

There is nothing subtle about the racial aspect of Duncan's social mythology. In Canada she shows the Scotch and their off-spring to be builders, men to usher in the future; the English are reactionary, cautious, conservative and ridiculously class-ridden in a society which sees itself as classless. In effect, Duncan polarizes the two racial strains to the point of substituting her own elite establishment, Scotch and Presbyterian, for the old colonial elitism of British and Anglican. Duncan's elitism, however, is always based on the ideals of moral probity and industry, buttres-sed and enhanced by education and given dynamic by the assu-rance she shares with Lorne, her hero—"the splendid conviction of resource" (65) in the land of Canada. Her own distance from home and her observation of the British Raj in India may well have fostered pride in her own people and prejudice against English colonialism. Nevertheless, her attitudes are far from idiosyncratic. A social mythology surrounding the Scotch in Canada had been evolving before her time and is potent still.

As the home is the centre and support of the Murchison family, so is the family the central institution of the town of Elgin. It is buttressed on the one hand by the Presbyterian church and on the other by John Murchison's successful hardware business. Home, business, church—in a series of introductory scenes, Duncan establishes their importance and shows us their interactions. In the prologue, we see the young Murchison family in the home, with the mother very much the ruler in her territory and the father worried about business, his territory. Chapter II has moved on in time by a decade: "We've seen changes, Mr. Murchison. Aye, we've seen changes," is Dr. Drummond's opening remark as he stands with John Murchison in the door of the hardware store, now established for thirty years. Next, we are shown an expanded view of the grown family and the home; then Dr. Drummond preaching a sermon; and finally, the scene-setting for the book's action climaxes with the ritual visit of Dr. Drummond to the Murchisons for supper (28)—this last perhaps the best description in Canadian fiction of good food and a company occasion ....

On the whole, business takes precedence over the church among the central business institutions of Elgin. The town had begun as the centre of trade for the farmers of Fox County. It had grown and prospered, but any ostentation along Main Street's business premises was suspect (15).

.... The religion that Duncan writes of centres in the church as an institution and it is a religion of ethics and social decorum before personal passion or "emotional lift." In Chapter VII, she describes it, certainly knowingly, in business terms:

> In Elgin religious fervour was not beautiful, or dramatic, or self-immolating; it was reasonable. You were perhaps your own first creditor; after that your debt was to your Maker. You discharged this obligation in a spirit of sturdy equity: if the children didn't go to Sunday School you knew the reason why. (50)

The law, the press and education are the other institutional components of Elgin, peripheral but very necessary to the central three. Early in the book the law, through the skill of Lorne Murchison, brings to justice the outsiders, Miss Belton and her accomplice, in their conspiracy to rob the bank and let the blame fall on Squire Ormiston's son. Lorne, then, comes to his candidacy for the Liberals through his reputation as a brilliant young lawyer. At the end of the book the law is called in to determine the legality of the election returns and finally Lorne is established as a figure of influence and future growth in Elgin through his acceptance of a partnership in Cruickshank's law firm.

Education provides the basic means for progress and advancement in Elgin. Duncan's ironic voice as she describes Lorne Murchison, Elmer Crow and the "potential melting pot" of the Collegiate Institute makes clear the gap between the rhetoric of education in a "classless" society and its realities. She first engages in the kind of Ontario educational rhetoric that has been familiar since Ryerson's day and is familiar still:

> [Lorne] and Elmore Crow, who walked beside him, had gone through the lower forms of the Elgin Collegiate Institute together, that really "public" kind of school which has so much to do with reassorting the classes of a new country .... The Collegiate Institute was a potential melting-pot: you went in as your simple opportunities had made you; how you shaped coming out depended upon what was hidden in the core of you. You could not in any case be the same as your father before you; education in a new country is too powerful a stimulant for that ....(67)

She then deflates her rhetoric by particularizing the cases of Lorne and Elmore:

> Neither Lorne Murchison nor Elmore Crow illustrates this point very nearly. Lorne would have gone into the law in any case, since his father was able to send him, and Elmore would inevitably have gone back to the crops since he was early defeated by any other possibility.

When she talks of the avid party press of Elgin, the Grit *Express* and the Tory *Mercury*, Duncan's ironic tone is at its broadest. She was a working member of the press herself for several years; she undoubtedly knew her types, the editors of small town papers, and as she shows their shrewdness, conceit, cunning, buf-

foonery and above all, party competition, her irony is very close
to Leacock's in *Sunshine Sketches* (published in 1913, nine years
later than *The Imperialist*):

> .... It was the *Express* that managed, while elaborately abstain-
> ing from improper comment upon a matter *sub judice*, to feed
> and support the general conviction of young Ormiston's inno-
> cence, and thereby win for itself, though a "Grit" paper, wide
> reading in that hotbed of Toryism, Moneida Reservation, while
> the Conservative *Mercury*, with its reckless sympathy for an old
> party name, made itself criminally liable by reviewing cases of
> hard dealing by the bank among the farmers, and only escaped
> prosecution by the amplest retraction and the most contrite
> apology. (70)

The institutions and the people of Elgin are bound together
into a community with a well-developed social hierarchy which
Duncan makes very explicit as she describes the Milburns' danc-
ing-party. Here too are the antecedents of Leacock's humour, particularly of his Peter Pupkin, the bank-clerk. In Elgin, she says,
"the young men were more desirable than the young women; they
forged ahead, carrying the family fortunes, and the 'nicest' of
them were the young men in the banks" (36).

What Duncan omits in her picture of Elgin is, of course, at
least as interesting as what she includes, because only by sensing
areas of omission can we really appreciate the social mythologies
which she records. There are no poor in her book—there are town-
folk and countryfolk, represented by the Crows, but one would
certainly not presume to call the Crows "poor." The Indians on the
reservation hardly count as people to the citizens of Elgin and they
only become visible, so to speak, when their votes become important in an election. Outside of Mother Beggarlegs, and she is
described as an exotic, there are none of any community's pathetic
outsiders, the so-called "shiftless" failures, or even of its wage-
earning working men and their families. The name of the game
pictured by Elgin and its society is "Opportunity and Progress,"
and its key-words are work, education and Protestant ethics.

Among the novel's major characters, the one misfit to everything Elgin represents is Advena Murchison, the oldest of the
family. Mrs. Murchison is shown often ironically, but on the
whole affectionately, to be the very epitome of the mother-house-

wife and her managerial role in the affairs of the family is given full weight. Daughter Abby has followed her mother's path, marrying well and early and swiftly becoming housewife and mother herself. Advena is, and always has been, "different," the despair of her mother as far as aptitude for housewifery is concerned. She only becomes the object of her mother's grudging pride when she is completely removed from the domestic sphere, a teacher in the Collegiate Institute. Advena, like Sara Duncan herself, is one of the first generation of women in Canada to be educated for a career beyond the home. In the novel's structure, she is a parallel for her brother Lorne: her idealism equals his; her intelligence equals his—but her opportunities and her future, by comparison, are circumscribed. Her romance with Hugh Finlay culminates in marriage, but only through the determined manipulation of Dr. Drummond. She and Finlay are to take up mission work in White Water, Alberta—there, the reader need not be told, Advena will certainly have to learn and practice the housewife's skills that she has resisted; there, also, the poetic conversations which she and Finlay have will be singularly incongruous. There is a kind of void surrounding Duncan's portrait of Advena—her characterization and her destiny do not seem falsely contrived, but all too real. She has had many sisters in Canadian fiction and in life, women who were trained and talented beyond the scope that their destined role as mothers and wives could possibly bring them. Duncan herself, after a short time as teacher, got away from the Elgins of Ontario and finally from Canada. Stella, the youngest of the Murchisons, is already a young lady of independent thought, action and speech, "well-equipped for society," and possessed of two qualities which are likely to take her far—"the quality of being able to suggest that she was quite as good as anybody without saying so, and the even more important quality of not being any better" (34). Stella, in fact, has many of the book's best ironic lines. But Advena is an outsider in Elgin, as she will be an outsider in White Water, and the necessity Duncan felt to write in her romance did not exclude a residue of sadness in its telling. For Advena, unlike Lorne, there can be no "splendid conviction of resource" and unlimited opportunity.

Politics is described by Duncan as one of the "controlling interests" (48) in Elgin (the other being religion), and politics is the activating force in *The Imperialist*'s central plot. People are as known and marked by their party as their church affiliations and a shift from one allegiance to another, as when Squire Ormiston moves from Tory to Grit during Lorne's campaign, is a serious business, providing great comment—and great satisfaction for the local Liberal leaders. Politics is, in fact, Elgin's "Great Game," a serious game, and taken very seriously. Beyond that, however, and most important, politics and the right of male suffrage bring excitement, colour, novelty, individual importance and above all, the thrill of contest, to the sober citizens of Elgin and Fox County around it.

.... Like Leacock, Duncan exposes the restricted vision, the corruption and the petty pork-barrel aspects of party politics. "Dash these heart-to-heart talks," says one of the men, after Lorne has left, "it's the only thing to do, but why the devil didn't he want something out of it? I had the Registrarship in my inside pocket" (260).

Throughout the book, Duncan has described Imperialism as a noble, but losing dream. In neither Canada nor England does it have the appeal to counteract the sheerly practical, short-term concerns of voters, and in Canada the party-men will not throw their weight in the direction of England at the expense of their precarious triangular balance between England and the United States.

Duncan's final concern, however, is not with her "political motif," but with Lorne as Hero and Builder. He is not crushed and he has learned—"Another time he would find more strength and show more cunning; he would not disdain the tools of diplomacy and desirability, he would dream no more of short cuts in great political departures" (261). He resists the offer of a friend, of a law partnership in Milwaukee, and after a short time in the west comes back to Elgin to be a partner in Cruickshank's law firm. Cruickshank has recognized Lorne's quality and so, by implication, will Elgin—and Canada.

The Canadian mythology of the Scotch was based, of course, on a solid ground of fact—on the numbers of Scotch who were prominent in the exploring and settling of the country, in its fur trade and later, on every level of government and financial enterprise; on the Presbyterian church, the Established Church of Scotland and so a prime and powerful institution to its people; and above all, on the pride of race and clan among the Scotch, a pride that distance from the homeland enhanced and fostered. What Carl

Berger says of the Loyalist is also true of the Scotch tradition: "[It] began, as did all myths of national origins, with the assertion that the founders of British Canada were God's chosen people" (Berger 99). The vastly popular novels of Sir Walter Scott, their heroes and their elevation of the common people were certainly a force in the propagation of the mythology. Phillipe Aubert de Gaspé, for instance, acknowledges Scott's influence in the text of *Les Anciens Canadiens* (1863), and his work celebrates the two races, Scotch and French Canadian.

The work of Carlyle, his philosophy of Heroes and his doctrine of work certainly played its part as well. In his instructions for the teaching of history in Ontario schools, Ryerson made a special point of the use of biography—by the time Duncan wrote her novel, three generations of students were undoubtedly familiar with the Carlylean Hero and the Carlylean work ethic which dovetailed so neatly with the actual necessities and opportunities of an expanding nation. In *Novels of Empire* (1949), Suzanne Howe did not deal with Canadian works—she did, however, deal with the influence of Carlyle on the novelists of British India (82ff), and her words apply equally to Duncan's *The Imperialist* and to all the novels of Ralph Connor.

The abundant lore of the Scotch in Canada began to cohere into a consciously promulgated mythology in the last quarter of the nineteenth century, as did the Loyalist tradition, and like the Loyalist tradition, its rise was partly defensive (Berger 99). According to census figures, from 1850 on the Scotch were always outnumbered by the Irish and the Presbyterians by both Anglicans and Methodists (Urquhart and Buckley 18). The pressure to be differentiated from Americans played its part in Scotch, as in Loyalist, myth-building, and individuals of influence, most notably George Munro Grant, were powers in its promulgation (Berger 23-33).

The social mythology of the Small Town is also based on a groundwork of historic fact—on a time when Canada was predominantly rural, and towns like Elgin were important centres of their agricultural districts, purveyors, for their areas, of education, religion and culture, as well as of the necessities of trade. The hey-day of the small town, in Ontario at least, was over by 1900, but for long after we were largely an urban people, Canadians liked to think of themselves as farm, not city-centred, and of the

town as a centre of society and commerce. Our writers have
followed, or led, our fantasies—even now, we have relatively few
urban novels—and they have also recognized in the small town
setting a manageable microcosm of our society as a whole.
Among our novelists, Duncan and Connor have given us the
"classic" statements of the Scotch Hero and Builder mythology;
Duncan and Leacock of the Small Town; all of these between
1901 and 1913. Lorne Murchison and his father John, for together
they make the complete hero, are unique in Duncan's seventeen
novels. By contrast, Connor rewrote the Scotch-Canadian hero in
different guises and situations in virtually every one of his thirty-
odd novels. In portraying their towns, Duncan and Leacock over-
lap enough in their selection of detail about persons or events so
that each provides a check on the validity of the other. There is
one massive difference between the towns, however—the captains
and the kings have departed from Mariposa; Leacock's narrator is
one of them. He remembers Mariposa from his arm-chair in the
Mausoleum Club, but the city, and the Mausoleum Club, are
where the real business of the country is done. The episodes begin,
rise and fall and, essentially, nothing in Mariposa changes. The
town stagnates. On the contrary, Elgin's influence reaches outside
of itself and its young are very much designated to be capably in
charge of a progressive future in Canada. Mariposa and its people
are broadly and briefly drawn; Duncan's portrayal of Elgin and its
people is replete with detail. She tells us much more than she
shows us in action and a certain slowness of pace and density of
fabric are the consequence. That fabric, however, is alive with
remembered detail and enlivened by remembered colloquial
speech, a source for nineteenth century Canadianism that has not
yet been explored.

There is no other social mythology so pervasive in our literature as that of the Scotch—and perhaps that is true of our histories
as well. Certainly the Laurentian thesis implies a great band of
Heroes and Builders and certainly the Scotch are paramount
among them. Among our major novelists Hugh MacLennan and
Margaret Laurence have both built on and revised our mythology
of the Scotch. In characters such as Neil Macrae and Alan Ainslie,
in the restricted Cape Breton community of *Each Man's Son*, and
in the essays collected in *Scotchman's Return*, MacLennan has
examined the burdens as well as the triumphs of the Scotch-Cana-

dian heritage. Margaret Laurence has worked with both the Small Town and the Scotch mythologies in all of her Canadian works. Like MacLennan she rejects superficial complacencies: Jason Currie, of *The Stone Angel*, is a builder indeed, but he has turned towards power, pride and the death of natural feeling—he is a "fledgling pharaoh in an uncouth land." The town of Manawaka symbolizes constraint far more than opportunity for its young. But her devotion to the old heroic myth of the Scotch is also evident in *The Diviners*, in Christie Logan's tales of Piper Gunn and the coming of the Sutherlanders to Manitoba. Both MacLennan and Laurence have written of a double Canadian heritage, however: French Canada has been prominent in MacLennan's work ever since *Two Solitudes*; and Christie Logan's tales share their mythic place in *The Diviners* with the Métis tales of Jules Tonnerre.

The Small Town mythology works towards the integration of individuals into a closely-knit community. For all Duncan's irony, Elgin is "The Good Place"; and for all Laurence's exposure of Manawaka's limitations and constraints, all her characters carry Manawaka with them always, and finally accept that they do. The Scotch mythology moves towards the separation of the individual from the group, towards an identification that is at once elite and egalitarian, based on privations and hardships overcome or, at the very least, endured with pride in the endurance. It is a Canadian mythic and secular doctrine of the elect and it retains its strength—or gains strength—in times of high Canadian nationalism such as our own.

Narrative Uncertainty in *The Imperialist* *

Peter Allen

In recent years a number of Australian films have won acclaim in Canada, as elsewhere, for their sympathetic and realistic depiction of colonial life in the years before World War I. The common theme of such films as *The Getting of Wisdom, My Brilliant Career, Picnic at Hanging Rock* and *Breaker Morant* is the process of maturation from colony to nation: they are preoccupied with Australia's ambivalent relation to British social traditions and Britain itself. These are notable examples of successful regional art—works that command an international audience for a subject that might have been of merely local interest.

English-speaking Canadians may well be jealous. We have so few films in English, apart from *The Wars*, that give a vivid sense of earlier Canadian life and almost none on our evolution from a colonial past. The Australians' success is not only a sad commentary on our film industry but reveals a curious gap in our cultural records. In this context, Sara Jeannette Duncan's *The Imperialist* appears as the remarkable achievement it is. Unlike the Australian filmmakers, Duncan did not have the benefit of historical hindsight. *The Imperialist* was published in 1904 and for the most part deals with the contemporary scene. In subject-matter and perspective, however, it is very similar to their films. Her theme is the ambiguity of Canadian identity and especially the mixture of excitement, scepticism and apathy with which we viewed our role in the British Empire. She vividly depicts that period of relative calm before the eruption of the modern age, a time in which British attitudes and customs were being slowly but unmistakably altered by the demands of a new country, and the Mother Country's political and cultural dominance was coming increasingly into question.

---

*Originally published in *Studies in Canadian Literature*. 9.1 (1984): 41-60. Minor revisions by the author. Reprinted by kind permission of *Studies in Canadian Literature*.

Like the Australians, Duncan sought to interest an international audience in a local issue, but unlike them her degree of success was very moderate (for some contemporary responses, see the "Reviews" section of this volume). In the last thirty years, however, her novel has become a standard text in Canadian studies, and a good deal of critical commentary has accumulated around it. With the spread of Canadian studies to other countries it may be hoped that Duncan will eventually earn the wider readership she deserves. In any case it seems likely that *The Imperialist* will be increasingly recognized as an unusual and accomplished testimony to an important stage in the development of our nation.

Whatever its historical significance and artistic merit, *The Imperialist* is not likely to win wide popularity, mainly because of the very considerable difficulties it presents to its readers. Duncan's narrative voice is the chief puzzle. Although her subject is a provincial way of life, she herself as narrator is notably cosmopolitan, sophisticated, witty, complex, altogether hard to catch and hold. The problem is partly a matter of tone—as is pointed out by Thomas (this edition, 357, 362), she alternates between an ironic and an objective mode of reporting—and we cannot always be sure how to take her. It is partly a matter of style: she has a penchant for clever obliquity that makes her a consistently demanding writer and occasionally a very obscure one (for a discussion of her style, see Tausky, *Novelist of Empire* 84-87). It is partly a matter of narrative method: she moves unpredictably and abruptly from one topic to another, sometimes with the explicit suggestion that her novel-writing is a spontaneous affair, a little uncertain and not entirely under her control. An affectation or simply the truth? The question is not easy to answer, though the narrator's cultivated sensibility and considerable intellectual self-confidence may make us suspect that we are in the hands of someone who knows what she is about, even when we don't.

Careful readers will discover that *The Imperialist* is tightly, indeed elaborately, organized, a fact that has been clearly established by its modern critics. But the published criticism, valuable as it is, has only begun to explain the curious mixture of artistic control and the apparent lack of it that we find in this novel. Several critical problems present themselves. The general tendency of the novel is well understood, but the detail of the pattern deserves more thorough treatment. A consideration of the way her central themes affect her treatment of minor characters and individual scenes will show something of the painstaking care with which she works. The inconsistencies in her narrative method become the more striking. Of these, the most obvious is the disparity in treatment between the main and the sub-plots. Her conclusion presents yet another problem. Finally, there is the general question of how far her narrative uncertainty constitutes an artistic flaw.

II

Duncan begins her novel in Elgin's market square, which is central to the town both literally and metaphorically. She repeatedly returns to this setting, always to suggest that it represents the unchanging fact of the practical, commercial spirit that rules the community. Her hero's misunderstanding of the market and its people is of a piece with his misunderstanding in general. In chapter nine, having become a young lawyer, Lorne Murchison looks out over the market from the passage-way to his office and dreams about its importance and his own. He feels an affinity with the people of the market, as indeed he should, considering that he is the privileged eldest son of a man who has struggled with great effort to a high place in the commercial world. He recognizes the market people as the foundation of the world he has inherited and is filled with a sense of his own power and purpose. But he and the narrator see the market in different terms. She stresses the harshness of the struggle it represents. It is a grim, joyless process, a "twisted and unlovely" tradition, "no fresh broken ground of dramatic promise, but a narrow inheritance of the opportunity to live which generations had grasped before" (64). Lorne overlooks the "sharp features" of the market and sees it in terms of its promise. He is seized with tenderness "for the farmers of Fox Country" or rather for "the idea they presented" (65) to him.

The narrator is not suggesting that Lorne is wrong in thinking Elgin has a promising future, at least commercially. She consistently presents Canada as a thriving, expanding and very North American enterprise, a place of new opportunities that subtly converts the British immigrant into someone who thinks in new and wider terms. Nor is Lorne wrong to think well of his own future. But he does not understand how far his world and he himself are controlled by the tradition of single-minded commercialism that the market represents. As his father later says, he takes too much for granted that other people are like himself. He fails to recognize the limitations of their minds, the dogged resistance to attempted amelioration with which he will be met.

In this particular scene Lorne's failure of understanding is dramatized by his confrontation with Elmore Crow and his mother. As is suggested by Gerson (77), Elmore is a cautionary parallel to Lorne himself. Having been Lorne's fellow student at the Collegiate Institute—a notable avenue to social advancement in a new country—he dreamed of making a new start out West, only to find that the frontier is governed by the same principles as Elgin itself. Now that he has returned he has become even more a victim of economic necessity. Since his father is old and his brother Abe is to become a dentist, Elmore must take over the family farm. He tries to ignore his mother's existence—"If you had been 'to the Collegiate,' relatives among the carts selling squashes were embarrassing" (68). But she and the life she represents are inescapable. She may be a "frail-looking old woman" (68), but she shows no signs of weakness whatsoever. She treats Elmore as though he were a child. She is shrewd, suspicious, a sharp businesswoman, impatient of "big ideas" (69) and utterly unimpressed by Lorne's claims to be treated as an unusual individual. If you don't buy Mrs. Crow's rhubarb at her price, you can do without rhubarb altogether.

Mrs. Crow is a pretty close parallel to Mother Beggarlegs, with whom Duncan began the novel. These characters represent the base fact of Lorne's community, and one he is never able to deal with effectively. Like the farmers of Fox County, Mother Beggarlegs is a traditional, indeed ancient, institution. Her antecedents are mysterious, and she is the subject of speculation, especially by Lorne, who sees her as a kind of dramatic possibility. The idea is typical: from the first pages of the novel we are led to think of Lorne's world as one that may inspire great ideas in children and other imaginative types but ultimately defeats them. Mother Beggarlegs' gingerbread comes without gilt, and no other is for sale in Elgin, a place where the only safe dreams are the ones you have in bed.

Mrs. Crow and Mother Beggarlegs are two of the many characters who personify the intractability of society in general. Like the punctilious Peter Macfarlane, most people are quite unvarying in their social routine. Lorne is perpetually disconcerted by this fact. In England he dreams of getting to know the working classes by talking to bus conductors, but he gets no further than he did with Mother Beggarlegs and Mrs. Crow. The little he does learn is not comforting. "There was the driver of a bus I used to ride on pretty often," he tells his family, "and if he felt like talking, he'd always begin, 'As I was a-saying of yesterday—' Well, that's the general idea—to repeat what they were a-sayin' of yesterday; and it doesn't matter two cents that the rest of the world has changed the subject" (124-25). As a result the imperial scheme makes headway slowly. Wallingham is able to convert some people in the upper reaches of society, but there is a problem with "the resistance of the base," and Lorne admits that at present the promoters of the scheme are "fiddling at a superstructure without a foundation" (121).

With the federal by-election Lorne has a chance to put his fine new ideas before the people themselves. In Chapter XXV, he again encounters Mrs. Crow, as much an inescapable fact in the political process as she was in the market, since the two are in fact different aspects of the same ruling principle. Perfectly set in her ways, the very picture of the social type she represents, she waits for the Liberal politicians in her parlour:

> She sat on the sofa in her best black dress with the bead trimming on the neck and sleeves, a good deal pushed up and wrinkled across the bosom, which had done all that would ever be required of it when it gave Elmore and Abe their start in life. Her wiry hands were crossed in her lap in the moment of waiting: you could tell by the look of them that they were not often crossed there. They were strenuous hands; the whole worn figure was strenuous, and the narrow set mouth, and the eyes which had looked after so many matters for so long, and even the way the hair was drawn back into a knot in a fashion that would have given a phrenologist his opportunity. It was a different Mrs. Crow from the one that sat in the midst of her poultry and garden-stuff in the Elgin market square; but it was even more the same Mrs. Crow, the sum of a certain measure of opportunity and service, an imperial figure in her bead trimming, if the truth were known. (184)

A key word here is "imperial." The title of the novel is of course ironic as well as literal. Lorne, the bearer of the imperial ideal, is presented as a kind of Canadian prince, receiving the admiration and acknowledgement of all as he passes through the market square. Ultimately, however, he is governed by the people he would lead. The emphasis on Mrs. Crow's limitations as a nurturing parent is also significant and typical of the novel as a whole. Like Mother Beggarlegs and the Mother Country she is certainly not going to take Lorne to her bosom. She may have given Elmore and Abe their start in life, but they, and anyone else like them, had better look after themselves now.

It is not simply that Lorne and his fellow-idealists are defeated by the lower orders, though they present the reality with which the idealist must contend in its starkest and most unmistakable form. Though Dr. Drummond is sympathetically portrayed, he is no less fixed and certain in his ways than Peter Macfarlane. His study is lined with "standard religious philosophy, standard poets, standard fiction, all that was standard, and nothing that was not" (150). He is a "beneficent despot," and Knox Church is his "dominion" (52). It is he who controls the action of the sub-plot, confronting Hugh Finlay with the inescapable fact of his love for Advena and, when Hugh will not be governed by him, marrying Christie Cameron himself. As a figure of authority he is very like John Murchison: both are kindly, thoughtful, dignified, imaginative but educated by the "discipline of circumstances" (20), preoccupied by the world of practical necessity and as perfectly inflexible in their own spheres as Mother Beggarlegs and Mrs. Crow in theirs. John Murchison is an excellent parent, but he cannot give his children money for their Victoria Day celebrations when he doesn't have it. If Mrs. Murchison is more forthcoming on this occasion she is no less resolute and unchanging in her views in general. As the sub-plot is controlled by Dr. Drummond, so the main plot is controlled by Henry Cruickshank. It is he who gives Lorne the chance to go to England, suggests his name for the Liberal nomination, and resolves his final dilemma by offering him a law partnership in Toronto. Like Dr. Drummond, Cruickshank is especially welcome in the Murchison home and bears some resemblance to John Murchison in character and social status. Thus Lorne and Advena grow up in a tightly-knit, stable social group that is closely supervised by a few highly respected and powerful elders. The newspaper editor Horace Williams takes not just his social announcements but his editorials virtually from Dr. Drummond's dictation, and public opinion tends to follow their lead respectfully. In short, the dominance of parents and parental figures is a major theme of the novel (which is dedicated, incidentally, to Duncan's father, the supposed original of John Murchison). Through her imagery the theme is extended to Britain and Canada. For Lorne the imperial idea means that "the old folks" in Britain will come to accept the leadership of "the sons and daughters" (113). The immediate response is that "England isn't superannuated yet." We Canadians are "not so grown up but what grandma's got to march in front" (123), Horace Williams later remarks.

To note the universality of this theme is not to deny the importance of the distinctions Duncan is careful to make among the various social groups she portrays and among the individuals within these groups. One of the strengths of the novel is the precision of her social analysis. Although the same principles are shown to prevail in Britain as in Canada, British and Canadian attitudes are carefully distinguished. Her main characters are drawn from Elgin's "polite society" (5), which is set off both from the factory workers of the town and from the farming community. As children, Lorne and Advena attended the lacrosse match on the twenty-fourth of May when they could afford the admission, unlike "the young Flannigans and Finnigans, who absolutely couldn't" (5), but went anyway. Within polite society there are marked contrasts between Dr. Drummond and Hugh Finlay or between the Murchison and Milburn families; within the Murchison family, between Advena and her sisters or between Lorne and his brothers. Even here there are differences: Lorne's brothers seem interchangeable, but Stella seems likely to become a more intelligent conformist than her sister Abby.

Differences in imaginative capacity are especially important. This is not a matter of social class: Elmore Crow is as capable of "big ideas" (69) as is Lorne. The members of the Murchison family are "all imaginative" (8), though in varying degrees, and are regarded as slightly odd by the townspeople, whose attention (says the narrator sardonically) is typically restricted to "the immediate, the vital, the municipal" (50). The Murchisons live at the very edge of town in the old Plummer Place, an unusually spacious house that is "in Elgin, but not of it" (19) and that had been built by an earlier settler with "large ideas" (18). Henry

Cruickshank, who becomes Lorne's mentor, is characterized as having "lofty but abortive views" (72). His opposite is Octavius Milburn, the "representative man" (41), who is incapable of imagining anything beyond the narrowest practical necessities. Lorne characteristically imputes his own imaginative sympathy to others and tends to assume that older people will all be as benevolent as those who dominate the little world he was raised in. He hopes that Milburn imagines him to be a suitable prospective son-in-law, when in fact Milburn is holding the garden gate open for him merely because it is more convenient than closing it (85-86). Once again Lorne is making his appeal to the wrong sort of parental figure. In a pleasant twist on this pervasive theme, Milburn is the "Father of the Elgin Boiler" (42) and of Dora Milburn, two products that have in common a certain hard, commercial quality. Lorne will be no more successful with the Milburns than he was with Mrs. Crow and Mother Beggarlegs or than Advena will be when she utters "her ideal to [the] unsympathetic ears" of the visiting Scotchwomen. She had "brought her pig, as her father would have said, to the wrong market" (216).

The elaborately particular social world that Duncan depicts thus appears to be the scene of a perpetual conflict between a romantic world of imagination and controlling world of hard fact (Tausky, *Novelist of Empire* 162, says that "the struggle of imaginative minds against their environment" is "the pervasive concern of her fiction" in general). From the first pages the world of children is associated with imagination, romantic dreams, the transmutation of the ordinary into the miraculous, the dramatic, the splendid. Against this tendency there is the steady pull of the mundane or market-place reality, bringing the imagination back to earth, containing and disciplining it. This is the pre-existing or parental world, into which the imaginative mind is born and to which (in this novel) it must ultimately accommodate itself. Not that the imagination is invariably subordinate: Lorne's legal career is launched when his imaginative sympathy for Walter Ormiston allows him to penetrate Florence Belton's hard, businesslike dignity and to score in the face of "probability, expectation, fact" (78). Nor are the townspeople in general without imaginative qualities, if of a somewhat opportunistic sort. Following his courtroom success, they see Lorne as a promising young fellow. But they desert him when he fails to deliver in the only terms they can really understand, just as his fellow Liberals are not willing to sacrifice their short-term interests for the sake of the imperial connection, though they were willing to "work it for what it was worth" (259). Having been defeated by the business community's distaste for the idea, they turn to the second-rate Carter as "the admitted fact" (260). Similarly, the Canadian delegation to Britain is forced to accept the fact of British apathy and misunderstanding. Hugh Finlay must accept that the fact of his relationship with Advena "is beyond mending" (155) and that the "whole fabric of circumstance was between them" (176). The Murchison parents "acknowledge their helplessness before the advancing event" (200) of Christie Cameron's arrival. She appears as "the material necessity, the fact in the case" (211). Advena finds it impossible to deny the fact of her physical passion, but it takes the hardheaded Dr. Drummond to strike the bargain that will set the lovers free.

In a characteristic passage Duncan begins with the everyday occasion of a Murchison family outing to church, sketches in a winter's night in Elgin and concludes by contrasting what an imaginative mind might have made of the scene and what the Murchison parents actually did make of it:

> Mr. and Mrs. Murchison, Alec, Stella, and Advena made up the family party; Oliver, for reasons of his own, would attend the River Avenue Methodist Church that evening. They slipped out presently into a crisp white winter night. The snow was banked on both sides of the street. Spreading garden fir-trees huddled together weighted down with it; ragged icicles hung from the eaves or lay in long broken fingers on the trodden paths. The snow snapped and tore under their feet; there was a glorious moon that observed every tattered weed sticking up through the whiteness, and etched it with its shadow. The town lay under the moon almost dramatic, almost mysterious, so withdrawn it was out of the cold, so turned in upon its own soul of the fireplace. It might have stood, in the snow and the silence, for a shell and a symbol of the humanity within, for angels or other strangers to mark with curiosity. Mr. and Mrs. Murchison were neither angels nor strangers; they looked at it and saw that the Peterson place was still standing empty, and that old Mr. Fisher hadn't finished his new porch before zero weather came to stop him. (198)

This passage is very like the novel as a whole. It is factual, precise and vivid. We are made aware both of the scene and of the narrator's literary sensibility. The key issue is the restraint placed on the human imagination by the social world she depicts. An angel or stranger might have found the scene dramatic, mysterious, symbolic, but their long years in Elgin have taught Mr. and Mrs. Murchison to restrict their vision to the ordinary. The idea of a limiting world is subtly reinforced by the detail of Mr. Fisher's failure to build the porch he had planned. Yet the general impression left by the scene is one of romantic potential—as is pointed out by Thomas (this edition, 357). Mr. and Mrs. Murchison may not be able to appreciate it, but the narrator does, and she keeps alive the hope that the young people of the novel (who are closer to being angels and strangers) will somehow make more of this world than their elders have.

This sort of teasing possibility pervades the novel and makes for persistent difficulties of interpretation. What precisely is the relationship of her idealistic young people to the parental world that surrounds them? Will they transform it, be defeated by it, merge into it? Duncan admired W.D. Howells, and in part *The Imperialist* proceeds by arousing and then undermining the reader's romantic expectations, as in *The Rise of Silas Lapham*. But only in part. Catherine Sheldrick Ross points out a major problem. The spinsterish Advena, with her nose in a book, is clearly a realistic foil to Dora Milburn, in whom Duncan parodies the appearance and manners of the conventional fictional heroine. Thus Lorne's love affair with Dora is treated in an ironic, anti-romantic way and comes to an appropriate conclusion. But "Advena is in fact involved in a plot with exactly the same structure as that which used to propel the old-time heroine from 'an auspicious beginning, through harrowing vicissitudes, to a blissful close' " (Ross 43-46). The disparity between the main and sub-plot is the most obvious example of Duncan's inconsistency. But even here it is no simple matter to explain why we are led to feel that an inconsistency exists.

III

The Imperialist is as elaborately constructed in terms of scene and plot as it is in theme and character. The scene in which Lorne is introduced to Mrs. Crow is a case in point. The situation will recur when Lorne introduces Hesketh to his father, but with the important difference that it is the person being introduced, and not the introducer, who is embarrassed. The scene with Mrs. Crow begins with Lorne looking out across the market and finding it good. At the end of the novel, after hearing he has been dumped by the Liberals, he is again in "the companionship of Main Street" (260-61), but finds the view not nearly so encouraging. At this point he encounters Hesketh, who caps his revelations with a line that Lorne himself had used in an earlier scene: "is this a time to be thinking of chucking the Empire" (115; 264)?

The correspondence among other scenes is equally striking and especially her careful paralleling of scenes from the two plots. As Lorne and his parents confer with their visitors, Drummond and Cruickshank, in the drawing room, Advena confers with hers, Hugh, in the library. The two parties meet at the front door, and we understand that the affairs of both Murchison children are prospering. Lorne returns with discouraging news from England, and in the next chapter discouraging news from Scotland arrives for Hugh. When he tells Advena about his engagement, she understands what is really happening, but he does not. In the next chapter, Lorne tries to become engaged to Dora; again the woman is the one who understands. Their secret engagement is both a parallel and a contrast to Hugh's, and both are ended by surprising marriages.

The correspondence of the two plots in theme and characterization is even more obvious. As Thomas points out (364), Lorne and Advena are alike in character, unlike in sex and hence in social destiny. The family expects much of Lorne, little of Advena, and would rather prefer that she conformed to the town's conventions for young women. Lorne's professional position makes him as prominent as Advena's makes her obscure. His prospects for advancement are excellent, hers are nil. It may seem a little odd that she sees a sunset as "a hateful reminder ... of how arbitrary every condition of life is" (61), but social frustration has been the main fact of her life. Hugh Finlay is perhaps too neatly paralleled to her as a sensitive soul who has been cooped up in a harshly unimaginative world of practical necessity and smallmindedness, but in fact he too is a realistically portrayed character—"a great gawk of a fellow" (96), as Mrs. Murchison says, with a flair for his profession that resembles Lorne's but even less understanding of life outside it. He is of course both paralleled and contrasted to the plausible Alfred Hesketh, another recent immigrant who eventually forsakes his old-world attitudes for the fresh prospects afforded by the new—as pointed out by Gerson (79); for other parallels and contrasts among the characters, see Gerson (75-79) and Zezulka (148-49).

The disparity in treatment between the main and sub-plots is thus not a matter of structure, characterization or the handling of theme. The main problem is of course the implausibility of the conclusion. Duncan works hard to make the conclusion seem realistic and in keeping with the novel as a whole, but the reader is unlikely to be convinced, largely because a shift in her narrative perspective has already been announced by a shift in her use of language.

Although Lorne is her hero, her view of him is sufficiently dispassionate to be in keeping with her generally ironic and realistic tone. We are aware of his faults and are certainly not asked to identify uncritically with him. Her view of Hugh is less consistently objective. "He was a passionate romantic," we are told, with "deep dreams in his eyes." "His face bore a confusion of ideals; he had the brow of a Covenanter and the mouth of Adonais" (58). Advena is fascinated by this mouth, which she takes to be evidence of his genius. The narrator ironically accepts her view, considering the "difficulty of proving anything else," but then adds, "he had something, the subtle Celt; he had horizons, lifted lines beyond the common vision, and an eye rapt and a heart intrepid" (59). The final phrase destroys the illusion of ironic and realistic commentary. She seems momentarily to have adopted Advena's overheated perspective, and this impression is sustained throughout the scene that follows, that of their first conversation. This is a meeting of souls, marked by much highflown and rather unlikely dialogue. The scene could only be saved for the cause of realism if the narrator made fun of her overly serious characters a little, as she will later do in describing their tryst at the Murchison home. But in this case all irony is forsaken, and the scene ends with Advena going on "into the chill, yellow west, with the odd sweet illusion that a summer day was dawning" (62). This uncritically romantic tone recurs in describing Advena's growing love for Hugh: "she walked beside him closer than he knew. She had her woman's prescience and trusted it. Her own heart, all sweetly alive, counselled her to patience" (99). All sweetly alive? Warned by this sort of language that we are not to take the subject of Advena's love ironically, we can only read the climactic scene between the lovers in Chapter XXXII as unrestrained melodrama: "Pitifully the storm blew her into his arms, a tossed and straying thing that could not speak for sobs; pitifully and with a rough incoherent sound he gathered and held her in that refuge ...." (245).

If we compare this with the climactic scene between Dorothea and Will in Chapter LXXXIII of *Middlemarch*, we will see the difference between subordinating melodramatic elements to the general design of the novel and failing to do so. What seems to have happened is that Duncan's intense sympathy for Advena's dilemma has subverted her narrative technique and created an unnecessary gap between the main and sub-plots. Though her deviations from the general tone of sophisticated social comedy are infrequent, they constitute a serious flaw, for they all concern Advena and serve to isolate her story from the main concerns of the novel.

IV

Even if we resolutely ignore such slips in narrative tone, the conclusion of *The Imperialist* is perplexing. The Milburn family seems to be central to the puzzle. Clara Thomas points to the racial element in Duncan's thought and suggests that the "pretension, time-serving and prejudice of such neo-colonialists as the Englishman, Octavius Milburn ... are clearly to be vanquished by the rising generation" of Scotch-Canadians represented by the young Murchisons (360). For Thomas Tausky the novel is more ambiguous: "she seems to have the Murchisons and Milburns in mind as two alternative directions for the evolution of a more advanced culture," and her conclusion is highly uncertain (*Novelist of Empire* 163, 171). Yet another possibility is that these families represent two contending social principles, neither of which can entirely prevail over the other.

There is no doubt that Duncan portrays a society in the process of change. She strongly emphasizes the passing of the seasons and the years, the rise to social dominance of such men as John

Murchison and Dr. Drummond, the emergence of a new generation in the young people of the novel. In a characteristic passage
the Murchison parents sit on their verandah talking over the development of their children's lives. Now that the Murchisons have
"overstamped the Plummers" (92) in the town's consciousness,
their home is known as the Murchison Place. The horse chestnut
blooms as it had done for thirty years; the "growing authority of
his family" (92) has led John Murchison to forsake shirtsleeves for
more formal dress; the coming of Abby's babies has led Mrs.
Murchison to take out her old patterns for children's clothes. Such
gradual developments are presented as part of a larger historical
pattern that will determine Canada's future. "[W]e are here at the
making of a nation" (37), Duncan remarks at one point.

It is also true that in treating this historical pattern she reveals
strong racial sympathies. She likes the Scotch and views Indians
with contempt. The Murchisons, who certainly have her sympathy,
are represented as part of a general movement that has supplanted
the Anglican colonial gentry. But she presents this change as political and social rather than simply racial, as a move from the Tory
centre to the Liberal provinces. The Anglican gentry were succeeded in political office by "young Liberals" and their "grandsons married the daughters of well-to-do persons who came from
the north of Ireland, the east of Scotland, and the Lord knows
where" (37). Octavius Milburn is not actually an Englishman but
a nationalistic and highly conservative Canadian, one who "was
born, one might say, in the manufacturing interest, and inherited
the complacent and Conservative political views of a tenderly
nourished industry" (41). His wife and his wife's sister ape the
manners of the British upper class and have taught his daughter
Dora to speak with an English accent. The family is Anglican as
well as Conservative and has links through the local rector with an
English family, the Chafes, whose social and political position
much resembles theirs. Thus the Milburns seem related to the tradition of British colonialism, and Duncan plainly views them with
distaste. But again the reason may be political. Wallingham and
Williams are not Scottish names, but their owners are liberals and
are sympathetically treated. Squire Ormiston is even more clearly
a remnant of a bygone era and is certainly of English descent, but
he is not viewed negatively, perhaps because he does not pose a
present threat to the liberal interest. Indeed the good old fellow

turns out to be a whig, deep down. Duncan's racial prejudices are undeniable, but her political prejudices are even stronger. One reason that the Milburns are treated as the villains of the novel is that they represent the continuing force of conservative opinion in Canadian society. Will the Milburns be supplanted by the Murchisons? No doubt Duncan hopes so, but her novel does not give much hope of it. Octavius and Dora Milburn are especially notable as being more clear-sighted in their views of what is going on in society than the characters whom we are expected to like, and at the end of the novel there is no sign that their powers are on the wane. Octavius Milburn has no illusions at all about the likely fate of the imperial ideal. His daughter is equally realistic. In her own drawing-room "she was very much aware of herself, of the situation, and of her value in it, a setting for herself she saw it, and saw it truly" (88). She has a calculating eye for Lorne's chances. Like the town in general, she begins by taking up with him as a very likely opportunity and ends by discarding him as not really to the purpose. When Lorne rhapsodizes about the English ("they're rich with character and strong with conduct and hoary with ideals"), Dora merely replies, "I don't believe they are a bit better than we are" (90). Of course she is right, as the career of Alfred Hesketh will show. Lorne discovers that narrow-minded materialism prevails as much in England as at home, and the idealistic Wallingham is ultimately helpless against it.

Catherine Sheldrick Ross says that Advena is "marked out by name and character as the heroine of the future" (44). But the novel concludes with Dora still ascendant over conventional society in Elgin while Advena and Hugh Finlay, having been set free by the grace of Dr. Drummond, are to bring their combined idealism to bear on life at the White Water Mission in Alberta. Why should we expect two such impractical dreamers to make more of life out West than Elmore Crow did (a point suggested by Thomas 364)? If the mission is to the Indians, we know too well what Duncan thinks of them. The ending of the main plot presents a similar problem. Duncan suggests that Lorne and Henry Cruickshank will sustain each other against the onset of cynicism and will continue to struggle for a better Canada. Why should we expect them to be any more successful in the future than they have been in the past? A modern reading of the novel is necessarily affected by the fact that we know the outcome of the imperial question. Octavius Milburn's skeptical predictions have proved to be the simple truth. It seems that Duncan has dramatized her fears for the future of Canadian society in the figures of the Milburns, her hopes in the Murchisons. In her final paragraph Cruickshank's offer of a partnership to Lorne is compared with the British government's moves towards imperial federation. Is it too soon for these to be accepted by Canada, she asks, or is it too late? The Milburn faction have won in the short run, but will they win in the long? Duncan tries to leave the issue open (Tausky, *Novelist of Empire* 160-61 points out that the future of the question was especially uncertain at the time the novel was written), but even to her contemporary readers it might well have seemed that the future of the social world she depicts is more likely to lie with Stella Murchison, who knows how to appear no better than other people (34), than it does with idealists such as Lorne and Advena. Our final image is of Lorne going "forth to his share in the task among those by whose hand and direction the pattern and the colours [of destiny] will be made." This is intended to assert his significance, but it also suggests his submergence in the crowd. Just as Lorne was "an atom in the surge of London" (109) and just as Canadians are "atomic creatures building the reef of the future" (143), so Lorne is powerless to do more than lend his hand to the building of a nation that is ruled, for the most part, by narrow-minded practicality. The Milburns represent a basic conservatism to which society, however liberal-minded it may appear, is always likely to revert. In fact Duncan's liberals are ultimately contained by conservatism. The Liberal party will take up with Lorne when he seems the coming thing, but will desert him just as surely as Dora does when the going gets rough. The Milburns are unattractive figures because they present in its purest form the values that actually prevail in society, without the sympathetic qualities that offset these same values in such figures as Dr. Drummond and John Murchison, and without the excuse of economic necessity that explains such lives as Mrs. Crow's.

As Thomas Tausky remarks, the action of *The Imperialist* "inspires pessimism," yet the work as a whole is not pessimistic (*Novelist of Empire* 160, 171). Rather it presents social life as a constant battle in which the human imagination must always be curbed and disciplined by circumstances but in which the heroic quality of life comes from the continued assertion of human ideals in the face of their continued defeat. Certainly human beings without ideals are an unattractive spectacle, as Duncan presents them. Yet idealism itself is ambiguously presented. Is her hero Lorne Murchison, as she says, or his father? John Murchison and Henry Cruickshank seem to represent the best that society has to offer. Perhaps Lorne's role is to become like them and in his turn to offer fatherly guidance for the idealistic impulse in others. Duncan does not tell us, and evidently she was not sure. She plainly believed in the progressive amelioration of society by liberal principles. Her experience of life and particularly of Canadian life had taught her that this process was at best an arduous and painful one, perhaps even futile. Yet she was not prepared to see the submergence of liberal principles as simply an unhappy ending.

Claude Bissell invites a comparison of Duncan and George Eliot (vi), and the idea is a useful one. The detached yet sympathetic analysis of a provincial community, the insistent theme of social determinism, the use of contrasting yet matched or paired characters (and especially the use of a pair of idealists, one male and one female, as central figures in separate plots)—in all these ways we may be reminded of *Middlemarch*. The correspondence in imagery is sometimes striking, as in Lorne's being "fast tied in the cobwebs of the common prescription" (43). Dora is very like Rosamund Vincy in her selfishness, her shallow materialism and her conventional beauty. But the pattern of causality in *Middlemarch* seems so complex and far-reaching that no one can grasp it, and certainly not Rosamund. Duncan is concerned with a simpler and more limited pattern, one that so acute and hard-headed a person as Dora has no trouble understanding. This quality of understanding also means that Dora cannot bring about so tragically destructive an outcome as Lydgate's eventual fate. Dora finds the right mate in Hesketh, and Lorne at least does not find the wrong one in her. Furthermore, such tragic potential as Duncan's material possesses is nullified by the intervention of kindly parental figures. The impossibly idealistic Finlay is saved from disaster by Dr. Drummond, just as Henry Cruickshank saves Lorne from the unhappy fate of trying to be become an American. The reader is led to identify with her idealistic young people but at the same time led to understand that there will always be someone around who knows how the world really works and can save the idealists from themselves. Duncan's allegiances are divided: she wants the idealists to win, but regards it as simply part of the social comedy when they do not, very likely because she has an underlying faith in the world of John Murchison and her own father. The result is a curious mixture: the social realism she had learned from George Eliot and others gives way ultimately—and yet not entirely—to the conventions of popular romantic comedy (see Ross 46 and Tausky, *Novelist of Empire* 73-75).

V

Duncan's narrative uncertainty is by no means simply a weakness. It can be an amusing affectation, as when she finds herself launched on "an analysis of social principles in Elgin" (36), despite her desire to get herself and her characters to the Milburn party. But it is not just an affectation, for the novel has a distinctly improvisational cast. A single final example will show how this quality contributes to its general character.

In describing Lorne's first meeting with Elmore Crow the narrator permits herself an aside on the subject of the Collegiate Institute's importance in the life of Elgin. Evidently thinking of her British readers, she identifies the Institute as "that really 'public' kind of school which has so much to do with reassorting the classes of a new country." She then develops this theme at a little length:

> The Collegiate Institute took in raw material and turned out teachers, more teachers than anything. The teachers taught, chiefly in rural districts where they could save money, and with the money they saved changed themselves into doctors, Fellows of the University, mining engineers. The Collegiate Institute was a potential melting-pot: you went in as your simple opportunities had made you; how you shaped coming out depended upon what was hidden in the core of you. You could not in any case be the same as your father before you; education in a new country is too powerful a stimulant for that, working upon material too plastic and too hypothetical; it is not yet a normal force, with an operation to be reckoned on with confidence. It is indeed the touchstone for character in a new people, for character acquired as apart from that inherited; it sometimes reveals surprises. (67)

At this point in the paragraph she turns abruptly back to the subject at hand:

> Neither Lorne Murchison nor Elmore Crow illustrates this point
> very nearly. Lorne would have gone into the law in any case,
> since his father was able to send him, and Elmore would inevit-
> ably have gone back to the crops since he was early defeated by
> any other possibility. Nevertheless, as they walk together in my
> mind along the Elgin market square, the Elgin Collegiate Insti-
> tute rises infallibly behind them, a directing influence and a
> responsible parent.

Clara Thomas suggests (362) that in the first part of this paragraph Duncan was being ironic. This is a charitable view, but it
seems just as likely that she was carried away for the moment by
her nationalistic sympathies, then remembered that her characters
did not fit her thesis and simply said so, rather than revising the
paragraph. She is concerned to present Canada as a young and
developing nation, and so she falls into rather conventional North
American rhetoric about educational opportunities in the new
world. But she has already made it clear that class distinction
remains all-important in Elgin, however much the traditional
barriers may have shifted, and the scene she is depicting turns on
this fact. Her apparent confusion on the point derives from her
ambivalence about the traditional or parental world. In part, the
dead hand of tradition lives on Elgin's hopes; in part, Elgin is
moving towards a brighter future. Thus the market is described
with notable ambiguity as containing Canada's heart—"the enduring heart of the new country already old in acquiescence … the
deep root of the race in the land, twisted and unlovely, but holding
the promise of all" (64-65). Canada is new but old, crippled but
flourishing, dominated by the past but the country of the future. In
any case, the Collegiate Institute is clearly "a directing influence
and a responsible parent" (67). But what kind of parent? One that
restricts its children or sets them free? Duncan knows it is the first:
much of what happens at the Institute is an extension of the social
principles that separate a Lorne Murchison from an Elmore Crow.
In fact, Elmore *will* be what his father was before him, and if
Lorne will not, it is because of his father's social position. Yet she
trusts it is somehow the second. After all, Elmore's brother will

become a dentist. Because of the Collegiate Institute? No doubt, but also because "the old folks are backin' him."

The confusion revealed in this passage is fundamental to the novel. Duncan's uncertainty about the Collegiate Institute is of a piece with her uncertainty about the imperial question and her uncertainty about Canada itself. Much of the work's complexity and richness derives from her not having been able to decide. She has dramatized her hopes and fears and at the same time has been seemingly compelled simply to tell the truth as far as she knew it. The unevenness and difficulty of the novel are part of its interest and ultimately reveal an imaginative mind grappling with the most perplexing and compelling of all questions to Canadians, that of their own uncertain nature. Will Canada become a major power through her association with the British Empire? Duncan sympathized with the youthful excitement and idealism that accompanied this idea but guessed shrewdly at the forces that would in time make it irrelevant. Will Canada's Lornes and Advenas transform the parental world as they inherit it? The question is left open, though the disparity in Duncan's treatment of her hero and heroine shows her unacknowledged disbelief in the likelihood of much improvement in the unconventional woman's lot. In both her certainty and her uncertainty, in her realism and occasional deviation from it, Duncan is an eloquent and important witness to the ambiguity of our developing national identity in the years before World War I.

A Portrait of the Idealist as Politician: The Individual and Society in *The Imperialist**

Francis Zichy

One of the most noteworthy features of Sara Jeannette Duncan's *The Imperialist* is the presence of the narrator herself, challenging our attention as she presents and evaluates her subject. An important object of her interest is, of course, Lorne Murchison, the main protagonist of the novel. In presenting Lorne, the narrator's attitude is for the most part sympathetic and affirmative. Her customary satire and wit, which often creates an impression that she is looking down on her subject, are in abeyance as she stresses the value of Lorne's idealism and affirms his vigour and his soundness of heart and mind. Nevertheless, partly because of the determination that seems necessary to sustain her affirmations, a note of underlying scepticism is heard, as if there were some uncertainty about Lorne's fulfilling the potential he so evidently possesses. In reciting Lorne's first action, the boyhood encounter with the enigmatic and intractable Mother Beggarlegs, the narrator expresses a hopefulness somewhat surcharged by its very air of conscious assurance:

> One prefers to hope he didn't [hurl the usual taunt at Mother Beggarlegs], with the invincible optimism one has for the behaviour of lovable people; but whether or not, his kind attempt at colloquy is the first indication I can find of that active sympathy with the disabilities of his fellow beings which stamped him later so intelligent a meliorist. (2)

This generous, fostering interest creates questions even as it seeks to set them aside. That interesting phrase, "invincible optimism," makes us pause to wonder what considerations might lie behind such an attitude. In spite of his fine qualities, in his first

---

*Originally published in *English Studies in Canada* 10 (1984): 330-42. Reprinted by kind permission of ACCUTE.

action the narrator cannot say whether or not Lorne did all that she thinks him capable of doing, but this only prompts her to make a larger allowance for him. It is striking, moreover, that the novelist introduces her protagonist in an action which to her mind expresses his best, his essential nature, but in which he is at least temporarily defeated.

Part of the excitement of reading *The Imperialist* is in realizing at this early stage in the story, that the young man of great promise may be the real thing, and that the narrator's magnanimous attitude towards him is a justified, attractive point of view. But another source of interest as we read on must be our curiosity to see how Lorne's fine potential may actually realize itself, or fail to do so, in an interaction with the particular community in which he is obliged to act. Our curiosity is sharpened by the fact that the narrator's unusual confidence is mingled with premonitions of difficulty and doubt. This tension between faith and curiosity, between hope and scepticism, where both seem equally imperative, gives *The Imperialist* its special urgency and suspense.

The encounter with Mother Beggarlegs is of course prospective in a straightforward way, since Lorne is only a boy when it occurs. The mature Lorne Murchison first comes into active contact with the Elgin community in his defence of Young Ormiston, the unfortunate youth accused of robbing the bank for which he works. In describing Lorne's response to his first significant challenge in public life, the narrator adopts a tone which is charged with sympathy and admiration for her protagonist, but also with an implicit recognition of the dangers he runs, given the circumstances in which he must work:

> Imagination, one gathers, is a quality dispensed with of necessity in the practice of most professions .... Lorne was indebted to it certainly for his constructive view of his client's situation, the view which came to him and stayed with him like a chapter in a novel .... It was a brilliant view, that perceived the young clerk the victim of the conspiracy he was charged with furthering; its justification lay back, dimly, among the intuitions about human nature which are part of the attribute [i.e., imagination] I have quoted. I may shortly say that it was justified; another day's attendance at the Elgin Courthouse shall not be compulsory here, whatever it may have been there. (77)

Yet although the narrator seems initially to brush aside the circumstances surrounding Lorne's courtroom triumph, claiming that what counts is his own quality of mind ("the thing which does matter, and considerably, is the special quality which Lorne Murchison brought to the task"—77), a great deal of attention is actually given to the public reception of Lorne's actions, and to the particular environment in which he is constrained to act. Lorne's performance in the Ormiston trial, like his later election campaign, is in public, before an audience with views and a will of its own. The developing irony of Lorne's situation is that although he wins his case partly because of his use of imagination, the townspeople do not understand what his victory owes to the exercise of imagination. Instead, they are merely mesmerized by the results. Ironically, Lorne's danger lies precisely in the distracting appeal through imagination, among a people so untutored and so fundamentally pragmatic as the citizens of Elgin. Their pragmatism does not protect them from binges of credulity, from which, however, they quickly recover. The seeds of later scepticism about Lorne's political ideas are contained in the credulous approval of his performance in defence of Young Ormiston. For the townspeople, there is no distinction between simple credulity (which can always swing round to disbelief) and thoughtful assent to the legitimate claims of imaginative intelligence:

> The fact that the defence was quite as extraordinarily indebted to circumstantial evidence as the prosecution in no way detracted from the character of Lorne's personal triumph; rather, indeed, in the popular view enhanced it. There was in it the primitive joy of seeing a ruffian knocked down with his own illegitimate weapons .... There was in it that superiority in the art of legerdemain, of mere calm, astonishing manipulation, so applauded in regions where romance has not yet been quite trampled down by reason. Lorne scored .... he scored not only by the cards he held but by the beautiful way he played them, if one may say so. (77-78)

This finely suggestive passage captures Lorne's personal qualities in a vividly dramatized context. Two points of view, two assessments of Lorne's performance, are subtly superimposed: that of the narrator, who knows his real value, and that of the audience, which has eyes only for the results obtained, and judges them in

a manner consistent with its own character. The "romantic" tendencies of the townsfolk are unreliable and ambiguous, for they
are entirely compatible with a dominant, unenlightened pragmatism. Because of the interaction between Lorne and his public, his
triumph is mixed, containing elements of misunderstanding, credulity, and potential scepticism. The implication that events are
being made for Lorne as much as he is making them is enforced
when Walter Winter steps forward among the first with his
congratulations, asserting his claim on the results: "Young man ...
didn't I tell you you ought to take the case? ... Now I'll tell you
another thing: today's event will do more for you than it has for
Ormiston" (78-79). Because of the unpleasant suggestion that
Lorne will benefit more from the trial than Ormiston, there is a
certain ambiguity in that "quick and friendly sense of opportunity"
which now spreads on Lorne's behalf. Walter Winter is an
embodiment of the public forces which will assert their own
interpretation of Lorne's intentions and actions, drawing him
down from the high- minded level on which he wishes to live. The
continuity between success and the compromising circumstances
in which it is won is underlined: there is not even a chapter break
between the trial episode and the meeting with Cruickshank which
launches the next phase of Lorne's career.

Having to absorb these unsettling implications, the narrator's
"invincible optimism" (2) regarding Lorne's potential must be
very different from the complacent estimate of his prospects
among the public at large: "Sanguine persons in Elgin were freely
disposed to 'bet on' Lorne Murchison, and there were none so
despondent as to take the view that he would not come out of it,
somehow, with an added personal significance" (71-72). This confidence recalls Dora Milburn's calculating assessment of Lorne's
future importance, her real reason for allowing him to court her.
It is precisely this sort of calculation which the narrator's informed
optimism wishes to rise above, and which Lorne radically challenges with his generous idealism, so little concerned with mere
results as the world normally judges them. Yet it is a requirement
of this portrait of the idealist that he not be unusual in any freakish
or unrealistic way. He is not to be a knight of romance, capable of
superhuman feats, or a romantic villain heroically at odds with the
normal decencies, but rather a believable citizen of a society
presented in recognizable detail. Lorne's special value is to rise

out of his deep affinity with his community, with which he holds many values in common: "Lorne meant to be a good lawyer, squarely proposed to himself that the country should hold no better" (24) and "his eye was full of pleasant, easy familiarity with the things he saw, and ready to see larger things" (66). Lorne will attempt to bridge the gap between what he sees in common with others, and the larger prospects he has imagination enough to apprehend, and faith enough to believe possible of achievement.

This effort at connection is badly needed, because the Elgin community as a whole suffers from a tendency to separate the everyday world and the larger vision. Few seem able to apply imagination to the working of day-to-day affairs. In some members of the community, this caution takes negative, complacent forms, becoming a withering scepticism concerning all challenging sentiments and prospects. One manifestation of this scepticism is the fun made of youthful sexual romance, which is generally "belittled and laughed at" (24). This shyness regarding sexual romance may explain why Elgin so greatly enjoys the shenanigans of the law and of politics, which may be felt to be a safer outlet for high spirits, because more readily controlled by pragmatic considerations. The scoffing attitude towards romantic sentiment creates the conditions in which a cold and merely conventional young woman like Dora Milburn can consider herself as holding sway over the social life of the town. Another prominent manifestation of Elgin's scepticism is the complacent political conservatism of Dora's father, the manufacturer Octavius Milburn. The novelist states near the conclusion of the story that there is a close connection between love and politics (258), and it can be said that Dora's stature in the world of love is complementary to her father's oppressive, inert weight in the councils of the Chamber of Commerce and the Conservative Party. It is a sign of Lorne's over-arching idealism that he wishes to prevail in both love and politics, to conquer both Dora and her father, and it is a mark of his generous (if partly unconscious) instinct for finding where the most difficult work is needed that he attempts to carry his case in their hearts and minds.

Unlike the Milburns, the Murchison family has a capacity for generous thoughts and feelings: "the Murchisons were all imaginative" (8). Yet even they do not often express the larger vision which they are capable of apprehending: "No one could say that the Murchisons were demonstrative" (10), and "they might believe everything, they would express nothing" (25). The reticence of the Murchisons is different from the complacency of the Milburns, in that it is the result of modesty and long habit rather than shallowness or conventional thinking, but it is even more restrictive for that. An example of this reticence is John Murchison's "shyness of an artist in his commercial success" (14). It is suggestive that in one of his first deeds of intelligent good will Lorne compensates for his father's parsimony by offering his own pittance to help his younger brothers celebrate the Queen's birthday (10). John Murchison's expressions of opinion regarding Lorne's political goals are sceptical and guarded:

> "He takes too much for granted."
> "What does he take for granted?" asked Mrs.Murchison.
> "Other folks being like himself," said the father. (144)

Yet towards the end of the election campaign, in the difficult days when Lorne feels most out of sympathy with the pragmatic leaders of his party, it is with his father that he has the most free and satisfying talk about the value of the British connection. John Murchison's heart is in the right place, yet he feels obliged to maintain a cautious attitude towards Lorne's attempt to argue the imperial cause. The event seems to justify his caution, yet perhaps this lack of confidence, even in John Murchison and others like him who are alive to the deeper appeal of imperialism, is one of the major obstacles to Lorne's success.

It is a large part of Lorne Murchison's importance that he strives to outgrow his father's caution, to live in the real world without guardedness or reticence, which can lead to inaction or resignation, and leave the field of public life to be dominated by the forces of mediocrity and expediency. In Elgin, complacent mediocrity and crippling reticence—the Octavius Milburns and the John Murchisons—accommodate each other in a manner which suppresses the larger potential of the individual and society alike. Yet reticence may be a mark of deep feeling and serious thought, and a measure of reserve and modesty is fundamental to Lorne's conscientious idealism (to such a degree is he his father's son). In Duncan's presentation, this endearing modesty is basic to the character of the Murchisons, and of Elgin as a whole. It is one of the sympathetic novelist's most important tasks to discriminate between the town's modesty and its complacency, even though both may result in caution and inaction. It is suggestive, in light of Lorne's struggle with the decisive problem of Elgin's relation to England, that the narrator's sympathy for the town seems especially alert when she speaks of the local feeling for the old country: "The common love for the throne amounted to a half-ashamed enthusiasm that burned with something like a sacred flame, and was among the things not ordinarily alluded to, because of the shyness that attaches to all feeling that cannot be justified in plain terms" (48).

Elgin's dilemma is that it can neither express nor repudiate its strong feelings regarding the old country. Its reticence, which is the very sign of the strength of its sentiment, prevents the town from coming to grips with one of its deepest concerns. Lorne tries to break free of this hampering reticence by fully expressing what has always been partly repressed by Elgin, the deep loyalty felt towards England. He seeks to make this the cornerstone of the Canadian identity—he realizes that it is both an aspiration and a concession to do so. His misfortune is that in pushing forward towards this particular self-affirmation, he uncovers a tangle of ambiguities and conflicts in Elgin's attitude, and even in his own attitude, towards the British connection. In his brave attempt to resolve these conflicts he is finally let down by those to whom he must appeal for confirmation if his hopes are to become policy.

The Ormiston trial is a rehearsal for Lorne's most sustained effort in the novel, his campaign for the Liberal Party and for Imperialism in the Fox Country by-election. When Lorne presents himself as a political candidate his idealism, and the narrator's optimism regarding his prospects, are obliged to operate under increasingly specific circumstances. Lorne's political affiliation is known; he has committed himself to certain controversial policies; and he is addressing the public which must support him if his hopes are to be realized. The views and responses of this public will therefore be even more crucial to his success than they were in the Ormiston trial.

In his activity as a campaigner, Lorne brings to bear the same qualities he showed in his first trial: imagination, sympathy, and moral fervour. These qualities give him a special appeal, but now as before they also oblige him to take special risks. By the very intensity of his appeal, Lorne risks being misunderstood, and may prod into life a scepticism equal to his powers of persuasion: "They listened with an intense personal interest in him which, no doubt, went to obscure what he said: perhaps a less absorbing personality would have carried the Idea further" (223). On the night of his final speech (the first occasion when we hear the protagonist's own voice at any length) the irony of Lorne's situation is sharply brought home. At a first glance, he is in a highly advantageous situation, surrounded by committed supporters: "the friendliness of the meeting was in the air .... he could feel completely at home .... Lorne did feel at home" (223). These advantages are real, but it is not clear that they help Lorne in the matters that concern him most deeply. In stressing his unwavering commitment to the imperial idea, the narrator's language suggests his isolation and the pitch of his excitement, so intense as to imply delusion: "His jehad it would be, for the faith and purpose of his race; so he scanned it and heard it, with conviction hot in him ... and intention noble" (224). Perhaps most unsettling of all is the repeated assertion that nothing in the campaign has mattered to him except his personal idea and the hope it arouses in him. For how is his idea to realize itself, if not through the actual circumstances and strategy of the campaign, to which he has after all been obliged to surrender his time and energy? Lorne has been forced to capitulate to goals and considerations which apparently can give him no real satisfaction. He has fought the campaign as he has been told to do, but this has meant slighting his real concerns. Even on the night of his final speech Lorne does not intend to raise the question of imperialism. When he does so, his previous allegiance to strategy falls away entirely and he is "hopelessly adrift from the subject he had proposed to himself, launched for better or worse upon the theme that was subliminal in him" (227). There appears to be no reinforcement between his personal current of thought and the circumstances within which he must work, and thus all the external advantages are only ironic reminders of his deeper frustration.

Yet Lorne does speak out unreservedly on this last night of the campaign. His Opera House speech gives his idea of Canada, and sums up the considerations which lie behind his advocacy of imperialism. The key to his conception of Canada is the reminder that Canadians are distinctive for having remained faithful to British tradition and ideas: "remembering that the greater half of the continent did remain faithful, the northern and strenuous half, destined to move with sure steps and steady mind to greater growth and higher place among nations than any of us can now imagine" (226). This is a special form of pride, in the qualities of faithfulness and moderation—a pride in having restrained inordinate pride and self-aggrandizement. An important aspect of Lorne's Canadian pride is the bitterness in what he says about the English of his day, even the English imperialists, to many of whom imperialism is merely "the after-dinner fantasy of aristocratic rhetoric" (226). Lorne emphasizes not only what the British connection has been worth, but what it has cost, and not only in money: "There are those who say that the impost has been heavy, though never a dollar was paid" (226-27). The loyalty of Canada is Lorne's burden, and the moral cost of that loyalty. Nevertheless, it is precisely by paying that tribute that Canada has forged its unique character as a nation:

> We from the beginning went in a spirit of amity, forgetting nothing, disavowing nothing, to plant the flag with our fortunes. We took our very Constitution, our very chart of national life, from England—her laws, her liberty, her equity were good enough for us. We have lived by them, some of us have died by them ... and thank God, we were long poor ....(229)

This self-definition, this inspirational invoking of a shared history, is paradoxical and volatile. Lorne is asking his audience to be grateful for poverty, to take pride in self-limitation. The final court of appeal for self-definition must always be, not Canada itself, but the English tradition to which Canadian loyalty defers. His emotional language (the feelings are all the stronger for his characteristic surface restraint) releases meanings which Lorne may not be entirely conscious of, may not have intended. His speech has a double message, for underlying his praise of loyalty there is a subdued and sometimes sorrowful calling into question of the very tradition being invoked.

That tradition, moreover, may be interpreted in ways very different from Lorne's; it may justify a quite different vision of the

Canadian future. It is worth considering the relation of Lorne's Canadianism, his sort of nationalism, to Milburn's complacent patriotism, "convertible into the language of bookkeeping, a balance struck with the profit on the side of the flag, the patriotic equivalent in good sound terms of dollars and cents" (42). Lorne's purpose and Milburn's are quite different, yet they sometimes appear to speak the same language, for Milburn too can say that Canada and the British tradition are good enough for him, "that he preferred a fair living under his own flag to a fortune under the Stars and Stripes" (41). Milburn is particularly angered by Lorne's campaign for a new Canada because it radically challenges the manufacturer's moderate and self-serving patriotism. Yet there is no doubt that Milburn's views are also an outgrowth of Canadian history and experience, also a manifestation of Canada's tradition of loyalty and restraint. This may make it unusually difficult for Lorne to combat Milburn's position, since both men call on the same heritage, but to such different ends.

Yet for all the obstacles to his purpose, in his Opera House speech Lorne achieves a kind of importance because of his willingness to speak out about important matters not usually discussed in Elgin. His grave candour reaches his audience; surprised at first, they nevertheless attend to his message: "He had them all with him, his words were vivid in their minds ... But he had done" (230). At the deepest level, his fellow citizens are doubtless alive to the concerns Lorne lays before them. Perhaps, too, they are heeding both parts of his double message, his frustration and sorrow as well as his vigour and optimism. It may be that only this audience could grasp that message and interpret it back to him. Lorne may not have anticipated the exact character of that response, as he could not foretell Walter Winter's insinuating speculations about the possible results of the Ormiston trial. Yet the full meaning of his actions can only be read in the interaction between his pressure and the answering response of the community. His vision of Canada is realized in his audience, in their strengths and limitations. For Lorne, this embodiment of his vision in his people is as much a qualification as it is a confirmation of his hopes. For his purposes, one decisive limitation is that his listeners will not suddenly abandon their usual caution and moderation. When it comes to action, they will remain loyal to their tradition of restraint and compromise; they will choose the path which lies between imperialism and Americanism.

In his final action of the campaign Lorne is seen as thoroughly immersed in the everyday life of the town, and it has always been the special purpose of Duncan's treatment to show that he can live in the world and contend with its pressures. There is something impressive and challenging about making the idealistic protagonist a practising politician. That is working in the world with a vengeance; it is letting oneself be defined by practical life, in connection with the most mundane issues. The Opera House speech is the climax to this effort, the moment in which Lorne's message is delivered, and his position as political idealist is focused in all its difficulty. The dénouement of the action comes after Lorne's narrow, contested victory in the election, when he is told that he must step down from the candidacy, a result more bitter than actual defeat at the polls. This unwinding of the plot is completed when Lorne hears that Hesketh is to marry Dora Milburn. The double story of love and politics is now complete, with Lorne apparently a loser in both.

The final encounter with Hesketh drives home the bitterness of Lorne's position, and ironically underlines the comparison between his prospects and those of his contemporary. It is harrowing and yet appropriate, as Duncan presents it, that the opportunist Hesketh should feel free to explain to Lorne the reasons for his setback. It is the people of Elgin who have delivered this check to Lorne's hopes, and the pragmatic Englishman, who has found a comfortable place in the community as Milburn's business partner, blandly volunteers his appreciative assessment of these people: "I'm beginning to have a great respect for the electorate of this country, Murchison .... They know what they want, and they're going to have it" (261-62). Lorne is obliged to assent to this, although he must see in it a more unsettling significance than does Hesketh: "Yes, I guess they are." Throughout this scene a distressing double perspective is maintained which pits knowledge against sympathy. On the one hand, there is Hesketh's glib assurance, which seems justified by the realities of life in Elgin; on the other hand, there is Lorne's subdued disillusionment, derived from his conscientious attempt to apply idealism in a major area of town life. The episode reminds us of Lorne's qualities, first affirmed in the encounter with Mother Beggarlegs, which "stamped him later so intelligent a meliorist" (2). But the reminder in this context is sharply ironic. Generous aspiration, active sympathy, and personal diffidence: these have been Lorne's instruments in the fight, and in this final crisis they appear to let him down more than ever. For Lorne, and for the reader, the gilt is indeed off Mother Beggarlegs's gingerbread cookies; the reality of life in Elgin stands revealed in unadorned grimness.

When Lorne hears of Hesketh's plan to marry Dora, his diffident resolve finally breaks, and he grasps for the ultimate solution, defection to the United States. By a harsh irony it is Hesketh who now chastises Lorne for thinking of "chucking the Empire," repeating the very words Lorne once used in pressing the case for closer ties between Britain and Canada (115; 264). In his facile, uncomprehending way, Hesketh is only suggesting that Lorne remain true to his own policy of loyalty to British tradition, the policy which, in his conscientious application of it, has brought him defeat and frustration. This too the idealist must face, to have his hopes parodied before him, and used to admonish him in his harshest trial. Lorne's own attitude has been a noble example of the diffident loyalty which he sees as central to the Canadian tradition. He has been true to this tradition in its highest form, but Hesketh has shrewdly grasped some of its less elevated tendencies, and now Lorne must confront a youthful contemporary who glibly parrots back to him a lower form of his own Canadian tradition.

Lorne's intemperate last word to Hesketh is the first action in which he departs from the exemplary behaviour associated with the intelligent meliorism he first gave sign of in his boyhood encounter with Mother Beggarlegs. The meeting with Hesketh replays that first encounter between Lorne and a representative of the Elgin world. In its elusive fashion, the final episode gives a kind of answer to the opening question whether Lorne did or did not strike back at Mother Beggarlegs for her rude response to his kindly interest in her affairs. Here Lorne does strike back with a mild curse, but he does so ineffectually and parenthetically, for Hesketh does not even hear his words. Even when Lorne drops his self-restraint and decency, he gets no easy satisfaction, and the narrator is moved to protect him from the possible results of his momentary lapse. The suggestion seems to be that even though the policy of intelligent meliorism will bring no certain victory over the forces of ignorance or complacency, Lorne cannot afford to depart from it. He must do as he has always done, and hope that his efforts will bring the good results he is intelligent enough to conceive and generous enough to wish to put into practice. We seem, then, to have fallen back on invincible optimism, although we now know something of the difficult conditions under which it must operate. For indeed the story as it has been told, under the pressure of a conscientious realism which promises to make the narrator's optimism more than wishful thinking, does not offer any evident rewards for her protagonist's high-minded policy. To the reader's discomfiture, the hopes of the protagonist and the narrator's invincible optimism are both shown to be at odds with the facts of life in Elgin.

After Lorne has paid for his exertions by a temporary physical and nervous collapse, from which he recuperates in the benign, alien sun of Florida, he is invited to return to Canada and take up his profession again under the sponsorship of his first mentor, Cruickshank. But this rescue of the still youthful but now deeply chastened protagonist is given only in an epilogue, and has all the marks of a contrivance to extract the narrator and her hero from a difficult impasse. Despite his role as rescuer, Cruickshank, as a leading Liberal party organizer, has always been in an ambiguous relation to the young man he favours. He has promoted Lorne's career, helping to pluck him from the safety of vague youthful projects and placing him in uneasy eminence. But the Liberal bosses have also used Lorne because they needed him, and have seen to it that he does not exceed the limits within which he can serve their immediate purposes. Lorne's sponsors have been prominent among the agents of practical life which have disappointed his idealism. Will it be any different in the future? The story suggests that if Lorne ever returns to pursue a political career in Elgin, it will have to be as a disillusioned idealist who, as Duncan presents the matter, looks like a beaten man—such is the force of pragmatic considerations in Elgin society.

There is at least as much in this narrative to encourage wariness at the end as there is to prompt confidence. Lorne cannot evade the final blow that it is Hesketh who gets the girl (such as she is) and the benefits of a comfortable place in the prudently "go-ahead" society of the day (such as it is): "Hesketh had sailed before Lorne left his [sick-room]. to return in June to those privileges and prospects of citizenship which he so eminently deserves to enjoy" (265). The force of this irony is to remind us of

Hesketh's limitations, and the limitations of the Canadian society which he has, in his fashion, joined. Yet this society is also the object of Lorne's love and solicitude, and it has bested him in a struggle to define the shape of its future. The equation drawn between Hesketh's merit and the prospects afforded by Canadian citizenship is unsettling, given the previous satiric treatment of Hesketh's character. If he is able to become such a good Canadian, so painlessly, what does this imply about Canada? The émigré Englishman becomes the successful Canadian of the moment, and the conscientious, lovable nationalist is left "stranded," undone by his very virtues. Despite the narrator's resolute spirit, it is a bitter ending to a vexatious enterprise.

There are some challenging elements of qualification in Sara Jeannette Duncan's rendering of personal and public life in Canada at the turn of the century. This qualification is implicitly registered in the mere facts of her career. Duncan spent most of her adult life outside Canada. Of her twenty or so novels only three deal to any great extent with Canada, and even in her earlier journalism her interests are often directed beyond her own country to the United States and the wider English-speaking world. In a letter to Lord Lansdowne, she referred to *The Imperialist* as "my Canadian novel," suggesting that her attention to Canada was indeed an aspect of a wider view (by the time of its writing, she had in fact published several novels, of varying degrees of seriousness, set in England, the United States and British India). Yet Duncan is of special interest to students of Canadian writing precisely because her experience and interests went beyond the borders of Canadian thought and geography in her day. If *The Imperialist* remains finally ambiguous about the prospects of its hero and his community, that might be the most significant comment the novel makes on Canada at the end of the nineteenth century. It is very clear that Lorne's imperialism cannot provide a basis for that more complete national existence he is concerned to promote. His policies have been too thoroughly discounted by indifference and scepticism, even more devestating in such a case than outright hostility. And there is real doubt about the actual soundness of Lorne's policies, on the practical level where they must finally be tested. Yet it is far from clear, in Duncan' account, that anything else in Elgin can spark the livelier and fuller national life which Lorne alone seems to think is necessary. This reasonable aspiration, both generous and moderate, is harshly frustrated. Duncan's final word on Elgin, and on the outlook for her protagonist within his society, is ambiguous: either the fuller community life to which he has dedicated his personal virtues is forming and will affirm itself one day, in "the enduring heart of the new country already old in acquiescence," or it is already too late for its development: "for that it is too soon, or perhaps it is too late." The country has shown both signs of endurance and of acquiescence; by an ironic twist of fate, which Lorne understands and which he seeks to break free of, it has endured largely by acquiescing. It is the mixed consequences of this shared history that Duncan explores in *The Imperialist,* and she leaves us at the end with an unanswered question about the shape of the future. In an early essay entitled "Colonialism and Literature" (*The Week* 30 September 1886; rpt Duncan, *Selected Journalism* 105-109), Duncan declared that "a national literature cannot be looked for as an outcome of anything less than a complete national existence" (109). This rather stringent equation between a youthful nation's politics and its imaginative life may help to explain why in Duncan's "Canadian novel," imaginative idealism is obliged to take a political turn, and lays itself open to a discouraging setback.

"This Little Outpost of Empire":
Sara Jeannette Duncan and the Decolonization
of Canada*

Ajay Heble

> Imperialism means ... the realization of a Greater Canada ...
> I ... am an Imperialist because I will not be a Colonial.
>
> Stephen Leacock

There is a two-cent stamp issued by this country for Christmas
1898 which bears the following inscription: "We hold a vaster
empire than has been."[1] The stamp displays a map of the world,
with North and South America prominently located in the centre
of the picture. All British possessions are marked in red, and
Canada, the reddest spot on the entire map, is given the distinct
privilege of being topped by a crown. Perhaps what is most striking about this stamp is its use of the term "we"—a term which
suggests a community of involvement, invokes a shared history,
and acknowledges, anticipates, and ultimately authorizes our participation and complicity in the process of imperialist expansion and
domination. The stamp reflects the prevailing sentiment of the
time, that of the English-Canadian majority, and is useful because,
among other things, it provides us with a possible explanation as
to why Canada and Canadian literature tend to be excluded from
so many important international studies of empire. The almost
non-existent status accorded to Canada in these studies[2] may, at
some level, be the result of the widespread impression, which our
stamp and its inscription certainly do nothing to mitigate, that
Canada had been part of the *dominating* group rather than the
oppressed and *dominated* one. What this impression refuses to
admit, in short, is that Canada was, and to a certain extent still

---

*Originally published in *Journal of Commonwealth Literature* 26.1
(1991): 215-28. Some omissions. Reprinted by kind permission of Hanz
Zell Publishers, an imprint of Bowker-Saur, a division of Reed-Elsevier
UK Ltd.

remains, a colony. The conflict between our colonial "victim status" and our desire to be a vital part of the Empire, to rally round
the British flag in times of need, played an especially important
role in the Canadian way of life during the period between 1884
and 1914.[3] It is this conflict which is dramatized in *The Imperialist.*

Much commentary on *The Imperialist* tends to praise the
author for her realistic presentation of life in a small Ontario town
at the turn of the century. Claude Bissell, in his "Introduction" to
the New Canadian Library edition of *The Imperialist*, insists that
"Duncan is not making a statement, or parading her own convictions ... which ultimately ran counter to the logic of her fictional
creation" (ix). Bissell commends Duncan for her ability to remain
critically detached from the events and issues which she describes
in her novel, especially since in "real life" she was an ardent
imperialist. We know about Duncan's convictions in "real life"
because she was a journalist as well as a writer of prose fiction,
and in the columns she wrote no attempt was made to disguise her
loyalty to the imperial cause in Canada. Why, then, should Duncan
write a novel which, as most critics would have it, ran counter to
the feelings which she so vehemently expressed in her non-fic-
tional writing? Or *is* this what Duncan was doing in *The Imperialist*? Despite Bissell's contention that Duncan is not parading her
own convictions, despite the attempt of another critic, Francis
Zichy, to maintain that Duncan, through Lorne Murchison's celebrated speech in praise of loyalty to Britain, is "calling into question the very tradition being invoked" (this edition, 397), I would
like to suggest that Duncan is as committed to the "imperial idea"
in her novel as she is in her journalism. One of the ways that Duncan reveals this bias, in *The Imperialist*, is through her manipulation of narrative technique. More specifically, as we shall see in a
moment, the *way* Duncan writes *The Imperialist* cannot finally be
separated from the novel's political content ....

The central proponents of imperialism in Canada—George R.
Parkin, George M. Grant, and George T. Denison—all believed
that Canada could achieve full status as a nation only by holding
onto its connection with Britain. The "imperial idea," then, was
irrevocably bound up with Canada's national development. As
Carl Berger has convincingly demonstrated, "Imperialism was one
form of Canadian nationalism" (*Sense of Power* 259). Far from
being concerned with the acquisition and exploitation of foreign

territories, Canadians who embraced the "imperial idea" saw it as a necessary prerequisite for the self-preservation of their nation. While there were those who still stood opposed to imperialism on the grounds that it was absolutely incompatible with Canada's national interests,[4] a vigorous attempt was made by its supporters to promote imperialism as the only means by which Canada would shed its colonial status.

This is precisely the attitude which Duncan attempts to promote in *The Imperialist*. The goal which Lorne Murchison espouses is explicitly linked with nationalism. Lorne "believed himself," Duncan writes, "at the bar for the life of a nation" (230). That Duncan herself believes this is made apparent when she intrudes—and I will return to the question of authorial intention in a moment—into her narrative and tells us "we are here at the making of a nation" (37). Imperialism, then, for both Lorne and for Duncan, means precisely what it meant for Parkin, Grant and Denison—a form of Canadian nationalism. Lorne makes the connection between the imperial idea and nationalism most evident in his speech given in the opera-house to the electors of South Fox:

> "The imperial idea is far-sighted. England has outlived her own body. Apart from her heart and her history, England is an area where certain trades are carried on—still carried on. In the scrolls of the future it is already written that the centre of the Empire must shift—and where, if not to Canada?" (225)

Though I will return to this quotation a little later, I would like here to point out that its prediction for Canada's future testifies to the nature of Lorne's appeal. The argument is clearly a nationalistic one and it smacks of nothing so much as Duncan's own article, "Imperial Sentiment in Canada" (*Sara Jeannette Duncan: Selected Journalism* 62), where she too sees Imperial Federation as prefiguring Canada's greatness.

Other aspects of Lorne's opera-house speech reinforce the notion that Canadian imperialism was the result of the conditions which I have been considering:

> "The question that underlies this decision for Canada is that of the whole stamp and character of her future existence. Is that stamp and character to be impressed by the American Republic

effacing—he smiled a little—the old Queen's head and the new King's oath? Or is it to be our own stamp and character, acquired in the rugged discipline of our colonial youth, and developed in the national usage of the British Empire?" (229)

Imperial Federation, then, was construed to be for the political advantage of Canada; it was a step necessary for our self-preservation. But its impact, as Lorne demonstrates, went far beyond the political realm. Part of what imperialism meant was a deeply felt devotion to the British heritage. "Belief in England," writes Duncan, "was in the blood, it would not yield to the temporary distortion of facts in the newspapers" (49). Before Lorne goes to England, he tells Dora Milburn that Canada has derived a "moral advantage" from its connection with Britain:

"But I'll see England, Dora; I'll feel England, eat and drink and sleep and live in England, for a little while. Isn't the very name great? I'll be a better man for going, till I die. We're all right out here, but we're young and thin and weedy. They didn't grow so fast in England, to begin with, and now they're rich with character and strong with conduct and hoary with ideals. I've been reading up the history of our political relations with England. It's astonishing what we've stuck to her through, but you can't help seeing why—it's for the moral advantage. (90)

The novel abounds in such speeches in praise of England; what I want to bring to our attention is the explicit shift in focus which takes place once Lorne Murchison, in his official capacity as secretary to the Cruickshank deputation, has returned from his trip to England. This shift, which has been noted by a number of critics, is important because it signals a crucial stage in the process of Canada's decolonization. Before Lorne sets out for Britain, he sees his fellow Canadians as "young and thin and weedy" (90). His hometown of Elgin, which operates as a microcosm for all Canada and which Duncan refers to early in the text as "this little outpost of empire" (11) is teeming with inhabitants who are more English than the English themselves. Elgin's attitude, or the attitude of a number of its inhabitants, towards the Mother Country, is delineated with precision in two passages which occur early in the novel. The first of these is Duncan's description of the enthusiasm with which Canadians celebrate the Queen's Birthday. "Here," Duncan writes, "it was a real holiday, that woke you with bells and cannon." This is the kind of enthusiasm, Duncan insists, which, in England, is only reserved for a "Bank holiday" (3). The second passage which announces the extent to which a loyalty to Britain dominated every-day life in Canada is a passage in which Duncan explains how the Murchison children came to receive their names:

> Lorne came after Advena, at the period of a *naive* fashion of christening the young sons of Canada in the name of her Gover-nor-General. It was a simple way of attesting a loyal spirit, but with Mrs. Murchison more particular motives operated. The Marquis of Lorne was not only the deputy of the throne, he was the son-in-law of a good woman, of whom Mrs. Murchison thought more, and often said it, for being the woman she was than for being twenty times a Queen; and he had made a metrical translation of the Psalms, several of which were included in the revised psalter for the use of the Presbyterian Church in Canada, from which the whole of Knox Church sang to the praise of God every Sunday. These were circumstances that weighed with Mrs. Murchison, and she called her son after the Royal representative, feeling that she was doing well for him in a sense beyond the mere bestowal of a distinguished and a euphonious name, though that, as she would have willingly acknowledged, was "well enough in its place." (7)

Both of these passages alert us to the fact that Elgin, when the novel begins, is steeped in a colonial tradition. The slavish imita-tion of British customs, to which these examples testify, goes hand in hand with Lorne's insistence on the superiority of the British race. Lorne, while still abroad, insists that England is "the heart of the Empire, the conscience of the world, and the Mecca of the race" (116).

Once Lorne returns to Canada, however, he demonstrates a significant change in attitude. Duncan, as if signalling the impor-tance of this turning-point in her novel, prepares us for this change by *telling* us that "what [Lorne] absorbed and took back with him is, after all, what we have to do with; his actual adventures are of no great importance" (106). It is here that I wish to return to Lorne's opera-house speech. While abroad Lorne has become aware of England's "unready conception of things," its "political concentration upon parish affairs," its "cumbrous social machine-ry," and its "problems of sluggish overpopulation" (117). When he returns to his homeland, these observations lead him to the conclusion that England has "outlived her own body" (225). Lorne becomes conscious of the advantages which Britain's decline could have for his own nation, and he accordingly posits a future with Canada as "the centre of the Empire." No longer a "little outpost" teeming with "young and thin and weedy" inhabitants, Canada "in the scrolls of the future," abandons its colonial position of dependency and becomes a full-fledged nation. This shift in focus from Britain as "the heart of the Empire" to Canada as "the centre of the Empire" is accompanied by a change in the rhetoric of imperialism. Not content to concern himself simply with the rhetoric of self-preservation, Lorne now feels compelled to introduce, if only by implication, the notion of power into the discourse of Canadian imperialism.[5]

Lorne's attempt to centralize Canada's position within the imperial scheme—by ascribing to his nation a future greatness—should remind us of the considerations with which I began this essay. The sentiment reflected in Canada's stamp of Christmas 1898 is very much the same sentiment which Lorne Murchison expresses in his opera-house speech when he envisions Canada as the centre of the Empire. In our stamp, we will recall, Canada occupies a central position in terms of both its prominent location on the map and its striking inscription. The "we" of this inscription testifies to the extent to which Canada felt great pride in its participation in the Empire. It is like the "we" which Duncan herself uses when she makes what seems to be an implicit comment on Canada's participation in the Boer War:

> Indifferent, apathetic, self-centred—until whenever, down the wind, across the Atlantic, came the faint far music of the call to arms. Then the old dog of war that has his kennel in every man rose and shook himself, and presently there would be a baying! The sense of kinship, lying too deep for the touch of ordinary circumstance, quickened to that; and in a moment "we" were fighting, "we" had lost or won. (49)

Here, Duncan seems to imply that our loyalty to Britain is ultimately more important for Canada than it is for the Mother Country. It is our participation in the Empire, she tells us, which will relieve us of our indifference, apathy and self-centredness. By coming to the aid of Britain, by helping fight wars for the Mother Country, we experience the sense of power which accompanies the enactment of our imperial duties and we move one step closer to an affirmation of our own national identity. Duncan, in other words, legitimizes our involvement in overseas wars by suggesting that such involvement is for our own good.[6] Her employment of the pronoun "we," like the use made of it in our stamp's motto, is indicative not only of the pride which many Canadians took in belonging to the Empire, but also of the pride which they felt in being at its very centre: " 'we' were fighting, 'we' had lost or won."[7]

Sara Jeannette Duncan contributes to this process of centralization by the very way she writes her novel. The point-of-view employed by Duncan in *The Imperialist* is a curious one. Much of the novel is presented from a third-person omniscient perspective. Frequently, however, Duncan will intrude into her narrative, usually with the use of a first-person narrator. Although Duncan's strategy clearly has literary precedents in much Victorian and some 18th century fiction, the specific political context of *The Imperialist* makes the manipulation of narrative perspective here particularly intriguing. For the most part, Duncan seems pretty comfortable with the conventions of a third-person narration, and she likes the fact that it allows her to see into the minds of her characters. Most of *The Imperialist* is written from this perspective presumably because Duncan wants to be able to transcend the limitations of a first-person point-of-view: she wants her characters to be knowable, and she, the narrator, wants the privilege of knowing and seeing all.

At various points in the text, however, Duncan also wants to present herself as the real-life author that she is, as someone who holds her own opinions and judgments—in short, as the writer of this history. The first-person narrator who interrupts what is primarily a third-person narration is not a character in the fiction, though she does, somewhat after the fashion of Thackeray's narrator in *Vanity Fair* and Fielding's in *Tom Jones*, frequently speak in a highly individualized voice. She is all too willing, when she finds it convenient, to enter into the text and offer her own views on what she has just been describing. Consider, for instance, the following passage in which Duncan makes explicit her own positive attitude towards her protagonist:

The characteristics of him I have tried to convey were grafted on an excellent fund of common sense. He was well aware of the proportions of things; he had no despair of the Idea, nor would he despair should the Idea etherealize and fly away. (258)

By using the first-person here, and in other passages in the novel, Duncan endeavours to validate the discourse of imperialism through the authority of her own self-presence. To put it another way, Duncan intrudes into the text and formally acknowledges the protagonist's "excellent" characteristics precisely in order to guide her reader's attitude toward Lorne and toward the imperial ideal which Lorne represents.

Duncan's authorial intrusions, in telling us how we should look upon her characters, remind us of the extent to which part of the "author-function"—if I may borrow Michel Foucault's term— is to restrict and limit meaning ("The author is the principle of thrift in the proliferation of meanings," Foucault 159). That Duncan's first-person remarks serve this purpose is quite evident. As one critic of her work has correctly pointed out, "Duncan's style emphasizes telling rather than showing, and ... [her] bemused and frequently astringent intrusions are clearly intended to guide the reader's response to Elgin society" (Zezulka 147). By *telling* us what to think through an appeal to her own authority, Duncan is attempting to limit our range of personal response.

But Duncan is not content with this. A world of only restricted meanings and first-person judgments is not perfectly compatible with her urge for narrative omniscience. When Lorne goes to Britain, for instance, Duncan wants to be able to tell us what he "absorbed" while he was there. Because she is not a character in the fiction, she cannot, in realistic terms, go abroad with him— though she would undoubtedly like to do so. If the novel were being written strictly in the first-person, Duncan would here be faced with a structural and epistemological problem: the inability of the individual perceiving mind to know about what went on when the Other was not in its presence. Duncan, of course, never encounters this problem because she maintains a third-person omniscient narration which, by its very convention, allows her to know what Lorne "absorbed" in Britain without our ever having to deal with the question of whether or not she, Duncan, was present. My point here is that Duncan's account of Elgin's, and by implication Canada's, history depends on and is determined by the imagination. And the novel, as we shall see in a moment, makes an explicit connection between the imagination and imperialism. But first, let me be more precise about what I mean here. In the omniscient sections of the narrative, which comprise, as I said earlier, most of *The Imperialist*, the whole problem of the first-person narrator, this "I" who appears every now and again, is essentially forgotten. We accept the conventions of the third-person narration so completely that we forget—except when Duncan sees fit to remind us—that the author of this history is, in fact, an "I" who has been positing herself as the centre of authority. What becomes evident, then, is that Sara Jeannette Duncan wants the best of both perspectives. She wants her status as a real-life author to count for something because of the authority that goes along with it; but she also, as we have seen, wants to have the totality of vision which accompanies omniscience. By combining the two points-of-view, Duncan enables herself to enjoy and exhibit power on both levels. The first-person point-of-view puts her at the centre of the text as its real-life writer—a writer with the power to guide and manipulate the response of her readers. The third-person perspective bestows upon her the power of the imagination—the power to recount events at which she need not have been present. That Duncan herself is aware of this power is made strikingly evident at one point in the novel. I am referring here to a passage in which Lorne has just encountered an ex-schoolmate named Elmore Crow. Suddenly, Duncan, in the first-person, admits that this entire episode is the result of her own invention:

> Nevertheless, *as they walk together in my mind* along the Elgin market square, the Elgin Collegiate Institute rises infallibly behind them, a directing influence and a responsible parent. (67; emphasis added)

Although this passage is interesting for a number of reasons, its most striking characteristic, it seems to me, is the very explicitness with which it signals its self-consciousness: nowhere else in the text does Duncan make such an overtly self-conscious gesture. Why should she, at this particular juncture in the narrative, suddenly decide to admit that this scene is constructed? Or, to put it another way, if Lorne can walk along Elgin market square "in [Duncan's] mind," is it not equally plausible for him to walk, say, through the streets of London "in [her] mind"? Far from incidental, Duncan's decision to privilege this moment in the Elgin market square as an instance of her imaginative capacity is indeed telling. By looking more closely at the positioning of the passage, we can begin to understand the logic behind her intrusion. In the same paragraph, for instance, just a few sentences earlier, we are given the following information about the Elgin Collegiate Institute:

> The Collegiate Institute was a potential melting-pot: you went in as your simple opportunities had made you; how you shaped coming out depended upon what was hidden in the core of you. You could not in any case be the same as your father before you; education in a new country is too powerful a stimulant for that .... It is indeed the touchstone for character in a new people, for character acquired as apart from that inherited; it sometimes reveals surprises. (67)

While, as the narrator goes on to point out, Lorne's choice of a career fails to illustrate her point about character acquired rather than character inherited, what she does not mention here is that Lorne's political ideals approximate her notion quite nicely. In calling for a more closely-linked Empire, and, in particular, by envisaging a more central role for Canada within that Empire, Lorne rejects the backward-looking notion of character based exclusively on inheritance in favour of a more forward-looking conception of a country which will soon come into its own.

Earlier in the same chapter, Lorne has a kind of epiphany in the Elgin market square, an implicit vision, even before he goes to England, of Canada's future greatness:

> This morning he had an elation of his own; it touched everything with more vivid reality .... the whole world invited his eyes, offering him a great piece of luck to look through. The opportunity was in his hand which, if he could seize and hold, would lift and carry him on. He was as much aware of its potential significance as anyone could be, and what leapt in his veins till he could have laughed aloud was the splendid conviction of resource. (65)

As Duncan herself is engaged in the same process of imagining the moment of her country coming into its own—indeed the whole novel constitutes such an act of the imagination—she selects this particular section in the narrative, following Lorne's vision in the Elgin market square, to signal her own powers of vision. Duncan's capacity to imagine, to recount an event which takes place solely *in her mind*, in other words structurally links her with Lorne Murchison, Elgin's central proponent of imperialism. Lorne, we are told, is gifted with the power of "imagination and energy and love." As Thomas Tausky reminds us in his analysis of Duncan's novel, Lorne has the ability to "conjure up an *imaginative* vision of Canada's future destiny" (*Novelist of Empire* 162; emphasis added). Tausky observes, quite correctly I believe, that an explicit connection between imperialism and the imagination is made by the novel. That Duncan, herself gifted with the power of the imagination—a gift which she significantly chooses to announce at the very moment that Lorne has his epiphany in the Elgin market square—favours imperialism for Canada is suggested by the fact that "the line dividing the proponents from the opponents of imperialism also divides the imaginative characters from the unimaginative" (*Novelist of Empire* 161-62). Unlike Lorne, who is concerned with the future destiny of his nation, the characters who stand opposed to imperialism are shallow and self-centred. They are, as Dora Milburn so aptly illustrates, leftovers of a colonial tradition. The imitation of British manners which we see in the Milburns—Dora "had been taught to speak, like Mrs. Milburn, with what was known as an 'English accent' " (39)—attests to what Tausky calls their "unthinking conformity" (as contrasted with the "independence of mind" [*Novelist of Empire* 165] which characterizes Lorne and Advena Murchison). There is very little doubt about where Duncan's sympathies rest.

Sara Jeannette Duncan, then, in *The Imperialist*, is herself implicated in two specific acts of creation which depend on and are determined by the power of imaginative vision. These two acts of creation, the creation of a novel and the creation of a nation, are linked in such a manner that Duncan's very method of writing becomes a reflection of the way she would like to see her country governed. By combining third-person omniscient narrative with first-person authorial commentary, she alerts us to the sense of power and influence which she exhibits in her own writing. It is precisely this sense of power and influence which Duncan wishes Canada to obtain through its participation in the imperial scheme. Although Lorne Murchison, Elgin's proponent of the imperial idea, fails in both his short-term political career and his affair with Dora Milburn,[8] Sara Jeannette Duncan, in her own way, succeeds in her attempt to promote Canadian imperialism.[9] She succeeds because her novel operates not only as a depiction, but also as a representation of an important stage in the process of Canada's decolonization. While Duncan does not advocate a total dismantling of dominant old world social practices, her commitment to national power within the Empire reveals the extent to which she is presaging the moment when Canada will be able to assert its difference from the inherited British tradition.

The problem here, as recent studies in the politics of national consciousness in settler-invader cultures have shown, is that the assertion of difference from inherited traditions runs the risk of leading to a dangerously monolithic construction and understanding of Canada. As Diana Brydon and Helen Tiffin suggest in *Decolonizing Fictions*, the discourse of nationality itself "depends on the suppression of oppositional voices and the smoothing over of differences for its construction of a unified identity" (64). In looking forward to a moment when Canada will come into its own as a nation, *The Imperialist*, then, represents an important, if problematic, stage in the process of national formation—the stage of power and centralization, the stage so incisively registered in the stamp which inaugurated this discussion—by enacting it through Duncan's very mode of presentation. Duncan, to put it another way, translates Lorne's idealistic conception of imperialism into the practical realm of her own writing. That she should do this, of course, comes as no surprise. The decolonization of Canada is, after all, a cultural process as much as it is a political one.

Endnotes

1 A version of this stamp is reproduced on the front cover of Berger, *The Sense of Power*.

2 See, for instance, Hobson, *Imperialism: A Study* and Arendt, *Imperialism*. Both writers make only passing references to Canada—Hobson to its "self-governing" status and Arendt to the fact that it was "almost

empty and had no serious population problem."

3   These thirty years before the First World War are cited by Professor Berger as being the most bitter years of the struggle between the advocates of Canadian imperialism and their opponents. See *Imperialism and Nationalism 1884-1914,* ed. Berger, 1-5.

4   Such opposition can be found in Ewart, *The Kingdom Papers* and Bourassa, *Great Britain and Canada.* See also Bourassa's "The French-Canadian in the British Empire."

5   This shift in attitude towards the Empire finds a parallel in the actual circumstances of Canadian history. See Berger, *Sense of Power* 259.

6   Such a view, of course, is perilously slanted towards the goals of the English speaking majority. French Canada, in Duncan's text, is conspicuously absent.

7   The "sense of power" which accompanied such a central position was expressed by Sir George Foster in 1901: "[With] the perception of increased power and influence, and the appreciation of future possibilities, there has arisen ... the sense of power to be exercised within the Empire, of responsibility to imperial duties, of attachment to imperial ideals, and co-operation in the achievement of imperial destinies." Quoted in Berger, *Sense of Power* 259-60.

8   Lorne, the idealist, is defeated—on both the romantic and the short-term political level—by pragmatism and self-interest. This is, of course, sharply contrasted with his sister Advena's successful romance with Hugh Finlay. In this relationship, Hugh's old-world conventional ideals are defeated by common-sense practical life in Elgin. In Hugh's case, this defeat of old-world ideals results in his attaining that which he most desires. In Lorne's case, however, the defeat is an indication of Duncan's ironic detachment—as an example of the way in which she refuses to parade her own convictions. But it is important to note that Lorne is not completely defeated. At the end of the novel he forms a partnership with Cruickshank, a partnership which is undoubtedly an analogy for Canada's relationship with Britain (see Zezulka 149).

9   "Imperialism," as I try to point out in this essay, had different meanings for different Canadians. The sense in which I am using it here is the one which Duncan herself promotes—imperialism as a form of nationalism which would lead to Canada's centrality within the Empire.

"There's a tremendous moral aspect": Imperialism and morality in *The Imperialist* *

Terrence L. Craig

Lorne Murchison is one of the most positive characters in Canadian literature. Lorne is *good*, for a variety of reasons which Duncan finds innate to the New World. His lack of class consciousness and his open and genuine nature are examples of the characteristics Duncan gives him in contrast with those of the Old World characters. His greatest quality is that of imagination—the ability to visualize a better future out of an acceptable present. Despite his enthusiastic imagination he is unable to inspire the electorate with his idealism, and this quality which raises him above the "masses" also plunges him into defeat and depression.

However idealism may be admirable, it is itself only a psychological conveyance for abstractions that eventually have to work in practice. Lorne's idealism is contrasted with the smug, defensive bean-counting of Mr. Milburn, and even with his own father's careful steadiness. These two men have in common that they resist the fast currents of Lorne's enthusiasm, and their successes in life thus far seem to be because of such resistance to imaginative risks. The novel is not entitled *The Idealist*. Lorne's idealism is merely a characteristic of the man. What his idealism has fastened upon is revealing, not just further into his personality but into Duncan's treatment of her main theme.

Lorne's idealism for imperialism is as unlimited as his understanding of its practical consequences is limited. He is actually a preferential trader (and behind that an anti-American), but neither phrase catches the imagination like "the imperialist." Lorne is supposed to have studied the statistics of empire, and to have incorporated them into the brief the committee takes to London. However, his studies of imperial commerce begin after his acceptance of the position of secretary to the committee. Looking at this impulsive acceptance statement, so emotionally loaded and yet so undefin-

---

*Commissioned for this edition.

able and even semi-mystical, it seems that Lorne has always been an imperialist, and that those qualities which make him "good" would inevitably lead him in this direction. Elgin, in producing Lorne, must also have produced his idealistic sense of imperialism. Other "good" characters—notably Dr. Drummond—have tended in that direction too, and might be expected to have contributed to Lorne's imperial motif, but they do not go as far as he does. With the naive idealism of youth and inexperience, Lorne follows his mixture of emotion and thought to an extreme, and is unable to convince others that he is right to do so. How, then, is Duncan to convince her readers?

Lorne's idealism, so ostensibly attached to imperialism, is actually grounded in morality. "Moral" is one of the key words in the novel, and is often indirectly referred to without the word itself being mentioned. Lorne's emphatic statement, "But it's the Empire!" (81) is a complete abstraction, and any understanding of it is predicated on an acceptance of the moral ascendancy of the British Empire over its competitors. It has been argued that Lorne's idealism is political while Finlay's is moral (Gerson 73). Rather, I see the idealism of both as primarily moral: while Lorne's operates in the political arena, where morality is often seen as a pose, Finlay's moral position is situated in the romance sub-plot where, in a late Victorian novel, it would be expected. Lorne assumes a moral position towards imperialism, sensing its integral morality, and follows the political consequences. Morality and imperialism are virtually equated, and the two plots complement each other to confirm the equation. In *Moral Vision in the Canadian Novel*, Dooley has described Lorne as confessing that "he is a politician secondarily, a man with an ideal, a vision of empire, a moral mission primarily," and Duncan as showing "moral idealism" to be the "salvation" of both Britain and Canada (33). Dooley re-articulates Duncan's premise that Canada was at a crucial decision point in its history, and would either prosper *and* be moral one way, or subside into a semi-Americanized lesser sense of morality the other way. ("Lesser breeds without the law?") The implications of this premise suggest explanations for some of the structural oddities of the novel.

Whether or not Duncan was a Social Darwinite, she certainly presents the British Empire, even with the weaknesses she exposes both of the centre and of the parts, as the pinnacle of human civilization. It is morality that distinguishes this empire, and makes its renewal worth fighting for. She can assume that her readers understand the moral nature of this conflict, as her narrator regularly raises it as an issue that *is* understood by Lorne as well as the reader.

Why should an empire be moral, or "good" like Lorne, at the expense of those outside it? An empire is a power structure supported by its citizens, who express in their support certain forms of xenophobia. Duncan had consciously made herself a citizen of the Empire, outgrowing the provincialism she describes so knowingly in the novel. To be conscious of being morally superior because of one's membership in a group is a mannered form of racism, particularly when one race is being discussed and others are excluded. Carl Berger has addressed the relationship of racism and turn-of-the-century Canadian imperialism in *The Sense of Power*, noting that "racial explanations were conventional as well as respectable within the cultural milieu of the later nineteenth century and imperialists had no monopoly over them. The familiar language of racism, however, frequently concealed confusion ..." (117). I expect what is confusing and vague to a modern reader about such explanations is that they were not ends in themselves nor were they intended as negative or discriminatory by people who prided themselves on fair play and British justice. Rather, this confused sense of racial enclosure provided Duncan with a positive, global frame for her xenophobic pride in her own power group, and for lack of any clearer terminology she expressed this as morality. It is a paradox that an abstract as morally tainted as racial pride should be the foundation of Duncan's rhetoric about her moral empire. She presents morality as linked to honour and chivalry, and accentuates its results without exploring its roots.

" 'Well, there's a tremendous moral aspect,' Finlay said, 'tremendous moral potentialities hidden in the issue' " (130). These potentialities and their bases remain essentially hidden; for all the debate and rhetoric staged throughout the novel, the moral base of the British Empire is presented as a given, and as an incontrovertible argument. Instead of discussing morality, Duncan has it acted out by her characters. They are manipulated as correlatives of the abstracts that contribute to her theme. As Victorian morality must have a clear dichotomy, Duncan provides this in her characterization, and lets the morality of characters influence the morality the reader will find behind the political rhetoric. Morality is a constant for the narrator, who expects the reader to share it, and thus be swayed towards imperialism. Morality is the controlling abstraction behind the novel's plot, driving its theme.

Yet because of its fuzzy racial associations when linked with empire, morality too is left dangerously fuzzy. This can be seen when Lorne tells Dora of his new-found ardour for the Empire:

> I've been reading up the history of our political relations with England. It's astonishing what we've stuck to her through, but you can't help seeing why—it's for the moral advantage. Way down at the bottom, that's what it is. We have the sense to want all we can get of that sort of thing. (90)

What exactly "that sort of thing" means is left hanging in the air when Dora (understandably) shows no interest in it. When Hesketh tries to help Lorne's campaign, he too lapses into vagueness: "Even proposals for mutual commercial benefit may be underpinned, I am glad to say, by loftier principles than those of the market-place and the counting-house" (191). What exactly are those "loftier principles" other than a claim of superior morality linked to a superior race? Lorne's own final election speech—the five-page rhetorical death ride he makes in Chapter 29—is as much an attack on the United States' rising position in the world as it is a defence of Canadian ties with Britain.

This is not a novel about winners. If Lorne and his family are shown to be too good for Elgin, it is Elgin which is at fault for not being good enough, just as the English are faulted for not following Wallingham. Lorne is associated politically with Wallingham in London and Cruickshank in Toronto. These three characters are brought together once, momentarily, for lunch in London. By the novel's end all three will have failed in the same enterprise, trying to gain support for an imperial federation. All three are depicted as morally better than those they tried to lead. Cruickshank is introduced in glowing, even heroic, terms as "an able man and, what was rarer, a fastidious politician. He had held office in the Dominion Cabinet, and had resigned it because of a difference with his colleagues in the application of a principle" (72). The implication is that politicians are unprincipled and that Cruickshank has been a shining exception. Wallingham is shown as having left his party (as Joseph Chamberlain had done, in fact) for the sake of a principle. And Lorne loses the election by promoting his principle. These politicians that Lorne admires and follows are history's losers; they may be *morally* right, but the public will not let that interfere with business. Lorne and his fictional defeat are not being contrasted with Dr. Drummond and his fictional success; rather, within the main plot Lorne's defeat because of society's weakness is contrasted with Hesketh's success which is due to Hesketh's personal weakness. Thus society rewards those least deserving of it, and the reader is invited to make a moral judgment about that.

It is possible to read *The Imperialist* as a social satire twisting back and forth between comic and tragic polarities; such a reading is largely dependent upon a deconstruction of Lorne's perfect character. Lorne has to be "good" enough to succeed or the plot has no point; equally, he has to be "good" enough to fail. His goodness, which is seen in his generous, unselfish nature and in his firm adherence to principle, is supposed to spill over on to imperialism, yet beyond the fact that Lorne seems to have been raised as an imperialist there is no clear connection. The Milburns, and eventually Hesketh as well, are accused of being unprincipled. Mr. Milburn condemns subsidies, although he was once glad to accept one. Hesketh first supports Lorne's campaign and then switches to the other side; Dora's engagement is equally transferable. Their hypocrisy contrasts obviously with Lorne's unselfishness. Yet in each case their switches are made for gains the reader can see, while Lorne remains constant with principles that are not seen but merely implied. Lorne's major principle is his constancy, which attracts attention away from the insubstantial nature of the ideal to which he is faithful. The ideal must be good if Lorne espouses it, yet Lorne fails to convince *his* audience, and this leaves Duncan depending on the hypothetical negative scenario to convince *her* audience.

Finlay and Lorne are both Romantics, each willing to suffer loss for the sake of the ideal, each so involved with abstract principles that the practicalities of life are avoided. Finlay is way-laid on his self-destructive voyage, but Lorne is not. It is Romanticism in the abstract that ties Finlay and Lorne, and the two plots together. Each plot focuses on a love interest, with Hesketh doing to Lorne what Dr. Drummond does to Finlay. Yet Dr. Drummond has been established as the voice of rectitude in the community, and in "cutting out" (252) Finlay he is surely doing no wrong. Both Lorne and Finlay are upholding moral principles in a world that is shown to care little for morality in practice. Their opposites, Dr. Drummond and Hesketh, are shamelessly unromantic and prosper accordingly in an unromantic society. Lorne and Finlay together demonstrate the problems that a Romantic attachment to abstracts can create in the real world, but ironically both characters gain strength for their unswerving adherence to their vague moral principles. Romanticism is so allied with morality in both plots that it is difficult to assess it as a problem. *The Imperialist* is no twentieth-century *Northanger Abbey*, yet Duncan, like Austen before her, demonstrates the tragic potential of Romantic excess. And also like Austen, she presents a common-sense foundation in contrast with the Romantic imagination. In moving her characters between these polarities, Duncan reflects the complexities of human nature while still asserting the moral, political and xenophobic *weltanschauung* of her class and time.

The Narrative Politics of *The Imperialist**

Frank Davey

The explicit political concerns of Sara Jeannette Duncan's *The Imperialist*—its cautious sympathy with Joseph Chamberlain's 1902-03 proposals to establish a British Empire customs union protected by tariffs from the potentially cheaper goods of non-Empire countries, and its extremely qualified endorsement of British institutions and traditions—have been evident since its publication in 1904. In recent years Duncan criticism has quite reasonably focused much less on interpreting these concerns than on recovering the context of Canadian and British "imperialist" politics of

---

*Commissioned for this edition.

the 1896-1904 period, and on considering what Duncan's own views of those politics might have been. The narrative structure of *The Imperialist*, however, does offer considerably more political meanings than those the novel explicitly indicates.

§

Most readers of *The Imperialist* imagine that the first character they encounter in it is the old black vendor of taffy and ginger-bread, Mother Beggarlegs, whose name occurs at the end of the opening sentence, "It would have been idle to inquire into the antecedents, or even the circumstances, of old Mother Beggar-legs." But she is actually only the second. The first is the narrator who insinuates his or her playful hypothesizing intelligence into this sentence, proposing that someone might indeed inquire into "the antecedents" or "the circumstances" of this street vendor, and firmly declaring such inquiry so unfruitful as to be "idle." And if there is anything that this narrative intelligence is not, it is "idle." It is instead active and assured, launching itself in this paragraph into a series of lengthy sentences each one of which begins with a main-clause assertion: "It would have been idle ...."; "She would never tell;" "Her occupation was clear;" "She came, it was under-stood, with the dawn;" and so on far into the opening paragraph. Not until the ninth sentence is this syntax varied, with the inverse structure of "And why 'Beggarlegs' nobody in the world could tell you."

It would be fairly easy and even reasonable to explain this narrator as a product of the omniscient narrator conventions of nineteenth-century English fiction: in most of her novels Duncan in fact uses fictional conventions familiar to her audiences to write commercially successful combinations of social satire and senti-mental romance. But because such a convention might well be transparent to those familiar with it does not mean that the con-vention itself does not carry ideological effect. And in a novel in which politics is such a major and explicit focus, such ideological effect is unlikely to be negligible.

Beyond its breezy and confident style, there are a limited number of things a reader can "know" about the narrator of *The Imperialist*. The narrator is familiar with both English-Canada and Britain, but seems to identify itself more with the latter than with the former. It uses both the first-person singular and the first-person plural to refer to itself in the first half of the book, with the plural form seeming to denote others who can share its cosmopolitan viewpoint. It is most familiar with the privileged classes of both countries; except for its attention to the Crow family, it views the lower classes only as crowds or groups. It is most comfortable with a socially dominant middle-class, a class it easily locates in Canada but does not find in Britain. Its perspective on Old Mother Beggarlegs is simultaneously that of a young middle-class Canadian boy and that of a mature cosmopolitan looking amusedly down on that middle-class boy. In religion, it is knowledgeable about various protestant churches but most comfortable with Presbyterianism—a church which is an influential one in nineteenth-century Canada but a minor one in the social structure of nineteenth-century Britain. It is knowledgeable about politics and economics, but satirically so; its political discourse is that of an observer rather than a participant. Its gender is unspecified. Yet the range of characters offered by the novel does operate to gender the narrator as female. Only two characters in the book speak in styles as breezy and confident and as politically unengaged as the narrator, and both are young women: the Murchison sisters Stella and Advena. And only a woman character—Advena—shares in any way the narrator's ability to stand outside the action and perceive its ironies and humiliations.

§

Misao Dean has argued that *The Imperialist*'s opening on a portrait of Mother Beggarlegs allows the narrator to affirm Canada over Britain: in the portrait "the narrator links the conventions of the literary biography and British society and then dismisses them as irrelevant, showing the inadequacies of the old view in creating a realistic portrait of a different place" (29). This argument overlooks the fact that the figure recurrently aggrandized by the rhetoric of this chapter, and the one on whom the emphasis falls, is not Mother Beggarlegs or any other character but the cosmopolitan narrator, with her verbal wit and superior social understanding. It is she who can look down on the unfortunate encounter between young Lorne and Mother Beggarlegs and see both characters' shortcomings, she who can comment ironically that for Elgin

May 24th was a "real holiday" because it began "with bells and cannon ... and ended up splendidly with rockets and fire-balloons and drunken Indians vociferous on their way to the lock-up." The "vociferous" "drunken Indian" figure here allows the narrator both to comment with mild satire on an Elgin that would perceive such Indians as one more element in the entertaining sounds that constitute a holiday, and to display her own cosmopolitan discursive cleverness, building the series of sounds (bells, cannon, and rockets) that culminate in the "vociferous" Indians, and building the ironic syntactic parallelism of rockets, balloons, and Indians. The cleverness in turn helps establish her as the reader's even more entertaining companion.

The secondary emphasis of this opening chapter falls not on its beginning, or on Mother Beggarlegs, but on its conclusion in which, after Mr. Murchison has refused to agree that his children have "rights" to spending money to attend the celebrations, Lorne, the oldest boy, volunteers to pool his money with the few pennies of the other five, and his mother quietly adds another twenty cents. In ideological terms, a general social policy of "guaranteed income" has been refused by Mr. Murchison, while a concept of charity and social duty to the less fortunate has been affirmed by Lorne, and endorsed by his mother. Reading the Murchison family here as a model for the state, one can read a rejection of interventionist government, and an endorsement of individual initiative and charity. "Go make yourselves some use," Mr. Murchison tells his children. The narrator's cheerful reporting of this incident as a heartwarming indicator of the nurturing dynamics of the Murchison family places her also on the side of charity, and thus on the side of ad hoc rather than systematic solutions to general social problems. It further aggrandizes the narrator for the reader, showing her to be someone who can create poignant moments, and unexpectedly happy endings. In terms of the arguments to come about imperial union, the incident suggests a narrator who may be bemusedly skeptical about any systematic "top-down" economic proposal, and understanding of those who, like Mr. Murchison, see society as a collection of individual interests. Like the chapter's emphasis on its cosmopolitan narrator, this economic message is also beyond nationalism, and beyond simple contrasts such as Dean's between Canada and Britain.

§

The accent in general use in Elgin was borrowed—let us hope tempo-
rarily—from the other side of the line. (39)

What also characterizes the arguably female narrator is the
audience she chooses to address. In part this audience is created by
what she deems it not to know. It most clearly does not know much
about Canada, or about the social customs of the Canadian middle-
class. The narrator spends much of her time in the first half of the
novel explaining things like Canadian meal times, the topics of
concern to Canadian newspapers, Canadian customs for celebrating
the 24th of May holiday, and Canadian styles of dress. When
explaining Canadian customs for naming their children, she comments "[w]e must take this matter of names seriously" (7) as if the
audience she is addressing, and identifying herself with, would most
likely not take it seriously. The implied audience knows a great deal
about Britain, and something about the United States, but only from
the perspective of an educated and somewhat worldly class. It
understands why Lorne's attempt to speak to a London bus driver
might fail. It knows the social implications of the Cruickshank
delegation's choice of a temperance hotel in Bloomsbury. It understands sufficiently the social implications of dress codes to follow
the narrator's observation that "in Fifth Avenue Lorne would have
looked countrified, in Piccadilly colonial" (66), and is even sufficiently urbane to find plausible the narrator's subsequent sardonic
observation that "Districts are imaginable, perhaps not in this world,
where the frequenters of even those fashionable thoroughfares
would attract glances of curiosity through their failure to achieve the
common standard in such things."

This audience is also constructed by numerous passages that
describe the cultural conditions of Canada and Britain. The tone of
the passages describing the slowness and narrowness of life in
Elgin—"a streetcar jogged by every ten minutes or so, but nobody
ran after it" (15); "[n]o one could dream with impunity in Elgin,
except in bed" (35)—is satiric and playfully figurative, and works
better to amuse a non-Canadian audience about the quaintness of
Elgin than to urge Elgin's citizens to change their lives. The tone
of the passages which describe the parochialism of British life—
"the political concentration upon parish affairs, the cumbrous
social machinery" (117)—is often ponderously lacking in wit and

irony. The language of Lorne's several outbursts on the slowness of England is also non-ironic and largely non-figurative. Both descriptions suggest a direct discourse of social commentary, a commentary intended for Britain itself, most plausibly to its leaders who within the plot of the novel need to be able to take this parochialism into account in drawing up public policy.

But while this implied audience is identifiable as British, cosmopolitan, and educated, there are no representatives of it among the characters in the novel. Apart from the politician Wallingham, who is present in the novel only through his policies, the British characters, who nearly are all upper-class, are parochial and in effect undereducated even when products, like Alfred Hesketh, of the best upper-class schools. This creates a somewhat unusual narrative situation in which a powerfully intelligent narrator has no community of its own or spokesperson within the narrative. In political terms, it suggests that the kind of intellectual and class power the narrator enjoys may not be available to the communities whose story she tells.

§

What perhaps most characterizes *The Imperialist* narrator is her apparent confidence that she possesses infinitely more knowledge than any character in the novel, regardless of country, class, or gender. She routinely presents herself as knowing more about the motivations of most of the characters than they do themselves, much more about Canada than most Britons and more about Britain than the Canadians (the narrator would clearly *not* take rooms in a London temperance hotel). Although such an assumption of authority is a convention of the satiric point of view adopted by the novelist, ideologically this assumption has a devastating effect on the values of the characters and the action that unfolds from these values. The largest presence and wisest authority throughout the novel remains the unnamed narrator, beside whom Wallingham and other powerful British politicians seem minor historical players, and the main characters Lorne and Advena Murchison naive children, even when the former is a 28-year old lawyer running for election to Canada's national parliament. This contrast is devastating because one of the novel's primary concerns is the nature of political authority and power—is there political authority that, as both Wallingham and Lorne Murchison believe, can make wise choices and foresee economic and cultural consequences? From the Canadian perspective, this emphasis includes the possibility of Canadians taking larger roles in the moral and economic leadership of the British Empire, perhaps even at some point becoming its seat of government. From the British perspective, this authority is constructed mostly as the carrying forward of long-achieved ethical principles (precisely what these principles are, beyond a few platitudinous phrases offered by Lorne about "the finest human product there is" [90] and the ennobling "ideals of British government" [226], the narrator pointedly does not specify). Yet the people who espouse these ideals, whether Lorne in Canada or Wallingham in Britain, are repeatedly shown to be obliged to work with the help of much less insight and much less knowledge than the narrator possesses—as when Lorne mistakes Alfred Hesketh as one of Britain's "best" and the narrator sardonically comments that Hesketh "[p]erhaps ... more properly represented the second best" (113).

Other politicians are portrayed by the narrator mostly as short-sighted and poorly informed pragmatists, wary of offending blocks of special-interest voters who may be equally-short-sighted and even less informed. The most vividly portrayed of these are the Elgin Liberal Party organizers Farqurharson and Bingham, for whom no political principle is worth jeopardizing a successful election campaign. The public at large in both Canada and Britain is portrayed as being as self-interested and limited as politicians like Farquharson and Bingham judge them to be. When Canadians visit Britain they are dismayed, the narrator suggests, by "[t]he unready conception of things," the "dull anachronism" of social practice, "the problems of sluggish over-population" (117). Even Lorne, ever eager to idealize things British, is struck by the intractable parochialism of ordinary Britons. He reports to his family that several things stand in the way of significant changes in British economic policy:

> "The conservatism of the people—it isn't a name, it's a fact— the hostility and suspicion; natural enough: they know they're stupid, and they half suspect they're fair game. I suppose the Americans have taught them that. Slow—oh slow! More interested in the back-garden fence than anything else. Pick up a paper, at the moment when things are being done, mind, all over the world, done against them—when their shipping is being captured, and their industries destroyed, and their goods

undersold beneath their very noses—and the thing they want
to know is—'Why Are the Swallows Late?' I read it myself in
a ha'penny morning paper, too, that they think rather dangerously go-ahead—a whole column, leaded, to inquire what's
the matter with the swallows. The *Times* the same week had a
useful leader on Alterations in the Church Service, and a special contribution on Prayers for the Dead. Lord, they need 'em.
Those are the things they think about!" (124)

The most positively portrayed characters, those of the Murchison
family, who are at best on the fringes of politics, and who in the
novel represent the potential "best" of the public, are also depicted
by the narrator as having serious limits on their perceptions. Mr.
Murchison is as bemused by Lorne's idealism as he was earlier by
another son's theory that he had "rights" to spending-money, and
sees constructive political action as difficult, if not impossible. His
view of the world is focused on the near at hand, and appears to
see each individual doing what they can do best within a private
sphere. He keeps his distance from Lorne's election campaign,
venturing only the comment that the outcome "remains to be seen"
(237). "You're a great man, John," his wife tells him in another
context, "for letting everything alone" (200). The narrator portrays
John Murchison's townspeople as virtually as conservative as
Lorne's Britons:

> Main Street expressed the idea that, for the purpose of
> growing and doing business, it had always found the days
> long enough. Drays passed through it to the Grand Trunk
> station, but they passed one at a time; a certain number of
> people went up and down about their affairs, but they were
> never in a hurry.... There was a decent procedure; and it was
> felt that Bofield—he was dry-goods too—in putting in an
> elevator was just a little unnecessarily in advance of the
> times (15).

§

Before she [Advena] had preferred an ideal to the desire of her heart;
now it lay about her; her strenuous heart had pulled it down to foolish
ruin ... (247)

The narrative structure of *The Imperialist* places emphasis
almost equally on two Canadian characters, Lorne and Advena

Murchison, and on their relationships with characters closely tied
to aspects of British culture: Advena's romantic entanglement with
the young Scottish clergyman Hugh Finlay, and Lorne's infatuations with the British politician Wallingham, the young British
gentleman Alfred Hesketh, and the vacuous young Canadian-born
anglophile, Dora Milburn. In each of these relationships the inade-
quacy of both the Canadian and British cultural fields is emphasized. The common features of the Lorne and Advena narrative
lines, one involving both public and private hopes, the other only
private ones, is evident in much more than their being interwoven
in the novel's chapter structure. Lorne and Advena are the exceptional members of the Murchison family, Lorne contrasted to his
less-ambitious brothers Alec and Oliver, and Advena contrasted to
her domestically-inclined sisters Stella and Abby. Both have
become educated beyond the norms of Elgin, Advena as a teacher
and Lorne as a lawyer. Both have become attracted to idealisms
that appear to originate in Britain, Advena to the Scottish Hugh
Finlay's Romantic vision of intellectual joys and passions that can
render the material world irrelevant, and Lorne to a vision of
British political equity that waits to be achieved in an evolving
British Empire. Part of the reason for this attraction is that both
have outgrown the potential of their home cultural fields—Advena
a culture that praises only a domestically skilled woman, Lorne
one that values political chicanery far above political principle.

Lorne's attraction to large abstract concepts that might have
the power to change unpleasant particulars has been evident since
the opening pages and his inept attempt to converse pleasantly
with Mother Beggarlegs—an attempt which the narrator indulgently described as "the first indication ... of that active sympathy
with the disabilities of his fellow beings which stamped him later
so intelligent a meliorist." The irony in the narrator's "so intelligent" will not become fully available until after Lorne has mistaken Alfred Hesketh for one of Britain's best and has trusted South
Fox electors to support the "noble" goal of customs union with
Britain even though it may bring them economic hardship. Lorne's
infatuation with "England—her laws, her liberty, her equity"
(229), despite his having witnessed and complained about its slowness, its paralyzing class structure, and its petty concerns with
"parish affairs" (117), is paralleled by his infatuation with Dora
Milburn, whom he pursues despite her affected English accent and

obsession with the trivia of fashion and courtship. Both of these infatuations are to a lesser extent paralleled by his trust in the Liberal Party organizers, Bingham and Farquharson, and by his willingness to look the other way on election day when they attempt to influence and buy votes to support his high-principled bid for a parliamentary seat. In all three cases Lorne displays an aversion to seeing what the narrator can plainly see: unpleasant Hobbesian particulars that contradict an ideal in which he would believe.

In Advena's relationship with Hugh Finlay, Lorne's several infatuations are brought together in one person. Advena not only mistakes Hugh to be someone who may want her love (not knowing of his earlier 'arranged' engagement in Scotland to Christie Cameron), as Lorne mistakes Dora as wanting his, but also misreads through him the intellectual traditions of Britain, as Lorne misreads these traditions through Wallingham and Hesketh. And as is usual in *The Imperialist,* the narrator knows better: "Advena Murchison thought him the probable antitype of an Oxford don. She had never seen an Oxford don, but Mr. Finlay wore the characteristics these schoolmen were dressed in by novelists ...." (59). For Advena, friendship with Finlay becomes an opportunity to discuss Victorian poetry and Greek philosophy, together with various ideals of personal and physical self-denial. At first tutored in these by Finlay, she becomes, like Lorne, more enthusiastic in her commitment to newly learned ideals than is the person from whom she believes she has learned. "I look forward to the time when this—other feeling of ours will become just an idea, as it is now just an emotion, at which we should try to smile," Advena says hopefully, once she and Finlay have managed to acknowledge their love for each other. "I used to feel more drawn to the ascetic achievement and its rewards," the mischievous narrator has Finlay reply, "than I do now" (180).

By the end of the novel the parallel romantic and cultural entanglements of Lorne and Advena have exposed both the shallow pragmatism of Elgin's Canada and the emptiness of British "principle." British characters like Wallingham and Hugh Finlay, no matter how sincere or well-meaning, have been incapable of reading and responding to the complexities of changing circumstances. Canada in turn has offered Advena no one with whom she can share her hopes and ideas, beyond the immigrant Finlay. It has offered Lorne neither a woman with whom he might converse nor a politics in which he could imagine honourably serving. What saves both of them are two apparently rare exceptions to cultural norms: the practical *and* honourable Dr. Drummond, who finds, by unconventional means, a way for Advena and Finlay to continue together, and an exception even "rarer, a fastidious politician," the similarly honourable Henry Cruickshank.

§

Mr. and Mrs. Murchison were indubitably of the elect, but he was singularly closed-mouthed about it ... (29)

If in the narrator's view ideals usually lead to misunderstandings, to mistakes in personal relationships, and to ignorance of the pettiness, inefficiency, corruption, and self-interest which forms the actual ground of political action, what is the alternative to them? The answer, *The Imperialist* hints, may lie in Presbyterianism's Calvinist theology, and in the role the narrator gives to Dr. Drummond, the minister of Elgin's Presbyterian church. The narrator allows the Calvinist concern with the conflict between divine foreordination and the human illusion of free will several appearances in the novel, and in most of these treats it playfully. The playfulness suggests both the presence of a shared field of allusion between narrator and audience—each understands the paradoxical aspects of foreordination—and some shared skepticism: Calvinist belief, that is, is here strong enough both to take for granted and to have fun with. One of the narrator's first allusions to it occurs in the first sustained conversation between Hugh and Advena, as they look upon a sunset. Advena fancifully protests against the sunset as a limitation on their freedom:

> "It's the seal upon an act of violence, isn't it, a sunset? Something taken from us against our will. It's a hateful reminder, in the midst of our delightful volitions, of how arbitrary every condition of life is." (61)

The fancifulness of her remark—"hateful reminder," "delightful volitions"—implies that for her the foreordination/free will debate may be as yet an intellectual concept, rather than something which actually does "take from" her life. Hugh replies with the conven-

tional Calvinist doctrine that life is foreordained but unknown, and
that human individuals must "work" in the belief that they may
have been foreordained to work and thrive. His metaphor is not the
romantic one of sunset but the more practical one of business, and
echoes the historic "work for the night is coming" connection
between English protestantism and commerce.

> "The conditions of business are always arbitrary. Life is
> a business—we have to work at ourselves till it is over. So
> much cut off and ended it is," he said, glancing at the sky
> again.
> .... "The world is wrapped in destiny, and but revolves
> to roll it out." (61)

In her following comment, the narrator also uses, most likely ironically, the freedom/foreordination figure: "They lingered together
for a moment talking, seizing the new joy in it, which was simply
the joy of his sudden *liberation* with her, *consciously pushing
away the moment* of parting ..." (my italics). The apparent irony
ambiguously places the knowing narrator both within and beyond
the Calvinist theology.

The next instance occurs when Dr. Drummond begins using
the foreordination concept to attempt to prevent Hugh's marrying
the stolid Christie Cameron and fulfilling the marriage contract he
had agreed to before leaving Scotland. Here the question becomes,
for both Drummond and Finlay, which woman is it whom God has
foreordained Hugh to marry? Drummond argues that this woman
is Advena. When Finlay acknowledges that the attraction between
him and Advena is beyond altering ("beyond mending"), Drummond replies "It's beyond mending, Finlay, because it is one of
those things that God has made. But it is not beyond marring, and
I charge you to look well what you are about in connection with
it" (155). The implication is that Hugh may be about to sin by
going against what "God has made." However, Drummond is still
left with the question of the extent to which he himself can personally intervene, and whether God has foreordained such intervention. A few chapters later his plight amuses the narrator: "Dr.
Drummond had his own method of reconciling foreordination and
free will" (201), she comments. Drummond has prayed publicly
in his church for God to

"clear the understanding ... of such as would interpret Thy
will to their own undoing: do Thou teach them that as happiness may reside in chastening, so chastening may reside in
happiness. And though such stand fast to their hurt, do Thou
grant to them in Thine own way, which may not be our way,
a safe issue out of the dangers that beset them." (201)

Still amused, the narrator reports that Advena has heard his prayer
as a providential coincidence, as a portent that carries "that mysterious double emphasis of chance words that fit." Finlay, however, has heard them as the meddling words of a wilful colleague,
and "furious, and more resolved than ever, had gone home by
another way."

Six chapters later, in the scene that resolves these conflicts,
Dr. Drummond again attempts to invoke foreordination. Noting
pragmatically that there has been no romantic relationship between
Finlay and Christie Cameron, that Christie is some years older
than Finlay but not inappropriately younger than himself, he suc-
cessfully proposes himself as a husband to her. "I think I see the
finger of Providence in this matter" (252), he exclaims to Miss
Kilbannon, Hugh Finlay's aunt and Christie's chaperon, near the
end of his proposal. Again the narrator appears amused by his
attempt to reconcile his own will and that of the divine, and gives
Miss Kilbannon rather than Providence the last word. " 'I think,'
she said, 'we'll just leave it to Christie.' "

Yet the narrator's amusement seems less at the concept of
foreordination itself than at Drummond's attempt to claim its
support for his own project. Throughout the novel the narrator has
shown that those who hope to impose large general models upon
society or individuals will eventually encounter numerous human
desires that are intractable to general models. Whether the specific
instance is Advena believing that she can love Hugh spiritually
from a distance while he is married to another, or Lorne believing
that he can achieve in Canada the "nobler ideal" of British equity
when even Britain has not achieved it, the narrator's message
seems to be that human life resists idealist interventions. Those
who succeed are those who can closely and accurately read a small
part of actuality—who can run a dry-goods store and foundry as
carefully as John Murchison, or analyze a set of social circumstances as skilfully as Dr. Drummond. These are empiricists rather

than imperialists. They take advantage of how events are "rolling out," to employ Hugh Finlay's figure, rather than attempting to alter the unrolling. Despite the various ironies, this understanding remains consistent with Calvinist theology. The future is not be changed but to be, as God's will, accurately read and comprehended. The social and material success that ensues from such reading—here Drummond's comical but successful arranging of desirable marriages for both himself and Hugh—can be both a sign that the individual is one of God's elect, and a consequence of the foreordained election.

§

The novel's final invocation of foreordination is made by the narrator herself, not as a possible limitation on her characters, but as a limit on her own narration. On the last page of *The Imperialist* a disillusioned Lorne Murchison, who has lost his parliamentary seat through deals made by his own election workers, and has discovered both his beloved Dora and his Liberal Party colleagues to be no more than self-interested opportunists, is offered a partnership by Cruickshank, the respected senior Toronto lawyer who had led the Canadian deputation to Britain. On its face, this offer seems to resemble in miniature the imperialist political proposal that Lorne has so recently wasted himself in supporting. The aging Cruickshank has invited a vigorous young Lorne Murchison to join with him, much as an aging Britain might have invited a vigourous young Canada to join it in political union. The narrator, mischievous as ever, hints broadly at the presence of this metaphor.

> Henry Cruickshank, growing old in his eminence and less secure, perhaps, in the increasing conflict of loud voices, of his own grasp of the ultimate best, fearing too, no doubt, the approach of that cynicism which, moral or immoral, is the real hoar of age, wrote to young Murchison ... and offered him a partnership. The terms were so simple and advantageous as only to be explicable on the grounds I have mentioned ... in which one is tempted to find the individual parallel of certain propositions of a great government also growing old. The offer was accepted, not without emotion, and there too, it would be good to trace the parallel, were we permit-

> ted: but for that it is too soon, or perhaps it is too late. Here,
> for Lorne, and for his country, we lose the thread of destiny.

But "we" the narrator are not permitted to trace a parallel, it seems, because, like the actions of great nations or people, what is narratable is also limited by destiny. Moreover, it may be less an ideal that has motivated Cruickshank here than aging and death, the blights of sublunary—and subnarrative—humanity. While the narrator has been able from her general viewpoint outside the action to see the forces that Lorne, Advena, Hugh, and Wallingham could not see, even when their lives were shaped by them, on this page the narrator's view has paradoxically become so general that it can see only the vague presence of destiny—its "shuttles" but not its cloth. Yet the narrator's playfulness about the conflict between foreordination and free will continues. The shuttles of destiny weave the "will" of nations, but human hands, including those of young Murchison, may also be directing the weaving shuttles:

> The shuttles fly, weaving the will of nations, with a skein for
> ever dipped again; and he goes forth to his share in the task
> among those by whose hand and direction the pattern and the
> colours will be made.

In the light of the empyrean position the narrator has enjoyed throughout the novel, and the limited power she has granted any of its characters to help "weave" the world, this ending seems at first glance somewhat disingenuous. Destiny rules, yet it in turn is created by human hands. But despite the playfulness, this is not entirely an optimistic reconciliation of contraries. For which of the weavers can see the pattern they are helping weaving? Here is perhaps the bleakest implication of *The Imperialist*'s narrative politics. The weavers of the human stories can weave, but not see. If they do have free will, they have but limited vision, whether contemplating through Lorne's eyes the fate of Britain or through Dora's the choice of a frock. And while the narrator has seemed throughout the novel to possess much more vision than her most ambitious characters, here her vision has proved to be at best retrospective. At the end of a known story, the narratable closes, and there is no theory or plan, for statesperson or novelist, to help shape the weaving to come.

§

Despite the whimsy with which the narrator of *The Imperialist* treats the foreordination/free will dilemma, there is little indication in the text that she ever gives up a belief in the predestined nature of human affairs. The whimsy never mocks the theology of the concept, but instead finds dramatic irony in the plights of characters who struggle mightily to find ways of action that somewhere are already known. The verbally mischievous concluding passage appears to allow the possibility of free will, but without granting humanity the vision to make such freedom meaningful, and without denying the continuing operation of destiny. From this theological viewpoint, if "the imperialist" politician has hoped to purposefully change the world, he has been seriously mistaken. If, in the form of Lorne Murchison, he has hoped to be a Calvinist agent of predestined change, then he has been a poor reader of the portents available in the commercial and political habits of Britons and Canadians. John Murchison's comment, "That remains to be seen," becomes in this understanding both the novel's political and narrative dictum. The narrator's sweeping power of vision has rested on what has already been seen. The imperialist's failure has rested on what he has not seen. The novel's own vision continues to rest on the play it and its narrator have created between fate and will, as Lorne "goes forth" as if knowing where he is going, and the shuttles of destiny covertly weave.

Excavating the Expendable Working Classes
in *The Imperialist**

Teresa Hubel

You can't get much more middle class than Sara Jeannette Duncan's turn-of-the-century novel *The Imperialist*. Its middle-classness calls out from virtually every page and through almost

---

*Commissioned for this edition.

every narrative technique the novelist employs, from her choice of theme—the debate over imperial federation, conducted some hundred years ago primarily in elite political circles—to her setting—the social world of the commercial classes who live in a prosperous southern Ontario town (which she names Elgin but which most critics suspect is Duncan's own hometown of Brantford in very thin disguise)—and finally to her protagonists, the Murchisons, whose middle-class values are proudly paraded at every opportunity and who are ultimately enshrined as a superior people, "too good for their environment" (34). Although *The Imperialist* criticizes certain kinds of middle-class behaviour, the Milburn variety, for example, it cautiously but warmly commemorates another. Even Duncan's penetrating and clever irony does not get in the way of her fondness, or ours, for the Murchison family and their fundamentally intelligent, honourable ways.

Duncan's celebration of the particular brand of middle classness that the Murchisons are made to represent has been echoed by many of the literary scholars who, in the last twenty years or so, have done valuable work in releasing her prose from obscurity. Their praise for her novel often centres on the novel's historical accuracy. So Peter Allen, for instance, insists that one of Duncan's strengths is "the precision of her social analysis" (this edition, 375) and predicts, in his 1984 article, that *The Imperialist* "will be increasingly recognized as an unusual and accomplished testimony to an important stage in the development of our nation" (370). Michael Peterman's applause is even louder. He asserts that the novel manages to construct the "typical Canadian experience" and "the generic Canadian character" (this edition, 354, 355) and seems particularly impressed by its faithful replication of Canadian life at the turn of the century: "The fact that it is being used increasingly on university courses in Canadian history and politics attests to the exactness of its detail and its ability to capture the mood of the time" (347). Allen and Peterman are reaffirming what Duncan herself believed she was doing in *The Imperialist*, that is, presenting one of the most fervent political arguments of the day from the perspective of "the average Canadian of the average small town" ("Letters" 310). Within the ever-circling areas of literature and literary studies, both of which are still much influenced by a liberal humanist ethos, claims of centrality invoked by such words as "generic," "typical," and "average" and the authenticity accorded a text by recourse to mainstream versions of history can hardly be underestimated. For a novel, these are the means to power. They ensure that it will appear on university English courses and they standardize its rendition of things.

That *The Imperialist* actually draws a specific image of life rather than a generalized one has not gone unnoticed. In an effort to deliver Duncan from one critic's idealized depiction of her as a rescuer of the destitute and ignorant, Thomas E. Tausky points out that there is no evidence that she was concerned with the advancement of those lower down on the social scale. He places her very firmly in the camp from which, he maintains, she never strayed: "Duncan was of the middle class, she wrote for and about the middle class, and her keen interest in the literary developments of her time was focused on the theory and practice of dealing with middle-class experiences in fiction" ("In Search ..." 98). Seeing this issue from an opposite vantage point, Clara Thomas notes that the social mythologies presented in *The Imperialist* are predicated on the near absence of the working classes: "There are no poor in her book ... there are none of any community's pathetic outsiders, the so-called 'shiftless' failures, or even of its wage-earning working men and their families" (this edition, 363). Tausky and Thomas offer us important insights on which to build a new interpretation. *The Imperialist* is a novel that lays claim to the territory of the typical in its recounting of an important Canadian moment: "we are here at the making of a nation" (37), the narrator announces early on in the text. Surely we have to ask ourselves why a novel so determined to tell a collective Canadian story—a story which, by the nature of its collectivity, we should all be able to recognize as our own, as about us—would alternately leave out and undermine such a prevalent portion of our population. If this is a narrative of nation-building, well, then, who constitutes the nation?

The complete omission in *The Imperialist* of some working classes and the marginalization of others is decidedly telling, especially when we consider the novel in light of a non-mainstream chronicle of Canada, the middle to late nineteenth and early twentieth century history of working-class experience and culture. It is only by paying attention to this history in its relationship to the issues that surrounded the middle class of that period that we can come to some understanding of class antagonism, which many historians now acknowledge was a major component of life in Canada in the era that comprised Duncan's writing career.[1] Most literary critics, taking their cue from Duncan herself who suppresses class conflict in *The Imperialist*, have ignored the way that she struggles to establish the middle class as the norm by which all of Canada is to measured, and the limits of her success in this effort. That she does this in a novel written at the turn of the century, when much of Canada and certainly her setting of southern Ontario had already seen forty years of organized and militant working-class protest against the very peoples that Duncan commemorates and would see twenty more, suggests that *The Imperialist* represents a contribution, possibly deliberate, to the greater movement of the middle class to dominate Canadian thought. I write this essay for the purposes of undoing that movement by exposing its existence in a canonized novel whose story paints a literary picture of that time. *The Imperialist* will undoubtedly continue to be taught on Canadian literature courses, and it should be, because it gives its readers a fascinating and finely constructed vignette of a vital moment in Canadian history. But to avoid complicity with Duncan's own political program, it is important to know the stories she does not or cannot tell us.

I should mention at this point that my definition of class, while it is grounded in some Marxist assumptions about the workings of class in an industrialized society, is much more indebted to feminist and postcolonialist ideas about the normalization effects caused by structures of dominance. So when I look for class in this novel, I take into account the labour and economic conditions that Marxism insists is fundamental to any attempt to categorize social groups into classes, and, putting into practice the theoretical insights of feminism and postcolonialism, I examine the questions surrounding such issues as voice appropriation, authority in representation, and the politics of subject positions: who gets to speak for whom in the text; whose definitions of self and the other are authorized and by what means is this supremacy established; and what are the limitations of the novel's perspective? While Marx gave us the beginnings of class analysis when he located class in the economic, he did not go nearly far enough. It seems to me that class, like womanhood and race, has no essence. Like them, it is, instead, experiential and diffuse, and it is experienced as a distinct set of values and expectations in life, as language, as acts of resistance to or complicity with systems of exploitation, and as internalized views of subordination or primacy.

Marxism tells us that class is determined by an individual's relation to the means of production. The middle class owns the means of production and members of the working classes must sell their labour to these middle-class owners in order to make a living. But Marxism also acknowledges that the middle class additionally consists of salaried professionals—lawyers, doctors, etc—who, while they are not actually owners of industry, nevertheless work as agents of the middle class, propagating certain values and ideology that ensure the continued dominance of this class. If we apply this paradigm to Duncan's *The Imperialist*, it becomes apparent that virtually every group, indeed every individual character discussed in any detail, belongs to this middle class, including the farmers of South Fox. Although the novel at times delineates what might appear (to late twentieth-century readers) to be hierarchical differences between the working classes and the middle class—in its depiction, for instance, of Lorne Murchison's encounter with Elmore Crow in Chapter IX and its description of the South Fox farmers as "big, quiet, expectant fellows" who "had the air of being prosperous, but not prosperous enough for theories and doctrines" (187)—these differences occur within the middle class itself, between its rural and its urban expressions.

The working classes in the novel are those characters and groups who exist outside the prosperity, respectability, decorum and authority of the middle class. They are the domestic servants who hover at the edges of many of the social events the Murchisons attend and the factory workers, the "corner loafers" (36), the drunks, and the poor who are mentioned only to draw a distinction between their values, labour, language, and economic circumstances, and those of the middle class that the novel privileges. Duncan attempts to define these socially-subjugated collectivities in terms of the middle class, according to its norms, and, consequently, they appear deviant or deficient. However, her success in doing so depends to a large extent on whether or not we choose to see through the filter that she provides. But if we read against her insistences, we are able to recognize that the middle-class perspective in the novel is not so much normal or natural as it is constructed and dominant. It is through the novel's representation of the working classes and its recording of their defiance in the face of middle-class expectations, then, that we can measure the limits of Duncan's version of middle-classness.

Duncan started writing *The Imperialist* in 1902 and completed it in 1903, when it was first published as a weekly serial in a British periodical called *The Queen* (see "The Writing of *the Imperialist* elsewhere in this volume). In his book *The Canadian Class Structure* sociologist Henry Veltmeyer states that at around that time in Canada the working classes comprised roughly 47 per cent of the labour force: about 8 per cent, most of whom were women, were engaged in the service sector, primarily occupying jobs as domestic servants, five per cent were paid farm labourers and the remaining 34 per cent consisted largely of industrial workers, who were employed in the basic industries in urban centres, and also of those who worked for wages in logging camps, quarries, and on fishing boats (71-99). While the middle classes—the small business owners, managers, clerks, professionals, and the independent commodity producers such as farmers who figure so prominently in Duncan's novel—certainly possessed a modest majority in the Canadian labour force at the turn of the century (a fact which is no longer true in the Canada of today where the middle classes stand at less than 20 per cent), at 47 per cent the working classes were hardly an insignificant minority.

And yet these classes barely appear in *The Imperialist*. Indeed there seems a concentrated effort to keep them out of Duncan's illustration of small-town Canadian life. The little mention there is of the people who occupy the working classes occurs early on in the text, principally in the first chapter when the narrator describes the holiday atmosphere and festivities that prevail in Elgin on the twenty-fourth of May, Queen Victoria's birthday. Here we learn about the impossibility of "social combination" (4). The narrator tells us that to commemorate the day the workers from the Milburn Boiler Company, in conjunction with the Grand Trunk railway, organize cheap trips from Elgin to the lakeside and "the Falls." However, to take advantage of the discount, middle-class travellers must not only consort with the workers but pretend to be them. The intended audience of this novel becomes abundantly clear when the narrator explains the impropriety implicit in mixing with the lower orders:

it was a question in Elgin whether one might sink one's dignity and go as a hand for the sake of the fifty-cent opportunity, a question usually decided in the negative. The social
distinctions of Elgin may not be easily appreciated by people
accustomed to the rough and ready standards of a world at
the other end of the Grand Trunk; but it will be clear at a
glance that nobody whose occupation prescribed a clean face
could be expected to travel cheek by jowl, as a privilege,
with persons who were habitually seen with smutty ones,
barefaced smut, streaming out at the polite afternoon hour of
six, jangling an empty dinner pail. So much we may decide,
and leave it, reflecting as we go how simple and satisfactory,
after all, are the prejudices which can hold up such obvious
justification. (4)

No doubt the tone we are hearing in the above passage is Duncan's
typically ironic one: she is, we are supposed to believe, merely
seeming to adopt the arguments of a respectable middle class,
afraid of losing its respectability by cavorting with the usually
messy masses, in order to make a point about the extent to which
the more fortunate people will go to maintain the established
social distinctions. But these statements are funny only to a reader
comfortably (meaning unselfconsciously) ensconced in the middle
class. A working-class reader knows that she or he is being
laughed at. The working classes, then, are not only devalued and
kept to the edges of the story, their degradation and marginalization are also confirmed by the process of reading itself, a process
in which they are constantly reminded that this novel is neither for
nor about them, unless, of course, they are willing to 'sink their
dignity' and play the clowns to Duncan's middle-class normality.

This strategy of undermining the importance of the working
classes is reiterated, again in the opening chapter, with the introduction of the novel's first domestic servant, Lobelia, who has run
off to enjoy the holiday rather than staying in the Murchison home
and doing the work Mrs. Murchison requires of her. There are a
couple of interesting aspects to Duncan's representation of domestic servants in *The Imperialist*. First, none of them ever actually
appear as characters in the novel. Instead, they are always only
talked about by the middle-class characters. So, for instance, we
never meet Lobelia but simply hear about her after she has departed from the scene. Considering that she does not speak at all

in the text, it is hardly surprising that the image we get of Lobelia has a decided class bias. Duncan is more concerned with airing the complaints of the Murchison family about Lobelia's behaviour than with sympathizing with a servant who wants her fair share of holiday fun. Hence the young Lorne, announcing to his sister Advena that "the girl's gone," which means that the Murchison children will have to do the chores normally assigned to her, adds, " ... I guess Lobelia's about as mean as they're made!" And Mrs. Murchison, who had told Lobelia that she could leave the house once she had done the dinner dishes and only if she had finished yesterday's ironing, is outraged to discover the ironing not done: "five shirts and *all* the coloured things. I call it downright deceit!" (6) Of course, this is meant to be an amusing moment in the novel—when the Murchison's "girl" leaves the family in the lurch —and we are not necessarily supposed to believe Lorne's or Mrs. Murchison's assessment of Lobelia. Nevertheless, the overall impression we are left with is that the Murchisons' servant has been remiss in her duties and even underhanded, and this impression is primarily the result of Lobelia's complete absence from the story and her consequent representation from the unmitigated perspective of her employers.

So unmitigated is this perspective that even Lobelia's quite justifiable resistance to the tyranny found in the Murchison household is swallowed up by a middle-class explanation. Advena suggests that the real reason Lobelia has run off is not the pull of the festivities so much as the presence of a rag carpet in her bedroom. Mrs. Murchison responds by soundly putting Lobelia in her place for us:

> Rag carpet—upon my word! . . . It's what her betters have to do with! I've known the day when that very piece of rag carpet—sixty balls there were in it, and every one I sewed with my own fingers—was the best I had for my spare room, with a bit of ingrain in the middle. Dear me ... how proud I was of that performance! She didn't tell *me* she objected to rag carpet! (6)

A lack of attention to class issues in analyses of literary works can often result in interpretations that seem oblivious to the political implications of a scene or a symbol. Thus Elizabeth Thompson in her reading of *The Imperialist* sees the rag carpet solely as an emblem of Mrs. Murchison's pioneering experience, an emblem which, given the current prosperity of the Murchison family in Elgin, suggests that she is engaged in "an outdated mode of perception" (64). Thompson overlooks the rag carpet's resonance as a class symbol. Even though "her betters" at one time used the carpet proudly (at least in their spare room), Lobelia gets it now because it is no longer in keeping with the family's thriving respectability and is, in fact, more suited, in Mrs. Murchison's eyes, to the servant's inferior status in the home. Furthermore, Lobelia's reaction to this rendering of her as an subordinate inhabitant of the Murchison house is made to seem ridiculous by Mrs. Murchison's outburst of nostalgic pride. Her defiance of this middle-class categorization of her is trivialized and explained away by the middle-class characters of the novel.

This complicated bit of footwork—that is, acknowledging working-class resistance only eventually to deflate it with middle-class explanations—is common in both Duncan's fiction and in her journalism. And she performs it frequently when she tries to address what she and many women of her class saw as a "problem" with the situation of domestic service in the late nineteenth and early twentieth centuries. This "problem" so concerned Duncan that not only did she broach it again and again in her various columns in the Montreal *Star* and the Toronto *Globe*, all of which she published in the 1880s, but she also raised it 15 years later in *The Imperialist*. Just prior to the kerfuffle over Lobelia's refusal to work on a "bank holiday" is the following not-entirely-relevant comment about the difficulty of finding and keeping good help: "Let a new mill be opened, and it didn't matter what you paid her or how comfortable you made her, off she would go, and you might think yourself lucky if she gave a week's warning" (5). She expresses a similar sort of combative bewilderment in a November 1886 column for the *Globe*, wondering why "girls" (the term she uses to designate all female domestic servants) seem to prefer the "hard routine, the long hours and the scanty remuneration of factory work" to the "safe comfortable life of the valued domestic servant, with all the pleasant relations it involves" (*Journalism* 30). And those who do go into service, she says, convey their dissatisfactions with it through "mutinous mutterings, and reckless smashings, and violent efforts to assert a somewhat exaggerated and top-loftical dignity" (31).

Not just those who choose or have in the past chosen domestic service as a profession but all working-class women are the targets of her class-biased criticism. In a later column for the same paper, dated 31 Jan. 1887, she castigates shop-girls for not being servants, even going so far as to blame them, rather than their obviously greedy and corrupt employers, for the oppressive conditions of their work, which consisted of having to stand on their feet for hours and hours six days of every week and even late into Saturday night: "so long as these young persons prefer being overworked and under-paid in a shop to being over-paid and underworked in a kitchen, with power to dismiss the mistress thereof at pleasure, it is nobody's fault but their own that they are." Duncan is not without sympathy for these shop-girls (nor for the servants), and she is willing to concede that the women who shop in these stores after 6 p.m. on Saturday are participants in the exploitation of "their sisters." But the apparent conspiracy among working-class girls and women to avoid domestic service so baffles her that the only answer she can provide—the girls are revolting against the "personal tyranny" of mistresses (*Journalism* 31)—is patently inadequate.

Clearly Duncan is able to admit that domestic servants are unhappy with the job and even to describe the manner of their rebellion—"mutinous mutterings" and a preference for work that appears to her to be much more onerous—but the only interpretation that she can come up with to explain their decision makes them seem stupidly short-sighted and irrational. Several labour historians have posited other grounds for the widespread reluctance of working-class females of the late Victorian and early Edwardian periods in Canada to take up domestic service in the homes of the women and men of commerce, the professions, and the manufacturing classes. They agree that there was a perpetual shortage of domestic servants and this existed despite the fact that many poor families were compelled by severe economic circumstances to send their daughters—often as young as twelve years—into the labour force, and despite the desperation of female workers, who could, according to the Royal Commission on the Relations of Labor and Capital of Canada (1889), be "counted on to work for small wages, to submit to exasperating exactions, and to work uncomplainingly for long hours" (qtd. in Palmer 116).

Bettina Bradbury suggests one reason why wage labour in a middle-class home was, if possible, shunned by these women and girls: "they toiled for long hours, got shelter, more protection than they may have wished for and minimal pay" (30). Susan Trofimenkoff, in an article that analyzes the few female voices that contributed evidence to the above-mentioned Royal Commission, points to a more sinister explanation.

Seeing themselves as the protectors of the chastity of working-class women, the male Commissioners of this 1889 investigation searched in vain for proof that female factory workers were being sexually compromised or molested by those men of their class with whom they mingled at the job site. In fact, the Commissioners heard no testimony whatsoever that substantiated their belief in the immorality of factory hands. But why the concern? Trofimenkoff argues that the middle-class Commissioners were actually revealing more about their own class's behaviour than about that of the lower orders. Moreover, they were looking in the wrong place and among the wrong women: "In the Canada of the 1880's there were far more women working as domestic servants than as factory workers and the domestics were far more susceptible to male (and middle-class) aggressions. Indeed, studies of the period indicate that most prostitutes began their careers as servants" (199). In light of Trofimenkoff's conclusions, I would contend that Duncan's consideration of the domestic service situation is insufficient because she is largely unwilling to question the moral basis and the economic motivations of the employing class to which she belonged. I do not mean to suggest here that she is wrong while Trofimenkoff and Bradbury are right, since the predicament of the domestic at the turn of the century is obviously a complicated one and the shortage of female workers in the middle-class home could be traced to a number of different causes. My point is that Duncan is reproducing a characteristic middle-class response to working-class practices of resistance. Rather than confront the class politics that have engendered a specific reaction to middle-class authority and exploitation, she searches among the working classes for some deficiency that would explain why these women and girls are reluctant to take on domestic service.

Certainly one of the reasons she is disinclined to hold her own people up to any kind of thorough moral scrutiny in *The Imperialist* is that this novel, though not without its criticisms of middle-

class self interest, is fundamentally committed to the establishment
of that class as the pre-eminent one in Canada. In pursuit of this
goal, the text uses a complex tactic to affirm the absolute centrality
of this class, represented by the supposedly typical merchants and
manufacturers of Elgin and the farmers of Fox County. Sometimes, the novel is quite candid in its deployment of this tactic, for
example, when it tells the cheerful tale of the dissolution of the
aristocracy.

This "little knot of gentry-folk" came to Fox County from
England years before, and they brought their social pretensions
and their determination to maintain class boundaries. But the rising middle class in Canada overcame them: "Prosperous traders
foreclosed them, the spirit of the times defeated them, young
Liberals succeeded them in office. Their grandsons married the
daughters of well-to-do persons . . ." (37). Later on in the text, we
are told that the parties seeking election in Fox County need not
bother with the "leisured class" (203) because its influence is
microscopic. Class, of course, is an entirely relational concept; any
specific class identity is constructed always with the other classes
in mind. Hence part of what it means to be middle class in *The
Imperialist* is not behaving in ways associated with the "gentry-
folk," namely, not keeping a groom, not dining late, not drinking
port regularly or playing whist. In Duncan's novel, these practises
are viewed as outmoded traditions, which are being supplanted by
the customs of the newer but no-less-respectable middle class.
This open confrontation, then, between the Canadian upper class
and middle class in *The Imperialist* results in the textual annihila-
tion of the former. The novel assures us that it is simply not a
group that amounts to much in Canada.

Occasionally, however, the passing of the Canadian aristocracy is equated with the elimination of class itself. So we hear Hugh
Finlay rhapsodizing on the new possibilities that Canada creates
for immigrants such as himself: "And the scope of the individual,
his chance of self-respect, unhampered by the traditions of class,
which either deaden it or irritate it in England!" (102). This notion
that Canada is classless, that it has no "traditions of class," is
typically Canadian; indeed, it is one of our most treasured myths.
We see ourselves, as Duncan's Finlay did before us, as a society
in which immigrants can escape from the strict class confines that
seriously restricted them in their birth countries, and this belief is

premised on the fact that, unlike the older nations, we do not have a landed aristocracy, the people who, because they seem to benefit from it the most, are often thought to embody class much more than everyone else. Get rid of the aristocracy, the linchpin of the class system, and you get rid of class altogether, this thinking seems to go.

But, of course, class exists even without the presence of the aristocracy. Written at a profoundly pivotal moment in Canadian history, when this national self-deception about our classlessness was only just beginning to take hold, *The Imperialist* knows that more than the middle class lives and works in Elgin. But it deals out that knowledge sparingly, and the traces of the working classes that are present in the novel are carefully contained within a rhetoric that ultimately ejects working people and the poor from this picture of Canadian life.

Where, then, do we see the working classes in *The Imperialist*? Often they appear in what seem to be throw-away lines. The Queen's Birthday celebration is described as ending "splendidly with rockets and fire-balloons and drunken Indians vociferous on their way to the lock-up" (3);[2] East Elgin, with its "tall chimneys and rows of little houses" is said to be the "invariable hunting ground for domestic servants" (53); and after hearing that newcomer Alfred Hesketh would like to be nominated to a provincial seat, Advena advises that he begin his political career with a less glamorous service: "There's a representative committee being formed to give the inhabitants of the poor-house a turkey dinner on Thanksgiving Day" (172). Drunken Indians, inhabitants of poor-houses, and domestic servants whose families live in close-fitting homes with tall chimneys—here are the working-class people of Elgin, relegated to the edges of the story as if they did not matter.

I am inclined, however, to believe that they do matter. Within the context of this novel, they matter because Duncan bothers to mention them at all and, further, because at other moments in the text she goes to great lengths either to camouflage their presence or to devalue their opinions. For instance, one of her earliest portraits of Elgin delineates it as a "thriving manufacturing town, with a collegiate institute, eleven churches, two newspapers, and an asylum for the deaf and dumb, to say nothing of a fire department unsurpassed for organization and achievement in the Province of

Ontario," but its economic achievement can be recognized only at noon, "when the prolonged 'toots' of seven factory whistles at once let off, so to speak, the hour" (16). Although the seven factories are clearly the basis of the town's middle-class affluence, neither they nor those who work in them are accorded a place in this text. Instead, whistles metonymically stand in for workers.

Similarly, in her discussion of the desirability of bank clerks (from the point of view of the prospecting bride), the working classes are not named, but they are present nevertheless. The bank clerks' privileges—their short working days, the "gentlemanly form" of their labour, and their finely tailored suits—make them the most eligible of bachelors among single middle-class women of Elgin. But not all of Elgin's residents are prepared to admire them: "envious persons and small boys" view the clerks as effeminate. And so the narrator informs us that the question " 'D'ye take me fur a bank clurk?' was a form of repudiation among corner loafers as forcible as it was unjustifiable" (36). Any working-class criticism of the middle class—evidence of which lies in Duncan's use of English vernacular language—is pre-empted by her designation of the critics as "corner loafers" or "envious persons and small boys," who would hardly be speakers the reader could be expected to take seriously.

Duncan's virtual erasure of the working classes in Elgin and her undermining of their opinions when they are allowed to be present in the text are both part of her tactic to construct the middle class as central and dominant. Still, though the working classes are suppressed in the novel, they are essential to the middle class's definition of itself. In her study of the class consciousness found in Dickens's novels, Pam Morris charts the progress of the middle class in England from its roots in obscurity to its domination of the Victorian social and economic scenes. Some of her observations are useful in this reading of Duncan's book. Morris notes that, although in the first stage of its bid for ascendancy at the end of the eighteenth century the middle class of England differentiated itself through comparisons with the aristocracy, eventually it had to confront those from below who posed a greater threat to its continued authority:

> Increasingly, after the French Revolution, the middle class
> defined its identity, not in opposition to the aristocracy, but

in marginalization of the working class ... it was ... upon
vociferous reiterations of the uncouth behaviour and moral
degeneracy of the 'vulgar poor' that the middle class depended to construct their sense of identity and worth. Rough
hands, uneducated speech, unpolished manners became ...
absolutely necessary ... to define and justify bourgeois hegemony. (8)

To know itself, to be able to distinguish its culture from others
in society, the middle class needs the working classes. And more
important, it needs them to be contemptible, envious, and inferior.
The brief glimpses of the poor and the working people that appear
in *The Imperialist* are, therefore, supremely meaningful, since it is
these glimpses that are supposed to convince the reader that, for all
its misplaced and self-centred loyalties, the middle class constitutes the only class morally, economically, and intellectually fit to
dominate and rule the nation.

But what Duncan neglects to tell us is that when she wrote her
novel, in 1902 and 1903, the sovereignty of the middle class in
Canada was not so incontrovertible an argument. In fact, many
Canadian labour historians now suggest that the twenty or so years
on either side of the century's turn were a period of extreme class
antagonism, as the employers' class fought to develop the economic system we live with today in Canada, monopoly capitalism,
and the workers united to retain the little power they had already
achieved, through the earlier establishment of trade unions and
other working-class organizations, and to demand a fairer share of
the economic pie and better working conditions. Because the
stakes were high on either side—the middle class sought political
power and continued profit while the goal of the working people
was personal and class autonomy—the battle was bitterly fervent.
On the one side were the business people and professionals who
considered the workers ungrateful and grasping, as this statement
from an 1891 *Journal of Commerce* suggests: "The spirit of trades
unionism ... is strangling honest endeavour, and the hard-working,
fearless, thorough artisan of ten years ago is degenerating into the
shiftless, lazy, half-hearted fellow who, with unconscious irony,
styles himself a Knight of Labor" (qtd. in Palmer 133). On the
other side were the workers themselves whose solidarity was
cemented through membership in associations such as the Knights

of Labor, where, as new initiates, they would vow to "rescue the toiler from the grasp of the selfish" and to "affirm the nobility of all who earn their bread by the sweat of their brow" (qtd. in Kealey and Palmer 223). This was a clash of immense proportions, involving enormously divergent ideologies, and it took up much space in the journals and newspapers of the day.[3] Moreover, the opposing visions of the future for Canada, separately espoused by the working classes and their employers, led again and again to strikes. In the thirteen year period, from 1901 to 1914, 421 strikes and lockouts, involving 60,000 working men and women, occurred in southern Ontario alone (Heron and Palmer 85). Considering the magnitude of this conflict between labour and capital, it is surely quite significant that Duncan chooses not to refer to it in the one novel she wrote that explores the political, social, and cultural issues and values of a typical Canadian town at the beginning of this century.

This missing information is especially telling given the novel's setting, Elgin-alias-Brantford, a town in southern Ontario. Brantford was one of the strongholds of the Knights of Labor in the late nineteenth century. Bryan D. Palmer notes in his 1983 book *Working-Class Experience: The Rise and Reconstitution of Canadian Labour, 1880-1980* that, along with Chatham, Brockville, and Ottawa, Brantford saw the success of a combined Knights of Labor-trades union force in its municipal council. It was also a major centre for the metal trades with additional industry in tobacco, textiles, and carriage construction (see Heron and Palmer 89). According to David Burley's recent study of mid-Victorian Brantford, labour agitation can be traced back to 1860 "when skilled craftsmen, especially in the metal trades, organized unions and struck against the town's major employers, conflict became a part of the fabric of community life and could no longer be easily dismissed as the acts of outside conspirators" (Burley 51). In the 1901 *Census of Canada* report, issued just a year before Duncan began work on *The Imperialist*, Brantford is said to have 44 manufactures, employing a total of 3,603 people and producing $5,564,695 worth of products (Heron and Palmer 88). The working classes in Brantford, therefore, were neither politically silent, as their presence on the municipal council indicates, nor small in number.

The men of these classes also certainly had the right to vote.

In an 1872 election speech, the Liberal candidate William Paterson told the working men in his audience: "Many of you would never have had the franchise if it had not been for the efforts of the Reform [Liberal] Party" (qtd. in Burley 198). We are left wondering, then, why the novel shows Lorne Murchison wooing the farmers of South Fox as well as the merchants and professionals of Elgin during his campaign to be elected to the provincial seat of Fox County, but does not depict him as at all interested in the votes of the working men. Burley says that "By the 1870s partisan politics in Brantford organized discernible class interests" (199). It could be argued that imperial federation, Lorne's campaign platform and his personal passion, was an issue that labour in Canada resisted (see Berger 2), committed as it was to the internationalism of the labour movement, particularly across the U.S./Canada border. Such a stance was in direct opposition to the ideal of imperial federation, which strove to enhance the commercial ties between Canada and England. But, in the Canada outside *The Imperialist*, the Canadian labour movement's lack of support for imperial federation did not prevent the Liberal party from addressing some of the favourite causes of the working classes. Because of the politicization of these people in the last two decades of the nineteenth century by means of class associations like the unions and the Knights of Labor, the Liberal party had learned to take the voices of labour seriously. Palmer goes so far as to assert that the Liberal hegemony in Ontario and Quebec, from 1896 through to the twentieth century, which is the political state we see existing in Duncan's Elgin, was indebted to labour. He writes, "It was obvious that workers had to be considered as a class with a unified voice and that the *ad hoc* manner in which they had been treated in the late nineteenth century was no longer applicable" (137). It was partly because the Liberals were willing to recognize that class was indeed a relevant and vitally important concern for many working Canadians that they found their way into power and then stayed there.

Middle-class narratives about the working classes, whether they emerge from Marxist perspectives, Duncan's turn-of-the-century Liberalism, or conservative assumptions, often tend to construct the working classes for the varied purposes of the middle class. Sometimes, these purposes are predicated on ignorance of or disdain for the working classes and their motivations, as is frequently the case in Duncan's novel; at other times they are charitable but condescending.[4] Usually, however, such constructions tell us more about the middle-class author and middle-class ideology than they do about the working classes. We cannot know the working classes through middle-class texts. Indeed, as a whole, they are not knowable at all, being far too enormous a population and far too diffuse in their political loyalties, cultural beliefs, and social behaviours. There is no neat package of working-classness that will license their easy consumption by the middle class. What we can know about the working classes must be rooted in specific contexts, events, and circumstances. And we can analyze the systems that exploit them and de-authorize their values and their own interpretations of their experiences. But in texts like *The Imperialist*, in which the working classes function as the classed Other, as a category that is generalized beyond any point of comprehensibility—the vulgar poor, the objects of charity, the mirrors that reflect and help define the middle-class—they always only slip away from outsiders' attempts to understand them or their realities.

In this essay, then, I use history cautiously, not in order to posit an alternative reading by which the working classes can be known but as an interrogator of Duncan's middle-class opinions about the working classes. Hence the above brief historical account of certain events, issues, and movements that affected numerous members of Southern Ontario's working classes in the decades surrounding the turn of the century is not meant to be complete, only suggestive. It is meant to give readers of Sara Jeannette Duncan's *The Imperialist* some idea of the complexities that get lost and the challenges that are suppressed when we allow the middle class alone to speak for all of us. It is incapable of doing so, though one of its defining characteristics seems to be the pretense that it does.

Endnotes

1   Gregory S. Kealey, Susan Trofimenkoff, Bryan D. Palmer, Peter Delottinville, Bettina Bradbury, and Craig Heron are just a few of the many historians in Canada who, since the late '70s, have been producing histories of the working classes that use class as a primary interpretive

category. Kealey, in his interesting article "Labour and Working-Class History in Canada: Prospects in the 1980s," even goes so far as to assert that "it is now necessary to locate class conflict and class struggle at the centre of modern Canadian history" (248). The paucity of class analyses in the discipline of literary studies in Canada is, I would suggest, indicative of a wider refusal to allow a working-class critique to radicalize our field, maybe even our places of work, in the way, for instance, that middle-class feminism has.

2   I regret that I cannot go into more detail about the construction of the native figures in Duncan's *The Imperialist*, but this subject is immensely complex and requires its own essay. Suffice to say, for now I have included the images of nativeness in my working-class category because Indians in the novel are, like the white working classes, held in contempt by the middle-class, white narrator and viewed as inferior and not typical of Canadian life.

3   Duncan herself frequently joined the middle-class fray ranged against such working-class institutions as unions. In a few of her columns she makes it clear that she is opposed to unions for women, arguing that they would not work to secure better wages for women as their proponents insisted they would. So long, she said, as the market is glutted with unskilled female workers, employers could not be convinced to pay them more (*Selected Journalism* 41). The idea that employers had a moral responsibility to pay their workers a living wage Duncan dismisses as "philanthropy," which she thinks should not be mixed with business.

The extent of her lack of sympathy for working-class women is especially evident in a December 1886 column for *The Week*. Here she insists that, contrary to what many middle-class reformers were saying, women workers are not paid unfairly. According to Duncan, women need to acquire the skills that employers appreciate and for which they are willing to pay highly. Her final point is colossally condescending: "It behooves us, therefore, to choose our work for its value to the world, and not for its agreeableness to ourselves . . . to think less of bewailing our injuries and more of repairing them . . ." ("Saunterings" 6). Duncan, of course, chose her own career as journalist and later as novelist because, we presume, of their "agreeableness" to herself. Blind to her own class bias, which assumes that people much less privileged than she is are accorded the same opportunities in life, she is unable to critique the ideology produced by her own class, which was designed to keep the working poor poor.

4   Most of the labour historians that I came across during my research for this essay were either thoroughly Marxist in their assumptions or unselfconsciously indebted to the insights of Marxism. This allegiance, particularly if it is uncritically held, is often problematic because some expressions of Marxism can be read as yet another

middle-class discourse about the working classes. Unable to imagine the triumph of the working classes except through the lens of revolution, Marxist historians frequently overlook the everyday victories and solidarities that constitute so much of working-class life in its constant interaction with middle-class domination.

"Was *This* The Course of Conduct That She Had Marked Out For Herself?": Advena as Self-Constructed Romantic Heroine[*]

Elisabeth Köster

In an 1888 review of *An Algonquin Maiden*, Sara Jeannette Duncan concentrates on the disparities between the co-authors. Firmly allying herself with G. Mercer Adam, whom she credits with the historical and political portions of the novel, she praises his "tact," "guiding and restraining hand" and strong portraiture. At the same time she highlights the stylistic excesses of Ethelwyn Wetherald, author of the romantic plotline, whose prose she gently ridicules (Duncan, *Selected Journalism* 112). Yet Duncan is herself accused of producing a similarly uneven work. John Moss states a common view of *The Imperialist* when he declares that the novel "steers ... between the poles of sophisticated political analysis and conventionally sentimental romance towards a coherent definition of society" (*A Reader's Guide to the Canadian Novel* 63-64). The very existence of the Murchison family, however, points to the fact that this society defies any easy definition. Meanwhile, just as Lorne's idealism blinds him to many of the political realities upon which *The Imperialist* elaborates, the sentimental nature of the sub-plot can be seen as a commentary on its central character and on the place of romance in a young society, rather than conventional writing on Duncan's part. This paper will

---

[*]Commissioned for this edition.

explore the degree to which Advena herself initiates the romantic plotline. If Duncan produces a "plot with exactly the same structure as that which used to propel the old-time heroine" (Ross 46), it is partly because Advena herself appropriates and manipulates it. Only through attempting to shape her character and her situation into the subject of a romance does she learn to value her true talents and desires.

As Elizabeth Morton points out, exclusion from the community values makes Advena into an outsider: because she cannot conform to the female role, she "withdraw[s] from the circles in which she cannot be useful" (102). Interestingly, Elgin mothers initially predict Advena's fate in terms of her besetting sin: the dreamer will come to "some dramatic end" (*Imperialist* 35) more suited to the novels in which she buries herself than to straightforward Elgin. Banished to her books, Advena first attempts to profit from this exile through teaching. While this practical occupation wins her some grudging approval, it is not enough to satisfy her romantic yearnings. Here literature remains her closest confidant.

Advena is the product of two radically opposed educational approaches. On the one hand, the world presided over by her mother is centred around such "feminine" pursuits and accomplishments as playing the piano, entertaining, preserving, sewing, and maintaining a clean home. While Abby follows her mother's ways unquestioningly, Advena attempts to negotiate the traditions passed on by both parents. She initially discards Mrs. Murchison's lessons with ease by retreating into the educational world her father has offered her. She uses books, with which he has surrounded himself and his offspring, as a means of gaining employment outside the domestic realm of the home. She then attempts to apply the concepts she has encountered in novels to define a place for herself in the "feminine" domain of love and marriage. Here she finds any self-expression inhibited by both aspects of her background: Mrs. Murchison may be voluble upon practical matters, while her husband maintains his characteristic reticence, but both are "shy of any affair of sentiment in terms of speech" (200). In the absence of a recognized discourse of love in Elgin, Advena adopts the discourse of novels.

Love, in Elgin, is by tacit agreement a forbidden subject: "These early spring indications were belittled and laughed at; ... usually, after years of 'attention,' a young man of Elgin found himself mated to a young woman, but never under circumstances that could be called precipitate or rash" (24). Mrs. Murchison, meanwhile, views marriage in strictly practical terms: she expresses sorrow for any man who might marry Advena because his house would never be properly managed. While other Duncan heroines move from such repressive situations to "the romance inherent in charming traditions" of such established centres as Quebec or London (Tausky, *Novelist of Empire* 94), Advena returns to the one locus in Elgin where romance is thoroughly expressed and examined: literature.

Advena, as Elizabeth Morton notes, is influenced by her reading of Plato, Buddhism and Yoga, which "preach the rejection of earthly considerations and physical desire as a means of release from suffering" (103). An even larger factor in shaping her imagination, however, is her reading of popular fiction. In her tribute to the disappearance of "The Heroine of Old-Time," Duncan examines the changing faces of this heroine—from passive beauty to blue-stocking to moody, freckled charmer, concluding that the modern heroine is created by women who "show themselves as they are, not as a false ideal would have them" (Daymond and Monkman 80). Duncan, Catherine Sheldrick Ross concludes, "pretends to regret the passing of the old-time romantic heroine, who has been pushed into oblivion by the new school of realists to which Duncan herself belongs" (43).

Duncan's mockery is not, however, unmixed with nostalgia, as when she reminds the reader of "your" own acquaintance with the "light reading" which "formed the solace of many an hour in the dusty seclusion of the garret, while the rain pattered on the roof, and the mice adventured over the floor, and the garments of other days swayed to and fro in dishevelled remembrance of their departed possessors" (Daymond and Monkman 79-80). This scenario closely parallels one in the Murchison attic, "where Advena on rainy days ... made an early acquaintance of fiction in *Ready Money Mortiboy* and *Verner's Pride*, while Lorne, flat on his stomach beside her, had glorious hours on *The Back of the North Wind*" (21).

As one of the two Murchison siblings most gifted with imagination, Advena later lives out such early germs of her imagination. She is first attracted to Hugh Finlay because his "passionate" appearance accords with that of the romantic hero; she "thought him the probable antitype of an Oxford don" because he "wore the characteristics those schoolmen were dressed in by novelists" (59). From one literary convention she rushes to another: that of love at first sight. As the "eternal habile feminine," she knows that her role is to wait quietly until the hero recognizes and reveals his love for her: "he was loved, and he was unaware" (60). While her own role does not exist in Elgin, it holds a clearly defined place in the "glorious, defensible, demonstrable sequence" (60) of popular fiction. "She found herself treating his shy formality as the convention it was, a kind of make-believe which she would politely and kindly play up to until he should happily forget it and they could enter upon simpler relations" (60). Here, she has already begun to confuse the reality that they are strangers with the literary situation which is more familiar to her. After several encounters with Hugh, she comforts herself with poetry which speaks of the moment of revelation, while "Her own heart, all sweetly alive, counselled her to patience" (99).

Peter Allan queries,

> All sweetly alive? Warned by this sort of language that we are not to take the subject of Advena's love ironically, we can only read the climactic scene between the two lovers as unrestrained melodrama .... What seems to have happened is that Duncan's intense sympathy for Advena's dilemma has subverted her narrative technique and created an unnecessary gap between the main and sub-plots. [Such] deviations from the general tone of sophisticated social comedy ... constitute a serious flaw. (this edition, 381)

Alternatively, such diction may be employed to point out the excesses of Advena's character. That it is most closely allied with Advena's perspective is suggested by comments in which the narrator expresses doubt regarding her wisdom: "It was Advena, I fear, who insisted most that they should continue upon terms of happy debt to one another ..." (176). The narrator regards Finlay as a "poor fellow" (176), rather than the exalted hero Advena chooses to see.

Offering insight into the day-dreaming of which Elgin disapproves, Advena finds it natural that a sensitive person "can't see a thing truly without feeling it; you can't feel it without living it

.... I experience—whole publisher's lists" (100). Upon Hugh's admission that he finds himself in accord with a novelist, she is quick
to suggest that he, too, "lives" novels. Hugh confesses a preference
for "old-fashioned" works, "old stories of pain," over "the highest
class of fiction" (100). It is not entirely surprising, then, that
Advena later finds a solution to their mutual problem in one of
these older popular novels banished to the attic.

Advena is initially silenced by Hugh's admission that he has
allowed his aunt to arrange a comfortable marriage for him.
Shocked by the disparity between his passionate appearance and
prosaic acceptance of a situation which falls "so lamentably short
of man's dignity" (134), she rapidly resolves to assist him in
overcoming his deep sense of humiliation. Just as Lorne turns to
a past political situation for guidance and inspiration, Advena returns, presumably unconsciously, to a novel that she "lived" years
earlier. Recognizing that Hugh has almost certainly fallen in love
with her while promised to another woman, she observes, on some
level, the similarities between his position and that of Lionel
Verner, hero of *Verner's Pride*. Ceasing to regard herself as part
of a "demonstrable sequence" of literature in general, Advena
begins to model her reactions on this particular plotline.

In Mrs. Henry Wood's novel, Lionel offers himself as
Sibylla's "protector" in an unguarded moment of pity that she is
"alone in the world" (189). It is only later that he recognizes fully
the depth of his love for Lucy Tempest, and his folly in having
engaged himself to a woman to whom he is no longer well suited.
In each of these particulars the present situation finds some correspondence. Lionel stubbornly defends his stated intention to
marry while recognizing that he has compromised his happiness
(197); likewise, Hugh maintains that it is more important to keep
his word than to give in to his true desires. Given that she cannot
change the circumstances which Dr. Drummond terms "pure cardboard farce" (156), Advena can only alter the way she "reads" or
interprets them. She and Hugh speak glowingly of their almost
mystic "ideal"; in fact, it merely echoes the "sacred feelings ... so
well hid from the world" (Wood 411) of a melodramatic, contrived text which she may have forgotten reading. It does, however,
offer her a "safe place" (35) in which to come to terms with her
own ability to experience passion.

Advena models her own behaviour upon Lucy's. Having

struggled with her grief, Lucy "strove to arouse herself to better things. She would meet him and others with a calm exterior and placid smile; none should see that she suffered, no, though her heart were breaking" (Wood 211). In this vein, Advena clings to her martyrdom. She emulates Lucy in communicating her secret to no one, continuing her meetings with Hugh, and making friendly overtures toward her rival. Just as Lucy and Lionel "knew that the love of the other was theirs, the punishment keenly bitter, as surely as if a hundred words had told it" (Wood 237-38), she determines to "leav[e] it, all unsaid and all undone" (180). Her bittersweet reward will be the secure knowledge that she is foremost in Hugh's heart. Just as Lucy and Lionel seem most alive, after his disastrous marriage, when encountering one another, she convinces Hugh that their friendship will provide "the greater part of whatever happiness life may have in store for us" (157).

Although Lionel consistently remains "true to the line of conduct he had carved out for himself" (Wood 399), Hugh is not sure that the role in which Advena has cast him truly "cover[s] him." He goes so far as to dismiss their chosen course as "Charming— literature" (181)! All the while, paradoxically, he and Advena are being drawn towards a more realistic appreciation of their situation. In the course of theorizing about their predicament as if it were indeed literature, they cease to discuss books. Instead, Advena begins to take interest in such practical matters as suitable overcoats, mended gloves, Hugh's weak chest, and appropriate living quarters. Emulating the domesticity of long-married couples they sit together in the library, she with her sewing, he with his pipe. Having initially escaped from her mother's prescriptions into novels, Advena is beginning to make her passage back to a place where romance and practicality can coexist. Mrs. Murchison "implicitly understands the emotional realities that Advena and Finlay try so hard to idealize away" (Gerson 74); now Advena's recognition that the pain inherent in living out exalted ideals cannot compensate for the day-to-day satisfactions of real life denotes her acceptance of some of her mother's basic precepts.

Advena signals her final repudiation of *Verner's Pride* on the night of the storm. During a similar rain storm, Lucy "timidly" asks whether Lionel will unburden himself to her, only to be told, "No, Lucy. If I could speak, it would only give you pain; but it is of a private nature." Far from challenging his resolve, "She looked up at him, puzzled; sympathy in her mantling blush" (Wood 310), and he sees her home with perfect correctness. Rejecting such submission, Advena allows the storm to propel her into Hugh's arms, then demands that they give in to their mutual love (245-46). To a degree, she may be acting out the melodramatic convention that lovers, like nature, can find release in unleashing their passionate emotions during a tempest. Advena may even be dramatizing herself in a new role, for example, the scene from *Ready-Money Mortiboy* in which the young women determine that men are too proud to give in to what is in their best interests, "so we have come to you" (Besant and Rice 509). Even if her actions take clichéd forms, the storm on another level signals that Advena no longer inhabits a vicarious dream world of publisher's lists. The rain wets her naked hands, the wind physically buffets her, and while experiencing these natural elements she is finally able to bare her soul. In a dramatic setting reflective of her "strong natur[e]," Advena accepts reality. Whereas in their initial outdoor scene both she and Hugh attempted to invest a sunset with symbolic and philosophic value, Advena's focus is now upon the realistic personal insight, confirmed by Dr. Drummond, "I have seen [Christie]; and oh! she won't care, Hugh—she won't care" (246).

Elizabeth Thompson contends that Advena is not as dissimilar from her mother as might be suggested by her inadequacies as a homemaker. Just as Mrs. Murchison fulfills most of Catharine Parr Traill's requirements for the ideal frontier woman (Thompson 62), Advena's "desire to change the world about her" and her "honesty and personal sense of freedom" (75; 76-77) place her in the same tradition. Both extend "the concept of the pioneer woman as a feminine ideal" (60). However, while Advena has pioneered a new career and accomplishments for women, she has compromised her pioneer honesty up till this point by emulating past models of romance which silence women.

From the moment she becomes aware of her attraction to him, Advena focuses upon Hugh's "lips," which will eventually release them both from an "auspicious" silence. Convention dictates that, as a woman, it is not her place to initiate romantic dialogue. Embarrassed and elated when Hugh for the first time publicly walks home from church in her company, "She heard, and hated the note of constraint in her voice. 'Am I reduced,' she thought, indignantly, 'to falsetto?' and chose, since she must choose, the betrayal of

silence" (130). Silence, at this point, is a temporary state which be-
trays her sense of wanting to be self-directed in love—her feeling
that once they have entered into terms of easy intimacy, she will
never feel exiled and alone in Elgin again. Together they will
pioneer a more explicitly passionate and self-revelatory attitude
towards romance than Elgin presently sanctions. Upon learning
that Hugh's romantic life has been managed by an elderly spinster,
however, she becomes motivated by the need to view him in more
heroic terms.

According to novelistic convention, the hero is one who can
live up to his promises, however distasteful. "I swore it. I must
keep my oath. It will be my life's work," Frank Melliship declares
in *Ready-Money Mortiboy* (Besant and Rice 171), and Grace
avows to love him more for this. Lionel Verner, similarly, schools
himself never to complain about his disastrous decision. Meanwhile, the good woman waits, silently and with infinite patience,
for the man to speak. In this way she aids him to maintain his
heroism. Only her paleness and thoughtful air betray her inner
agitation (Besant and Rice 179). In contrast to Lucy Tempest,
Decima Verner and Mary Elmsley, whose silence is rewarded in
the conclusion of *Verner's Pride*, Sybilla's unheroic cast of mind
is marked by her inability to hold her tongue:

> "I won't be silent!" she reiterated, her voice rising to a
> scream. "Who is Lucy Tempest, that you should care for her?
> You know you do! and you know that you meant to marry
> her once!" (Wood 428)

Although she is on one level revealing the truth, Sybilla is treated
as though she were willfully making false accusations, because she
voices what neither Lionel nor Lucy has ever verbally acknowledged. She is the one who is punished. Her death—the price of giving utterance to her distempered imagination through such "un-
wifely word(s)"—is soon foreshadowed by the "blood pouring
from her mouth" (430).

It is appropriate that Advena treats Hugh like a character in a
novel, since he feels himself to be bound by words. "He cherished
in secret an admiration for the young men of Elgin ... but he could
not translate it in any language of sympathy" (99): past codes of
speech and behaviour, his Scottish accent, his upbringing—all set

him apart from other men as much as his profession of preaching "the Word." Although he wishes to "yiel[d] to the words" (155) of Dr. Drummond's advice, he will not be known as a man who has broken his promise. He "lock[s] his lips" (245) against any utterance of love to Advena, rather "clinging to the sound and form of [his own] words" (247). In a new world whose customs and "freedom of conversation" seem "extraordinary" (213), Hugh's word is the only ongoing marker of personal identity left to him. He clings to it as a secure touchstone.

Fictional heroines gain their status by curbing any "hasty, thoughtless, impulsive words ... ere they [are] spoken" (Wood 211) and bolstering the dictums of their men in silence. Initially modelling her behaviour upon them, Advena bitterly chides Hugh in her thoughts, "but something else came to her lips" (134). She must "wait for his words to explain" (178) and "listen[s] with submission and delight" to Hugh's description of her "intimate nature" (181). In finally verbalizing her desire—"Send [Christie] away!"—Advena rejects both the reticence regarding love which prevails in Elgin and its alternative, the feminine standard of modest silence imposed by the romantic novel. The "life script" (Dean 74) which she provided for her relationship with Hugh twice distanced her from genuine self-expression, both because it was based upon events arising from another author's imagination, and because it suppressed her own voice. Casting off her dependence on the written word, "She spoke timidly, in a voice that should have been new to him, but that it was, above all, her voice" (246). There is no shame in speaking as impulsively as Sybilla, or virtue in remaining as reckless of her future happiness as Lucy. Like Duncan's "woman of to-day," she is finally prepared to show herself as she is by forgoing such a "false ideal" (Daymond and Monkman 80).

Many characters in the novel cannot express dichotomized emotions which remain in tension. Mrs. Murchison takes pride in her eldest daughter and in her home, but disguises her fear that both are too far outside the norm to be acceptable in Elgin with loud complaints against them, while Mr. Murchison and Dr. Drummond feel an "obscure ... undercurrent of the old allegiance" (12) beneath their loyalty towards Canada. As Francis Zichy asserts, Lorne's primary difficulty is that he verbalizes what Elgin "can neither express nor repudiate," and in uncovering "a tangle of ambiguities and conflicts in Elgin's attitude, and even in his own attitude towards the British connection" (Zichy this edition, 395), he both overstates and undermines his political position. After recapitulating and confessing her need for Hugh, Advena finds herself in a similar position. In voicing what Hugh dare not give in to, she threatens to destroy his identity. If Hugh were to acknowledge the truth of who he has become, he would reshift the balance he has established between possibly contradictory elements of his past and present. Thus, his word must remain paramount.

After his political defeat, Lorne initially considers "chucking the Empire" (264). Similarly, when Advena's "broken world of hapless defeat" goes unheeded, she renounces her new-found voice. She interprets herself as lying "abased" and "ashamed" for having unsaid her original words and Hugh as standing "erect and full of the deed they had to do" because he has refused to recant. She returns to the realm of melodramatic fiction, marking her disappearance from his life with the words "remember this—I was ashamed" (248). Speaking to the fact that neither sibling is, in fact, totally alien to the community, Henry Cruikshank and Dr. Drummond then step forward to prevent such wasteful lives of exile. As Drummond retains Hugh's integrity by arranging that he and Christie "giv[e] back" one another's word, Hugh's lips relax, and "the chambers of his brain seemed empty or reiterating foolish sounds" (253). For an instant, he returns to a pre-verbal infantile stage which augurs well for a new start in a new land—and the possibility of a new language. Hugh's dilemma is not however entirely resolved, since he is again bound by an earlier promise: to move with his bride to an Alberta mission. Thus, although Advena attains a position which is acceptable to the community, by embracing a new locus for her married life she transcends the sentimental novel's happily-ever-after assumptions about marriage and Elgin's premature complacency in predictable social routes. Advena's subjectivity has been suppressed both by the dominant emotionally sterile discourse, and by texts whose construction of romance entail silencing women. Duncan's discretion about the further development of the relationship accentuates the fact that it is Advena's choice whether she will continue to "live" existing texts, or articulate the alterity of her own experience. It is to be hoped that her relationship with language will continue to be infused by the pioneering spirit of her parents.

"It is the very life of our people":
the audiences of *The Imperialist*

Thomas E. Tausky

The contemporary West Indian writer Caryl Phillips makes some fascinating comments in an interview with Eleanor Wachtel that are surprisingly relevant to Duncan's situation as she worked on *The Imperialist*. Born in St. Kitts, Phillips was taken to England when he was twelve weeks old and did not return to the island until he was 22 and had developed the ambition of becoming a novelist:

> Going back to St. Kitts was almost a way of saying that if I'm going to write, if I'm really going to take this seriously, I have to find a way to go back to where it all began .... I want to feel it for myself, I want to see it for myself, I want to attempt to begin to tell the experience myself .... There was a kind of historical imperative to tell it.

Contributing to this sense of urgency was Phillips's consciousness of the absence of any definition of the island in literary terms:

> I looked around at the life that I would have led if I had grown up in the Caribbean. I looked around at the people my parents left behind, and I realized I was in a country in which nobody had ever published a book, I was amongst a people whose story—whose myriad of stories about their lives—had never been told. And their lives were at least as rich as the lives of the people that I had grown up with in England.

Duncan in mid-career retained the idealism and ambition, as well as the sense of commitment to a fictional setting, that permeates Phillips's remarks, but at the same time as an experienced writer she was well aware of the need to impress publishers and reach readers. The present essay applies various concepts of audience to *The Imperialist*, beginning with Duncan's acute consciousness of specific national audiences for her work, as revealed in her letters.

Duncan's letter to the American magazine publisher R.W. Gilder shows her as an author selling her work to a particular market, and trying, rather desperately, to find an American "angle" to arouse Gilder's interest. But Duncan's obvious desire in this letter to make a sale is not at all inconsistent with a sincere account of her own intentions. What she calls "a sense of difference"— distinctions based on nationality—is fundamental to all her fiction. The final sentence of the letter displays an eager anticipation of the role of being a literary and cultural pioneer: "It is untouched material and if I can only treat it as I imagine it, should work up well." It is sad to read a letter from the American publisher of Duncan's next novel which bluntly reveals that in the United States at least, her hopes of reaching an audience were doomed to failure, with the humiliating consequence for Duncan of a reduced royalty for her next book. H.W. Lanier of Doubleday, Page writes Duncan's agent, A.P. Watt:

> I want to tell you frankly that "The Imperialist" has not left a good impression among the booksellers here, who are the best arbiters of a new novel's fate: they did not succeed in selling it as well as they expected and the next book would come out under a distinct handicap from this point of view. (Letter of 4 April 1905: A. P. Watt papers for Mrs. Everard Cotes, Wilson Library, University of North Carolina).

Duncan's initial letter to John Willison, an old friend and the publisher of the Canadian serialization of the novel, communicates the joy of creative anticipation. Dated a year before *The Imperialist* began its first serialization, it combines a high sense of purpose with a powerful and in some ways unusual focus on her Canadian audience. She had published thirteen books by this time, but, she writes Willison, "I am trying very hard to make it my best book." The reason for this resolve is perhaps to be found in the letter's very direct first sentence: "I have taken upon myself to write a Canadian novel, with a political *motif*, and I am rather anxious that none of you shall be ashamed of it." She had written novels with a political theme before, though probably none were on an issue that meant as much to her. She had not, however, previously written "a Canadian novel," and Canada remained for her, despite over a decade of exile, a permanently attractive place to which it was necessary to do full justice. She wrote Willison in 1898, "I have quite succumbed to the charms of our own Toronto as a haven for my old age" (qtd. in Fowler 237); in her unsuccessful 1901 attempt to interest him in serializing her autobiographical work *The Crow's Nest*, she assumes that Canadians might constitute an audience especially interested in her as a person: "It ... is very personal, so much so that I venture to think my fellow Canadians might regard it with a special interest" (qtd. in Fowler 248).

In that letter, Duncan underplays the serious side of what in many ways is a sombre work. In writing about *The Imperialist*, however, Duncan calls attention to the seriousness of her task both by using a verb that suggests a momentous responsibility ("take upon myself") and by confessing that she is "rather anxious" that it should result in a novel worthy of the setting. It is curious that she should state as her concern that "none of you shall be ashamed of it," rather than that "I shall not be ashamed of it." She is, after all, addressing one individual, who would have no reason to be ashamed regardless of how the novel turned out. What this phrasing suggests to me is that Duncan is in this instance nervously aware that her potential audience includes Canadian journalists and intellectuals, some of them her former colleagues, to whose judgment she is submitting herself. Duncan might be vulnerable to criticism from this imagined audience if she were to fail to gauge accurately the political mood of Canada—the climate created in large measure by some of these same intellectuals. The same collective expression occurs again at the end of the letter, in which Duncan announces that she expects to be in Canada by the following June and says that "It will be a pleasure to see you all again in Toronto."

Duncan's concern about her Canadian audience turned to disillusionment in the aftermath of the publication of *The Imperialist*. Her expression of thanks for Archibald MacMechan's praise of the book shows how much what she interprets as the critical rejection of her book had troubled her:

> I confess I *had* wondered, a little here on my remote hill top, whether anybody had listened to me in Canada and had come rather to the conclusion that I had been too far away to be well heard, or perhaps I had forgotten my country's note. But that anyone should write like this reassures me quite, and

that you alone should feel the book as you do justifies me
very happily in having written it.

Duncan seems unsure as to whether her apparent failure to
communicate with her Canadian audience was their responsibility
("whether anybody had listened to me"), an inherent condition of
exile ("I had been too for away" whether she got those *Globe*
issues from Willison or not) or an inability on her part to bring
back the past ("I had forgotten my country's note"). The statement
that MacMechan's enthusiasm alone redeems the book in her eyes
is extraordinary, yet the context establishes that it is not just
embellishment to please an admirer. She goes on to speak with
renewed artistic energy of the Canadian character, its regional
basis and its value as a subject: "I share with you the conviction of
the individuality of the Canadian type. The spirit of place always
seems to me strong in the land. I want to come back and work at
it from closer range, and soon I think this will be possible." For
whatever reasons, neither re-settlement in Canada nor a second
exploration of the Canadian setting turned out to be "possible."

Duncan also could not afford to ignore her British audience,
which had been the chief market for her books. No doubt in planning a novel which invoked imperial allegiances and commented
directly on the immediate events of British politics she had an
investment in the English response that was more than financial.
She had a new publisher in England for *The Imperialist*, but no
letters to that publisher, Constable, appear to have survived.
Nevertheless, a letter to her previous publisher, Chatto & Windus,
shows a keen awareness, in very detailed financial terms, of the
market that had London as its centre and India, Australia and
Canada at its edges (qtd. in Fowler 206-207).

There is reason to believe, therefore, that Duncan set for
herself the complicated task of addressing three different national
audiences in the work she so eagerly wished to be her "best book."
The evidence as to how well she succeeded with the first readers
of her book is complicated and requires careful interpretation.

§

In her letter to Willison of 24 November 1903, written after
the first version of the novel had been completed, Duncan an-

nounces an event that might well have seemed to be an opportunity for the audience of Canadian literati to express itself upon the novel: "It appears that I am again to visit Toronto at the benevolent bidding of the Authors' Society..."

Heralding that event, Willison, or perhaps Duncan's friend Marjory MacMurchy, who was the literary editor of the *News,* paid tribute to Duncan in an editorial on "Canadian Literature," the main theme of which was that Canadian writers needed to go abroad to find a suitable audience:

> On Saturday night the Canadian Society of Authors will honor itself by honoring an expatriated Canadian who has won an enviable reputation in Europe. The novels and short stories of Mrs. Everard Cotes (Sara Jeannette Duncan) possess very distinctive qualities. In point of literary finish, insight and humor, they represent the highest reach to which Canadian fiction has yet attained.

The occasion itself provides some clues as to the identities of the collective "you" waiting for Duncan in Canada. She had reason to be pleased at the turnout, which was estimated by the Toronto *Star* to be two hundred. The *Globe* reporter was certainly impressed, claiming that "one of the most charming entertainments ever given in Toronto was the reception in honor of the brilliant Canadian authoress, Mrs. Everard Cotes." Each account of the occasion gave a list of guests, which included Goldwin Smith, Duncan's former employer at *The Week*; Pelham Edgar, an influential English professor at the University of Toronto, and his pioneering colleague in political economy, James Mavor. In general, professors and ministers were thick upon the ground. Smith, as a tireless anti-imperialist, would not have been enthralled by Duncan's reading of Lorne's passionate pro-imperialist speech. Whatever intellectual sparks flew were not, however, observed by the reporters, each of whom felt it necessary to describe Duncan's gown. The *Star* account confined itself to an enthusiastic survey of several ladies' dresses, followed by the guest list.

Yet the "honour" paid to Duncan that night may have been deceiving. Certainly some of the reviews of *The Imperialist* in England were not only the most negative Duncan ever received in her career but also often insufferably patronizing. Her former employer, the Toronto *Globe*, was not much kinder, and the *Canadian Magazine*'s verdict echoed the British comments about women novelists: "if the reader finds difficulty in seeing clearly what Mrs. Cotes is trying to say, he will kindly remember that a woman attempting politics must be judged leniently."

The British reviews displayed some interesting imperial attitudes towards their former colony. The *Daily Telegraph* reviewer found the periphery inherently contemptible: "the serious student of politics will regard the very commonplace love stories of some very commonplace persons in a remote Canadian townlet as an unworthy setting." Yet the *Times Literary Supplement* reviewer, while objecting to political didacticism, recognized and welcomed the novelty, in fictional terms, of the Canadian small town:

> The setting demands a good romance. Those good Scotch settlers, many of them staunch Presbyterians, who form so large a part of some of the townships in Ontario, and the U.E. Loyalists, still very "stark to traitors" to the imperial sentiment; the busy jealousy of the United States and the strengthened pride in the superiority of Canadian liberty; the keenness, even the corruption, of the elections are new and good material ready to the hand of any novelist of knowledge.

The point of view expressed here has much in common with the outlook we could find in some passages of the narrator's reflections—there is an almost sociological view of categories of settlers and a mixture of respect and condescension.

As events turned out, Duncan had many more Canadian than British or American readers. The Toronto *News* gave her 20,000 potential readers, and in contrast to the publication history of her previous work, in this case she secured a separate Canadian edition, with its own publisher (Copp Clark). The large turnout for her Toronto reception may have been a tribute to her longstanding reputation with the Canadian reading public, or perhaps an indication of the interest the novel was awakening in its serialized form.

She certainly found two sympathetic Canadian readers in the reviewers for the Toronto *News* and *Saturday Night*. Of course, it is hardly surprising that her friend, Marjory MacMurchy, writing in the newspaper in which the novel was serialized, should choose to give *The Imperialist* a favourable review; perhaps, indeed, she had no choice. What matters is that the review is written with intelligence, and that it finds a special value in the novel for the Canadian reader: "Nowhere else but in Canada can the book be entirely understood; and anyone who goes without reading it will miss a part of present Canadian life which in its own way is as useful as it is inspiring." "J.G." in *Saturday Night* makes exactly the same point, at greater length and with remarkable vividness:

> It is not "about" or "concerning" us, but here is an Ontario town, with its everyday trials and triumphs, its local ambitions, and its national significance. Elgin, the town described, is said to be Brantford, but it might be Guelph or Stratford or Goderich. We all know the Murchisons, the family circle into which Mrs. Cotes so warmly welcomes us; in fact, I know I have had tea at the Murchisons ...

What has made these two readers feel this way? It is possible that as patriotic Canadians eager to praise Canada's leading novelist in her first Canadian work they simply chose to find something that wasn't there. Yet their sense of identification with Duncan's evocation of a nascent Ontario urban culture seems to go beyond mere boosterism. What they recognize in the novel—and here we may recall Caryl Phillips's ambition, quoted at the beginning of this essay—is that Duncan has given a literary life to a society that had previously lacked any such recognition.

Fundamental to the criticism of *The Imperialist* for nearly twenty years has been a consciousness of an unusual narrator's voice in the novel. Within this volume, the exceptionally fine critical essays by Thomas, Peterman, Allen, Zichy, Heble, and Davey all address this issue in one way or other.

It is Frank Davey who is most explicit in noticing that a particular kind of narrator may well be implicitly addressing a particular kind of audience. He persuasively argues that "the implied audience is identifiable as British, cosmopolitan and educated," as well as strongly in need of enlightenment about Canadian customs. As he remarks, a "somewhat unusual narrative situation is created" by the absence of such traits among the actual characters of the novel. In his view, the result is that the narrator is firmly established as "the largest presence and wisest authority throughout the novel," claiming that role at the expense of the characters.

Yet we can imagine Duncan's narrator addressing other audiences—not in place of the cosmopolitan readers she sought to cultivate but in addition to them. Though in general Duncan's narrator tells us of Elgin that "the arts conspired to be absent" (50), Duncan herself must have known that a novel dealing with many facets of Brantford life including its heated political controversies would probably find some curious readers there. We should not be surprised, therefore, to find certain indications in the narrator's commentary of an awareness of this audience. Then there were the sophisticated Toronto readers who, we recall, were not to feel ashamed of the book.

An intriguing context for the complexities of the relationships between Duncan's narrator and her various audiences is afforded by the efforts of other local authors, with less experience of the wider world as well as less talent. The historian David G. Burley, in his distinguished study *A Particular Condition in Life: Self-Employment and Social Mobility in Mid-Victorian Brantford, Ontario*, suggests that "a surprising amount of biography and autobiography, and other instructive literature, was written or published in Brantford [in the 1880s]" (4). Like *The Imperialist*, these documents apparently communicated an awareness of dramatic social change, though obviously in a more naive way. Burley offers an interesting explanation of the underlying meaning of these works:

> ... each *apologia pro vita sua* also sought understanding and validation from others. By suggesting that what they had achieved could be attained by others, they denied that their lives had been exceptional and sought to reduce the social distance which their success had produced between themselves and others. (5)

A comparison of the narrator's remarks on the "controlling interests" of Elgin (Chap. VII) with her account of Dr. Drummond's ministry in the same chapter and the "analysis of social principles in Elgin" (Chap. V) may serve to show that the narrator's "social distance" from Elgin is quite variable.

When, in Chapter VII, Duncan writes of the Elgin outlook that "like other movements of the single mind, it had something of the ferocious, of the inflexible, of the unintelligent; but it proudly wore the character of the go-ahead" (50), she seems almost to be flaunting her intellectual distance from those within the community for whom economic progress meant everything and cultural pursuits meant nothing. In passages like these, she is affirming, to borrow the terms of Burley's summation, that her life *has* been exceptional, that what she has achieved could not be attained by others.

The chapter opens with an account of Elgin's indifference to British foreign policy and indeed to Britain altogether under the conditions of "ordinary circumstance." The implied audience here is very much the educated British reader posited by Davey. Such a person needs to be informed as to the precise reasons why the "theatre of European diplomacy," a drama of deep significance in British eyes, "had no absorbed spectators here." Duncan's narrator seeks to redeem Elgin by theorizing that the town displays proper reverence for "the monarch" and will rush to Britain's aid in times of military crisis, for "belief in England was in the blood." "Beauty and poetry" is claimed for Elgin's attachment to royalty. It is clear from external evidence that Duncan herself was very enthusiastic about the monarchy. Here, however, this attitude is described as a worthy characteristic that the unimpressed British reader must pause to contemplate: "*when you consider* [emphasis mine], beauty and poetry can be thought of in this."

The characterization of religion, a little later in the chapter, is transitional in tone as well as content; it acts as a bridge between the impersonal generalizations of the previous paragraphs and the more intimate portrait of Dr. Drummond that follows. By comparison with the other religious feelings the narrator claims to understand, the "reasonable" spirit of Elgin worship seems mundane. But as the narrator continues to describe the functions religion fulfills in Elgin, its value becomes more apparent: it may have "prescribed limitations," but at the same time it is "the backbone of life," and it also offers an undefined "thing that was more than any of these"—a sense of community solidarity perhaps, the "repressed magnetic excitement" she describes two sentences later —which can only be appreciated by those who have direct experience of it, "which you can only know when you stand in the churches among the congregations" (50). The narrator here continues to address an audience outside of Elgin, but at this moment she is conveying to that audience an Elgin emotion that she herself has felt.

The account of "the minister" begins in very general terms, with some of the anthropologist's distance with which the narrator started the chapter. As soon as Duncan begins discussing Dr. Drummond's sway over his congregation, however, a kind of sympathetic irony displaces the former aloofness. Dr. Drummond is said to combine dedication and idealism with autocratic tendencies; he would have been suited, the narrator suggests "to rule an Eastern province"—to be a district officer in India (a reader with a long memory will recall that in Chap. II, Dr. Drummond is said to have contributed his "labour" and his "life" to "this little outpost of Empire"). He is, therefore, not only a guardian of his flock, but also engaged in a praiseworthy imperial mission, and his obsession with the size of his congregation is both gently mocked and implicitly excused as a by-product of his zeal.

The controversy about a new minister for Elgin takes the form of a lively narrative in which the events are largely allowed to speak for themselves (the fictional episode is based on a real incident; see "The Writing of *The Imperialist*"). "Human nature in its Presbyterian aspect" is shown to be vigorous in correcting an inequity (Dr. Drummond faces an "unexpected rally" against him) and yet tactful in attempting to assuage his wounded feelings. The narrator is at ground level, as if herself a member of Knox Church: she admits, "I do not know who was found to broach the matter to Dr. Drummond." She seems to be attending the general meeting of the church rather than floating in the intellectual firmament above Elgin. The "social distance" between her and the natives has vanished, and the narrator's position recalls "J.G." 's claim in *Saturday Night* that Duncan "will probably be known to the end of the chapter among her Canadian friends as a Brantford girl, and no doubt will be content with the description, since she has not forgotten her Ontario home."

Similarly the narrator informs us in Chap. V that "there is a party at the Milburns, and some of us are going" (36) The remark occurs in a particularly self-conscious sentence in which the narrator defends the elaborateness of her protracted "analysis of social principles" on the grounds that such a task is "an adventure of difficulty." She will persist with "a clue or two more for the use of the curious." Who does she have in mind as her audience of "the curious"? Not her Brantford readers, who would not require such an explanation. But the condensed explanation of Canadian political and social patterns which follows, while it does not exclude an English audience, does not necessarily direct itself to such readers either. What the narrator suggests, in half a page, is that Elgin was representative of the province as a whole in being controlled in its early days by a local version of the Family Compact; this aristocratic elite was then eroded by political and economic change, and by inter-marriage with the offspring of self-made immigrants. All of this flashes by a little too quickly for a totally uninformed reader; an Ontario native would certainly be better placed to decode the narrator's message.

The paragraph ends with the memorable phrase, "we are here at the making of a nation." Does this "we" imply an audience of some sort? The tone of the statement is serious, even (for a narrator who is often facetious) solemn. One can imagine two possible interpretations—that the narrator is seeking to claim importance for Elgin and Canada in the eyes of skeptical international readers, or that she is showing to Canadians, many of whom would be startled by the daring of the claim, that their own country was on the way to nationhood. Perhaps this assertion is directed at both audiences simultaneously. In any event, it alerts the reader, wherever she may be placed, to the momentous goal that is the outcome of seemingly confused social processes.

The next paragraph returns to the topic which had been introduced two paragraphs before, the question of what makes for social desirability in a community such as Elgin. The narrator provides a minute investigation of the distinctions among the professional and merchant sub-categories of the middle class. Elgin's "little prejudices" are scrutinized in a lightly ironic way ("Groceries, on the other hand, were harder to swallow, possibly on account of the apron ...") that suggests the narrator's superiority to those within the community—Mrs. Milburn is named—who consider themselves to be superior. Yet in the midst of what seems like a condescending enumeration, we come across a sentence which undertakes a serious defence of Elgin: "The valuable part of it all was a certain bright freedom, and this was of the essence." The discriminations within the community are apparently of less importance to the narrator than the opportunities that present themselves within a relatively fluid social world.

For the two Canadian reviewers who greatly admired the entire novel, the opening chapter was especially complimentary to Elgin, and therefore especially significant for a Canadian audience. Marjory MacMurchy assumes that "everyone" (in Canada, presumably) will share her enthusiasm for this chapter:

> But how charming to everyone are the early chapters, written with the unhasting geniality of one who remembers very well. The Queen's Birthday—the Twenty-fourth of May—in Elgin is one of the prettiest, most humorous and touching things that have been written for our own country.

The last four words indicate that she has no doubt that Duncan was primarily concerned with addressing her own people.

"J.G." of *Saturday Night* specifically differentiates between the English or American reviewers who may not have the inside knowledge to appreciate the book, and Canadians who can find in the book a mirror of themselves: "The English critic or the United States reviewer may say what he likes about the book, but we know, before we have finished the first chapter, that it is the very life of our people."

Both Frank Davey and Michael Peterman have used the word "cosmopolitan" in describing the posture of the narrator in this chapter. It is clear that the narrator can on occasion invite an amused response to the unsophisticated celebrations that take place in Elgin on the holiday. At the same time, however, the narrator can also enter into the spirit of a "real holiday, that woke you with bells and cannon"—the following sentences that provide concrete details of the festivities manage to combine a sense of participation (conveyed by the breathless rhetoric and exclamation marks) that is no doubt founded upon childhood memories with a more detached perspective that regards these rituals as "humorous" as well as "touching."

Davey accurately points out that the second half of the novel contains far fewer instances of the narrator's intrusions than the first half. Such comments on Elgin as do occur are closely related to the political calculations of the opposed factions, and the longest such account, in Chap. XXVII, is cleverly cast in large measure as Walter Winter's reflections.

Much more than most Canadian novels ever since, *The Imperialist* is a work built around public actions—most dramatically, speeches, but also the trial in which Lorne Murchison shines, sermons, the work of a Canadian delegation to England and ultimately the formation of a legal and political partnership which is the final event of the novel. Such public acts are not performed in a vacuum. They depend upon a willing response from the audiences to which they are directed, and often those engaged in a public arena of any sort will seek to base their conduct, to some degree at least, upon a prudent calculation of the policy or manner that will be most acceptable to a prospective audience. The dilemma Duncan faced in her letters—whether an ambitious idealism could win popularity—is shared by several of her characters. The interaction between the leaders of the community and the audiences whom they address is fundamental to the portrait of a society which one finds in *The Imperialist*.

Duncan is at her most sardonic in showing that a complete miscalculation of one's audience can lead to utter disaster. Alfred Hesketh, Lorne Murchison's English friend, in the course of addressing an audience of pragmatic, democratically inclined farmers uses the views of various noble English lords to impress his rural audience and impress upon them very high-flown arguments. " 'Had ye no friends among the commoners?' suddenly spoke up a dry old fellow ... and the roar that greeted this showed the sense of the meeting" (192). On this occasion, Lorne repairs the damage caused by Hesketh precisely because he has a more precise awareness of his audience: "He did it by the simple expedient of talking business."

In Knox Church, public support is much more equally divided between Dr. Drummond and Hugh Finlay, despite the fact that the former is much more conscious of his audience than the latter. We see the sermons of Finlay, a "passionate romantic" (58) through the eyes of Drummond, who knew as soon as the text was announced "what the young fellow there would be at" (56-57) and criticizes Finlay for not looking up from his notes: "The man loses half his points" (59). Here novelty has a charm that is at least a match for professionalism; after twenty-five years of Dr. Drummond, the congregation finds itself attracted, not to different doctrines, but to a different presentation.

Finlay's appeal to his parishioners has something in common

with Lorne's initial appeal to Elgin; in both cases an idealist is valued more for the freshness associated with youth than for the substance of his ideas. As the narrator comments when Lorne is about to make his first court appearance in a prominent case: "Youth in a young country is a symbol wearing all its value. It stands not only for what it is. The trick of augury invests it, at a glance, with the sum of its possibilities" (71).

Lorne's political defeat by the end of the novel is all the more dispiriting, for him and for the reader, because he begins his career with the favourable climate created by this appreciative audience for the young man of promise. At the beginning of the novel, his feat of standing first in the provincial law examinations is seized upon by Horace Williams, the editor of the *Express*, who proclaims in his newspaper, "Elgin congratulates Mr. L. Murchison upon having produced these results, and herself upon having produced Mr. L. Murchison" (17). The community defines itself through its capacity to nurture rising young men.

Until the moment of his crucial election speech, Lorne's ascent is the main direction taken by the plot. When he "scored" with the lawyer's favourite audience, a jury, in the court case, his future political opponent proclaims that "today's event will do more for you than it has for [the defendant] Ormiston!" and the wider community audience of "friends and neighbours ... and people who hardly knew the fellow" concur—"they were all of that opinion" (79), the narrator states. When Lorne is appointed secretary to the Cruickshank delegation to England, once again the community audience applauds: "It was the talk of the town, the pride of the market-place, Lorne Murchison's having been selected." (83). When he becomes a federal candidate at the age of 28, only five chapters from his downfall, Lorne's destiny is positively linked to his role as the "spirited advocate" of imperialism; "his political future was assured" (173) whether he won or lost the election. Francis Zichy has very perceptively noted that there are danger signals in Elgin's enthusiasm for its young hero: "Two points of view, two assessments of Lorne's performance, are subtly superimposed: that of the narrator, who knows his real value, and that of the audience, which has eyes only for the results obtained, and judges them in a manner consistent with its own character" (this edition, 391-92). Yet the broad structural pattern throughout much of the novel is the apparent alignment of protagonist and community. All this endorsement on the part of the community adds greatly to the poignancy of Lorne's ultimate fate.

Lorne's zeal in the cause of imperialism is responsible both for his ascent and his downfall. Until the moment of Lorne's major speech it appears that he will not have to choose between keeping his audience with him and expressing his imperial sentiments. The waning popularity of the cause creates the necessity to confront such a choice. Before the fatal night, Lorne succeeds in compelling assent by the force of his oratory: "his talk had been so trenchant, so vivid and pictorial, that the gathered farmers listened with open mouths, like children, pathetically used with life, to a grown-up fairy tale" (221). Espousing imperialism appears to be no handicap. Then in response to the changing political climate and the entreaties of his handlers, Lorne "submitted," leaving the issue "in the background of debate" at joint meetings. "He submitted," the narrator confides ominously, "but his heart rebelled" (222).

The speech itself, in which Lorne's heart emphatically wins out over his head, is imagined with remarkable subtlety. It is only in the aftermath of the election that it becomes clear that the speech contributed to Lorne's demise. It is important to realize that it is given to two audiences. In the opera house itself is a picked audience of fellow Liberals; when he make his "bad break," in the words of a back-room analyst, and takes up the imperialist theme in earnest, they give "a half-comprehending burst of applause" to his blunt assertion that "England has outlived her own body" and his leap of faith that "the centre of the Empire must shift—and where, if not to Canada?" In words reminiscent of the description of Lorne's early triumphs, the narrator suggests that "They applauded Lorne himself; something from him infected them; they applauded being made to feel like that" (225). Even after Lorne goes on to argue that Canada should choose loyalty to the Empire over prosperity, and hotly attacks American infiltration of the country, "They cheered him promptly," and when he returns to the theme of Canada's role as a world leader, this time in a future "union of the Anglo-Saxon nations of the world," the response goes beyond party loyalty: "He had them all with him, his words were vivid in their minds; the truth of them stood about him like an atmosphere" (230). Most of Lorne's immediate audience have been captivated as much as the Fox County farmers were before them. As readers, we respond appropriately to many of the signals sent out by the narrator if we consent to become part of that appreciative audience, surrendering to the eloquence of the arguments Lorne advances in favour of both the "nobler ideal" (229) of "our [British] heritage" (226), and of Canada's opportunity to find an enlarged identity within the Empire.

But there is another audience outside of the hall, the unpersuaded, pragmatic voters of Elgin. Their representatives inside, paradoxically, are Lorne's own political backers. They know this wider audience better than Lorne does, and as he gives his speech, the narrator pans to their anguished features: "Bingham, doubled up and clapping like a repeating rifle, groaned aloud under cover of it to Horace Williams, 'Oh, the darned kid!' " (225). This audience has the last word when Lorne barely wins the election, and after allegations of corruption on both sides, fails to secure the nomination for a second election. As Farquharson, the outgoing member, tells Lorne, "The popular idea seems to be ... that you would not hesitate to put Canada to some material loss ... for the sake of the imperial connection" (259). Even before this verdict is pronounced upon him, Lorne knows he has said the right thing to the wrong community audience: "He himself observed himself with discontent, unable to fathom his extraordinary lapse from self-control on the night of his final address" (256). Ultimately, therefore, we are led to share his conviction that in tactical terms he has made a political mistake. As many critics have rightly observed, Elgin's pragmatists win the day. Zichy shrewdly comments that "the full meaning of his [Lorne's] actions can only be read in the interaction between his pressure and the answering response of the community.... It is the people of Elgin who have delivered this check to Lorne's hopes" (398-99).

Yet if Lorne has miscalculated, it has not been by much. Before we condemn Elgin too severely, we might perhaps reflect that idealism has not exactly predominated in Canadian history, either in our politicians or in our electorate. Nor does Canada have a monopoly on political sluggishness, either in reality or in the world of *The Imperialist.* Duncan's narrator speaks of "the slow British consciousness" (111) and Lorne, even more bluntly, condemns "the conservatism of the [British] people ... they know they're stupid" (124). Lorne's previous successes, even in his passionate advocacy of his cherished cause, provide some justification for his ill-timed surrender to idealism.

Yet he *has* lost, and it is fair to ask why. Could Lorne be guilty of the misjudgment for which Duncan blamed herself? Has he, in the words of her letter to MacMechan, "forgotten [his] country's note," or perhaps did he not want to hear it? For all the differences—gender, age, role in and experience of the world—there are between Lorne and Duncan herself, the grief he suffers in feeling rejected for his idealism is, in significant respects, the grief Duncan expressed to MacMechan. Lorne, "a dramatic figure, standing for the youth and energy of the old blood" (224) is, to adapt the narrator's phrase about Finlay's view of Advena, Duncan's "idea incarnate" (102). His wish to use the legacy of the past as a basis to build a glorious future for Canada is Duncan's own formula, as revealed in her letter to MacMechan. In seeking to assess the responsibility for Lorne's political setback, we find ourselves turning to the same kinds of questions that Duncan asked herself in that letter when she sought to explain *The Imperialist*'s apparent failure with its Canadian audience. Was she (or Lorne) guilty of a miscalculation? Was her audience (or Lorne's) incapable (not "listening") of understanding what she (or Lorne) had to tell them?

In taking on herself to write a Canadian novel with a political *motif*, Duncan showed herself to be as much of an idealistic risk-taker as her protagonist. Her ambition in combining Howells-like social realism with a remarkably up-to-date political theme matches Lorne's ambition to make the gospel of imperialism prevail; both ultimately suffered for their failure to find a means of adapting their purpose to find favour with their chosen audiences. In deciding to read Lorne's extremely controversial speech before her Toronto audience of admirers, Duncan was repeating the daring she ascribed to Lorne in delivering the speech. Of course she could not know when she was composing the novel that she would encounter a hostile reception for it, but her anxieties about the book are quite evident in her pre-publication letters. In writing a novel about the difficulties an idealist encounters in finding a well-disposed audience and in striving to link a new country with its old roots, Duncan was creating her finest art out of the subjects that were most vital to her.

Bibliography

Editor's Note: This bibliography documents all works cited throughout this edition. As well, criticism of *The Imperialist* not cited in the edition is included. It is not, however, a comprehensive bibliography of Sara Jeannette Duncan's works or of the writing about her, apart from *The Imperialist.*

Writing by or about Sara Jeannette Duncan

Allen, Peter. "Narrative Uncertainty in Duncan's *The Imperialist.*" *Studies in Canadian Literature* 9.1 (1984): 41-60.

Bailey, Alfred G. "The Historical Setting of Sara Duncan's *The Imperialist.*" *Journal of Canadian Fiction* 2.3 (1973): 205-10.

Bissell, Claude. "Introduction." *The Imperialist.* New Canadian Library. Toronto: McClelland & Stewart, 1961. v-ix.

—. "Literary Taste in Central Canada during the Late Nineteenth Century." *Canadian Historical Review* 31 (1950): 237-51.

Burgin, G.B. "A Chat with Sara Jeannette Duncan." *The Idler* Sept. 1895: 113-18.

Dean, Misao. *Sara Jeannette Duncan: A Different Point of View.* Montreal and Kingston: McGill-Queen's UP, 1991.

—. "Duncan's Representative Men." *Canadian Literature* 98 (1983): 117-19.

Donaldson, Florence. "Mrs. Everard Cotes (Sara Jeannette Duncan)." *The Bookman* June 1898: 65-67.

Dooley, D.J. "Sara Jeannette Duncan: Political Morality at the Grass Roots." *Moral Vision in the Canadian Novel.* Toronto: Clarke, Irwin, 1989. 25-35.

Duncan, Sara Jeannette. "Bric-a-Brac." Montreal *Star* 19 April 1888.

—. "Imperial Sentiment in Canada." *Indian Daily News* 7 Oct. 1896; rpt. *Sara Jeannette Duncan: Selected Journalism.* Ed. Thomas E. Tausky. Ottawa: Tecumseh Press, 1978. 60-62.

—. *The Imperialist.* London: Constable, 1904; New York: Appleton, 1904; Toronto: Copp Clark, 1904. Rpt. Toronto: McClelland & Stewart, 1961, 1990. Rpt. Ottawa: Tecumseh Press, 1988.

—. "The Heroine of Old-Time." Rpt. in Daymond, Douglas and Leslie Monkman, eds. *Canadian Novelists and the Novel.* Ottawa: Borealis Press, 1981. 78-80.

—. "*An Algonquin Maiden.*" Rev. of *An Algonquin Maiden.* By G. Mercer Adam and Ethelwyn Wetherald. *Sara Jeannette Duncan: Selected Journalism* 109-12.

—. "Saunterings." *The Week.* 21 Oct. 1886: 756-57.

—. "Saunterings." *The Week.* 2 Dec. 1886: 5-6.

—. "Woman's World." *The Toronto Globe.* 4 Feb. 1887.

Fowler, Marian. *Redney: A Life of Sara Jeannette Duncan.* Toronto: Anansi, 1983.

Gerson, Carole. "Duncan's Web." *Canadian Literature* 63 (1975): 73-80.

—. *A Purer Taste: The Writing and Reading of Fiction in English in Nineteenth-Century Canada.* Toronto: U of Toronto P, 1989.

Goodwin, Rae. "The Early Journalism of Sara Jeannette Duncan, with a Chapter of Biography." M.A. Diss. University of Toronto, 1964.

Heble, Ajay. " 'This Little Outpost of Empire': Sara Jeannette Duncan and the Decolonization of Canada." *Journal of Commonwealth Literature* 26.1 (1991): 215-28.

Hospital, Janette Turner. "Afterword." *The Imperialist.* New Canadian Library. 2nd ed. Toronto: McClelland & Stewart, 1990. 311-16.

Keith, W.J. *Canadian Literature in English.* London: Longman, 1985. 47-49.

Kelly, Darlene. "Rewriting *The Imperialist*: Duncan's Revisions." *Canadian Literature* 121 (1989): 26-38.

M.E.R. [Mrs. Sandford Ross]. "Sara Jeannette Duncan: Personal Glimpses." *Canadian Literature* 27 (1966): 15-19.

Macdonald, R. Douglas. "Rereading Duncan's *Imperialist* In the Light of Free Trade." *Dalhousie Review* 68.4 (1988-89): 428-44.

MacMechan, Archibald. *Headwaters of Canadian Literature.* Toronto: McClelland & Stewart, 1924.

MacMillan, Carrie. "The Figure of the Artist in Late Nineteenth Century Canadian Fiction." *Studies in Canadian Literature* 5.2 (1980): 63-82.

MacMurchy, Marjory. "Mrs. Everard Cotes." *The Bookman* May 1915: 39-40.

Merrett, Robert James. "Signs of Nationalism in *The History of Emily Montague, Canadians of Old,* and *The Imperialist*: Cultural Displacement and the Semiotics of Wine." *Recherches Semiotiques/ Semiotic Inquiry* 14: 1-2 (1994): 235-50.

Morton, Elizabeth. "Religion in Elgin: A Re-evaluation of the Subplot of *The Imperialist* by Sara Jeannette Duncan." *Studies in Canadian Literature* 11.1 (1986): 99-107.

Moss, John. "Colonial Exile." *Patterns of Isolation in English-Canadian Fiction.* Toronto: McClelland & Stewart, 1974.

—. *A Reader's Guide to the Canadian Novel.* Toronto: McClelland & Stewart, 1981.

New, W.H. *A History of Canadian Literature.* London: Macmillan, 1989. 107-11.

Peterman, Michael. "Humour and balance in *The Imperialist*: Sara Jeannette Duncan's 'Instinct of Presentation.' " *Journal of Canadian Studies* 11.2 (1976): 56-64.

Roper, Gordon, S. Ross Beharriell, and Rupert Schieder. "Writers of

Fiction, 1880-1920." *Literary History of Canada: Canadian Literature in English.* Ed. Carl F. Klinck. Toronto: U of Toronto P, 1976. 1: 327-53.

Ross, Catherine Sheldrick. "Calling Back the Ghost of the Old-Time Heroine: Duncan, Montgomery, Atwood, Laurence and Munro." *Studies in Canadian Literature* 4.1 (1979): 43-58.

Slonim, Leon. "Character, Action and Theme in *The Imperialist.*" *Essays in Canadian Writing* 3 (1975): 15-19.

Tausky, Thomas E. *Sara Jeannette Duncan: Novelist of Empire.* Port Credit: P.D. Meany, 1980.

—. "In Search of a Canadian Liberal: The Case of Sara Jeannette Duncan." *Ontario History* 83.2 (1991): 85-108.

—. "Introduction." *The Imperialist.* By Sara Jeannette Duncan. Ottawa: Tecumseh, 1988. ix-xxxix.

—. *Sara Jeannette Duncan and Her Works.* Canadian Writers and Their Works. Toronto: ECW, 1988.

Thomas, Clara. "Canadian social mythologies in Sara Jeannette Duncan's *The Imperialist.*" *Journal of Canadian Studies* 12.2 (1977): 38-49.

Thompson, Elizabeth. *The Pioneer Woman: A Canadian Character Type.* Montreal and Kingston: McGill-Queen's UP, 1991.

Waterston, Elizabeth. "Canadian Cabbage, Canadian Rose." *Journal of Canadian Fiction* 2.3 (1973): 129-31.

Zezulka, Joseph M. "*The Imperialist*: Imperialism, Provincialism, and Point of View." *Beginnings.* Ed. John Moss. Toronto: NC Press, 1980. 143-57.

Zichy, Francis. "A Portrait of the Idealist as Politician: The Individual and Society in *The Imperialist.*" *English Studies in Canada* 10 (1984): 330-42.

Other Works Cited

Adam, Graeme Mercer, and Ethelwyn Wetherald. *An Algonquin Maiden. A Romance of the Early Days of Upper Canada.* Montreal: Lovell, 1887.

Amery, Julian. *Joseph Chamberlain and the Tariff Reform Campaign. The Life of Joseph Chamberlain Volume Five: 1901-1903.* London: Macmillan, 1969.

Arendt, Hannah. *Imperialism.* New York: Harvest/HBJ, 1968.

Bercuson, David Jay. *Confrontation at Winnipeg: Labour, Industrial Relations, and the General Strike.* Montreal and London: McGill-Queen's UP, 1974.

Berger, Carl, "Introduction." *Imperialism and Nationalism 1884-1914: A Conflict in Canadian Thought.* Toronto: Copp Clark, 1969. 1-5.

—. *The Sense of Power: Studies in the Idea of Canadian Imperialism* 1867-1914. Toronto: U of Toronto P, 1970.

Besant, Walter and James Rice. *Ready-Money Mortiboy: A Matter-of-Fact Story.* London: Chatto and Windus, 1887.

Bourassa, Henri. "The French-Canadian in the British Empire." *The Monthly Review* 9 (1902): 53-68.

—. *Great Britain and Canada.* Montreal: C.O. Beauchemin et Fils, 1902.

Bradbury, Bettina. "Women and Wage Labour in a Period of Transition: Montreal, 1861-1881." *Canadian Labour History: Selected Readings.* Ed. David J. Bercuson. Toronto: Copp Clark, 1987. 27-42.

Brydon, Diana, and Helen Tiffin. *Decolonising Fictions.* Sydney: Dangaroo Press, 1993.

Burley, David G. *A Particular Condition in Life: Self-Employment and Social Mobility in Mid-Victorian Brantford, Ontario.* Kingston and Montreal: McGill-Queen's UP, 1994.

DeLottinville, Peter. "Joe Beef of Montreal: Working-Class Culture and the Tavern, 1869-1889." *Canadian Working Class History: Selected Readings.* Eds. Laurel Sefton MacDowell and Ian Radforth. Toronto: Canadian Scholars' Press, 1992. 245-68.

Ewart, John S. *The Kingdom Papers.* Ottawa, 1912.

—. *Report of the Canadian Club of Winnipeg together with the Inaugural Address of the First President, Mr. J.S. Ewart, K.C., 1904-1906.* Winnipeg: n.p., n.d.

Foucault, Michel. "What is an Author?" *Textual Strategies: Perspectives in Post-Structuralist Criticism.* Ed. Josué V. Harari. Ithaca: Cornell UP, 1979. 141-60.

Frye, Northrop. *The Secular Scripture.* Cambridge, Mass.: Harvard UP, 1976.

Grant, R.N. *Life of Rev. William Cochrane, D.D.* Toronto: Briggs, 1899.

Gwyn, Sandra. *The Private Capital: Ambition and Love in the Age of Macdonald and Laurier.* Toronto: McClelland & Stewart, 1984.

Halévy, Elie. *Imperialism and the Rise of Labour. A History of the English People in the Nineteenth Century.* Vol. 5. 1926. London: Ernest Benn, 1961.

Heron, Craig. *The Canadian Labour Movement: A Short History.* Toronto: James Lorimer, 1989.

— and Bryan D. Palmer. "Through the Prism of the Strike: Industrial Conflict in Southern Ontario, 1901-14." *Canadian Labour History: Selected Readings.* Ed. David J. Bercuson. Toronto: Copp Clark Pitman, 1987. 85-115.

Hobson, J.A. *Imperialism: A Study.* London: George Allen and Unwin, 1938.

Howe, Suzanne. *Novels of Empire.* New York: Columbia UP, 1949.

Hyde, Francis R. *Cunard and the North Atlantic 1840-1973: A History of Shipping and Financial Management.* London: Macmillan, 1975.

James, Henry. *The Letters of Henry James.* Ed. Leon Edel. Vol. 4. Cambridge: Harvard UP, 1984. 131-32.

Kealey, Gregory S. "Labour and Working-Class History in Canada: Prospects in the 1980s." *Canadian Labour History: Selected Readings.* Ed. David J. Bercuson. Toronto: Copp Clark Pitman, 1987. 232-56.

Kealey, Gregory S. and Bryan Palmer. "The Bonds of Unity: The Knights of Labor in Ontario, 1880-1900." *Canadian Working Class History: Selected Readings.* Eds. Laurel Sefton MacDowell and Ian Radforth. Toronto: Canadian Scholars' Press, 1992. 205-43.

Leacock, Stephen. *Greater Canada: An Appeal.* Montreal: Montreal News Company, 1907.

—. *May Court Club Lectures: McGill University Lectures. Six Lectures on the British Empire by Stephen Leacock.* Montreal: n.p., n.d., n. pag.

Lewis, R.W.B. *Edith Wharton: A Biography.* New York: Knopf, 1975.

Macleod, A.C. [Lady Wilson]. *Letters from India.* Edinburgh: Blackwood, 1911.

Marsh, Peter T. *Joseph Chamberlain: Enterpreneur in Politics.* New Haven: Yale UP, 1994.

Masterman, C.F.G. *The Condition of England.* Ed. J.T. Boulton. 1909. London: Methuen, 1960.

Montgomery, Malcolm. "The Six Nations Indians and the Macdonald Franchise." *Ontario History* 67.1 (1965): 13-25.

Morris, Pam. *Dickens's Class Consciousness: A Marginal View.* New York: St. Martin's, 1991.

Morton, Desmond. *A Military History of Canada.* Edmonton: Hurtig, 1985.

Palmer, Bryan D. *Working-Class Experience: Rethinking the History of Canadian Labour, 1800-1991.* Toronto: McClelland & Stewart, 1992.

—. *Working-Class Experience: The Rise and Reconstitution of Canadian Labour, 1800-1980.* Toronto and Vancouver: Butterworth, 1983.

Partridge, Eric. *A Dictionary of Slang and Unconventional English.* 5th ed. New York: Macmillan, 1961.

Reville, F. Douglas. *History of the County of Brant.* 2 vols. 1920. Brantford: Hurley Printing Company, 1967.

Said, Edward W. *Culture and Imperialism.* New York: Knopf, 1993.

Shortt, Adam. *Addresses Delivered Before the Canadian Club of Toronto, Season 1903-1904.* Toronto: Canadian Club, n.d.

Trilling, Lionel. *The Liberal Imagination.* New York: Viking, 1950.

Trofimenkoff, Susan. "One Hundred and Two Muffled Voices: Canada's Industrial Women in the 1880s." *Canadian Working Class History: Selected Readings.* Eds. Laurel Sefton MacDowell and Ian Radforth.

Toronto: Canadian Scholars' Press, 1992. 191-201.

Urquhart, M.C. and K.A.H. Buckley, eds. *Historical Statistics of Canada.* Cambridge: Cambridge UP, 1965.

Veltmeyer, Henry. *The Canadian Class Structure.* Toronto: Garamond, 1986.

Wood, Mrs. Henry. *Verner's Pride.* 1863. London, Melbourne & Toronto: Ward, Lock & Co., 1910.

Marquis Book Printing Inc.

Québec, Canada
2008